NAPLES &
CAMPANIA

NAPLES & CAMPANIA

Martha Pichey

A & C Black · London

© Martha Pichey 1994

Photographs by Peter Wilson
Maps and plans by John Flower

A & C Black (Publishers) Limited,
35 Bedford Row, London WC1R 4JH

ISBN 0-7136-3823-0

A CIP catalogue record for this book is
available from the British Library

Typeset in 9 on 11pt Linotron Optima
by Rowland Phototypesetting Ltd, Bury St
Edmunds, Suffolk

Printed in Singapore by Imago

To my parents, Alberta and Raymond Pichey,
the most enthusiastic travellers I know.

For all their help and encouragement I'd like to thank

Simon Gavron, Ann Pichey, Imelde Sello,
the Toledo Family and Conrad Williams.

CONTENTS

FOREWORD
by John Julius Norwich

Here be dragons, they used to write on the old maps, whenever they got to a bit of *terra incognita*: not only a warning to the impetuous traveller, but a comforting reminder of the infinitely preferable state of things back home. To this day, every native of northern Italy instinctively feels something of the kind about the south: he will mentally cross himself at the very mention of Campania, let alone Naples. For him, real civilisation stops at the southern border of Tuscany: even Rome is hopelessly beyond the pale. Anyone venturing still further into the wilds will do so at his peril, and is unlikely to be seen again.

The North Italians have, of course, a perfect right to their own opinions, which – having held them since the early Middle Ages – they are anyway unlikely to change. But they do not know what they are missing; for the region covered by this book is among the most rewarding of all Italy. It can boast, in Pompeii and Herculaneum, the first sites ever to be subjected to serious archaeological investigation; in Vesuvius, what is perhaps the world's most famous volcano; in Paestum, three of the earliest, best-preserved and most moving Doric temples anywhere; and in the Sorrento Peninsula and its off-shore islands, some of the most spectacularly beautiful scenery that the world has to offer.

And then there is Naples; and Naples is, of course, the problem. Does it deserve its reputation? Is it really the running sore on the shin of Italy, the malignant ulcer that nothing can cure? Or is it in fact a noble, historic city, still bearing the scars of centuries of misgovernment but preserving at the same time a strength of character, and a power to fascinate, that many another European metropolises might envy? I myself have loved it since my first visit over thirty years ago when, at the instigation of an old Neapolitan friend, my wife and I found our way to the convent of San Gregorio Armeno and, sitting in the cloister garth among a riot of baroque statuary, watched the nuns – their black habits slashed down the middle by a broad band of scarlet – teetering on the tops of their ladders while they picked oranges and threw them down to their colleagues below, who held out their skirts to receive them. Later, one of their number took us into the treasury, where she treated us to our own private miracle: the liquefaction of the blood, not of San Gennaro but of Santa Patrizia, which took place – unmistakeably – a foot in front of our eyes.

And there are plenty of other memories too: Capua on its hilltop, commanding the great loop of the Volturno, and the almost palpable presence there of Frederick II, *Stupor Mundi*, the first Renaissance prince, two hundred years before his time; the breathtaking frescoes at Sant' Angelo in Formis nearby; the tremendous Roman arch of Benevento; the sulphurous gurglings of Solfatara; and the excitement of finding, at Sessa Aurunca, a superb 12th-century cathedral of which I had never even heard, with a majolica dome above and a mosaic floor below wrought in that wonderful technique known as *opus alexandrinum* – my first, unforgettable introduction to the Romanesque architecture of the south.

All this and much, much more came flooding back into my memory when I first read the typescript of the book that you now hold in your hand. Its author has travelled every inch of the territory that she describes with such infectious enthusiasm, and she knows its history as well as she knows the land itself – no small achievement with a history as tortuous and tormented as that of Southern Italy has been. But she writes not only with knowledge: she also writes with love – a love that is not limited to Capri, Amalfi and the obvious delights of the coast but which extends, sincerely and genuinely, to Naples itself. When I came upon the title of the chapter 'Naples Explained', I confess to a momentary feeling of misgiving, if not of actual alarm: can anyone explain Naples? Well, they can; and she has.

For the first secret of understanding Naples is not to be afraid of it, as nearly all first-time visitors are. This does not mean to tempt fate, leaving your wallet sticking half out of your hip pocket, or swinging your handbag carelessly from your shoulder; but there are, after all, very few large towns anywhere in which such conduct is to be recommended. What it does mean is that you should forget all those horror stories you have heard and approach the city as you would any other: ready to enjoy it, to seek out its hidden treasures – which are there in plenty, if you know where to look for them – and, quite simply, to give it the benefit of the doubt. Even then, you may not immediately like the place; but Naples – like Marseilles, or Liverpool, or Barcelona, or many other great cities, especially if they happen to be great ports as well – does not set out to seduce. Some people, try as they may, will never see its charm; but there will be others for whom, one day, the veil will suddenly lift, never to fall again.

If Naples is an acquired taste, the rest of Campania is more usually a question of love at first sight. Even there, however, we need somone to direct our steps; not only to the sights that we have come to see, but also – and every bit as important – to the hotels and restaurants and bars where we can suitably reward ourselves after a long, hard day. Hence the very proper stress that is laid on the food and the wine of the region in the pages that follow – aspects of the local culture in which the author of this book is no less an expert than in matters of art and architecture. Put yourself, therefore, confidently in her hands. You will not regret it.

John Julius Norwich

1. INTRODUCTION

Everyone seems to know something about Italy's southern region of Campania. They've seen a picture of the cliff-hugging town of Positano, been transfixed by the casts made of Pompeiians killed by Vesuvius, and perhaps heard the phrase 'See Naples and die'. But how many people, even the Italophiles among them, realize what a vast amount of history, art and architecture lies waiting to be discovered throughout Campania? How many travellers have seen the ancient mosaics in the Archeological Museum in Naples, traversed the underground chambers of Italy's best preserved amphitheatre at Santa Maria Capua Vetere or explored the Greeks' first mainland city of Cumae?

Visitors to the region will be following in illustrious footsteps: Virgil settled in Naples; Giotto, Boccaccio and Petrarch were courted there by King Robert the Wise; Dickens, Ruskin, Shelley and Goethe all criss-crossed this territory. As in other parts of Italy, religion is one of the region's strongest threads. Here in Campania it is responsible for temples to Greek and Roman gods, for Romanesque, Gothic and Norman churches scattered throughout the countryside, and for brightly tiled church domes along the coast which attest to sailors' fascination with Eastern trading posts. Amalfi's cathedral and Padula's monastery are two of the region's most lavish examples of the church's power throughout the centuries. And superstitious beliefs reach the height of frenzy when San Gennaro's blood liquifies each year in Naples, though each town boasts its little miracles and sacred stash of saints' bones.

Campania Felix was what the Romans called this place, because it appeared so blessed with fertile soil and superb scenery – bay after bay on the blue Tyrrenhian Sea, hills covered with olives and oranges, flat green fields full of tobacco and vegetables, wheat harvested by the ton. Hot sun, little rainfall and an average temperature of 60 degrees certainly added to a Roman nobleman's enjoyment.

But the Romans weren't the only ones to appreciate the region. Greeks settled here eight centuries before the birth of Christ; then came Oscans and Samnites, followed by Romans, Lombards, Saracens and Normans. At the end of the 12th century the royal houses of Hohenstaufen, Anjou and Aragon ruled the region, though were finally succeeded by the Bourbons. After 1860, Italy was united under the House of Savoy, which begat its own set of problems for a warm and resilient people now officially part of the arid Mezzogiorno south of Rome.

Italy's dividing line between north and south is, geographically speaking, the Garigliano river. This is Campania's northern border, separating the region from

1

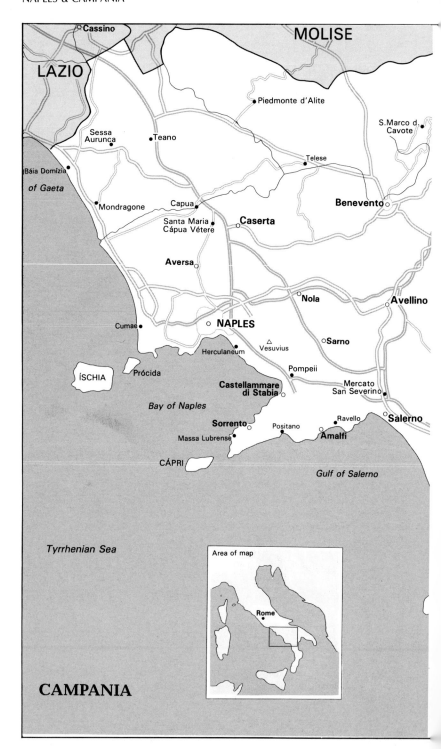

MOLISE

LAZIO

Cassino

Piedmonte d'Alite

S.Marco d.
Cavote

Sessa
Aurunca

Teano

Telese

Báia Domízia
of Gaeta

Mondragone

Capua

Santa Maria
Cápua Vétere

Caserta

Benevento

Aversa

Nola

Avellino

Cumae

NAPLES

Vesuvius

Sarno

Herculaneum

Pompeii

ÍSCHIA

Prócida

Mercato
San Severino

**Castellammare
di Stabia**

Bay of Naples

Ravello

Salerno

Sorrento

Positano

Amalfi

Massa Lubrense

CÁPRI

Gulf of Salerno

Tyrrhenian Sea

Area of map

Rome

CAMPANIA

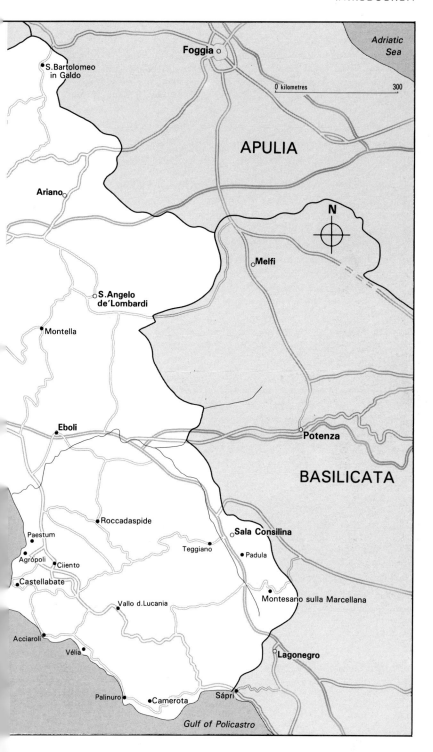

Lazio, while its southern limits extend to the Gulf of Policastro, shared with Basilicata. Borders to the east are adjacent to the regions of Molise, Apulia and Basilicata. Campania's inland villages and hill-towns sit low in the valleys or are poised high above them, while the rugged limestone coast is lined with villages tumbling down to the edge of the sea. The islands of Procida, Ischia and Capri encircle the Gulf of Naples, which has struggled with volcanic activity for centuries.

Then there is Naples. A sizeable section of this book is devoted to this raucous city, and with very good reason. Naples is like a huge and dusty antique shop, which initially appears to be unappreciated by its owners. But Neapolitans can quickly, and keenly, catalogue their rich selection of stock for you, and will be happy to show you what is behind a locked door or around the next corner (while also bemoaning the lack of money available to restore their fine buildings). The city is a fascinating study in history, architecture and social custom; the historic centre is a vital and absorbing place to explore.

Naples was a royal capital for almost 600 years, and today's inner cityscape was much influenced by the reign of the Bourbon dynasty from 1734 to 1860. Baroque and Rococo more than flowered: they burst into full exotic bloom. From painters such as Caravaggio and Luca Giordano to architects like Vanvitelli and Fanzago, the city is a rich testimony to the royal courts' patronage of the arts. The museums are outstanding, from the National Picture Gallery at Capodimonte to the National Archeological Museum with its sculptures, wall paintings and mosaics from Pompeii and Herculaneum.

Other parts of Campania are home to similar treasures, and the effort spent tracking them down is a rewarding experience. Caserta Vecchia is a charming walled town north of Naples; the caves and coves along the Cilento coast make beautiful private bathing pools. The landscape is not everywhere an aromatic patchwork of lemon groves and grape vines however, as industrial plants have sprouted like nasty weeds outside the five main provincial cities of Naples, Caserta, Benevento, Avellino and Salerno. To avoid these blights, I have suggested when it's best to drive down the motorway instead of slowly winding through the countryside.

To help get a sense of this region's history and its people, I suggest three 20th-century travelogues: H. V. Morton's *A Traveler in Southern Italy*, Norman Douglas's *Siren Land*, and *Naples '44* by Norman Lewis. I add this guidebook to the list in the hope that I can help you discover the best of what Campania has to offer. But trust the people of Naples and Campania to be your guides as well. If the church door is locked, a restaurant closed, if the street signs seem too confusing, help is always at hand – literally. Italians are famously inventive when it comes to communicating without a common language, and Campanians are no exception.

2. THE FOOD AND WINE OF CAMPANIA

Despite the diversity of the region's geography, and the foreign influences which have played on the Neapolitan's palate, Campanian tastes remain simple and straightforward when it comes to their choice of food and wine. This is partly because they have been blessed with an abundance of flavourful crops in a region of rich soil. But Campania is also part of Italy's Mezzogiorno, the demarkation zone between north and south which implies a peasantry toiling under hot sun for centuries. Historically, this lack of money and its pretensions has meant that Campanians have been forced by necessity to exploit their natural resources to the fullest.

Food

Fruit and Vegetables

Tomatoes grow full of flavour on the volcanic slopes of Vesuvius; fruit and vegetables are planted on the inland plains awash with mineral silt from rivers criss-crossing the region. The food is fresh; most shoppers prefer choosing their own produce at the local seller's stall to the anonymity of convenience stores where they can't chastise a vendor for selling unripe apricots. Their Mediterranean diet is a healthy mix of grains, pulses and vegetables, with seafood eaten far more often than meat. Many families still press their own olives for oil, and their grapes for wine (which is good enough to wash down the midday meal, but rarely of a standard high enough to export).

But the region's fruit and vegetables are shipped throughout the country, with as many as four crops harvested annually on the fertile slopes of Vesuvius. The small San Marzano tomatoes are the stars of any southern sauce. Cherries, figs and apricots are among the best in Italy, along with pungent lemons grown on the islands of Procida and Ischia. Native artichokes, aubergines, broccoli and courgettes are cooked in every conceivable style, bottled and pickled too. They are also breaded and deep fried for what's called the *fritto misto*, an assortment brought hot to the table. Little red peppers are strung to shrivel in the sun, and in early autumn you might come across a caldron of stewing tomatoes outside a family's kitchen – this season being the perfect time for bottling the rich red sauce.

The tomato came to southern Italy by way of South America, by courtesy of the Spanish explorer Hernando Cortes in the 16th century (though some give Christopher Columbus the credit). Other foods came much earlier, and all were made use of by peasants inventively managing with what they had. Grape vines and olive trees had been planted hundreds of years before by the Greeks; later trade with the East brought nuts and spices to the area. Though Campania was under the domination of so many different rulers – Greek, Roman and Byzantine, then French Normans, Hohenstaufens, and Angevins followed by the Spanish Aragonese – those in control of the kitchen kept on a steady course by serving the region's freshest produce, fish and the daily portion of pasta.

Pizza, pasta and gelato

Southern Italy is famous for pizza, pasta and ice cream, and Naples has distinguished itself in all three categories. Where would we be if Neapolitans hadn't had the courage to taste the *pomi d'oro*? Tomatoes were the ideal topping for the flat bread baked in a brick oven, *picea* being a word used since the 11th century to describe this circular bread. Sailors improved upon the recipe by creating *pizza alla Marinara* – not by adding fish but by topping it with garlic, oil and oregano in the 1500s. Then in 1889 the food received the royal stamp of approval with the invention of the Regina Margherita pizza. When Queen Margherita, wife of Italy's King Umberto I, summered at Capodimonte, a pie-maker named Raffaele Esposito was invited to experiment for her. He added mozzarella to the standard tomato pie, along with sprinkling leaves of basil over the top: a celebration of Italian unity in red, white and green.

At its simplest, pizza is just *bianca*, freshly baked dough sprinkled with salt and sold by the etto (one hundred grams, or one-tenth of a kilogram). It's a favourite snack available from bakeries and bars. Also popular in Naples are *taralli*, crusty bread rings flavoured with pepper and a hint of almond. Another bread-based dish is *panzanella alla Napoletana* – a salad layered with bread at the bottom, and piled with tomatoes, onions, anchovies and basil. Then there is the *calzone*, or 'trouser-leg', a crescent-shaped pizza that has been folded in half so that its contents are hidden inside. The choice of toppings for pizza or calzone is endless: mushrooms, olives, anchovies, eggs, clams and artichoke hearts to name a few. The Margherita is still a popular choice, but the more elaborate Quattro Stagioni is often ordered. Divided into four sections to represent the seasons, the pizza is normally topped with black olives, hard-boiled egg, artichoke hearts and either clams or mussels. The Neapolitan pizza is not a thick crusted variety; it is thin and crisp, still baked on wooden pallets in round ovens.

Pasta needs no introduction. But what distinguishes this southern staple from its northern counterpart is that it is most often made with durum wheat and without eggs. Naples and its surrounding towns were once famous for exporting hundreds of varieties of dry pasta, but Campania's wheat is no longer harvested for the factories of Torre del Greco and Torre Annunziata. The traditional image of the *mangiatore di maccurune*, a street urchin slurping up strings of pasta, made its way on to postcards and into theatre scenes, and Neapolitans today are no less passionate about their pasta. It's eaten at least once a day, and more often than not with a simple Neapolitan sauce like this one:

> **A Sarza cu 'a Pummarola** (as the Neapolitans say)
> **Salsa al Pomodoro** (as other Italians would say)
> **Tomato Sauce** (for the rest of us)
> Fry a small, chopped onion in oil, and when it begins to turn golden add one kilogram of fresh, peeled tomatoes which have also had their seeds removed (done by immersing the tomatoes in boiling water for about 30 seconds, then peeling and slicing them when cooled). Also add about six sweet basil leaves. Cook over low heat for about half an hour. When the sauce thickens, add salt and pepper to taste. Pour generously over *al dente* (slightly chewy) portions of vermicelli, and sprinkle with freshly grated parmesan.

Lasagne is a dish traditionally eaten during *Carnevale*, while *maccheroni* pie is another reserved for festive occasions. This is usually made with a pasta such as *rigatoni*, layered with eggs, sausage and mozzarella and smothered in a ragu tomato sauce. Another local favourite in the pasta department is called *Strangolapreti*. As the story goes, a greedy priest ate so many of these little potato dumplings that he suffocated. Commonly called *gnocchi*, the ribbed pasta shapes are made with mashed potato and flour, removed from boiling water as soon as they rise to the surface, and doused with a tasty meat sauce (eat slowly).

Mozzarella

This soft cheese is one of the region's prized specialities, made from the milk of buffalo raised on the plains north of Naples. Don't think you know what it tastes like if you've been subjected only to the plastic-packed version bought outside Italy. Mozzarella is practically impossible to export successfully, since it must soak in a mixture of milk and water in order to remain fresh. But taste mozzarella in Campania and you will be hooked for life. Slightly salty and just a bit spongy, it is at its best when dressed with a rich olive oil. The *insalata Caprese*, slices of fresh tomato and mozzarella with basil, olive oil and salt, originated on Capri but is now found on lunch menus all over Italy. Try it, and try it again.

Another version of mozzarella is called *fior di latte*, made with cow's milk. It doesn't have quite as much flavour as that made with buffalo's milk, but is still very good. *Bocconcini*, or 'little bites', are the smallest forms of this delicious cheese, found in shops called *latterie* and *salumerie* (and good for picnics). One of the best sandwiches in the world is mozzarella combined with a salty prosciutto on a crusty round *rosetto* roll. When mozzarella is fried between two pieces of bread it's called *in carozza* (in carriage), a starter seen on most menus in Campania. Any variation on the theme is bound to be delicious!

Meat and fish

You won't often find Campanian families cooking a roast for Sunday lunch – most meat is reserved for making sauces. Traditionally, meat (especially lamb) was eaten a few times a year during Carnevale in February and other holidays. But today financial constraints have lessened, and you will find veal and pork, as well as lamb and chicken, served at home more regularly. They are always to be found on restaurant menus however, along with regional specialities such as rabbit and wild boar.

The local *salumeria* has always had a varied and tasty stock of sausage and salami. The sausage called *cervellata* is one of the best, made with red wine and packed with fennel seeds. *Morsello* is one of the strongest, with its biting red peppers. The Neapolitan salamis tend to be highly flavoured, full of pepper and somewhat fatty. *Prosciutti* are also fatty, though flavourful – certainly not like the delicate slices from the northern regions that go so well with sweet melon. You'll find that the thick *prosciutto* is used to flavour a variety of pasta sauces.

Fish has been a staple part of the coastal diet for hundreds of years, though surprisingly few seafood recipes have ever made their way inland. Hilltop farmers stayed far away from seafaring pirates, and didn't want to have anything to do with their food either! But in Naples and along the Amalfi coast, housewives and restaurant chefs have always been on the lookout for what's *pescato della mattinata* (caught fresh this morning).

Mussels, clams, squid and octopus make their way into pasta sauces, as well as being stewed in the rich *zuppa di pesce*, which also includes the strongly flavoured scorpion fish. Anchovies, called *acciughe* or *alici*, are cooked in a variety of ways: marinated as a starter, fried with *prosciutto* into fritters called *pizzelle alla napoletana*, and often added to deep-fried courgette flowers called *pasta cresciuta*. They also find their way into stuffed peppers and on to the top of the pizza pie.

Common fish dishes include poached octopus, peppered mussels and *calamari* (squid) with raisins and pine nuts.

Sweets

Most of the region's *dolci* are to be found in Naples, a great place for pastry tasting as you hop from café to café. Coffee is strong, the perfect antidote to light, sugar-covered sweets. At the top of my list come *sfogliatelle*, crispy shell-shaped puff pastries that are stuffed with ricotta cheese and fruit such as candied cherries. Another favourite – though by no means confined to Campania – is a caramel-coloured cone-shaped sponge called the *baba*. This is soaked in rum, a common mid-morning snack for stall sellers and students. Along the Amalfi coast you will find *sproccolati*, deliciously skewered sticks of dried figs stuffed with fennel seeds.

Festivals and holidays have a host of treats centered round them. At Christmas time, one traditional cake made with almond paste is called *Divino Amore*. Another, which makes a popular present among friends and relatives during the holiday, is *struffoli* – fried pastry rings coated in honey and decorated with coloured almonds and candied peel. But Naples is probably most famous for the *pastiera*, or Easter pie, a recipe that dates back to the 14th century. The basic ingredients are ricotta cheese and corn, symbols of well being and family prosperity. The Easter pie has become so popular that you can usually find it throughout the year in this region, as well as in other parts of Italy during the Easter season.

Wines of Campania

'The human body was designed as a funnel for pouring wine' is what Pompeiian wine producers used to say. They saw an awful lot of it being drunk, and when the city was destroyed so was Rome's wine supply. Pompeii was part of the area known to Romans as Campania Felix, so rich was its soil for cultivating grapes and other fruits. The wines, supplied in heavy terracotta amphorae, were called Falernum and Caecubum, deep coloured and full-bodied. Were they better than most produced in the region today, as some wine writers suggest? It's hardly an argument one can prove, though certainly worth debating over a bottle or two on a sun-washed terrace. Certainly Caligula would have been on the side of pessimism: he called the wine of Sorrento 'respectable vinegar'.

It has taken Campanian vintners decades, if not centuries, to overcome prejudice against their wines. Norman Douglas showed very little enthusiasm for them in *Siren Land*. Eighty years ago he described those from around Naples as 'inky fluid . . . the grapes clamber up to heaven out of sight of the peasant, who periodically forgets their existence and plants hemp and maize in their earth. No vine will endure this treatment; personal contact is the first requisite for good results.' As for the wine of Capri, he wrote 'it has now become a noisome sulphur-and-vinegar compound that will etch the bottom out of a copper cauldron.'

Campania's annual wine production is close to 30 million cases, though that's less than four per cent of Italy's total annual output. The region's most outstanding producer is Mastroberardino, in a town called Atripalda near Avellino. This vineyard's wines are among the only ones that meet the standards of Italy's DOC (*denominazione di origine controllata*) label. Less than 15 per cent of all Italian wines are classified as such, but the percentage for Campania is less than one per cent. The red and white Lacryma Christi wines, made from grapes grown on Vesuvius, are also known outside Campania. Other wines of the region with a good reputation come from Ischia, known for its dry whites, and from Ravello, known for its reds.

9

The Mastroberardino wines are all made from local varieties: the red Aglianico, and white grapes called Greco di Tufo and Fiano di Avellino. The family were wine merchants in Naples during the 16th century; in 1720 they moved inland to Avellino and began producing their own. The vineyard was damaged in the 1980 earthquake, but fortunately their stock of 500,000 bottles survived unharmed in a hillside tunnel. Mastroberardino's red Taurasi is the region's, and one of Italy's, best. Aged for three years, it is a rich and velvety wine always worth ordering if seen on the wine list. When the season has been exceptionally good, the family also bottles a Taurasi Riserva.

Another regional red worth noting comes from Mandragone, on the coast near the northern border. The wine is called Falerno, from the ancient Falernum so popular in Imperial Rome. It's a full-bodied, DOC classified wine. Ravello has also had some success with its reds, produced from Per'e Palummo, Aglianico and Merlot grapes. The best of these is called Episcopio, produced by the Vuilleumier family who own the Hotel Palumbo in Ravello. Competition in the category is with another Ravello hotel family. The Caruso family's Gran Caruso red is not quite of the same standard, but still better than most reds in the region.

For Campania's best white wine, we turn again to the Mastroberardino family near Avellino. Their very dry and weighty Fiano di Avellino ranks with the country's best. Running a close second (and three times cheaper) is the same vineyard's Greco di Tufo, of which they bottle up to half a million per year. The only other Campanian whites that can stand up to Mastroberardino are from Ischia and Ravello. In that gorgeous hill-town, the same two hotel families, the Caruso and the Palumbo, compete again, though both vineyards are less successful with white than red.

Of Ischia's wine, the Don Alfonzo, from the Perrazzo vineyard, is good, along with Biancolella from D'Ambra Vini d'Ischia. Norman Douglas was uncharacteristically enthusiastic when describing the wines of the island. 'Large heart in small grape,' he noted, 'a drink for the gods that oozes in unwilling drops out of the dwarfed mountain grapes.'

3. NAPLES EXPLAINED

One fine morning a northerner was walking along the port, when he saw a fisherman stretched out in the shade by the sea-wall, enjoying his rest.
'What are you doing, lying there?' asked the northerner. 'It is only ten o'clock.'
'I have done my fishing. I have sold my fish. Now I am resting,' replied the Neapolitan.
'If you did a little more work, you would catch more fish,' said the northerner.
'And then?' enquired the Neapolitan.
'Then you would have more money.'
'And then?'
'Then you would be able to buy a net.'
'And then?'
'Why then, my good man, you would get a bigger catch.'
'And then?'
'Well, you would have the money to buy a bigger boat.'
So question followed answer until the exasperated northerner explained the end of all this practical exertion.
'Then you would own a beautiful villa, with servants and everything you could possibly want!'
'Yes, and then?'
The northerner was by this time thoroughly nonplussed.
'Then you could lie down and rest.'
'But that is just what I am now doing,' replied the astonished Neapolitan.

I dare anyone to defy the logic in this Neapolitan's world view. Peter Gunn set down this fable thirty years ago in his *Naples: A Palimpsest*. Today, Neapolitans still give one the impression that despite their city's frenetic pace and grimy exterior, they know how to appreciate life and their city's hidden riches. Neapolitans are survivors: most have not benefited in any material way from the seven dynasties which ruled their city; they managed, barely, through dismal conditions during World War II; yet another earthquake devastated buildings in 1980; present-day poverty and unemployment (as high as 25 per cent) seem to give northern Italians and foreigners grounds to express strong prejudice against the local population.

Clichés here run fairly true to form: Neapolitans really are often like actors who relish their roles in street theatre. Everyone seems to live out of doors; on Friday and Saturday nights, midnight traffic jams are not uncommon. And on a Sunday morning, typically quiet in many parts of the world, Naples is bustling as usual. The park grounds at Capodimonte are chaotic – children bicycling, girls doing handstands, and boys playing football while dodging bicycles are just a few of the acts on view.

The city's architecture – so striking and full of contrast – is an invitation to perform. Encrusted Baroque obelisks are tall defenders of small squares; façades of huge crumbling palazzi give no hint of the soaring staircases within; churches are so numerous that you could find one to visit for almost every day of the year (except that nearly half are usually closed). The Castel dell'Ovo remains a placid extension into the sea which Turner painted so softly in 1819. And the Bay of Naples is the same wide blue arc which beckoned Virgil, Goethe and Dickens, while the wide cone of Vesuvius and the twin peaks of Capri are still part of the ancient backdrop.

Why do today's travellers need to be convinced that Naples is worth the trip? It is an insult to its rich heritage merely to 'pass through' on the way to Campania's more favoured spots, and it is a plain mistake to skirt its wealth all together. I know a Swedish woman who was on her way to Rome by train for a holiday twenty years ago. She slept through her stop at Rome's Termini and two hours later awoke to find herself at the Naples station. Two Neapolitan husbands and four children later, she is still there. Naples can do that to a person.

Neapolitans will welcome you happily if you are prepared to explore its riches with an open mind (and, unfortunately, with a tightly clasped purse). Chapter four is devoted to five walking tours, and you'll find that the city will wrap itself around you like a net of hectic energy, charming you with architectural surprises. Its sights and sounds will engage you completely, and perhaps unnerve you at times. In either case, this city and its vibrant people refuse to be ignored. That is part of what makes a city great, and I for one add Naples to an Italian list that includes Rome, Venice and Florence.

Naples through history

Greco-Roman times

The first references to Naples – Neapolis to the Greeks – are found in the Homeric legends of the sirens, who lured smitten sailors to their unsuspecting deaths. But death comes to beautiful sea creatures too, and legend has it that the siren Parthenope threw herself into the waves over unrequited love for Odysseus. Her body was washed ashore in Naples near the Castel dell'Ovo, and the city is said to have sprung from her burial ground. Surprisingly, no crafty tour guide has invented a geographical resting place for the siren, though Neapolitans often refer to themselves as Parthenopeans.

The oldest inhabitants of Neapolis, or New City, built the port in 6BC just a few kilometres to the east of their first Magna Graecia colony of Cumae. The name Neapolis was chosen to distinguish it from Palaepolis, an older city whose foundations merged with the new. Greek culture was so strong along these shores that the language was spoken in some parts until 1450; linguists studying Neapolitan dialect have found traces of Greek within their language today. The whole of Campania has Greek colonists to thank for the introduction of the olive and the vine.

But Greek culture was challenged by the invasion of Samnites from the northern interior who first captured Cumae in 420BC. Then the Romans expanded southwards. After a series of wars from 343BC to 290BC, they gained control over the Samnites and Campania became part of the Roman Republic. Rome's success during the Punic Wars with Carthage between 264BC and 146BC secured their stronghold of the south. Neapolis had fallen after a three-year seige in 326BC, and was a satellite city to Rome for centuries. Her emperors turned this area into a royal playground. Lavish villas were built at Baia, a town which still exists on the Misenum Peninsula west of Naples. The city itself was considered a relaxed place of high culture. Augustus, Tiberius and Nero travelled down from Rome; Virgil spent his last years here while writing the *Georgics* and the *Aeneid*. He was buried in Naples, and guides are fond of pointing out an historically unproven site for this tomb.

Vesuvius erupted in 79AD and Neapolis to the north east escaped the fates of Pompeii and Herculaneum, thanks to a prevailing south west wind. The city was covered with a thin layer of ash and was rocked by tremors.

The Roman Empire itself was officially extinguished in Naples with its last western emperor, Romulus Augustulus. He died in exile in the Castel dell'Ovo in 476AD, after being humiliatingly deposed by the barbarian Ostrogoths. (They considered him too unimportant to be put to death in public, and banished him with an annual pension of 6000 gold pieces.) During the next century, the Byzantine general Belisarius recaptured Naples; the city was firmly in the hands of Byzantium by 533 and for almost six centuries was ruled by exarchs, Byzantine provincial governors.

City-states and dynasties

As in other parts of Italy, a unified Roman Empire gave way to small city-states throughout Campania during this period. The Franks invaded from the Rhine Valley; Lombards from Hungary (then called Pannonia) made Capua and Benevento their strongholds. Saracen invaders from eastern Europe terrorised the coastal regions. The church was also a gradually strengthening force during these centuries, responsible for controlling Byzantine territory. Finally, it was the Norman crusaders who unified the region in the 11th century. From Palermo, they reigned over a land mass equal to the size of Portugal which became the richest state in Italy.

The royal parade began in 1197, and continued until the unification of Italy in 1860. Seven dynasties ruled from Naples, their histories elaborate and sometimes entangled. In the early 11th century, Norman pilgrims, soldiers and their leaders came to Italy from France; by 1053 Norman warrior Robert Guiscard was awarded the whole of southern Italy and Sicily as a papal fief. Palermo fell to Robert's younger brother Roger in 1072 and his son, Roger II, was named founder in 1127 of what was to become the Kingdom of the Two Sicilies. Naples officially became part of this Kingdom in 1139, and the Normans remained in power until 1194.

They were followed by the Germanic Hohenstaufens, Ghibelline supporters of the Holy Roman Empire who were caught in a struggle with the Guelph-supported Papacy. Frederick II came to power in 1208, an enlightened ruler whom Dante called the father of Italian poetry. He founded the first Italian state university at Naples. But when he died in 1250, the Guelphs began to gain the upper hand. Frederick's son Conrad tried to claim the throne in 1252, but was killed. His illegitimate brother Manfred tried to do the same, and was crowned King of Sicily in 1258. But he was killed in 1266 by troops led by Charles of Anjou, who had been goaded by the papacy to oust the House of Hohenstaufen from Naples.

Manfred's younger brother Conradin then tried to reclaim the throne in 1269. At the age of 15, with 10,000 men and the backing of Ghibellines in Pisa, Verona, Siena and Pavia, Conradin moved south through Italy to Naples. But most of his troops were slaughtered before getting close, and Conradin himself was captured and brought before Charles of Anjou who had him beheaded in the Piazza del Mercato. In 1631, when the Church of the Carmine was being built in that same square, a lead coffin inscribed R.C.C. was found. The letters are thought to refer to Conradin: Regis Corradini Corpus. Inside was found the skeleton of a young man, with its severed skull.

So Charles of Anjou, the brother of King Louis IX, became the first in a line of Angevin kings who ruled Naples for almost 200 years. However, he lost Sicily to the Spanish Aragonese in 1282 after a famous struggle known as the Sicilian Vespers. A conspiracy by Sicilians to undermine the French king's power turned into a massacre after a Frenchman insulted a young Sicilian woman. The Sicilians rose up in revolt at the signal of the evening vespers and killed close to 8000 Frenchmen.

Charles of Anjou's successor was Charles II, who ruled from 1285 to 1309. But it was Robert the Wise, ruling from 1309 to 1343, who helped to cleanse the family name, for the Angevin dynasty was criticised for its ruthless tactics and lack of compassion for Naples' people. Robert was a patron of the arts who encouraged poets, writers and artists to find inspiration in his city. Giotto came here to paint in 1328, though only fragments of his work have been discovered; Petrarch visited twice, and was given the sought-after royal seal of approval from Robert the Wise as a poet fit to receive the laurel crown from the Roman Senate; Boccaccio arrived from Tuscany ostensibly to study banking, but spent his time at court collecting material for some of the wonderful tales of The Decameron which he wrote in the 1350s.

After 1343, the Angevin dynasty was gradually weakened by power struggles within the family that lasted for almost 100 years. This opened the way for the House of Aragon. In 1442, Alfonso the Magnanimous captured Naples, and reunited Sicily with the mainland. The Aragon dynasty was decidedly less enlightened than Naples' previous rulers. Alfonso celebrated his victory by inserting a tall marble arch into the entrance of the Castel Nuovo. 'Pious, merciful, unconquered,' he modestly commissioned stone carvers to inscribe upon the arch. His bastard son and successor was Ferdinand I, who ruled from 1458 to 1496. He had an even worse reputation than his father, for he exploited women, killed feudal barons in revolt, and even mummified his enemies.

Naples was then ruled by a long line of viceroys from Spain, the most influential of whom was Don Pedro de Toledo (1532–54). The city was greatly expanded during this period, the Via Toledo (also called Via Roma) running in a long ribbon from north to south. The narrow streets branching off it first held barracks for Toledo's soldiers; today they are known as the poverty-stricken Spagnolo quarter, full of small and airless homes called *bassi*.

Vasari came to work in Naples in the 1540s; Caravaggio reached Naples in 1606. The first performances in which the famous, earthy, tragi-comic Neapolitan character of Pulcinella appeared occurred around 1620. A brief revolt over increasing taxes started by a fishmonger named Masaniello led to Naples' only popular uprising, in 1647; citizens were freed from Spanish rule for nine whole days . . . before the Spanish viceroy had Masaniello shot. The Count of Onate, viceroy in 1651, is credited with introducing opera to the city of Naples. But staged tragedy became reality in 1656 when a plague hit the city and close to one half of the city's population of 450,000 died.

The Bourbons

After the War of the Spanish Succession, Naples came under the rule of Archduke Charles of Austria through the Treaty of Utrecht. But in 1734, with 27 years of uninspired Austrian viceroys behind it, the city became autonomous under the Spanish Bourbon Charles III. The Bourbon dynasty was to remain in power until 1860, except for 15 years (1799–1815) when Naples was proclaimed the Parthenopean Republic by the French. The early Bourbon kings were considered honourary Neapolitans, speaking dialect and behaving the way the citizenry thought they ought to – holding court as royal patrons and parading in finery through the city streets.

Charles III gave Naples many of its most lavish buildings. He was well versed in the history of architecture, and practised drafting and design. He took a keen interest in the commissions he initiated. Capodimonte and its famous porcelain factory were built; the San Carlo Opera House rose in the city's centre; Dutch architect Vanvitelli (Van Wittel) was commissioned to design the Palace of Caserta; excavations at Herculaneum and Pompeii were begun. Charles III's mother was Elizabeth Farnese, and it is thanks to her inheritance that the Farnese collection now rests in the National Archeological Museum here.

When Charles was called back to rule Spain at the age of 43 in 1759, his third son Ferdinand was crowned King of Naples at the age of seven. (The eldest, Philip, was declared insane and the second son, Charles, later became Charles IV of Spain.) Ferdinand IV was known as 'King Nosey' by affectionate attendants because of his most prominent feature. He grew up relatively uneducated, and spent more time hunting for boar and wildfowl than in caring for the Neapolitan people. By 1760, the population of Naples had reached 347,000 – one of the largest and poorest cities in Europe. Ferdinand's wife Maria Carolina was Marie Antoinette's sister, far more politically astute than her husband. When Napoleon's army was marching from Rome to Naples in 1799 she was convinced that the guillotine would be her fate as well. But the royal family sailed to safety in Palermo, thanks to the help of British Ambassador Sir William Hamilton and Admiral Horatio Nelson (who was infatuated with Hamilton's young wife Emma). This was probably the most dramatic event in the reign of King Ferdinand IV.

Ferdinand returned to Naples after the Peace of Amiens in 1802, choosing the new title of Ferdinand I, King of the Two Sicilies. But in 1805, the king fled again, when by Napoleon's decree his brother Joseph Bonaparte regained the throne, which was then passed to French marshal Joachim Murat (married to Napoleon's sister Caroline). French rule was brief and chaotic; the Bourbon King Ferdinand returned in 1815 after the Congress of Vienna restored order in Europe.

His grandson Ferdinand II inherited the throne in 1830, known unpopularly as 'King Bomba' for his bombardment of Messina to show the Sicilians what he thought of their demands for a Constitution. But a fair account of King Bomba's reign would show that he constructed the fantastic Amalfi Coast drive, built the first iron suspension bridge in Italy and repeatedly saved the San Carlo opera house from bankruptcy. His successor was Francis II, who ruled Naples until Garibaldi entered the city in September, 1860.

This last Bourbon king fled north to Gaeta; Garibaldi arrived with his troops by train from Salerno the morning after. Neapolitans were on the streets to greet them, waving banners and handkerchiefs, though they didn't seem to have any more or less faith in this new band of rulers than the last. Turin was made the new capital of a united Italy in 1861, and the House of Savoy now ruled with Victor Emmanuel II as the first king. Naples was never again looked upon as a royal capital, though upper class travellers did continue to make a pilgrimage there as part of the obligatory Grand Tour for at least another thirty years.

Grand Tour travellers

Naples was host to a steady stream of travellers well before the 1800s, and its appeal (and in some cases, lack of it) was recorded by many. One Englishman, a member of the Royal Society called John Ray, published his observations of daily life in 1673:

This City is well served with all provisions, especially fruit which is very cheap heer . . . Macarones and Vermicelle (which are nothing but a kind of paste cut into the figure of worms or thongs) boil'd in broth or water, are a great dish heer as well as at Messina, and as much esteemed by the vulgar, as Frumenty by the Countrey people in England.

Elizabeth David has done a better job since in describing the delights of Italian food, but it is interesting that even then a traveller found it worth noting. Observations took on a more cultural aspect in the 1700s, when Sir William Hamilton's presence drew many English travellers to the city. As British Ambassador, he lived in Naples for 35 years, well-known for his serious studies of volcanoes and classical antiquities – an early archaeologist whose family would have inherited valuable treasure if most of it had not sunk in a storm off Sicily on its way back to England. In the 1780s, his young wife-to-be, Emma, was famous for her drawing room performances called 'Attitudes'. Goethe described them during a visit in 1787:

> . . . letting her hair loose, and taking a couple of shawls, she exhibits every possible variety of posture, expression and look, so that at last the spectator almost fancies it is a dream . . . Standing, kneeling, sitting, lying down, grave or sad, playful, exulting, repentant, wanton, menacing, anxious – all mental states follow rapidly one after another.

When Stendhal visited in 1817, finding it hard to find a hotel room, he remarked that, 'there must have been two or three thousand English in the city.' Lady Blessington, who published two volumes in 1839 titled *The Idler in Italy*, observed

> The more I see of the Neapolitans, the more I like them. I have not detected among the individuals of the lower class that have fallen in my way, a single instance of the rapaciousness so generally, and I am inclined to think so unjustly, attributed to them by strangers.'

Travelogues took on a negative tone in the late 1800s. The Bourbons had left, and there were no longer Court balls and hunting parties to overshadow the city's poverty. John Ruskin described Naples as 'the most loathsome nest of human caterpillars I was ever forced to stay in'. At the turn of the century, an American millionaire named Dan Fellows Platt wrote that Naples was 'a motorist's hell'. In that he is right to this day, but Ruskin must have been wearing blinkers.

Naples since Garibaldi

During centuries of royal rule, the average Neapolitan was living in anything but palatial quarters. The citizenry's plight became more obvious after Unification in 1860, and received nationwide attention with the outbreak of cholera in 1884. Soon Naples was involved in a massive urban renewal programme to unweave the tight web of airless slums, and to transport cleaner water to the centre. But the divide between northern and southern Italy, which had always

17

existed, continued to widen in economic terms. Various government programmes meant better health and a higher rate of literacy, but northern industry
was steaming ahead of the agriculturally-based south. Campania and the rest
of southern Italy were virtually ignored when Mussolini was in power, except
as a place to which fascists exiled the likes of Carlo Levi.

The city was bombed during World War II – first by the advancing allies in
August, 1943, when Italy was still aligned with Germany, and then attacked
and captured by the Germans after the armistice was signed that September.
The American 5th Army ousted them, but not before the Germans had destroyed
hotels, the port area, and gas and electricity supplies for the city. Because of
a drastic lack of food and other services, Neapolitans earned a well-deserved
reputation for imaginative cunning and enterprise during World War II.

American soldiers were charmed by the boisterous warmth of Neapolitan
families, and when visiting them would bring welcome gifts of flour, cigarettes
and chocolate. What the soldiers didn't realise was that 'selling Americans' was
one way to make a little extra cash: a Neapolitan family would introduce their
soldier to another local family – for a fee, of course. You've only to read Norman
Lewis's wonderful book, *Naples '44*, to understand the true meaning of the
verb *arrangiarsi*, to 'get by'. In one passage Lewis describes being

> 'drawn into a corner by a priest, white-lipped and smiling. He opened a
> bag full of umbrella handles, candlesticks and small ornaments of all
> kinds carved out of the bones of saints, i.e. from bones filched from one
> of the catacombs. He, too, had to live.'

Despite the fact that Naples has always been dominated by foreign rulers,
some of its citizens still believe that they were better off before a 'unified'
national government had a guiding hand in their affairs. Masses of development
money from the *Cassa del Mezzogiorno* has not successfully addressed their
problems. One typical opinion was expressed by a Neapolitan woman I know:
'Where are all the macaroni factories we used to have? Out of business. Where
do we buy our pasta from now? The north. Yes, they give us money, but we
spend all of ours on goods produced by them.'

Us versus them, and she even has relatives in northern Italy. Her son has a
Bolognese friend who braved Naples to visit him, under the impression that
Federico was unusually educated and amiable for a Neapolitan. When his
cultured northern friend saw that Federico's sister Maria Teresa had rings on
her fingers he was horrified. 'Won't they cut your finger off to steal the ring?'
he asked. Stories such as these abound, and they astonish me.

The city's population now numbers more than 1,200,000 and the labyrinthine
Spaccanapoli section of Naples is still crowded with many who just manage to
scrape by. Old men sell eggs from straw carts, lined with sprigs of sage.
Widowed women in black sit on wooden chairs behind their makeshift counters,
selling contraband cigarettes in open and accepted transgression of the law.
And always there are gangs of young boys, *scugnizzi*, about, making you
wonder when on earth school is open in this city. I remember one eight-year-old
who took time out from his football game beside the Duomo to have a chat

with me. Could he help with my map reading? No? Then he'd go back to score a goal for me. Saying goodbye, he chucked me under the chin with unnerving confidence. Older gangs of Neapolitan boys are not so innocent, however. To pay for drugs, they will steal your bag with speed and efficiency.

The devastating earthquake of 1980 has forced the city to re-examine its programme to overhaul many old buildings. A group of concerned citizens, led by Baroness Mirella Barracco, created the Fondazione Napoli '99, an organisation founded in 1984 to focus world-wide attention on the city's plight. Private donations, and patrons such as Mario Valentino, Mobil Oil and the CIGA hotel chain have enabled the foundation to restore a number of important monuments, including the Castel Nuovo's marble entrance arch and frescoes within the San Gennaro Chapel. Neapolitans have embraced the foundation's philosophy with fervour. 'Open Door' weekends, to view many monuments often closed to the public, have drawn crowds of up to 500,000. Schoolchildren have proudly 'adopted' monuments throughout the city.

The business of constructing new buildings is not conducted with such noble intentions, however. The construction industry is booming, especially in the suburb of Fuorigrotta, but the Camorra, Naples' mainland version of the Mafia, plays an all too visible role in raking off billions of lire. Many of the city's shops and businesses, an estimated 50,000 of them, pay protection money to the Camorra just to be left alone. (Aptly, Camorra is a corruption of the Spanish word *gamurra* meaning extortion money.) Highest stakes are in the drugs game: the sale of cocaine and heroin is masterminded by the Camorra, and sadly the number of drug addicts has risen in proportion to the organisation's ability to sell. And the criminals' tactics are just as sinister as those of the Sicilian Mafia – in 1988 the severed head of Naples' chief prison psychiatrist was found in a tin biscuit box. He had been testing the mental health of jailed Camorra bosses with too much skill.

That is the darkest side of Naples' character, and is not denied by anyone living there. As with the Mafia, the organised clout and control of the Camorra has remained stable in part because national government has been so unstable. Recent arrests of Mafia and Camorra bosses, as well as of corrupt politicians, have left citizens feeling unsettled, yet hopeful. They remain passionately proud of their city, and of themselves. And, *grazie a Dio*, San Gennaro's blood is still reputed to liquify with reassuring regularity.

4. NAPLES EXPLORED

The five walking tours that follow will take you past almost all of Naples' most famous sights. I stress *walking* tours, for except in the case of Hilltop Museum-Hopping, you will be able to see everything easily on foot. The city's oldest and most evocative quarter is Spaccanapoli, with its tight alleys and many famous churches. Then heading toward the sea and radiating out from the Piazza Trieste e Trento are the city's municipal and cultural monuments: the Palazzo Reale, Castel Nuovo, the Galleria and the San Carlo Opera House. Another walk takes you down to the seafront, by the Villa Communale and the port area of Mergellina. On the hills above you will find some of Naples' most treasured art – in the San Martino Monastery and at Capodimonte. An important part of Naples' history is also underground, but unfortunately very few of these subterranean tunnels, grottoes and building foundations are accessible to the public yet.

Above ground, it isn't difficult to make your way around Naples. Bus and tram lines are good, and a ticket purchased for 1000 lire (then cancelled by inserting into the small red machine at the back where you enter the bus) will take you from one end of the city to the other. Tickets can be purchased from many newsstands, and from shops with a black and white sign saying 'T' for *Tabacchi*. Buy a detailed map of the city from a bookshop or newspaper stand. The map published by Studio F. M. B. Bologna is a very good one.

Do not take a car into Naples if you can help it. Even if it isn't stolen, you'll find it difficult to make your way through city streets. Traffic laws were made to be ignored here, and only at the major intersections (with a traffic warden present in crisp uniform) will cars consistently stop for a red light. An estimated 800,000 cars are on the move in the Naples area daily, and half of them invade the historic centre. If you've rented a car, drop it off at the Capodichino airport 7km out of town and take the bus or taxi in. (The coach service runs reliably every 40 minutes and costs 3000 lire, whereas a taxi costs anywhere from 30000 to 50000 lire.) If you are driving, choose a hotel with a parking garage, though this can be a costly option – negotiate with the hotel's management before handing over the keys or you might be in for an unpleasant surprise when paying the bill.

While walking in Naples, on no account assume that a driver will stop if you set foot on a zebra crossing. Every part of the pavement is dodgem territory for cars and bodies alike. My tactic is to cross with an old man or woman, or a mother and child, but I can't say this is successful in every case. I should add, however, that not once have I seen an accident in Naples. When taking a cab, always check to see whether or not the meter works, and ask about the supplement charged at night and on weekends. Try to establish a fee, if only roughly, for the length of your journey.

From first-hand experience, I also caution you (as will many Neapolitans) not to carry valuables when touring city streets. Leave credit cards, traveller's checks, passports and cash in the hotel safe, and take with you only what's needed for the day's outing. I found it impossible – what with books and camera and notepads – not to carry a bag the last time I was there but Neapolitans will tell you not to roam around with one. If you must, strap the bag across your chest so that it doesn't dangle from the shoulder, and make a record of your credit card numbers. I learned this the hard way, or rather my sister did. She was pushed to the pavement while two teenage boys on a motorino tried to yank my bag away. (They didn't get it.)

The five sections of Naples explored in the following walking tours cover a total area of about six kilometers from east to west, and five kilometers from north to south. Each tour takes about three hours, and you will by no means have exhausted the city's possibilities by walking them. On the other hand, I have tried to fashion them in a flexible way so that you could visit a museum in the morning and then do a portion of one walk in the afternoon. I must stress that if you are only in the city for a few days, do not miss Spaccanapoli and the National Archeological Museum (Walk 1).

In general, museums open from 09.00 until 14.00. Churches open from 08.00 to 12.00 and/or from about 17.00 to 20.00 in the evening, but these hours are notoriously inconsistent; one of the best times to view churches is on Saturday morning. Shops will close in the afternoon from about 13.00 to 16.00, and then open again until about 20.00. The sign *Chiuso per Restauro* (closed for restoration) might hamper you at times, but it's best to look on the bright side when a monument has been 'closed for restoration': Naples is trying to stop the decay of its architectural history, and is hard at work restoring those buildings most badly in need of repair. Where possible, I have been more specific about opening times for major sites, listed alphabetically in the information section at the end of the chapter.

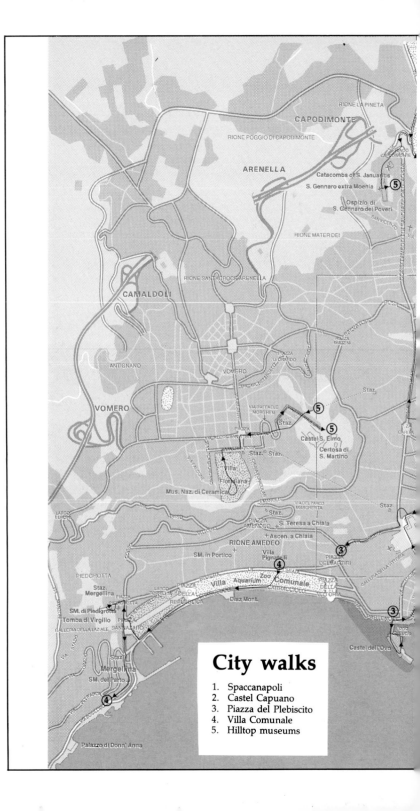

City walks

1. Spaccanapoli
2. Castel Capuano
3. Piazza del Plebiscito
4. Villa Comunale
5. Hilltop museums

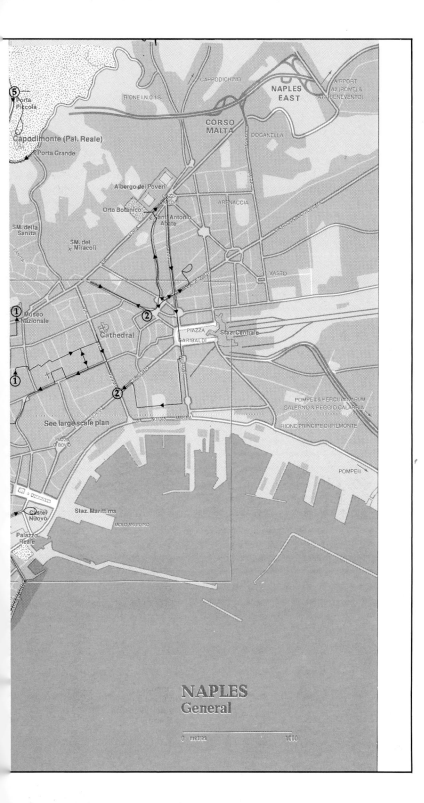

Porta Piccola ⑤

Capodimonte (Pal. Reale)

Porta Grande

CAPODICHINO

RIONE I.N.C.I.S.

NAPLES EAST

AIRPORT
A2 (ROME) &
(BENEVENTO)

CORSO MALTA

DOGANELLA

Albergo dei Poveri

Orto Botanico

Sant'Antonio Abate

ARENACCIA

S.M. della Sanità

S.M. dei Miracoli

VASTO

① Museo Nazionale

Cathedral

②

PIAZZA GARIBALDI

Staz. Centrale

①

②

POMPEII & HERCULANEUM
SALERNO & REGGIO CALABRIA

RIONE PRINCIPE DI PIEMONTE

See large scale plan

PIAZZA G. BOVIO

POMPEII

Castel Nuovo

Staz. Marittima

MOLO ANGIOINO

Palazzo Reale

NAPLES
General

0   metres   1000

WALK 1
The inner square: Spaccanapoli

Greco-Roman Naples is almost non-existent if you are looking for ruins to mark the period. What survived best is the original street pattern of the old city, and the section of Naples called Spaccanapoli is right at its heart. This quarter derived its name from the view of Via Roma from the Monastery of San Martino on the hill above. This main street seems to 'split' the city in half, for the verb *spaccare* in Italian means just that; Spaccanapoli is directly east of where the split occurs. The paths of the old city within the quarter can be traced to their Greek nomenclature: the *decumanus major* is Via Tribunali, and *decumanus minor* are Via Forcella and San Biagio dei Librai. This walk is bounded by the superb National Archeological Museum to the north, the Duomo to the east, by the Piazzas Amore and Carità in the southern corners, and by Piazza Dante to the west. The quarter is jam-packed with sights, and though the walk covers the major monuments, there is always more to see. The National Archeological Museum, for example, is worth a full morning's viewing if not a return visit.

The Via Roma cuts through the centre of Naples from south to north into **Piazza Dante**. Many buses begin and end their run here; it's a lively square that serves as a good introduction to the quarter of Spaccanapoli. The high statue of Dante has been watching over the populace since 1872, and the Doric semicircle with statues of twenty-six not very inspiring Virtues was created by Vanvitelli under Charles III. The Port' Alba on the northeast corner of the square is your way in to the quarter. Streets are narrow – a *via* suddenly becomes *vico*, and even this word (meaning alley) takes on its dimunitive in *vicolo*.

People say that you can never really know a Neapolitan until he invites you into his home, and part of Spaccanapoli's irrepressible charm lies in the feeling that you have indeed been invited in. Doors are open wide to the street; people sit in ground floor kitchens having a chat or a game of cards. A girl on a second floor balcony lowers a basket for the red peppers and pasta her mother has bought. Ask for directions and an old man wants to practise the English he picked up from soldiers during World War II. Laundry is draped from one side of the street to the other – like strips of pasta hanging to dry from on high. Plants flourish on balconies, but they'd never survive at street level. All the while cars are edging past *motorinos* which are trying to avoid the passers-by, who are either totally oblivious or suspiciously eyeing anything on wheels.

East to San Lorenzo

Via Port' Alba travels east through the arch and then for a short distance becomes Via San Pietro a Maiella before reaching **Piazza Miraglia**. It might be too early yet for lunch, but make a note of Pizzeria Bellini near the corner of Via Santa Maria di Costantinopoli. It's one of the best in the city, and great fun when lively students from the surrounding university faculties pack it out at lunchtime (though this can make for surly waiters).

The statue of Dante looks down over the Naples piazza that bears his name

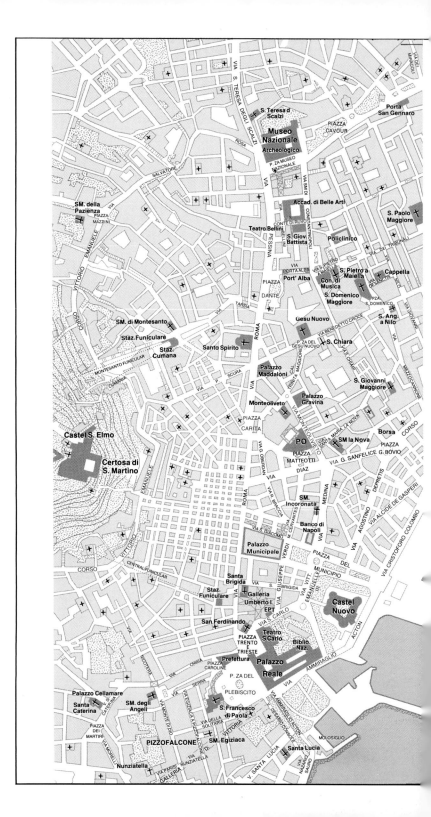

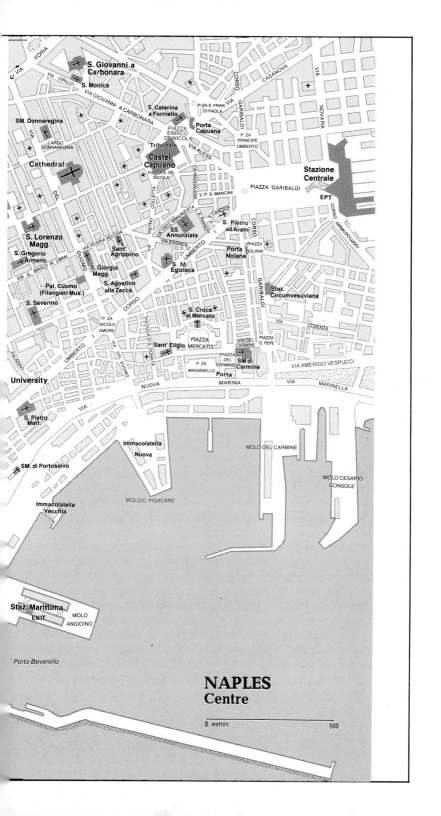

S. Giovanni a Carbonara
S. Monica
VIA CIRILLO
FORIA
VIA
VIA GIOVANNI A CARBONARA
S. Caterina a Foriello
P.ZA S. FRAN. DI PAOLA
VIA GARIBALDI
CORSO
CASANOVA
VIA
NOVARA
SM. Donnaregina
VIA
LARGO DONNAREGINA
PIAZZA ENRICO DE NICOLA
Porta Capuana
P. ZA PRINCIPE UMBERTO
Tribunale
Cathedral
Castel Capuano
PIAZZA E. DE NICOLA
VIA ALESS
DEL
V. P. S. MANCINI
Stazione Centrale
PIAZZA GARIBALDI
EPT
VIA MADDALENA
S. Lorenzo Magg.
VIA VICARIA VECCHIA
PIETRO
VIA DELL'ANNUNZIATA
SS Annunziata
VIA A. RANIERI
VIA CANDIDA
S. Pietro ad Aram
CORSO
CORSO ARNALDO LUCCI
S. Gregorio Armeno
AI LIBRAI
Sant' Agrippino
VIA EGIZIACA
UMBERTO
Porta Nolana
PIAZZA NOLANA
S. BIAGIO
DUOMO
S. Giorgio Magg.
S. M. Egiziaca
VIA
Pal. Cuomo (Filangieri Mus.)
S. Agostino alla Zecca
Staz. Circumvesuviana
S. Severino
CORSO
GARIBALDI
S. Croce al Mercato
COSENZA
VIA
P. ZA NICOLA AMORE
UMBERTO
VIA DEL CARMINE
PIAZZA G. PEPE
PADDONO
VIA DEL DUOMO
VIA DUCA DI S. DONATO
Sant' Eligio
PIAZZA MERCATO
VIA AMERIGO VESPUCCI
University
P. ZA MASANIELLO
PIAZZA DEL CARMINE
SM di Carmine
Porta
NUOVA
MARINA
VIA
MARINELLA
S. Pietro Mart.
VIA
Immacolatella Nuova
MOLO DEL CARMINE
SM. di Portosalvo
MOLO CESARIO CONSOLE
Immacolatella Vecchia
MOLO C. PISACANE
Staz. Marittima
ENIT
MOLO ANGIOINO

Porto Beverello

NAPLES
Centre

0 metres   500

On the north west corner of Piazza Miraglia is the elegant **Cappella Pontano**, constructed in 1492 as a funerary vault for Giovanni Pontano's wife Adriana Sassone. The small, simple interior is offset by its beautifully detailed majolica floor. Just beyond the chapel is the church of **Santa Maria Maggiore detta La Pietrasanta**. Building began on Roman foundations under the Bishop Pomponio in the first half of the sixth century, and was among the first four parishes in Naples. But it was rebuilt beginning in 1653, partially redesigned by Cosimo Fanzago. Pietrasanta, or holy stone, refers to the name added in the late 17th century, when a stone within began to attract followers. It was carved with the sign of the cross, and those who kissed it were said to receive plenary indulgences. The fantastic, swirling cotto and majolica patterned floor was restored in 1992. The church's medieval bell-tower is one of Naples' oldest, dating from the 11th century. It is separate from the church and standing to the south east.

A small church with a long name – **Santa Maria delle Anime del Purgatorio ad Arco** is next on the left, at the beginning of Via Dei Tribunali. You are greeted by three bronze skulls on stone columns at street level. Begun in 1604, its façade was reworked by Fanzago in 1652 and again refurbished in 1716. Climb the stairs to a church rich in marble and mother-of-pearl tarsio decoration. The side chapels are as richly decorated with artwork: in the third chapel on the left is Andrea Vaccaro's *Transito di San Giuseppe*, painted in the middle of the 17th century; in the third chapel on the left is an early work by Luca Giordano, *Sant'Alessio Moribondo*, signed and dated 1661.

Farther along on the **Piazza Gaetano** (under which part of the ancient Forum lies) is the church of **San Paolo Maggiore**, built in 1603 by Francesco Grimaldi. The inlaid marble work within is beautiful; frescoes by Massimo Stanzione are on the ceiling, though I think overshadowed by those done by Francesco Solimena in the sacristy. There is a very pretty cloister. This was first the site of the Temple of the Dioscuri, and its two Augustan columns with Corinthian capitals extend out from the church's façade.

San Lorenzo Maggiore

Across the piazza is the entrance to a more interesting church – **San Lorenzo Maggiore**, erected at the end of the 13th century. It is named for the martyred saint who was literally grilled to death over an open flame. The visiting Florentine Boccaccio met his love Maria here in 1334, whom he immortalised as Fiametta in many of his works, including the *Decameron*:

> I found myself in a gracious and beautiful church in Parthenope named after him who, to make himself immortal, endured to be offered on the gridiron. Now while I stood there . . . there appeared to me the marvellous beauty of a young woman . . . my heart began to flutter so strongly that it was as if I could feel it throbbing in the smallest pulses of my body.

I can't guarantee that anything similar will happen to you, but visit San Lorenzo just the same. Erected by the Franciscans, a mix of architectural styles, (thanks to successive earthquakes) is obvious at the entrance, and even more so once inside. The Gothic doorway is set into a Baroque exterior by Sanfelice; within, the Gothic nave with its trio of arches before the high altar has been restored to its simple state, while the apse and its nine radiating chapels were never modernised. In the first chapel to the left of the altar is a *Crucifixion with St Francis and Franciscan Saints* painted by Mattia Preti in 1660; his *Madonna and Child with Franciscan Saints* is on the adjacent wall. The high altar is by Giovanni da Nola, with its statues of Sts Lorenzo, Anthony and Francis; relief panels of the saints are below. Directly to the right is the tomb of Catherine of Austria. With its twisting columns and delicate figures, it is said to be Tino di Camaino's first work done in Naples, commissioned by the Angevin court in 1323.

The 18th-century cloisters of San Lorenzo are entered through doors to the right of the altar, or through a separate door beside the entrance. The four side passages are raised about 2m above the sunken grassy centre, where a forsaken well sits amid toppled columns and broken capitals. This seems an odd and lonely place, but perhaps the thought of Petrarch suffering through an incredible storm here in 1345 aided my impression: 'What a deluge! What trembling of the earth and roaring of the sea! What human shouts!' he wrote. He and the Franciscan monks might have been safest of all in the subterranean passages beneath the church which reveal traces of Greek structures and Roman walls. (Ask the sacristan to lead you down.)

Via San Gregorio Armeno

From Piazza Gaetano, **Via San Gregorio Armeno** runs south, and is worth a detour for its 16th-century church of the same name. Before reaching the church, the entrance to the cloisters is on the right (ring the bell set just within the gate). After Santa Chiara, these are my favourite cloisters in Naples – overflowing with greenery, the yellow-and-green tiled cupola of the church poking up beyond the far wall. Though the Benedictine nuns live in the building above the cloisters, the atmosphere here does not feel confining. In the nineteenth century, girls were sent here to atone for unacceptable behaviour in the eyes of their noble families, and their spirits live on. The nuns here have their own miracle to rival San Gennaro, when the blood of Santa Patrizia liquifies seemingly on request.

The Benedictine nuns have been blessed with visits by restoration experts from Rome; their meticulous work on a cycle of frescoes was finished last year. You will see their handiwork upon entering San Gregorio Armeno – the walls and gilded arched ceiling are covered with the story of the life of the saint. Frescoes between the windows are by Luca Giordano; the Baroque organs here are the most elaborate I've ever seen.

This street is a delight to walk down, filled with the workshops of Neapolitans who sculpt the figurines which fill the Nativity scene of the Christmas creche. In Naples it is known as the *presepio*, a famous part of the holiday tradition. Some churches are renowned for elaborate creche scenes devised 200 years ago. They inspire ordinary citizens to do their best by coming to this street at

Via San Gregorio Armeno, Naples

all times of the year to buy clay and plaster fishmongers, bakers, cheese sellers, wise men, hovering angels and the ubiquitous Christ child in a basket of hay. You can purchase a whole pizzeria in miniature, or a basket of mussels the size of a coin. These delightful representations of daily and divine life make their way to all parts of Italy for sale before Christmas (at many times the Neapolitan price!).

The Duomo

Head back up to Via dei Tribunali, turn right, and walk until you reach Via Duomo. Turn left, and the **Duomo** will be just up on the right. This is not one of the city's most impressive architectural monuments, but the patron saint of Naples, San Gennaro, calls it home. Charles I of Anjou began the French Gothic cathedral in 1294 and Robert the Wise finished the work in 1323. The earthquake of 1456 shattered all but the façade, which had already been rebuilt after an earthquake in 1407.

To the left above the central doorway is the tomb of Charles of Anjou, but the original was destroyed in the earthquake and it's unlikely that any of the man's bones found their way back to his resting place. The ceiling was painted by Fabrizio Santafede in 1621; Luca Giordano and pupils frescoed the 46 saints on the walls above the arches. The third chapel on the south side, with its intricate gilded bronze gates by Cosimo Fanzago, is dedicated to San Gennaro. This is High Baroque at its zenith. The dome was frescoed by Lanfranco; the altarpiece to the right is by Ribera. The head of the saint is stored within a tabernacle behind the altar, along with two phials of his blood.

The cathedral's famous patron saint proves himself worthy by producing a miracle not once, but three times, each year for it is claimed that San Gennaro's blood liquefies within the small phials stored in the chapel. If the ceremony happens quickly, this is a sign of good luck for the city. But if it happens slowly – or, God forbid, not at all – then times will be hard for the Neapolitans. (Ten minutes is quick work; a half hour is agonising.) The head of the saint must always be near the capsules for the miracle to work. Since 1398, the miracle has been documented in this way: on the Saturday before the first Sunday in May the blood liquefies in the church of Santa Chiara (the phials and head taken by procession from the Duomo), then in the Duomo on 19 September and again on 16 December. The churches are packed, but very few people are ever close enough to see whether the hard red substance has turned into liquid. In the late 19th century, a Professor Albini declared the liquid to be a kind of chocolate, but he and his kind were hushed up.

Art experts might argue that the devastating earthquake of 1980 actually produced a different kind of miracle in the Duomo. Strangely enough, the violent tremors uncovered early art works within the side chapels of Santo Spenno and San Massimo on either side of the high altar. Much older frescoes were discovered for the first time and have since been restored, resulting in the layered look of both chapels' walls. One of the most beautiful Renaissance works in Naples lies beneath the main altar. This is the crypt or Capella Carafa, its ornamental work and statue of Cardinal Carafa done by Tommaso Malvito from 1497 to 1506.

Leaving the Duomo, head south on Via Duomo past Via San Biagio dei Librai until you see the **Palazzo Cuomo** on your right, close to the corner of Via D'Alagno. This dark and aggressive façade conceals the **Museo Filangieri**, full of eclectic treasures collected by Prince Gaetano Filangieri. The 17th-century scale model of Naples is one of the most interesting pieces. The model shows that there was slightly more breathing room three hundred years ago, but you'll be able to identify many of the monuments dotted around the city. The museum houses everything from Greek coins and Sevres vases to delicate works in lace.

West along Via San Biagio

Return by Via Duomo to Via San Biagio dei Librai and turn left there. At No.81 you'll come to the **Doll Hospital**. The man who calls himself the doctor here is Luigi Grassi. His grandfather, who designed scenery for the San Carlo Opera House, developed this business as a sideline almost one hundred years ago. But the state of the shop attests to the fact that repairing dolls is no longer a sideline. Signor Grassi is happily entrapped in the limbs of porcelain, wax and wooden creatures. It is a highly 'animated' scene – these dolls, puppets and broken busts all seem to be in the midst of conversation – but you will always be welcome to enter and add to the confusion.

A detour you must take is to the **Cappella Sansevero**, now a private museum. Walking down Via San Biagio, turn right on Via Nilo and then left to 19 Via Francesco de Sanctis. The building (down on the right) was founded in 1590 by Prince Raimondo di Sangro as the family burial chapel, but over the entrance is a sculptural relief of one family member who refuses to be interred. Don Cecco di Sangro is climbing out of his coffin in the hope of heading off to another military campaign.

The chapel's most impressive Baroque work is the *Veiled Christ* by sculptor Giuseppe Sammartino, worked from a single block of marble. Lying in the centre of the chapel, the shroud actually looks like a thin, translucent cover for the body laying beneath; the crown of thorns is at his feet near a pair of pliers with the pulled nails that have released Christ from the cross. The other powerful piece of sculpture here is by Francesco Queirolo from Genoa. Called *Disillusion*, it shows a man said to represent Prince Raimondo's father struggling to free himself from vice, which takes the form of a net incredibly worked in marble. In the chapel's crypt are very strange examples of the Prince's alchemical experiments: the upper bodies of two human skeletons, covered with wires meant to show how and where blood travels through the heart and lungs.

From the chapel's entrance, turn right and return to Via San Biagio by way of **Vico San Domenico Maggiore** to visit the Gothic church of that name. In the piazza to the right, San Domenico was built in the late 13th century and the adjoining monastery, where St Thomas Aquinas once stayed, is run by

The Doll Hospital, Via San Biagio dei Librai, Naples

Dominican friars. Once you have climbed the steps to the basilica, you will find yourself behind the high altar. There are many tombs within, and very good examples of Renaissance sculpture by Malvito, Camaiano and followers, and Jacopo della Pila.

The little church of **Sant' Angelo a Nilo** is nearby, on the square's south east corner. Naples' first Renaissance work is here – the tomb of Cardinal Brancaccio beside the high altar. It was done in Pisa by Donatello, Michelozzo and Pagno di Lapo Portigiano, and shipped here in 1428. Donatello was definately responsible for the delicate relief panel on the side of the tomb facing the altar, called *Assumption of the Madonna*, but art experts no longer think he sculpted the cardinal's head.

Naples never yearned to be the Florence of the south, and its architects were unapologetically more enthusiastic when it came to creating monuments in the Baroque style. Personally, I try to limit my exposure to it, but not when it comes to the city's obelisks. One of the three in Naples is in nearby **Piazza Domenico Maggiore**. Called a *guglia* in Italian, this obelisk was actually started in 1658, two years after Neapolitans voted to put one there after the plague of 1656. But it wasn't finished by Vaccaro until 1737 when a bronze statue of San Domenico was added as the finishing touch at the top.

Piazza Gesù Nuovo and Santa Chiara

The way west now becomes Via Benedetto Croce. On the left, at No.45, you pass the once sumptuous **Palazzo Carafa**, built at the end of the 16th century but modified to accommodate the popular Baroque style at the beginning of the 18th century. Two gryphon-like dogs of stone stand guard at the entrance. You soon reach **Piazza Gesù Nuovo** with its own encrusted *Guglia della Immacolata*, erected in about 1750 through a public collection. On the north side of the square is the church of **Gesù Nuovo**, and its overblown Baroque interior has kept me from entering more than once, despite the appeal made by an old man on the local bus: 'To me it is the most beautiful church in the world. I am only saddened that our city doesn't take better care of it.' Every inch of gold and bronze gleams within, so I'm not sure what he was complaining about. The most interesting thing about the church is the contrast between its stark Renaissance exterior (like that of Palazzo Cuomo) and the completely unexpected explosion of colour inside.

At the southern end of the square is **Santa Chiara** and its famous majolica cloisters (one place you should not miss seeing). The early 14th-century church was badly bombed in World War II but the city wisely decided to return the interior to its original Gothic simplicity. Walk behind the high altar for a look at the tomb of Robert the Wise. Though damaged, Florentine brothers Giovanni and Pacio Bertini sculpted this impressive piece in 1343–45, with the six Virtues upon pillars which support the sarcophagus. On the front and sides are figures representing the king and his family.

Before visiting the cloisters, it is worth spending the small fee to see the presepio nearby. It's a finely crafted representation of the Wise Men visiting

The cloisters of Santa Chiara, Naples

the Christ Child. Exotic animals are crowded next to Neapolitans carrying on with daily life; people hang over balconies or do their shopping, with the requisite ruins in the background. Hanging from the star of Bethlehem is the very thing needed to keep evil spirits away – the *cornuto*, a small horn-shaped amulet hanging from the star's bottom point. What better place for this Neapolitan good luck charm than here?

The **cloisters of Santa Chiara** are a true oasis in the heart of old Naples. The walls, benches and octagonal columns are lined with brightly coloured land and seascapes depicted on majolica tiles. (The name majolica derives from the island of Majorca, where this pottery with its brownish-red base and richly coloured, glossy glazes has been made since the 12th century.) Some of the thickest vines I've ever seen wind their way up toward the overhead arbour, and even the weeds which surround the four-square pathways are lusciously green. The Rococo architect Domenico Vaccaro finished these unusual cloisters in 1742 and they have been used regularly by Neapolitans ever since. To spend a Sunday morning here is to be invited into an eccentric Italian's garden. Children skip rope or help push a younger sibling's pram; some adults read the newspaper while others just meet to exchange local gossip.

Monteoliveto and north to Piazza Dante

The church of **Monteoliveto**, or **Sant' Anna dei Lombardi**, is not far away, and after a trek here you'll be rewarded with a stop at one of Naples' most famous

35

bakeries. On the southeast corner of Piazza Gesù, take the Calatà Trinita Maggiore south, crossing the main road up to Piazza Monteoliveto. But before visiting this church, let me just digress (at the risk of decreasing your appetite) to list the odd assortment of relics kept within **Santa Maria Donnalbina**. The relics of a saint are important to any church's sanctity and identity, but priests here have been more conscientious than most. The following relics are said to lie within: a thorn from the crown worn by Jesus; one of Saint Sebastian's arms; a thighbone from the martyred Saint Arsenio; a breast of Saint Agatha the Virgin; and finally a piece of skin from the body of San Lorenzo said to liquify each year on his birthday. (The church is reached by going south on Via Monteoliveto and taking a left on Via Donn' Albina, but it has been closed *per restauro* for some years now.)

But back to Sant'Anna dei Lombardi, one of the most interesting in Naples for its Renaissance sculpture. The best work here is a terracotta Pietà, with eight figures, in the Chapel of Santo Sepolcro, reached by going right before the high altar and walking to the end of the corridor. The group is by Guido Mazzoni, done in 1492. In the Piccolomini Chapel to the left of the entrance is a lovely sculptured relief, *Adoration of the Shepherds*, by Antonio Rossellino dated 1475. Frescoes by Giorgio Vasari in the vault only convince me that he was better off devoting himself to writing about the lives of the artists than to competing with their talent.

From Piazza Monteoliveto take Via Caravita out to Via Roma and walk north toward Piazza Dante. On your right at No.13 you'll come to a wonderful old pastry shop called Fratelli Cappuccio. Stop in to fortify yourself before making your way to see the Greek statuary and treasures from Pompeii and Herculaneum at the National Archeological Museum. Coffee at Cappuccio is excellent, not to mention the finger-like almond cakes called *cartucci* and the *sfogliatelle* filled with cherries and ricotta cheese.

Via Roma becomes Via Pessina north from Piazza Dante, and you'll see the large building housing the National Archeological Museum up on the far right hand and corner. Walk through the **Galleria Principe di Napoli** on the eastern side of Via Pessina. This three-armed, glass-domed gallery is the oldest in the city, constructed in the 1880s. Like London's Crystal Palace, it was a technological breakthrough with its use of iron struts and glass. But it was never as popular as the Galleria Umberto I built ten years later; most of its original shops now serve as municipal offices.

The Museo Nazionale Archeologico

The northern entrance of the Galleria Principe di Napoli takes you out to **Piazza Museo Nazionale** – not really a square but the beginning of a wide avenue. The 16th-century building, used as a barracks and then as part of the university, was remodelled as a museum in 1790. It houses one of the richest collections of antiquities in the world. When all of its rooms are open it is a huge place to roam around in, with so many important works that it's worth spending quite a bit of time here or coming more than once. I'd suggest that it is worth purchasing the pictorial English guide to the museum in the little shop just inside the entrance. This is mainly to locate objects visually, because some are poorly labelled, if at all, and due to earthquake damage works are occasionally moved as rooms are still being renovated.

The main hall on the ground floor, the *Grande Atrio dei Magistrati*, is full of astoundingly large pieces of sculpture. The marble sarcophagus (No.6705) is from Pozzuoli and carved by Roman sculptors in the third century. Prometheus is at the centre on the bottom row, moulding man from clay, and deities such as Psyche and Zeus surround him. It's an animated scene with an amazing amount of detail in relief. The galleries to the right of the main hall contain a number of fine Greek works: the muscular Farnese Hercules; the Farnese Bull (one of the largest surviving works from ancient Rome, taken from the Baths of Caracalla); a Roman copy of Doryphoros, a boy carrying a spear; the headless statue of Nike; and the Aphrodite Sossandra from Baia, inspired by the original bronze done by Kalamis for the Acropolis in Athens. The Farnese collection has been beautifully restored; an added benefit to visitors is that the process has been well documented and explained, in Italian and English, on side panels beside the works.

On the left hand side of the mezzanine floor are some of Italy's finest treasures – the spectacular mosaics from Pompeii. They are all so well executed and, in most cases well preserved, that I'm hard pressed to single any out. The largest mosaic, of Darius and Alexander at the Battle of Issus, is probably the most dramatic, but not my favourite. I think the Nile scenes, the winged boy on a lion, and the marine creatures are far more compelling. But the most endearing mosaic is by far the least elaborate, that of the small skeleton in black and white. This symbol appeared in many Pomeiian kitchens as a reminder to eat, drink and be merry while in good health because, as the skeleton signifies, life all too soon wastes away. The artist's simple work reminded me a child's efforts to draw the human form. I love the way the artist got away with omitting the hands by having the skeleton carry jugs instead.

The *Gran Salone del Atlante* on the first floor has been under restoration (for its highly decorated ceiling) but should now be open and is the best way through to the wall paintings from Pompeii and Herculaneum. Most were taken from the walls of houses there and many represent scenes from the Greek myths. In room LXXI is Hercules and his son Telephus, who is being suckled by a deer – full of symbolism and strong detail; in the next room is the Sacrifice of Iphigenia being carried away by Ulysses and another young hero while Iphigenia's father, Agememnon, turns his back on the scene; in the same room is Perseus and Andromeda, as he frees her after killing the sea monster. Wall paintings from Stabia, a town south of Pompeii which was also destroyed by Vesuvius, are in room LXXIV. They are much more delicate depictions of lighter subjects, especially the personification of Spring – a young girl, with her back to us, daintily gathering flowers.

WALK 2
Edging beyond ancient boundaries: Castel Capuano and east

This eastern section of Naples is just as dense with people and alleys as Spaccanapoli. Expansion here was more gradual, however; this area does not have the overwhelmingly consistent character that Spaccanapoli does. But the working-class neighborhood here is steeped in history, and in some ways is even more representative of the Neapolitan population as a whole (though you'll see more foreigners in this part of the city, which is full of cheap hotels). Portions of this walk are not pretty; traffic is heavy and persistent. But the churches are well worth viewing, the newly restored English cemetery is a worthy place of pilgrimage, and the market stalls lining Vico Sopramura are a typical part of daily life in Naples.

Castel Capuano to San Giovanni a Carbonara

The walk begins at the immense, white **Castel Capuano**, which doesn't look much like a castle. It was built during the second half of the 12th century, was adapted for use as a royal residence by Frederick II, was restored by Charles I of Anjou in 1266, and was the scene of the assassination of Caracciolo (Joan II's lover) in 1432. Since 1540, it has been the seat of the Court of Justice, but the castle's nickname of La Vicaria represents an unjust act practised just beyond the walls. La Colonna della Vicaria was a marble pillar where debtors were forced to strip and stand naked to declare bankruptcy and to hear the insulting accusations of their creditors. The pillar is gone now, taken to the San Martino Monastery (a museum in Naples' Vomero district) in 1856, but the name lives on. Walking across the bustling Piazza Enrico de Nicola you'll see the slightly less oppressive **Porta Capuana**. This triumphal arch between two squat Aragonese towers was designed by Giuliano da Maiano and erected in 1484. Market stalls and cars encircling the arch are dwarfed by the bulk of the two towers, christened 'Honour' and 'Virtue'. On the north side of this square is the elegant Renaissance church of **Santa Caterina a Formiello**. It was finished in 1593, its design attributed to Florentine Romolo Balsimelli and considered one of the most Tuscan churches in Naples.

Walk north on the Via Carbonara until it becomes Via Cirillo. On the left is the church of **San Giovanni a Carbonara**. The long curving steps up to the Gothic chapel of Santa Monica were designed by San Felice in 1708, but the church's original structure dates to 1343 and was then enlarged by King Ladislas in the early 15th century. Behind the high altar is the king's tomb, erected by his sister Joan II who succeeded him to the throne. Four colossal statues of Virtue hold up the 18m megalomaniac structure. There is some fine sculptural work by Marco and Andrea da Firenze in this piece, but King Ladislas' sister surely went over the top with this commission. Just behind this piece is the Cappella Caracciolo del Sole with a very pretty majolica floor, but the Cappella Caracciolo di Vico to the left of the chancel is really the most interesting part

The vast 15th-century archway of Porta Capuana, Naples

of the church. This unusual circular structure, laden with sculpture, might have been based on a design by Malvito in 1517; but the architect is unknown.

South West to Piazza Garibaldi

Retrace your steps to reach the **English cemetry**. Walk past the Castel Capuano and through Porta Capuana. Then head northeast on Via Martiri d'Otranto until you reach Via S. Maria di Fede on the left. You will come to Piazza S. Maria di Fede, and the cemetery sits on the northern side of the church of the same name. (The bigger Protestant cemetery is just to the east.) Abandoned for decades, this quiet outpost began life as a resting place for illustrious foreigners in 1826 through the efforts of the British Consul Sir Henry Lushington. Its nine statues and funerary munuments have been restored, thanks to the Comune di Napoli and the Fondazione Napoli '99 (see p. 19). The mathematician and physicist Mary Somerville, founder of the Oxford college, is buried here, along with celebrated archeologist Sir William Gell and botanist Friedrich Denhart.

From here, head south on Corso Garibaldi until you reach **Piazza Garibaldi**. Or, if the **Botanic Garden** is open (on Wednesdays and Thursdays from 09.00 until 14.00) head north on Via San Antonio Abate and then left on Vico San Antonio Abate; the garden is directly in front of you. Founded in 1807 by Joseph Bonaparte, it is a rare haven of green, with a gorgeous Neo-Classical greenhouse designed by Giuliano De Fazio. The University of Naples' Science Department has labs and a library here; 8000 species of Mediterranean flora continue to thrive. Beyond the Botanical Garden on the Via Foria is Piazza Carlo III, an uninspiring square dominated by the Albergo dei Poveri which opened in 1829 to house and educate orphans and invalids. It has been wrongly attributed to

A detail of the carving on the Porta Capuana

Vanvitelli, but was in fact initiated in 1751 by Carlo III's second official architect, Ferdinando Fuga. If you've come this far on the walk, hop on a bus that will take you down Corso Garibaldi to the piazza of the same name. **Piazza Garibaldi** is the centre of Naples' transportation network. Incessant traffic snakes in a figure of eight around the rectangular square. Buses from here will take you to any part of town; the Metropolitana stops here and in four other places in Naples, while the Circumvesuviana will take you to points east and west beyond the city. The square is lined with Italian and African vendors selling everything from braided bracelets to cheap mechanical toys. The area around almost any city's train station is insalubrious; Naples is no exception.

South towards the marina

On the south west corner of the square, Corso Garibaldi continues down to the new marina. Stop at Piazza Nolana, where the round towers (these two christened 'Faith' and 'Hope') mark the position of city gates constructed in the 15th century. Walk under the arch and then turn immediately left down Vico Sopramuro. The daily **market** here is a busy one: everything from fresh fish and wine to coconuts and dinner plates are on display. Heading south, turn right on Via del Carmine until you are in the busy Piazza Carmine – more of a parking lot than an open public square. The large ruins on the southern end are what remains of the Castello del Carmine, built in 1382 but for the most part demolished in 1906.

The grey and ochre-coloured church of **Santa Maria del Carmine** is at the square's northeast corner, there since the 12th century but enlarged between 1283 and 1300. Conradin is buried where his statue is displayed on the church's left side; the letters RCC mark the spot behind the high altar where he was first interred. When the coffin was discovered by workmen in the 1600s, it is said that the severed head and a sword were lying beside the body. But if the coffin were opened today, no sword would be found. Legend has it that Conradin's mother travelled to Naples and stole the sword (long after she died apparently, as Conradin died three centuries earlier . . .).

The church, with its pretty onion-domed bell-tower and cloisters, is dressed in fireworks for a fantastic spectacle on 16 July in honour of the Madonna 'Bruna' of the Carmine. She is pictured above the entrance, and many Neapolitans have a relationship with this Madonna that rivals tributes to the city's patron Saint Gennaro. On a Wednesday, Santa Maria del Carmine is filled with those praying for miracles because it was on a Wednesday, they say, that the Madonna Bruna healed the sick and wounded who filled her church.

Walk west now toward the Piazza del Mercato, where a small obelisk marks each corner. It is hard to imagine that this large car park was once Naples' most popular square – popular mainly because it was where public executions took place. It is where Conradin, last of the Hohenstaufens, was beheaded in 1268, after trying to recapture the throne at the age of 17. And this is where crowds who had supported Masaniello during a nine-day uprising in 1647 came to jeer as his dead body was dragged around the square.

41

Continue to walk west along the south side of the square until you reach the church of **Sant'Eligio**. Its original 13th-century structure came to light after the bombing of 1943, and was the first church constructed by the Angevin kings in Naples. That influence is especially seen in the French Gothic entrance, which is just beside the wonderful 14th-century bell-tower with its big round clock – now working again after a silence of fifty years.

South of Piazza Mercato is the new dock area, not especially picturesque unless you thrill to the sight of large ships unloading cargo, and boats ferrying passengers to and from Capri, Ischia, Sorrento and Amalfi. Our walk ends north of here, in the heart of the Rettifilo district. From Via Sant'Eligio, turn right on Via Duca di San Donato and walk north until reaching Corso Umberto I. To the left is Piazza Amore, where trams and buses travel east and west on the wide Corso, and north on Via Duomo.

WALK 3
The political centre: Piazza del Plebiscito and surroundings

If Spaccanapoli is the ancient heart of Naples, then the area around Piazza del Plebiscito is the modern centre of a city that has its share of political emergencies and journalists' deadlines masterminded by upwardly mobile professionals. Bank clerks, café waiters, civil servants and high-ranking public officials all make their way here daily. Via Chiaia, with its elegant shops, is Naples's answer to London's Bond Street, and the stylish cafés in and around the Galleria Umberto Primo cater to a crowd that aspires to be the most cosmopolitan in the city. But the seafront and its salty heritage is not far away, where the Castel dell' Ovo has planted its thick walls in the sea. The quarter of Santa Lucia faces the sea here, a traditional outpost for beached fishermen and fast women, but no longer the colourful scene it once was.

The Castel dell' Ovo

This area of Naples, from Castel Nuovo past Palazzo Reale down to the seafront, is just as full of history as any other. Start your walk by taking the causeway from Via Partenope out to the **Castel dell' Ovo** on the Borgo Marinaro. You are standing in front of the oldest fortress in Naples, the Castle of the Egg. I prefer to call it the Castle of the Enchanted Egg, being charmed by the legend of its foundation. This is where the siren Parthenope was said to have been washed ashore, and in the Middle Ages the legend spread that Virgil built this castle upon a submerged egg that was balanced on the seabed. Official record books tell a more straightforward story: the castle was constructed in 1154,

The imposing fortress of Castel dell' Ovo, Naples

used as a prison, as the site of duels and as a military barracks until recently. Robert the Wise commissioned Giotto to fresco the Chapel of the Saviour in 1309, but no traces of his work have been found by restoration experts.

The castle is now open to the public, though some halls are used for private conferences and lectures. The view of the bay from its upper terraces is superb, and to take a walk through the arched alleyways is to imagine yourself a citizen of an 800-year-old city-state. Appropriately, the Italian Castle Institute has an office here, along with the Alpine Hiking Club. The last time I wandered through I was amazed to see a sign for a poster shop. When I found the room, it was hardly the repository for picturesque landscapes that I thought it would be. The first poster read: 'Contribution of chest X-ray to the functional evaluation of patients with atrial septal defect'. It was the showcase for a European Conference of the International Society of Noninvasive Cardiology. I decided to be noninvasive myself, and went to sit on one of the large paved terraces in the sun.

The borgo surrounding the castle is home to a handful of lucky Neapolitans who have the sea lapping at their islet on three sides. Restaurants line the northern edge, my favourite being a simple little place sandwiched between two fancier ones. The sign above the back door simply says Cucina (kitchen), with a bar counter within and six or seven tables outside by the water. The owner was born 76 years ago in what is now the kitchen, and he'll serve you whatever is brewing on the stove that day – steamed mussels, fried calamari, pasta with those small, rich tomatoes from the slopes of Vesuvius. The fare isn't exceptional, but the setting is and you can't beat it for the price. Looking north from here, you'll see the more expensive restaurants of Ciro and Bersagliere that are packed on Saturday night and Sunday lunchtime. Just beyond, the city's best hotels line the Via Partenope.

From the seafront to the Palazzo Reale

Back on the mainland, turn right and walk to the end of Via Partenope before turning left on Via Console. On the corner here is the three-arched Baroque **Fontana dell' Immacolata**, worth seeing for its statues by Bernini, a fitting entrance to the city's yacht and rowing club, Rarinantes, below. Via Partenope now becomes Via Nazario; fishermen and swimmers clamber over huge volcanic boulders at the water's edge. (To avoid the traffic on this stretch you could cut through the Santa Lucia district in to the left.) Via Sauro bears left into Via Console, and the faded red façade of Palazzo Reale stretches out far to the right. You are now walking up to Piazza del Plebiscito, built during the brief reign of Joachim Murat in the early 1800s. The sweep of this large semicircular piazza is hard to appreciate with so many cars parked within inches of its Doric columns, but the statues of the Bourbon kings Charles III and his son Frederick IV on horseback manage to rise above the modern turmoil. In the centre of the curving colonnade is the church of San Francesco di Paola, an imitation of the Pantheon in Rome which was designed by Pietro Bianchi in 1817.

Immediately to your right is the façade of the **Palazzo Reale** built from 1600–1602 by Domenico Fontana. Eight Neapolitan kings stand guard in their niches along this wall, but the huge building was not inhabited by royalty until the Bourbons came to Naples in 1764. It had been used by Spanish viceroys before that time. The National Library is on the second floor; the Royal Apartments, now a museum, are on the first floor. The picture galleries at Capodimonte are so much better that I wouldn't recommend spending a lot of time viewing pictures here. However, *Patron Saints of Naples Adoring the Cross* by Luca Giordano, the *Annunciation* by Artemisia Gentileschi, and *Return of the Prodigal Son* by Mattia Preti are all powerful works. The beautiful marble Staircase of Honour on the left side of the inner courtyard is your way up to the museum.

Continue north beyond Palazzo Reale, across Piazza Trieste e Trento, to the **San Carlo Opera House** on Via San Carlo. The opera house is the largest in Italy and second in reputation only to La Scala in Milan. The season runs from September through to June, and you shouldn't leave Naples without attending some event here. (It's open from 09.00 to 12.00 weekdays, except Monday, so you can have a look inside without paying to see a performance, if you prefer.) It was first constructed in 1737 by Medrano, but the theatre was completely rebuilt after a fire gutted the interior in 1816. Verdi, Rossini and Donizetti composed operas for San Carlo; later the famous Caruso sang here for his fellow Neapolitans. Suffice to say that he wasn't well received, and vowed never to sing there again.

Castel Nuovo

Before walking through the famous Galleria Umberto I across from the opera house, continue down Via San Carlo to the **Castel Nuovo**. Neapolitans call it the Maschio Angioino, meaning Angevin fortress or keep. It was built for Charles

I of Anjou in 1279–82, but the structure changed many times in succeeding centuries. The most impressive part of its façade is the triumphal entrance arch – restored and unveiled in the autumn of 1988 with much ceremony. The marble arch was not erected until 1453–67, when Alfonso I of Aragon wanted to remind his subjects how lucky they were that he entered their city. This is one of the finest Renaissance monuments outside Tuscany.

The castle was host to Angevin and Aragon, to the abdication of Pope Celestin V, and to an unexpectedly bloody affair arranged by King Ferdinand I in what is now called the Hall of the Barons. Today it is used as the meeting place for both the City Council and the Regional Council of Campania, but in August, 1486, a different kind of political spirit was at work. King Ferdinand had crushed a revolt of the kingdom's princes, who had banded together and appealed to the Pope to dethrone the tyrants of Aragon. But the king negotiated with such goodwill that the princes were undermined, and to show them that there were no hard feelings Ferdinand suggested that the Count of Sarno hold the reception for his son's wedding at the castle. What a kind invitation! All the rebellious bigwigs were invited, and during a merry feast the drawbridge was lowered and the princes taken to the dungeons.

The Hall of Barons is across the large inner courtyard, up a staircase to the left. In the centre of the courtyard's far side is the gothic Church of Santa Barbara, or Palatine Chapel. It is now part of a civic museum which also includes a first floor picture gallery. The single-naved church was built in the 14th century; frescoes done by Giotto in 1330 once covered the walls. Unfortunately, his *Scenes from the Old and New Testaments* have not survived, save for thin fragments along the window frames. Other frescoes of the late fourteenth century line the walls, done by the Florentine Niccolo di Tommaso, and by lesser painters of the Florentine school. Sculpture done by artists who worked on the castle's entrance arch is also here, notably that of Domenico Gagini, who was an apprentice to Donatello and Brunelleschi.

The Crypt of the Barons is beneath the church, but it is closed to the public. The museum's custodian insists that mummified bodies are still there, but my own demands for proof proved worthless. Traveller Arthur Norway, writing in 1901, described what he found in the crypt:

> Within lies the mummy of a man, fearfully distorted by his agony, his cramped hands clutched desperately . . . the man was strangled, there can be no doubt of it; and there he lies to this hour, fully clothed in the garments which he wore when he came down that little winding stair, hose, buttons, and doublet intact.

The custodian tells a slightly different tale: of four adults and two children who starved to death, chained together but far enough apart so that they would not eat one another. My morbid curiosity was only partially satisfied when the custodian unlocked the rear door to a fantastic, tight spiral staircase. Standing beneath it, dead centre, I felt as if I was being swept up inside a stone cyclone.

Relief scenes on a set of massive bronze doors, recently restored, show Ferdinand of Aragon's victory over the rebelling barons in 1462. Oddly enough,

The triumphal entrance arch, Castel Nuovo, Naples

The soaring arcade of the Galleria Umberto Primo, Naples

a cannonball is embedded in one of the relief panels. One explanation for this mystery was a sudden assault on Castel Nuovo by the Spanish under Consalvo of Cordova, with the French desperately firing at the advancing troops from within. Another hypothesis has the doors sailing to France with other Neapolitan treasures looted by Charles VIII, and caught in the crossfire during the Battle of Rapallo between the French and Genoese. The victorious citizens of Genoa then returned the doors to their rightful owners.

Pizzofalcone

Walk back up the Via San Carlo and directly across from the opera house you will see the entrance to the Galleria Umberto Primo, one of the symbols of the city. The soaring arcade is in the shape of a cross, with four entrances. It opened to the public in 1900, but was badly damaged during World War II when thousands of panes of glass from the roof lay broken on the floor. Now it is full of shops at ground level, with offices on another four. Heading left out to Via Toledo, you are across from the popular café called Caflish, a great place for pastries and a *granita di caffe con panna*, iced coffee with cream.

A break from history and architecture takes you past the shopfronts of such fashionable designers as Armani and Valentino, so from the south-western corner of nearby Piazza Trieste e Trento head down Via Chiaia. This is the place to window-shop, one display vying with the next. Naples' famous chocolate maker, Gay-Odin, is in a wonderful old wooden-fronted shop at No.237 (their factory is open to the public at 12 Via Vetriera). Not much further on, men's shirts are made to order by Giuseppe Buccafusca at No.43; the next shop is Aldanese, selling ribbon, lace, and gorgeous strips of sequins, coral

47

and mother-of-pearl. A wonderful dressmaker, Concettina Buonanno, is at No.30 Piazza dei Martiri.

The funny thing about this district, between Piazza dei Martiri and Piazza del Plebiscito, is that it was once the site of Naples' only volcano, and the crater still exists. The area is known to Neapolitans as Pizzofalcone (falcon's peak), and part of the first Greek colony is said to have risen on its promontory. The spent volcano of Mount Echia has not erupted for centuries, but mineral waters surged through the ground for many decades. The impotent crater is now just a large hole filled with vegetation, suffocated by the surrounding houses near Vico Santa Maria a Cappella Vecchia.

WALK 4
On the waterfront: From Villa Comunale to Mergellina

Naples opens wide on this walk, an area much less dense than those covered in the first three walks. The greenery of the Villa Comunale and the wide avenue of Riviera di Chiaia are centuries removed from a quarter such as Spaccanapoli. The grand sweep of the Bay, the view which inspired the phrase 'see Naples and die', dominates this walk. The city's layout will become more apparent, with the Castel dell'Ovo to the east, and the hills of the Posillipo and Vomero districts above. The walk itself is less than two kilometres from east to west, and takes about three hours.

Villa Pignatelli and Villa Comunale

Your first stop is the **Villa Pignatelli Museum**, half-way down the Riviera di Chiaia. It was built in the 1820s for Ferdinand Acton, who distinguished himself by being in the right place on the family tree, having a famous father in the admiral and a famous son in the author and historian. The villa was later owned by the Rothschild family and then by the Aragonese family of Pignatelli. It was bequeathed to the state in 1952 and became a museum in 1960. Lush gardens of palm and pine surround the white Neo-Classical villa; I think this is one of the prettiest and most peaceful areas of greenery in all of Naples. Many rooms of the museum have been restored to reflect early 19th-century interiors: ornate mirrors and settees, high candelabras, sumptuous silver tableware, and porcelain from Naples and other parts of Italy and Europe. This isn't a museum for picture viewing; the best works are the stately carriages shown in five large rooms near the back of the garden.

Back on the Riviera di Chiaia, cross over to the **Villa Comunale** which runs along the seafront. Spanish viceroys paraded along this leafy stretch, and gathered with other members of the aristocracy. But Ferdinand IV proclaimed

Lush gardens surround the Villa Pignatelli Museum, Naples

it a public park in 1780. It now has a neglected air: its fountains empty and scribbled with graffiti, with traffic whizzing by north and south. The Villa Comunale's best feature is its newly restored aquarium in the centre, said to be the oldest in Europe and founded in 1872 by German Antonio Dohrn. Small tanks, flanked by columns, hold 200 species of marine life which swim in salt water pumped from the bay. A highly regarded marine biology laboratory operates here, and hopes are that its research professors will find a way to counteract the horrendous pollution of the Mediterranean; twelve countries are involved in the effort.

Just to the west of the aquarium is the a statue of Philosopher Giambattista Vico, and this seems a good time for a short philosophy lesson in honour of one of Naples' most famous citizens. The son of a bookseller, he lived from 1668 to 1744 and revived the theory of recurring cycles in history. He was a professor of rhetoric at the university in Naples; his famous *Scienza Nuova* studies and describes the imaginative faculty, along with the nature of poetry and the origins of language. Vico was not well understood during his lifetime, remained in obscurity for decades after his death and is still an unfamiliar name to most people. Yet his ideas helped to shape some of Croce's philosophy, and his writings have continued to influence modern thinking about history and literature.

Santa Maria di Piedigrotta and 'Virgil's Tomb'

From the Villa Comunale, walk toward the seafront and head west on Via Carracciolo for about one kilometre. The walk will end at the Mergellina port area farther along the avenue, but turn right on Via Sannazzarro, and walk through the piazza of the same name up to Piazza Piedigrotta. Up on the left you will see the church of **Santa Maria di Piedigrotta**. Though the church was built in the 14th century, it was completely remodelled in the 1800s and the interior gives no hint of its earlier architectural heritage. Santa Maria di Piedigrotta is famous for its festival in early September. Fireworks, colourful streamers and excited children are all part of the revelry, as well as Neapolitan songs composed especially for the occasion. Naples' second largest train station, Mergellina, is just north.

If you would like to pay tribute to both Virgil and the poet Giacomo Leopardi, author of the lyrical *I Canti*, climb up to the Parco Virgiliano. The little park was created in 1930 to commemorate Virgil's birth two thousand years before, though this spot has been well known to literary travellers since the 16th century. To get there, walk along the church's north side, under the railroad tracks near the tunnel entrance of the Galleria Quattro Giornate. You'll see the entrance to the small park on your left. After walking through the gate and up a steep alleyway you'll come to Leopardi's tomb, moved here from a demolished church in 1939. (Leopardi was from the northern Italian town of Recanati, but died of cholera here in 1837. His devoted friend Antonio Ranieri is said to have saved him from burial in a mass grave, carrying his body through the streets of Naples at midnight to the church of S. Vitale a Fuorigrotta.)

The so-called **tomb of Virgil** (no one seriously believes he is buried here) is above, a niche with its sepulchral urn. A Latin inscription reads: 'Ravaged the tomb, and broken the urn. Nothing remains. Yet the poet's name exalts this place.' Just beyond is the Grotta Romana, a long tunnel now closed which connected Naples to Pozzuoli in Roman times. Neapolitans add to the myth of Virgil as magician by saying that in his wizardry he excavated the grotto himself. The view is excellent, one that must have been very familiar to romantic landscape painters of the Scuola di Posillipo, such as Vanvitelli's father Gaspar van Wittel and Jakob Philip Hackert, who worked not far from here.

Mergellina

Retrace your steps and head for the port area of **Mergellina**. Bow to bow, bumper to bumper, the humble fishing boats here are moored in such a haphazard way that only a Neapolitan could be in charge. Fishermen's shacks line the docks, and they are full of families having their pasta, sorting the day's catch and repairing nets and conical cages. One of Naples' best maintained shrines to the Virgin is near the docks, protected from the elements by a Perspex cover – as if to remind her that sailors need similar protection when braving the sea. Stalls lining the sidewalk sell an array of squirming, silvery fish which I'm sad to say has a reputation for looking better than it tastes. I'd stick to souvenirs of shells and coral.

Panoramic views of the Gulf of Naples can be enjoyed from Posillipo

This part of Naples has a festive atmosphere as the sun sets. Strings of coloured bulbs hung from the restaurant façades blink on like so many stage lights, illuminating various entertaining places for pizza and pasta which are absolutely packed in the summertime. The building behind, which houses the funicular to Posillipo, looks like the entrance to a turn-of-the-century fairground. This is a good spot for people-watching, strolling along the port past stalls that sell salted nuts, coconut slices and cups of lemon ice. The carnival atmosphere is alive and well with sellers of cheap little treasures such as the plastic *cornuto* and shell-covered vases. By bus or funicular, you can climb up to the expensive residential quarter of Posillipo for the famous postcard panorama of the gulf and, at one of the outside bars on Via Petrarca, sip a *cappuccino* with the city spread out below and Vesuvius standing silent guard beyond.

WALK 5
Hilltop museum hopping: Capodimonte and the Vomero

This tour involves walking, but not through narrow streets seeking churches and Renaissance palazzi. Walk 5 is actually two separate tours, within museums mostly, and because they are both on hills above the city you will need to take a cab or public transport to reach them. If you've only got one morning to devote to seeing art then I'd recommend heading for the Museum and National Galleries at Capodimonte, where you can expect to spend about two hours. I especially like the galleries here because you are not overwhelmed – on exhibit are ten to twelve excellent works from each important period of Italian painting with examples by Masaccio, Botticelli, Titian, Carracci and Caravaggio, among others.

The second tour, a bit longer and taking in three sights, is in a residential district called the Vomero. The Carthusian Monastery of San Martino is the main attraction. Portraits, landscapes and maps in its museum elucidate Neapolitan history while giving you a fantastic view of the city. Above the monastery is the huge Castel Sant'Elmo and about one kilometre away is the Villa Floridiana, a ceramics museum surrounded by a park.

Capodimonte

Capodimonte is just that – the top of the hill. This big park and its galleries are in the north central section of the city, and the best way to get there is to take Bus No.24 or 110 from Piazza Garibaldi, or No.160 or 161 from Piazza Dante, then turn left up the hill to the Porta Piccola gates which take you into the park. This is a popular setting for wedding photos, and on weekends hundreds of Neapolitan families come to picnic and relax.

The Bourbon King Charles III commissioned Medrano, the same architect who designed the opera house, to begin the rather severe Neo-Classical **palace** in 1738. He liked this plot of land because it was a good place to hunt, and he wanted a suitable home for the Roman Farnese collection which came to him through his mother, Elizabeth Farnese. It has been said that the paintings suffered while they waited for a home: stacked in hallways and stairways at the Palazzo Reale, visitors complained that bratty delivery boys peed on the Titians and Caravaggios. Carlo also initiated the porcelain works on the grounds of Capodimonte, rivalling his father-in-law Frederick Augustus, Elector of Saxony and King of Poland's factory at Meissen. (The factory no longer produces any porcelain, but some buildings are used as an art college.)

The palace became a museum in 1957. Before viewing the paintings, take time to see the Chinese-style Salottino di Porcellana in room No.94 on the first floor. Everything but the floor and black marble skirting board is made of porcelain, designed by German artist Johann Sigismund Fischer in 1757 for Charles III's wife Maria of Saxony. The white background is festooned with delicate but colourful relief decoration: fruit baskets, birds and butterflies are interspersed with scenes of Chinese men and women. The factory staff was employed full-time for two years on producing the 3000 porcelain pieces needed to decorate the room. Also displayed on the first floor are objects that furnished the Royal Apartments during the 18th century: tapestries, landscape paintings, small ivories, jewellery, gilded chairs and tables, along with more porcelain from the Bourbon collection (though most pieces were taken to Spain by Charles III).

The second floor is where it is worth spending most of your time. (A word of warning however: ongoing renovation has meant that a selection of paintings was moved temporarily to the first floor while the second floor was closed. To avoid confusion, I have not referred to the room number in which a painting hangs.) Notwithstanding, works are displayed in a chronological order and well marked by period, so that one of the first set of rooms you enter is of 14th and 15th-century Sienese and Florentine paintings. The best among them is Masaccio's grief-stricken Mary Magdalen in the *Crucifixion*, a small but very powerful work done in 1426 for the Church of the Carmine in Pisa. Botticelli's *Virgin and Child with Angels* was painted in 1470 when he was just 26. Mantegna is represented by his beautiful soft portrait of *Francesco Gonzaga* who became cardinal at the age of 16, and by his long, dark painting of *Saint Eufemia* holding a white lily. An outstanding work is Bellini's *Transfiguration*.

Parmigianino's restored *Portrait of Antea*, is among the best paintings by the Emilian Mannerists. It's a strange scene – she with the small head, and the ferret baring its teeth. A superb work by El Greco, done in 1577, is called *Youth Blowing on Hot Coals*, with its rich and eerie shades of brown. The *Annunciation* is the first Titian we see at Capodimonte, and one room is devoted to his works – take a close look at his sexy *Danaë* and his unfinished portrait of *Pope Paul III* with his Farnese nephews. There is a change of scene with Flemish Masters, and I didn't expect to be so moved by Pieter Brueghel the Elder's *Blind Leading the Blind* and his allegorical *Misanthrope* which depicts corruption of the church through a boy cutting the money bag (shaped like a heart) from beneath a priest's robe. These paintings seem strangely modern to me, smoky and disturbing scenes painted a year before his death in 1568.

Take time to see Claude Lorrain's large evocative painting of the Roman countryside, *Landscape with the Nymph Egeria*, and my favourite paintings in this museum: Carlo Saraceni's scenes of the life of Icarus – *Flight*, *Fall*, and *Burial*. Art experts don't single this Roman painter out, except to say that he was influenced by Caravaggio. But his touch here is, thankfully, so much lighter than Caravaggio's, full of delicate whimsy and a sensitivity for the tragic folly of Icarus. They are offset by Caravaggio's stormy *Flagellation*, though his *Seven Acts of Mercy* is no longer here, but back in its original position at the church of Monte della Misericordia near the Duomo. Artemesia Gentileschi, one of the few recognised women artists of the period, is represented by her strong portrayal of *Judith* painted in 1630.

The only element I found lacking in the galleries was adequate seating; there is practically nowhere to sit and view the paintings unless you dare to steal a guard's seat for a few minutes. But across from the gates of the park I found an unpretentious place to sit and have a good meal, a pizzeria at No1 Via Bosco di Capodimonte. This was cheap and cheerful at its best, and I had the one of the most delicious pizzas I have ever eaten.

The **Catacombs of San Gennaro** are down Via di Capodimonte (take the stairs and then turn right), behind the Church of San Gennaro Extra Moenia. They are viewed by guided tour (mornings only), a fascinating walk through some of the excavated passages of underground Naples. They were built in two storeys during the second century; the city's patron saint, San Gennaro, is buried within, along with bishops and dukes. The mosaics here are some of the best examples of early Christian art, especially the half-body portraits in the Crypt of the Bishops.

The Vomero

On another hill to the southwest of Capodimonte is the Vomero district, and three funicular railways travel up and down its slope throughout the day. Don't go by bus, because the route skirts the city on the outer highway and takes a long time. Take the Montesanto Funicular west of Piazza Dante, getting off at the second station. (You might be tempted to hum a few bars of the song, 'Funiculi-funicula', written by Neapolitans Peppino Turco and Luigi Danza in 1880. Their song is a wonderful example of the traditional, melodramatic *canzoni napoletane* which are famous the world over.)

If you're interested in ceramics and would also like a walk through dense gardens, make the **Villa Floridiana** your first stop on the Vomero. Walk straight out of the station and down the two sets of steps into Piazza Vanvitelli. Turn left on Via Bernini and right on Via Cimarosa. The entrance to the park will be up on your left.

The Villa Floridiana is a reflection of its neighbourhood – calm and solidly middle class. Young mothers and grandmothers are preoccupied by babies, old men balance canes and cigarettes as they shake hands with friends, and teenage couples steal kisses in more secluded sections of shrubbery. The pathways to the villa are lined by cedars, cypress and pine (and explode with camellias in springtime). From the long terrace at the park's farthest point, you get a fantastic view of the Bay of Naples, and – on a clear day – of Capri.

The **National Ceramics Museum** is housed in the Pompeian-style villa built in 1817 by Ferdinand I for his wife, who took the unlikely name of Duchess of Floridia. The Duke of Martina began to amass his porcelain collection in the second half of the 18th century, with pieces from China, Japan and Europe. The collection of 6000 pieces was donated to the state by the widow of the duke's nephew in 1931.

The next stop on the Vomero is the **monastery of San Martino**. Retrace your steps until you are again in front of the Montesanto funicular station. Facing the station, turn left on Via Morghen, which changes to Via D'Auria. Then take a right on Via Tito Angelini, and up on your left at the end of the street you'll see stairs leading down to San Martino, which lead to a sloped road with the entrance to the monastery at its end. **Castel Sant'Elmo** looms on your left, built in the early 14th century by Robert of Anjou. It was restored in the 1970s and no longer keeps political prisoners within; various cultural organisations for Naples and the province have offices here, and the castle is used frequently for receptions and conferences.

The San Martino Monastery is just below, founded in the 14th century by the Angevin dynasty. The monks became so rich that in the 18th century the

Bourbon King Ferdinand threatened to check their books and cut down on their 'grant'. In the meantime, however, the monks were spending thousands of pounds on paintings, frescoes and sculpted marble, turning the San Martino monastery into an artistic treasure trove.

The lavish Baroque church is just past the entrance on the left. The ribs of the Gothic vaults reveal the character of the original interior, but Baroque was then incorporated and in a much more careful way than in other Neapolitan churches. The best works within are by Ribera, dubbed Il Spagnoletto or Little Spaniard, a court painter who settled in Naples. His twelve larger-than-lifesize *Prophets* are in the spandrels of the arched nave. On the left wall of the choir is the painting some consider his masterpiece, *Communion of the Apostles*, done in 1651. To complete a short study of his best paintings, behind the high altar head to the left through a number of rooms. The last one you come to is the Cappella del Tesoro where Ribera's tender *Deposition* hangs above the high altar.

From the church, pass through the small cloisters and the hallway beyond to enter the museum. The collection in the monastery's museum is eclectic, well displayed and well labelled. If you are interested in the history of the city through art – street scenes, portraits of regal personalities, works of Neapolitan and Campanian masters – then this is the best place in Naples to spend your time. But I have found the museum to be less than illuminating, with too many rooms closed. Room No.25 is one small room that doesn't close, however; it is famous for its exceptional view of the city below. The museum is also known for its Nativity scene called the Cucimiello Crib. It has recently been restored, apparently because the crib had been sent to the Metropolitan Museum of Art in New York City for a special display where harsh lights had wrought havoc on the figurines. 'Mai piu,' explained the custodian sadly. Never again would they let that happen.

From the small cloisters, a long narrow hallway leads to the Grand Cloisters. Sixteen columns line each side, with grey and cream-coloured marble ornamentation above. A well sits in the middle, and only five lonely fruit trees grow in the open square. Its original plan was developed by Giovanni Antonio Dosia at the end of the 16th century, but Cosimo Fanzago had a hand in adding the level above the high arches and completing the decoration. The small cemetery on one side of the cloister with its 16 marble skulls was also his idea.

Fanzago was a prolific artist – an architect, sculptor and decorator – contracted to carry out this work in 1623, which landed him with a lawsuit initiated by the monks. He apparently attacked one of his masons on the job there and was then suspected of murdering him two years later. He always had a hard time working to deadline, and the six-year contract for the Grand Cloisters beginning in 1623 was not completed by 1631. Fanzago had so many commissions throughout Naples that he constantly juggled materials and workers. Employers accused him of taking their materials to another job; he used sculptures meant for the monastery, for example, in a chapel at San Lorenzo instead. And strong as his influence was upon 17th-century Naples, he didn't always receive very good press. But he was an expansive, creative personality who spent generously to entertain his friends. Where were they at the end of his life? He died in poverty, at the age of 87, in 1678.

Practical Information

When to go

The so-called 'tourist season' doesn't exist in Naples, so you don't have to worry about running across busloads of foreigners there. In my opinion, Naples needs and deserves more tourists. But I must caution you to be 'street-wise'. Do not walk around Naples with a wallet or purse which could be stolen. If you can, carry enough cash for the day's outing in a pocket and leave everything else at your hotel. I would also advise against women travelling alone; it is best to travel in company as most Neapolitan men believe themselves to be irresistible and will try their best to convince you of this. And lastly, if you are driving do not stop the car for anyone who appears to need your assistance. This is most likely a ploy to disorient you in order to steal your belongings.

To enjoy the best weather while walking the city streets, choose late spring or early autumn. The sun will often be shining and rain will be a only minor irritation. July and August can be stifling, but September and October can still be very warm. December, January, February and March can be cold and wet with occasional strong winds.

Getting there

Most visitors fly into the Capodichino Airport outside the city, but you could instead fly to Rome and drive down through the Campanian countryside. Naples is only 200km from Rome; alternatively, the train ride from Rome's Termini to Naples' Stazione Centrale takes two hours. A hydrofoil service also runs from the Rome airport to Capri and Sorrento (see 'Getting there' information at the end of Chapter Six).

British Airways flies direct from London Gatwick to Naples twice daily, but Alitalia does not fly direct. A British Airways flight doesn't come cheaply, and is more expensive than flying to Rome. The low season Apex fare is about £180 return. But there are very good charter flight deals from companies such as Adelphi Travel, Pegasus and Quo Vadis. Their fares recently ranged from £110 to £140 return, and these agents will often help with hotel reservations, car hire and insurance. A coach runs every 30–40 minutes from Capodochino Airport into Naples, at a cost of 3000 lire. The bus stops at the main train station of Piazza Garibaldi, at the Piazza Municipio in the city centre, and at the main dock of Porto Beverello where boats leave for the islands. It makes sense to use this service, as taxi rates can fluctuate outrageously!

If you decide to rent a car, always book from home – rates within Italy can be twice as expensive. If you want to hire a car when you're already in Italy,

I would still recommend that you telephone a car hire rental company in the UK; believe me, it's worth the price of the phone call.

Tourist Information Offices

The main tourist office in Naples, called the Ente Provinciale per il Turismo, is on 10 Via Partenope, (tel. 081 406 289). They also have a number you can call at the central railroad station: 081 268 779. Another tourist office is located in the lobby of the airport and another is located at the entrance of the causeway to Castel dell' Ovo.

Students looking for less expensive places to stay should contact the Associazione Alberghi per la Gioventú at 9 Via del Chiostro (tel. 081 551 3151). There is also a tourist centre for students at 35 Via De Gasperi 35 (tel. 081 522 0074). The only youth hostel in Naples is behind the Mergellina train station, across from the entrance to Virgil's tomb, on Salita della Grotta 23 (tel. 081 761 2346).

Guided tours are run almost every Sunday between 10.00 and 11.00 from the tourist information office called the Azienda Autonoma di Soggiorno, Cura e Turismo. One office is located at Piazza del Gesù, open 09.00–15.00 every day except Sun (tel. 081 552 3328). The office also has a mobile unit in front of the station in the middle of Piazza Garibaldi, open 08.00–20.00 Mon-Sat; 09.00–13.00 Sun.

Get yourself a copy of the free monthly *Qui Napoli*, written in Italian and English, which is full of useful information – hydrofoil and ferry schedules, sightseeing tours, sports facilities, exhibitions and concerts, church and museum schedules.

Fondazione Napoli '99

If you'd like more information about what this energetic group is doing to help save Naples, or how you can help, write to the foundation at Riviera di Chiaia 202, Naples, 80121 (tel. 081 412 948).

Consulates

Great Britain: 122 Via Crispi (tel. 081 633 511).
United States: Piazza della Repubblica (tel. 081 660 966).

Hotels

Naples is not exactly famous for opulent, old world charm when it comes to hotel interiors. But there is a good deal of choice in both price and location.

I would put GIGA's *Excelsior*, Via Partenope 48 (tel. 081 417 111) at the top of the list for comfort, elegance, services and location. But the superlatives don't come cheaply – room rates start at about £150 for a double. On the corner of the Via Partenope overlooking the Castel dell' Ovo, views from most of its rooms are superb. Special services give you an indication of the clientele: interpreters on request, jet rental, dock space for private boats. Very expensive.

Two other hotels along the waterfront are a bit less posh, and slightly less expensive. Prices at the **Santa Lucia**, Via Partenope 46 (tel. 081 416 566) include breakfast, and this place has a friendly atmosphere.

The **Vesuvio**, Via Partenope 45 (tel. 081 417 044), is right next door, and has gone through some unfortunate modernisation to accommodate more conference business. Its Ristorante Caruso on the 9th floor is this city's answer to Manhattan's 'Windows on the World', with a wonderful view out across the bay. Expensive.

The simply furnished, unpretentious **Hotel Rex**, Via Palepoli (tel. 081 416 388), is around the corner in the Santa Lucia quarter. There is no restaurant, so you have to go out to the local coffee bar for breakfast. Ask for a room with a small balcony, and you'll enjoy a sideways glimpse of the sea. Moderate prices.

The **Britannique**, 133 Corso Vittorio Emanuele (tel. 081 761 4145), has long been a favourite with travellers, halfway up the hill which rises to become the Vomero. It is quiet, with a very pretty garden; moderate to expensive prices.

I can recommend one hotel situated on the central Piazza Garibaldi; make sure you get a room on one of the top floors, some of which have their own terraces with very nice views. The **Hotel Cavour**, Piazza Garibaldi 32 (tel. 081 283 122), has recently been carefully restored, having been a hotel for 100 years; room rates here are moderate. The restaurant attached to the hotel is very good, but expensive.

Restaurants

I have never failed to eat a decent meal anywhere in Campania, and Naples is no exception. Very rarely is dining a three-star experience with a *nouvelle cuisine* platter looking like an underpainted canvas, and that's fine with me. Most often, what you'll get is a one-star meal full of fresh ingredients, from the first-course pasta to a steaming cup of espresso. Trust the waiters' opinions. They've usually had an early meal of the day's specials.

Amici Miei, Via Monte di Dio 78 (tel. 081 405 727), is known for its fresh pasta, especially the lasagna, and ravioli stuffed with ricotta and mozzarella. Moderate.

Bellini, Via Santa Maria Costantinopoli 80 (tel. 081 459 774) is a justly famous pizzeria in Spaccanapoli, though service was poor the last time I ate there. Inexpensive.

La Cantinella, Via Cuma 42 (tel. 081 405 375) is one of only two restaurants in Naples with a Michelin star. It is near the seafront in the Santa Lucia district. Pasta is superb, especially those dishes served with seafood. Closed Sunday and during the month of August; moderate to expensive.

Also in the Santa Lucia district is a good pizzeria called **Da Ettore**, Via Santa Lucia 56, very simple with a warm atmosphere. Inexpensive.

The **Casanova Grill** at the Hotel Excelsior, Via Partenope 48 (tel. 081 417 111), is a very good, though very expensive, restaurant. If you're not staying at this swanky hotel, at least splash out for a meal (or a drink at the bar) if you are looking for some peace and quiet.

The **Cavour**, Piazza Garibaldi 32 (tel. 081 264 730) is an elegant antidote to the chaotic Piazza Garibaldi just outside its doors. *Risotto agli scampi* and pasta with *frutta di mare* are excellent; this is also the place for a tempting array of desserts. Expensive.

At the other end of the port area is a Neapolitan favourite, **Ciro a Mergellina**, Via Mergellina 21 (tel. 081 681 780). Nearby, just beyond Piazza Piedigrotta, is **Il Vicoletto**, Via Piedigrotta. This relaxed, old-style place will be full of Italians who heard about it through word of mouth, and they'll be ordering the fresh pasta made on the premises. Moderate prices.

High up in the Posillipo district is Naples's second Michelin-starred restaurant, **Giuseppone a Mare**, on Via Ferdinando Russo 13 (tel. 081 769 6002). Its speciality is seafood, at very moderate prices, and the position above the gulf can't be beaten.

Price Ranges

Hotel (double room)	*Restaurant (per head)*
Inexpensive: under 60,000	under 25,000
Moderate: 60–120,000	25–50,000
Expensive: 120–200,000	50–90,000
Very expensive: 200,000+	90,000+

Museums and other public sites

Aquarium: Villa Comunale (tel. 081 406 222). 09.00–17.00 Mon–Sat; 10.00–19.00 Sun and hols.

Botanic Gardens: Via Foria (tel. 081 449 759). 09.00–14.00 Wed and Thurs only, or by request through Science Faculty, University of Naples (tel. 081 449 759).

Catacombs of San Gennaro: Via di Capodimonte. Guided tours Fri, Sat and Sun only 09.30, 10.15, 11.00 and 11.45.

Capodimonte Museum and Picture Gallery: Parco di Capodimonte (tel. 081 741 0881). 09.00–14.00 Tues–Sat; 09.00–13.00 Sun and hols. Summer opening hours 09.00–19.00 Tues–Sat; 09.00–14.00 Sun and Mon.

Cappella Sansevero: 19 Via de Sanctis. 10.30–13.30 Mon–Sat, 11.00–13.30 Sun and hols.

Cloisters of Santa Chiara: Via B. Croce (tel. 081 205 561). 09.00–12.30, 16.00–18.30; 09.00–12.30 Sun and hols.

Doll Hospital: 81 Via San Biagio dei Librai (tel. 081 203 067). 09.00–14.00, 16.30–20.00 Mon-Fri.

Filangieri Museum: 288 Via Duomo (tel. 081 203 175). 09.00–14.00 except Mon; 09.00–13.00 Sun and hols.

National Archeological Museum: 35 Piazza Museo (tel. 081 440 166). 09.00–

14.00 Tues–Sat; 09.00–13.00 Sun and hols. Summer opening hours 09.00–19.00 Tues–Sat; 09.00–13.00 Sun and hols.

Palazzo Reale: Piazza Plebiscito (tel. 081 413 888). 09.00–14.00 Tues–Sat; 09.00–13.00 Sun and hols. Summer opening hours 09.00–19.30, 09.00–13.00 Sun and hols.

San Carlo Opera House: Via San Carlo (tel. 081 417 144). Tours 09.00–12.00 Tues–Sat. Ticket office for evening performances open 10.00–13.00, 16.30–18.30 daily except Mon.

San Martino Monastery and Museum: Largo San Martino 5 (tel. 081 377 005). 09.00–14.00 Tues–Sat; 09.00–13.00 Sun and hols. Summer opening hours 09.00–19.00 Tues–Sat; 09.00–13.00 Sun and hols.

Tomb of Virgil: 09.00–13.00 daily. Guided tour by request (tel. 081 413 888, ext. 51).

Villa Floridiana (Duca di Martina Ceramics Museum): Vomero district in park (tel. 081 377 315). 09.00–14.00 Tues–Sat; 09.00–13.00 Sun and hols.

Villa Pignatelli Museum: Riviera di Chiaia (tel. 081 669 675). 09.00–14.00 Tues–Sat; 09.00–13.00 Sun and hols.

5. WEST OF THE BAY OF NAPLES

The Phlegrean Fields

This fascinating part of Campania, less than 16km west of Naples, claims more classical mythology and ancient history per acre than any other place in Italy outside Rome and Sicily. Yet few travellers seem to know much about it. Full of secrets barely concealed, it's as if by putting an ear to the ground you'll hear the whispered prophecies of the Cumaen Sibyl, the Greek recitations of Virgil's *Aeneid*, or Nero's confession to the murder of his mother at Baia. Roman villas have sunk beneath the sea, Cumae's amphitheatre is overgrown with weeds, and the land still rises and falls with underground volcanic activity. This is a mystical land, still so full of hidden promise for the classical archaeologist.

But hidden promise also translates as hard to find in some cases, and other sites, as steeped in myth and history as they are, can no longer be found at all. But with patience and imagination the pieces begin to fit neatly together as you trace your way around the bay. The area's three most important sites, the baths at Baia, the ruins at Cumae and the amphitheatre at Pozzuoli, are all open to the public.

This wide arc of land around the Gulf of Pozzuoli, extending to the tip of Cape Misenum, is called the *Campi Flegrei* – the Burning Fields. You can see why if you visit the crater known as the Solfatara near Pozzuoli. Mud still bubbles up from the ground and many small fumaroles emit sulphuric gases, though this active crater hasn't erupted violently for 36,000 years.

The area's main sights can be seen in a full day, but if you've got less time I would whittle these down to two: the amphitheatre at Pozzuoli and the Italian mainland's first Greek colony of Cumae. Wonderful views await you from Pozzuoli around the bay to Baia, then out to Cape Misenum and up past Lake Fusaro to Cumae. The best plan is to pack a picnic lunch, or buy sandwiches while in Pozzuoli, for a late lunch on the summit at Cumae. Train lines from Naples extend to the Phlegrean Fields (the Ferrovia Cumana e Circumflegrea), but most sights are too far from the stations for the line to be of much use. I would suggest either renting a car (making this a day trip from Naples) or touring with a group arranged by the tourist office in Naples.

The Solfatara and Pozzuoli

The English guidebook for sale on site describes the Solfatara as one of the area's 'innumerable beauties'. Hmmm. Some might prefer to omit this stinking bed of clay in favour of more romantic spots but the Solfatara should be experienced, as it is an extraordinary phenomenon. The Greek geographer Strabo, who lived in Rome after 14AD, described the place in his *Geographica* as the workshop of the god Vulcan, the entrance to the Underworld. A massive eruption 36,000 years ago created this area, 12km wide, and there is record of an eruption in 1198 which poured forth a stream of lava. As you walk across the ash-laden ground, it feels hollow and is hot to the touch. Small rooms have been built to capture the sulphurous steam that is emitted by a number of *fumarole*. A campsite near the Solfatara bills itself as one of the few in Europe to be 'inside a volcano', and many come for the soothing effects of therapeutic steam baths and thermal springs.

If sulphuric fumes have an unpleasant effect on you, travel directly to **Pozzuoli** instead, where the old market area and amphitheatre are worth seeing. The town of 60,000 inhabitants has almost completely engulfed most of the older ruins, and its present troubles are unfortunately the most fascinating aspect of its modern-day character. Pozzuoli has been described as a 'potential apocalypse', very seriously affected by thousands of tremors – a condition called bradyseism. In 1983 about half the population fled as buildings began to crumble. The moving earth, rising over a metre in two years, pushed the piers up so high that ferries from the islands of Procida and Ischia had difficulty docking.

One would have hoped that the past presence of saints (along with being the birthplace of Sophia Loren) could have protected Pozzuoli. St Paul stepped ashore here after the Alexandrian ship 'Castor and Pollux' carried him to Italy from Malta, and San Gennaro survived beastly trials in the amphitheatre. But early warnings by the scientific community seem to be the only cause for hope. Two giant underwater fumaroles were recently discovered offshore, and some scientists think that is a good sign: pressure is being released slowly over a wider area than they had thought. Though the crisis of the early 1980s has passed and Pozzuoli's citizens have returned, other scientists believe it is only a matter of time before mud and lava explode to cover the Phlegrean Fields.

One area that demonstrates the changing sea levels through history is right in the middle of Pozzuoli. Romans came to 'Puteoli' in 194BC, and it became an active trading port. A large marketplace, or *macellum*, still exists near the seafront behind the Via Roma, and its so-called **Temple of Serapis** is the circular area with columns in the centre. But even Serapis, god sacred to merchants, couldn't keep the water from flooding the market square periodically. Three columns standing by the entrance show traces of water marks at different levels along their lengths. In one section they are perforated for a length of about 3m by a species of boring shell which lives underwater.

The amphitheatre, the third largest in Italy after Rome's and Santa Maria Capua Vetere's, is on the hillside behind Pozzuoli off the Via Domiziana (also the way to the Solfatara). You can take the Cumana railroad line from Naples in this case, and walk up the steps behind the Pozzuoli station.

The **amphitheatre of Flavius** was constructed in the second half of the first century, not far from an earlier and smaller amphitheatre. Three tiers of arches define the perimeter (149m x 116m), with a wide entrance at either end and a smaller one on either side. A garden of fragments now surrounds the amphitheatre – headless statues, bodiless heads, portions of a freize, a huge marble foot. What makes this amphitheatre so worth seeing is that it gives visitors a clear idea of how any Roman amphitheatre functioned as a showplace: the floor's middle section opened wide to allow scenery to be drawn up from below, and the extensive underground passages are incredibly well preserved. These can most easily be seen by peering through the sixty openings on the amphitheatre's floor. But the amphitheatre is often fairly empty and you can usually find a way beneath ground level, though due to recent earth movement in the area many passages have been blocked to visitors.

The rectangular openings on the amphitheatre's floor were constructed so that caged animals could be raised through them on a pulley system to the level of the floor. As the cage doors opened, lions and tigers sprang out roaring. In one instance, when Nero was entertaining the Armenian king Tiridates, the emperor became so excited by the fighting that he jumped into the ring and killed several of the animals himself, including two bulls that he speared with one javelin. This is perhaps not surprising when one considers Nero's track record as a pathological killer.

Baia, Bacoli and Cape Misenum

From the main road by the port of Pozzuoli, head west to Baia. Only one main road will take you there, although the Cumana rail line does stop at Baia also. The views here, as you round the bay, are as pretty as those in Naples and once past Bacoli and around the point they are better still. To the east, blocking the Bay of Naples from sight, is the little island of **Nisida**. It is an ancient crater, like so many lakes and lumps in this region. Cicero says that Brutus retired here after Caesar's assassination, in a villa built by the son of the Roman general Lucullus. But no traces remain of this – nor of the delicious wild asparagus described by the naturalist Pliny. This island is nowadays a state-run home for juvenile delinquents.

Before reaching Baia make a detour inland (a right turning off the main road) to **Lake Avernus**, known through Homer's *Odyssey* as home of the Cimmerians and entrance to Hades. It isn't the lake itself but the so-called **Sibyl's Grotto** on the south side which is the attraction here. An overgrown path leads to this long dark tunnel, best seen with a guide who is normally there on weekdays. Legend has it that the cave led the way to a mysterious prophetess similar to Cumae's sibyl, but it is far more likely that the tunnel was built by the Roman general Agrippa around 37BC to escape the advancing troops of Sextus Pompeius.

As a safe harbour for his fleet, Agrippa connected Lake Avernus to the sea by a canal which also ran through the smaller Lucrine Lake nearby. Another tunnel on the northwest side of the lake was dug to Cumae (called the Grotta di Cocceio or della Pace), and ruins on the west side were probably a ship-yard. On the lake's eastern edge are ruins of an octagonal building called the **Temple of Apollo**, thermal baths built by the Romans. And the Sibyl's Grotto, despite romantic legend, was part of Agrippa's overall defence plan – perhaps a place to hide his army and their supplies.

Baia

Drive back out to **Baia**, a picturesque fishing port with so many ruins beneath the sea that fishermen have to be careful where they anchor their boats. Stretched along the hillside are the extensive remains of Roman baths, but there is hardly a foundation wall left to show that Caesar and Pompey, Hadrian and Livy all built luxurious holiday homes along this coastline. Seeing what Vesuvius has preserved at Pompei and Herculaneum, I can understand turn-of-the-century travel writer A. H. Norway's plea, though he isn't exactly sympathetic towards potential human suffering: 'If only the ashes had rained down a trifle harder at Misenum and Baia, what noble Roman buildings might have survived unto this day, conserved by the wisdom of the mountain!' Today the town just seems like a quiet working people's port with modest homes along its shores, hardly a place where midnight orgies raged in damp caves.

The **Roman baths** are reached by a staircase beside the railroad line (to the left as you face the station). Crossing the bridge, you'll see the Temple of Diana down to your right behind the tracks – probably just an extension of the baths at one time. The ingenious Italian who farms this land has created an intimate garden of vegetables among the ruins, with tools and tomato sticks stacked neatly within a subterranean gallery to the side – a typical yet powerful image of an Italy that blends the illustrious past with the ordinary present.

The baths are farther along on your left at the top of the stairs. The **Archeological Park** begins with a long avenue, with ruins far below and just above. This huge Imperial Roman complex was built between the first and fourth centuries, and staircases still connect the different levels. Some rooms were for hot baths, others for cold plunges. Small chambers and pipes supplied and drained water from all over the hill; sulphuric springs were tapped for soothing soaks. Large buildings still stand that were used to collect warm mineral water, the best preserved being the so-called Temple of Mercury. The large circular chamber, with its vaulted roof, is reminiscent of the Pantheon. Because of the water at its base, the building is like an echo chamber – if you whisper on one side your secret will be carried to the other. Directly to the east of this temple are small rooms in a semi-circle, thought to be a theatre. Just below is a large area that served as a swimming pool.

The villas that once lined the shore below the baths are about 4m beneath the sea at Baia, but it wasn't until the early 1970s that archeologists seriously considered excavating. That's when a local fisherman discovered amongst his catch a marble hand holding a cup. Since 1981 about 22 marble statues have been raised from the depths, though progress is slow and government monies hard to procure. Recent discoveries show that more remains of the ancient town are about 1km beyond the shore, but at least 15m below the surface. These finds are exhibited in the 16th-century Aragon castle seen on the hill when travelling out of Baia toward Cape Misenum.

Bacoli

Bacoli is the next stop, a small unpretentious town up beyond Baia. It has two attractions to recommend it. One is the **Cento Camerelle**, or Hundred Little Rooms, a two-storeyed combination of tunnels and arcades near the church of Sant'Anna. The other is the **Piscina Mirabilis**, a big cistern in five sections used to supply water to the Roman fleet at the port of Misenum. The Piscina is a haunting and wonderful experience; a high vaulted ceiling towers above and hundreds of plants hang from the ruins like mossy stalactites.

Bacoli is also supposed to be the scene of the murder of Nero's mother Agrippina. (A ruin known as the Tomb of Agrippina is nearby.) It was a commander of the fleet at Misenum who first helped Nero plan his mother's murder, according to historian Charles Merivale. The commander had designed a boat with movable bolts that could come apart in the water like a broken toy. Persuading his suspicious mother to board the vessel was no easy task for Nero, but she finally assented one moonlit night. Out on the water, however, the boat didn't fall apart as planned. Agrippina jumped overboard and managed to survive. So Nero resorted to more direct tactics. That same night the commander raided her villa and she was murdered in her bed. Perhaps Agrippina deserved her fate, for she is said to have poisoned her husband Claudius so that her son Nero would become emperor.

Nero hardly deserved to enjoy the good life at his villa near Baia. As emperor from 54 to 68AD, he poisoned his stepbrother Brittanicus, killed his wife Octavia and a second wife Poppaea by kicking her when she was pregnant. When his offer to marry Claudius's daughter was refused, he had her put to death. He gained his third wife, Statilia Messallina, after killing her husband. But these incidents were mere trifles when contrasted with his massacre of thousands of Christians and the burning of Rome. To save himself from execution, he committed suicide in 68.

The road which climbs from Bacoli to Cape Misenum affords spectacular views across the Gulf of Pozzuoli, and down into wide blue **Lake Miseno**. This was once linked by a canal to the port area, used as a base for the Roman fleet.

The spectacular view from Cape Misenum

Now the American military has a base here, and long grey metal ships sit like bobbing hippos in the gulf. As you wind slowly inland via Monte di Procida, umbrella pines crown the hills on either side. Scrubby patches of sloping land are cultivated for grapes, olives and tomatoes.

The lives of Campanian citizens here are far removed from those of their cousins in Naples, or even in the busy port of Pozzuoli. Small and somewhat messy rural towns line the twisting road to Lake Fusaro. On a recent autumn visit I was surprised to find myself driving behind a uniformed brass band and a line of decorated wooden carts in one of these little towns. It was a procession to celebrate the *vendemmia*, the season's grape harvest. Vines had been curved to form graceful side arches on the carts, laden with boxes of freshly picked grapes and little girls in frilly dresses. They waved slowly and confidently to the crowd of parents and shopkeepers who lined the streets. The band made its way to a small central square where a platform had been set up for the day's speeches. Neapolitans complain that their festivals and customs don't seem to mean much anymore, but out here on Cape Misenum they still take their harvest traditions very seriously.

Follow the road up past **Lake Fusaro**, stopping briefly at the park bordering the lake if you'd like to see the charming hunting lodge, or *casino*, that Vanvitelli built for Ferdinand IV in 1782. It seems a true folly now, sitting out in the lake with nothing to hunt for miles around. The lake might have been the port for Cumae, 1km north. Until recently, the lake was known for its oyster beds. The fact that it was the crater of an extinct volcano was proven in 1838 when such noxious gases were emitted that all the oysters were destroyed. Vanvitelli's lodge, with a wooden bridge connecting it to the mainland, was restored in 1981 after being neglected for thirty years. It was being used as an outpost to a marine biology station in the big house nearby on the mainland, but both now look empty and neglected, a disappointing example of local restoration efforts wasted through an unclear policy of how to make best use of them.

Cumae

There's nothing more exciting than exploring ruins with no one else around. Although it's completely irrational, whenever this happens I get the feeling that I'm the first to have laid eyes on such a place. I wholeheartedly agree with H. V. Morton in his opinion of Cumae:

> I have not seen a more romantic classical site in Italy. Anyone who is even remotely interested in the classical world who comes to Naples yet fails to visit the Grotto of the Sybil is missing a great experience; should it be a matter of time, I would rather see what is left of Cumae than Pompeii.

The grotto he mentions wasn't uncovered until 1932. In reading older guide-books which are unable to locate the cave I have felt very happy to be a modern traveller, for I can now walk down its long, eerie passage. Cumae was founded about 800BC by Greek colonists, one of their first outposts in a foreign land. The Roman historian Livy has written that these colonists were driven here from Ischia by frequent earthquakes, however; other historians claim it was from the island of Procida due to lack of water. Classical mythology tells the story of the inventor Daedalus escaping from King Minos and landing here on his wings of wax. His son Icarus didn't make it that far, melting his wings by flying too close to the sun and falling to a watery grave. Daedalus rested at Cumae, and then made his way to Sicily where King Minos unsuccessfully pursued him.

Cumae was a powerful port city for centuries. The Etruscans, jealous of her influence, tried unsuccessfully to take the city in 474BC with the help of Umbrian allies. But the Romans did defeat the Cumaeans 140 years later, and it then became a colony of the empire under Augustus. Cumae continued to decline; Saracens sacked the city in the ninth century. Four hundred years later it was such a notorious hideout for pirates and brigands that angry Neapolitans came to burn what was left of the city.

To reach the ruins of Cumae today, you climb a path that leads to a wide tunnel carved in the rock. Just past it, on the left, is the entrance to the **Grotto of the Sibyl**. On either side of the dark entrance are verses from Virgil describing how Aeneas came to consult the Sibyl who he called Deiphobe. In the sixth book of the *Aeneid* Virgil writes:

> On one side of the Eubean rock
> Is cut a huge cavern. To it lead
> A hundred broad ways, a hundred mouths
> From which there tumble out as many voices,
> The Sibyl's answers. As they all arrived

> *Upon the threshold of the cave the virgin*
> *Cried out: 'The time to question fate is now!*
> *The god is here, the god!' As she spoke*
> *Before the temple doors her countenance*
> *Changed suddenly, her colour changed, her hair*
> *Fell loose about her shoulders and she panted*
> *Violently, her wild heart grew great within her,*
> *She seemed taller, her voice was not a mortal's*
> *Because the god's power had breathed upon her*

This scene is not hard to imagine as you walk down the corridor of the Sibyl's Grotto, almost 50m long and over 2m wide. The whole passage is hewn from the rock; its angled walls create the shape of an inverted V with its point lopped off. Six galleries allow light to filter through on the west side, but this is hardly an airy place. When walking through the dank grotto I felt like a citizen of Cumae coming to consult the Sibyl, spooked by whatever fate she had in store for me. She sat in a small room at the end of the tunnel, waiting for her wary customers.

The Cumaean Sibyl was one of the three most venerated oracles in the ancient world, along with those of Delphi and Erythrae. After willing herself into a trancelike state, she was said to make her utterances in perfect Greek hexameters. Her prophecies were written on palm leaves, and collected later into what were called the Sibyline Books. Pliny tells a tale of Tarquinus Priscus coming from Rome to buy the books. The Sibyl offered him the nine books and when he questioned the price she ruined three, offering him the remaining six at the same price. When he continued to quibble three more books were destroyed; the sale was concluded when Tarquin bought three books at the original price. Who knows what wisdom the Roman Senate lost in that transaction! The books Tarquin bought were burned when the Forum was destroyed in 82BC and a committee was elected to go and gather a new collection in Asia Minor. This was safely stored on the Palatine Hill but disappeared after the year 400.

Across from the entrance to the grotto is the puckered rock face of the **Roman Crypt**, a deep underground gallery almost 230m long. The last time I was there it was closed to the public, and the custodian at the entrance had no idea when it might reopen. It is thought that the tunnel continues even deeper through the hills, perhaps connecting Cumae with Lake Avernus to the southeast where the Grotto of Cocceio would be the tunnel's logical exit.

A winding stone staircase above the Grotto of the Sibyl leads to the Acropolis, and the temples of Apollo and Jupiter. A belvedere is on your left, with remnants of statues found in the excavations. From here one has a perfect view out to Ischia and Procida. Now the **Via Sacra** begins, flanked by laurel and oak. The **Temple of Apollo** is just up on the right, with two headless statues at the entrance. Tufts of grass and clover have grown between the big tufa blocks; an interesting section of column rests at one end, constructed in a trefoil pattern. In the sixth or seventh century the temple's foundation was used to construct a Christian basilica.

A series of hewn arches lead to the Sibyl's Grotto

The Via Sacra continues up the hill to the **Temple of Jupiter**. This is the perfect place for lunch – quiet, with a soft breeze coming in off the sea over the summit. Small wildflowers grow between the crumbling brickwork, and the hill is covered with thyme, clover and pine. Arched sections of the Christian basilica built on the temple's remains stand at chest height, and tombs have been discovered beneath the pavement. Amongst the scattered ruins is a circular baptism font in the centre.

Through a small group of trees on the steep hill is a flat area allowing for an expansive view out to sea and south to Cape Misenum. Neatly framed green fields are stretched out far below. Looking closely you will notice just how many low rounded, grassy walls there are in all directions. No larger vegetation has been able to root itself along these humps, for they are all ruins that were once part of the city. If archaeologists resumed excavation here, Cumae would be shown to be much more extensive than just the additional outcropping of ruins (baths and forum) uncovered below to the north-east.

The remains of the city's **amphitheatre** (probably constructed in the first century BC) are beyond the excavated area of the city. Turning right out of the entrance, the hidden oval is near the corner and marked only by a battered yellow metal sign. The site is fairly buried in bushes and high weeds, but with persistence you can find your way through brush and olive groves to the amphitheatre. Many tombs have been discovered nearby, the oldest dating back to the seventh century BC, but they have been badly pillaged for their valuable sarcophagi and other ornaments. The road from the amphitheatre now leads north on the **Via Domiziana** to the elegant **Arco Felice**. This tall triumphal brick archway is squeezed into the hillside to the east, built by the Emperor Domitian in 81–96 to link Cumae with Pozzuoli. Its dark polished Roman paving is still intact beneath, and your way back to modern civilisation is through this lovely arch.

Practical Information

Getting there

Travelling west of Naples to Pozzuoli, Baia and Cumae is best done by car. Avis, Europcar, Hertz and InterRent car rental agencies are all located on Naples's Via Partenope, and also at the airport. If you'd like to go by coach, the following companies in Naples run tours to the Solfatara and Cumae: CIT (Piazza Municipio 70, tel. 081 552 54 26); Cima Tours (Piazza Garibaldi 114, tel. 081 22 06 46); and Tourcar (Piazza Matteotti, tel. 081 552 33 10). By train, the Ferrovia Cumana will stop at Pozzuoli and Baia, leaving from the Montesanto or Corso Vittorio Emanuele stations in Naples. The Metropolitana from Naples's Piazza Garibaldi also stops at the Pozzuoli Solfatara station.

Tourist Information Offices

POZZUOLI   Azienda Autonoma di Soggiorno, Cura e Turismo: 3 Via Campi
Flegrei (tel. 081 867 2419).

Hotels and Restaurants

To see the sites here it's really best to stay in Naples, or even base yourself on
Procida or Ischia and take the ferry over to Pozzuoli.

BAIA   The place to eat is **Dal Tedesco**, Via Temporini 8 (tel. 081 868 7175),
with local pasta dishes served with *frutti di mare*. It's nicest here when you can
sit outside on the terrace full of flowers; there are also nine simple and inexpensive bedrooms available if you'd like to stay in the area, though it doesn't open
until early June. Inexpensive.

POZZUOLI   Neapolitans will drive out to dine at one of the many restaurants
here, since it's well known for fresh fish specialties. The **Castello dei Barbari**,
Via Fascione 4 (tel. 081 867 6014) is good, with a nice view to boot and
moderate prices.

Price Range
Restaurants (per head)
Inexpensive: under 25,000 lire
Moderate: 25−50,000
Expensive: 50−90,000
Very expensive: more than 90,000

Museums and other public sites

BACOLI   Cento Camerelle: 09.00−16.00; obtain key from custodian at 16 Via
Santa'Anna; small fee.
Piscina Mirabile: 09.00−16.00; obtain key from custodian at 16 Via Creco;
small fee.
Tomb of Agrippina: Via della Marina.

BAIA   Parco Archeologico, Roman Baths: 09.00−16.00; closed Mon and hols.

CUMAE   09.00−16.00; closed Mon and hols; free parking, snack bar.

POZZUOLI   Amphitheatre: (tel. 081 867 6007) 09.00−16.00; closed Mon and
hols.
Solfatara: (tel. 081 867 2341) 09.00−dusk; free parking, snack bar.
Macellum: part of the market place behind Via Roma, seen at any time of day
from above, though gates sometimes open 09.00−13.00.

71

6. NORTHERN CAMPANIA

The fertile fields of the territory north of Naples still deserve the name given to them by the Romans: Campania Felix. Lush soil enriched by river silt, volcanic ash and mountain spring water yield tobacco and olives, fruit and vegetables. The Garigliano River is Campania's northern border with Lazio, and the Matese Mountains separate it from the small region of Molise to the north east. Towns along the Mediterranean coast are packed with holiday visitors in summer, and then completely quiet during winter months.

Inland are many small hill-top towns once protected by now-crumbling castles, whose ancient ancestors saw the likes of Hannibal and Manfred march through on their way to war. Though these foreigners' exploits are part of their history very few towns, even the larger ones such as Caserta and Benevento, are geared to tourism. This certainly adds to their charm, but sometimes also leads to frustration. Streets and historic sites are not always well sign-posted; shops might close just when you're feeling peckish. But if you're interested in architecture and ancient history, and don't need the typical tourist's trappings to keep you satisfied, then this part of Campania is well worth trooping through.

The land area covered in this chapter totals not more than 80km from east to west, and about 50km from north to south. Architectural gems are hiding not far from the main roads. The small Romanesque church of Sant' Angelo in Formis with its complete cycle of frescoes is now totally restored, a jewel polished to perfection. And to paraphrase American writer F. Scott Fitzgerald, a diamond as big as the Ritz sits sparkling in Caserta – the palace and garden complex designed by Vanvitelli for the Bourbon King Charles III. Other less well appreciated sites include the walled town of Caserta Vecchia, Santa Maria Capua Vetere's amphitheatre, the cathedrals of Sessa Aurunca and Teano, and small mountain villages of the Matese.

It's easy enough to make a day trip from Naples out to Caserta, but you'll need a car to reach other smaller towns nearby. With one or two exceptions, the area does not have much to offer when it comes to hotels with character and ambiance. If you'd like to spend a few nights in northern Campania, (and when travelling south from Rome this makes a good place to stop) I recommend staying in the coastal town of Baia Domizia at an unusual hotel called La Baia. Run by three sisters with wonderful taste, it has a distinctive atmosphere with excellent food. I'm sure that warm impressions of northern Campania stem in part from my stay at La Baia. The drive from the hotel to places such as Teano and Sessa Aurunca is less than 45 minutes, to Caserta and Capua just over an hour. And when you're not touring, Hotel La Baia is a great base for eating, drinking and soaking up the sun. During the summer months, a boat takes visitors from Baia Domizia out to the islands of Capri and Ischia.

Sessa Aurunca, Roccamonfina, Teano and Matese Mountains

A short drive east on route 430 from Baia Domizia will bring you to state road No.7, a wonderful stretch of the Via Appia which leads to Sessa Aurunca. The Appian Way, starting in Rome, crosses the whole region of Campania. The Roman official known as Appius Claudius Caecus began the road in 312BC and for about 150 years it simply stopped at Capua. The finished road to Brindisi, passing through Benevento and east on to Potenza, was constructed in 190BC.

The flat road to Sessa Aurunca reminds me of a rural avenue in the south of France where tree tops arch gently to create a leafy tunnel. Low limestone mountains rise in the distance, but beside the road fields are filled with low tobacco plants, and row after row of peach and apple trees. In late autumn nets are cast below limbs to catch olives as they fall, and long tobacco leaves are drying in makeshift sheds.

Sessa Arunca

The hillside town of **SESSA AURUNCA** is 2km north of the main road. Sessa's oldest sight is an arched bridge called the **Ponte degli Aurunci** or Aurunco. It is named for the local population who made this their capital under the Latin name Suessa. The long bridge is just south of the small city, in a solitary place crowded by vegetation, but with portions of Roman paving intact on the road. (Turn left coming into town. Then turn right on Via Adrianea where the Roman paving begins, and the bridge will be at the end of this road.) Built between the first and second centuries, the 21 arches are tall and elegant. It's hard to believe that the bridge has managed to survive this long, considering man's insensitive attempts to domesticate the scene: the archways have been lived in by squatters, and are still used as animal stalls and storage sheds for rusting farm machinery.

The Aurunci fought both the Romans and the Samnites, but were eventually dominated by both. From the influence of Imperial Rome sprang baths and an amphitheatre. Walking along Sessa's medieval streets, you will come across builders' inventive use of old fragments – columns encased in corners and busts protruding from walls, though many have been painted over in recent years. Luckily though, the façade of the **Duomo of San Pietro**, on the Piazza del

Duomo, has remained untouched. It is studded with stone monsters and animals such as wolves, goats and sheep, interspersed with masks from the old theatre. The church's central arch is flanked by lions, who are in the midst of devouring a meal.

The Romanesque cathedral was under construction in 1103, using the remains of the temples of Mercury and Hercules, along with those of the theatre. The portico in front of the church shows St Peter in bas relief above its middle arch. The cathedral's central nave is flanked by 18 columns which separate it from two aisles; the mosaic floor running down the nave is a rich geometric pattern of Arab influence.

The best part of this church's interior is the lovely pulpit. Raised up by six columns riding on the backs of little lions, it is reminiscent of those in both Ravello and Salerno. (Five of the six columns face the centre of the aisle, but the sixth faces the other way. According to locals, the builders were so tired they didn't notice, and didn't have the energy to correct their mistake when it was pointed out to them!) The tight, pieced marble work on the pulpit was done in the 13th century by Taddeo and Pellegrino, masters of their trade. Pellegrino also created the Pascal candelabra nearby, lit for high mass at Easter. A painting by Luca Giordano, *Communion of the Apostles*, is in the Baroque Chapel of the Sacrament.

Roccamonfina and Teano

Back on the road still heading north, you'll be traversing the valley which leads to **Roccamonfina**. The whole group of hills in this area is called Rocca Monfina, the oldest volcanic territory in Campania. It is thought that the hills once rimmed a large crater, which has not been active for thousands of years. On the edge of the highest peak, called Monte Santa Croce, are remains of lava walls that might have been part of a temple in the original settlement of Aurunca. Historians think that the Aurunci abandoned this site in 337BC and moved down to what is now Sessa.

The next stop in this part of Campania is at **Teano** on the slopes of Roccamonfina. Narrow streets wind through the historic centre but the population now numbers 15,000. Its history has seen the Aurunci, Samnites and the Romans file through, along with Lombard domination in the ninth century. Teano is known to modern Italians as the place where, on 26 October, 1860, Garibaldi encountered Victor Emmanuel II – but the position was actually 4km northeast. It is reached by heading north east out of Teano on Route 608 where a granite column was erected in 1960, symbolising the country's unity by a handful of soil from each region buried beneath a plaque.

Teano's Duomo, built in 1116 but renovated on a design by Andrea Vaccaro in 1630, is worth a look for its Crucifix painted on wood above the high altar. The grave, dark cross of the Gothic School is thought to have been painted in 1330 by Maestro di Giovanni Barrile. The church was badly damaged by bombs in World War II, and townspeople say that when its renovation was complete they discovered that the crucifix had been used as a lunch table by the workers!

Just outside Teano, on the way to Capua, is the **Roman amphitheatre**. Excavations there have not been exactly systematic, and the addition of a local family's two-storey home in the middle of the site doesn't add to its appeal.

Matese Mountains

From Teano, heading south means a concentration of rewarding sites in Capua and Santa Maria Capua Vetere. But if you are feeling adventurous, a drive through the slow back roads of Campania takes you north and then west to the beautiful Matese mountains. To find one of the most characteristic villages, Piedimonte Matese, take State Road No.608 north from Teano for about 8km. Then turn right and west on No.372 for 30km until reaching a left turning north on No.158 to Piedimonte.

This territory is dominated by three peaks north of Piedimonte: **Colle Tamburo**, **Monte Gallinola** and the highest, **Monte Miletto** (2050m). They are reflected in the large, clear Lago del Matese below. In the isolated towns just north of here, such as Gallo and Letino, many women still wear the traditional *mappelana*, a headcovering coloured according to marital status: green for the single, red for married women, and black for widows.

But **Piedimonte**, with a population of 12,000, is one of the best places to visit, with interesting churches. And townspeople are used to outsiders – this is becoming a popular day-trip out of Naples for those who want to hike in the mountains, and buy local wine and olive oil. The town was already inhabited during the neolithic age, and almost certainly by the Samnites (who fought their last battle with the Romans on Mount Miletto.)

On Piazza d'Agnese is the Church of San Tommaso d'Aquino, or San Domenico, built in 1414. It sits on the site of the earlier San Pietro, which was built above the ruins of a Roman temple. The church's bell-tower has beautiful green and yellow majolica tiles. On Via d'Agnese is the Baroque church of San Salvatore, designed by Cosimo Fanzago. The majolica paving within is reminiscent of the style found in many Neapolitan churches; the ornately gold-plated organ is an amazing instrument. Just beyond on the left is San Biagio, notable for its cycle of Gothic-inspired frescoes by an unknown artist, Scenes from the Old and New Testament, and the Life of San Biagio, which were completed in the middle of the 15th century. The town's biggest and most Baroque construction is the cathedral of Santa Maria Maggiore, built between 1725 and 1773.

Just north of Piedimonte is the small village of **Castello del Matese**, worth a sinuous sidetrip for its view out to the valleys and down to Piedimonte before heading south toward Teano.

Capua and Santa Maria Capua Vetere

The road south from Teano leads back to state road No. 27, and crosses the motorway which also takes you the 25km down to Capua. The only advantage in taking the slower route 7 instead is that it will lead directly into Capua, and then to Santa Maria Capua Vetere farther south.

Capua

Capua is on a bend of the Volturno River, but the town is not situated to take advantage of the scenery. From the centre of town you'd hardly know the river existed at all, but in fact the Volturno is just behind the Duomo. The draw here is the Museo Campano, with a very good acheological collection housed in the 15th-century palazzo of the dukes of San Cipriano. Walking around, you'll find that Capua is a somewhat sleepy place – typical of so many Campanian towns which have more to tell about their past than future.

Capua was founded in the middle of the ninth century, after the Saracens destroyed the old town further south in 840. Lombard domination is particularly evident; no other city in Campania can boast as many high medieval churches. Restoration experts are struggling to obtain funds in order to reopen the dozen or so that are still intact, some of which have been closed for fifty years. The Duomo itself has mainly been rebuilt, though its elegant bell tower has been standing since 861.

The **Museo Campano** is at the end of Via Duomo; enter a pretty garden through a large stone doorway and climb the steps to the first floor. The museum houses works dating from the Hellenistic to the medieval period. The monumental busts in the first room to the left are strong, severely simple pieces done in the thirteenth century. They once adorned a triumphal arch in Capua, now destroyed, which was built by Frederick II in about 1230. Room No.28 has a small collection of pictures from the 15th, 16th and 17th centuries; the best by far is the *Deposition* by the Venetian painter Bartolommeo Vivarini done in the late 1400s.

The museum's most important works are the strange and solid tufa sculptures on the ground floor. This collection of ancient fertility figures, called Madri (Mothers), represents a rich chapter in Campanian popular art. The statues were uncovered in 1845 near ancient Capua (Santa Maria Capua Vetere) and span the 6th–1st centuries BC. They are *ex voto* offerings to a divinity called Mater Matuta who represented both dawn and birth. When someone offered one of these statues to the divinity, it was in the hope of becoming pregnant, of giving birth to a healthy baby, or offering thanks for the safe birth of a sound child. These sombre women of stone are seated with bundled infants – sometimes as many as five or six – nestled on each arm.

Santa Maria Capua Vetere

Capua's ancient counterpart is a few kilometres south. The drive is down a dreary-looking avenue bordered by signs, shops and petrol stations, which probably once formed part of the Via Appia. Is this really where Hannibal marched into the town that revolted against Rome during the Second Punic Wars and opened its gates to him? I would have had second thoughts about entering the city if the outskirts looked anything like they do today.

The scenery improves once you've passed through the vestiges of Hadrian's Arch at the city's northern edge. (The Appian Way passed through the arch, which was probably dedicated to the Emperor Hadrian who restored the amphitheatre nearby and was a generous patron of the city.) In 215 BC, Hannibal and his Carthaginian troops rested here in style, and exaggerated reports of the perfumed and willing women of Capua have survived the centuries. When I asked the women of Santa Maria Capua Vetere about this reputation, they snorted and said, 'Ridiculous'. When I asked the men, they replied, 'We wish!' Whatever transpired during that period of winter rest is still something of a mystery; some historians have claimed that Hannibal and his troops were then prepared to wage battles throughout Italy while others claim the city's charms softened him for good. Still, it wasn't until the great Roman general Scipio held Spain and its Carthaginian strongholds (defeating Hannibal's brother Hasdrubal) that Hannibal was given marching orders back to Carthage 12 years later.

On the outskirts of Santa Maria Capua Vetere is Italy's second largest **amphitheatre**, a wonderful relic of the town's illustrious past. When H.V. Morton visited here with an Italian professor in the early 1960s, they wandered 'all over the grassy giant as if we were solitary figures in some print by Piranesi, an unusual experience these days when ladies from Bradford and Kansas City are so often to be found seated upon the most remote altars'.

I share the impression; one is often left alone here to explore beneath and around the great shape, 170m long by 140m wide. The amphitheatre sits in its underclothes these days – so much stone has been stripped from the four-tiered façade that it's now more brick than marble. Some of the statues are in the National Archeological Museum in Naples. The best thing about the amphitheatre is the freedom to explore the curving tunnels beneath the floor, trying to imagine the chaos as lions and other beasts were funnelled through as gladiators scrambled into position. Cicero records that it seated 100,000; others claimed it was the model for all other amphitheatres in Italy because Rome's Colosseum was constructed almost 100 years later. A number of fragments are on view in a garden below the ticket entrance, but unfortunately the gladiators' school beyond the amphitheatre (where a slave revolt led by Spartacus is said to have started) is no longer in evidence.

Santa Maria Capua Vetere was originally settled by Oscans, a highly civilised Italic tribe inhabiting the region. But they were overpowered by the Etruscans and Capua became one of the most important cities in southern Italy. It was once the capital of Campania, but that distinction was absolutely out of the question after the citizens' hospitality to Hannibal. To avenge their disloyalty,

Italy's second largest amphitheatre, at Santa Maria Capua Vetere

leading citizens were killed or imprisoned by the Romans; Livy says that some took poison at elaborate banquets to outwit their captors. After the fall of the Roman Empire, the city was under attack by a series of invaders during the next five centuries. First came the Goths, then Vandals and Lombards, and old Capua was finally destroyed by the Saracens in 856.

The small city you drive through today is an amalgamation of many building periods; some structures have survived from the 16th and 17th centuries, especially the brown stuccoed walls bordering the streets. Tall portals with their heavy wooden gates along these dusty walls lead to small courtyards; most of the houses within have, at least in part, been rebuilt to accommodate 20th-century amenities. Streets are narrow and dark; shopkeepers advertising their goods by placing them outside the shop door risk having their fruit and brooms swept away by passing cars.

Life spills out into the squares, and the main one in town is **Piazza Mazzini**. Hundreds of years ago this was the Piazza Seplasia, a market for the famous perfumes distilled from Capuan roses. Just down Via Mazzocchi is the **Duomo**, or the Church of Santa Maria, which survived the Saracen raids. It was first built in 432, enlarged in 787, transformed in 1666, 1700 and 1884. The façade is now Neo-Classical; many of the internal columns are taken from ancient temples in the surrounding countryside. The polychrome marble altars are colourful and well-wrought works of Campanian art, but the dark religious paintings are not the most inspiring of their genre.

More interesting than the Duomo is the **Mithraeum** northwest of Piazza Mazzini off the Via Morelli. This temple to the Persian god Mithras was discovered in 1922. (To enter ask the ticket collector at the amphitheatre to take you there.) This rectangular underground room was the scene of rituals dedicated to Mithras in the second and third centuries centuries AD.

Roman soldiers brought this religion back with them from the Middle East; Mithras was a god ordered by Apollo to kill a bull, symbol of fertility. He wasn't supposed to spill a drop of blood while performing this task. But a scorpion intervened, and the dripping blood from the slain bull represented evil in a then-perfect world. To symbolise this scene, initiates into the cult of Mithras were sprinkled with bull's blood, and promised a better life to come.

A fresco of *Mithras Killing the Bull* is on the back wall of the chamber, a well preserved depiction of the god re-enacting the mythic scene. The stone seating on each side is for members – all male – and the frescoes on the side walls represent the seven stages of initiation into the cult. It wasn't a sinister organisation, though members were sworn to secrecy and always met in underground chambers. The cult was popular enough to arouse the suspicion of Roman politicians, however, who banned members from practising their pagan religion in 395.

Sant' Angelo in Formis and San Leucio: Frescoes, Silk, and a Social Experiment

Two small towns are worth the short detour north from old Capua before heading south to Caserta. One is to Sant' Angelo in Formis, celebrated for its Romanesque church with an incredible cycle of medieval frescoes. The other spot is San Leucio, still producing beautifully embroidered silks in modern, out-of-the way factories. San Leucio is now a rather isolated place but with such an interesting past that it is worth noting. Besides, you should not miss Sant' Angelo in Formis, and from there you will pass San Leucio on your way south to Caserta.

Sant' Angelo in Formis

When leaving Santa Maria Capua Vetere, head directly north out of town on Via Galatina from the Piazza San Francesco. About 10km on, at the foot of Monte Tifata and just after passing beneath an old archway, is the church of **Sant' Angelo in Formis**. (The caretaker's house is just beyond the arch on the right. He will escort you to the church; a small fee is recommended.)

This beautiful little Lombard Romanesque basilica was known to exist as early as 925, built on the ruins of a large ancient temple dedicated to Diana Tifatina, protectress of the forests. The church you see today was finished under the supervision of the abbot Desiderius from the Abbey of Montecassino in 1073. (That famous and once powerful Abbey is just 20km north in Cassino, in the region of Lazio.) The 1980 earthquake so badly damaged the church that state monies were earmarked for a complete restoration of the structure and frescoes.

The façade of Sant' Angelo in Formis is graced with a delicate portico of five arches, upheld by four Corinthian columns probably taken from the original temple. Inside, the church floor is thought to be from the temple also. The central nave is divided from its side aisles by 14 columns – some granite and others of veiny white cipollino marble. Earthquake damage led architectural experts to realise that the high arched windows were not of the original fenestration; they have been restored as longer lites without as many frames. It was also discovered that the basilica had been fitted with a false ceiling in 1926, and the original ceiling's design has now been duplicated.

Despite its being one of the best examples of medieval ecclesiastical architecture in Campania, Sant' Angelo in Formis is even more important for its cycle of frescoes. Ten experts from the Istituto Centrale del Restauro in Rome came to work on the frescoes for three years. These expressively depicted stories are clearly influenced by Byzantine models. Both those done in the portico and on the walls within were finished in the second half of the 11th century, most likely painted by artists who had also worked at Montecassino. The Life of Jesus is depicted above the arches in the central nave; in the central apse above the altar is Christ Giving His Blessing and opposite, on the back wall above the church's entrance, is a chilling scene of the Last Judgement.

The unattached bell-tower is at least as old as the church, and the big white travertine blocks used in part to construct the tower were taken from the amphitheatre at Santa Maria Capua Vetere. Behind the church are steps leading down into the remains of the temple, soon, we hope, to be open to the public. From the church's forecourt you are treated to a wonderful view: Campania's fertile fields lay below, with Capua straight ahead and Monte Roccamonfina off to your right.

San Leucio

To reach San Leucio, return to the main road travelled on from Santa Maria Capua Vetere, but then turn right on Road No.87 which travels south past Vaccheria. About 2km past the turning for Vaccheria you will come to **San Leucio** and the Piazza della Seta (Silk Square) – more of a roundabout than a proper town square. A left off the piazza leads up the hill on Via Planelli; proceed through the arch and drive up to the parking lot beneath the abandoned palace. On the street to either side are what remains of King Ferdinand's bold social experiment: the 18th-century homes of his silk workers, still inhabited today.

In 1789, the Bourbon King Ferdinand IV had visions of a new town, and with all due modesty planned to call it Ferdinandopoli. Two hundred people would be employed in reviving the manufacture of damasks and brocades, beautifully embroidered silks to be used in the Palace at Caserta and sold to the upper classes. A set of egalitarian laws would be followed, fair to both sexes. Most of this happened, though the town was never called Ferdinandopoli.

It became San Leucio instead, named after a church there dedicated to the saint who was bishop of Brindisi.

Ferdinand's ideas were certainly progressive, though some suspected that San Leucio was merely a playground for the king as benevolent dictator who frolicked there with local peasant girls. King Ferdinand claimed that he was only trying to put into practice the philosophical ideals of Gaetano Filangieri and the social reforms of Bernardo Tanucci. To that end, public health services and education were available to all (school commencing at the age of six); merit was to be the only way of earning individual distinction; people were free to dress however they wished; parents were not allowed to intervene in their children's choice of marital partners; and each factory worker gave a portion of his earnings over to the *Cassa della Carità*, a fund to care for the sick and the aged.

King Ferdinand and members of court came often to San Leucio, a weekend retreat just north of the Palace at Caserta. They stayed in the huge yellow-and-white edifice called the Casino Reale di Belvedere. From the promenade in front there is a wonderful view of Caserta beyond the rooftops of San Leucio. The Belvedere was constructed in 1776. The German painter Jakob Phillip Hackert was invited to reproduce the Campanian countryside on the walls within, and to paint the ceiling of Ferdinand's bathroom where he had requested a bathtub 'big enough to swim in'. A sign tells you that this decaying beauty is now the headquarters of a Scholastic Institute, but I saw no evidence of anyone learning anything. The clock at the top of the façade has stopped; the tall arched windows are broken. The interior must be in a similar state of disrepair.

To King Ferdinand's credit, the manufacturing colony at San Leucio thrived for more than half a century; silks produced here were sought after by wealthy patrons all over Europe. The factories were built behind and to the right of the Belvedere. These buildings are no longer used, as the modern Palazzo dello Stabilmento Serico is in operation just south. The cloth is still highly prized, though it is now made of artificial silk. The Italian government sent state gifts of San Leucio silk to both Queen Elizabeth upon her ascension to the throne and to Jacqueline Onassis when she was First Lady. The only little shop on the Piazza della Seta, called the Bottega della Tessitura d'Arte, sells fantastically intricate bolts of silk in an atmosphere reminiscent of 18th-century workshops.

Caserta and Caserta Vecchia

Caserta is the provincial state capital, dominated by the grand Palazzo Reale designed by Vanvitelli. I highly recommend a visit, for its gardens as well as the sumptuous interiors, despite the fact that there is little else to see in the town of Caserta. As compensation though, the small town of Caserta Vecchia 10km north east is one of the most charming villages in all of Campania. You will have had a very fulfilling day if you visit the Palazzo Reale in the morning, stroll through its gardens, and then drive to Caserta Vecchia in the afternoon.

The gardens at Caserta rival those of Versailles

While Caserta has little to recommend it in the way of restaurants, Caserta Vecchia has a surprising number of good, unpretentious places to eat.

The Palazzo Reale

If you're arriving at Caserta from the direction of San Leucio, state road No.87 continues the five or six kilometres south. But if coming up to Caserta from Naples it's a quick trip north by train or bus, or by car up the A2 motorway. You'll see signs for the **Palazzo Reale**, or **Reggia** as it's also called, when reaching Caserta. You can't miss it, for it's the biggest building for miles around.

The Bourbon King Charles III was again the mastermind behind this impressive architectural centrepiece for the region, and the court architect Luigi Vanvitelli threw himself into planning its construction in 1752. Charles wanted a royal palace and seat of government away from congested Naples, but he never had the opportunity to spend a single night there. He was called back to rule Spain in 1759 before work was completed, and it was then up to King Ferdinand to finish the job in 1774. The palace has been likened to Versailles, and is said to have been influenced by it. I know mine is a minority opinion, but I think Vanvitelli more than satisfied the king's wish to rival Versailles. He positively outdid the French architects – the dramatic staircases and floor plan within, as well as the multitude of diversely planned landscapes behind the palace make it a far more exciting and much less predictable place to explore than Versailles.

The Reggia at Caserta was US General George S. Patton's headquarters after the Allied invasion of Italy, and the scene for Field Marshal Lord Alexander's acceptance of the unconditional surrender of the German forces on April 29, 1945. (2km north east of Caserta is the British Military Cemetery.) I was told

The impressive grand staircase at Caserta, flanked by lions

that the American Army, upon leaving the palace of Caserta, paid to have the marble floors re-polished since so many pairs of heavy boots had detroyed the finish. With 1200 rooms, there is a lot of marble to polish and with 1790 windows, plenty of work for those who wash them.

The main façade of the yellow stucco and travertine building is almost 250m long; the utterly symmetrical, Neo-Classical plan has four identical inner courtyards. The gardens stretch for three kilometres north beyond the back façade of the palace – sculptures, fountains and cascades, along with an English garden and man-made lake with an island are all part of the impressive landscape.

Italian military and other government offices occupy almost half of the Reggia, with one wing open to the public. The second of three front entrances leads to the centre of the building, and at ground level the eye travels straight through to the garden cascades beyond. To the right is the grand staircase, where you are greeted by the stone lions of Clemency and Fortitude, and then led to a wonderfully marbled vestibule – the red star in the middle of the floor is the palace's geometric centre.

The thirty rooms open to the public are entered through the **Hall of the Halbardiers**, where visitors were once discreetly frisked and royal bodyguards would stand in line when the king passed. I found the ornamentation in most of these large rooms overwhelming. The **Appartamento Vecchio** in the left wing is prettier than the Royal Apartment rooms to the right. Allegorical frescoes adorn four rooms named for the seasons, their walls lined with silk from the factories at San Leucio. At the end of this wing are three rooms comprising the library: marquetry borders repeat around the shelf tops and some books are shelved in the lovely conical glass bookcase in the last room. A wonderful, large *presepio* also rests here, with more than 1000 figures and buildings adorning the nativity scene. The **Chapel** and the beautiful 18th-century *Court Theatre*, if open, are worth seeing more than the upper rooms. Ask one of the guards to take you to see them.

At the back of the palace is a bus that travels to the top of the park, for an additional fee of 1000 lire each way. I suggest taking the ride up; you can always walk back. At the top is a snack bar where you can buy a sandwich or slice of pizza, along with illustrated guides and souvenirs. The park is at its best on Wednesday, Saturday and Sunday from about 11.00 to 14.00, when the fountains are on and the long terraced canal is filled with water. Since this is drinkable water, coming from a superbly designed aqueduct in Maddaloni devised by Vanvitelli, the commune decided to limit the supply of this precious commodity to certain days of the week – very sensible, but not so gratifying for the visitor who comes on the wrong day.

Vanvitelli also supervised the park's landscape, which was laid out by Martin Biancour. The most famous set of fountain statues at Caserta is that of **Diana and Actaeon** at the top of the hill beneath a high waterfall. Diana and her nymphs are bathing on one side, while on the other Actaeon has stumbled upon the divine naked figure while hunting. For this innocent accident, Diana punishes him severely; Actaeon sprouts horns and is attacked by his own dogs. To my mind, the dogs are more animated than the other figures in this landscape, but the harmony of composition in such a natural setting more than compensates.

Facing the back of the palace, the **English Garden** will be on your left, and a guide will take you through this section of the park. It was laid out by the Englishman John Andrew Graeffer in 1782, and has many delightful elements. Cedars of Lebanon, palms, pines, and the first camelia imported from Japan to Europe are among the rich variety of botanical species here. The mock ruins are my favourite part of the English Garden. Arched walkways wind around a pond – portions of the vaulted roof and tufa walls are missing while frescoes continue to fade beneath moist brown moss. Another favourite is the **Castelluccia** or miniature castle, a Vanvitelli folly closer to the palace on the west side. It is found past the old fish pond with its central island. The big fishpond, half a kilometre long and forming the first pool before ascending north to the Grand Cascade, was always stocked with fish for the royal kitchens. The way back to the Reggia is along the central avenue with its wide water path of twelve little waterfalls.

The Medieval Borgo of Caserta Vecchia

A winding corniche road to the northeast of Caserta takes you up to the walled town of Caserta Vecchia. Views along the way give you a good idea of what this farming country is like, and what mining has done to the limestone mountains beyond. Stark white patches have exposed whole sides of these mountains, and the regional government no longer allows companies to be so rapacious. But one thing that remains entirely intact in this area is the charming town of

Caserta Vecchia. It's a pleasure to walk its cobbled streets and stand in the unchanged main square with its cathedral and bell tower, with 9th-century castle ruins on a neglected hill above. No more than 300 people live here, and most of the mini Fiats are parked on the town's edge. Unless you're making a delivery to one of the local restaurants, don't try to take a car through these narrow streets.

The town was probably founded in the 8th century by the Lombards, but the oldest existing buildings date from the 11th and 12th centuries when the Normans controlled the region. The **cathedral of San Michele**, finished in 1153, is a fine example of Southern Norman architecture, which in some ways is a blend of styles. The central cupola, added 100 years later, has a Moslem feel to it – a rounded roof, with chequered squares of brown and yellow between delicate intertwined arches on two levels. The bell-tower was built in 1234; Gothic influence means that it's less ornamental but again has the rounded roof of a Middle Eastern dwelling. One of the roadways into the main Cathedral square runs through it.

The cathedral's façade is simple and joyful: two small stone lions jut out on the sides of the main central portal with a little bull above. Over the right-hand entrance are two horselike creatures, and on the left are centaurs. The interior has recently undergone renovation, remaining simple and solemn, and very similiar in plan and proportions to Sant' Angelo in Formis. Eighteen Corinthian columns divide the nave from the aisles; the pulpit and altar are good examples of intricate mosaic marblework.

During the second half of September the town sponsors exhibits and games to celebrate its patron saint of San Michele. I happened upon the *spettacolo* one warm evening when the walled square beside the Duomo was filled with children in splendid silk costumes. Their outfits were half one colour and half another, to represent different teams competing in their version of the *Palio*. The four squads went by the names of the Towers, Walls, Cathedral and St Michael. Before the festivities began, the children sang their way through a half-hour mass. Then they tore back into the square, some hugging the young priest around his middle, imploring him to get the show on the road. The first race began: one runner from each team bore a torch and ran off through the streets, their silken tunics flapping in the breeze. This was followed by more foot-races, and many tries at tug-of-war in the twilight.

I wandered up and down the streets, thinking what a safe and sheltered life they must lead in this perfectly preserved outpost. To grow up in a town that nobody can remember ever having looked any differently – what must that feel like? Perhaps only the names of restaurants here have changed. The five or six here now will beckon you with the smell of roasted peppers and simmering tomato sauce. (Try wild boar too – the local speciality.)

East to Benevento and south to Avellino

Benevento is the capital of Campania's smallest province, important for its place in ancient history. It is surrounded by small, insular towns whose people don't appear to be as open as those in towns and cities along the coast. South of Benevento by about 30km is Avellino, hit so hard by the 1980 earthquake that it's still trying to build itself back into shape. Benevento has more to recommend it than Avellino but, frankly, I wouldn't make a special trip to either place unless you are in search of something of specific interest, or unless your route takes you conveniently past either city.

Avellino and Benevento are quickly reached by motorway from Naples, or by the slower route 7 when coming from Caserta. Route 7, though busy and unattractively lined with small factories just outside of Caserta, traverses interesting countryside before reaching Benevento. Two towns worth stopping in along the way are picturesque **Airola** (with the Church of the Annunciata's façade designed by Vanvitelli) and **Montesarchio** with its Baroque fountain in Piazza Umberto I and a solid 15th-century castle at the top of the windswept hill. You'll drive through a ravine known as the Caudine Forks, where the Samnites trapped the Romans in 321BC, though historians still debate its exact location: between Arienzo and Arpaia, or between Sant' Agata de' Goti and Moiano?

Benevento

Benevento's old town sits on a hill between the Calore and Sabato Rivers, still a throughfare for those travelling between Naples and Apulia. Its Latin name was Malaventum, ascribed to bad air flowing through. Either the air or attitudes changed dramatically, for the Romans renamed this place Beneventum in 268BC. In 571 it became the first independent Lombard duchy, and the remains of walls built during that time are among the oldest in Europe. Benevento was the site of Manfred of Hohenstaufen's defeat by Charles of Anjou in 1266, and the city gained yet more battle scars during World War II when it was badly bombed by the Allies. Benevento is probably best known throughout Italy as the home of Strega, a bitter liqueur made from walnuts. *Strega* means witch in Italian, and the famous yellow mixture takes it name from the superstition that witches gathered around a walnut tree here to celebrate rites on the Sabbath.

Benevento's main sights are grouped closely together, most on or close to the Corso Garibaldi. The 13th-century Romanesque Duomo sits at one end, the church of Santa Sofia and its museum at the other, while Trajan's Arch is down the Via Traiano halfway along the Corso. The **Roman theatre**, built during Hadrian's reign in the second century, is just south east of the Duomo. It is engulfed by homes and apartments, another sad example of how lack of planning can damage an ancient monument. But to the city's credit the amphitheatre is still used for open-air performances.

Trajan's Arch here in Benevento is one of the best preserved in all of Italy, erected across the Appian Way by Trajan in 114. 17m high, it's made of Parian marble and covered with rich bas relief scenes. All the figures are intact, save two on one high outer edge. Those that remain are somewhat hard to identify, but they all depict scenes from the life of the emperor – his coronation, in counsel with Roman senators, and ceremonies of worship, along with mythological scenes. Though the arch is dirty, the only real distraction here is the information booth ridiculously placed in the centre which spoils the arch's lofty proportions.

Benevento's other highlight is the church of **Santa Sofia** and its **Samnite Museum** in the cloister behind. The small church on pretty Piazza Matteotti was built in 762. The internal plan is unusual – semicircular behind the high altar, with six-sided wall sections connecting front to back. The church's central nucleus consists of six columns connected by arches, and a second outer ring of eight pilasters. The overall effect produces a simple and intimate interior, one of the oddest and most pleasing I've ever experienced. Behind the high altar, in the two outer apses, are fragments of an 8th-century cycle of frescoes depicting the Life of St Zacchary.

The cloisters of Santa Sofia are just as delightful as the church. The Samnite Museum is set in airy rooms off this courtyard, and from each is yet another view of the cloisters and its fanciful columns. Each capital, carved in the first half of the 12th century, is full of detail and not a little Arab influence: a camel with driver along one side, a trellis of grapes along the other. On another horsemen gallop and a deer is being attacked. I found every single scene captivating. The museum itself is formed from a provincial archeological collection initiated by Talleyrand in 1806, absentee ruler for nine years who was given the title of Prince of Benevento by Napolean when the French briefly ruled Naples. Statues from Domitian's Temple of Isis are among the most interesting in the collection, but there are also Magna Grecia coins, 6th-century bronze jewellery, ceramics, and paintings by Francesco Solimena, Andrea Vaccaro and Giacomo del Po.

Avellino

The most scenic route from Benevento to Avellino is by winding state road No.88, which takes about an hour. The route wends through a green valley full of small farms. Tobacco is grown here in abundance, and stepped gardens are planted with grape vines and tomatoes. A faster route is by motorway running south east and parallel to state road No.7, and then directly west by motorway A16 to Avellino.

The city of Avellino is capital of its province, with a population of 60,000. It has had the worst luck of any city in the region, being drastically shaken by earthquakes from 1456 until the present day. Perhaps this helps to explain why a high number of Italians from this area have emigrated to other countries, especially the US. After the earthquake in 1980, Italians from many other parts of the country came here to help restore some degree of normality to peoples' lives.

Avellino's medieval nucleus, from the Duomo to the castle ruins just east, is the most interesting section to explore. The cathedral, with its Neo-Classical façade, was originally built in the 12th century but rebuilt in 1868. Beneath the Duomo are remnants of the original Lombard church – **Santa Maria dei Sette Dolori**. Near the Piazza Amendola in the streets around the church are a number of Baroque fountains, along with a clock-tower designed by Fanzago. Avellino's only other attraction is the **Irpino Museum** on two floors of the modern Palazzo della Cultura on Corso Europa. Its archeological collection of prehistoric Irpine, Samnite and Roman objects embraces a period from the neolithic age to the sixth century. There is also a small but valuable selection of Neapolitan paintings, along with a section devoted to the Risorgimento.

Practical Information

Getting there

Travelling north of Naples to Caserta and Benevento is easy to do by train, from either the main station in Naples or Rome. The tour companies listed in the information section at the end of chapter three also run day trips to the palace at Caserta. However, for outlying towns and the coast you must go by car. The A2 motorway is a fast connecting route from Rome to Naples, and many exits along the way are close to the towns mentioned in this chapter.

Tourist Information Offices

AVELLINO   50 Piazza Libertà (tel. 0825 35175).

BENEVENTO   34 Via Giustiniani (tel. 0824 21960).

CASERTA   The main provincial tourist office is located within the central area of the palace complex (tel. 0823 326832). A more accessible office is located on the corner of Piazza Dante at 39 Corso Trieste (tel. 0823 321137).

Hotels and restaurants

AVELLINO   Jolly Hotel, 97a Via Tuoro Cappuccini (tel. 0825 25922) is comfortable but lacking in character. Expensive. Close to the hotel is a very good restaurant called **La Caveja**, 48 Via Tuoro Cappuccini (tel. 0825 38277). Moderate.

BAIA DOMIZIA   In the province of Caserta, my first choice is always **Hotel della Baia**, Via dell'Erica, 81030 Caserta (tel. 0823 721344). In the north west corner of Campania right on the Mediterranean, the small town of Baia Domizia itself is characterised by uninspired post-war buildings, but the hotel is set apart from all that, with a view out to sea. It is a low, cool white stucco building, the floors paved with large glazed terracotta tiles. A tennis court is shared with the hotel next door; the food here is wonderful; taking full or half board is very good value. If it weren't for the fact that the hotel is closed from October to mid-May, the restaurant would undoubtedly be awarded a Michelin star. Moderate prices.

BENEVENTO   The Hotel President, 1 Via G.B. Perasso, 82100 Benevento (tel. 0824 21000), is in a good position near the church of Santa Sofia. Clean and moderately priced, though without any atmosphere. The basic and inexpensive **Hotel Traiano**, Viale dei Rettori, is just up the street from Trajan's magnificent arch.

Benevento is filled with pizzerias, as well as more formal places such as the expensive **Antica Taverna**, Via Annunziata 41 (tel. 0824 21212), closed Sun; and the moderately-priced **Pascalucci** in the Piano Cappelle district (24548); closed Mon.

CASERTA   The large Reggia Palace Hotel, Viale Carlo III, PO Box 20, 81100 Caserta (tel. 0823 458500), is clean and comfortable, though impersonal and without character. It is on a main road just south of the palace, 2km from the Caserta Sud exit off the motorway. Food here is good, but the modern décor in the dining room is appalling; there's a pool and a clay tennis court. Expensive. (The hotel is technically in San Nicola La Strada, and other smaller hotels are also on Viale Carlo III, such as the **Pisani** and the **Serenella**.)

One good restaurant in the centre of Caserta is the **Antica Locanda-Massa 1848**, Via Mazzini 55 (tel. 0823 321268), open for lunch, and on Saturday nights. Moderate prices.

CASERTA VECCHIA   Unfortunately, there is no accommodation in this charming town, but five or six small and simple restaurants have a long tradition of serving good local fare. They are so close to one another on the town's few walking streets that you can easily survey menus and prices as you stroll along. One I'd recommend is **Al Ritrovo dei Patriarchi** (tel. 0823 371510); closed Wed. Moderate.

TELESE   In the region of Benevento, I came across another hotel like della Baia, unusual for its elegance and amenities. It's called **Grand Hotel Telese**, 1 Via Cerreto, 82037, Telese Terme (tel. 0824 940500), located in the small town of Telese about 25km north west of Benevento. It's surrounded by woods, and a large complex of thermal baths are nearby. Reception rooms with floor to ceiling windows are furnished with antiques; bedrooms are plush and inviting, with thick terry-cotton robes supplied. Ask for a room overlooking the front drive and gardens. Full board only; expensive.

Price Ranges

Hotel (double room)	*Restaurant (Per head)*
Inexpensive: under 60,000	under 25,000
Moderate: 60–120,000	25–50,000
Expensive: 120–200,000	50–90,000
Very expensive: 200,000+	90,000+

Museums and other public sites

AVELLINO Irpino Museum, Corso Europa, Palazzo della Cultura. Open 08:30–14.00 Mon–Fri, 08:30–12.00 Sat, closed Sun and hols.

BENEVENTO Samnite Museum, Corso Garibaldi (tel. 0824 21818). Open 09.00–13.00 Mon through Sat; closed Sun and hols.
Trajan's Arch, Via Traiano, viewed at all hours.

CAPUA Museo Campano, Palazzo Antignano, Via Roma (tel. 0823 971402). Open 09.00–14.00 Tues through Sat, 09.00–13.00 Sun, closed Mon and hols.

CASERTA Palazzo Reale and gardens (tel. 0823 321127). State apartments open 09.00–13.30 Tues through Sat, 09.00–13.00 Sun, closed Mon and hols. The park is also open until 16.30 during the months of July, August and September.

SANTA MARIA CAPUA VETERE Amphitheatre, at the top of Piazza Primo Ottobre from Corso Umberto Primo. Open 09.00–16.00, closed Mon and hols. **Mithraeum**, Vico Mitreo off Via Morelli. Same hours as amphitheatre, whose custodian will escort you on the ten-minute walk from there.

7. SOUTH WITH HISTORY: Vesuvius, Herculaneum and Pompeii

'Blow on a dead man's embers and a live flame will start,' wrote poet Robert Graves. Is there anywhere in the world where this is more true than at the ancient sights of Pompeii and Herculaneum? Vesuvius wrought molten havoc in 79AD, but 1900 years later the tragically encased bodies are still telling us their tales.

Pompeii has been more systematically excavated than Herculaneum, mainly because the fallen volcanic material was not as dense and rock-like as that at Herculaneum. The town's layout is so extensive that you can spend hours in Pompeii wandering from house to shop to temple, getting a good idea of what life must have been like in this market town. But Pompeii is so famous that perhaps people expect too much from it, and some travellers express disappointment with what they find – and don't find. An endless number of unmarked, half-height walls running in all directions appear daunting at first; I do recommend hiring a guide who speaks English to some degree. An important point to remember is that the best works of art found in Pompeii are now in the National Archeological Museum in Naples, except for the cycle of frescoes at the Villa of the Mysteries.

Many more travellers find their way to Pompeii than to Herculaneum and the summit of Vesuvius. If you can devote at least two days' sightseeing to this area of the Campanian coast, it's really best to see all three (along with a trip to the museum in Naples). More than Pompeii, Herculaneum's excavations are a compact and primarily residential quarter which help shed a different shade of light on the period. If you climb to the summit of Vesuvius, wander through Herculaneum, and then spend a day at Pompeii you will have as complete a picture of life suspended in 79AD as anyone possibly can.

After the volcano smothered both towns, they lay hidden for centuries. Rumours of buried treasure at the foot of the mountain were often heard, but nothing was found; in 1503 a cartographer named Ambrogio Leone marked Herculaneum fairly accurately when drawing a map of Campania. But that didn't stimulate enough interest to start digging, perhaps a blessing in disguise considering the amount of damage done by excavating in the 1700s. In the 1590s, an aristocrat who needed water for his villa's fountain at Torre Annunziata dug a channel across the site of Pompeii, and came across inscriptions which named the town. But still nothing was done; he left all stones unturned because he thought the carving referred not to the city but to Pompey the Great, a popular general who conquered the army of Spartacus.

Then in 1709 the building of a monastery well at Resina led to the accidental discovery of Herculaneum. A workman revealed splendidly coloured marbles when he hit seats in the town's theatre, and many objects were then plundered for the nearby villa of an Austrian prince. The theatre was identified correctly only in 1738, and Charles III financed the first excavation, headed by a Spanish engineer. His methods weren't exactly scientific, until a Swiss architect named Weber arrived on the scene. He discovered the famous Villa of the Papyri, still buried under 20m of volcanic matter. Weber diligently tunnelled through many areas, drawing systematic plans of what he found. (These invaluable, though incomplete, floor plans were used for the J. Paul Getty Museum replication in Malibu, California.)

Finally, it was the famous Italian archeologist Amedeo Maiuri who carefully directed the first comprehensive modern excavations of both sights. Past discoveries, especially during the 18th and early 19th centuries, had done their damage – in some cases worse than that inflicted by Vesuvius over the centuries. But Maiuri's work in the 1920s, based on solid research carried out by Giuseppe Fiorelli in the 1860s, has carefully yielded the most fascinating tale of two cities ever told.

Vesuvius

Before visiting Pompeii and Herculaneum, acquaint yourself with their annihilator by climbing to the top of Vesuvius. Still deceptively active, the volcano has erupted eighty times since Pompeii and Herculaneum were buried, though it has been relatively quiet since 1944. While driving up to the summit you'll be able to see where the last lava flow in March, 1944, left its wide dark mark.

The ascent of Vesuvius takes about forty minutes if you're walking up the west face path, reached after passing villages on a winding road that ends at the car park. The trip up Vesuvius can easily be combined with a visit to Herculaneum on the same day, but don't try to fit in Pompeii too; save that experience for a full day's outing.

For the climb up the west face, wear a pair of sturdy, flat-bottomed shoes. The path consists of uneven bits of hard lava and you can lose your footing. Even if it's a warm day, take a sweater or windproof garment because it does get cool on the way up. While climbing, you won't question the position of the cone looming above. But from Naples and the north east, Vesuvius with its two lopsided peaks looks as if it harbours two volcanoes. Before 79AD, the summit was wider and taller, encompassing both peaks as one large mass; but the eruption that wiped out Pompeii and Herculaneum blew away the mountain's top. From the Sorrento side, you can tell which portion of the mountain is a peaked ridge, and which is the cone.

When you get to the summit, at 1277m, you'll be looking down into a cone with a flat barren bottom. In its present state it's hard to believe that this volcano has been capable of spewing forth lava and ash, along with sending low banks of superhot gases and sliding debris toward villages miles away. Vapour continues to escape from cracks along the inner sides and bottom, but fencing prevents anyone from walking down inside for a closer view. Snack bars mark the beginning and end of the trail, selling postcards and garish bits of painted lava.

Vesuvius is an otherworldly place. How could anyone judge its force as the volcano slumbers within and the landscape below looks so tranquil? When Vesuvius is as still as it is today, and was before the great eruption, it's easy to see why Pompeiians were unaware of its destructive power. Tales were told of orange light once escaping from Vesuvius, and in 30BC, the geographer Strabo thought the rocks on the top looked as if they'd been subjected to fire. But this mountain dedicated to Bacchus yielded succulent tomatoes, and its grapes still produce a fine white wine known as Lacrima Christi. This soil full of nutrients was a symbol of plenty rather than ruin.

Even the naturalist Pliny the Elder initially thought the eruption merely curious on that day in August, 79. According to his nephew's account, Pliny sailed closer and closer to Pompeii, both to get a closer look and with the thought of saving people along the shore. Upon arriving at Castellamare di Stabia south of Pompeii, he thought he had time for a little rest and relaxation, and dozed off into a sound sleep. But when he awoke the walls around him were shaking violently; Pliny and his friends were forced to flee with pillows tied to their heads for protection. The air was thick and black with smoke, and Pliny suffocated from the vapours he couldn't help inhaling. Hundreds of people in Pompeii and Herculaneum must have suffered the same fate.

Pliny's nephew's eyewitness account from the shores of Cape Misenum across the bay earned him a scientific honour: the first stage of eruption (fall-out of pumice and ash from a high cloud) has been named the 'Plinian phase'. He recorded that this cloud was

> in appearance and shape like a tree – the umbrella pine would give the best idea of it. Like an immense tree trunk it was projected into the air, and opened out with branches. I believe that it was carried up by a violent gust, then left as the gust faltered.

Sir William Hamilton gives us a light-hearted account of Neapolitan behaviour during a lesser eruption in 1767 in his *Campi Phlegraei*:

> The ashes, or rather small cinders, showered down so fast that the people in the streets were obliged to use umbrellas or flap their hats, these ashes

being very offensive to the eyes. The tops of the houses and balconies were covered above an inch thick with these cinders . . . In the midst of these horrors the mob, growing tumultuous and impatient, obliged the Cardinal to bring out the head of San Gennaro and go with it in procession to the Ponte Maddalena, at the extremity of Naples toward Vesuvius; and it is well attested here that the eruption ceased the moment the Saint came in sight of the mountain.

I have no doubt that Neapolitans would try that ploy again if Vesuvius threatened them. What are the chances of an eruption occuring today? Nobody knows for sure. Many volcanologists are troubled by the disturbances at nearby Pozzuoli – are they a sign that pressure beneath the earth's surface is escaping in a less disastrous way, or is another volcano building up far beneath the flat plain of Vesuvius we see today? The only reassurance is that trained eyes and instruments record every belch and rumble these days, and that there should be plenty of warning before anything drastic happens.

Herculaneum

Herculaneum sits on the western hem of Mount Vesuvius, and on a full day's outing can be combined with an ascent to the summit. The town was named for Hercules by Greek settlers, though the city's origins are not entirely clear to scholars. An Italic people called the Oscans certainly dominated the area 500 years before Christ, building the original walls at Pompeii. But the Oscans were then ousted by another stronger, native tribe called the Samnites who made their way south from the region bordering Campania and Lazio. It wasn't until 89BC that Herculaneum was taken with other Campanian towns by the Roman general Sulla.

As it was part of the Roman Empire, life was relatively peaceful, and Herculaneum was really no more than a satellite to Naples. It was never a commercial centre like Pompeii, and a population of 5000 inhabitants was deduced by counting the seats through tunneling down into the amphitheatre. Large villas were built by the sea, an exclusive suburban enclave similar to Baia which lies west of Naples.

Herculaneum's fate was very different to Pompeii's, due to its position upwind and to the northwest of Vesuvius. After an initial explosion, pumice fell lightly on the town; about 20cm accumulated in 18 hours. But then it was hit by ground surges (clouds of ash and hot gas that hug the ground) and pyroclastic flows (avalanches of pumice, ash and gases). Six successive waves of thick, hot volcanic matter soon flowed into Herculaneum, and the town was buried to an average depth of 22m.

Archeologists had assumed that most of the residents had had time to escape, since less than 12 bodies had ever been found. But in 1980, while workmen were digging a drainage ditch near the marina, they came across a skeleton. Soon they dug up dozens more and in 1982, a capsized boat 10m long. A new theory emerged. Had hundreds of frightened townspeople made their way to the beach, hoping to escape by sea? Groups of up to seven people were found huddled together in vaulted chambers, probably built to store boats. A Roman soldier was found face down with his sword beside him. A 25-year-old woman had been seven months pregnant, her unborn baby's bones as fragile as eggshell. Many had contorted jaws, as if trying to fight the fumes that must have asphyxiated them.

Although much of Herculaneum remains unexcavated, there are important sights to see. (Underground tunnels still lead to the buried amphitheatre and the fantastic Villa of the Papyri, but aren't open to the public and would be difficult to get through even if they were.) The area of the city which has been uncovered comprises five quarters and three main streets, similar to the earliest inner Greek-planned district of Naples. Houses are in a very good state of preservation, including a second storey in some cases. It has been much harder work to uncover ruins here than in Pompeii, but the tough shell of tufa-like material that encased Herculaneum's structures has meant that even some wooden beams and household objects are still in place.

The houses within the excavated area show a variety of different building methods, for a populace which ranged from merchant to patrician. The rich laid claim to the best positions by the seafront, and their homes were filled with decorative frescoes and mosaics. All the public elements of a Roman town are present in Herculaneum: the baths, forum, market, basilica, palestra and theatre. For a lively and informative account of life in the town, I recommend getting hold of a copy of *Herculaneum: Italy's Buried Treasure*, by Joseph Jay Deiss, first published by Harper and Row in 1966 but revised in 1985.

Across from the entrance to the site is a shop selling a detailed visual guide to the ruins, worth purchasing, but I've also outlined highlights here. From the entrance gate, walk south down the avenue and around to your right. The excavated area sits down within high walls, somewhat claustrophobic compared to the open plain of Pompeii.

At the western edge, where you enter, is the **House of the Inn** (Casa dell'Albergo) to the right. This is one of the biggest houses in the southern quarter, and just before Vesuvius erupted had been undergoing renovation to add an apartment and a shop.

Heading up Cardo IV, the first dwelling on the right is the **House of the Mosaic Atrium** (Casa dell Atrio a Mosaico). It once had a beautiful view of the sea, but the shore has since retreated by about 500m. The mosaic in the large atrium is a bold black-and-white geometric design, yet the most amazing thing about it is the floor itself: rippled waves of tile are what you now walk on, caused by the forceful flow of volcanic material beneath the surface. The house is in two sections, with a garden between, and most of the wood in the portico – window sashes, frames and beams – is original. To the left of the entrance was the doorkeeper's area: his mosaic sign to beware of the dog, *Cave Canem*, is similar to the famous Pompeiian version now at the Archeological Museum in Naples.

Just up the same street on the left is the **Wooden Trellis House** (Casa a Graticcio or Opus Craticium, which is the Latin term for this type of construc-

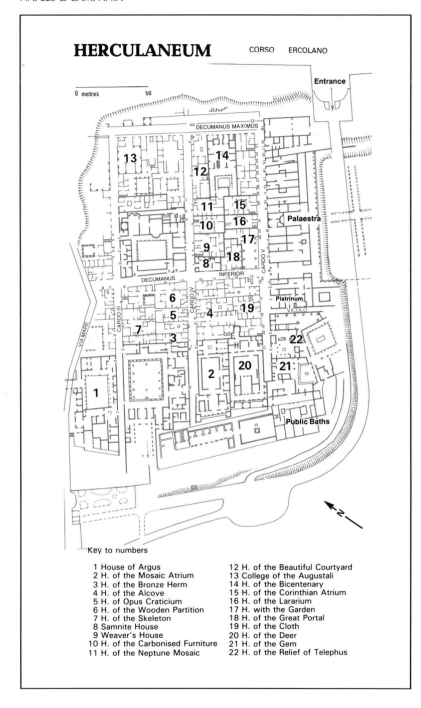

HERCULANEUM

CORSO   ERCOLANO

Entrance

0 metres   50

DECUMANUS MAXIMUS

Palaestra

DECUMANUS

INFERIOR

Pistrinum

VICOLO

Public Baths

N

Key to numbers

1 House of Argus
2 H. of the Mosaic Atrium
3 H. of the Bronze Herm
4 H. of the Alcove
5 H. of Opus Craticium
6 H. of the Wooden Partition
7 H. of the Skeleton
8 Samnite House
9 Weaver's House
10 H. of the Carbonised Furniture
11 H. of the Neptune Mosaic

12 H. of the Beautiful Courtyard
13 College of the Augustali
14 H. of the Bicentenary
15 H. of the Corinthian Atrium
16 H. of the Lararium
17 H. with the Garden
18 H. of the Great Portal
19 H. of the Cloth
20 H. of the Deer
21 H. of the Gem
22 H. of the Relief of Telephus

tion). Its square wooden frame is simple, consisting of small rooms and a balcony protruding from the second storey. The inexpensive wood and plaster construction was used for poorer dwellings, and the technique was called *opus craticium*. The building has a shop, a back workroom and two apartments; some of the steps to the upper storey are original, and the bedrooms above still contain furniture.

Next door is the patrician **House of the Wooden Partition** (Casa del Tramezzo di Legno), whose façade is one of the best preserved in Herculaneum. Inside, ceilings are high, and traces of fresco decoration are evident from floor to ceiling. The house is named for the wooden screen on bronze tracks used to close off the living room (*tablinum*) from the atrium. Two small bedrooms still have their wooden bed frames.

On Cardo IV's opposite corner is the **Samnite House** (Casa Sannitica), built at least three centuries before Vesuvius erupted and one of Herculaneum's oldest. The atrium is a large airy space dominated by the entranceway, which is flanked by two Corinthian columns. The second-storey gallery is divided by small Ionic columns between a perforated rail. Interior walls were delicately painted in shades of red and sea-green, along with many frescoes.

Across the street are the **Baths** (Terme del Foro), very well preserved and probably constructed between 30 and 10 BC. The men's section is entered at No.7 Cardo IV, the women's at No.8. It's not a luxurious place, but well equipped; some mosaics still survive, along with the characteristic phallic graffiti on some of the walls. In the center of the Baths is the Paleastra, or gym, where both men and women would exercise – perhaps fencing, or playing *pila*, a game in which players would toss a ball (an inflated animal's bladder) to each other. Walking through the Baths, you'll come across separate cold, tepid and hot rooms, as well as waiting rooms and toilets for men and women. Skeletons, perhaps of bath attendants, still remain in the men's waiting room, trapped there when Vesuvius erupted.

Look into two other houses along Cardo IV across from the Baths. The **House of the Carbonised Furniture** (Casa del Mobilio Carbonizzato) still contains its dining couch and a three-legged table.

The **House of the Mosaic of Neptune and Amphitrite** (Casa di Nettuno ad Anfitrite) had its front walls destroyed and lies open to the street, with a shop and its shelves close to the street. The living quarters are toward the back, and the pretty blue-and-green mosaics in the open dining room are only outstripped by the stunning mosaic of a nude golden Neptune and his wife Amphitrite.

Up at the top of the street, turn right on Decumano Massimo. The **House of the Bicentenary** (Casa del Bicentanario) will be on your right, so-called because it was excavated in 1938, 200 hundred years after organised digging started. It was a beautiful house, one of Herculaneum's richest, and lies at the centre of a controversy as a result of a curious discovery within. A wall in one of the upper floor's rooms is marked with the shape of a cross on a patch of white stucco, as if someone had ripped a wooden crucifix from the spot. A small wooden cabinet had been positioned beneath, with a platform in front that might have been used for kneeling in prayer. If that's the case, this would be

The mosaic of Neptune and Amphitrite at Herculaneum

the oldest evidence of the Christian cross in use as a symbol for the group then known by Romans as the cult of the Jew Christus. The Apostle Paul had landed at Pozzuoli 18 years earlier. Was this room's tenant a convert after listening to his radical teachings?

Now turn left into limestone-paved Cardo V, walking past merchant's shops to the **Bakery** (Pistrinum) at No.8. This shop was owned by Sextus Patulcus Felix, as seen by the inscription. Two stone flour mills are intact within, along with bronze baking tins. Over the baking ovens at the back is an upright phallic emblem, a humorous symbol employed to ensure that cakes would rise successfully while baking.

Behind this section of the street is a large gym and exercise area called the **Palaestra**, only partially uncovered among the weeds. But you can see the cross-shaped swimming pool that's been excavated.

Stop into the **House of the Gem** (Casa della Gemma) for a look at the famous graffiti in the loo. Inscribed on the wall is: *Apollinaris medicus Titi imperatoris hic cacavit bene.* In other words: Apollinaris, physician of the Emperor Titus, crapped well here.

The **House of the Deer** (Casa dei Cerveri) is just opposite, named for two little marble statues found inside. It's the last house on the right at the end of the street, and decoration dates it to about 25 years before the eruption. The lavish house is divided into two long sections, and at one time overlooked the bay. Walls were decorated in the black-and-red style of Pompeii; in the enclosed portico are charming paintings of cupids playing hide-and-seek and other games; black-and-white mosaics pattern the hallways, and pots and pans still sit on the charcoal stove. Most of the house's treasures are in the National Archeological Museum in Naples, but the wonderful drunken Hercules, trying to pee, is in one of the little rooms off the garden.

Modern-Day Herculaneum

Excavation continues at the main site, though the extraordinary Villa of the Papyri still remains underground. One of Italy's biggest challenges is to come up with enough money to excavate the site (the J. Paul Getty Museum in Malibu near Los Angeles makes up in part for what we can't see, as it is a modern replica of the structure). Though the villa was partially tunnelled through in the 1750s, archeologists today are still thwarted by the heavy matter encasing it. This amazing suburban villa was named for the papyrus documents retrieved from the library. In total, 1787 volumes were brought to light, and careful unrolling of the scrolls revealed an almost complete collection of the works of Philodemus, the Greek philosopher. Trying to decipher the texts has been a painstaking process for papyrologists at the International Centre for the Study of Herculanean Papyri. But sophisticated microscopes, cameras and computers have all helped to yield interesting results. Ninety pieces of sculpture have come from the villa, among them Hermes at Rest, the Sleeping Faun, and Drunken Silenus, all now at the museum in Naples. It seems a travesty that work to rescue the villa has gone this slowly. When so many valuable works have been uncovered, who knows what remains to be revealed?

Beyond the ruins, Herculaneum has other treasures to offer in the form of elaborate 18th-century villas which have been renovated and opened to the public. These Vesuvian villas are a ten-minute walk south from the excavations, well sign-posted. They were constructed when Bourbon King Charles III was in power and his summer court was transferred to Portici, just north of Herculaneum. Neapolitan noblemen followed suit, and the 'golden mile' was a patch of real estate glittering with 121 late Baroque villas designed by Vanvitelli, Fuga, Vaccaro and Sanfelice. When Charles left Naples for Spain, however, the area lost its appeal and the aristocratic owners began renting these luxurious quarters to local families. Many of the villas were lost through fire and neglect, or subdivided into numerous apartments; the frescoes and elaborate mouldings fell into disrepair.

In 1977, the regional government purchased one of the best examples in the form of Villa Campolieto, designed by Vanvitelli and now beautifully restored. It is a surprising sight after passing crumbling palazzi and auto mechanics' shops. The villa, an elegant Neo-Classical structure in pale yellow and white, is used for conventions and events such as summer theatre. The swirling staircase within is a Vanvitelli trademark, and rooms on the first floor are absolutely covered with floral frescoes. It is the 18th-century answer to the first century's luxurious and elaborately decorated Villa of the Papyri.

Pompeii

The town of Pompeii, originally a native Oscan settlement founded in the 7th century BC, is 16km south of Herculaneum. The city was conquered by Greeks, Etruscans and Samnites, and finally became a Roman colony in 80BC along with Herculaneum. Pompeii was a thriving, noisy market town of about 20,000 inhabitants, filled with shops and bars and small family factories. Traders constantly came and went, while wine and a potent fish sauce were Pompeii's most popular exports.

On the day Vesuvius erupted, Pompeii was the scene of a different but no less deadly series of catastrophes. Many more pumice stones showered down here than at Herculaneum, while dense layers of ash settled at the rate of about 15cm per hour. Roofs began to collapse, and the town was in almost total darkness. The people who died waited too long inside their homes, trapped by fallen timbers or barred from leaving by the pumice still falling. Then they were unable to breathe from the gases and ash surging southward early the next morning. But archeologists think that only one-tenth of the population died that way; many more might have suffocated, like Pliny the Elder, on the roads outside the city while trying to flee. If some of the population did in fact survive, it still isn't clear where they went.

The excavated city today is much larger than Herculaneum, covering an area of about one kilometre east to west, and about half a kilometre north to south. Plan on spending at least four hours here. Apart from the amphitheatre, however, you won't find many places to sit and rest and the site is not well shaded. Wear flat-soled shoes too, since the pavement is uneven. I recommend spending the morning in Pompeii, having a meal outside the gates at lunchtime (or a picnic in the amphitheatre), and then exploring the Villa of Mysteries north of the main excavations in the afternoon.

Though the 1980 earthquake damaged some buildings, many have now been re-opened. And, ironically this most recent earthquake was the catalyst for renewed enthusiasm, and funding, for Pompeii. The Soprintendenza Archeologica di Pompeii was founded in 1981, and an exciting interdisciplinary approach to restoration has evolved: archeologists, biologists, art historians, botanists, climatologists, physicists and computer scientists are all working to maintain and enhance the ancient city of Pompeii.

The most important sites are accessible to the public, and others can be entered with a guide. You'll see the guides milling around looking for business, and you should consider paying their small fee as they'll also take you to see the licentious wall paintings hidden to the general public (listen to their entertaining tales with a historical grain of salt, as many guides can't resist embellishing the facts).

When Goethe visited the site in 1787, he wrote:

> the city still manages to demonstrate, even in its utter desolation, that all its inhabitants had a love of painting and the arts which today's would-be dilettante is incapable of understanding or appreciating.

The excavated city of Pompeii

Add to that Percy Bysshe Shelley's impression of the whole scene in 1818:

> I had no conception of anything so perfect yet remaining. They lived in a perpetual commerce with external nature, and nourished themselves upon the spirit of its forms. Their theatres were all open to the mountains and the sky.

When Pompeii was uncovered in the 1700s, it sparked a resurgence of the four 'Pompeian Styles' of painting found in the town's villas, baths and theatres. The first style is really just a wall covering without any human figures – swirls of colour to represent marble, or simple squares of colour on stucco slabs. The second style, dating from the first century BC, is illusionistic figure painting of religious and mythological scenes. The third is more complex and was popular about one hundred years later – bands or tablets of intricate mythological scenes and landscapes with more figures, the edges often festooned with colourful decorative motifs. The fourth style followed from this, often employed after the earlier earthquake of 63AD. Large panels are of a more impressionistic nature so that decorative elements are less well-defined, best seen in the Villa of Mysteries outside the main area where its cycle of frescoes is still in place.

Enter Pompeii from the west entrance at the Porta Marina near the railroad stations. Close to sixty sites have been excavated, most of them open to the public, and 12 of the most interesting are highlighted here. As in Herculaneum a thorough descriptive guide, with photos, is helpful.

The **Antiquarium**, a museum just inside the western gate, opened in 1948. Recently closed for extensive renovations, it should re-open by the end of 1994. The museum's most famous objects are the plaster casts of bodies caught in

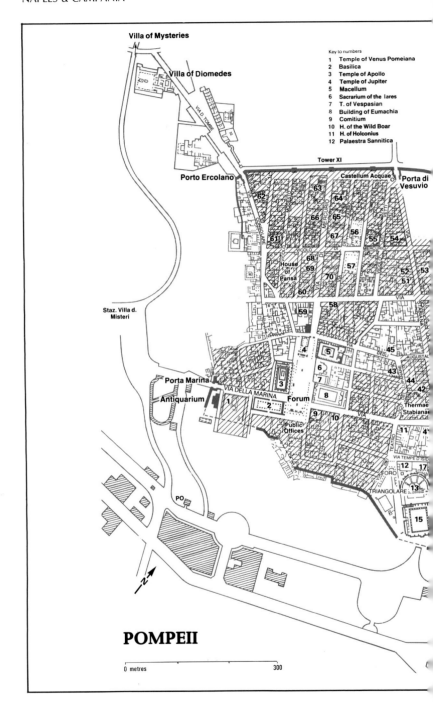

Villa of Mysteries

Villa of Diomedes

Key to numbers
1 Temple of Venus Pomeiana
2 Basilica
3 Temple of Apollo
4 Temple of Jupiter
5 Macellum
6 Sacrarium of the lares
7 T. of Vespasian
8 Building of Eumachia
9 Comitium
10 H. of the Wild Boar
11 H. of Holconius
12 Palaestra Sannitica

VIA D. TOMBE

Tower XI

Porto Ercolano

Castellum Acquae

Porta di Vesuvio

62

63

64

66

65

61

67

56

55

54

VICOLO DI

MERCURIO

House of Pansa

68

69

57

52

53

70

51

60

58

59

Staz. Villa d. Misteri

45

AUGUSTAL

4

5

DEGLI

6

43

Porta Marina

7

44

42

3

Antiquarium

1

Forum

8

Thermae Stabianae

2

VIA DELLA MARINA

9

10

11

4

VIA TEMPE D'ISID

Public Offices

FORO

12

17

PO

13

TRIANGOLARE

15

N

POMPEII

0 metres   300

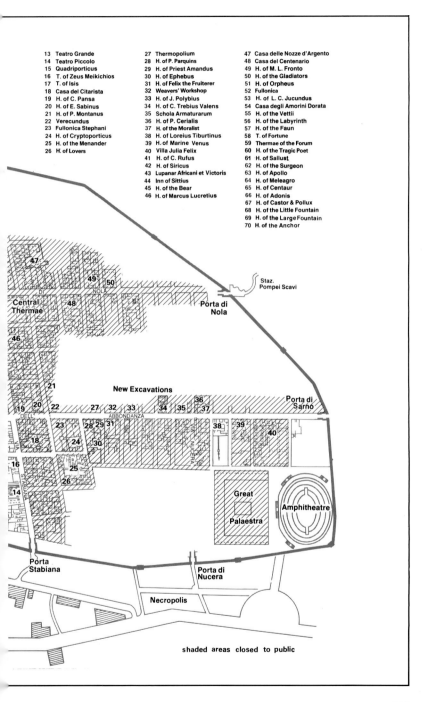

13 Teatro Grande	27 Thermopolium	47 Casa delle Nozze d'Argento
14 Teatro Piccolo	28 H. of P. Parquins	48 Casa del Centenario
15 Quadriporticus	29 H. of Priest Amandus	49 H. of M. L. Fronto
16 T. of Zeus Meikichios	30 H. of Ephebus	50 H. of the Gladiators
17 T. of Isis	31 H. of Felix the Fruiterer	51 H. of Orpheus
18 Casa del Citarista	32 Weavers' Workshop	52 Fullonica
19 H. of C. Pansa	33 H. of J. Polybius	53 H. of L. C. Jucundus
20 H. of E. Sabinus	34 H. of C. Trebius Valens	54 Casa degli Amorini Dorata
21 H. of P. Montanus	35 Schola Armaturarum	55 H. of the Vettii
22 Verecundus	36 H. of P. Cerialis	56 H. of the Labyrinth
23 Fullonica Stephani	37 H. of the Moralist	57 H. of the Faun
24 H. of Cryptoporticus	38 H. of Loreius Tiburtinus	58 T. of Fortune
25 H. of the Menander	39 H. of Marine Venus	59 Thermae of the Forum
26 H. of Lovers	40 Villa Julia Felix	60 H. of the Tragic Poet
	41 H. of C. Rufus	61 H. of Sallust
	42 H. of Siricus	62 H. of the Surgeon
	43 Lupanar Africani et Victoris	63 H. of Apollo
	44 Inn of Sittius	64 H. of Meleagro
	45 H. of the Bear	65 H. of Centaur
	46 H. of Marcus Lucretius	66 H. of Adonis
		67 H. of Castor & Pollux
		68 H. of the Little Fountain
		69 H. of the Large Fountain
		70 H. of the Anchor

Staz.
Pompei Scavi

Porta di
Nola

Central
Thermae

New Excavations

Porta di
Sarno

Great
Palaestra

Amphitheatre

Porta
Stabiana

Porta di
Nucera

Necropolis

shaded areas closed to public

103

the volcano's destructive path. The casts were made in the 1800s by injecting plaster into the hollows left by the decayed corpses, though epoxy resin is now used. The bodies are a moving if macabre sight. Other outstanding pieces in the museum are the lifesize statue of Livia taken from the Villa dei Misteri and the simple household objects such as tools and terracotta vessels.

The **Basilica**, Pompeii's largest building at 67m long and 25m wide is just down the Via Marina. Probably built in 200BC, it had nothing to do with religion, but was where judicial affairs were conducted. The large central courtyard is divided by two long rows of 28 Ionic columns, and the Law Courts were in the raised portion at the back. Much of the Basilica was badly damaged in the serious earthquake 16 years earlier, and Pompeiians had not restored it. Its main entrance to the northeast opened on to the Forum.

The **Forum** (Foro), perfectly planned and positioned, lies in what was once the centre of town. This was a large and active meeting place, lined with emperors' statues up on pedestals and paved with marble flagstones. Pompeiians would come here to vote, to have documents notarised, to buy goods at market stalls or at auction. Undoubtedly one would bump into a neighbour or a friend – this was the best place in Pompeii to catch up on local gossip and government scandal. The Forum was almost completely enclosed by the provisions market (Macellum), the voting hall, Chief Magistrate's office, temples, a cereal market and a fuller's hall for woollen-cloth merchants who sold their goods to foreign buyers.

The **Temple of Apollo** (Tempio di Apollo) runs along the western side of the Forum. This revered god was honoured with official cult status, and his temple was one of the first buildings restored after the earlier earthquake. The rectangular area is surrounded by 48 columns; copies of the statues of Apollo and Diana are in the southern corners (the originals are now in the museum in Naples). A travertine altar, where offerings were presented, sits in front of wide steps. These lead up to the sacred shrine (cella), bounded by six frontal columns, where a statue of Apollo was once placed.

The **Temple of Jupiter** (Tempio di Giove) is at the Forum's northern end, at the top of a wide set of 15 steps, once flanked by two equestrian statues. The temple was constructed in the second century BC, covered by a high roof and enclosed by tall white Corinthian columns. The cult that worshipped here venerated three divinities called the Capitoline Triad: Jupiter, Juno and Minerva. The huge marble head of Jupiter now in the Naples Museum was found upon the shrine here.

Walking north from the Forum up the Via di Mercurio, you'll be leaving civic and religious Pompeii and entering one of the town's residential districts. Turn right on Via della Fortuna and stop at nos 2–5, one of Pompeii's most interesting houses.

The **House of the Faun** (Casa del Fauno) was a luxurious dwelling, named for the little bronze statue found there. The original of this and other treasures from the House of the Faun are among the best pieces in the Naples museum. This includes stunning mosaics: the Battle of Alexander, the Nile Scene, and

The Temple of Apollo with its travertine altar, at Pompeii

that of doves pulling a pearl necklace out of a vessel. To think that Pompeiians trod on these works of art!

Before entering the house, look down at the word *HAVE* inscribed in the pavement, a Latin salutation meaning 'Welcome' (*salve* in Italian). The house is large, covering a whole block, but most of the rooms within are small and intimate. Bedrooms surround the first open courtyard and in the middle of its far end is the tablinum, a room where the nobleman Signor Cassia conducted his business affairs. The first peristyle, or columned courtyard, behind this section of rooms was decorated with a fine pavement and surrounded by 28 stucco covered columns. The largest peristyle is behind, surrounded by Doric columns to include the garden area.

The **House of the Vettii** at No.1 Vicolo dei Vettii is probably Pompeii's most famous, rich in decoration of the Fourth Style. From the House of the Faun, go north and take your first right on Vicolo ai Mercurio, and then left on Vicolo dei Vettii. This grand house belonged to the Vettii brothers, Restitutus and Conviva. They were rich merchants who owned a large estate, selling wine and other agricultural products. The wall decoration here is superb, and when you see these paintings you'll probably recognise them immediately. The house is notorious for its pornographic wall paintings, especially that of a man weighing his huge appendage on a pair of scales. Guides love to attract men to this sight for a few hundred lire extra, while with dark looks and hand signals they try to deter women from coming along for the private view.

The first room you enter is the atrium, with its delightful set of Cupids painted along a black band on the wall; I especially like the one of Cupid riding a fat crab. This room opens onto a beautiful rectangular garden (peristyle) with asins, statues and classical flowers that probably grew there. Public spaces in Pompeii were not full of greenery, and the House of the Vettii is one of the best surviving examples of how gardens came to dominate homes' interiors.

Facing the atrium, take a look at the rooms which exhibit better than any other in Pompeii the role that classical mythology had in art of the period. Off to your right is the Pentheus Room, a dining room named for the god who is being torn limb from limb by maenads, frenzied females who were followers of Bacchus. Also here is a painting of the baby Hercules strangling two snakes, the first of 12 tasks he had to perform. Off to your left in the other corner of the peristyle is another small dining room; the fresco is of Daedalus presenting a lifesize wooden cow to Pasiphae, wife of King Minos of Crete. (Poseidon has made her fall in love with a bull, and a trap door in the wooden cow's hollow back allowed her to mate with it.) The Queen looks slightly sceptical as the cow is wheeled up to her, but she must have managed somehow, as she later gives birth to the Minotaur, a monster with the head of a bull and the body of a man who is eventually killed by Theseus.

You should see one other dining room off the peristyle, the Sala Dipinta in the middle of the northern wall with rooms along its length. It was probably used for special occasions, and little Cupids are up to all sorts of tricks on a black band running around the room. They gather flowers, distil perfume, race chariots, make bread, harvest grapes and sell wine. The rooms beyond are servants' quarters and the kitchen, where bronze pots are still waiting to come to a boil on the hearth.

Walking south on Via del Vesuvio, which then becomes Via Stabiana, turn right on Via dell 'Abbondanza to enter the **Stabian Baths**. Four public bath houses were built in Pompeii, and these are the best preserved, divided like most into separate sections for men and women. People gossiped, had a swim, ordered a drink or snack at the bar, relaxed with friends, and perhaps did a little politicking between a massage and a cold plunge.

After entering the baths, you immediately come upon a large gymnasium surrounded by columns; dressing rooms and a swimming pool are on the left. The stucco reliefs and paintings here show Daedalus fixing the wax wings on his son Icarus; Hercules and a Satyr; and Jupiter with his eagle. In the lower right-hand corner are the men's baths, with pretty pale blue-and-cream coloured stucco decoration on the ceiling in the vestibule. The women's baths, in the upper right-hand corner, are not as big or well-decorated as the men's, but the mosaic floor of the triton with sea creatures in the changing room (apodytarium) is wonderfully intact.

Heading down the Via dei Teatri, turn left on the Via del Tempio d'Iside.

The **Temple of Isis** is farther down this street on your right, dedicated to the Egyptian goddess who was the wife of Osiris. She was the patron goddess of navigation. In one ceremony, called the Adoration of the Sacred Water, the high priest blessed water from the Nile which was thought to have miraculous healing powers. Egyptian forms abound in the temple – even the candelabra were lotus-shaped.

The inscription along the entrance door's architrave announces that a man named Ampliatus paid for the complete rebuilding of the temple after the earthquake in 63. To the left of the entrance are the rooms where the priest lived. Inside, steps lead up to the temple, with broken columns lining the front and niches on the sides which once held statues. The main altar was at the bottom of the steps. Behind the raised temple were a meeting hall and a chamber for initiates into the most popular of foreign cults at Pompeii.

The small theatre, or Odeon, is reached by following the Via del Tempio d'Iside and turning right on the Via Stabiana. It is adjacent to the Great or Large Theatre, which was an open-air complex accommodating 5000 spectators. The smaller Odeon, built about 80BC, held only about 800 people and originally had a wooden roof. Pompeiians attended more intimate musical performances here, along with very popular poetry readings.

From the small theatre head back up the Via Stabiana and turn right on the Via dell'Anfiteatro, which becomes the Vicolo Meridionale.

Here on the right you will find the entrance to the **House of Menander** (Casa del Menandro), a large patrician villa that had servants' quarters and its own private baths. The name of the house comes from a wall painting of the seated Greek poet. The atrium is beautifully decorated in the Fourth Style, and in a room to the left are three paintings of Trojan scenes. Off the peristyle is a green reception room with a Nile scene mosaic, and the house's best mosaic is in the caladarium of the bath area: swimmers are surrounded by eels, crabs and other fish on a black-and-white floor. In 1930, a rich cache of silver kitchen and tableware was found in the cellar here; most of these pieces – more than 100 of them – are now in the Naples museum.

The last stop within the confines of the town is the Amphitheatre (Anfiteatro), reached by walking all the way down the Via dell'Abbondanza and turning right. The large grounds of the palestra are nearby, where gladiators and athletes trained. This Roman amphitheatre, built in 80BC, is the oldest ever uncovered but it doesn't appear to have had underground chambers. It held at least 12,000 spectators; people would often come from the neighbouring towns of Stabia, Nola and Naples for wrestling matches and other spectacles. The lower walls of the arena were decorated with animal and combat scenes. Men sat closer to the action while the upper galleries were reserved for women and children.

In 59AD, a bloody scene ensued in the stands. It began with name-calling and stone-throwing between the citizens of Nuceria and Pompeii, but escalated into a full-scale riot. Many people were killed in the fighting. The Roman Senate was so outraged that they ordered the amphitheatre to be closed for ten years, and all the chief magistrates were removed from office. But Nero became emperor during this ten-year period and it is thought that he lifted the ban, which seems highly likely considering his bloodthirsty love of combat.

To the north west lies the **Villa of the Mysteries**, one of the highlights of a visit to Pompeii, beyond the excavated area of the main town. The most interesting way to reach the villa is via the Porto Ercolano Gate in the north west corner.

Floor mosaics in the House of Menander, Pompeii

You will be on the Via delle Tombe, a suburban byway once flanked by shops, villas and family tombs. Pass both the Villa of Diomedes and that of Cicero. The Villa of Mysteries is about 200m beyond.

The villa was built during the third century BC and belonged to various patrician families. Its position was carefully planned, surrounded by terraced grape vines with views to Vesuvius and out to Capri. But the building was not uncovered until 1909, and it was the remarkable discovery of a complete cycle of frescoes in 1930 which gave the villa its name.

Just inside the entrance to your right is the Sala del Grande Dipinto where the frescoes were found. These lifesize figures confounded art historians for years, though most experts now agree that the panels represent initiation rites into the cult of Dionysus. Legend has it that this cult spread quickly in Greece, especially among women. The devoted, called Maenads or Bacchae, left their homes to roam through the countryside, whirling in dance and cavorting with woodland spirits. At the height of ecstasy and with superhuman strength, they seized an animal and tore it to pieces, devouring it in a sacrificial meal to Dionysus.

An inscription found at Cumae, dating back to the fifth century BC, orders those who are not members of the cult to be buried in a separate place. Later, in 186 BC, the Roman Senate suppressed their frenzied *Bacchanalia*, which were reported to accompany a crime wave in the city! The Senate blamed citizens of Campania for 'bringing much disorder under the cover of religion'. We can't know how spirited or disruptive the Pompeiian cult might have been, but the owner of the Villa of the Mysteries was certainly a member of the cult, and perhaps one of its ministers. These ceremonial scenes, painted on a background in the Second Style, fill the whole room. The famous colour of 'Pompeiian red' features heavily in this panoramic frieze.

On the north wall, an initiate or bride walks toward a young boy who is reading the rites from a sacred text; in the second scene a seated priestess takes cloth from a basket while a female attendant pours water over her right hand, thought to be a sacrificial ceremony. An old Silenus strums his lyre, looking toward the next scene.

On the east wall a cloaked woman seems to be warding off evil. Some interpret this as a fleeing, frightened initiate who looks toward the woodland spirits of satyrs and Silenus, as well as Dionysus who lies sprawled on the lap of a woman who many think must be his wife, Ariadne. The next scene is somewhat unclear: a kneeling woman, the initiate, reaches to unveil (or protect?) a purple object – probably the sacred phallus which represents the god's fertility – in the ceremony's climax. An angel (or demon with wings?) stands ready to chastise her with a whip.

In the first scene on the south wall, the initiate is being flogged as she lies in the lap of her companion. No pleasure without pain, these scenes seem to say. But the initiation ceremony is finished, and a naked woman clashes her cymbals as if to announce 'Let the dance begin'. The cult's newest member can now perform the ritual dance of joy. The frescoed scenes end on a peaceful note, perhaps signifying purification and total acceptance.

The panoramic frieze in the Villa of Mysteries, Pompeii

Practical Information

How to get there

By car, take the A3 autostrada from Naples to Salerno. The exit for both Vesuvius and Herculaneum is the Ercolano exit (13km from Naples); for Pompeii the exit is marked Pompeii Scavi (25km from Naples). The Circumvesuviana Railway runs from Naples' main station at Piazza Garibaldi to both Ercolano and Pompeii at regular intervals. To reach Vesuvius, get off at the Ercolano station, where a bus (summer months only) or taxi (best shared) will make the 15-minute drive to the parking lot below the final walking path to the summit. At the same station, a ten-minute walk south down the main road leads to the entrance gates of the excavations. (Beware: pickpockets have a reputation for stalking this stretch.)

To reach Pompeii by railway, depart at the Villa dei Misteri station on the west side (the Pompeii Scavi station is on the east side).

Tourist Information Offices

POMPEII 1 Via Sacra (tel. 081 8631040) and at the excavations at Piazza Esedra (tel. 081 8610913).

Hotels and restaurants

Unless it's absolutely necessary, I don't recommend spending a night in the vicinity of either Herculaneum or Pompeii. It's better to head farther south along the Amalfi coast (see information section in Chapter 9).

HERCULANEUM No hotels to recommend, but quite a few good, inexpensive trattorie like **Corso IV Novembre** on its bottom half closest to the entrance of the excavations.

POMPEII The **Villa Laura**, 13 Via della Salla (tel. 081 8631024), is a pleasant enough hotel with just twenty rooms and free parking. Moderate prices. Across from the railway station in modern Pompeii is **Hotel Bristol** (Tel. 081 8631625) – somewhat noisy, but very clean and serving meals; moderately priced.

The American fast-food restaurant **MacDonald's** is open, after much controversy, on Via Roma near the Duomo in Pompeii.

Price Ranges

Hotel (double room)	Restaurant (per head)
Inexpensive: under 60–000	under 25,000
Moderate: 60–120,000	25–50,000
Expensive: 120–200,000	50–90,000
Very expensive: 200,000+	90,000+

Museums and other public sites

HERCULANEUM Excavations (tel. 081 7390963) open 09.00–15.00 except Mon and hols; until 18.00 during summer months. Vesuvian Villas such as Campolieto open 09.00–14.00 daily unless a conference or other function is in session.

POMPEII Excavations (tel. 081 8621181) open 09.00–15.00 except Mon and hols; until 18.00 at height of summer.

VESUVIUS Best climbed in the morning, catching an early train from Naples' main train station (Piazza Garibaldi) to Ercolano, then by bus or taxi from there; the road to the top of Vesuvius is often blocked after 14.00.

8. CAMPANIA'S ISLANDS: Procida, Ischia and Capri

Islands, simply by virtue of being surrounded by water, have always exerted a soothing influence on the traveller. Campania's islands remain among the most beautiful in the Mediterranean, though they haven't remained untouched. Inevitably, some will reminisce about past unspoilt charm and bemoan the age of mass tourism, but to my mind the sheer numbers of people who have already discovered the islands of Ischia and Capri (while Procida awaits them) do little to diminish their beauty. You just have to know when to go – if you like tourists and café society then travel during the summer months when the sun is strongest; if you prefer your sites less peopled, then the months of April, May, September and October are ideal.

Ischia, Campania's largest island, is in many ways just as dramatically beautiful as Capri, and has had a large number of summer residents for decades. Many Germans own homes here, and even more come as tourists. In fact on Ischia you'll find that most of its citizens have acquired a basic knowledge of German to oil the wheels of tourism, whereas Capri has traditionally been the province of the English. In recent years Americans have chosen Capri as a holiday haven too, and this island has the most 'international' character of the three. Small Procida, however, is still very much a fisherman's island, unchanged and proudly planning to remain so. They don't court tourists here – in summer months you'll find mainland Italians mixing with the locals along with day-trippers from Ischia and Capri.

Procida and Ischia share the same geological history: volcanic islands that were once connected, and broke away from the mainland near the Phlegrean Fields thousands of years ago. No volcanic activity has been recorded on either island for centuries, though Ischia is famous for its hot springs and thermal baths. Their beach sands are dark, whereas Capri shines brightly on sheer cliffs of dark creamy limestone, having the same geological makeup as the Sorrentine peninsula and Amalfi coast.

It's easy to reach all three islands, either from Naples, Pozzuoli, Sorrento or Positano. Cars with Campania license plates aren't allowed on the ferries during summer months, but rental cars, or those with foreign plates and from other Italian regions, can book passage at any time. However, you cannot take a car on to Capri unless you are a resident (it would be more of a hindrance than a help anyway) and though Ischia is larger, the bus service around that island is extremely good and will probably meet your needs unless you've rented a villa off the beaten track. Procida has a less efficient bus service which will probably prove frustrating if you aren't staying in one of the main towns. Micro-taxis at the port will take you to the few hotels on the island, but some streets are so narrow that you risk scraping side walls if driving anything wider than a small Fiat. Either take a small car to Procida or, if relying on taxis and your own two feet, stay at the port or the areas of Chaia or Chiaiolella.

Procida

The approach to Procida is a lovely sight. The Bay of Naples and Cape Misenum recede into the background, and a charming streetscape of yellow, white and pink houses stretches along the island's seafront. The port area is divided into two short sides, Marina Grande and Marina di San Cattolico (or Sancio'), where all ferries arrive and depart. The tourist office, bars, and three or four good restaurants are all along the port area's main street here.

The island is made up of four low, partially eroded craters. It's less than 4km long, and about 2km broad at its widest point on the northern side. But Procida is packed with people – more than 10,000 inhabitants – which makes it one of the most densely populated places on earth. The statistic makes it surprising that life here is not more chaotic. Fishing is still one of the island's main sources of income; almost one-fifth of the islanders employ themselves this way, with a centuries-old reputation in Europe's ports for being among the best sailors and fishermen. Procida is also known for its tangy, fragrant lemons, so don't leave the island without trying a fresh iced *granita di limone*.

One other point about these islanders: they are steadfast in their wish to keep Procida as it is, with no desire to compete with Ischia or Capri for tourists' dollars, pounds and deutschmarks. Their respect for the island's beauty borders on passion, and if you can't understand that then don't come to Procida. The beautiful islet of Vivara (attached by a walking bridge to the mainland) is a case in point. A well-known vacation club company tried to buy this island some years ago, and islanders answered, 'You want to buy our *isoletto*? Have you taken a good look at it? Please, open your eyes: wild olives, capers, berries . . . do you realize that the only foreigner permitted there was Ferdinand IV, King of the Two Sicilies? It was his hunting ground, but after others hunted there we are left without falcons, and now you want to take away the olives, the capers. Please, go back to your own country.'

The ancient history of Procida, once called Prochyta, is similar to Ischia's. It is thought that Greeks settled here too. The Romans were the first to use the island as a hunting ground, making day trips from Baia and Naples. An abbey was built by Benedictine monks in the 11th century, and the small number of inhabitants supported themselves by cultivating vines, olives and lemons. In the 13th century, the island was the property of Giovanni di Procida, a Ghibelline nobleman born in Salerno who liked his domain so much that he named himself after it. But the island was confiscated by Charles I of Anjou after he entered Naples with the victorious Guelphs. (John of Procida then took revenge in helping to instigate the Sicilian Vespers in Palermo, the revolt which killed close to 8000 Frenchmen.)

By 1340, two shipyards were constructing vessels in the port area and the population continued to grow. But the island wasn't without enemies, and during the 16th century marauding pirates such as Barbarossa, Dragut and Bolla all stormed the island. It was also occupied by the English in 1799 when Napolean proclaimed the region a republic, from 1806–9 against Napolean and Murat, and then again in 1813 for a brief period. It was during this time of French influence and upheaval that the poet Alphonse de Lamartine came to Procida and fell in love with a girl named Graziella. She renounced her island fiancé for him, but Lamartine went back to Paris never to return. Graziella didn't survive such treatment; she died two months later. Yet her name, and her island, became known throughout Europe after the success of Lamartine's novella entitled *Graziella*.

The island's three main centres are the port area, Corricella on the northwest coast, and Marina di Chiaiolella on the island's southern end near the islet of Vivara. There are a number of dark sandy beaches, but none are very long due to the nature of this rugged and sometimes high coastline. It juts in and out for 14km around the island, but that also means that you're apt to find a secluded though somewhat rocky spot for sunning. Procida's main beaches are Ciraccio, Ciraciello and the Lido on the southeastern side, and Chiaia near Corricella to the northwest.

The island's prettiest area to walk through is *Corricella*, with its fishing boats moored in the harbour beneath the abbey walls. This is Procida's oldest village. If you walk up the Via Madonna delle Grazie to the island's highest point of Terra Murata, you get a wonderful view back down to the beach with old houses rising above it. Faded pastel facades in pink, yellow and blue, arched entryways and outer stairwells are all reminiscent of Greek island architecture. Men on the beach sort their catch, fix nets or scrape the bottoms of wooden boats while women chat from balcony to balcony and children tumble in the sand. Down to the left are the abandoned ruins of a church built in 1586 called Santa Margherita Nuova. A long bay sweeps in a gorgeous band south here, from the Punta dei Monaci to the Punta di Pizzaco.

The Via Madonna delle Grazie leads up further through an archway called the Porta Mezz'Olmo, where you pass what was once a castle and is now an abandoned prison. (The whispered rumour is that Gianni Agnelli of Fiat fame is trying to buy the complex from the state in the hope of turning it into a big hotel, much to islanders' chagrin.) Turning right up a steep and narrow street leading to a small enclave of houses, you'll come to the island's most interesting church, **San Michele Arcangelo**. The richness of its marbled altars, tall candelabra and indented coffered ceiling of gold leaf is matched in literary terms by the number of expressive notes left in strategic places by the priest for his congregation. By the pews: 'Kids! Keep Quiet!' On the side wall: 'Please! The church . . . is not a museum. Do not offend the faith of God and your brothers.'

But, God forgive me, it is hard not to see the church as a museum; the objects on view here seem part of an eccentric curator's collection. The small church is stuffed with old statues, dark religious paintings badly in need of restoration, and glass cases filled with votive offerings made from scrap metal. Two important paintings are housed in the church: on the main ceiling is Luca Giordano's *The Glory of San Michele*, painted in 1699, where the Archangel is battling with Lucifer. Even more interesting is Nicola Rosso's painting in the apse: *San Michele Defending the Island*. The monumental figure with fiery sword and shield is surrounded by helpful putti, while the perfect toytown of Procida below is surrounded by ominous shiploads of Turks.

Chiaolella is the small fishing port on the island's southern end, where buses end their routes and modest restaurants line the beach. From here you can head south west for two beautiful walks. The first is to the promontory of Santa Maria Vecchia, where you'll find the ruins of a church with its Benedictine convent that was abandoned in 1586. The view back to Procida is superb.

The other walk takes you over the little bridge that leads to crescent-shaped **Vivara**, now a nature preserve protected by the state. No one lives there, but rabbit hunting is still allowed so it is open to the public. (If the chain appears to be wrapped around the gate, give it a yank because it probably isn't padlocked.) One path leads up the hill to a number of walking trails that twist around the summit, one of which leads to the arched ruins of what was probably a hunting lodge. Other routes stop at the edge of high cliffs affording wonderful views. To the south east is the mountainous island of Ischia, and to the east is Procida's southernmost tip of Punta Solchiaro, so-named because the island receives its first rays of the day's sun here (another good place for walking).

Heading through the island's centre from Chiaolella in the direction of the northern port area (a distance of about 4km), you wind through narrow streets flanked by the stuccoed walls of small houses. Fields behind are full of olive and lemon trees, as well as grape vines. You'll come to a small quarter known as Olmo, with a square by the same name. Near here is the 17th-century church of St Anthony of Padua, with its pretty cupola. Head off to the left while going north, and you'll end up at Punta Serra, with the little beach of Pozzo Vecchio beyond. Going inland again leads to the Annunziata quarter, named after the church overflowing with votive offerings to its miraculous Madonna. From here, follow the Via del Faro north to Punta Pioppeto, with its lighthouse and a good view up to Cape Misenum. To the north east, sunlit ferries and hydrofoils carry islanders and visitors in and out of the marina, back to the mainland or off to the shores of Procida's neighbour.

Ischia

Green and mountainous Ischia easily holds its own when compared with the natural beauties of Procida and Capri. Pine and olive groves seem to cover what isn't home or street, while pink and purple bougainvillea curls and hangs from every post and gate. An extinct volcano rises high in the middle of the island, and villagers close to the summit cultivate the grapes that have given the island its famous white wine, named after Monte Epomeo. The coast-line rises and falls with each bay and creek, especially dramatic on Ischia's southern edges. Much as on Capri, what you can be sure of is that each fantastic view will be surpassed by another as you make your way around the island.

Was the first Italian Magna Graecia colony here on Ischia? The prevailing theory is that Pithecusa, as it was called, was a settlement as far back as the 9th century BC but that volcanic eruptions sent the Greeks, originally from the island of Euboea, fleeing to Cumae on the mainland. According to legend, the giant Typhoeus fought Jupiter's thunderbolts with flowing lava and quaking earth from his seat on Monte Epomeo. Eruptions were recorded as early as 500BC, but not since 1301 has there been any cause for alarm.

Ischia was the province of Hieron of Syracuse, then of the Neapolitans, and by 326 belonged to the Romans. The emperor Augustus had owned the island, but exchanged it for Capri in 6AD. It was sacked by Saracens in the 9th century, and then by Pisans on their way to Amalfi. It's as if these sailing invaders sighted land and decided to give their troops drill practice before the main event elsewhere.

In the late 13th century the islanders, with Sicilian help, opposed Charles I. But Charles II recovered the island in 1299 and punished the citizens of Ischia by sending soldiers in to cut down their trees and vineyards. In another tragic episode, Barbarossa landed with his pirates in 1541 and is said to have taken away 4000 prisoners. Kings, queens and consorts came and went, whose fortunes are connected to the Aragon Castle. Ischia, like Procida, played a part in the Napoleonic Wars by serving as Nelson's base, and in 1815 was a refuge for Murat on his way out of Naples when the shortlived Parthenopean Republic was overthrown.

Ischia is now an island with a population of about 45,000. The island is 9km from east to west and six from north to south. Inland it's high and hilly, but there are quite a few good stretches of dark sandy beach. Many of the islanders work in the tourist trade – in hotels, restaurants, thermal baths and boutiques. The season runs well beyond the summer months because of the many Scandinavians, as well as Germans, who come for thermal treatment from April to October. But some of Ischia's citizens still make a living through growing grapes, olives and fruit; fishing is a viable occupation for very few.

Visitors arrive by boat at **Ischia Porto**, a perfect ring of a harbour that's packed with all the amenities a tourist might need: information office, bus terminus, restaurants, pharmacy, T-shirt shops, and ice-cream vendors. Small boats line

The island of Ischia

the shore; there's always a ferry or hydrofoil disgorging passengers. The main shopping street in Ischia Porto is Via Roma, heading south, and this is the place for people watching during the evening *passeggiata*. The square where almost all the island's buses begin and end their routes is just up the street from the harbour, and a cable-car to take you to the extinct crater of Montagnone – a short trip affording fantastic views – is a five-minute walk from there.

A far more interesting little town on the island is **Ischia Ponte**, a ten-minute bus ride south of Ischia Porto. Once a fishing village, this quarter is dominated by the **castle** on its rocky hilltop, connected to the mainland by a causeway built in 1438.

One of my favourite hotels in Campania is within this castle complex. It is called Il Monastero, after the monastery it once was, and some of the best sunset views in Campania can be enjoyed from its terrace. It is a simple place (accommodation is in small bedrooms that were once monks' cells) and the spartan setting leaves one feeling tranquil, serenely able to relish the island's history and landscape.

The castle is surrounded by thick stone walls, and tall arched passages lead to structures in various states of ruin. Ferdinand II retired here in 1495 after abandoning Naples to Charles VIII, but he almost didn't get on to the island. When he sailed up to the castle with 14 galleys, the Catalonian castellan refused him entry. At last he acquiesced – the king and queen could enter, but Ferdinand would have to send his retinue back to Naples. When the king entered the castle, he drew his sword and killed this huffy castellan, whereupon the whole

117

crew came ashore. Six years later Ferdinand's uncle and successor also retired to Ischia, where he stayed until he travelled to France to surrender to King Louis. So ended the Aragon dynasty.

But the castle's most celebrated inhabitant was the 16th-century poetess Vittoria Colonna. She was from a famous Roman family whose ancestors included cardinals, generals and Pope Martin V. Betrothed at the age of four, she married the Marquis Pescara Ferrante D'Avalos in the castle's church in 1509 when she was 17. Widowed at the age of 33, she turned to poetry and her *Rime spirituali* were widely praised, especially by the poet Ludovico Ariosto. But she was probably best known for her warm friendship with Michelangelo, who composed sonnets to her.

The church, dedicated to the Assunta, where Vittoria Colonna was married lies in the heart of the complex, built in 1301. This romantic expanse is nothing but arched ruins now, with a Gothic substructure and remnants of Baroque renovation in the 1700s. The church was completely destroyed in 1809 by the English fleet when they were chasing the French.

Farther along the wide stepped passages is the Gothic arched entrance to the Abbey of Basiliani di Grecia, also ruined. At the castle's high southern edge is the small hexagonal church of San Pietro a Pantaniello, built in the 16th century. This out-of-the-way sanctuary has a wonderful view. The abandoned prison above held prisoners such as Carlo Poerio, Nicola Nisco, il Settembrini and other patriots from 1851 to 1860. Continue up the cobbled pathway to a secluded, terraced café, a fantastic place to contemplate the lives of those who were walled within.

Once you've descended and crossed the castle's bridge, you will be on the Via Mazzella in Ischia Ponte. On the side closest to the sea is the island's **cathedral**, also called the Assunta, first built in 1300 and renovated in the Baroque style. Within are lavish marble *intaglio* altars. The Church of Santo Spirito, almost opposite, is more interesting however. Its cupola of green-and-yellow tiles is much like those on the Amalfi coast, built with the money of sailors who were keen to inject an Eastern influence into their architecture. The sacristy in this church is charming: the ceiling is a beautiful faded fresco in shades of olive green; on the wall is another fresco of a tall ship in the port by the still recognisable causeway, probably done in the early 16th century.

If you continue to walk north on Via Mazzella, and then turn right on Via Pontano, you'll come to a good beach called the **Spiaggia dei Pescatori**. The **Lido**, on the same stretch of coast but farther north, is one of Ischia's nicest beaches. It is best reached by one of the side streets leading from the main avenue of Corso Vittoria Colonna.

Heading down toward the southern edge of the island, follow road No.270 through mountain villages, many of which are untouched by the tourists crowded into the seaside towns. You'll pass through Fontana (not to be confused with Serrara Fontana), the highest town on Ischia. This is the best place to start the ascent of **Monte Epomeo** (788m), either by a challenging one-hour walk or by hiring mules well used to making the trip. On a clear day, and for those with very good eyesight, the view extends to 100km from the top. (The iron

Punto Sant' Angelo, Ischia

crucifix towering above was erected in memory of 44 people killed in an air crash.) Far to the north are Lazio's Pontine Islands; closer to Ischia are the Gulf of Gaeta, the Phlegrean Fields, Vesuvius and the Sorrentine Peninsula. The whole island is spread below, ringed by water of cobalt blue. You don't have to return by way of Fontana – a two-hour descent down the other side leads to either Forio or Casamicciola.

After stunning mountain-top views the next best are witnessed while following road No.270 south to **Punto Sant' Angelo**, a teardrop of land descending into the Tirrhenian Sea. Buses and cars stop at the top of a hill where a wide paved path then leads to the village. This fishing port, though very crowded in summer, is a great place to hire boats for a tour around the island, or for a drop-off at either Maronti Beach or Ischia's oldest hot springs of **Cavascura**. A series of baths cut into the hillside is said to have been used by the Romans, and I'm not sure hygiene standards have improved much since then. I'd choose one of the island's newer establishments on the hill above the town, such as the kitsch **Thermal Gardens Tropical** which sports lots of healthy vegetation and masses of monstrous white statuary.

Back on route 270, heading northwest now, you'll come to another pretty village called **Forio**. Here too are boutiques and restaurants, but one gets the feeling that these villagers have better things to do than simply cater to passing tourists. Kids run off to school, while adults head to the vineyards, for this is the island's most important wine-producing centre.

This area of the coast was plagued by marauders more than any other, and

119

Model ships rest on columns in San Soccorso, Ischia

12 towers were constructed along the shore to guard the sea and relay messages. The largest, and one of the few still standing, is the **Torrione** near the Piazza Matteotti. It was reconstructed in 1480 and now serves as a gallery to exhibit the work of many artists who work here in Forio. The Baroque church of Santa Maria di Loreto is nearby, erected in the 14th century with two tiled bell-towers.

Even more picturesque is the small, white sanctuary of **San Soccorso** down by the water. This church is unusual for its harmonious blend of architectural elements: a Gothic bell-tower, Renaissance portal, a Baroque pedestal for the cross. The outer stairway is decorated with majolica tiles. This is where fishermen and their families have been praying for centuries. Beautifully carved model ships rest atop columns; above the side chapel are 15 highly-varnished *putti* carrying crosses, chains, arrows, and crown of thorns – all symbols of the Passion and Crucifixion.

Just below San Soccorso, on its southern side, is the Pensione Umberto a Mare. This is a clean and quiet place to stay, also serving lunch and dinner to travellers on its enclosed terrace overhanging the sea. One of the finest gardens in the region (open to the public) is just north, toward Punta di Caruso on Via Francesco Calisa. Called **La Mortella**, the late Sir William Walton and his wife Susanna began building their home and garden in 1956. The extensive plantings cover a fertile valley, filled with palm, magnolia and tulip trees, along with water lilies and lotus, tree fern and camellia. Along with overseeing the garden, Lady Walton runs a foundation for promising young musicians who come here to study.

On Ischia's northern side are the towns of **Lacco Ameno** and **Casamicciola Terme**. Lacco Ameno still retains a personality strongly linked to its past, while Casamicciola is best left to the patrons of hotels and hot springs.

In Lacco Ameno, the pink-stuccoed church of **Santa Restituta** and its underground museum are worth a detour. Santa Restituta is the island's patron saint, a North African Christian whose body was found on the nearby shore of San Montano in 304. She'd apparently survived many forms of torture in Carthage before being forced out to sea, but while her captors tried to set fire to the boat they were engulfed in flames instead. She died at sea but when her boat landed here, lilies sprang up on the beach, and the saint's remains were buried in the house of a woman who claimed to have dreamed of Restituta's arrival. Villagers still celebrate the coming of the saint each year on May 17th. The church is filled with the white lilies that bear her name; fireworks and symbolic bonfires are part of the festivities.

The sanctuary of Santa Restituta is really two churches: the more modern one was reconstructed in 1800 with a façade that dates to 1910. Within this church are ten paintings telling the story of the life of the saint. The smaller church dates from 1036, built on the remains of a Paleo-Christian basilica. Behind the altar here is a statue of Santa Restituta, dating from the early 16th century. Below is the excavated crypt, only discovered in 1951. These ruins, with tombs and old sections of pavements, form part of the underground museum. Glass cases displaying ceramic fragments and iron tools attest to Greek colonisation, along with Egyptian and Syrian objects that must have been traded when Ischia's port was included in the sailors' route from the eastern Mediterranean.

The pretty inlet beach of **San Montano** (no lilies growing here now) is just west of Lacco Ameno. Seven kilometres east along the northern shore is the town of Casamicciola Terme. Greek colonists probably settled here first, and legend has it that the Sibyl of Cumae prophesied the coming of Christ while in Casamicciola. (Does this mean that she practised here, and left for Cumae on the mainland with the other settlers?) Henrik Ibsen began *Peer Gynt* here in 1867, but this area was devastated by an earthquake in 1883 and was completely rebuilt at the turn of the century.

As in Lacco Ameno, many hot springs bubble forth in Casamicciola, accounting for the large number of hotels. These waters, high in carbonate and muriate of soda, are said to relieve symptoms of rheumatism, arthritis and sciatica, while Lacco Ameno's waters are purported to be the most radioactive on the island. *Murray's Handbook* of 1855 recommended these waters for 'scrofulous swellings' and 'gunshot wounds'. If you're sensitive to smells, these springs just might do your system more harm than good; near the famous Gurgitello spring in Casamicciola is another called *Agua di Cappone* because it's supposed to smell like chicken broth.

The next town along the coast is lively Ischia Porto again – the completion of a clockwise tour around the island.

Capri

Whenever I go to Capri I find myself thinking that surely this time it won't be the same. I'll find more crowds than before, or yet another useless boutique, and will vow never to return. But the island remains alluring. The Blue Grotto has lost none of its ultramarine glow; the Faraglioni stand as solid and serene as ever; the whitewashed homes of the islanders have been coated anew, their gardens overflowing with flowers.

However, thousands of other travellers are attracted to Capri for all the same reasons. Be warned: it becomes very crowded during the summer months. As inaccessible as its tall cliffs seem, thousands of tourists scramble on and off the island each day in the months of July and August. If you are able to travel during low season (there is consistent sun as early as April and as late as October), you'll find a seat on Piazza Umberto, and will be able to take splendid walks without others bumping into you from behind. Let me add one other word of warning, depending on your state of health: you'll do a lot of walking on this island, especially from the main town of Capri itself. Make sure to check just how far your hotel is from the main square, because some are quite a steep hike from the centre.

The island seems bigger than its ten square kilometres suggest, due to an undulating landscape upon sheer limestone cliffs. Ferries and hydrofoils dock at the **Marina Grande** on Capri's northern side; fishermen and those in smaller private boats sometimes dock at the **Marina Piccola** on the southern coast. Above the Marina Grande is Capri's main town, also called Capri, arrived at from the port by taking the quick funicular railway, or by taxi up a steep winding road. The island's only other main town is Anacapri, connected to Capri by a high corniche road that affords beautiful views down to the sea. Anacapri sits on a flat plateau, and is therefore less strenuous on the legs and lungs.

Capri and Anacapri have traditionally been involved in a tug-of-war for power and prestige, and have evolved distinct personalities. Capri is more pretentions, seemingly more elegant with the Quisisana Hotel, designer boutiques and the much photographed main square with its tall clock-tower. Anacapri is best known for quieter pleasures such as Axel Munthe's Villa San Michele, the small enchanting church of San Michele and Monte Solaro. The connection between the two towns can be made by riding in some of the best taxicabs I've ever seen – gleaming bulbous convertibles, circa 1950, proudly maintained by their owners.

Tourists are constantly transported back and forth between Capri and Anacapri, a hard job for the small local buses in high season. The thousands of day trippers I mentioned are mainly from Naples, along with tourists from coastal resorts such as Sorrento and Positano. Islanders would like to put a stop to this heavy influx of tourists, and the police force has started to levy fines on those who wear too little clothing, carry noisy radios or are judged to be making a general nuisance of themselves. I doubt this method will deter many day-trippers, but the suggested addition of much higher boat fees, and restricted ferry schedules, probably would. That tactic might not seem fair to mainland Italians, but locals are finding it harder and harder to cope with so many people on such a small island.

This love for Capri is nothing new. First came the Greeks, then Emperor Augustus built villas and baths as a retreat from a stressful life in Rome. He was followed by Tiberius in 26AD, who ruled Rome from Capri for the last 11 years of his life. He gave Capri its racy reputation, highly exaggerated to entice the tourists. It's said that he constructed 12 villas on Capri, one for each deity (or one for each mistress depending on who's doing the telling). Some historians would have us believe that Tiberius spent his days in orgiastic pleasure, contrasted with the pain of tortured prisoners who were then thrown over the cliffs at his hilltop palace of Villa Jovis.

But about Tiberius I side with Norman Douglas, the English writer who immortalised his adopted home of Capri and other parts of southern Italy in *Siren Land* and *South Wind*. He came to the emperor's defence in *Siren Land*, writing in one passage that:

> Tiberius at Capri is supposed to have suffered from the mania of persecution, ending in senile dementia. In proof of his madness is adduced the fact that he complained of the debauched habits of his (adopted) grandson Nero. As if Tiberius had not been making complaints of this kind, and with perfect justice, all his life!

When the Roman Empire fell, Capri belonged to Naples, and then to powerful Amalfi during the ninth century. The Saracens terrorised these islanders too, until the Normans came to power in the 11th century. The island's fate shadowed that of Naples for many centuries – changing hands from Anjou to Aragon – and during the Napoleonic War was occupied by both the British and the French. In 1813, Capri was back in the hands of the Italians under Ferdinand I of the Two Sicilies.

The island's history as tourist attraction blossomed with the so-called discovery of the Blue Grotto in 1826 by a German poet called August Kopisch. But islanders certainly knew that it existed; it was marked on a 1696 map with the name of Grotta Gradola and the district above is still sometimes referred to by the same name. As Norman Douglas points out in *Siren Land*, 'Beezlebub himself could never keep a Capri fisherman out of a sea cave if there were half a franc's worth of crabs inside it.' And as for the romantic names of so many caves cut into Capri's coastline, Douglas wrote:

> The foreigners liked colour in caves. The foreigners brought money. Colour in caves is cheap. Let them have it! Therefore, in a twinkling, the two-mouthed Grotta del Turco became the green grotto; the venerable Grotto Ruofolo put on a roseate hue sufficient to justify the poetic title of Red Grotto . . .

And no harm's been done. The island's caves are definitely worth viewing, whatever they may be called and, if you've got the time and money, hire a boat with knowledgeable guide for a trip along these 17km of coastline. The lovely island landscape, at sea level and above, is home to more than 800 species of plant life. It's not at all surprising that Capri has been found agreeable by every sort of traveller – from politicians and philosophers such as Lenin, Rilke and Nietzsche, to writers such as Turgenev, Conrad and G. B. Shaw. The Swedish doctor Axel Munthe added to the island's fame with his *Story of San Michele*, and more recently the music-hall legend Gracie Fields made her second home here.

Some of these famous characters are buried in the foreign cemetery, a short walk from Capri's Piazza Umberto Primo down the Via Marina Grande. Norman Douglas was buried here in 1952. The consolatory inscription on his tombstone, a quotation from Horace, reads *Omnes Fodem Cogimur* (We are all in the end driven to the same place). This small, scruffy cemetery begs so many questions: what were they like, the foreigners who chose to live here? How in the world did Dr Ludwig Schroeter, a physician born in Poland who practiced in Buffalo, New York, end up here in 1912? One couple from Pontiac, Illinois, engraved on their joint monument: 'Within this bit of foreign earth there lies the dust of two who loved this Italy.' The best inscription of all belongs to both Salvatore Vuotto and his wife Irma Schwarze: 'Citizen of the world and free thinker'. The island's Catholic cemetery is stepped above; graves are carefully tended by island relatives who are near enough to pull the weeds and repot the flowers.

Walking up the Via Marina Grande to the enclosed **main square** brings you back to the center of life on Capri. The cafés here are see-and-be-seen venues, and you pay highly for the privilege. Narrow walking streets radiate off the square, leading to shops, hotels and restaurants. Right on the piazza is the 17th-century Baroque church of **San Stefano**, interesting for its mosiac floor at the foot of the high altar. The inlaid marble pavement was taken from the Villa Jovis, Tiberius' most elaborate dwelling. In the chapel to the right are the tombs of Vincenzo and Giacomo Arcucci, both sculpted by Naccherino. Count Giacamo is the one holding the little church, for he founded the island's monastery.

Near the church is the **Palazzo Cerio**, named for the physician and amateur archeologist who dedicated so much of his time to studying the island's history. This small museum was originally a 14th-century castle, now housing various artefacts and fossils. Even Augustus, according to the historian Suetonius, found 'tremendous limbs of huge monsters and wild animals', attesting to the accepted view that Capri was once part of the mainland near Sorrento. When the Hotel Quisisana was enlarged in the early 1900s, Cerio was there to help label the skeletal remains of an elephant, hippopotamus and a rhinoceros from the quaternary era.

Not far from the main square is the Carthusian monastery, the **Certosa of San Giacomo**. Follow the Via Vittorio Emanuele down to the Hotel Quisisana, and then go right on Via Federico Serena to Via Certosa. The monastery, at the end of this street, was founded in 1371. Though it was destroyed by Torgud in 1553, monks restored it soon after. As a religious retreat it was supressed in

1807, then used as a prison and a hospice throughout the 1800s. Today the convent buildings are occupied by a secondary school as well as a library.

The cloisters and the dark Gothic church are open to the public. The church's most interesting feature is the 14th-century fresco above the outer doorway, called *Madonna and Child Enthroned Between Sts Bruno and Giacomo*. To the right of this central panel is the fresco *Founder with Two Sons*; to the left of the central panel is *Three Praying Women*, the first of whom is Angevin Queen Joan I, who died here on the island.

The Great Cloister here does not impress me. This is a bleak open space carpeted with cement, such a contrast to the abundance of flowers hidden in the back garden just over the walls. The Small Cloister nearby is much prettier, with 18 columns and a well at its centre. There's also a permanent art gallery attached to the monastery, called the **Museo Diefenbach**. This space exhibits about thirty dark and crusty oils painted by the German artist Diefenbach who died on Capri in 1913. I found nothing inspiring in these large works, but the first room on the left after entering the gallery is worth a look. It holds a painting by American genre scene painter C. Caryl Coleman called *Sorrow*, very much influenced by the Pre-Raphaelites. (Coleman is another lover of Capri buried in the foreign cemetery, having died in his Villa Narcissus in 1928.) Here also are pitted sculptures dredged up from 20m below the surface of the Blue Grotto, which help to support the hypothesis that this cave was used to worship nymphic divinities in Roman times.

From the monastery, walk back up the Via Certosa, turning left on Via Matteotti. On your right is one of Capri's two perfumeries – a pretty little shop for truly Caprese gifts, such as one of their small jars of cream, wrapped with exquisite care. The Monastery of San Giacomo began producing perfume on the island in 1380. This industry flourished for a few centuries, but died out as the monastery lost its prestige in the late 18th and 19th centuries. In 1948, inspired islanders began to produce these old formulas once again.

Past the perfumery are the **Gardens of Augustus**. More gorgeous views await you from the terrace here, this time down to Marina Piccola and the Faraglioni rock formations. The winding path below is Via Krupp (also called Augusto), excavated from the rock by German arms manufacturer Friedrich Krupp. The easy walk down, of about one-half hour and highly recommended, leads to the Marina Piccola, a much prettier port area than Marina Grande. Small beaches along the shore are connected to restaurants, called *stabilmenti* because you pay a small fee for beach chairs, mattresses and shower. A bus or taxi is available for the trip back to Piazza Umberto Primo.

One of the island's most spectacular walks is from Capri's main square to the **Faraglioni** and the **Arco Naturale**. Steps and steep pathways are positioned high above the southeastern coast, and the walk takes about an hour. From Via Vittorio Emmanuele, turn left on Via Camarelle past the Hotel Quisisana. After shops and a scruffy sort of animal farm over the wall on your right, you'll be passing private villas on Via Tragara, along with another luxury hotel called La Scalinatella. Rounding a bend, you'll see a sign pointing down to the Faraglioni, the three tall rock sentinels beyond the Punta di Tragara. One of the three is said to harbour a species of blue lizard – the *Lacerta caerulea Faraglionensis* – found nowhere else in the world. It would be hard to check the accuracy of this statement, as it is thought that the lizard may now be extinct.

You can cut this walk short by spending a day at the beach, climbing down the steps here (a long way down and no other way up), but fisherman from the Marina Piccola will also take passengers by boat. This is a popular spot for sunbathing, so if you want to assure yourself a prime position, head down early. Rocky sections have been connected by flat cement areas; you can rent chairs or foam mats, and dive into clear deep pools. Two restaurants with terraces make it very easy to spend a day lazing around.

Back at the top of the stairs, continue along the well-tended pathway past private homes in enviable positions. The flora bordering the walkway is astonishing for its variety – rosemary, heather, juniper and myrtle – one or another plant is fragrant and flowering. You will see a long, rectangular red house on a rocky plateau below, but without any way of reaching it. This was the home of Italian writer Curzio Malaparte, author of *The Skin* and other books about Neapolitan life. Designed in 1940 by Adalberto Libera, the building is a strong simple shape, and its position is astonishing – if not stupefying.

The path now climbs up and down constantly, sometimes through dense pine woods, and then suddenly open to sun and sea again. You'll pass the **Grotta di Matromania**, a damp cave with a semicircular apse. This is believed to have been a Roman sanctuary for those dedicated to the cult of the Cybele, a fertility goddess also known as the Mater Magna. From here it's a 15-minute climb to the Arco Naturale, a tall arch which has eroded its way through craggy golden limestone. In the distance are Punta Campanella and the Sorrentine Peninsula on the mainland, 6km away. Just beyond this beautiful spot is a small terraced bar, very welcome after a long climb. Soon the path evens out and, flanked by islanders' homes with their welcoming ceramic plaques, you'll be descending to the main square.

From the town of Capri, there is one other site to see before heading to Anacapri. This is the **Villa Jovis**, the biggest and best-preserved Imperial villa on the island. It's high on a hill, at the end of one of the walking streets passed on the way back from the Arco Naturale. (If you're refreshed enough after a rest at the bar mentioned above you could head up to the villa before returning to the main square.) From Piazza Umberto Primo, however, the Via Delle Botteghe climbs to become Via Fuolovado and then Via Croce, which takes you left to the Via Tiberio (ceramic signs will also help point the way). Just before reaching the villa's entrance the street becomes Viale Amedeo Mauri. I suspect this stretch has been named as an avenue not for its size but for the great amount of respect Italians have for this famous archaeologist. He supervised the villa's excavation from 1932–35.

You won't find elaborate mosaic floors or statues in place here, and at first glance the site might seem disappointing. Many of the villa's treasures were plundered in previous centuries, but the sheer extent of the ruins in such a superb setting makes them worth a visit. Built in the first century, Villa Jovis was apparently 12 storeys high but only partial remnants of three remain. A

The towering rock sentinels of Faraglioni, Capri

warren of passages leading to many small rooms makes it clear that this villa functioned almost as a mini city, with baths, stores and servants' quarters. The remains of a tower, called il Faro, are near the entrance gate. It's thought that Tiberius sent signals (smoke by day, fire by night) from here to the mainland when urgent answers were needed on political matters in Rome. Nearby is il Salto, or the Leap, where the emperor may have tossed his enemies to their death.

The walls and pavement of the villa are interesting for their methods of construction, now stripped bare of stucco and marble facings. In the middle of the villa was a huge cistern, mainly to supply the extensive baths in the front section. On the upper terrace stands a small ugly chapel called Santa Maria del Soccorso, along with a bronze statue of the Madonna flown in by US Navy helicopter in 1901. But these odd elements are easily ignored when you consider the incredible panoramic view from this terrace. At the villa's northern edge is the **Imperial Loggia**, reached by a path covered with some of the only original mosaic pavement remaining at the site. The loggia is almost 100m long, enough uninterrupted space for Tiberius to stroll along while pondering problems of state.

Anacapri

The town of Capri is on the slope of the island's east mountain; Anacapri lies west at the foot of Monte Solaro. Until the 1870s, the only way to reach Anacapri was by way of 881 steps cut into the rock, called the Scala Fenicia; donkeys scrambled up and down them more quickly than people did. The steps were probably first formed by the Greeks to connect the marina to this town, then reconstructed by the Romans. But now the Scala Fenicia is impassable, and the corniche road connects Capri to Anacapri. A bus or taxi will drop you at Anacapri's main square, Piazza Vittoria. From here small streets fan out leading to the Villa San Michele and the church of San Michele. Just above the piazza is a chairlift to the top of Monte Solaro. Once away from the main square, you'll find that Anacapri is a quieter town than Capri, especially if you wander through the maze-like back streets past whitewashed homes cascading with bougainvillea.

The **Villa San Michele**, the famous home of Swedish doctor and psychiatrist Axel Munthe, is what draws most tourists to Anacapri. His charming *Story of San Michele* was published in 1929. A profitable practice in Rome allowed Munthe to buy land here in the 1890s, though throughout his life he devoted time to the poor. His reputation for generosity was sealed after his work in Naples during the cholera epidemic there in 1884, and he was also a volunteer doctor with the British Red Cross during World War I.

The villa is reached by Via San Michele, a flat path about 1km long, from steps at the top of the main square. You might wonder, as you pass shops filled with straw donkeys, mohair jumpers and stuffed blue bears, what all this has to do with Axel Munthe, but it seems quite acceptable to the islanders who manage to sell so many silly trinkets. Don't despair, you are well rewarded

The Villa San Michele, former home of Swedish doctor Axel Munthe, Capri

at the end of the trail when you enter the beautiful whitewashed villa on a promontory.

When Munthe was building his dream house the ruins of a much older villa were discovered. It's possible that this was the site for one of the 12 villas of Tiberius, though there's no substantial proof. The elegant interior, cool and dark, is filled with small swirling columns, arched windows, Latin inscriptions and other spoils inserted into the walls. One piece of sculpture to look for is the Roman original of Medusa, along with another thought to be Tiberius or his nephew Germanicus. In the outer courtyard is a beautiful table of exquisite inlaid marble in the Cosmati tradition. Everywhere is green, surrounded by cypress, pine and palm.

I couldn't help envying Axel Munthe his discovery of so many island 'treasures'. Though he bought numerous antiques in Rome and Naples, some of the precious objects here were found on Capri at a time when one didn't have to turn every shard and fragment over to the state department of archeology.

The gardens here are gorgeous, and so are the views. Walk through the sculpture garden to the pergola by the granite sphinx (another little 'find' from a villa on the Calabrian coast). Looking below you'll see a section of the Scala Fenicia, now boarded up. Just above is a small chapel, with the Roman figures of mother and child beside the door. On the hillside above is the Barbarossa Castle, raided by the pirate Red Beard (Kheir-ed-Din) in 1535. However, unless you're keen to view the surroundings from a bit higher up, it's not worth trekking to these ruins.

Once back in the main square, head for the island's most interesting church, **San Michele**. It's reached by taking Via Orlandi and then turning right on Via San Nicola. This street leads to a small enclosed square; the octagonal church with its beautiful tiled floor is on the left side.

San Michele was built in 1719 to a sober Baroque design by Domenico Antonio Vaccaro. The high altar (not so sober Baroque!) and those in the side chapels are worth viewing for their soft colours, but it is the floor that overwhelms. Walking around its edges on wooden planking, you can see the story of Adam and Eve unfold in colourful detail. The sinister snake has wrapped itself around the central tree; monkeys, unicorns, camels and dozens of other creatures fill the scene. Climb the spiral staircase up to the choirloft (with its pretty wooden-cased organ) from where the floor can be fully appreciated. The majolica tiles were made in 1761 by Leonardo Chiaiese, and shipped to Capri from Naples. Chiaiese was also responsible for the beautiful tiled cloisters in the Neapolitan church of Santa Chiara, worked from a design created by Francesco Solimena.

By returning to the Via Orlandi and turning right, you come to the **Piazza Diaz** and the Baroque church of **Santa Sofia**. It has three assymetrical cupolas and a surprisingly soothing interior in the softest of yellows. The piazza is surrounded by majolica-tiled benches, a good place to rest and read though it lacks shade. Little streets from here lead to Anacapri's most typical neighbourhoods.

One of the island's highlights awaits if you take the chairlift to the top of **Monte Solaro** from Piazza Vittoria. This is easily equal to a trip into the Blue Grotto below, because sitting atop this summit plants you in one of the world's prime picnic spots. (Buy sandwiches from the Salumeria on Via Orlandi near the corner of Via San Nicola.) Gazing down on the Faraglioni while munching on a mozzarella and prosciutto *panino* is an unforgettable experience. The chairlift is a one-seater; feet dangle above grape vines, tomato plants, ferns and chestnut trees on the 12-minute ride to the top. Bring a windbreaker or a jumper even if it's a sunny day, because even though there are many spots to choose from for your picnic, it's scrubby ground without many trees for protection from sun and wind.

Last but not least, drop to sea level to row inside the **Blue Grotto** on the northwestern coast. It's close to Anacapri, by bus or a walk down the Strada della Grotta Azzura. From the bottom you can hire a small boat with sailor to take you into the grotto. Or, from the Marina Grande, motor boats carrying from four to twenty people ply from the harbour to the cave. Most guidebooks suggest reaching the grotto between 11.00 and 13.00, but Norman Douglas (who certainly visited more than once) insisted that the afternoon hours are really when the light within is best. I wonder whether the morning rule recommendation has anything to do with the Italian rite of a large lunch and an undisturbed siesta . . .

If you're in a boat with lots of people, you'll be transferred to a smaller rowboat outside the mouth of the cave. The entrance through a rocky arch is very low, so you must sit on the bottom while the boatman (on his back now) leads the boat in by pulling hand over hand on a length of fixed chain above. The blue light inside is close to indescribable – the sun's rays enter beneath the water and anything in it shimmers with this light when submerged. Don't foolishly deny yourself the joy of this excursion for fear of being labelled a 'typical tourist'. It's a wonderful treat on an island that has more than its fair share of them.

Practical Information

My preference is to see the islands during the months of May or September. These are both reliably sunny months, and even mid-October can be warm enough to spend a few hours of the day on the beach. From October to March, some hotels and restaurants will be closed, but all three islands have much to offer to fewer tourists during the quiet months.

Getting there

You won't be sorry if you bring a small car to Procida, and it's also easy to manoeuvre with one on Ischia (though not at all necessary). On Capri, however, visitors' cars are not allowed. A reliable and frequent ferry and hydrofoil service is available from Naples at both Mergellina and the Beverello port areas; less extensive service during high season is maintained from Pozzuoli, Sorrento and Positano. There is also a twice-daily hydrofoil service from Rome's Fiumicino airport to Capri from 15 June until 30 September, calling at Ponza, Ventotene and Sorrento en route. The trip takes 4½ hours and costs about £35. Tickets are purchased in Rome from Med Mar, Piazza Barberini (tel. 081 4828579). The dock near Fiumicino is on Viale Traiano (tel. 081 6521577).

If you're island hopping, the only connections you can't make are between Procida and Capri, and between Ischia and Capri from late September to May. Take a ferry to Ischia from Procida and connect to Capri during summer months, or travel via Naples from Procida and Ischia to Capri. The trip from Naples to Capri, the island farthest from Naples, takes about forty minutes by hydrofoil and 1½ hours by ferry. The cost of transporting a car by ferry, one-way, varies from about £10 to £30 depending on size.
The main boat companies are:
ALILAURO Via Caracciolo 13, Naples (tel. 081 682017).
CAREMAR Molo Beverello, Naples (tel. 081 5515384).
SNAV Via Caracciolo 10, Naples (tel. 081 7612348).

A helicopter service is available from Naples's Capodichino Airport to Ischia and Capri during the summer months, an expensive 15-minute trip. Contact Società Eliambassador, Naples (tel. 081 8370644).

Tourist Information Offices

CAPRI AAST offices at Marina Grande where ferries dock (tel. 081 8370634), in Piazza Umberto I under the clock (tel. 081 8370686) and in Anacapri at 19A Via G. Orlandi (tel. 081 8371524). Close to the town of Capri's main square are agencies that will book island tours and excursions for you.

ISCHIA AAST, Via Iasolino (tel. 081 991146); bordering the port area near ferry line ticket offices.

PROCIDA 138 Via Roma (tel. 081 8969594 or 8969624).

Hotels and Restaurants

CAPRI Many hotels and pensione are scattered down side streets off Capri's main square of Piazza Umberto Primo. The doyen of high-class hotels here is the very expensive **Quisisana**, 2 Via Camarelle (tel. 081 8370788). If you don't stay here, splash out by ordering drinks on the raised terrace. Much smaller but almost as expensive is **La Scalinatella**, 8–10 Via Tragara (tel. 081 8370633), and nearby is the expensive **Hotel Punta Tragara**, 57 Via Tragara (tel. 081 8370844), built as a private villa by Le Corbusier in the 1920s. On a more moderate scale and up the street from the Quisisana is the **Gatto Bianco**, 32 Via Vittorio Emmanuele (tel. 081 8370203), with its vine-covered terrace and décor that harks back to the 1960s. The very pretty and peaceful **Villa Sarah**, 3a Via Tiberio (tel. 081 8377817), is a whitewashed home with a newly added wing of comfortable rooms, situated a steep ten-minute ascent from the main square, also moderately priced.

ANACAPRI, the **San Michele**, Via G. Orlandi 1/3 (tel. 081 8371427), is in a villa just off the main square; moderate.

The island had one restaurant accorded a Michelin star, but it has recently been demoted to 'two fork' status – **La Capannina**, 14 Via delle Botteghe (tel. 081 8370732), near Piazza Umberto Primo in Capri town; Its *ravioli alla caprese* and *linguine* with fish sauce are very good, and now they are working harder than ever to rejoin the upper ranks; expensive. Just up the street is the **Aurora Grill**, 46 Via Botteghe (tel. 081 8377642), good for pizza and grilled meats and fish; moderate.

One of Capri's most elegant eateries is probably **Ai Faraglioni**, 75 Via Camarelle (tel. 081 8370320), with a dining room overlooking the Faraglioni; very expensive. Have a swim, and take in lunch, at the delicious but pricey **Canzone del Mare** (tel. 081 8370104) down at Marina Piccola. Back near the main square **Da Gemma** is a sound choice, with its mouthwatering display of *antipasti* in the room's centre; 6 Via Madre Serafina (tel. 081 8370461); moderate.

In ANACAPRI, try two inexpensive places: **La Rondinella**, 295 Via Orlandi (tel 081 8371223), on a continuation of the street after it forks to left. A more unusual restaurant is **Da Gelsomina**, 6 Via Migliera (tel. 081 8371499). It is found near the Belvedere di Migliara, a thirty-minute walk south of Anacapri, where the family offers home-made wines, sausage and tasty mushrooms from the slopes of Monte Solaro.

ISCHIA   This island has more than 200 hotels, so you won't be left out in the cold, whatever the season. My favourite place is **Il Monastero**, 3 Castello Aragonese, Ischia Ponte (tel. 081 992435). Accommodation is simple but comfortable, and the view is fantastic. There is a lift for which you'll get a pass, though there's still some climbing to do before reaching the hotel entrance. The price includes breakfast and dinner (which is nothing special) but the room rate is low enough to warrant skipping the evening meal here to dine elsewhere; closed mid-Oct to mid-March. Inexpensive.

A small moderately priced place I recommend is **Pensione Umberto a Mare** in **Forio** on the island's western side, 2 Via Soccorso (tel. 081 997171). All 14 rooms have lovely views, as the hotel practically hangs over the sea. Prices are for full board (slight reduction for half), but food is good, and the terraced restaurant is pretty; closed Nov–March. On to more superior places: in Lacco Ameno, the **Regina Isabella e Royal Sporting**, Piazza S. Restituta (tel. 081 994322), closed mid-Oct to mid-Apr, and the **San Montano**, Via Monte Vico (tel. 081 994033), closed mid-Oct to late March. Both have tennis courts, a pool, pretty gardens, hot springs and spa, and both are very expensive.

In PORTO D'ISCHIA, the **Excelsior Belvedere**, 19 Via Gianturco (991522), is the plushest, out on a spit protruding from the ringed harbour, surrounded by pines and pretty gardens, along with a heated pool; closed mid-Oct to mid-April. Very expensive. Not far from this hotel is a less expensive alternative hidden in lush gardens with a small pool, **La Villarosa**, 5 Via Giacinto Gigante (tel. 081 991316); closed Nov-late March; Moderate.

Better known for hot springs than haute cuisine, Ischia doesn't have any outstanding restaurants. But like Procida, fresh seafood is plentiful and pasta never disappoints.

In the port area, **Gennaro**, 66 Via Porto (tel. 081 992917), is good, and close to where boats come in and out of the harbour; closed Nov to mid-Mar. Moderate.

Near the castle at Ischia Ponte is **Di Massa**, 35 Via Seminario (tel. 081 991402), for typical southern Italian dishes; closed mid-Nov to mid-Feb. Inexpensive.

Another inexpensive restaurant good for seafood is **Dal Pescatore** in tiny Sant'Angelo (tel. 081 999206); closed Dec–Mar.

In **Forio**, **Lacco Ameno**, **Casamicciola** and **Ischia Porto**, you'll find many pizzerias and trattorias offering modestly priced meals.

PROCIDA   The island has three fairly basic, clean hotels. **The Riviera**, 36 Via G. Da Procida (tel. 081 8967197), is south near the eastern beach of Ciraciello, and less than 1km from the small bay of Chiaolella. Nice views from some of the rooms here; closed Nov–Mar; moderate.

The **Savoia**, 32 Via Lavadera (tel. 081 8967616), is near Chaiolella and has six bedrooms, none with bath. The small, family-run pensione was one of the first to open on Procida many years ago. They are open year round and offer full board during the summer months. Inexpensive.

The **L'Oasi**, 16 Via Elleri (8967499), is northwest, down a very narrow street and somewhat cut off from island life, open year-round; moderate.

You'll find small restaurants and trattoria throughout the island, though mainly at the port area, Corricella and Chiaolella. You'll get a good meal if you opt for island specialities of seafood or rabbit. Along the Via Roma in the port area are five or six places – try **La Medusa** (Inexpensive). In Chiaolella, try **Da Crescenzo** (they've also got a few bedrooms), 33 Marina di Chiaolella (tel. 081 8967255); inexpensive.

Price Ranges

Hotel (double room)	*Restaurant (per head)*
Inexpensive: under 60,000	under 25,000
Moderate: 60–120,000	25–50,000
Expensive: 120–200,000	50–90,000
Very expensive: 200,000+	90,000+

Museums and other Public Sites

CAPRI Carthusian Monastery of San Giacomo: Open 09.00–14.00 except Mon and hols.

Church of San Michele: 10.00–18.00 Mon–Sat, 10.00–14.00 Sun April–Oct.

Foreign Cemetery: 07.00–17.00 daily except Thurs 07.00–13.00, and hols 08.00–12.00.

Monte Solaro Chairlift: 09.30–sunset daily.

Villa San Michele: 10.00–sunset daily.

Villa Tiberio (Jovis): 09.00–one hour before sunset daily except mon and hols.

ISCHIA Aragon Castle, Ischia Ponte: open 09.00–18.00 daily except during months of Jan, Feb and Mar.

La Mortella Gardens, Via Francesco Calisa, Punta Caruso: open 09.00–19.00 Tues, Thurs and Sat from Easter until end Oct. Entrance fee of about £4.

Santa Restituta Museum, Lacco Ameno: 09.00–12.00, 15.00–18.00 except Sun, March–Oct.

9. THE AMALFI COAST: From Sorrento to Salerno

The Amalfi coast road is the best known drive in Italy, a geographical wonder separating the Bay of Naples from the Bay of Salerno. The road winds, climbs and swoops relentlessly from Sorrento to Salerno, flanked by tenacious groves of lemons, oranges and olives. From the top of limestone cliffs which edge the Lattari Mountains, you catch glimpses of fishing villages beside the sea, and pass through towns crammed precariously onto the high ridges. Some, like Positano, have terraced themselves into a set of solid white steps down to the water's edge, whereas Amalfi is serenely situated on a gentle slope. Ravello, one of the prettiest towns I've ever seen, sits back in proud isolation high above sea level.

The ride along the coast can be hair-raising, but I offer the following advice for safe passage: allow yourself to be overtaken, sound your horn around corners, and prepare to reverse when an oncoming coach needs room to manoeuvre. Don't try making the trip from Sorrento to Salerno in one day – there are enough bends on the Amalfi Drive to send you round one. It's a distance of about 80km, closer to 100 if you include the northern section from Castellammare to Sorrento. With so many picturesque towns to stay in, and hotels of a high standard, plan to spend at least three or four days exploring the Amalfi coast. In high season you must book well ahead and be prepared for crowded resorts; spring and autumn are a more pleasant alternative, as the weather can still be glorious, though a number of hotels will be closed.

Like Naples and Capri, towns along the Amalfi coast – especially Sorrento – have a well-established tradition of attracting travellers. Initially, this popularity was partly because of the bad press Naples received from guidebook writers during the 1800s, but it developed quickly due to Sorrento's superb position above the Gulf, within easy reach of Naples, Pompeii, the islands and Paestum. Charles Dickens came here in the 1840s, Tolstoy and Longfellow too, while Henrik Ibsen worked on *Peer Gynt* here in 1867.

English writer Norman Douglas evoked the Sorrentine peninsula's past in *Siren Land*, published in 1911. His tales of the elusive sirens and their rocky

The Amalfi coastline is one of the most famous in the world

homes on the outlying islets of li Galli conjure up images of helpless sailors struggling back to Amalfi's safe harbour. And indeed, when one explores the coast by boat, a host of pirates and sea-monsters seem to beckon from the hills and hidden sea caves. Regional myths abound – from capricious gnomes called *monicelli* to golden lambs and chickens buried in the hills near Punta Campanella.

Sorrento

Sitting 50m above the sea, Sorrento is one of the most popular towns on the Amalfi Coast. In an enviable geographic position, it possesses superb views, with the Sorrentine Gulf below and the islands out to sea. Hotels perch on the edge of the cliff, and a sliver of beach rims the bay far below. Small streets wind through the town's historic centre, easily explored in a day. Though Sorrento has become increasingly devoted to tourism and its more tawdry trinkets, local craftsmen still create beautiful objects of inlaid wood (their method is called *tarsia*), leather, and jewellery of coral and cameo in side-street workshops.

Many travellers base themselves here when touring the area, as it has scheduled ferry and hydrofoil services to Naples and the islands. Sorrento has lost some of its character simply because there are too many hotels, and too many foreigners staying in them. But it is a very pretty town, and the hotels above the marina have unbeatable views from windows and balconies. Most offer lift service to the north-facing beach below, which consists mainly of deck chairs and mattresses lined up along cement piers. Sorrento also has a good choice of restaurants, despite a proliferation of English 'pubs' (or poob as the Italians call them).

Sorrento was known as Syrentum to the Greeks, cementing its connection to the place where Odysseus resisted the call of the Sirens by tying himself to his ship's mast. Then, for the Romans, Surrentum was a pleasant escape, a colony during the reign of Augustus. From 830 to 1109 the town was an independent republic. Its citizens repelled a series of Saracen raids, and battled against Amalfi seafarers for the right to remain independent in 892. Conquered by Normans in 1133, Pisans helped them rebel four years later. But in the 16th century, Sorrentines could not hold back the bloodthirsty Turks, who carried off 2000 citizens; only 120 ever returned. The population constantly allied itself with groups trying to overthrow the monarchy, but eventually came under the power of the dukes and kings of Naples.

Sorrento's main square is **Piazza Tasso**, named after its most famous son, the poet Torquato Tasso (1544–95) whose best known work is the epic poem *Jerusalem Freed*. Two years before his death he composed *Jerusalem Conquered*, about the First Crusade. If he had stayed in Sorrento he might have led a happier life; for seven years he was confined in the northern city of Ferrara, declared insane. In later years, after much restless wandering, he was summoned to Rome by Pope Clement VIII to be crowned Poet Laureate, but he died in the capital before receiving the honour. His home is now part of Hotel Sirenuse along the town's eastern edge.

Sorrento's main street, Corso Italia, runs north and mainly south from the Piazza Tasso. The town's prettiest tourist attraction is the 14th-century **Cloister of St Francis**, south of the square near the corner of Via Vittorio Veneto. Attached to the Baroque church with its big bell-tower, the arched cloister is filled with palms and tumbling purple bougainvillea. The surrounding walls are often used for local art exhibits, as the convent is now an art school.

On nearby **Piazza Antonino** is the church of the same name, dedicated to the city's patron saint. Traces of the original 11th-century basilica have been uncovered, but the present features are mainly Baroque. The church's three most interesting elements have little to do with the grander aspects of ecclesiastical architecture: a beautiful pulpit crafted in the Sorrento style of inlaid *tarsia* by the Fiorentini Brothers in 1938; the animated *presepio* created in the 1700s by the Neapolitan school of Solimena in a room to the left of the high altar; and, in a chamber beneath the high altar, an amazing collection of ex-voto offerings from sailors to the saint buried here. These paintings and metal decorations read like a logbook of divine intervention.

Sorrento's **Cathedral**, located on the southern half of the Corso Italia, is not much to look at. Its pale, plain façade was unfortunately rebuilt in the early 1900s, but at least the bell-tower on the left, unattached to the Duomo, retains its graceful Romanesque arch. More Sorrentine *tarsia* work is displayed in the choir stalls inside. Behind the Duomo are the remains of a Roman arch, at the end of the Via Sersale off Corso Italia. Also near the Duomo, heading south

The cloisters of St Francis, Sorrento

this time off the Corso down Via Tasso, is a strange corner building called the **Sedile Dominova**. Recognisable by its bright green-and-yellow tiled dome, this was the seat of the Sorrentine nobles in the 15th and 16th centuries; their coats of arms are displayed within. The dark forecourt is now the *Società Operaia*, a men's social club where a lot of serious card-playing takes place beneath the faded frescoed ceiling. The Via San Cesareo runs to one side of the building, filled with fruit and vegetable stalls on most mornings.

Sorrento's only museum is in the 18th-century **Palazzo Correale**, recently reopened after extensive earthquake damage forced curators to close it in 1985. It is reached by walking north on Via Correale off the Piazza Tasso. The works within were donated to the town by Alfredo Correale, Count of Terranova, and his brother Pompeo. The museum houses an impressive collection of furniture and Neapolitan paintings, as well as other Campanian works of art – porcelain, majolica tiles, more Sorrentine *tarsia* work – from the 15th to 18th centuries. Some of Tasso's manuscripts are kept in the library here, guarded by his death mask poised on a corner pedestal.

Excursions from Sorrento

Sorrento is ringed by many small hill towns worth exploring, such as Sant'Agata, Vico Equense and Massa Lubrense. The area is especially good for long walks with spectacular views to coves and coastline far below, such as the highly recommended trek to the abbey of Il Deserto south of Sorrento. If you haven't climbed Vesuvius, or been to the summit in either Ischia or Capri, spend half a day on top of Monte Faito north of Sorrento. Or take to the open sea – hire a boat in Sorrento and visit the hidden fishing village of Marina di Puolo just south.

Sant'Agata sui Due Golfi and Il Deserto

The old monastery of Il Deserto, with its many terraces and spectacular views, is best reached by first driving to **Sant'Agata sui Due Golfi** south of Sorrento. This small town, inland off state road No.145, sits high between the Gulf of Naples and the Gulf of Salerno. Park near the church of Santa Maria delle Grazie, built in 1622, and peek inside if you're lucky enough to find the doors open. The high altar here is a magnificent example of Florentine inlaid marble work. Mother-of-pearl, malachite and lapis lazuli are swirled in intricate patterns on all four sides. The altar was made in the 1500s, and moved here from a church in Naples in 1845.

A road climbs north from the left side of the church, a walk of less than 2km up to the abandoned site of **Il Deserto**. (This is a good place for a picnic, almost sure to be free of other travellers.) Suppressed by the French, the Franciscan monastery's red buildings are crumbling now. But their fading beauty only helps to enhance the impact of the view – especially to the north, as the convent was built on the Sorrentine side of the ridge.

Marina di Puolo and Massa Lubrense

The small fishing village of **Marina di Puolo** is just around the Punta del Capo, also south of Sorrento. In a protected cove, it is one of the Amalfi coast's unspoilt havens where life simply carries on regardless of tourists. If you take a boat from the Marina Grande in Sorrento, you'll pass the ruins of the Roman villa of Pollio Felix on the way around the point. Nearby is the **Bagno della Regina Giovanna**; light enters the sea pool through a cleft in the rock, causing the water to be tinted with hues of blue, green and violet.

Marina di Puolo is enclosed in a gorge between Punta del Capo and Capo di Massa. The faded red, white and pink façades of fishermens' homes are squeezed together along the shore. It's a good place to come for lunch if you're skirting the coastline by boat (though the village can also be reached by parking above and walking down). There's a small beach for sunbathing, and a few modest restaurants serving fish guaranteed to be fresh.

The town of **Massa Lubrense** is about 5km south, and if driving from Sorrento you'll have many open views of the sea. The town is situated on a cliff, with homes stepped gently down to the small harbour which is still an active fishing port. Massa is of Lombard origin, recorded in the first half of the 10th century as Massa Publica; the name Lubrense then came from the church of Santa Maria della Lobra. This church was probably built upon the remains of a Roman

139

temple, though no one knows for sure who the temple was dedicated to – perhaps Minerva or Jupiter.

The town's history is similar to Sorrento's, but when Massa was incorporated under the domain of that bigger town in the 1300s, its townspeople successfully rebelled and regained their independence. The Turks ravaged this town in 1558 too, capturing many prisoners. Murat watched his French troops take Capri from here in 1808.

Massa Lubrense's two churches both have pretty majolica-tiled floors. Santa Maria delle Grazie, built in 1512 but reconstructed in 1760, has 18th-century paving in the transept and in the presbytery. Santa Maria della Lobra, dated 1512, is the second built on this site. Its tiled floor is also from the 18th century, and the organ here is unusual: supported by two antique columns that were possibly salvaged from the original temple. A peaceful cloister lies beside the church, part of the small Franciscan convent built here in the 17th century.

From Castellammare di Stabia to Vico Equense

Castellammare lies over the ancient ruins of **Stabia**, about 12km north of Sorrento. Stabia was also engulfed by the eruption of Vesuvius in 79, and on the shore here is where Pliny the Elder met his death. Stabia's uncovered sites have been overshadowed by the excavations at Pompeii and Herculaneum, and though the town does offer ruins dating from the period they are more spread out and many of them are best left to keen lovers of archaeology. Vico Equense and its little port of Marina di Equa are about halfway between Sorrento and Castellammare di Stabia.

In Stabia, visit the Antiquarium. It is within walking distance of the train station in Castellammare, near the corner of Via Denza on Via Mario Marconi. Eleven rooms are filled with artefacts found in the excavated baths, villas and burial ground – frescoes, pavement fragments, terracotta busts, bas relief sculptures and sarcophagi.

Between Castellammare di Stabia and Vico Equense is **Monte Faito**, worth the climb if you haven't had your fill of the view from other points. For a trip to the summit (1131m), return to Castellammare di Stabia. A small railway (open April–Oct) runs to the top, taking eight minutes from the Stazione Circumvesuviana. A more challenging route by car starts from the old Hotel Quisisana, reached from state road No.145 at Castellammare. If coming from Sorrento, pass the towered Angevin castle on the left and bear right on the Via Quisisana about 1km farther on. A sharp right again will start your serpentine climb of 15km up the mountainside. The surroundings of tall oak, cedar and chestnut trees mean that the view will not open out fully until you reach the top, but it's an absolutely magnificent one when you do. From the Belvedere of Monte Faito, the Gulf of Naples is spread below, with Vesuvius just north and Punta Campanella and Capri stretched south. The word Faito stems from the Italian *faggeti* for beech trees, and there are soothing walks beneath them which circle the summit.

Heading back down the coast again, southwards out of Castellammare di Stabia on state road No.145, **Vico Equense** makes a pleasant place to stop. At its centre is Piazza Umberto I, and on the nearby Via Corso is a small museum called the Antiquarium. It has a few interesting pieces, particularly from a necropolis found in the area which dates to the 7th century BC. At the end of Via Corso is the church of Sts Ciro and Giovanni, topped by a colourfully tiled cupola, one of the Amalfi coast's trademarks. Another pretty church is that of the Annunziata, poised above the sea at the very end of Via Vescovado. Its square bell-tower rises in three sections over an arch. Within the church is the tomb of Gaetano Filangieri, a Neapolitan economist and jurist who died in the Angevin castle here in 1788. Below is the small cove of Marina di Equa, a popular spot for swimming and relaxing. From Vico, a turning on Route No.269 inland provides a shorter alternate route to Positano. You'll pass through the town of **Moiano**, well-known for its creamy **fior di latte** cheese, the cow's milk version of buffalo mozzarella.

Positano and li Galli

The journey to Positano is almost as enjoyable as reaching your destination. From Sorrento through Sant' Agata the 'Strada del Nastro Azzurro', or Blue Ribbon Road, takes you over hills clothed with olive and orange trees. All the while the road remains true to its name: a wide band of blue never disappears as you drive south toward Positano. But the town itself plays a game of hide-and-seek while you wind along State Road No.163. Moorish-style houses glint like uneven stacks of white cubes in the distance, but suddenly you've rounded yet another bend and the vision is temporarily out of sight.

Positano

Positano has remained unchanged for centuries, and retains a unique atmosphere because of its Moorish architecture and terracing. What land was available has already been built upon, and there doesn't appear to be a single hectare left to develop. The town has far more steps than streets, so check how high above sea level your hotel is if you're concerned about too much climbing. (The less expensive pensioni tend to be higher up.) Apart from the small church of Santa Maria Assunta, there isn't another site to see in Positano, but this may come as a relief, and the town makes a good base from which to view other towns and ruins. (You just have to be prepared for the coast drive back and forth.)

Positano is first and foremost a great place to relax: marvel over its position, read on your hotel's terrace, drink *cappuccini*, or just soak up the sun while deciding where to eat the next meal. Of course, no one will deny that Positano has been 'discovered'. So fashionable are the boutiques that even the clothes-conscious Romans come here in May to buy their summer wardrobes. But

Moorish terracing characterises the town of Positano

Positano attracts all sorts of people. I have one friend (so oblivious to fashion that he can't match his socks) who is in love with this town, happy as a drunken sailor to read his book in a beachside bar all day, the quintessential Englishman Abroad.

Positano doesn't really have a town 'centre'. The town's only main street of Via Pasitea is one-way, but even so it is tight enough when buzzing motorinos and pedestrians crowd the pavement. This system does mean that if you need to come through town again you've got to go all the way down, around and out before re-entering. If you're driving and don't have a place to stay, or haven't yet located it, leave the car at the bottom of Via Pasitea in one of the car parks there. People congregate at the lower end of Via Pasitea where buses stop, but one of the few open areas immune to traffic (reached on foot only) is the Marina Grande. The other is Fornillo beach, reached by a cliffside walkway from Marina Grande or from steps higher up Via Pasitea. Both beaches are extremely crowded in summer, but it's the Marina Grande that hums from morning to midnight, lined with bars and restaurants.

Just above the Marina Grande is the church of **Santa Maria Assunta** with its brightly tiled cupola. The dark Madonna and Child over the high altar is a 13th-century Byzantine work. The local legend of this Madonna is illustrated in the painting to the right of the altar. Hostile Turkish sailors were ready to attack, whereupon the Madonna spoke to them, repeating the soothing word 'posa', meaning rest or lay down. This miracle of speech apparently converted them: they came peacefully to shore and christened their town Positano. A more widely accepted theory has it that citizens of Paestum founded Positano after fleeing from the Saracens, and that the town's name is also a corruption of the Greek Poseidon.

Li Galli

From Positano you can rent a boat to explore the coastal caves and the rocky islets of **li Galli** about 6km west. By tradition, these three outcroppings are the home of the Sirens, made so famous by Homer in the trials of Odysseus. The largest one was the summer residence of Rudolf Nureyev. He carried on a tradition of Russian ownership, after Diaghilev at the turn of the century. The other two, with barely a flat surface upon them, are uninhabited except for scrub pines and seagulls.

Li Galli, or the Roosters, hardly seem attractive enough to lure lovesick fishermen. What then did the Sirens make of their homes? Perhaps they only frolicked around and beneath them in large hidden caves, which my boatman told me do exist if you're willing to hold your breath and dive deep enough. And who were these so-called Sirens? I refer to Norman Douglas in *Siren Land*, who knows how to keep a reader within the realm of myth:

> The Sirens, says one, are the charms of the Gulf of Naples. No, says another; they were chaste priestesses. They were neither chaste nor priest-esses, but exactly the reverse. They were sunbeams. They were perilous

cliffs. They were a race of peaceful shepherds. They were symbols of persuasion. They were cannibals.

Whatever the mysterious Sirens were made of, it's obvious that their islands are chunks of Appenine limestone. They must have broken from the mainland thousands of years ago, but still seem to be sliding down into the sea with their long laminated sections of rock poised at such high angles. The first one viewed from Positano, il Gallo Lungo, is the largest. Close by is the smallest one named la Castelluccia for the remains of a tower on its edge. Locals prefer to call this island il Brigante, saying that brigands used this spot for hiding themselves and their stolen treasure. The third islet, la Rotonda, is . . . well, just a little bit rounder than the other two.

Point your boat in the direction of Nerano, about 4km farther west. You'll pass two more outcroppings on the way – the rock called Scoglia Vetara and another closer to shore called Scoglia dell'Isca, which was the summer home of Neapolitan actor Eduardo di Fillipo and is now owned by his son. The protected cove of Nerano, a quiet fishing village, has a couple of good restaurants on stilts by the water's edge. (Anchor off-shore by either one and the restaurant owners' sons will pick you up in a rowing boat.) Feast on fresh fish and the day's pasta, helped along by a local white wine.

Heading back toward Positano you'll pass secluded coves ideal for swimming, along with small grottoes emitting loud groans when the waves pound up against them. The limestone cliffs rise like an immense sea wall to restrain the land above, and the remains of towers – said to have signalled from one to the next all the way to Sicily in case of Saracen raids – are scattered on the grassy hills. One of the best things about this boat trip is being able to return to Positano and admire it from the sea, especially as the sun is setting. Tiny golden lights glimmer from houses that now look like so many tiers of theatre boxes, and soon you're back on the stage of Marina Grande.

South of Positano

The Amalfi drive continues its snakelike path south of Positano, full of hairpin turns and deep ravines. The **Punta San Pietro**, with its small church, is your first reference point out of town. The San Pietro, a luxurious cliffside hotel, is built below the upper terrace; hidden from view are sumptuous bedrooms with views back to Positano. From here, state road No.163 becomes a series of sharp curves intersected by small deep valleys; the view out to sea includes Capri and its Faraglioni rock formations. Three kilometres from Punta San Pietro is the small town of **Vettica Maggiore**, followed by **Praiano**. As the local saying goes, 'Whoever wants to live a healthy life spends the morning in Vettica and the evening in Praiano.' These are both simple villages, their homes scattered on the slopes down to the coast. They aren't as overrun with tourists as Positano and Sorrento, but the beach areas are small (though it's a nice sandy one at Marina di Praia) with a limited amount to do in each place.

You'll be driving through tunnels here, as the rock face juts out and falls in a sheer drop to the sea. Just past Praiano is a huge fissure in the limestone cliffs, a deep valley called the **Vallone di Furore**. The sea laps its way to a pebbly beach under the viaduct, a pleasant place to swim if you can find a safe place to park the car above. Steps beside the viaduct lead down to the beach, while a much longer set leads up to the windswept outposts of Sant' Elia and Furore. The valley and the village probably owe their name to the furious noise created when stormy weather sends the wind and water rushing into this deep gorge.

The **Emerald Grotto** is not far from the Furore Valley, and it's worth taking the lift or steps down to this huge cave (then entered by boat) if you won't have a chance to see Capri's Grotta Azzurra. The Emerald Grotto was discovered in 1932, and the eerie green light in the cave enters just as it does in Capri – filtered through indirectly and beneath the surface of the water. The emerald light also plays on the mineral formations in the cave – stalactites have dripped down to join stalagmites in columns that reach a height of 10m.

The coast road then swings past the small fishing villages of Conca dei Marini (once the most active sea-trading town on the coast) and Vettica Minore before introducing you to the whitewashed shapes of Amalfi, a total distance of about 6km from the Emerald Grotto.

Amalfi

This famous town's importance as a maritime power faded centuries ago, but sea trade has been effectively replaced by the tourist trade. Instead of the tall-masted sailing ships that once anchored in the small bay, double-decker coaches sit in the seafront parking lot. If you're driving the car must be left here, unless you're staying at one of the beautifully situated converted monasteries up on either edge of Amalfi, the Cappuccini Convento or the Luna. The town itself, with its impressive mass of a cathedral squeezed onto one side of the inner main square, climbs up the steep curved slope behind the bay. As in Positano, most streets are narrow lanes of stairs winding from house to house.

Despite constant sea-front traffic and the great number of tourists paying homage to the town that gave the coast drive its name, Amalfi is still one of the most picturesque spots on the Tirrhenian Sea. The Corso Roma above the beach area is the scene of the *passeggiata*, the evening stroll down the avenue performed in every town in Italy. You can continue up the Via Amendola near the remains of the Torre di Amalfi; the view back to town is the only one needed to prove why so many people visit Amalfi. Narrow streets off the Piazza Duomo, full of little restaurants, are reminiscent of a medieval town. Covered passageways lead to staircases which then open onto small squares as you climb higher into the town's residential quarters.

Amalfi was populated as early as the fourth century, possibly by shipwrecked Romans who had been trying to make their way to Constantinople but instead stopped at Palinuro to the south, then inland near Eboli and finally settled here.

Another version of the town's founding tells of a settlement in 320 headed by an official in Emperor Constantine's army called Amalfo. But Amalfi was a Byzantine dominion in the sixth century; then slowly, due to the distance and weakening state of Constantinople's governing power, it began to enjoy semi-independence. In 812, it was able to fend off Saracen invaders, and smaller towns along the coast depended on it for protection.

Amalfi became a republic in about 850, and until the 11th century rivalled the ports of Venice and Genoa in its ability to attract wealth and power through sea trade. Its population today is about 7000; but 1000 years ago it totalled 60,000 and was governed by enlightened doges. Amalfi owned warehouses and banks in Byzantine and Islamic ports; Amalfi sailors and merchants set up shop in such places as Cyprus, Jerusalem, Beirut and Alexandria. Its influence in Italy extended from Naples and Benevento down to Syracuse in Sicily. Amalfi became famous for devising the *Tavole Amalfitane*, said to be the world's oldest maritime code, a set of regulations for shipowners, merchants and seamen which was in use until the 1500s. But Amalfi was annexed to the Kingdom of Sicily under Roger II in 1131, then plundered twice by the Pisans. Until 1582, it was under the dominion of the Colonna, Orsini and then the Piccolimini families, and was never again able to regain its former power and prestige.

Little remains in Amalfi of its illustrious past – most historians will tell you it lies buried beneath the sea. Powerful storms in 1013 and 1343 destroyed most buildings along the seafront. The ruins of the **Arsenal**, two halls with Gothic arches, can still be seen on Via Camera near the bayside Piazza Flavio Gioia (named for the presumed inventor of the compass in the 11th century). The arsenal is where ships were constructed, some with as many as 116 oars. Amalfi's maritime laws are preserved in the Municipio near the Piazza Duomo.

The town's great architectural treasure, the **Cathedral of St Andrew**, over-whelms the central square. Its best features are the façade, the attached Cloisters of Paradise and the top level of the bell-tower. The cathedral is faced in striking bands of black and white, with small intertwined arches and alternating squares patterned with stars, crosses and animals. At the top is a bright gold-and-blue mosaic, *Christ Enthroned by Symbols of the Evangelists and Earthly Powers*, designed by Neapolitan artist Domenico Morelli. From the piazza, 56 wide steps lead to the cathedral's arched porch.

The Duomo was first built in the ninth century, reconstructed in 1203, and then again in 1701 in keeping with its earlier Lombard-Norman style. It partially collapsed in 1861, and was then heavily restored from 1875–94. Among its most impressive monuments are the carved bronze doors, inlaid with silver and made in Constantinople before 1066 by Simeon of Syria. Unfortunately, the designs have worn and are difficult to decipher.

The cathedral's interior is Baroque, divided into three naves on the plan of the Latin cross. The marble pulpit and the tall Easter Candelabra are interesting for their intricate Cosmati mosaic style; the only other objects within that I found worthy of inspection were the relics of St Andrew, which were brought from Constantinople in 1208 and are buried beneath the high altar. (He is missing one important body part though, since his head has been in the Vatican since 1462.) A sort of oily liquid is said to have oozed from his body in the 14th century, called the 'manna' of St Andrew. Amalfi's cathedral was a place of pilgrimage for such luminaries as St Francis of Assisi and Pope Urban IV in the 13th century, but when word spread about the 'manna' many more Christians came to pay their respects. Up until the 1500s, miracle health cures were attributed to the manna of St Andrew.

The **Cloisters of Paradise** are reached through a door from the left-hand side of the porch. They form an intimate courtyard, graced with slender double columns which are surmounted by tight pointed arches. Frescoes, sarcophagi and coats of arms along each aisle make it feel like an open-air museum; the Cosmati mosaic work embedded in the walls is the best I've seen, and the only opportunity I know of to see these fine geometric patterns displayed in daylight.

The Campanile, to the front of the church and on the same side as the cloisters, was completed in 1276 and is the only remaining portion of the earliest building work. Its central tower at the top, with four corner turrets, is criss-crossed with playful arches in tiles of yellow and green. I love everything about it but the bells. Perhaps being a manual bell ringer is not a very prestigious job, but was it really necessary to install an electrical system that allows these bells to ring every quarter hour?

Amalfi's quietest locale is up beyond the highest residential quarter, in the **Valle dei Mulini** or Valley of the Mills. About 150 years ago there were 16 paper mills (among the oldest in Europe) and 15 macaroni factories operating in Amalfi; many were based in this part of town. In fact, the only papermaker left, by the name of Cartiera F. Amatruda, still operates in a 14th-century mill near here. They produce beautiful stationery which you can purchase at the mill, a five-minute walk north of Largo Marini on Via delle Cartiere.

From Piazza Duomo, follow Via Genoa up to Via Capuano which leads you into the valley. The rushing stream is below, the way lined with gardens and citrus groves. In about an hour's time you reach the walk's prettiest point at the ruined mill, or *mulino rovinato*. The head of the valley is reached after another 45-minute walk, but most people make the ruined mill their stopping point.

Amalfi's other treasured and peaceful spot is on its western hillside: the Cappuccini Convento Hotel. Even if you're not staying at this 12th-century former monastery, it's worth the trek up a long flight of steps (or by lift) on the Via Camera. The view is superb; the restored cloisters and flower-covered loggia are soothing spots. On the other side of town is another hotel with a gorgeous 13th-century cloister called the Luna Convento. Part of the whitewashed hotel is in the Saracen Tower by the sea, Amalfi's last landmark on the eastern edge of town before the road rejoins the coast drive south to **Atrani**. This small town, so close to Amalfi that it seems like a beachside extension, is well known for its production of colourful ceramics. The bronze doors on the church of San Salvatore de' Bireto here (just off Piazza Umberto I) are as well-wrought as Amalfi's, and were made in Constantinople at about the same time.

Ravello

The steep turning left uphill to Ravello is just past the town of Atrani. This picturesque road off the Amalfi Drive ascends for about 7km, through the vineyard-laden Valley of the Dragon. The small villages of Pontone, Minuto and Scala (this last worth a detour for its views) can be seen in the distance on flat patches among the hills.

When you reach **Ravello** much of its beauty will be hidden from view until you leave the car and stroll up the narrow streets around Piazza Vescovado. One of the town's central avenues is simply a path of wide stone steps beside the Duomo which leads to the top of the hill. You're apt to pass schoolchildren whom the local priest is admonishing to slow down, and always a handful of other travellers who have discovered that this is a worthy place of pilgrimage. Ravello has some excellent hotels, amongst them my own favourite: the friendly, old fashioned Caruso Belvedere. A more formal (and more expensive) alternative is the Hotel Palumbo. The town's two most elaborate villas, the Rufolo and the Cimbrone, are set among gorgeous gardens and open to the public.

Ravello was probably established by the Romans in the sixth century, but the first accurate records point to settlement in the ninth century when this area of the coast was under Amalfi's rule. It became an independent episcopal seat in 1086, and by then had 13 churches and 4 monasteries. The ruins of these are hard to find, and many of Ravello's houses have been built upon them. Despite the town's isolated position, it came under very heavy attack by Pisans in 1135. Roger the Norman came to the citizens' aid, but Pisa retaliated two years later when the town was decisively destroyed by the northern invaders. Ravello recovered, however, and its period of greatest wealth was during the 13th century when rich merchant trading families had ties with Sicily and the Orient. The town retained its independence until the early 1800s, when it then became part of the diocese of Amalfi.

In 1086, Ravello's first bishop, Orso Papirio, founded the **Cathedral of San Pantaleone** that dwarfs the town's only piazza. The church was rebuilt in the 12th century, probably around the time when the justly famous bronze doors were brought here from the Apulian city of Trani in 1179. They were made by Barisano da Trani, divided into 54 panels depicting the lives of the saints and Christ's Passion. (Since they are protected by wooden doors inside and out, appeal to the Sacristan within the church to open them for you.)

Inside the cathedral (well restored in the 1970s when the 18th-century Baroque additions were dismantled), the floor slopes slightly upward. When I asked the Sacristan whether I was imagining this, he solemnly said, 'No, it slowly makes its way to God's altar.' (A less pious explanation is that it makes it easy for the water to run out when the floor is being washed.) Along the walls of the right nave are traces of ancient frescoes and two Roman sarcophagi. The raised pulpit in the central nave is a real beauty, created by Niccolo di Bartolomeo da Foggia in 1272. It is supported by six twisted columns encrusted with bands of mosaic resting on the backs of lions.

The mosaic pulpit in the cathedral of San Pantaleone, Ravello

Pantaleone is the town's patron saint, a doctor who was the favourite physician of Emperor Maximian. The saint was beheaded in the year 206, on 27 July, and Ravello claims for him an annual miracle on a footing with San Gennaro in Naples. An ampoule of San Pantaleone's blood is stored in the chapel to the left of the high altar; it's said that every year on 27 July it also becomes liquid. (According to H. V. Morton, the marble floor of this chapel was paid for by an Englishman named Captain John Grant, because he was so impressed by the ceremony in 1925.)

To the right of the church off the piazza is the **Palazzo Rufolo**. The rich Rufolo family elaborated on its earlier construction in the second half of the 13th century. Did Boccaccio's Landolfo Rufolo, hero of one of his stories in the *Decameron*, live here? As the story goes 'this Rufolo was a very rich man indeed. But being dissatisfied with his fortune, he sought to double it, and as a result he nearly lost every penny he possessed, and his life too.' By the story's end, after selling his cargo at bargain prices in Cyprus, turning to piracy and then being shipwrecked, Boccaccio has our hero 'secure at last in Ravello . . . no longer interested in commerce . . . living in splendour for the rest of his days.'

Once inside the walls of the Villa Rufolo, it is obvious to see how easy that would be. Wagner found inspiration for his *Parsifal* in the tropical gardens here (in summer still the scene of wonderful concerts); the villa was occupied centuries earlier by Pope Adrian IV, Charles of Anjou and Robert the Wise. In the late 1800s it was owned by Scotsman Francis Neville Reid, but is now the property of the Italian State. One of the two remaining towers can still be climbed, and the small enclosed Moorish cloister nearby is dark and quiet. Paths lined with palms and cypress trees lead to a wide terrace with a wonderful view along the coast.

149

The garden of **Villa Cimbrone** is slightly wilder and even more stunning, reached by Via San Francesco from the same side of Piazza Vescovado. The palazzo was built in the late 1800s by Lord Grimthorpe, a wealthy English lawyer and an authority on architecture and horology, who designed Big Ben. He had his ashes buried here beneath the Temple of Bacchus near the cliffside Belvedere. Villa Cimbrone is now owned by the Swiss Vuilleumier family, hoteliers who have run the Hotel Palumbo since 1875. They claim that not even a generous offer from Fiat magnate Gianni Agnelli has enticed them to sell the villa. One can't blame them: this has to be one of the most spectacular properties in southern Europe. (The American author Gore Vidal has managed to purchase one cliffside patch; inevitably though, animosity has developed over foot-path rights.)

Acres of lush garden are unevenly and sporadically pruned, which only adds to their charm. This is a place for lingering along paths lined by roses, camellias, begonias and hydrangea – and those are just the most easily identifiable plants in this flowering paradise. To the north, the ground slopes down to a wooded area covered with pine and chestnut trees, where the Temple of Bacchus is hidden. Within is the seductive bronze statue of the god, rubbed to a high sheen by appreciative hands. Just beyond is one of the highlights of the Amalfi Coast – an astounding view from the Belvedere, a clifftop balcony 350m above the sea. The railing at the outer edge is interspersed with busts of emperors, set bravely on pedestals; stone benches line the inner boundary. The panorama beyond is breathtaking – this is another perfect place for slicing the cheese and sausage, and uncorking the wine of Ravello . . .

Towards Salerno

The coast road continues to convolute, winding past the two seaside resorts of Minori and Maiori. The ruins of a **Roman villa** were uncovered in Minori during the fifties, found on the Strada S. Lucia before heading down into the main part of town. Built in the 1st century, only the villa's ground floor remains though some of the rooms are very well preserved. The villa was constructed around a central courtyard which once had a swimming pool. In the barrel-vaulted hall are faded frescoes and stucco decoration. In the course of excavation here, two other villas were uncovered. They are not open to the public but their existence points to the fact that Minori has been a holiday resort for almost 2000 years.

Minori is – as the name implies – smaller than Maiori, and so is its beach. **Maiori** draws more crowds in summer, and hotels line its long, grey, sandy beach. The church of Santa Maria a Mare is a pretty one, its golden-tiled cupola dominating the low skyscape and reached by climbing 108 steps from Corso Reginna Maior (the town's original name). Originally built in the 12th century, it was modified for the second time in 1836 and has a small, idiosyncratic museum in the sacristy. A beautiful ebony and ivory casket, used to store relics, dates from the 16th century. There are silver crosses, collection plates from the 1400s, even 15th-century English art in the form of an alabaster altar-frontal with Gothic bas reliefs of Gospel scenes. The little balcony with its view out to sea is unusual in a church. If you are down by the shore here, take a quick boat trip to the Pandona Grotto – much bigger than Capri's Blue Grotto but with similar light effects.

From Maiori, you'll round the **Capo d'Orso**, the last point along the drive to really get a good, long view back along the coast. This chunky spur of oddly shaped rock separates the valleys of Tramonti and Cava de'Tirreni. Driving out toward the lighthouse, the view will include Punta Campanella and Capri. Rounding this point, the view east now takes in the wide Gulf of Salerno. Below is one of the Amalfi Coast's best beaches at the **Marina di Erchie**, guarded by the square Saracen tower at its far end. Farther on is **Cetara**, a small fishing village which hasn't embraced tourism in a big way. I'm not sure why – all the requisite elements are there to exploit. Maybe it hasn't quite shaken off the reputation acquired in the late 1700s of being a 'nest of pirates'.

Vietri sul Mare is the next town along the coast, and marks the end of the Amalfi Drive. It's a popular holiday resort, but without the charm of a place like Positano. It's well known for ceramics that are produced in many factories among the inland hills, and buying in bulk means you'll easily slash chainstore prices in half. Another beautifully tiled dome is part of the landscape here, attached to the hilltop church of San Giovanni Battista built in 1732.

Up in the hills behind Vietri is a strange and interesting monastery, the **Abbazia dell Trinità**. It nestles in a deep, green valley, and the strong harsh lines of the buildings here don't seem in keeping with the soft surroundings, which only serves to emphasise the power and prestige this monastery once had. From the coast road in Vietri, a sharp left turn takes you on to a wide road which climbs for about 8km. Follow signs for Corpo di Cava, and also yellow signs for the 'Badia'. Once in Cava, you'll pass a small monument to Pope Urbano II who consecrated the abbey in 1092; the road from here (a distance of 3.8km) will lead down to the piazza by the monastery's church.

The powerful Benedictine abbey was founded in 1011 by Sant'Alferio Pappacarbone, a nobleman from Salerno who was the monastery's first abbot, and who apparently died here in 1050 at the age of 120. It is also the resting place for King Roger of Sicily's second wife Sibylla who died in Salerno, and the antipope Theodoric who died here in 1102 living as simple monk. The monastery was most powerful under its third abbot, Alferio's nephew San Pietro, with jurisdiction over about 500 abbeys, priories and churches from Rome to Salerno. It even maintained a fleet for commercial trading in the Orient, and along with artistic treasures the monks amassed an impressive and important collection of documents. Many are still preserved in the archives and library, including a Bible in Visigothic script and the *Codex Legum Longobardorum* (a complete survey of Lombard laws, dated 1004).

The abbey's church was first constructed toward the end of the 9th century, enlarged in the 11th, and then renovated in a Baroque style in the late 1700s. The façade is a restrained version of the style, but the interior is too modern for my taste. Highlights here are the 13th-century ambo, or pulpit, another beautiful example of Cosmati mosaic work and the Easter candelabra with its trunk in a spiralled mosaic pattern.

Passing through a massive hall to the left of the church, doors at the end lead to the vast and varied monastery complex. (Visitors are taken through by guided tour only, in English if requested.) The small Romanesque cloisters is one of the first areas within, with delicate marble columns marking the four sides. To the left is the Gothic Sala Capitolare, paved with majolica tiles and decorated with frescoes that portray celebrated popes, monks and emperors. The Lombard cemetery, a 12th-century crypt beyond the Chapel of the Crucifix, is below ground, supported by columns that are even older. A museum is located along one side of the cloisters, with some fine pictures by Andrea da Salerno, Luca Giordano, and the school of Lorenzo Monaco.

Though thoroughly diminished in power, it appears that the monastery has enough money for extensive and careful renovation work. Glassed balconies lead to monks' quarters; floors are highly polished; restoration experts have been called in to renew frescoes. The complex of buildings seems to extend indefinitely up the valley, some low passages from one room to the next are carved right out of the rock face. Despite the vast number of rich works accessible to the public here, Trinità di Cava feels extremely remote and hauntingly still, as if it has refused to come to terms with its lowered status in the eyes of the outside world.

Salerno

This sprawling industrial city is the capital of the province also called Salerno, built in a wide arc on the hillside above the gulf. It is in a pretty position, but a population of more than 150,000 creates planning problems, and the town's medieval quarter is almost hidden within an ugly urban sprawl. Salerno was badly damaged during World War II and much was rebuilt along the waterfront during the 1950s. On 9 September, 1943, the US Army landed just south of here, and with British commandos launched their attack on mainland Europe which signalled the turning point in the war.

The city's past is illustrious: a famous School of Medicine founded in the 11th century and capital of the Kingdom of Naples under Norman ruler Robert Guiscard. But in my opinion Salerno's present state doesn't warrant a lengthy visit. I wouldn't choose this city as a base for touring the Amalfi coast or for visiting Paestum and Campania's southern coastal region.

Yet the town's small medieval quarter is wonderfully intact, and the **Cathedral** here is one of the best examples of Norman architecture in southern Italy. From the Lungomare Trieste (very pretty along its western section closest to Amalfi), the tight Via Duomo cuts up left to the old quarter and you are at the back of the big church. Dedicated to St Matthew, the Duomo was begun in 1076 under the orders of Robert Guiscard near a previous church founded in 845; it was consecrated in 1085 by Pope Gregory VII, who is buried here. It was completely remodelled in the early part of the 18th century. The recent earthquake damaged the church, but surprisingly revealed Norman columns hidden inside the Baroque piers.

The Duomo's atrium is a delight, entered through the Romanesque Porta dei Leoni up a short flight of steps. It is surrounded by columned arches on all four sides and has a small fountain in its centre. The 28 marble columns were taken from Paestum long before one needed permission for such plundering, and there are some very well-preserved sarcophagi in the side galleries. The 12th-century bell-tower rises on the right, its decorative upper storey similar to Amalfi's.

It is thought that part of the medical school existed here, in what are now side rooms off the atrium. Its origins are obscure, first mentioned in documents dating from the early 9th century. Benedictine monks had a directing hand in the school's growth from the 10th century; but it reached its zenith in the 12th and 13th centuries. Students came from all parts of Europe (their teachers from as far afield as Africa), and no one could practise medicine in southern Italy without the school's certificate: seven years of study with public exams, and a year practising under a qualified physician. La Scuola Medica Salernitana also gave students a firm grounding in theology, and the philosophy and laws of medicine. Its Code of Health was a standard reference guide throughout the Middle Ages.

The cathedral is entered from the atrium through a tall bronze door of 54 panels, another import from Constantinople in 1099 and once also inset with silver. The decorated pulpits within are superb works, especially the bigger one on the right side of the middle aisle. It rests on 12 granite columns with exquisitely carved capitals. The Easter candlestick nearby was also made in the early 13th century; at more than 5m it's the tallest I've ever seen.

Though the Duomo is loaded with Roman sarcophagi and other monuments to the dead, the most splendid tomb was carved for Margherita di Durazzo. She died in 1412, the mother of Angevin King Ladislau and wife of Charles III of Durazzo. Supported by four symbolic figures of Prudence, Regality, Faith and Fortitude, the tomb is in the last chapel in the left aisle, just before the steps which lead to the high altar area. It was completed in 1435 by Alessio di Vico and Antonio Baboccio da Piperno (who also worked on Milan's Duomo).

The **Museo del Duomo** is nearby at No.2 Via Monterisi, and houses an interesting collection of art commissioned in Salerno through the centuries. Its best works are a large set of ivory relief tablets showing scenes from the Old and New Testaments. Four of the 54 panels are missing, one exhibited at the Louvre, another in Berlin, a third in Budapest and the fourth at the Museum of Metropolitan Art in New York. They were carved by various artists in the 12th century, probably made as the large frontispiece of an altar. A painting by Ribera, *St Peter and St Jerome*, is worth viewing in Room II; the museum's first room displays diplomas from the School of Medicine.

Via Mercanti, south of the Duomo, is the best street for absorbing the atmosphere of the medieval quarter. On the Piazza Matteotti at the street's eastern end is the **Church of the Crucifix**, first constructed in the 10th century. A

14th-century fresco under the altar in the right apse is a real oddity, *The Martyred Saints Clemente, Paolina and Cassiano*. The remains of each saint are said to be contained in the gold urns beneath the figures. At the other end of Via Mercanti is the Arco di Arechi, all that remains of a palazzo built in the 8th century by Lombard Prince Arechi.

The **Castello di Arechi**, stronghold of the same family, was constructed by the Byzantines, enlarged by the Lombards, and then reinforced by the Normans and Aragons. It sits on the hill above Salerno, and the view from here takes in the city and the gulf beyond, with the Cilento mountains to the south. The city plans to turn this site into a museum, but restoration of the castle ruins continues slowly.

Practical Information

Getting there

The Amalfi coast road, about 70km from Sorrento to Salerno, is reached by car from Naples on the A3 Autostrada. The motorway stops at Castellammare di Stabia, and parts of the coast road (No.145) from there to Sorrento can be just as breathtaking and time-consuming as the drive past Sorrento. An alternative route is to drive directly to Salerno on the A3, and make your way back up the coast in the opposite direction. Trains from Naples's central station leave often for Sorrento (the Circumvesuviana line), and blue Sita buses along the coast will connect one town to the next.

Tourist Information Offices

AMALFI   Azienda Autonoma di Soggiorno e Turismo: Corso Roma 19 (tel. 089 871107).

CASTELLAMMARE DI STABIA   Piazza Matteotti 34 (tel. 081 8711334).

POSITANO   Via del Saracino 2 (tel. 089 875067).

RAVELLO   Piazza Vescovado 10 (tel. 089 857096).

SALERNO   Piazza Amendola 8 (tel. 089 224744) or Piazza Vittorio Veneto at the train station (tel. 089 231432).

SORRENTO   Via Luigi De Maio 35 (tel. 081 8782229).

VICO EQUENSE   Corso Umberto I (tel. 081 8798343).

Hotels and restaurants

AMALFI   Cappuccini Convento Hotel, Via Annunziatella 46, 84011 (tel. 089 871877), has a wonderful situation above town in a 12th century monastery (lift from Via M. Camera, or with car follow signs up hill on town's western side); cloisters and columned dining room; private car park below at road level; expensive.
Luna Convento Hotel, Via P Comite 19, 84011 (tel. 089 871002). This old hotel has been in the same family for five generations, with claims that St Francis of Assissi stayed here in the 13th century. Beautiful Byzantine cloisters and nice swimming pool, private garage; expensive.
Hotel Fontana, Piazza Duomo 7 (tel. 089 871530), right across from the cathedral, clean and friendly, but you'll have to put up with the constant clang of church bells. Inexpensive.
Hotel Lidomare, 5 Largo Piccolomini (tel. 089 871332), a small hotel with friendly owners, right by the sea; clean, simple décor and inexpensive.
La Caravella Restaurant, Via Nazionale (871029), near the tunnel by the beach, very popular and known for tangy seafood sauces over generous helpings of pasta; closed Tues and Nov. Moderate.
Da Barracca, Piazza dei Dogi (871285) is on a side street west of the Duomo, with a pleasant outdoor terrace. Inexpensive.

CONCA DEI MARINI   Hotel Belvedere (tel. 089 831282) just beyond Amalfi on the way to Positano. Terraced rooms lead down to the water, tucked under the coast road with calming sea views; great swimming pool and private parking; moderate.

MASSA LUBRENSE   Antico Francischiello-da Peppino Restaurant, Via Villazzano 27 (tel. 081 8771171), on the coast road connecting Sorrento to Massa. (A number of clean and simple bedrooms available, private beach, moderate prices.) The restaurant's antipasto offerings are outstanding, cannelloni superb, good house wines. Expensive.

POSITANO   Casa Maresca, Viale Pasitea, 84017 (tel. 089 875140), simple, whitewashed hotel not far from the water. Run by an Englishwoman and her Italian husband, it's inexpensive, with good food to boot.
Conca D'Oro, (tel. 089 875111), 16 Via Boscariello, off upper end of Via Pasitea above Fornillo district. Rooms here have balconies with views over town, and the covered terrace is a crazy-quilt pattern of coloured tile chips. A long walk down many steps to beaches and town, but comfortable and inexpensive.
Palazzo Murat, 23 Via dei Mulini (tel. 089 875177), just behind the Duomo in a fantastic Baroque palazzo with profusely flowering plants; a new addition has rooms with bigger balconies. The architecture and atmosphere are worth the price. Expensive.
San Pietro Hotel, Via Laurito 2 (tel. 089 875455) just beyond Positano on a spur off the coast road. This is one of southern Italy's most luxurious hotels, its

suite-like rooms cut into the cliff with views across the bay to Positano. The formal dining room with very good food is for guests only; a lift serves the hotel's private beach and tennis court. Very elegant and understated; extremely expensive.

Buca di Bacco Restaurant, 8 Via Rampa Teglia (tel. 089 875699), right on the beach and also with rooms available from April to mid Oct. All sorts of tempting specialities are displayed in the dining room; the pasta is made fresh daily, for seafood try the *zuppa di cozze*. Moderate.

La Cambusa (875432), again on the beach, but up steps and set in a small square. I liked the *risotto pescatore* here, and pasta with zucchini which is a popular offering on this coast. Moderate.

RAVELLO Hotel Bonadies, 5 Piazza Fontana Moresca, 84010 (tel. 089 857918). A pleasant, family-run hotel with 33 rooms; its restaurant has stunning views to the south. A minibus runs guests to the seaside. Moderate prices.

Hotel Caruso Belvedere, Via San Giovanni del Toro 52, 84010 (tel. 089 857111). Opened in 1903 by the Caruso family, this is a relaxed old-fashioned place with loads of atmosphere. Comfortable rooms come in all shapes and sizes, some with arched windows and small balconies. A terraced garden affords marvelous views; Caruso family wines and delicious local specialties are offered at dinner. Expensive.

Hotel Palumbo, Via San Giovanni del Toro 28 (tel. 089 857244), closed Feb. This hilltop hotel has been host to such luminaries as Humphrey Bogart and D. H. Lawrence; it's more pretentious and more elegant by modern standards than the Caruso down the street. Most bedrooms have their own terrace; the Moorish-style courtyard is cool and quiet. Very good food, and Episcopio wine produced since 1860. Very expensive.

Hotel Toro, Viale Wagner 3 (tel. 089 857211), is near the piazza, entered through a pretty garden. The converted villa is small, and bedrooms are unexceptional, but food here is good, fresh fare (open to non-residents for dinner); moderate.

Villa Cimbrone (tel. 089 857459) is a moderately expensive but special place to stay, with only ten rooms – splash out if you can. Half the rooms have spectacular sea views, and breakfast is served on the lovely terrace; closed Nov to April.

Compa 'Cosimo Restaurant (tel. 089 857156), closed Mondays from November to March; also a pizzeria in the summer months and always a friendly relaxed atmosphere. The Bottone sisters make their own pasta, as well as ice cream.

Garden Restaurant (tel. 089 857226), also has ten bedrooms, each with terrace. Wonderful place to eat in warm weather, on shaded terrace with fine views. Moderate prices.

SALERNO Unfortunately, nothing to be recommended in the medieval quarter, but the **Jolly Hotel**, Lungomare Trieste 1 (tel: 089 225222) is a known quantity as it's part of a chain – high in services and low on character – in a very good location. Expensive.

Antica Pizzeria del Vicolo della Neve in the old quarter (at No.24, tel: 089

225705) serves excellent pizza evenings only. Closed Wed; inexpensive.

La Brace, Lungomare Trieste 11 (tel. 089 225159), closed Sun and two weeks late December, is near the Jolly Hotel. Good local dishes, moderate prices.

SORRENTO Bellevue Syrene Hotel, 5 Piazza della Vittoria, (tel. 081 8781024), positioned on the cliff edge, originally a private villa built in the 18th century, garden terrace and lift down to beach, along with over-the-top décor of the attached Villa Pompeiana (great for drinks on its far terrace), expensive prices.

Grand Hotel Excelsior Vittoria, Piazza Tasso 34 (tel. 081 8071044), is also on the edge of the cliff, its large, comfortable rooms in four grand villas. Beautifully frescoed breakfast room, a long terrace with sweeping views, pool behind and private beach below reached by lift, very expensive.

La Tonnarella, Via del Capo 31 (tel. 081 8781153), heading out of town toward Massa Lubrense but with good views of the sea. Also a popular restaurant, and gardens filled with lemon and eucalyptus trees. Lift to the beach, but only 16 double rooms; inexpensive.

Bar Santa Anna at the Marina Grande is a very simple trattoria by the sea. But you've got to go down and place your order in advance so there's enough time for them to fish it out of the sea. The nearby **Taverna Azzurra** operates under similar conditions. Both inexpensive.

Davide Ice-Cream Parlour, Via P. R. Giuliani 39 (tel. 081 8781337) is justly famous, to the extent that they even print their own brochure offering 'the largest range of sweetness in Italy'. You'll bump into lots of foreigners here, but what's the difference – it's fantastic stuff.

La Favorita-o'Parrucchiano, Corso Italia 71 tel. 081 8781321), closed Tuesdays November to May, is one of Sorrento's best restaurants. Try the amazing mozzarella rolled in lemon leaves, the *panzarotti* (little pies stuffed with mozzarella, tomato and basil), and the house speciality of *gnocchi alla sorrentina*. Moderate prices, but it could get expensive if you go all out on every course.

La Pentolaccia, Via Fuori Mura 10, (heading north off Piazza Tasso) prepares excellent regional dishes in unpretentious surroundings; a local favourite with moderate prices.

Price Ranges

Hotel (double room)	*Restaurant (per head)*
Inexpensive: under 60,000	under 25,000
Moderate: 60–120,000	25–50,000
Expensive 120–200,000	50–90,000
Very expensive: 200,000+	90,000+

Museums and other public sites

AMALFI Arsenal: corner of Via M. Camera. 10.00–13.00, 16.00–20.00
Municipio: entrance on the square behind the Municipio, off Corso Roma. 09.00–14.00, closed Sun.

CASTELLAMMARE DI STABIA   Antiche Terme Stabiane: Via Sorrentina, by Piazza Amendola at port. 09.00–sunset.
Antiquarium: Via Marco Mario 2. 09.00–15.00, (09.00–13.00 Sun), closed Tues.

CAVA DE' TIRRENI   Abbazia della Trinità di Cava, in the hamlet of Corpo di Cava. Guided tours and museum 09.00–12.30 weekdays, 09.00–11.00 Sun and hols.

MONTE FAITO   By cable car from Piazza Circumvesuviana in Stabia from 1 April to 31 October; 8-minute ride timed to leave after arrival of trains en route from Naple to Sorrento.

RAVELLO   Villa Cimbrone: fee; 09.00–sunset.
Villa Rufolo: fee; 09.30–13.30, 15.00–sunset.

SALERNO   Museo del Duomo; Via Monterisi. 09.30–12.30, 16.00–20.00, closed Sun and hols.

SORRENTO   Museo Correale di Terranova: Via Correale. 09.30–12.30, 16.00–19.00 Apr-Sept; 09.30–12.30, 15.00–17.00 Oct-Mar; 09.30–12.30 Sun, closed Tues.

10. PAESTUM AND THE CILENTO PENINSULA

The Cilento is Campania's least appreciated area, steeped in contrasts between its rocky coastline and mountainous inland areas. It is criss-crossed by rivers and wide valleys – its fertile plain a patchwork of greens, the mountains terraced with hundreds of olives trees. The name Cilento stems from the name Alento, one of the territory's central rivers.

It's hard to compare this part of Campania with any other. Remote hill-towns here have more in common with Basilicata to the east than agricultural areas closer to Naples and Caserta. Coastal resorts like Palinuro resemble those of nearby Calabria more than those on the Amalfi coast. What the Cilento does share with the rest of Campania is its western boundary on the Tirrhenian, and a host of mythical associations.

Then there are the wondrous temples at Paestum, the best examples of classical Greek architecture outside modern-day Greece. Two of the three massive temples are older than the Parthenon, all standing within the ruins of a city founded nearly 2500 years ago. It would be a great mistake to miss them, just 40k south of Salerno. Between Paestum and Palinuro are the rarely visited ruins of Velia, famed in antiquity for its school of philosophy. And about 60km inland, near the Basilicata border is the architecturally stunning monastery at Padula called the Certosa of San Lorenzo. North of here are the strange caves of Pertosa, more than 2km long and full of stalactites and stalagmites.

The town of Eboli, which just touches the northern tip of the Cilento, southeast of Salerno, was made famous by the title of Carlo Levi's book, *Christ Stopped at Eboli*. But it is the people from hill-towns south of Potenza, in the region of Basilicata who are the subject of Levi's book, which is well worth reading. When travelling through the Cilento though, one realises that Levi could just as easily have been describing the rural Italians here in southern Campania. Mountain trails traversed on the back of a mule are still favoured over paved versions, and small villages offer only the community comforts of a church and local coffee bar.

Travelling through the Cilento is easily worth three or more days of your time, perhaps based in Palinuro where hotels are of an acceptable standard. The A3 autostrada from Salerno zips down the eastern side of the Cilento, and the fairly good state road No.18 passes Paestum and then cuts inland (in part tortuously sinuous) toward the Gulf of Policastro. In the high season, you're less likely to run up against the large number of visitors to be found on the islands or Amalfi Coast, and more of them will be Italian than British, German or American.

Paestum

The temples at Paestum are overwhelming in their sheer size and beautiful simplicity. When staring up at them I feel an even stronger sense of the awe felt when visiting the city of Cumae near Naples. They are part of the same mysterious pattern etched on this landscape by Greek settlers. After their centuries of slumber, we now gaze at these monuments like children introduced to a new sibling. How in the world did they get there, and what secret knowledge is stored within their massive ancient columns?

It is not true to say that these Doric temples were 'rediscovered' in the 18th century. Italians in the hilltop town of Capaccio always knew they were there, though the ruins were partially covered in riotous vegetation. Small columns were carted away to Salerno in the 11th century; the troops of Ferdinand I fought Neapolitan barons on the Sele river banks nearby during the 15th. What guidebook writers condescendingly mean is that foreign travellers were not apprised of the temples' existence by their Italian contemporaries. What they were told was that this area was a nasty malarial swamp and a route for bandits, all true enough. Paestum was still slightly infested in 1944, when travel writer Norman Lewis (then a soldier) was admitted to hospital here.

The Latin poets Virgil, Ovid and Ausonius make no mention of malaria in their verses dedicated to Paestum, and we have no records to show that Greeks in the 6th century BC had to contend with the disease in their city. It was then called Poseidonia, City of Neptune, founded by the citizens of a settlement farther south called Sybaris (who were supposedly so decadent and unenterprising that they begat the term 'sybaritic'). Two hundred years later, the town's name was changed to Paestum when ruled by a local tribe called the Lucanians. It was then taken by the Romans in 273 BC, remaining loyal to the Empire when Hannibal charged through in the 3rd century. But malaria did finally cause the town to collapse, after a savage attack by the Saracens in 877. Paestum's dwindling population headed for the hills, where they founded the village of Capaccio in fresher air.

Along with the temples, the outlines of the old city of Paestum can be covered in a few hours, and the small museum across the street can be seen in the space of an hour or so. The site is about 1km long, and half that from the main street back to the farthest edges of excavated buildings. Old Paestum is surrounded by thick walls of travertine and is a fairly open site, though shade is supplied by the temples' huge round columns and the square blocks of stone

The Doric temples at Paestum

connecting them. The highest buildings are the temples of yellow limestone; most of the walls of other city dwellings, behind and between the temples, are less than waist high. It is a pleasure to wander in this open landscape: lizards bask on crumbling stone foundations and snails cling to the stems of flowering rosemary bushes. In the distance, people become Lilliputian as they make their way around the temples.

After walking through the entrance gates, the **Temple of Neptune** dominates the scene before you – the largest and best preserved, built about 450BC. Its 36 fluted columns are 9m high, those in the corners slightly more elliptical to counterbalance the thinning effect of light hitting them from more than one angle. The Basilica to the left was built 100 years earlier, with a single row of columns down its central space. Both temples were probably dedicated to the goddess Hera, Queen of Heaven and venerated symbol of fertility.

About 200m to the right of the Temple of Neptune is the wide open space of the **Forum**. It was once surrounded by a variety of Roman buildings; on the southern edge are ruins of baths and the Senate's Curia, to the north are the Roman Temple of Peace, a Greek theatre and an amphitheatre which, sadly, the modern main road has ploughed through. Also on this side of the Forum is a round area called the Bouleterion, thought to be where the city Senate (or Boule) met.

Farther north and to the right of the Forum is the **Temple of Ceres**, built about 500BC. It was in fact not dedicated to this goddess of tillage and corn (known to the Greeks as Demeter) but to Athena – or Minerva as the Romans called her – the goddess of wisdom. It is surrounded by 34 fluted columns, its interior more open than the other two large temples. In the Middle Ages it was turned into a Christian church: three tombs have been found near the south wall.

161

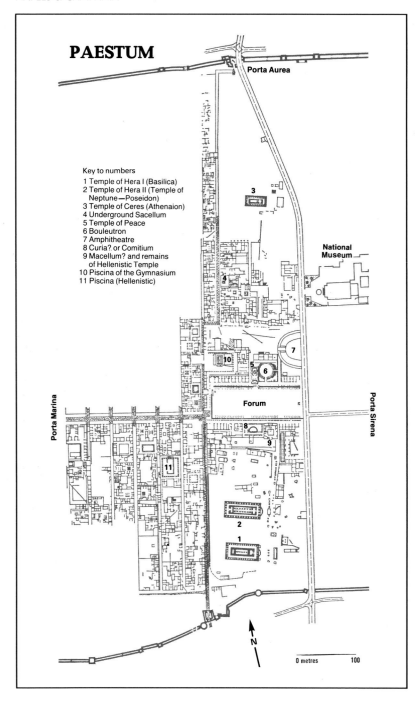

PAESTUM

Porta Aurea

Key to numbers
1 Temple of Hera I (Basilica)
2 Temple of Hera II (Temple of
  Neptune—Poseidon)
3 Temple of Ceres (Athenaion)
4 Underground Sacellum
5 Temple of Peace
6 Bouleutron
7 Amphitheatre
8 Curia? or Comitium
9 Macellum? and remains
  of Hellenistic Temple
10 Piscina of the Gymnasium
11 Piscina (Hellenistic)

National Museum

Porta Marina

Porta Sirena

Forum

N

0 metres   100

The Tomb of the Diver, Paestum

Across the street near the Temple of Ceres is the **museum**, containing objects found in and around Paestum, including a series of metopes uncovered in a sanctuary devoted to Hera outside the city walls. (Metopes are the bas relief depictions found on a frieze between the triglyphs, which are the stone blocks decorated with three vertical bands so evident on the Temple of Neptune.) These richly carved scenes date from between 800 and 480BC, the pre-Classical Archaic age in Greece. The metopes are in the first three rooms, presented as if still intact on a frieze, and are delightful episodes from Greek mythology and illustrations from poems by Stesichorus.

But the museum's highlight is in Room VIII at the back: the **Tomb of the Diver**. It was discovered in 1968, and is thought to be one of the few existing examples of Greek mural painting ever found. This amazingly serene cycle of internal tomb paintings was done in the 5th century BC, and most art from this period is intact only on vases and is rarely seen in a larger format like this. The diver appears to plunge untroubled into the pool beneath him; other sides of the tomb are banquet scenes which add to the sense of carefree transfer from one world to another.

On the same side of the street is the Ristorante Museo, a shaded terrace and inner dining room well placed for a snack or lunch. The modern town of Paestum is little more than a cluster of hotels and campsites, and the railway station is about half a kilometre from the entrance to the ruins, just outside the Sirena Gate which formed part of the city's eastern boundary.

From Paestum to Velia

Two routes lead 50km south to the Roman ruins of Velia. Inland is by way of state road No.18, a more rewarding alternative if you've spent a lot of time driving along the coast already. This road climbs east and then south through hilly country to the small towns of Ogliastro and Rutino, which were even smaller when mule tracks were the only routes of transportation here. Beside old stone homes are newer buildings in various states of completion, and more and more roofs are now topped with TV antennae. But the landscape hasn't changed that much. Hills are covered with olive groves, nets cast below each tangled tree to prevent the oily green fruit from rolling away.

From on high, an occasional glimpse of the sea near Agropoli is a perfect foil to the scrubby green hills surrounding you. West of Rutino are ruins of the castle at Rocca Cilento. The state road finally flattens out on the Salento Plain after passing through Omignano Scalo, and before joining the coast road you must turn right at the T junction. Velia will then be viewed up on the left, most notably the tower on the hill. A left turn on the main road leads to the ruins.

An alternative route is by coast road No.267, passing through Agropoli, Santa Maria di Castellabate and Acciaroli. The fishing villages strung along the coast here have been taking in summer visitors for some years now, mainly in July and August. Many Italians come to camp in this area, spending most of their time on the beach and exploring the coastline by boat.

The coastal resort closest to Paestum is **Agropoli**. It was probably founded in the 5th century by the Byzantines, and its oldest quarter is one of the more interesting and best preserved of any to be found along the coast. This area on the top of town is dominated by a castle, constructed by the Byzantines but enlarged by the Aragon dynasty. If you're looking for a place to eat lunch or dinner, good pizzerie and trattorie are to be found on the narrow streets here, but it's difficult to take a car all the way up. The rest of Agropoli is a modern sprawl of nondescript buildings, though bayside hotels near the port are clean and reasonably priced.

Farther along the coast is smaller **Santa Maria di Castellabate**, with a fine sandy beach on its northern side. The small marina of San Marco a little to the south also has a good beach and a short side trip of about 4km off the main road from San Marco takes you to **Punta Licosa**, one of the best places on the coast for a view out to sea. The name stems from Leucosia, one of the sirens whose legend says that she threw herself into the sea here after her failed attempts to lure Ulysses. The tiny island of Licosa, with its lighthouse and ruins of ancient walls, is just beyond the point. It's a beautiful walk up to the headland by mule track, but a paved road also leads there by way of Hotel Castelsandra – one of the nicest hotels the Cilento has to offer, though its position is the main draw.

About 15km south is the seaside town of **Acciaroli**, where Ernest Hemingway is reputed to have stayed. If so, he picked one of the prettiest resorts on the coast. The small harbour is packed with colourful fishing boats, dominated by a thick square Angevin tower. Acciaroli makes very few concessions to tourists, though they come just the same. There's not much to do here once you've walked its streets and studied the 12th-century Church of the Annunziata (much remodelled) at the marina. But it's a fairly quiet and unpretentious spot; the Hotel Scogliera with its view of the port serves a good meal in its terraced restaurant even if you aren't spending the night.

Pioppi is the only other place of interest passed on route No.267 south to Velia. Positioned on a small inlet protected by the surrounding hills, it retains a Saracen tower and a 17th-century castle. The Church of Santa Maria dei Pioppi was first built in 994, though you wouldn't know that from the unfortunately modern façade. There's a great view from here down to Cape Palinuro as the road climbs and continues on to Velia, flanked by fig and olive trees.

Velia

The sprawling hillside ruins of **Velia**, or Elea to the Greeks, are all that remain of what was once a thriving community 2000 years ago. They were discovered in the 1880s, and various archeological projects undertaken in fits and starts since then (notably by Amedeo Maiuri in the 1920s) have uncovered more areas of the city. But by scanning the hillside and walking its borders today, one realises that there is much more excavation to be done at Velia. This is a little visited site well worth exploring; very few of its walls and foundations are off limits, and you'll find yourself playing amateur archaeologist by sweeping sand away from a mosaic floor to find out whether there's anything worth seeing beneath. Though enough areas have been uncovered to give one a sense of Velia's overall plan, it's what is still buried that stimulates the imagination here.

Velia was founded in the 6th century BC by immigrants from Phocaea in Asia Minor who, first fleeing from Persian invaders by landing on Corsica, were then driven south by the Etruscans and Carthaginians. The town had strong trading ties with Marseilles, which was also settled by Phocaeans. Within 100 years, Velia was highly regarded for its Eleatic school, founded by Xenophanes who emigrated from Colophon. The school was then headed by one of his followers, the philosopher Parmenides. He stated that nothing changes, that one can logically only affirm existence and say 'it is'. Aristotle described him as the founder of 'the science of truth'.

The school continued to flourish under Zeno, one of Parmenides's favourite pupils. His four arguments against motion, 'Achilles and the Tortoise' (portrayed in one of the metope fragments in the museum at Paestum), 'The Flying Arrow', 'The Stadium' and 'The Row of Solids', are his best known contributions to philosophy, hotly contested by Aristotle.

By the 3rd century BC, Velia was a *municipium* under Roman rule. Villas sprang up as wealthy Romans discovered its beautiful setting by the sea – the orator and statesman Cicero and the poet Horace both came to stay, though

165

no villas have yet been uncovered. The two harbours slowly silted over, reducing the town's importance, and it was probably completely destroyed by the Saracens during the 8th or 9th century. A village called Castellamare della Bruca sprang up along the ridge in the early 12th century, but was abandoned some time in the 1600s.

The extensive ruins first seen on the right after entering from the car park were part of the lower city at the south marina, once on the shore but now half a kilometre away. The waist-high walls of homes and shops fill this area; to the south is a necropolis where the Romans buried their dead. A wide road of paving stones leads up the hill, past baths on the left. Constructed in the first half of the 2nd century, the floor of the frigidarium retains its mosaic design. On the right side of the road is a vast cistern.

At the crossroads beyond, the simple and stunning Porta Rosa finally comes into view, having been hidden by a high side wall until now. A left turn leads to the Acropolis. As you walk up toward the castle tower, down to the left are ruins of houses built in the 6th century BC. Farther on is a semicircular theatre from the Hellenistic period. On the summit near the castle are the remains of an Ionic temple. The castle dates from Norman times, though some of its foundations are the city's earliest; the circular tower was built during the Angevin period. This is where, according to H. V. Morton, the Scottish writer Ramage was so beseiged by fleas in 1828 that he ran to the sea, tore off all his clothes, and dived in. After reading that story, I was convinced I saw a fair number still jumping around.

Walking back through the Porta Rosa and along this path for about 300m, you turn left to the north marina with a good view down to the theatre and acropolis. If you head straight on instead, the path is flanked by tower ruins which once stood above the city walls. On your right are the excavated remains of a sacred area with its terrace and long altar; a few hundred metres beyond is the city's north-eastern boundary at the Castelluccio tower.

Palinuro

State road No.447 continues south from Velia along the sea, and views from this portion of coast road are among the best in the Cilento. The pretty town of **Pisciotta**, with its large church of Saints Peter and Paul, dominates one prominent hilltop. Winding down to the marina from the eastern edge of town, you pass grove after grove of olive trees, for Pisciotta produces more olives per square acre than almost any other town in the region. The small port area has a fine stretch of beach to one side, a popular place for summer boaters and campers.

Twenty kilometres south is **Palinuro**, named for the pilot of Aeneas in Virgil's *Aeneid* who legend says was buried here. The ruins of what is called his tomb are at the entrance of the harbour by the beach. Palinurus died while at the helm, and Book V closes with the ship drifting along Italy's coast:

The fleet ran its course none the less
Safely and without fear, for Father Neptune's
Promises held. Borne onwards, it drew near
The Sirens' rocks, so dangerous in old time
And white with the bones of many men.
(Meanwhile the rocks moaned hoarsely as the salt
Constantly flooded round them.) But Aeneas
Sensed that the pilot was gone and his ship was drifting.
And himself steered her through the waves of night,
Sighing and numbed at what had befallen his friend:
'Trusting too much to clear skies and calm seas,
The end is, Palinurus, you will lie
Naked upon an unfamiliar shore.'

Palinuro is famed for its position on a small bay, and though the modern town has grown for the sake of tourists with nothing to recommend it to those interested in history and architecture, the coast has remained rugged and wild. The town has two main streets: the Via Pisacane runs along the hillside; the Via Indipendenza runs parallel, closer to the sea. Both are lined with small hotels and restaurants, crowded in summer. But the grottoes and sandy inlets just north and south of Palinuro are this area's best features, and most can only be reached by boat (always for hire at the small port). Scuba divers come here by the dozens, attracted by the clean clear water and the abundance of marine life.

'From here the storms are born,' say fishermen in these parts. Winter winds whip fiercely around Cape Palinuro, and their erosive powers have created ragged natural arches and tall pointed cave openings. Heading down the coast near the cape is the **Grotta Azzurra**, not quite as splendid as Capri's but with big stalactites and still a beautiful shimmering blue. The **Cala del Ribatto** is farther on, a cove that opens on to four grottoes. There are yet more grottoes to explore in the **Cala del Salvatore**, **Cala della Lanterna** and **Cala Fetente** (dubbed the 'stinking' cove for its spring of sulfurous water). Just east is the natural arch called the Archetiello; farther south is the **Cala del Buon Dormire** (Cove of Good Sleep), so-called after a group of foreigners who once spent the night here for some odd reason. Out to sea is a rocky outcropping called **Il Coniglio**, though its shape hardly resembles the rabbit it's named after.

The vast cave beyond, **Grotta delle Ossa**, is interesting for the bone particles encrusted in stalactites and stalagmites and even in the cave walls. For a long time it was thought that these were the bones of shipwrecked victims of both the Second Punic War's Roman fleet and of seafarers during the reign of first Roman Emperor Augustus. But more recent studies conclude that these are the Neolithic remains of bears and horses – either trapped here or eaten by prehistoric man.

On the hillside above are the remnants of a town once called Molpa, thought to be an outpost of Velia. The river Lambo meets the sea here, once known as the Melpio. The city was sacked by Goths and then Saracens, and completely

destroyed by Barbarossa. Built on what was once an acropolis are the ruins of
a castle, and the view from this deserted spot is wonderful if you walk the half
hour needed to get there. (From state road No.447, head toward Centola until
it crosses the river, then turn right on No.562 for a short stretch, turning right
again toward the sea and the ruins.)

The Gulf of Policastro and north to Padula

Once out of Palinuro, state road No.447 becomes No.562 along the coast.
Around the headland of Cape Palinuro lies a gorgeous stretch of sandy beach,
belonging to the town of Marina di Camerota just south. The Touring Club
Italiano has a holiday village here, along with six campsites and a host of hotels
and bungalows. The old town of **Camerota** rises on a hill 300m from the marina,
known since the 11th century for producing ceramics, especially the long terracotta amphorae used to store wines and other liquids. Oddly enough, the town
also produced vast amounts of fishing line. It must have been a profitable
venture considering the number of Cilento fishermen who still make their living
from the sea.

But Camerota is not a charming place, nor are the towns of Policastro, Villamare and Sapri surrounding the beautiful blue Gulf of Policastro. They look as if
they sprang up when the tourists came to town, lacking character and saved
only by the scenery. Just before reaching them, state road No.562 heads inland,
climbing through green hills that make one forget that the sea is sometimes less
than a kilometre away. The road snakes on, reaching degrees of intestinal
intensity matched only by sections of the Amalfi Coast drive. Then at Scario
you are suddenly on the wide Gulf of Policastro, its colour an intense blue
even on a grey day.

Padula

The Carthusian monastery of San Lorenzo in Padula is the Cilento's architectural
wonder, about 35km north-east of Sapri. The drive from the Gulf of Policastro
through the inland hills is beautiful, cutting through the heart of rural Cilento.
Farmers tend olives and grapes, slow carts are piled high with produce. Mule
tracks trace their way up and over the hills, while cows and goats always take
precedence over cars as they cross the main roads.

Vibonati

From the coast road between Villamare and Sapri, turn left on the secondary
road that climbs toward **Vibonati**. Within a few kilometres you'll see this charming hill-town, its stone homes clustered around the church and bell-tower. Stop
here for a walk around, for this is one of the province's most evocative small

The charming hill-town of Vibonati

towns. Hundreds of years ago Vibonati provided shelter away from the coast for those escaping Saracen incursions. Streets are narrow and steps lead from one terraced home to the next. Some of their portals retain elaborately carved stone surrounds dating from the 16th and 17th centuries. The church of **St Anthony Abbot**, with three asymetrical naves, was built upon the ruins of the Carafa castle built in the 15th century.

Leaving Vibonati, and after successive bends and dips for about 12km, the road near Caselle in Pittari joins state road No.517. From here, the climb is slow to Sanza; the road then forks right toward Buonabitacolo. Within 15km after this town, the A3 autostrada and state road No.19 running north to south are reached (the exit off the A3 is Padula/Buonabitacolo). You are now in the lush Valley of Diano, but it won't really appear as such until viewed on high from such hill-towns as Teggiano farther north. To reach the monastery at Padula, yellow signs off cluttered state road No.19 will point the way east.

Certosa di San Lorenzo

Today the recently restored Certosa di San Lorenzo in Padula appears totally out of context in its 20th-century setting. When it was founded in 1306 by the feudal lord Tommaso da Sanseverino, the valley was a rich source of agricultural income in a strategic position between Naples and Reggio di Calabria. Surrounded now by modern homes not far from the highway, the monastery sits like some majestic remainder on a deserted film set whose size overwhelmed

The Certosa di San Lorenzo in Padula, one of the most elaborate and extensive monasteries in Italy

the carpenters sent to dismantle it. One finds it hard to imagine the monastery as a concentration camp, which it was during both world wars.

Tommaso set out to construct the most elaborate and powerful monastery in southern Italy, and he certainly succeeded. With a total area of 52,000 square metres, the Certosa's architectural statistics are staggering: 600 rooms, 13 cloisters, 41 fountains, 51 internal staircases, and lavish quarters for the monks. This is one of the biggest monastic complexes in the world, and flourished as the Order of San Bruno until it was supressed by the French in 1866.

The monastery was continually embellished until the end of the 18th century; the Baroque interiors are outstanding examples of the period. This was always an obligatory stop for the aristocracy and in 1535 Charles V just happened to drop by with his army, for which an omelette of 1000 eggs was said to have been made. (The size of the kitchen attests to the probability.) Painters, sculptors and architects from Naples and other parts of the south were commissioned to decorate altars, ceilings, cloisters and pavements.

The gridiron pattern appears everywhere, most obviously in the overall plan (which mirrors Spain's Escorial). The gridiron is a symbol of St Lawrence, who was burned to death while chained to the frame of iron bars. The symbol appears over the entrance, on the majolica tiles, and is always in the saint's hand or by his side in a number of sculptures and paintings.

The most noteworthy interiors are close to the monastery's entrance. The **small cloister** dating from 1561, paved in a delicate herringbone pattern with

The Fathers' Choir and high altar in the church at San Lorenzo in Padula

a central fountain, is to the right after entering the complex. The **church** is off to the right side; its Gothic doorway with bas relief scenes from the life of San Lorenzo is one of the only remaining elements from that period. The choir stalls within are remarkable. The section of the Lay Brothers has a grey-and-white geometric floor; wooden inlay scenes on the stalls are the early 16th-century work of Giovanni Gallo. The more elaborate Fathers' Choir with the faded majolica-tiled floor has 36 scenes from the New Testament on the seat backs. The high altar is a florid testimony to the Baroque, encrusted with mother-of-pearl, lapis lazuli and coloured marbles.

Farther along the main corridor is the kitchen, as big as a church hall and housing a hefty stove with a chimney that must be nearly 3m wide. The walls are skirted in scallop-shaped tiles of brilliant green and yellow, and on the far wall a fresco of the Deposition of Christ was uncovered during the course of restoration. When I visited recently, a group of old-age pensioners from Salerno was being taken through by a tour guide. They were most animated in the kitchen, excited by the length of the worktables and musing over the famous omelette they'd mistakenly increased to 10,000 eggs!

The monastery's most beautiful room is the **library**, reached by a spiral staircase near the edge of the Great Cloister. The floor is a pattern of soft blue-and-cream majolica tiles, and the curved ceiling painted in the 18th century by Giovanni Olivieri has recently been restored. When the monks were not praying or sleeping, many were to be found here. The Carthusian order (founded in Grenoble in 1084) was among the most cultivated and literate in Europe. The monks collected and studied classical Greek and Latin works, transcribed laws and manuscripts, as well as studying medicine and natural science.

Just beyond the library is the monastery's most outstanding attraction – the

171

Great Cloister, finished in 1690. The rectangular quadrangle is surrounded by 84 pilasters supporting arches which are topped by a covered walkway. The monks' cells are off the courtyard, six on each side, de luxe suites by an ascetic's standards. Each cell consisted of a small sitting room, bedroom, study and a covered walkway leading to a back garden. The monks' cemetery is just outside their doors, its low walls carved with skulls. At the opposite end to the cemetery is an elegant elliptical staircase designed in 1761–63 by Vanvitelli's pupil Gaetano Barba. This takes you to the upper walkway around the Great Cloister, built so that the steps would lead somewhere.

Teggiano

The 15km drive from Padula to Teggiano along state road No.19, following the course of the Tenagro river, is nothing but a line of shops, petrol stations and badly built modern houses. But once off the main road (follow signs left to Teggiano) you will find the Cilento's agricultural riches all around you. Fields stretch out along the long valley, filled with fruit trees, tobacco plants and vegetables. It's about 12km to the pretty town of Teggiano, seen on high before the climb round the hill's rim.

This is one of the region's best preserved towns, called Tegia when it was a municipality under Roman rule. After the 4th century it was known as Diano, taking the name of the valley it towers above. In 410 the town was destroyed by the Visigothic King Alaric I, who wrought havoc from Rome to Sicily. There is little left to discern the town's role during the Dark Ages, but in subsequent centuries it came under the jurisdiction of the monastery at Padula, and then shared the territory's fortune under Aragon and Angevin rule.

By the 15th century, a baronial family had planted itself here. Baron Antonello Sanseverino, Prince of Salerno, refused to be removed by Frederick of Aragon after the Rebel Barons conspiracy of 1485. His family had built the 13th-century **castle** which still dominates the town (now privately owned). With its arched and crenellated details, the stone castle is a rather heavy-handed reminder of feudal times.

Teggiano's **Cathedral of Santa Maria Maggiore** on Via Roma is a testament to the town's rich history. Its carved portal by Melchiorre di Montalbano dates from 1279, though the church was basically rebuilt after an earthquake in 1857. Within are an elaborate Pascal candlestick springing from a lion at its base, and a marble pulpit with symbols of the Evangelists carved in 1721. The other noteworthy work is the sculpted tomb of Enrico Sanseverino (on the wall of the internal façade up to the right), done in 1336 by followers of Tino di Camaino.

The Angevin church of **Sant' Andrea** is farther along the Via Roma, constructed on the remains of an ancient temple dedicated to Juno, wife of Jupiter. It's interesting for the two 14th-century triptychs done by disciples of Andrea da Salerno. The nearby church of San Pietro was also built on the remains of a temple, probably dedicated to Aesculapius, god of healing. The church is now a civic museum, exhibiting fragments of Roman capitals, coats of arms and tombs from medieval and Renaissance times. San Pietro has a very pretty bell-tower, and the nearby church of **Sant' Agostino** boasts a 16th-century cloister. The Gothic **Church of the Pietà's** small cloister was built in the 1400s.

Teggiano packs a lot of churches into a town of 8000 people. Its narrow streets are flanked by ancient homes that have been squeezed side by side for centuries; the winding alleyways make for a wonderful walking tour, past stairwells terraced with flower pots and lengths of red peppers hanging to dry from stone balconies. The one annoying thing about Teggiano is that though there's a bar or two on Via Roma, there isn't a single trattoria or pizzeria in town. But one hotel, the Eldorado, is situated above the castle. It's run by a very friendly family who make their own wine and sausages, and typically keep the TV on in the dining room during lunch and dinner. Most rooms have a view of either the castle or the valley below. The one view that can't be ignored before leaving Teggiano is from the Belvedere at the end of Via Roma to one side of the castle. Six hundred metres below is the Valley of Diano – immense rectangles of green and brown punctuated by the ochre-coloured dots of old farmhouses.

Pertosa

These long caves are extraordinary for the number of stalactites and stalagmites hidden within. You begin by boat, and continue on foot; the interior caverns are illuminated by artificial light. Round and twisted shapes distend from the ceiling and sprout from the floor, conjuring up the oddest images – one can become immersed in creating a fantasy world peopled by these formations.

From Teggiano, state road No.19 continues north (as well as the A3 auto-strada) past towns such as Sala Consilina, Atena Lucana and Polla. These are among the Cilento's oldest towns, dating back as far as the 4th century BC. But though they harbour churches and ruins of some interest, they have lost their charm due to modern development. Driving through them from Teggiano to the caves of Pertosa is not a very uplifting experience, and I don't recommend taking the time to search out the one or two hard-to-find sites they offer to travellers.

However, **Pertosa** is such a strange and magical place that it's worth the trip if you're heading back north. (The A3 then shoots up to Salerno, about 80km to the northwest.) The Grotte di Pertosa are about 3km off state road No.19; signs will send you down the valley past a handful of houses to the car park. From here you walk up past a small hotel and bar to the cavernous entrance. Once inside you step into the boat that travels slowly through a man-made canal. The underground caves are almost 3km long.

It is thought that these grottoes were inhabited during the Bronze and Early Iron Ages, but most recently only bats have found refuge here. Our guide

173

revelled in disclosing the amount of excavation work carried out in the 1930s: thirty tons of bat faeces removed, he claimed. He also prided himself on knowing their nocturnal schedule: out at 9pm and back at 4am. Whatever the creatures' habits, the caves seemed very clean and relatively bat free during the daytime.

The only other living things within are the stalagtites and stalagmites, some joined over centuries of steady dripping to create damp white columns up to 4m long. The process starts with soluble bicarbonate of calcium within the rock. When it reaches the surface, higher temperature and lower water pressure combine to change the bicarbonate into a hard material which adheres to the rock face. Over the centuries, strange forms have taken shape and the guides have identified a fantastic array of characters for their visitors – from the Sphinx to the Madonna of Lourdes and a garden of smurfs. You pass through the Throne Room, the Tabernacle, the Sponge Room and on to the Castle and the Waterfall. This is certainly fertile ground for the imagination, provided you have no fear of sleeping bats and dark spaces!

Practical Information

Getting there

Trains run from Naples and Salerno into the Cilento, stopping at Paestum and Palinuro on a fairly frequent basis. However, without a car you are confined to the coast and a limited number of towns, so it's best to drive through this area. Rent a car from either Naples, Sorrento or Salerno. The A3 autostrada, from Naples or Salerno, runs down the eastern border of the region. Choosing that route, you would then turn inland down state road No.517 to the Gulf of Policastro before heading north along the coast. Alternatively, follow the coast road from Salerno south, or state road No.18 which takes you inland before reaching Agropoli.

Tourist Information Office

PAESTUM   Via Magna Grecia 151/156 near the Archeological Zone (tel. 0828 811016).

Hotels and restaurants

ACCIAROLI   La Scogliera Hotel and Restaurant, port area, (tel. 0974 904 014). Clean and pleasant hotel; 14 rooms with good views of port and sea; nice terrace restaurant. Closed 15 Dec–15 Jan. Moderate.

AGROPOLI   Carola Hotel and Restaurant, near port at 1 Via Carlo Pisacane (tel. 0974 826422). Closer to the old town than the stretch of dull modern establishments on Agropoli's northern beach edge. Most rooms have small balconies, though some without views. Closed Nov through March. Moderate.

CASTELLABATE   Castelsandra Hotel at San Marco, Via Piano Melaino (tel. 0974 966021), 5km south overlooking the bay. Bigger rooms here are best; all have terraces. The hotel's position is wonderful, but it's a modern place and not as cosy as it could be. Closed Nov to late March. Expensive. **Palazzo Belmonte** (tel. 0974 960211) is a remarkable find in this part of Italy. Originally a 17th-century hunting lodge, the villa is on the outskirts of Castellabate, with a pool and five-acre garden bordering the sea. The Principe di Belmonte still lives in one wing; 19 self-contained apartments are on the first and second floors, along with a separate 18th-century cottage for rent called Eduardo's House. All have sitting rooms and kitchens. Highly recommended; expensive.

PADULA   Certosa Hotel, 57 Viale Certosa, across from the monastery (tel. 0975 77046), is an undistinguished place but valuable if you just don't want to get back into the car. Has a tennis court and pool. Moderate.

PAESTUM   Park Hotel, in the Linora district (tel. 0828 811134). Set in a small pine grove, with tennis and beach access. Moderate prices.
Schuhmann Hotel, on the sea in the Laura district, Via Laura Mare, (tel. 0828 851151) with slightly lower prices than the Park Hotel. Closed Nov. Moderate.
Nettuno Restaurant, Via Principi di Piemonte 1 (tel. 0828 811028), has unpretentious, fresh dishes, with a good view of the temples. Closed Mon, and dinners only in July and August. Inexpensive.
Ristorante Museo, in archeological zone near the museum (tel. 0828 811135). Simple dishes, taken either inside or on shaded terrace. Inexpensive.

PALINURO   King's Residence, Via Piano Farrachio (tel. 0974 931324) is one of the town's top hotels, with a great view of the coast and a nice pool. Closed Oct–March. Expensive.
Grand Hotel San Pietro, Corso Carlo Pisacane (tel. 0974 931466) is less posh, but still with good views and all modern amenities. Closed Nov–March. Moderate.
Hotel La Torre, 5 Via Porto, Capo Palinuro (tel. 0974 931107) is a friendly unpretentious place tucked into the hillside down by the port. All rooms have their own terrace with view, and the family-run restaurant here is good. Moderate.
La Pergola Restaurant, Corso Pisacane, is one of Palinuro's best examples of a typical, family-run restaurant. Tables are set on a shaded terrace, and the friendly family cooks are known for their pastas, *fusilli* and *orecchiette* especially. Inexpensive.

TEGGIANO   The Eldorado, 14 Via Castello, (tel. 0975 79044) is the only hotel in town, situated above the castle. Nothing fancy here, but it's a very clean and friendly family-run place (their own kitchen is just off the guests' dining room). Since there are no restaurants in town except the local bar for snacks, the hotel offers full board at inexpensive prices.

175

Price ranges
Hotel double room   *Restaurant per head*
Inexpensive: under 60,000   under 25,000
Moderate: 60–120,000   25–50,000
Expensive: 120–200,000   50–90,000
Very expensive: 200,000+   90,000+

Museums and other public sites

PADULA   The Carthusian Monastery of San Lorenzo: Open daily 08.00–sunset, by guided tour only, conducted hourly.

PAESTUM   Archeological Zone: two entrances, open daily 09.00–16.00 but closed on major hols. Entrance fee. **Museum**: open 09.00–14.00 Mon–Sat; 09.00–13.00 Sun. Closed hols. Entrance fee included in ticket to archeological zone.

PERTOSA   The caves are open 09.00–17.30; in low season closed for lunch 12.30–14.00. The guided tour lasts about one hour; entrance fee.

VELIA   Open 09.00–one hour before sunset. No entrance fee.

INDEX

Exploring Literature

Steven Croft and Helen Cross

OXFORD

Oxford University Press is a department of the University of Oxford.
It furthers the University's objective of excellence in research, scholarship,
and education by publishing worldwide in

Oxford New York

Auckland Cape Town Dar es Salaam Hong Kong Karachi
Kuala Lumpur Madrid Melbourne Mexico City Nairobi
New Delhi Shanghai Taipei Toronto

With offices in

Argentina Austria Brazil Chile Czech Republic France Greece
Gautemala Hungary Italy Japan South Korea Poland Portugal
Singapore Switzerland Thailand Turkey Ukraine Vietnam

Oxford is a registered trade mark of Oxford University Press
in the UK and in certain other countries

British Library Cataloguing in Publication Data

Data available

ISBN 978 019 832586 4
10 9 8 7 6 5 4 3 2 1

Printed in Great Britain by Bell and Bain Ltd., Glasgow

Contents

Acknowledgements

The authors and publisher are grateful for permission to reprint the following copyright material:

Maya Angelou: 'Still I Rise', 'Phenomenal Woman', 'Just for a Time', 'A Kind of Love, Some Say', 'Where We Belong, a Duet', 'Through the Inner City to the Suburbs', and 'Woman Work' from *And Still I Rise* (Virago, 1986), reprinted by permission of Little, Brown Book Group Ltd.

Margaret Atwood: extracts from *The Handmaid's Tale* (Cape, 1986), copyright © O. W. Toad Ltd 1985 and 'The Page' from *Good Bones* (Bloomsbury, 1992), copyright © O. W. Toad Ltd 1992, reprinted by permission of Curtis Brown Group Ltd, London.

Simon Armitage: 'Hitcher' from *Book of Matches* (1993), reprinted by permission of the publisher, Faber & Faber Ltd.

W. H. Auden: 'Twelve Songs IX' ('Funeral Blues') from *Collected Poems* (1986), reprinted by permission of the publisher, Faber & Faber Ltd.

Laurence Binyon: 'For the Fallen (September 1914)' from *Collected Poems 1869-1943* (Macmillan), reprinted by permission of The Society of Authors as the Literary Representative of the Estate of Laurence Binyon.

Alison Brackenbury: 'School Dinners' from *Christmas Roses and Other Poems* (Carcanet, 1988), reprinted by permission of the publishers.

Malcolm Bradbury: extract from *The Modern British Novel* (Secker & Warburg, 1993), reprinted by permission of the Random House Group Ltd.

Vera Brittain: extracts from *Testament of Youth* (Victor Gollancz, 1933) and 'Perhaps' from *Verses of a VAD* (Erskine MacDonald, 1918), reprinted by permission of Mark Bostridge and Timothy Brittain-Caitlin, Literary Executors for the Vera Brittain Estate, 1970.

Rupert Brooke: letter from Rupert Brooke to Katharine Cox, March 1915 from *The Letters of Rupert Brooke* edited by Geoffrey Keynes (1968), reprinted by permission of the publisher, Faber & Faber Ltd.

Angela Carter: extract from 'The Snow Pavilion' from *Burning Your Boats* (Chatto & Windus, 1995), copyright © Angela Carter 1995, reprinted by permission of the Estate of Angela Carter, c/o Rogers Coleridge & White Ltd, 20 Powis Mews, London W11 1JN.

Leonard Cohen: extract from lyrics of 'The Window' (1979), copyright © Bad Monk Publishing, administered by Sony/ATV Music Publishing, reprinted by permission of Sony/ATV Music Publishing. All rights reserved.

Wendy Cope: 'Engineer's Corner' from *Making Cocoa for Kingsley Amis* (1986), reprinted by permission of the publishers, Faber & Faber Ltd.

Richard Curtis: extract from 'Sons and Aztecs' from *The Faber Book of Parodies* edited by Simon Brett (Faber, 1984), reprinted by permission of PFD (www.pfd.co.uk) on behalf of Richard Curtis.

Kiran Desai: extracts from *The Inheritance of Loss* (Hamish Hamilton/ Atlantic Monthly Press, 2006), copyright © Kiran Desai 2006, reprinted by permission of Penguin Books Ltd.

Emily Dickinson: 'After great pain, a formal feeling comes' from *The Poems of Emily Dickinson: Variorum Edition* edited by Ralph W Franklin (The Belknap Press of Harvard University Press), copyright © 1998 by the President and Fellows of Harvard College, copyright © 1951, 1955, 1979, 1983 by the President and Fellows of Harvard College, reprinted by permission of the publishers and the Trustees of Amherst College.

Margaret Drabble: extract from 'Hassan's Tower' in *Winter's Tales* (Macmillan, 1966), copyright © Margaret Drabble 1966, reprinted by permission of PFD (www.pfd.co.uk) on behalf of Margaret Drabble.

Carol Ann Duffy: 'Anne Hathaway', 'Salome', 'Pilate's Wife', 'Demeter', 'Frau Freud', 'Mrs Darwin' and 'Delilah' from *The World's Wife* (Picador, 1999), reprinted by permission of Macmillan, London, UK; and 'Havisham' from *Mean Time* (Anvil, 1993), reprinted by permission of the publisher.

Gavin Ewart: 'Ending' from *No Fool Like an Old Fool* (Victor Gollancz, 1976), reprinted by permission of Margo Ewart.

Sebastian Faulks: extract from *Birdsong* (Hutchinson, 1993), reprinted by permission of the Random House Group Ltd.

Brian Friel: extract from *Making History* (1989), reprinted by permission of the publisher, Faber & Faber Ltd.

Stephen Fry: extract from *Moab is My Washpot* (Hutchinson, 1997), reprinted by permission of David Higham Associates Ltd.

Paul Fussell: extract from his introduction to *The Bloody Game: An Anthology of Modern War* (Scribners, 1981), reprinted by permission of W. W. Norton & Co.

Graham Greene: 'I Spy' from *Collected Stories* by Graham Greene (Bodley Head, 1972), reprinted by permission of David Higham Associates Ltd.

John Hersey: extract from *Hiroshima* (Hamish Hamilton, 1966), copyright © John Hersey 1966, 1973, 1985, reprinted by permission of Penguin Books Ltd.

Susan Hill: extract from 'Missy' and extract from 'Halloran's Child' in *A Bit of Singing and Dancing* (Long Barn Books, 1973), copyright © Susan Hill 1971, 1972, 1973, reprinted by permission of Sheil Land Associates Ltd.

John Holloway: extract from 'Literature' in *Cambridge Cultural History of Britain, Vol. 7 Victorian Britain* edited by Boris Ford (Cambridge, 1989), reprinted by permission of Cambridge University Press.

Ted Hughes: 'Wind' from *New Selected Poems 1957-1994* (1994), reprinted by permission of the publisher, Faber & Faber Ltd.

David Jones: extract from *In Parenthesis*, part 7 (1937), reprinted by permission of the publisher, Faber & Faber Ltd.

Bon Jovi: extract from lyrics of 'Burning for Love' (1983), words and music by Bon Jovi, reprinted by permission of the Hal Leonard Corporation. International copyright secured. All rights reserved.

Brian Keenan: extract from *An Evil Cradling* (Hutchinson, 1992), reprinted by permission of the Random House Group Ltd.

Philip Larkin: 'The North Ship XXIV' from *Collected Poems* (1990), reprinted by permission of the publisher, Faber & Faber Ltd.

F. R. Leavis: extracts from 'Hard Times: An Analytical Note' in *The Great Tradition* (Chatto & Windus 1948), reprinted by permission of the Random House Group Ltd.

Andrea Levy: 'Small Island' from *Headline Review*, September 2004, reprinted by permission of Hodder.

Felicia Hardison Londre: extract from 'A Streetcar Running Fifty Years' from *Cambridge Companion to Tennessee Williams* edited by Matthew C. Roundane (Cambridge, 1997), reprinted by permission of Cambridge University Press.

Edna St Vincent Millay: 'Time Does Not Bring Relief' from *Collected Poems* (HarperCollins), copyright © 1917, 1945 by Edna St Vincent Millay, reprinted by permission of Elizabeth Barnett, Literary executor, the Millay Society.

Grace Nichols: 'The Fat Black Woman Goes Shopping', from *The Fat Black Woman's Poems* (Virago, 1984), copyright © Grace Nichols 1984, reprinted by permission of Curtis Brown Group Ltd, London.

Wilfred Owen: letter from Wilfred Owen to Susan Owen, 19 January 1917 from *Collected Letters* edited by Harold Owen and John Bell (OUP, 1967), reprinted by permission of Oxford University Press.

Gilbert Phelps: extract from 'Literature and Drama' in *Cambridge Cultural History of Britain, Vol. 9 Modern Britain* edited by Boris Ford (Cambridge, 1989), reprinted by permission of Cambridge University Press.

John Pilger: extract from 'Video Nasties' in *Distant Voices* (Vintage, 1992), reprinted by permission of David Higham Associates Ltd.

Sylvia Plath: 'Frog Autumn' from *Collected Poems* (1981), reprinted by permission of the publisher, Faber & Faber Ltd.

Willy Russell: extracts from *Educating Rita* (Methuen, 1985), copyright © Willy Russell 1985, and from *Stags and Hens* (Methuen, 1986), copyright © Willy Russell 1986, reprinted by permission of Methuen Drama, an imprint of A&C Black Publishers Ltd.

Siegfried Sassoon: 'Base Details' and 'Attack' from *Collected Poems 1908-1956* (Faber, 1984); extract from *Memoirs of An Infantry Officer* in *Complete Memoirs of George Sherston* (Faber 1937), reprinted by permission of Barbara Levy as agent for George Sassoon.

Vernon Scannell: 'The Great War' from *New and Collected Poems 1953-1993* (Robson Books, 1994), reprinted by permission of the author.

Owen Sheers: 'Mametz Wood', 'Night Windows', 'Marking Time', 'Valentine', 'The Wake', 'Skirrid Fawr', 'Farther', and 'Drinking with Hitler' from *Skirrid Hill* (Seren, 2005), copyright © Owen Sheers 2005, reprinted by permission of the author, c/o Rogers Coleridge & White Ltd, 20 Powis Mews, London W11 1JN.

Edith Sitwell: 'The Dancers (During a Great Battle, 1916)' from *Collected Poems* (Duckworth, 2005), reprinted by permission of David Higham Associates Ltd.

Elizabeth Walter: 'Dual Control' from *Dead Women and Other Haunting Experiences* (Collins Harvill, 1975), copyright © Elizabeth Walter 1975, reprinted by permission of A. M. Heath & Company Ltd.

Peter Whelan: extract from *The Accrington Pals* (Methuen, 1982), copyright © Peter Whelan 1982, reprinted by permission of Methuen Drama, an imprint of A&C Black Publishers Ltd.

Oscar Wilde: extract from 'De Profundis', letter to Lord Alfred Douglas, from *The Letters of Oscar Wilde* edited by Merlin Holland and Sir Rupert Hart-Davis (Fourth Estate, 2000), letters copyright © The Estate of Oscar Wilde 1962, 1985, 2000, reprinted by permission of HarperCollins Publishers.

C. K. Williams: 'Love, Beginnings' from *New and Selected Poems* (Bloodaxe Books, 1995), reprinted by permission of the publisher.

Tennessee Williams: extracts from *A Streetcar Named Desire* (New Directions), copyright © 1947, 1953 by Tennessee Williams, renewed 1975, 1981 by The University of the South; and extracts from *A Glass Menagerie* (New Directions), copyright © 1945 by Tennessee Williams, renewed 1973 by The University of the South, both reprinted by permission of Methuen Publishing Ltd on behalf of The University of the South, Sewanee, Tennessee.

We have tried to trace and contact all copyright holders before publication. If notified, the publishers will be pleased to rectify any errors or omissions at the earliest opportunity.

Introduction

Reasons for choosing to study English literature at A level or AS level can vary tremendously. Some students choose the subject because they have always loved English and want to go on to study it at higher education level. Others choose it simply because they enjoyed English at GCSE level and achieved a reasonable result.

However, English is also a popular choice with 'mature' students. Very often the circumstances under which these students study are rather different from those of the school-based student. They might be studying the course over one year by attending an evening class at the local college or they might be attending workshop sessions at a college, or studying at home on a distance learning or correspondence basis.

Whatever your individual circumstances, though, the work that you will need to complete and the demands of assessment will be exactly the same. Obviously, everyone is an individual and one of the great strengths of English is that it encourages and requires the development of that individuality through studies that are stimulating, challenging, and enjoyable. This 'enjoyment' factor should not be dismissed lightly. Of course it does not mean that you will 'like' every text that you read. After all, it is possible to enjoy studying a text purely because of the academic challenges it presents. Enjoyment is important for another reason – students who enjoy their studies tend to be the ones whose motivation is highest and who ultimately achieve the best results.

Your past experience of studying English will probably have shown that it differs from other subjects. Unlike most other subjects, English literature does not consist of a body of knowledge that you can 'learn' in the conventional sense. Instead, you need to develop your own ideas and responses to the texts that you study and to base these responses firmly on evidence that you have gathered from your own readings of these. The development of these informed, independent opinions and judgements will underpin everything that you do in your study of literature at A level or AS level.

This text is specifically linked to the AQA Specification A (1741 and 2741). The specification is designed to encourage students to develop an interest in and enjoyment of English literature through reading widely, critically and independently, across centuries, genre and gender and through experience of an extensive range of views about texts and how to read them.

The general aims of the specification at AS and A level are to:

- encourage students to develop interest and enjoyment in literary studies through reading widely, critically and independently
- introduce students to the tradition of English literature.

More specifically, AS and A level courses based on this specification should encourage candidates to develop their interest in and enjoyment of literature and literary studies as they:

- read widely and independently both set texts and others that they have selected for themselves
- engage creatively with a substantial body of texts and ways of responding to them

- develop and effectively apply their knowledge of literary analysis and evaluation in speech and writing
- explore the contexts of the texts they are reading and others' interpretations of them
- deepen their understanding of the changing traditions of literature in English.

It is worth considering these aims carefully because the Assessment Objectives which are at the heart of your studies stem directly from them.

The Assessment Objectives are set our below. Study them carefully because everything you do in your study of English literature will relate directly to these objectives.

Assessment Objectives (AOs)

The Assessment Objectives are common to AS and A level.

- **AO1** Articulate creative, informed and relevant responses to literary texts, using appropriate terminology and concepts, and coherent, accurate written expression
- **AO2** Demonstrate detailed critical understanding in analysing the ways in which structure, form and language shape meanings in literary texts
- **AO3** Explore connections and comparisons between different literary texts, informed by interpretations of other readers
- **AO4** Demonstrate understanding of the significance and influence of the contexts in which literary texts are written and received.

In addition, you must be able to:

- ensure that your writing is legible and that spelling, punctuation and grammar are accurate so that meaning is clear
- select and use a form and style of writing appropriate to purpose and to complex subject matter
- organize information clearly and coherently, using specialist vocabulary when appropriate.

Reading, talking, and writing

Your studies will involve a good deal of reading, with your set texts forming the heart of this. However, the most successful students are those whose reading takes them beyond the texts that they must study. Such students read widely around the texts and the subject, building up a knowledge and understanding of literature that is not restricted simply to set texts. This background reading is the key element in developing an appreciation of literature and often is the difference between those students who achieve the higher grades and those who do not.

Discussion is also an important way in which to develop and test out your ideas about literature. Although your teachers or lecturers will give you guidance, they will not tell you what to think. They will encourage you to weigh various views and interpretations against each other and to formulate your own ideas. Talking to others about your ideas is an important (and enjoyable) way of doing this, so you will probably find yourself involved in a good deal of discussion work, in class, small groups, or with a partner.

If you are studying literature through a distance learning or correspondence course you are at a disadvantage here in not having the same opportunity to exchange ideas with others on a regular basis. It may be a good idea to find yourself a 'mentor' who can help you by talking through the work with you.

As far as writing goes, the course will involve writing about a whole variety of texts in many different forms. There will be essays on the set texts, 'unseen' pieces to be tackled, coursework pieces to complete, and notes of different kinds to be made.

Certainly this book will provide a full complement of spoken and written activities and will introduce you to a wide range of texts to help prepare you for your final assessment.

Summary

The work that you do will require you to:

- analyse texts
- explore and express your views on them
- work independently
- take a major responsibility for your learning
- develop and articulate independent opinions and judgements on the material you study
- be aware of different interpretations of the literary texts you study.

Aims of the book

With the Assessment Objectives in mind, *Exploring Literature* has been devised to guide you through your AS and A level courses.

Section I introduces the main types of writing that you are likely to study during your course. It offers approaches and strategies for tackling each genre.

Section II looks particularly at the skills required in writing about texts. Its aim is to help you write confidently and effectively about set texts and unseens. It also gives insights into how to write about context, how to compare texts and how to study themes.

Section III looks at the units that you will cover for your AS course and focuses on examining texts in context, the thematic and poetry options and the Creative Study element of the course.

Section IV examines the A2 units you will cover, focusing on Reading for Meaning and the Extended Comparative Essay, including the study of Shakespeare texts.

Section V looks towards the examinations and focuses on approaches to revision and a consideration of what the examiner will be looking for in your responses.

Throughout the text you will find a range of activities which are designed to help you consolidate your knowledge and understanding of English literature at AS and A level. Some of these activities may be based on texts that you are studying as part of your course. Others may be on texts that you have not read or studied. The completion of these activities will help you to develop your ideas and skills in a variety of ways and may introduce you to new ways of looking at the texts that you are studying.

Above all we hope that you will enjoy your study of literature at AS or A level, and that this book will add to that enjoyment and contribute to your success.

1 Studying Prose

Objectives

- To gain an overview of the different forms of literary prose, fiction and non-fiction
- To consider particular features of the novel, the short story and non-fiction texts
- To examine examples of prose works by writers often studied at AS or A level
- To gain skill in analysing specific aspects of prose texts, such as characterization and narrative viewpoint
- To prepare to study prose texts in relation to their context, period, or theme

What is prose?

Literature students sometimes wonder what we mean by 'prose', expecting it to be something more specific than it is. In fact, 'prose' is used to refer to almost anything that is not poetry, and so it includes a huge range of forms of writing. One dictionary definition has it as simply 'ordinary writing as distinguished from verse' and links it with the adjective 'prosaic', which means 'not fanciful, imaginative or challenging; dull; lacking wit or excitement.' However, as you explore some of the great prose texts in literature, you will find that they are rarely ordinary or prosaic. They are much more likely to be fanciful, imaginative, challenging, exciting, and even witty.

Studying literature for AS or A level, the prose texts you read will include works of fiction, usually novels and short stories, as well as examples of non-fiction material, such as memoirs, biographies or essays. This chapter introduces you to a selection of prose texts from each of these categories and provides you with some ways to approach studying them.

The novel

The word 'novel' usually means something new – a novelty. Some of the earliest novels, written in the seventeenth and eighteenth centuries, would have been just that. One dictionary definition describes a novel as:

> a fictitious prose narrative or tale presenting a picture of real life, especially of the emotional crises in the life-history of the men and women portrayed.

Jane Austen's view was that a novel was:

> ... only some work in which the greatest powers of the mind are displayed, in which the most thorough knowledge of human nature, the happiest delineation of its varieties, the liveliest effusions of wit and humour, are conveyed to the world in the best chosen language.

A 'novelty' suggests something fairly lightweight, entertaining, and perhaps not of lasting significance. Nowadays we tend to make a distinction between 'literary' novels and popular fiction – but this dividing line can be blurred. As part of your A level literature course, you will be expected to study novels which are 'literary' and to develop the ability to recognize the differences. However, it can also be interesting to study popular, mass market novels and to consider how the conventions of writing fiction are applied in them.

The Victorian novelist Anthony Trollope once wrote that novels should be written because writers 'have a story to tell', not because they 'have to tell a story', but literary novelists have almost always intended to do something more. Early novels, like those of Samuel Richardson, tended to preach strong moral messages, although they could be rather sentimental; in the nineteenth century, Victorian novelists often used their work to expose social or political injustice, while novels of the present day may demonstrate the questioning of almost every previously accepted belief. All along, writers have set out not just to tell stories, but to convey messages or explore ideas.

Activity

In a small group, discuss some of the novels you have already read. How well do they fit the definitions on page 1? Do you think they are 'literary' novels or not? How do you know? Create your own definition of a novel and compare your ideas with those of others in the whole group.

Studying the novel

Every AS or A level literature specification will require that you study at least one novel for the examination. This will probably be chosen from a list of texts recommended or set by the exam board. You may focus on the novel as an individual text, but you are also likely to study it in context, as part of a wider exploration of the literature of a particular period or theme. This approach is explained more fully in Sections III and IV. For coursework tasks, such as the extended essay, where you are asked to compare two or more texts, you may also have the opportunity to study and write about other novels you have chosen yourself. (For more about this, see Chapter 14.)

At the outset, studying a novel can seem a daunting prospect. If you are asked to read a novel by Dickens, or George Eliot's *Middlemarch*, for example, it may well be the longest book you have ever read. If it is a twentieth-century novel which does not follow realistic conventions or a novel from an earlier period where the language is unfamiliar, you may feel that you will struggle to master it. Some novels are difficult, but usually they are rewarding and a 'good read' too, once you become engaged with the plot and characters and more familiar with the author's language and ideas. In this unit we will develop strategies for approaching them and identify the most important things to pay attention to.

One concept we need to keep in mind is that there are two main attitudes or positions we can take when we study a novel. The first attitude we can hold is that what is important is the content or the 'world' which the author has created. This is a world we can enter into, full of people, places, things, and events, to which we respond with liking or hatred, pity or criticism, as we do to the real world. Studying from this position, we will discuss the characters almost as if they were beings with the ability to choose their actions.

The second position we can take is to see the novel as a 'text', as a created work of art, and to look at it in a much more detached and analytical way. Characters are devices which the author uses and manipulates to create a particular effect.

Their only existence is in the precise words on the page. Studying with this attitude, we will be more likely to consider what a character's role is in the construction of a plot, or the effect of using particular language to describe a place or person.

As you study a novel for AS or A level, you will most likely begin by responding from the first position, but you will also develop your understanding of the more analytical viewpoint. You will always need to know *how* the text is written as well as what it says.

Whether you are studying novels for the examination or for coursework, there are various aspects which you will need to know well. Questions or coursework tasks may be angled or worded in different ways, but they will expect you to demonstrate your knowledge of one or more of the following.

- **An overview.** You need to have a clear understanding of the plot and central ideas, how events follow on and are related, and how the novel is structured. Questions might ask you to show how the novel's structure affects the reader's response, particularly if it is not a straightforward chronological narrative.
- **Narrative viewpoint.** Who tells the story? Why has the writer chosen this viewpoint? How does this affect the reader's response?
- **Characters.** Questions often focus on one or more characters, their development or their relationships.
- **Setting.** The place, society or 'world' in which the story takes place. Questions may centre on this, or may ask about the relationship between a character and the society in which he or she lives.
- **Language and style.** There may be distinctive qualities in the writer's choice of language, for example in the use of imagery or comic exaggeration. Questions will almost always expect you to consider why the writer has made these choices. What is their purpose and effect?
- **Context.** What is the historical or social background to the novel? In what ways is it typical or not typical of the time when it was written? Does it belong to a particular literary period?
- **Extracts.** Questions may ask you to write in detail about a key passage and to place it in context by relating it to the whole text or to other texts from the same period. You may also be asked to compare several extracts on a similar theme.

Approaching the text

With a large text like a novel, we need to become familiar enough with it to 'find our way around' easily. We need to be able to locate incidents and important passages quickly. Here are some strategies that will help you to gain this familiarity.

- If you have time, read through the novel fairly quickly before you begin to study it. This gives you the opportunity to gain an overall impression of the novel and to read it, as it was intended, for entertainment. It will also help you to see how different aspects of the novel fit together when you begin to study it in depth. You will see how the plot is constructed and have an idea about what form of novel it is.
- Do some research. Find out what you can about the author and what was going on when the novel was written. If you are reading your novel as part of your study of a particular period, you will do this anyway, but even if you are not, knowing something about the historical and social background and about the conventions

and beliefs of the time can help you to understand things which may otherwise seem strange or incomprehensible.

- Keep a separate 'log' for your work on each text. Try dividing a notebook into sections, one for each important aspect of the novel. You will need pages for each of the main characters, the setting, the narrator, themes and ideas, and language and style. As you work through the novel, jot down your observations about each aspect in the appropriate places. Include important quotations and page references. Then, when you need the information for a discussion or an essay on one of these topics, it will be easy to locate.

- You may find it helpful to annotate your copy of the text, marking important passages so that you can find them again easily. It is important, however, to be aware of the regulations for the specification and paper for which you are studying. In some examinations, you are permitted to take your copy of the text with you on condition that it is a 'clean copy' and has no notes or markings written on it. In others, you are not allowed to have access to the text and must work from memory. These two situations require rather different revision strategies, and there is some advice on this in Chapter 16. If yours is a specification which does not permit access to the text, then annotation can be a great help when you are revising. It is also useful if you are preparing for a coursework assignment. More guidance on effective annotation appears in Chapter 4.

Let us turn now to exploring some texts. As we examine different aspects of novels in this unit, we will look at examples from these three very different novels by writers often set at AS or A level:

- *Emma* by Jane Austen
- *Hard Times* by Charles Dickens
- *The Handmaid's Tale* by Margaret Atwood

Jane Austen, writing at the beginning of the nineteenth century, published six major novels concerned with the issues of love, marriage, social class and money at a time when choices and opportunities, particularly for women, were much more limited than they are now. *Emma* is one of the best-loved examples of her work.

Hard Times, first published in 1854, is a typical example of Victorian literature. It can be placed in the category of 'Condition of England' novels, works written after the Industrial Revolution to draw attention to social and political issues, such as the gulf between wealthy, powerful businessmen and their employees, the poor living conditions and limited opportunities of factory workers, or the corruption of institutions such as the legal system.

In *The Handmaid's Tale* (1985), Margaret Atwood explores questions of gender and identity in an age of nuclear threat and environmental disaster. Exaggerating the inequalities of her own time, she creates a dystopia, an imaginary future world where women (and men) are confined to specific roles in order to ensure the survival of a human race endangered by chemical pollution and warfare.

Activity

Use reference books and other sources to find out more about each of these authors, their work and their different eras.

An overview

Novels come in many shapes and sizes, from short novellas (more like long short stories) with a few characters and fairly simple plots, to enormously large and complex works, with numerous characters, plots, and subplots and with many different strands which may or may not be interconnected.

There are also different genres or forms of novel. For example:

- **Fictional biography or autobiography** focuses on the life and development of one character.

- **Picaresque novels** follow a central character on a journey through life in which he or she encounters a series of 'adventures' which form separate episodes.

- **Social or 'protest' novels** use the characters and the world they inhabit as a way of criticizing or protesting about social or political issues.

The plot, or storyline, of a novel can also be constructed in different ways. The simplest strategy is to relate events in straightforward chronological order, from the point of view of a single narrator. Jane Austen usually adopts this approach. However, there have been many variations on this. For example:

- *In Hard Times*, Dickens moves from one group of people in Coketown to another. The connections between them all are not completely clear until the end, when we realize he has constructed a network of threads which link them.

- Emily Brontë, in *Wuthering Heights*, another Victorian novel, uses two narrators and departs from chronological order by plunging us into the middle of a mysterious situation and then going back in time to explain how it has come about. She then repeats this process to show how the situation is resolved.

- In *The Handmaid's Tale*, the narrative alternates between chapters which tell the story in the 'present' of the novel and others which are flashbacks. Entitled *Night* or *Nap*, these are times when the narrator has a chance to reminisce, dream or daydream about the past.

Activity

1 Discuss the structure of a novel you are currently reading or have read recently.

2 Widen your discussion to compare any other novels you know which have interesting structures.

Opening pages

Usually, we can learn quite a lot about a novel by looking closely at the first few pages. The writer will be trying to engage our attention so that we want to read on. So it is quite likely that some of the important situations, characters, and themes will be presented right from the start.

Activity

1 Here are the opening pages of the three novels. Read them carefully.

2 Working with a partner, choose one of these and discuss it in detail, making notes on the following points:

- Who is the narrator and what, if anything, can you find out about him or her? Is the narrative in the third person or the first person?

- What characters (including the narrators) are introduced? What do you learn about them?

- What situation is presented? Does the story begin in a particular place? If so, how is it described? What atmosphere is generated?

- Does the writer begin by explaining clearly who is who and what is what? Or are you plunged into the middle of a situation and left to work out what is going on from hints the writer gives you?

- Can you get a sense of the author's tone or attitude? Is the writing straightforward? Might there be hidden messages or other levels of meaning?

- What do you notice about the writer's style? Is the language simple or figurative? What sorts of imagery, vocabulary and sentence structures are used?

- What do you think this novel is going to be 'about'? Can you get a sense of any important ideas or themes that may be central to it?

- In what ways does the writer arouse your curiosity? Do you want to read further? Why?

3 Present and compare your notes in the whole group. What similarities and differences are there between the three passages?

4 Try working on the opening pages of any other novel you are studying in the same way.

Emma

Chapter 1

Emma Woodhouse, handsome, clever, and rich, with a comfortable home and happy disposition, seemed to unite some of the best blessings of existence; and had lived nearly twenty-one years in the world with very little to distress or vex her.

She was the youngest of the two daughters of a most affectionate, indulgent father, and had, in consequence of her sister's marriage, been mistress of his house from a very early period. Her mother had died too long ago for her to have more than an indistinct remembrance of her caresses; and her place had been supplied by an excellent woman as governess, who had fallen little short of a mother in affection.

Sixteen years had Miss Taylor been in Mr Woodhouse's family, less as a governess than a friend, very fond of both daughters, but particularly of Emma. Between them it was more the intimacy of sisters. Even before Miss Taylor had ceased to hold the nominal office of governess, the mildness of her temper had hardly allowed her to impose any restraint; and the shadow of authority being now long passed away, they had been living together as friend and friend very mutually attached, and Emma doing just what she liked; highly esteeming Miss Taylor's judgement, but directed chiefly by her own.

The real evils, indeed, of Emma's situation were the power of having rather too much her own way, and a disposition to think a little too well of herself; these were the disadvantages which threatened alloy to her many enjoyments. The danger, however, was at present so unperceived, that they did not by any means rank as misfortunes with her.

Sorrow came – a gentle sorrow – but not at all in the shape of any disagreeable consciousness. Miss Taylor married. It was Miss Taylor's loss which first brought grief. It was on the wedding-day of this beloved friend that Emma first sat in mournful thought of any continuance. The wedding over, and the bride-people gone, her father and herself were left to dine together, with no prospect of a third to cheer a long evening. Her father composed himself to sleep after dinner, as usual, and she had then only to sit and think of what she had lost.

Jane Austen

Hard Times

Chapter 1: The One Thing Needful

'Now, what I want is, Facts. Teach these boys and girls nothing but Facts. Facts alone are wanted in life. Plant nothing else, and root out everything else. You can only form the minds of reasoning animals upon Facts: nothing else will ever be of any service to them. This is the principle on which I bring up my own children, and this is the principle on which I bring up these children. Stick to Facts, sir!'

The scene was a plain, bare, monotonous vault of a schoolroom, and the speaker's square forefinger emphasized his observations by underscoring every sentence with a line on the schoolmaster's sleeve. The emphasis was helped by the speaker's square wall of a forehead, which had his eyebrows for its base, while his eyes found commodious cellarage in two dark caves, overshadowed by the wall. The emphasis was helped by the speaker's mouth, which was wide, thin, and hard set. The emphasis was helped by the speaker's voice, which was inflexible, dry, and dictatorial. The emphasis was helped by the speaker's hair, which bristled on the skirts of his bald head, a plantation of firs to keep the wind from its shining surface, all covered with knobs, like the crust of a plum pie, as if the head had scarcely warehouse-room for the hard facts stored inside. The speaker's obstinate carriage, square coat, square legs, square shoulders – nay, his very neckcloth, trained to take him by the throat with an unaccommodating grasp, like a stubborn fact, as it was – all helped the emphasis.

'In this life, we want nothing but Facts, sir; nothing but Facts!'

The speaker, and the schoolmaster, and the third grown person present, all backed a little, and swept with their eyes the inclined plane of little vessels then and there arranged in order, ready to have imperial gallons of facts poured into them until they were full to the brim.

Charles Dickens

The Handmaid's Tale

Chapter 1

We slept in what had once been the gymnasium. The floor was of varnished wood, with stripes and circles painted on it, for the games that were formerly played there; the hoops for the basketball nets were still in place, though the nets were gone. A balcony ran around the room, for the spectators, and I thought I could smell, faintly like an afterimage, the pungent scent of sweat, shot through with the sweet taint of chewing gum and perfume from the watching girls, felt-skirted as I knew from pictures, later in mini-skirts, then pants, then in one earring, spiky green-streaked hair. Dances would have been held there; the music lingered, a palimpsest of unheard sound, style upon style, an undercurrent of drums, a forlorn wail, garlands made of tissue-paper flowers, cardboard devils, a revolving ball of mirrors, powdering the dancers with a snow of light.

There was old sex in the room and loneliness, and expectation, of something without a shape or name. I remember that yearning, for something that was always about to happen and was never the same as the hands that were on us there and then, in the small of the back, or out back, in the parking lot, or in the television room with the sound turned down and only the pictures flickering over lifting flesh.

We yearned for the future. How did we learn it, that talent for insatiability? It was in the air; and it was still in the air, an afterthought, as we tried to sleep, in the army cots that had been set up in rows, with spaces between so we could not talk. We had flannelette sheets, like children's, and army-issue blankets, old ones that still said U.S. We folded our clothes neatly and laid them on the stools at the ends of the beds. The lights were turned down but not out. Aunt Sara and Aunt Elizabeth patrolled; they had electric cattle prods slung on thongs from their leather belts.

Margaret Atwood

Narrative viewpoint

You will have noticed that in *Emma* and *Hard Times* the authors have chosen to use third-person narrative, while Margaret Atwood uses a first-person narrator for *The Handmaid's Tale*. There are advantages and disadvantages, and different possibilities in each.

Writing in the first person, the author takes on the role of a character (or characters) and tells the story 'from the inside'. This can strengthen the illusion that the novel is 'real', by making us, the readers, feel involved and able to empathize with the character. However, this usually also limits our perspective to this one character's perceptions: we only see other characters through his or her eyes. We cannot know of events the narrator does not witness unless they are reported by another character, for example in conversation.

As we have only this narrator's words to go on, we need to ask how far we can trust the narrator. He or she might be biased, deluded, blind to the true significance of events, or even deliberately deceiving the reader. Often, this very question adds interest to a first-person narrative.

The narrator in *The Handmaid's Tale* is Offred, a woman living in a future society in which people are restricted to very narrow, specific roles. Offred is a handmaid. Her job is to 'breed' to ensure the survival of her nation, while other women are responsible for domestic chores and some carry out the formal duties of a wife. Much of her narrative is in **stream of consciousness**, a form in which the writer aims to give a sense of how a character's mind works by tracking her thoughts as they flow from one topic to another. We have to piece together our impressions of Offred from what she reveals of her thoughts and feelings, her actions, and her attitudes to other characters.

Activity

Here, early in the novel, Offred describes her living quarters and ponders on her situation. Read the extract and make a note of everything that you learn about her as a person and as a storyteller. Consider also how far she engages your interest and sympathy.

The Handmaid's Tale

Chapter 2

A window, two white curtains. Under the window, a window seat with a little cushion. When the window is partly open – it only opens partly – the air can come in and make the curtains move. I can sit in the chair, or on the window seat, hands folded, and watch this. Sunlight comes in through the window too, and falls on the floor, which is made of wood, in narrow strips, highly polished. I can smell the polish. There's a rug on the floor, oval, of braided rags. This is the kind of touch they like: folk art, archaic, made by women, in their spare time, from things that have no further use. A return to traditional values. Waste not want not. I am not being wasted. Why do I want?...

A bed. Single, mattress medium-hard, covered with a flocked white spread. Nothing takes place in the bed but sleep; or no sleep. I try not to think too much. Like other things now, thought must be rationed. There's a lot that doesn't bear thinking about. Thinking can hurt your chances, and I intend to last. I know why there is no glass, in front of the water-colour picture of blue irises, and why the window only opens partly and why the glass in it is shatterproof. It isn't running away they're afraid of. We wouldn't get far. It's those other escapes, the ones you can open in yourself, given a cutting edge.

So. Apart from these details, this could be a college guest room, for the less distinguished visitors; or a room in a rooming-house, of former times, for ladies in reduced circumstances. That is what we are now. The circumstances have been reduced; for those of us who still have circumstances.

But a chair, sunlight, flowers: these are not to be dismissed. I am alive, I live, I breathe, I put my hand out, unfolded, into the sunlight. Where I am is not a prison but a privilege, as Aunt Lydia said, who was in love with either/or.

Margaret Atwood

- -

Probably you will have noted the following points.

- She notices and describes her surroundings in detail and specific details spark off trains of thought about her life in an interior monologue. She pays attention to these things because there is plenty of time to do so and nothing else to occupy her.

- She separates herself from the people in authority by referring rather anonymously to 'they' and 'them'.

- She feels limited by her life and is not satisfied living by the maxims she has been taught. She longs for something more – 'Waste not want not. I am not being wasted. Why do I want?'

- She is determined to survive, even if this means denying the truth sometimes– 'Thinking can hurt your chances, and I intend to last.'

- She is optimistic enough to recognize what is good in her surroundings – 'But a chair, sunlight, flowers: these are not to be dismissed.'

- Her language is usually simple and she does not use specific imagery. Many of her sentences are short or incomplete. Their confiding quality suggests we already know what she is talking about and who 'they' are, when in fact we know nothing about the regime in which she lives. She likes to play with words and double meanings in a wry, humorous way – 'The circumstances have been reduced; for those of us who still have circumstances.'

Third-person narrative offers different possibilities. The author or narrator adopts a position which is 'godlike', or becomes a 'fly on the wall' reporting everything to us, the readers. This omniscient (all-knowing) narrator, from a vantage point outside the action, can relate events which may occur in different places, at different times, or even simultaneously. Often we are told how different characters feel so we see things from more than one perspective. Sometimes the author might tell the story dispassionately, without commenting or judging. Usually, however, authors make their presence felt. This might be through obvious authorial intrusion, where the writer butts into the narrative to express an opinion or comment on a situation, or it might be more subtle. For example, a character may be described in language we recognize as sarcastic, 'tongue-in-cheek', or ironic, making it clear that the author is critical or mocking; or positive or negative judgements may simply be revealed by the writer's choice of vocabulary.

We can easily detect Dickens's opinion of 'the speaker' in the opening page of *Hard Times*: describing his forehead as a 'square wall' and his voice as 'inflexible, dry, and dictatorial' is only the beginning of his portrait of the rigid Mr Gradgrind. A few pages later, when he concludes his description of Stone Lodge, Mr Gradgrind's 'matter of fact home' and his fact-ridden 'model' children, his bitter sarcasm is clear:

> Iron clamps and girders... mechanical lifts... everything that heart could wish for.

A moment later Dickens 'intrudes' in his own voice to express his doubts:

> Everything? Well I suppose so.

Jane Austen does something similar, but rather more gently. Primarily, her opening paragraphs in *Emma* introduce her central character. Little in the way of judgement can be detected except where she informs us that:

> The real evils, indeed, of Emma's situation were the power of having rather too much her own way, and a disposition to think a little too well of herself.

She does create characters who are 'types', such as Emma's father Mr Woodhouse, the anxious hypochondriac, and Miss Bates, the non-stop talker. Their traits are exaggerated, but her mockery of them tends to be affectionate, without the ferocity of Dickens. Often, she comments ironically with the voice of 'society', when it is clear that her own intention is to question or poke fun at the conventional view as she does in the famous opening lines of *Pride and Prejudice*:

> It is a truth universally acknowledged, that a single man in possession of a good fortune must be in want of a wife.

This question of the writer's stance towards characters or situations can be quite complex. Even in third-person narrative, things are often filtered through the perceptions of one particular character. We may need to consider carefully whether the author's views match those of this character or not. Alternatively, the author may choose to write with a 'voice' which is neither his or her own nor that of one of the characters in the novel.

Most of *Emma* is told from Emma's point of view, with her values and prejudices, but it is also possible to detect that Jane Austen shares some of her views and not others. Emma disapproves of two characters whose social status is inferior to her own. First, the self-satisfied Mrs Elton, who fails to recognize her position in Hartfield society and is much too familiar with Emma and her friends. Emma finds that she is:

> a vain woman, extremely well satisfied with herself, and thinking much of her own importance; that she meant to shine and be very superior, but with manners which had been formed in a bad school, pert and familiar; that all her notions were drawn from one set of people, and one style of living; that if not foolish she was ignorant, and that her society would certainly do Mr Elton no good...

> Happily it was now time to be gone. They were off; and Emma could breathe.

On the other hand, she also disapproves of respectable young farmer Robert Martin, whom she considers a bad match for her young protégé, Harriet Smith:

His appearance was very neat, and he looked like a sensible young man, but his person had no other advantage; and when he came to be contrasted with gentlemen, she thought he must lose all the ground he had gained in Harriet's inclination ...

'He is very plain, undoubtedly – remarkably plain: – but that is nothing, compared with his entire want of gentility. I had no right to expect much, and I did not expect much; but I had no idea that he could be so very clownish, so totally without air. I had imagined him, I confess, a degree or two nearer gentility.'

In the novel, it is clear that we are expected to agree with Emma about Mrs Elton. She is indeed an awful woman. However, where Robert Martin is concerned, we come to see that Emma is snobbish and misguided and that Jane Austen intends us to question her opinion.

Activity

1 Look once more at the openings of *Emma* and *The Handmaid's Tale*. Working with a partner, rewrite the first paragraph of *The Handmaid's Tale* in the third person and the first two paragraphs of *Emma* in the first person (with Emma as the narrator). Discuss the results. What is lost and what gained from changing the narrative viewpoint?

2 Think carefully about the narrative viewpoint in the novel you are studying. Who is the narrator? Can you trust his or her narrative? How aware are you of the author's presence? Look for examples of authorial intrusion.

Characters

Much of the interest in a novel lies in the characters whose world we enter and in whose lives we share. We usually respond to them first as people. We can analyse their personalities, trace how they are affected by events and empathize or disapprove of them. However, we do need to remember that they do not have lives outside the pages of the novel and so it is rarely useful to speculate about their past or future experiences. More importantly, we need to pay attention to how they are presented.

It has already been suggested that it is useful to keep a 'log' to record key passages and quotations for each important character which can be built up as you work through the text.

Characters are revealed to us in various ways:

- **Description.** The author often provides an introductory 'pen-portrait' and then builds up our knowledge with details as the narrative proceeds. Key passages describe main characters or make us aware of how they change and develop.

- **Dialogue.** Other characters often give important clues when they discuss the character concerned. We may also find out a lot about someone from his or her own speech.

- **Thoughts and feelings.** The 'inner life' of a character can be revealed directly, particularly in a first-person narrative.

- **Actions and reactions.** How characters behave in various situations will inform our view of them.

- **Imagery and symbols.** Characters may be described using simile and metaphor, or may be associated symbolically with, for example, a colour or an element. In Emily Brontë's *Wuthering Heights*, Heathcliff is frequently linked with fire and with the colour black. Similarly, in Thomas Hardy's *Tess of the D'Urbervilles*, Tess is associated with the colour red, which suggests danger or marks her out as a 'fallen woman' from the beginning.

Activity

Here are some introductory character sketches from *Emma, Hard Times* and *The Handmaid's Tale*. Working in a small group, make notes on these points:

- What kind of information does each author provide about the character in question?
- Do you learn anything of the character's inner life, or just factual or superficial information?
- How does the writer use language in each case? Consider sentence structure, vocabulary, use of imagery and other effects.
- What can you detect of the author's attitude to this character?

1   Mr John Knightley was a tall, gentleman-like, and very clever man; rising in his profession, domestic, and respectable in his private character; but with reserved manners which prevented his being generally pleasing; and capable of being sometimes out of humour. He was not an ill-tempered man, not so often unreasonably cross as to deserve such a reproach; but his temper was not his great perfection; and indeed, with such a worshipping wife, it was hardly possible that any natural defects in it would not be increased.

2   The Commander has on his black uniform, in which he looks like a museum guard. A semi-retired man, genial but wary, killing time. But only at first glance. After that he looks like a midwestern bank president, with his straight neatly brushed silver hair, his sober posture, shoulders a little stooped. And after that there is his moustache, silver also, and after that his chin, which really you can't miss. When you get down as far as the chin he looks like a vodka ad, in a glossy magazine, of times gone by.

His manner is mild, his hands large, with thick fingers and acquisitive thumbs, his blue eyes uncommunicative, falsely innocuous.

3   [Mr Bounderby] was a rich man: banker, merchant, manufacturer, and what not. A big, loud man, with a stare and a metallic laugh. A man made out of a coarse material, which seemed to have been stretched to make so much of him. A man with a great puffed head and forehead, swelled veins in his temples, and such a strained skin to his face that it seemed to hold his eyes open and lift his eyebrows up. A man with a pervading appearance on him of being inflated like a balloon, and ready to start. A man who could never sufficiently vaunt himself a self-made man. A man who was always proclaiming, through that brassy speaking-trumpet of a voice of his, his old ignorance and his old poverty. A man who was the Bully of humility.

4   Moira, sitting on the edge of my bed, legs crossed, ankle on knee, in her purple overalls, one dangly earring, the gold fingernail she wore to be eccentric, a cigarette between her stubby yellow-ended fingers. Let's go for a beer.

5   Harriet certainly was not clever, but she had a sweet, docile, grateful disposition; was totally free from conceit; and only desiring to be guided by any one she looked up to. Her early attachment to [Emma] herself was very amiable; and her inclination for good company, and power of appreciating what was elegant and clever shewed that there was no want of taste, though strength of understanding must not be expected.

Development of a character and a relationship

Now let us look at a character in more detail. If you are asked to explore the way a character is presented and how he or she changes and develops in the course of a novel, it is a good idea to choose a few passages or episodes from different parts of the novel, which feature the character, to examine in detail. These may be descriptive passages, moments of dramatic action, episodes where the character contrasts or is in conflict with others, or where he or she faces a decision.

Louisa Gradgrind

Dickens created the bleak world of Coketown, the setting of *Hard Times*, to expose and mock the philosophy of utilitarianism. This set of beliefs saw people only in terms of their usefulness as workers or tools for industry and wealth-creation. No allowances were made for people having imaginations or emotional lives.

Many of Dickens's characters, such as Mr Bounderby, are caricatures whose traits are exaggerated in the extreme. The effect is comic, but they also allow Dickens to make serious points and express his anger. Sometimes, he is accused of creating only caricatures, unrealistic people without depth, but this is by no means always the case. In *Hard Times*, the caricatures are usually recognizable by their comical names, while the central characters who develop as 'real' people are allowed to have ordinary names. Louisa Gradgrind, a victim of her father's belief that facts are 'The one thing needful', is one of these. The account of how her life and development are distorted, and of how her father learns to regret his rigid methods, is very moving.

Activity

We first meet Louisa when her father is appalled to have discovered her with her brother Tom, spying on the local circus, a forbidden entertainment. Study the passage closely, and make notes on how Dickens presents her and her relationship with her father. Consider in particular:

- the imagery used to describe Louisa's manner
- what is revealed about each of them by the dialogue.

Hard Times

Chapter 3: A Loophole

'In the name of wonder, idleness, and folly!' said Mr Gradgrind, leading each away by a hand; 'what do you do here?'

'Wanted to see what it was like,' returned Louisa shortly.

'What it was like?'

'Yes, father.'

There was an air of jaded sullenness in them both, and particularly in the girl: yet, struggling through the dissatisfaction of her face, there was a light with nothing to rest upon, a fire with nothing to burn, a starved imagination keeping life in itself somehow, which brightened its expression. Not with the brightness natural to cheerful youth, but with uncertain, eager, doubtful flashes, which had something painful in them, analogous to the changes on a blind face groping its way.

She was a child now, of fifteen or sixteen; but at no distant day would seem to become a woman all at once. Her father thought so as he looked at her. She was pretty. Would have been self-willed (he thought in his eminently practical way), but for her bringing-up.

'Thomas, though I have the fact before me, I find it difficult to believe that you, with your education and resources, should have brought your sister to a scene like this.'

'I brought *him*, father,' said Louisa, quickly. 'I asked him to come.'

'I am sorry to hear it. I am very sorry indeed to hear it. It makes Thomas no better, and it makes you worse, Louisa.'

She looked at her father again, but no tear fell down her cheek.

'You! Thomas and you, to whom the circle of the sciences is open; Thomas and you, who may be said to be replete with facts; Thomas and you, who have been trained to mathematical exactness; Thomas and you here!' cried Mr Gradgrind. 'In this degraded position! I am amazed.'

'I was tired. I have been tired a long time,' said Louisa.

'Tired? Of what?' asked the astonished father.

'I don't know of what – of everything I think.'

'Say not another word,' returned Mr Gradgrind. 'You are childish. I will hear no more.'

Charles Dickens

Louisa is presented in opposition to her father and his world of facts, but as yet the conflict is mostly within her, as her thwarted imagination fights for life. The images of light and an inward 'fire with nothing to burn' will recur frequently. She often gazes at the smoking chimneys of the Coketown factories which she knows must contain flames which have been suppressed, like her own imagination, and which burst out when darkness falls.

The dialogue reveals just how little capacity Gradgrind has for understanding his children. Notice the contrast between Louisa's short answers and her father's pompous, wordy style. She seems sullen, but also honest and very self-controlled. Her dry education has rendered her incapable of tears or emotional displays. His final accusation, that she is childish, is ironic. She has never been allowed to be a child. The passage does mark the first time Gradgrind is surprised by his children. Later it will be Louisa's tragedy which jolts him out of his complacency.

Now let us examine two further passages which reveal something of how their characters and their relationship alter.

Activity

1 Study the following extracts carefully, together with the one on the previous page. Discuss how the characters and their relationship are presented in each case.

2 Write a detailed comparison of the three passages. In what ways does Dickens convey the changes in Louisa's and Gradgrind's characters and in their relationship? Remember to consider:

   • the imagery used to describe the setting

   • characters dialogue, actions, and reactions.

Hard Times

Chapter 15: Father and Daughter

[Mr Gradgrind has just proposed that in the name of reason, Louisa should undertake a loveless marriage to the appalling Mr Bounderby, a rich banker and merchant.]

'I now leave you to judge for yourself,' said Mr Gradgrind. 'I have stated the case, as such cases are usually stated among practical minds; I have stated it, as the case of your mother and myself was stated in its time. The rest, my dear Louisa, is for you to decide.'

From the beginning, she had sat looking at him fixedly. As he now leaned back in his chair, and bent his deep-set eyes upon her in his turn, perhaps he might have seen one wavering moment in her, when she was impelled to throw herself upon his breast, and give him the pent-up confidences of her heart. But, to see it, he must have overleaped at a bound the artificial barriers he had for many years been erecting, between himself and all those subtle essences of humanity which will elude the utmost cunning of algebra until the last trumpet ever to be sounded shall blow even algebra to wreck. The barriers were too many and too high for such a leap. With his unbending, utilitarian, matter-of-fact face, he hardened her again; and the moment shot away into the plumbless depths of the past, to mingle with all the lost opportunities that are drowned there.

Removing her eyes from him, she sat so long looking silently towards the town, that he said, at length: 'Are you consulting the chimneys of the Coketown works, Louisa?'

'There seems to be nothing there, but languid and monotonous smoke. Yet when the night comes, Fire bursts out, Father!' she answered, turning quickly.

'Of course I know that, Louisa. I do not see the application of the remark.' To do him justice, he did not, at all.

Charles Dickens

Hard Times

Chapter 28: Down

[Long since married to Bounderby, Louisa has discovered and is tempted by the possibility of real love with another man. She returns to her father in great distress.]

When it thundered very loudly, [Mr Gradgrind] glanced towards Coketown, having it in his mind that some of the tall chimneys might be struck by lightning.

The thunder was rolling into distance, and the rain was pouring down like a deluge, when the door of his room opened. He looked round the lamp upon his table, and saw, with amazement, his eldest daughter.

'*Louisa!*'

'Father, I want to speak to you.'

'What is the matter? How strange you look! And good Heaven,' said Mr Gradgrind, wondering more and more, 'have you come here exposed to this storm?'

She put her hands to her dress, as if she hardly knew. 'Yes.' Then she uncovered her head, and letting her cloak and hood fall where they might, stood looking at him: so colourless, so dishevelled, so defiant and despairing, that he was afraid of her.

'What is it? I conjure you, Louisa, tell me what is the matter.'

She dropped into a chair before him, and put her cold hand on his arm.

'Father, you have trained me from my cradle.'

'Yes Louisa.'

'I curse the hour in which I was born to such a destiny.'

He looked at her in doubt and dread, vacantly repeating, 'Curse the hour? Curse the hour?'

'How could you give me life, and take from me all the inappreciable things that raise it from the state of conscious death? Where are the graces of my soul? Where are the sentiments of my heart? What have you done, O father, what have you done, with the garden that should have bloomed once, in this great wilderness here!'

She struck herself with both hands upon her bosom.

'If it had ever been here, its ashes alone would save me from the void in which my whole life sinks.'

Charles Dickens

Activity

1 Choose a character from a novel you are studying. Then select three or four passages from different parts of the novel which show 'key' moments for that character.

2 Analyse the passages carefully, paying close attention to how language and imagery are used to present the character at different times.

3 Using examples from these passages, write a short essay about the development of your chosen character.

4 Alternatively, choose an important relationship from a novel you are working on and follow steps 1 to 3.

The setting

The imaginary 'world' of a novel, into which the reader is invited, is often more than simply 'the place where the story happens'. The physical environment may be important in itself or as a backdrop to the action but it can also be used to reflect the characters and their experiences. It can be symbolic of the ideas the writer wishes to convey. However, the 'world' of a novel will also portray a society with its own culture, politics, and values. Characters may exist comfortably in their worlds, but often, the whole thrust of a novel depends on the central character being a misfit, or being in conflict with some aspect of their 'society', whether this is their family, their social class, a religious group, or a state.

The world of a novel can be as small as a household or as large as a nation. Jane Austen set herself tight limits, saying that 'Three or four families in a country village is the very thing to work on.' *Emma* is set in Highbury, a 'large and populous village almost amounting to a town'. London is only sixteen miles distant, but far enough in those days to seem out of easy reach. The action concerns only a few of the 'best' families in the village – those with whom the Woodhouses, at the top of their social ladder, can associate, and one or two others of lower status who provide material for comedy.

Although Jane Austen is quick to make fun of hypocrisy and snobbery, she does not challenge the rigid class boundaries of Highbury; in fact in this novel she endorses them. Emma's attempts to disregard them are definitely seen as misguided. Her matchmaking with Mr Elton on behalf of her 'friend' Harriet Smith, who is pretty, but illegitimate and penniless, causes only pain and embarrassment.

In *Hard Times*, the world Dickens creates is that of a northern English industrial town, a larger world than Jane Austen's Highbury. Like some of his characters, the setting is a caricature. It is based on a real town, but has exaggerated features. His intention of protesting against the deadening effects of utilitarianism is never clearer than when he introduces us to Coketown. He presents us with an environment where the physical surroundings reflect the social conditions. Read his description and then consider it through the activity which follows.

Hard Times

Chapter 5: The Key-note

Coketown, to which Messrs Bounderby and Gradgrind now walked, was a triumph of fact; it had no greater taint of fancy in it than Mrs Gradgrind herself. Let us strike the key-note, Coketown, before pursuing our tune.

It was a town of red brick, or of brick that would have been red if the smoke and ashes had allowed it; but, as matters stood it was a town of unnatural red and black like the painted face of a savage. It was a town of machinery and tall chimneys, out of which interminable serpents of smoke trailed themselves for ever and ever, and never got uncoiled. It had a black canal in it, and a river that ran purple with ill-smelling dye, and vast piles of building full of windows where there was a rattling and a trembling all day long, and where the piston of the steam-engine worked monotonously up and down, like the head of an elephant in a state of melancholy madness. It contained several large streets all very like one another, and many small streets still more like one another, inhabited by people equally like one another, who all went in and out at the same hours, with the same sound upon the same pavements, to do the same work, and to whom every day was the same as yesterday and tomorrow, and every year the counterpart of the last and the next.

Charles Dickens

Activity

How does Dickens present Coketown? Make notes on his use of:

- simile and metaphor
- colour and the senses
- the rhythm of the passage
- sentence structures.

The world of *The Handmaid's Tale* is wider again. It is set in the future, in an imaginary state in America, the Republic of Gilead. Fearful about declining population, due to man-made environmental disaster, a dictatorship has assigned roles to all people, but particularly to women. Wives are idealized, non-sexual beings. They wear virginal blue, while those women capable of the all-important child-bearing are assigned to them as handmaids or breeders, dressed in red. This symbolizes blood, sex, and childbirth. It marks them out as 'fallen women'. Gilead is a state ruled by terror, in which it is highly dangerous to ask questions or to assert one's individuality in any way. We do not even discover the narrator's real name: she is merely the handmaid 'Of-Fred'.

None of this is made clear to us at the start of the novel. Only gradually as we read Offred's stream of consciousness narrative do we piece together enough information to understand what is going on. It is quite a way into the text before we are provided with some 'historical background'. Here, Offred, waiting to assist at a birth, remembers some of the teaching she received at the Red Centre, where the handmaids are trained.

The Handmaid's Tale

Chapter 19

The siren goes on and on. That used to be the sound of death, for ambulances or fires. Possibly it will be the sound of death today also. We will soon know. What will Ofwarren give birth to? A baby, as we all hope? Or something else, an Unbaby, with a pinhead or a snout like a dog's, or two bodies, or a hole in its heart or no arms, or webbed hands and feet? There's no telling. They could tell once, with machines, but that is now outlawed. What would be the point of knowing, anyway? You can't have them taken out; whatever it is must be carried to term.

The chances are one in four, we learned that at the Centre. The air got too full, once, of chemicals, rays, radiation, the water swarmed with toxic molecules, all of that takes years to clean up, and meanwhile they creep into your body, camp out in your fatty cells. Who knows, your very flesh may be polluted, dirty as an oily beach, sure death to shore birds and unborn babies. Maybe a vulture would die of eating you. Maybe you light up in the dark, like an old-fashioned watch. Death-watch. That's a kind of beetle, it buries carrion.

I can't think of myself, my body, sometimes, without seeing the skeleton: how I must appear to an electron. A cradle of life, made of bones; and within, hazards, warped proteins, bad crystals jagged as glass. Women took medicines, pills, men sprayed trees, cows ate grass, all that souped-up piss flowed into the rivers. Not to mention the exploding atomic power plants, along the San Andreas fault, nobody's fault, during the earthquakes, and the mutant strain of syphilis no mould could touch. Some did it themselves, had themselves tied shut with catgut or scarred with chemicals. How could they, said Aunt Lydia, oh how could they have done such a thing? Jezebels! Scorning God's gifts! Wringing her hands.

It's a risk you're taking, said Aunt Lydia, but you are the shock troops, you will march out in advance, into dangerous territory. The greater the risk, the greater the glory. She clasped her hands, radiant with our phony courage. We looked down at the tops of our desks. To go through all that and give birth to a shredder: it wasn't a fine thought. We didn't know exactly what would happen to the babies that didn't get passed, that were declared Unbabies. But we knew they were put somewhere, quickly, away.

Margaret Atwood

Activity

Read the passage carefully and discuss in a small group what you learn about the following points.

- What has happened in Gilead in the past.
- What conditions are like in Gilead now.
- The laws and customs of Gilead in respect of pregnancy and childbirth.
- How propaganda and religion are used to ensure the women fit in with the needs of the regime.

In *Hard Times* and *The Handmaid's Tale*, the settings are very important. In both cases the writers have presented aspects they dislike about their own societies in an exaggerated form. This enables them to draw attention to these and to protest in an indirect way while being thought-provoking and entertaining. While Dickens demonstrates in Coketown the terrible results of extreme utilitarianism, Margaret Atwood writes as a feminist, concerned about the environment and about women being defined and limited by their traditional roles. Both writers create worlds where people are reduced to particular functions. However, both have a hopeful note in that the 'human spirit' is not entirely crushed despite such repressive regimes. 'Fancy' and imagination may be buried and distorted in *Hard Times*, but they do not die completely. Similarly, through the very telling of her story we know that Offred is far more than just her 'viable ovaries'.

Activity

Study and make notes on the setting of the novel you are studying.

- What sort of 'world' is it? How large or small, open or restrictive? What are its rules, values, beliefs, and customs?
- Locate passages where the author describes the physical surroundings, comments on the social order, or where characters act or speak in a way which represents their society.
- Do the characters fit comfortably in their world or are they in opposition to it? Is this shown to be a good or bad thing?

Language and style

Unless we are studying linguistics, we do not usually discuss a writer's use of language in isolation from its content. What we are concerned with is how effectively language is used to create worlds or present characters, situations, and ideas. So you probably will have noticed that as we have looked at each of these aspects of the novel, we have always examined the writer's language and style at the same time.

Here are some of the features of language we have considered.

- **Narrative voice.** The choice of first-person or third-person narrative; the tone of voice and how it is achieved.
- **Imagery.** The use of simile and metaphor. Look particularly for recurring images or patterns of imagery.
- **Sentence/paragraph structure.** The use of sentences which are long or short, complete or incomplete, complex or simple.
- **Vocabulary.** The selection of one word or group of words rather than another. For some examples, look again at the extracts from *Hard Times* which present Louisa Gradgrind and Coketown.

The short story

What is a short story?

In one sense the answer to this question is so obvious it hardly seems worth a thought. A 'short story' is clearly a story that is short! Perhaps we need to rephrase the question and pose the question that the critic, Norman Friedman, once asked – 'What makes a short story?'

Friedman answers this question by identifying two key features.

- A short story may be short because the material itself is narrow in its range or area of interest.
- A short story may be short because although the material has a potentially broad range the writer cuts it down to focus on one aspect and maximize the story's impact or artistic effect.

Many short stories do focus on a single incident, moment in time, or experience, but that is not always the case. Not all short stories are deliberately crafted by the writer as a vehicle for a single effect. In fact some stories gain their impact because they do not operate on a 'single effect' structure. Indeed, in some instances the 'single effect' type of story can appear contrived.

For many years the short story has suffered a good deal of critical neglect and has been regarded as an academically lightweight genre when measured against the much 'weightier' and more prestigious novel form. However, recently there has been a recognition that the short story is something more than the novel's poor relation and it is not now uncommon to find a range of short stories on A level specifications. Collections of short stories can also make interesting choices for coursework or for wider reading when you are studying a particular topic or theme.

If you are studying a short story text there are a number of areas that you will need to consider. These are very similar to the aspects of the novel that we explored earlier.

- **Plot and structure.** You will need a clear understanding of what happens in the story, the basic ideas that it deals with, how it is structured, and how the various elements of it relate to one another. How the story is structured can be of particular interest if it varies from a straightforward chronological pattern.
- **Narrative viewpoint.** The question of who is telling the story is a very important one and raises questions about why the writer has chosen to present the story from this particular viewpoint and what effect this has on the reader's response.
- **Characters.** This is a favourite area for A level questions. They often focus on one or more of the characters in the story or stories and may ask you to examine how the writer presents or develops the characters or to explore how they relate to each other.
- **Language and style.** You will also need a clear idea about the distinctive qualities of the writer's style. This will involve focusing closely on the specific detail and the writer's choice of language (the way this is used, and the effects that it creates).
- **Connections and comparisons.** If you are studying a collection of short stories, you will also need to be aware of links between the stories, such as common themes and patterns, or contrasts between them.

Plot and structure

One thing you may have noted about short stories is that very often the story focuses on a single character in a single situation rather than tracing a range of characters through a variety of situations and phases of development as novels often do. However, often the focus for stories is a moment at which the central characters undergo some important experience which represents a significant moment in their personal development. It can be seen as a 'moment of truth' in which something or some perception, large or small, changes within the character. In some stories, though, this 'moment of truth' is evident only to the reader and not the characters.

Not all stories reach a climax, though. Some stories may offer a kind of 'snapshot' of a period of time or an experience – a 'day in the life of...' kind of story might be like this. Other stories end inconclusively leaving the reader with feelings of uncertainty, while other kinds of story do not seem to have a discernible plot at all. This may lead the reader to feel completely baffled by what he or she has read and subsequently to tentatively explore a range of possible interpretations in his or her head. This might, of course, have been exactly the response that the writer intended.

This diagram presents one way of thinking about how alternative plots and structures of short stories work:

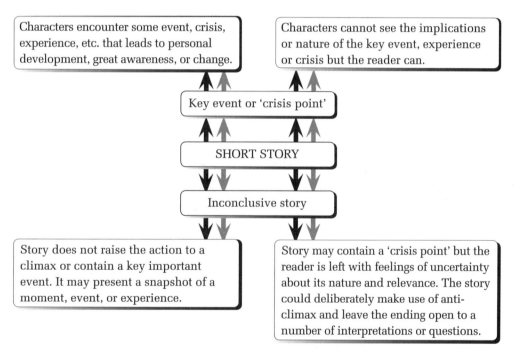

Beginnings

Our very earliest experiences of stories (the fairy tales we listen to, and then the vast range of stories that we hear, read, and see presented in film and television as adults) teach us one thing – stories have a 'beginning', a 'middle', and an 'end'. Strictly speaking, though, it is not entirely true. There are stories that do not seem to have a beginning or an ending in the conventional sense. We will look at stories like these, which seem to be 'all middle', so to speak, a little later. The vast majority of stories, however, do have some kind of beginning or opening section; a middle, where the characters, situation, and ideas are developed; and an ending that draws the story to a conclusion.

Here are some possible ways in which stories can open:

- the writer launches straight into the narrative
- the writer sets the scene by giving explicit background information
- the writer informs the reader using suggestion or implication rather than direct description
- the opening is direct and holds the reader's attention, perhaps capturing attention with a word or short phrase.

Activity

Read the following openings to three short stories. Then, in a small group, discuss your responses to them. Think carefully about how each writer approaches the opening to their story and try to identify the techniques that they use.

1   In Memoriam Brian Rosenfeld

'1939. It wasn't just the outbreak of war to us, but the fact that my mother decided to leave my father that week. Just like that. A personal holocaust. Fear was in the air, muted excitement; the measured tones of Neville Chamberlain oozed out of the dark brown canvas-webbed wireless set, gently, softly. He was an appeaser, like my ma, but he'd lost patience, as she had. The future would be different now.'

Elizabeth Troop

2   The Snow Pavilion

The motor stalled in the middle of a snowy landscape, lodged in a rut, wouldn't budge an inch. How I swore! I'd planned to be snug in front of a roaring fire by now, a single malt on the mahogany wine-table (a connoisseur's piece) beside me, the five courses of Melissa's dinner savourously aromatizing the kitchen; to complete the décor, a labrador retriever's head laid on my knee as trustingly as if I were indeed a country gentleman and lolled by rights among the chintz. After dinner, before I read our customary pre-coital poetry aloud to her, my elegant and accomplished mistress, also a connoisseur's piece, might play the piano for her part-time pasha while I sipped black, acrid coffee from her precious little cups.

Angela Carter

3   Dual Control

'You ought to have stopped.'

'For God's sake, shut up, Freda.'

'Well, you should have. You ought to have made sure she was alright.'

'Of course she's alright.'

'How do you know? You didn't stop to find out, did you?'

'Do you want me to go back? We're late enough as it is, thanks to your fooling about getting ready, but I don't suppose the Bradys'll notice if we're late. I don't suppose they'll notice if we never turn up, though after the way you angled for the invitation ...'

'That's right, blame it all on me. We could have left half an hour ago if you hadn't been late home from the office.'

'How often do I have to tell you that business isn't a matter of nine to five?'

'No it's a matter of the Bradys, isn't it? You were keen enough we should get asked. Where were you anyway? Drinking with the boys? Or smooching with some floozie?'

Elizabeth Walter

- -

Obviously the opening of a story is vital. If readers' attention is not captured immediately the story contains no initial impact to encourage them to continue, to draw them into the story. However, bearing in mind the constraints of length under which the short story operates, it is also important that the opening compresses information that might have taken some time to explain so that the reader quickly and effectively gains a picture of what is going on. Short story writers are often faced with this question of how much they can omit while at the same time creating the impression of completeness and continuity in their stories.

Going back to the extracts that you have just discussed, you may have noticed that Extract 2 launches straight into the narrative. The car getting stuck in the snow captures the reader's attention straight away. This opening paragraph goes on to give quite a bit of information to set the scene very economically as the narrator reflects on the plans he had made for his evening.

In Extract 3, on the other hand, we are told very little directly and we have to work out for ourselves what is happening or what has happened using clues suggested through the narrative. This approach can provide us with just as much information as straightforward description. In this instance we learn about the characters – what they are doing and what has happened – through the dialogue, but it leaves a good deal to the reader's imagination too. (In fact, this story is told entirely through dialogue with no direct description.)

In contrast, Extract 1 begins with the arresting '1939', which immediately captures our attention. The short and direct paragraph clearly sets the context for the story and indicates to us the personal and domestic scene reflected against the magnitude of world events.

Narrative line

Short stories, like other fictional works, order the events that they describe in a particular way. Through the story-line the writer can create a wide range of effects, such as creating suspense, raising the action to a climax point, resolving problems, leading (or misleading) the reader in particular ways, and leaving endings open to a variety of interpretations.

Very often the narrative structure is a straightforward progression with one event following another and moving towards a conclusion where all is resolved. However, sometimes a writer might play around with this structure to create particular effects. Here are some points to consider when you focus on the narrative structure of a story.

- Make a list of the key events in the story.
- Look at the order in which these events are related by the writer.
- Look at the time structure of the story – is it told in simple chronological order or is there use of flashbacks or cutting back and forth?
- Are there any details or pieces of information that the writer omits or particular points that are emphasized?

Short stories often have a moment in the plot upon which the whole structure of the story turns and which affects the outcome of the tale. Sometimes this trigger can be a quite trivial incident or experience but it signifies a moment of revelation to the central character. *Hassan's Tower* by Margaret Drabble contains just such a moment for newly married Kenneth on honeymoon with his wife, Chloë, in Morocco. They are a wealthy couple who appear to have everything that they could want in life but Kenneth is disappointed in his new wife and disillusioned with life in general. He is ill-at-ease in Morocco and goes about in constant fear of being robbed. Against his will his wife takes him to Hassan's Tower and wants to climb to the top to see the view. Reluctantly, he accompanies her and during the course of this seemingly unremarkable excursion he experiences a revelation that changes his whole outlook on his wife, his life, and those around him.

Hassan's Tower

The more he looked, the more he realized that the people on top of the tower were in their own way as astonishing a view as the more evidently panoramic vistas. The whole of the top of the tower was thick and covered with people: small children were crawling about, mothers were feeding their babies, young men were holding the hands of girls and indeed the hands of other young men, boys were sitting on the very edge and dangling their feet into space, and old women who would need a day to recover from the climb were lying back in the sun, for all the world as though they were grandmothers on a beach in England... and as he gazed he felt growing within him a sense of extraordinary familiarity that was in its own way a kind of illumination... He saw these people, quite suddenly, for what they were, for people, for nothing other than people; their clothes filled out with bodies, their faces took on expression, their relations became dazzlingly clear, as though the details of their strangeness had dropped away, as though the terms of common humanity (always before credited in principle, but never before perceived) had become facts before his eyes.

Margaret Drabble

Endings

There are as many ways of ending a story as there are of beginning it and the ending is clearly a very important element in the overall structure of a piece. In a short story it is often the ending which reveals meaning, points up a significant theme, or provides a resolution. This kind of ending should leave the reader contented and satisfied with a sense of a tale completed.

Equally though, a writer might create an 'open' ending, one that does not provide answers, an ending that might leave readers pondering on what it all means or unsettle them. This could be, of course, just the kind of response that the writer is aiming for.

The ending with 'a sting in the tail' has become quite common in recent years, being popularized through the short stories of Roald Dahl. It is worth noting, though, that with this kind of ending we need to distinguish between a device which is merely used as a kind of 'trick', and a twist at the end which causes us to see something fundamental in the story as a whole.

Activity

Choose three short stories that you know and re-read them. Discuss the ending of each story with a partner, thinking about the following questions:

- Does the story have what you would recognize as a definite ending?
- How does the ending relate to the rest of the story?
- Does the writer draw attention to any specific points in the ending?
- How would you have ended the story?

Viewpoints

You are already familiar with the term narrative viewpoint, in the sense of 'from whose point of view we see the events of the story' in relation to the novel (see page 8). However, it is perhaps useful to be reminded that this term can encompass two related but distinct ideas. In addressing viewpoint we need to consider the question of who is actually seeing the events described and who is narrating them. They may be one and the same or quite separate and the question is rather more complex than it might first appear.

It may be possible to approach the question of viewpoint by distinguishing between narrators who seem to address the reader directly from within the story (**internal narrators**) or those who have a more **external** narrative viewpoint. As a reader you need to be aware of how writers use viewpoint within their stories, be sensitive to subtle shifts and aware of the effects this can have on the narrative and your perception of it.

Activity

Look at these two extracts and think about the narrative viewpoints used in each.

1 Missy

'There you are, Mrs Ebbs, hold the cup steady. Can you manage, dear? Whoops! That's it. Now sit up properly, you'll slip down in the bed again, sit up against your pillows. That's it. Don't nod off again, will you? Now careful, Mrs Ebbs, I haven't got all day, dear. That's it, good girl.'

The voice came roaring towards her. The face was bland as suet. The face was a cow's face. An ox.

'Ox-face,' she said, but she had not said it.

She tipped the spoon and sucked in her soup, little bits of carrot and soft lentil sieving through the spaces between her teeth.

'All right now, Mrs Ebbs?'

Ox-face.

'I'm not deaf.'

Was she?

Susan Hill

2   A Tradition of Eighteen Hundred and Four, Christmas 1882

The widely discussed possibility of an invasion of England through a Channel Tunnel has more than once recalled old Solomon Selby's story to my mind. The occasion on which I numbered myself among his audience was one evening when he was sitting in the yawning chimney-corner of the inn-kitchen, with some others who had gathered there, and I entered for shelter from the rain. Withdrawing the stem of his pipe from the dental notch in which it habitually rested, he leaned back in the recess behind him and smiled into the fire. The smile was neither mirthful nor sad, not precisely humorous nor altogether thoughtful. We who knew him recognized it in a moment: it was his narrative smile. Breaking off our few desultory remarks we drew up closer, and he thus began ...

Thomas Hardy

- -

In Extract 2 you will notice immediately that Hardy is writing in the first person. He is recounting a particular evening when he heard a story told by Solomon Selby. You obviously cannot tell from this brief opening, but the bulk of the story is told as if by Solomon Selby as reported by Hardy. Think about what effect this has on the narrative. Notice too how Hardy economically sets the context of the story through implication – the title providing the date, 1804, coupled with the idea of an invasion through a 'Channel Tunnel', clearly sets the story against the background of the Napoleonic Wars. Hardy also economically sets the story in its more immediate context – the cosy inn of 1882, sheltering from the rain with others gathered round the fire, and the anticipation of a good story well told – all these details help to set the mood and draw the reader into the narrative.

Compare this with the approach adopted by Hill in Extract 1. She chooses a quite different way of telling her story. It is written in the third person and we are launched, without any preamble, into a 'situation'. It is not immediately clear what that situation is but it seems that someone, perhaps a nurse, is feeding soup to Mrs Ebbs. Although Hill partially adopts the stance of external narrator, some of the narrative views the scene through the eyes of Mrs Ebbs as she sees the face of the nurse peering towards her.

Activity

Look at three or four short stories that you have studied. With a partner, discuss the narrative viewpoint that the writer adopts in each. Now write a short essay, illustrated by examples, on the way in which narrative viewpoint contributes to the overall effect of these stories.

Characters

Earlier, we considered ways in which characters can be revealed to us in novels, and these also apply to the short story. It would be useful to look back at these points to refresh your memory (see page 11). There are also some differences, though. In a novel, the writer has many pages and chapters in which to present and develop characters in detail. Some novels have a timescale of years, in which we see characters grow and change. In a short story, which may only last a few pages and is more likely to focus on a particular incident, or a few days in a character's life, the writer needs to quickly and economically give us enough information to understand the features of the character which are essential to the story. It is a bit like the difference in art between a detailed painted portrait and a quick pencil sketch. The sketch tells us what we need to know and our imagination provides the rest.

Although some critics argue that it is absurd to consider fictitious characters as if they were 'real' people, when we read stories we do tend to create our own mental images of them based on our experiences of real life. However, we must not lose sight of the fact that they are creations of the writer and do not have an existence outside the text. In many cases writers create their characters to serve particular functions within the narrative and present them in ways that give particular impressions. Therefore, we should look carefully at the kinds of characters the writer portrays, how they are presented, which of their features are stressed, and what role they perform. We must also think about how the characters interlock with all the other elements of the story to create a unified whole and how we respond to them as readers.

Activity

Read the following extract and think about how the two characters are presented. What impressions do you get of Nelson and Nate Twomey? Use specific references from the passage to support your ideas.

Halloran's Child

He was eating the rabbit he had shot himself on the previous day, separating the small bones carefully from the flesh before soaking lumps of bread in the dark salt gravy. When they were boys, he and his brother, Nelson Twomey, used to trap rabbits and other animals too, weasels and stoats – it was sport, they thought nothing of it, it was only what Farley the gamekeeper did.

Then, Nate had gone by himself into the wood and found a young fallow deer caught by the leg, and when he had eventually got it free the animal had stumbled away, its foot mangled and dropping a trail of fresh blood through the undergrowth. Nate had gone for his brother, brought him back and shown him. 'Well, it'll die, that's what,' Nelson had said, and shrugged his thin shoulders. It was the first glimpse Nate had of his brother's true nature, his meanness. 'Die of gangrene. That's poison.'

He had wept that night, one of the few occasions in his life, and got up at dawn and gone out to search for the wounded animal, remembering the trembling hind quarters and the sweat which had matted its pale coat, the eyes, where the sticky rheum had begun to gather in the corners. He found only the blood, dried dark on the bracken. It led him towards where the bank of the stream fell away at his feet, and he could not follow further.

Susan Hill

One of the first striking things about this passage is the way that Hill emphasizes Nate's sensitivity and concern for the suffering of an innocent and helpless creature. He does, however, continue to shoot and eat rabbits and to kill chickens for food but these things are all part of the natural order of things and do not involve unnecessary or drawn-out suffering. What seems significant here is that it is not the killing but the pointless suffering of the innocent animal in the trap that appals him. In this respect he is quite different from his older brother Nelson, who not only appears indifferent to the suffering of the animals but actually relishes the cruelty inherent in his work as a rat-catcher. There is a violence within Nelson that seems to simmer below the surface and that makes Nate in some way afraid of him. One of the effects of the description of the two brothers in this passage is to focus attention more closely on the characteristics of Nate. If you were to read the rest of the story you would find that Nate is the central character.

Activity

1 Now look back at the two extracts on pages 25–26 that you considered in terms of narrative viewpoint. Read them again, but this time focus on any clues or hints that they might give concerning the characters. Discuss your ideas with a partner and jot down the main points of your discussion.

2 Choose two stories that you have read and studied and write brief notes on how the writers reveal and present the central characters.

Language and imagery

The style in which a story is written – the choices that writers make in the language they use and the ways in which they use it – is a key element in the overall effect that is created by a story in the mind of the reader. It might be written quite plainly using little figurative language, or the writer might use imagery to help create the desired effect.

In *Halloran's Child*, Hill very often uses groups of images to build up a particular effect. Look at this passage, for example, which describes the Hallorans' daughter, Jenny.

Halloran's Child

They had only one child, the daughter, Jenny. She had never been truly well since the day she was born, and when she was a year old and began to walk her limbs seemed incapable of holding her up, she was unsteady and sickly. At the age of four she had rheumatic fever and almost died, and Halloran had said in public hearing that he wished for it, wished to have it over with, for who wanted an invalid for a child and how could he bear the anxiety? She had been forbidden to run or even walk far, though she went to school when she was five and there was treated like a fragile doll by the others, who had been put in awe of her. She played with no one, though sometimes, as she sat in a corner of the playground, one of them would take pity on her and bring pick-sticks or a jigsaw and do it with her for a little while. But she seemed to be separated from them, almost to be less than human, because of the transparency of her skin and her thin, delicate bones, because of the fine blueness tingeing her lips and the flesh below her nervous eyes.

Susan Hill

Activity

Read this extract carefully and pick out any images that are particularly effective. Describe what impressions are created by each of these and them compare your ideas with a partner.

Notice how Hill emphasizes the frailty of Jenny through a variety of images that build up to create a vivid impression of the sick child. She tells us that Jenny '... was treated like a fragile doll' and that she seemed '... almost to be less than human, because of the transparency of her skin and her thin, delicate bones, because of the fine blueness tingeing her lips and the flesh below her nervous eyes'. This creates an image of a fragile, young, featherless baby bird and gives an impression of vulnerability, of someone with a tenuous grip on life.

Later on in the story Jenny goes into hospital, and when she comes out the fragility of her body is re-emphasized by Hill who describes her '... small legs poking out like sticks', her '... neck bent like a stalk', and introduces the idea that she is dying as Nate sees '... the deadness within the child's eyes'.

Nate goes to visit Jenny, and again Hill uses description relating to skin and eyes and bones to show the child's deteriorating condition:

> ... she seemed to have shrunk, her flesh was thinner, scarcely covering her bones, and the skin was tight and shiny. Her eyes were very bright and yet dead, too.

Again Hill uses imagery suggestive of a helpless creature:

> He looked down at her hand, resting on the sheet. It was like a small claw.

and again images that hint of death:

> Her lips moved and there was no blood in them, they were thin and dry and oddly transparent, like the skin of a chrysalis.

This technique of using recurring images to build up a picture or atmosphere is a feature typical of Hill's style.

Activity

Choose two or three stories that you have studied and think carefully about how they are written. Note down what seem to you to be particular features of the style of each. Include examples to illustrate your points.

The whole story

Annotation can be a very useful aid to exploring a text. It allows you to record those tentative first responses or ideas that are suggested to you as you read a text. Indeed, the process of noting points on the text itself can help you to focus on the meaning and implications of individual words and phrases.

Often these 'first impressions' tend to be lost or forgotten later, but they do play a very important part in the development of your ideas about a particular text. Here is an example of a second-year student's notes around the short story *I Spy* by Graham Greene. In this instance the student read the story and then began annotating it prior to a small group discussion in which students compared their ideas. Read *I Spy* for yourself and think about the annotations made around the text.

I Spy

Sense of secrecy

Charlie Stowe waited until he heard his mother snore before he got out of bed. Even then he moved with caution and tiptoed to the window. The front of the house was irregular, so that it was possible to see a light burning in his mother's room. But now all the

Searchlight
– airships
– wartime

1st World War

windows were dark. A searchlight passed across the sky, lighting the banks of cloud and probing the dark deep spaces between, seeking enemy airships. The wind blew from the sea, and Charlie Stowe could hear behind his mother's snores the beating of the waves. A

Cold – out of bed! – darkness emphasized

Not modern

draught through the cracks in the window-frame stirred his nightshirt. Charlie Stowe was frightened.

'Manly' to smoke – grown up

But the thought of the tobacconist's shop which his father kept down a dozen wooden stairs drew him on. He was twelve years old, and already boys at the County School mocked him because he had never smoked a cigarette. The packets were piled twelve

Brands of cigarettes

deep below, Gold Flake and Players, De Reszke, Abdulla, Woodbines, and the little shop lay under a thin haze of stale smoke which would completely disguise his crime. That it was a crime to steal some of his father's stock Charlie Stowe had no doubt, but he

Why?

did not love his father; his father was unreal to him, a wraith, pale,

Father does not seem to bother with him – different from mum

thin, indefinite, who noticed him only spasmodically and left even punishment to his mother. For his mother he felt a passionate demonstrative love; her large boisterous presence and her noisy charity filled the world for him; from her speech he judged her the

Zeppelins – bombing raids

friend of everyone, from the rector's wife to the 'dear Queen', except the 'Huns', the monsters who lurked in Zeppelins in the clouds. But his father's affection and dislike were as indefinite as his movements. Tonight he had said he would be in Norwich, and yet you never knew. Charlie Stowe had no sense of safety as he crept down the wooden stairs. When they creaked he clenched his fingers on the collar of his nightshirt. —— A sign of fear

Fear of discovery builds up atmosphere of tension

At the bottom of the stairs he came out quite suddenly into the little shop. It was too dark to see his way, and he did not dare touch the switch. For half a minute he sat in despair on the bottom step with his chin cupped in his hands. Then the regular movement of the searchlight was reflected through an upper window and the boy had time to fix in memory the pile of cigarettes, the counter, and the small hole under it. The footsteps of a policeman on the

Panic

pavement made him grab the first packet to his hand and dive for the hole. A light shone along the floor and a hand tried the door,

Relief

then the footsteps passed on, and Charlie cowered in the darkness.

Sense of mystery, menace, potential danger, etc.

Sleeping mother – repetition of snore

What is Charlie up to?

Mention of father

More info about Charlie

Pressure from peers

A 'crime', stealing, guilty conscience

What does all this mean?

Contrast with father

Something mysterious about father

A sense almost of surprise

What to do next?

Fear of his 'crime' being found out

Tension

Recovers — At last he got his <u>courage back</u> by telling himself in his (curiously) (adult) way that if he were caught now there was nothing to be done
Why 'curiously' adult? – he is realistic about what is happening

Gone so far, might as well go through with it — about it, and he <u>might as well have his smoke</u>. He put a cigarette in his mouth and then remembered that he had no matches. For a while

Still afraid — he <u>dared</u> not move. Three times the (searchlight) lit the shop, while he muttered taunts and encouragements. |'May as well be hung for a sheep,' 'Cowardy, cowardy custard,' <u>grown-up</u> and <u>childish</u>
Mixture of adult and child

Why this word? — <u>exhortations</u> oddly mixed.

Tension again — But as he moved he heard footfalls in the street, the sound of several men walking rapidly. Charlie Stowe was <u>old enough</u> to feel surprise that anybody was about. The footsteps came nearer, stopped; a key was turned in the shop door, a voice said: 'Let him

'Gentlemen' – very polite and formal — in,' and then he heard his (father,) 'If you wouldn't mind being quiet, (gentlemen.) I don't want <u>to wake up the family</u>.' There was a note
Supposed to be in Norwich

Something out of the ordinary happening — (unfamiliar) to Charlie in the (undecided) voice. A torch flashed and
Why not?
the electric globe burst into blue light. The boy held his breath; he wondered whether his father would hear his heart beating, and he
Fear of being caught
clutched his nightshirt tightly and prayed, 'O God, don't let me be
Like Charlie clenching his nightshirt
caught.' Through a crack in the counter he could see his father where he stood, one hand held to his high <u>stiff collar</u>, <u>between two</u>
Is he under arrest?

Police? — <u>men</u> in <u>bowler hats</u> and <u>belted mackintoshes</u>. They were strangers.
Fear, uncertainty

'Have a cigarette,' his father said in a <u>voice dry as a biscuit</u>. One of the men shook his head. 'It wouldn't do, not <u>when we are on duty</u>.

Police again — Thank you all the same.' He spoke (gently,) but (without kindness:) Charlie Stowe thought his father must be (ill.) —*Why ill?*
Why 'gently'/ 'without kindness'? – an unusual combination

Stocking up – may not be back for some time — 'Mind if I put <u>a few in my pocket</u>?' <u>Mr Stowe asked,</u> and when the man nodded he lifted a pile of Gold Flake and Players from a shelf
Has to ask permission – under arrest?

Why 'caressed'? — and (caressed) the packets with the tips of his fingers.

A bit like Charlie, 'if he were caught now there was nothing to be done about it' — 'Well,' he said, <u>'there's nothing to be done about it,</u> and I may as well have my smokes.' For a moment Charlie Stowe feared discovery, his father stared round the shop so thoroughly; he might have been seeing it <u>for the first time</u>. 'It's a good little business,' he
Or the last!
said, 'for those that like it. <u>The wife will sell out</u>, I suppose. <u>Else the</u>

Why would the neighbours do that? — <u>neighbours'll be wrecking it</u>. Well, you want to be off. A stitch in
The end of his family life
time. I'll get my coat.'

Daren't let him out of their sight – serious charges maybe — <u>'One of us'll come with you, if you don't mind,'</u> said the stranger

'Gently' again — <u>gently</u>.

'You needn't trouble. It's on the peg here. There, I'm all ready.'

Doesn't want to say goodbye – afraid, ashamed?

The other man said in an embarrassed way, 'Don't you want to speak to your wife?' The thin voice was decided, 'Not me. Never do today what you can put off till tomorrow. She'll have her chance later, won't she?' —— When?

Feels awkward

'Yes, yes,' one of the strangers said and he became very cheerful with it and encouraging. 'Don't you worry too much. While there's life...' and suddenly his father tried to laugh.   ... There's hope – could suggest long sentence or worse

Trying to jolly him along

Sounds serious

When the door had closed Charlie Stowe tiptoed upstairs and got into bed. He wondered why his father had left the house again so late at night and who the strangers were. Surprise and awe kept him for a little while awake. It was as if a familiar photograph had stepped from the frame to reproach him with neglect. He remembered how his father had held tight to his collar and fortified himself with proverbs, and he thought for the first time that, while his mother was boisterous and kindly, his father was very like himself, doing things in the dark which frightened him. It would have pleased him to go down to his father and tell him that he loved him, but he could hear through the window the quick steps going away. He was alone in the house with his mother, and he fell asleep.

We see everything through Charlie's eyes

What had he done?

Just like Charlie

Something has happened to change Charlie's view

Returns to the beginning

Graham Greene

Activity

1 With a partner, discuss your own responses to *I Spy* focusing on these points:
   - the kind of atmosphere that Greene creates and how he achieves it (use specific examples to support your comments)
   - the techniques that he uses to give you an impression of character.
   Write up your comments in a short essay (1–2 pages in length).

2 Choose a short story that you have not read before. Make notes around the text as you read it (use a photocopy of it if the text is not your own) thinking about all the short story elements we have considered so far.

3 In a small group, exchange your notes and discuss each of your responses to the stories you have chosen.

Non-fiction prose

So far, you have been introduced to the main prose fiction genres which are usually set for A level, but there is one further category of prose texts still to consider: non-fiction prose. You are very likely to study examples of non-fiction prose writing if you are preparing for a theme-based paper. Non-fiction prose texts can also be rewarding to study for coursework, and they can help us to build up our understanding of the historical, political, or cultural context in which other forms of literature are produced.

Writers of non-fiction prose can have many different purposes. These may include:

- describing or reporting events
- propounding new ideas or points of view
- teaching or explaining
- reflecting on or expressing opinions about people, events, or situations
- raising awareness of social issues or injustices
- persuading or influencing readers on political issues; for example, by presenting arguments from a particular point of view
- entertaining or amusing by presenting topics in original or clever ways, using satire, or allegory, for example
- reviewing, criticizing or reflecting on the work of other writers.

When studying non-fiction prose texts, our approach is not necessarily any different from when we study novels or even poetry. We still need to ask the same key questions: What is the text about? How has the author chosen to write about it? We may also ask: *Why* is the author writing this? In more specific terms, we need to examine the following.

- The surface and deeper meanings presented.
- The writer's purpose or aim.
- The audience/reader the writer has in mind.
- The author's viewpoint. Is the text written in the first person or the third person? The effects of this choice in fiction texts were explored earlier (see pages 8–11 and 25–26), but in non-fiction prose, they can be even more important. Writing in the third person suggests a more objective viewpoint, while writing in the first person tends to give a more opinionated or subjective view. Some texts will need careful thought to determine where the author stands in relation to the material and to the reader.
- The structure of the text. In argumentative writing, for example, both sides of the issue may be presented in a measured way before making a judgement, or the author may be concerned only with building up the evidence one-sidedly. In contrast, personal, reflective writing may be loose, informal, or even quite unconventional in the way it is structured.
- The tone of the writing and the emotions behind the words.
- Use of imagery and vocabulary.
- Other stylistic features, such as length and construction of sentences.

These aspects all need to be borne in mind as we go on to consider types of non-fiction that you may encounter at A level: essays, autobiography and diaries, documentary writing, journalism and literary criticism. However, you may find that it is sometimes difficult to put texts into categories in this way: essays can be journalistic and a diary can 'document' events.

The essay

In its pure form, the published essay is relatively rare nowadays. However, it used to be a popular way for an author to explore a topic of interest or to convey opinions about current affairs. From the seventeenth century, essays were circulated in pamphlets or published in magazines. These remained very popular forms of mass communication until radio and television took over as more powerful vehicles for the expression of personal or political views, while nowadays almost anyone can communicate ideas or opinions to a global audience through the Internet.

Essays are written in many styles: they can be witty, angry, and satirical or gentle and thoughtful, but they usually present a personal or subjective view of a topic, and do not pretend to be objective. Earlier essay writers often paid great attention to the way they used language, balancing their sentences and weighing their words, so that their writing can be quite stylized and formal. There is an example of an essay in Chapter 13, page 245.

Biography, autobiography and memoirs

These forms of writing provide fascinating insights into the lives of people, past and present. Biographies document or celebrate the lives of famous – or infamous – people. They may be the product of the author's friendship with his or her subject, or the result of extensive research. For example, two biographies of Charlotte Brontë, one by her contemporary and friend Elizabeth Gaskell which is personal and anecdotal, the other by the twentieth-century scholar Winifred Gerin which is scholarly and more objective, present very different insights into the life of this Victorian writer.

Autobiographical writing or memoirs might review a whole lifetime, or may focus on particular events or a significant period in the author's life, as Brian Keenan does in *An Evil Cradling*, his account of the years he spent as a hostage in Beirut.

Activity

1 Read the following extract in which Keenan invites us to share his experience of confinement and isolation, something which most of us would fear.

2 Discuss the text with a partner and make notes on how Keenan uses language:

- to involve the reader in his experiences
- to convey the monotony of life in the cell
- to describe how he is affected by captivity and how he copes with the situation.

In particular, consider:

- the sentence structures and patterns Keenan uses
- the effect of his strong use of the first person and the present tense.

An Evil Cradling

Come now into the cell with me and stay here and feel if you can and if you will that time, whatever time it was, for however long, for time means nothing in this cell. Come, come in.

I am back from my daily ablutions. I hear the padlock slam behind me and I lift the towel which has draped my head from my face. I look at the food on the floor. The round of Arab bread, a boiled egg, the jam I will not eat, the slice or two of processed cheese and perhaps some houmus. Every day I look to see if it will change, if there will be some new morsel of food that will make this day different from all the other days, but there is no change. This day is the same as all the days in the past and as all the days to come. It will always be the same food sitting on the floor in the same place.

I set down my plastic bottle of drinking water and the other empty bottle. From bottle to bottle, through me, this fluid will daily run. I set the urine bottle at the far corner away from the food. This I put in a plastic bag to keep it fresh. In this heat the bread rapidly turns stale and hard. It is like eating cardboard. I pace my four paces backwards and forwards, slowly feeling my mind empty, wondering where it will go today. Will I go with it or will I try to hold it back, like a father and an unruly child? There is a greasy patch on the wall where I lay my head. Like a dog I sniff it.

I begin as I have always begun these days to think of something, anything upon which I can concentrate. Something I can think about and so try to push away the crushing emptiness of this tiny, tiny cell and the day's long silence. I try with desperation to recall the dream of the night before or perhaps to push away the horror of it. The nights are filled with dreaming. The cinema of the mind, the reels flashing and flashing by and suddenly stopping at some point when with strange contortions it throws up some absurd drama that I cannot understand. I try to block it out. Strange how in the daytime the dreams that we do not wish to remember come flickering back into the conscious mind. Those dreams that we desperately want to have with us in the daylight will not come to us but have gone and cannot be enticed back. It is as if we are running down a long empty tunnel looking for something that we left behind but cannot see in the blackness.

The guards are gone. I have not heard a noise for several hours now. It must be time to eat. I tear off a quarter of the unleavened bread and begin to peel the shell from the egg. The word 'albumen' intrigues me for a while and I wonder where the name came from. How someone decided once to call that part of the egg 'albumen'. The shape of an egg has lost its fascination for me. I have exhausted thinking about the form of an egg. A boiled egg with dry bread is doubly tasteless. I make this meaningless remark to myself every day and don't know why.

Brian Keenan

Letters and diaries

Reading letters or diaries can be a very direct and fascinating way of entering into a writer's experience. They are informal autobiography, not necessarily written for publication. We are an audience the writer may never have imagined, reading material that was intended to be private. There is often controversy when writers die, or even during their lifetimes, about whether their personal diaries or letters should be made available for other people to read. However, some writers (if they are sure of their own importance!) do expect that their 'private' papers will be made public.

The following brief extract is from another account of the experience of captivity, by Oscar Wilde, who was imprisoned in 1895 for homosexual 'offences'. He wrote at length about his experiences in a 'letter' explaining his actions and motives, and expressing his feelings of betrayal to his young friend Lord Alfred Douglas, who was planning to publish some of the intimate letters he had received from Wilde. It seems likely that he expected this letter to be published, and it later became known as *De profundis*, which means 'Out of the depths', echoing Psalm 130, which is a cry for God's help and forgiveness in a time of sorrow and despair.

From *De Profundis*

All this took place in the early part of November of the year before last. A great river of life flows between me and a date so distant. Hardly, if at all, can you see across so wide a waste. But to me it seems to have occurred, I will not say yesterday, but to-day. Suffering is one very long moment. We cannot divide it by seasons. We can only record its moods, and chronicle their return. With us time itself does not progress, it revolves. It seems to circle round one centre of pain. The paralysing immobility of a life every circumstance of which is regulated after an unchangeable pattern, so that we eat and drink and lie down and pray, or kneel at least for prayer, according to the inflexible laws of an iron formula: this immobile quality, that makes each dreadful day in the very minutest detail like its brother, seems to communicate itself to those external forces, the very essence of whose existence is ceaseless change. Of seed-time or harvest, of the reapers bending over the corn, or the grape gatherers threading through the vines, of the grass in the orchard made white with broken blossoms or strewn with fallen fruit: of these we know nothing, and can know nothing.

For us there is only one season, the season of sorrow. The very sun and moon seem taken from us. Outside, the day may be blue and gold, but the light that creeps down through the thickly-muffled glass of the small iron-barred window beneath which one sits is grey and niggard. It is always twilight in one's cell, as it is always twilight in one's heart. And in the sphere of thought, no less than in the sphere of time, motion is no more. The thing that you personally have forgotten, or can easily forget, is happening to me now, and will happen to me again tomorrow. Remember this, and you will be able to understand a little of why I am writing, and in this manner writing…

Oscar Wilde

Activity

Re-read the extracts by Brian Keenan and Oscar Wilde on the theme of imprisonment, making notes on the ways in which they can be connected or contrasted.

Documentary writing

Sometimes authors use recorded facts and figures and the words of writers, experts, or witnesses (i.e. 'documentation') to produce their own interpretation of events. The maker of a television documentary works in a similar way.

In *Hiroshima*, John Hersey traces the experiences of six survivors of one of the first atomic bombs, dropped by the Americans on the Japanese cities of Hiroshima and Nagasaki at the end of the Second World War. He introduces each person individually, describing everyday details of their lives very precisely so that we can picture them in the moments before the bomb fell. He then goes on to track each of them through the year that follows. He originally wrote the book in 1946, only one year after the destruction of the city. Forty years later, he returned to Hiroshima to find out how the same six people had coped with the aftermath of the catastrophe, and added a further chapter to his book. This extract from the opening of the book begins the tale of Toshiko Sasaki.

Hiroshima

Miss Toshiko Sasaki, the East Asia Tin Works clerk… got up at three o'clock in the morning on the day the bomb fell. There was extra housework to do. Her eleven-month-old brother, Akio, had come down the day before with a serious stomach upset; her mother had taken him to the Tamura Paediatric Hospital and was staying there with him. Miss Sasaki, who was about twenty, had to cook breakfast for her father, a brother, a sister, and herself, and – since the hospital, because of the war, was unable to provide food – to prepare a whole day's meals for her mother and the baby, in time for her father, who worked in a factory making rubber earplugs for artillery crews, to take the food by on his way to the plant. When she had finished and had cleaned and put away the cooking things, it was nearly seven. The family lived in Koi, and she had a forty-five minute trip to the tin works, in the section of town called Kannonmachi. She was in charge of the personnel records in the factory…

Miss Sasaki... sat down at her desk. She was quite far from the windows, which were off to her left, and behind her were a couple of tall bookcases containing all the books of the factory library, which the personnel department had organized. She settled herself at her desk, put some things in a drawer, and shifted papers. She thought that before she began to make entries in her lists of new employees, discharges, and departures for the Army, she would chat for a moment with the girl at her right. Just as she turned her head away from the windows, the room was filled with a blinding light. She was paralyzed by fear, fixed still in her chair for a long moment (the plant was 1,600 yards from the centre [of the explosion]). Everything fell, and Miss Sasaki lost consciousness. The ceiling dropped suddenly and the wooden floor above collapsed in splinters and the people up there came down and the roof above them gave way; but principally and first of all, the bookcases right behind her swooped forward and the contents threw her down, with her left leg horribly twisted and breaking underneath her. There, in the tin factory, in the first moment of the atomic age, a human being was crushed by books.

John Hersey

Journalism

You may have noticed that several of the prose texts in this chapter deal with disturbing or disastrous events. This seems particularly true when we look at journalistic writing, because typically it focuses on 'bad news'. Indeed, the exposure of injustice or suffering seems to inspire journalists to produce their most powerful work. Journalism can, of course, be very humorous, satirical, or entertaining, but it is often intended to alert us to some form of wrongdoing.

John Pilger, an Australian journalist, has written bitingly about injustices all over the world. He has a particular concern to expose the ways in which the media and propaganda are used to distort people's perception of events. In the extract below, he shows how the language used by those responsible for bombing campaigns in Vietnam and in the First Gulf War blunted people's awareness of the human suffering involved.

Video Nasties

In 1972, I watched American B52s bombing southern Vietnam, near the ashes of a town called An Loc. From a distance of two miles, I could see three ladders of bombs curved in the sky; and, as each rung reached the ground, there was a plume of fire and a sound that welled and rippled, then quaked the ground beneath me.

This was Operation Arc Light, described by the Pentagon as 'high performance denial interdiction, with minimized collateral damage': jargon that echoes today. The B52s were unseen above the clouds; between them they dropped seventy tons of explosives in a 'long-box' pattern that extended several miles. Almost everything that moved inside the box was deemed 'redundant'.

On inspection, a road that connected two villages had been replaced by craters, one of them almost a quarter of a mile wide. Houses had vanished. There was no life; cooking pots lay strewn in a ditch, no doubt dropped in haste. People a hundred yards from the point of contact had not left even their scorched shadows, which the dead had left at Hiroshima. Visitors to Indo-China today are shocked by the moonscape of craters in Vietnam, Laos and Cambodia, where people lived.

The B52s now operating over Iraq are the same type of thirty-year-old aircraft. We are told they are bombing Saddam Hussein's Republican Guard, and the 'outskirts' of Baghdad. Before the introduction in Vietnam of military euphemisms designed to make palatable to Congress new hi-tech 'anti-people' weapons, the term used was carpet-bombing. This was vivid and accurate, for these aircraft lay carpets of death, killing and destroying comprehensively and indiscriminately. This is what they were built to do; and that is what they are no doubt doing in a country where most people neither have shelters nor are 'dug in'. The other night, on television, a senior ex-RAF officer included the current B52 raids in his description of 'pinpoint strikes... part of the extraordinary precision work of the Allies'. John Major and Tom King constantly refer to this 'remarkable precision' and, by clear implication, the equally remarkable humanitarian benefits this brings to the innocent people of Iraq, although further information about these benefits is curiously unforthcoming.

... The principal weapons used against Iraq, such as the Tomahawk cruise missile, have a 'circular error probability'. This means they are targeted to fall within a circle, like a dart landing anywhere on a dart board. They do not have to hit, or even damage, the bull's-eye to be considered 'effective' or 'successful'. Some have hit the bull's-eye – the Tomahawk that demolished the Ministry of Defence building in Baghdad is the most famous – but many, if not most, clearly have not. What else have they hit? What else is within the circle? People, maybe? The numerous autocues say nothing. General Powell has also referred to 'minimized collateral damage'. Like 'circular error probability' this term was invented in Vietnam. It means dead civilians: men, women, and children. Their number is 'minimized', of course...

John Pilger

Activity

1 Look at paragraphs 1 to 3. In what ways do Pilger's language, style and attitude in the second paragraph differ from those of the first and third? What is his aim here? Find other examples of this in the text.

2 Pilger talks about 'military euphemisms'. A *euphemism* is a word or phrase which we use when stating the truth baldly would be too painful or embarrassing. Examine the words and phrases in quotation marks – the official jargon. What is their purpose and effect? Devise substitute phrases which would express the truth more graphically. Create some euphemisms of your own for the effects of warfare.

3 'The... remarkable humanitarian benefits this brings to the innocent people of Iraq, although further information about these benefits is curiously unforthcoming.' How would you describe Pilger's tone in this extract? Find other examples in the text to support your views.

4 Make notes on both the Hersey and Pilger texts, then write a short essay in response to the question which follows.

John Pilger and John Hersey are both concerned about the civilian casualties of modern warfare, although they tackle the theme in very different ways. Write about the connections and contrasts between the two extracts, examining in detail the ways in which each writer treats the subject. Consider:

- the writers' aims and attitudes

- their use of language

- the tone of the writing

- the 'focus' of each extract: are we seeing a 'close-up' or a 'distance-shot'? Why might this be significant?

- the effect each piece has on you as a reader – and why.

Literary and cultural criticism

One more type of prose writing you are likely to come across in the course of your studies is critical writing, in which authors or scholars discuss the work of their fellow writers, past and present. This sort of writing can vary widely, from the detailed analytical comment and debate you might expect to find in critical books by respected academics, to the highly opinionated or even wildly judgemental views you might find expressed in newspaper columns or reviews.

One interesting angle is to look at reviews or critical material written close to the time when a text was published. This can throw light not only on the text itself, but also on what was going on and how people thought at that time. Some writers also include literature in commentaries on the social and cultural life of a particular time. They may discuss how literature reflects politics, philosophy, or artistic trends.

There is much more on how to approach this type of writing in Section III, chapters 8–11.

Activity

Read the two extracts A and B which follow. They are both examples of critical writing on Dickens's *Hard Times*, one of the novels featured earlier in this chapter. With a partner, discuss the extracts and any similarities and differences between them.

- To what extent is each piece an expression of the author's opinions?
- What do you learn from each extract about Dickens, his ideas or his style?
- What do you learn from each extract about the Victorian era?

A The first extract is by the highly influential Victorian writer and philosopher, John Ruskin, a contemporary of Dickens. It is taken from a major political and philosophical essay which was first published in the *Cornhill Magazine* in 1860, six years after the publication of *Hard Times*.

Unto This Last

Ad Valorem

The essential value and truth of Dickens's writings have been unwisely lost sight of by many thoughtful persons, merely because he presents his truth with some colour of caricature. Unwisely, because Dickens's caricature, though often gross, is never mistaken. Allowing for his manner of telling them, the things he tells us are always true. I wish that he could think it right to limit his brilliant exaggeration to works written only for public amusement; and when he takes up a subject of high national importance, such as that which he handled in *Hard Times,* that he would use severer and more accurate analysis. The usefulness of that work (to my mind, in several respects, the greatest he has written) is with many persons seriously diminished because Mr Bounderby is a dramatic monster, instead of a characteristic example of a worldly master; and Stephen Blackpool a dramatic perfection, instead of a characteristic example of an honest workman. But let us not lose the use of Dickens's wit and insight, because he chooses to speak in a circle of stage fire. He is entirely right in his main drift and purpose in every book he has written; and all of them, but especially *Hard Times,* should be studied with close and earnest care by persons interested in social questions. They will find much that is partial, and, because partial, apparently unjust; but if they examine all the evidence on the other side, which Dickens seems to overlook, it will appear, after all their trouble, that his view was the finally right one, grossly and sharply told.

John Ruskin

- -

B   In this passage, the major twentieth-century critic F.R. Leavis comments on a passage which is the continuation of the opening chapter of *Hard Times*, which we looked at earlier (page 7). It is from a controversial essay published in 1948. He quotes a considerable amount from the text here, which allows you to see what he is talking about.

Hard Times: An Analytic Note

Dickens's art, while remaining that of the great popular entertainer, has in *Hard Times,* as he renders his full critical vision, a stamina, a flexibility combined with consistency, and a depth that he seems to have had little credit for. Take that opening scene in the school-room:

'Girl number twenty,' said Mr Gradgrind, squarely pointing with his square forefinger, 'I don't know that girl. Who is that girl?'

'Sissy Jupe, sir,' explained number twenty, blushing, standing up, and curtsying.

'Sissy is not a name,' said Mr Gradgrind. 'Don't call yourself Sissy. Call yourself Cecilia.'

'It's father as calls me Sissy, sir,' returned the young girl in a trembling voice, and with another curtsy.

'Then he has no business to do it,' said Mr Gradgrind. 'Tell him he mustn't. Cecilia Jupe. Let me see. What is your father?'

'He belongs to the horse-riding, if you please, sir.'

Mr Gradgrind frowned, and waved off the objectionable calling with his hand.

'We don't want to know anything about that here. You mustn't tell us about that here. Your father breaks horses, don't he?'

'If you please, sir, when they can get any to break, they do break horses in the ring, sir.'

'You mustn't tell us about the ring here. Very well, then. Describe your father as a horse-breaker. He doctors sick horses, I dare say?'

'Oh, yes, sir!'

'Very well, then. He is a veterinary surgeon, a farrier, and a horse-breaker. Give me your definition of a horse.'

(Sissy Jupe thrown into the greatest alarm by this demand.)

'Girl number twenty unable to define a horse!' said Mr Gradgrind, for the general benefit of all the little pitchers. 'Girl number twenty possessed of no facts in reference to one of the commonest of animals! Some boy's definition of a horse. Bitzer, yours.'…

'Quadruped. Gramnivorous. Forty teeth, namely, twenty-four grinders, four eye-teeth, and twelve incisive. Sheds coat in the spring; in marshy countries, sheds hoofs too. Hoofs hard, but requiring to be shod with iron. Age known by marks in mouth.' Thus (and much more) Bitzer.

[D. H.] Lawrence himself, protesting against harmful tendencies in education, never made the point more tellingly. Sissy has been brought up among horses, and among people whose livelihood depends upon understanding horses but 'we don't want to know anything about that here'. Such knowledge isn't real knowledge. Bitzer, the model pupil, on the button's being pressed, promptly vomits up the genuine article, 'Quadruped. Gramnivorous', etc; and 'Now, girl number twenty, you know what a horse is'. The irony, pungent enough locally, is richly developed in the subsequent action. Bitzer's aptness has its evaluative comment in his career. Sissy's incapacity to acquire this kind of 'fact' or formula, her unaptness for education, is manifested to us, on the other hand, as part and parcel of her sovereign and indefeasible humanity: it is the virtue that makes it impossible for her to understand, or acquiesce in, an ethos for which she is 'girl number twenty', or to think of any other human being as a unit for arithmetic.

This kind of ironic method might seem to commit the author to very limited kinds of effect. In *Hard Times,* however, it associates quite congruously, such is the flexibility of Dickens's art, with very different methods; it cooperates in a truly dramatic and profoundly poetic whole. Sissy Jupe, who might be taken here for a merely conventional *persona,* has already, as a matter of fact, been established in a potently symbolic role: she is part of the poetically-creative operation of Dickens's genius in *Hard Times*. Here is a passage I omitted from the middle of the excerpt quoted above.

The square finger, moving here and there, lighted suddenly on Bitzer, perhaps because he chanced to sit in the same ray of sun-light which, darting in at one of the bare windows of the intensely white-washed room, irradiated Sissy. For, the boys and girls sat on the face of an inclined plane in two compact bodies, divided up the centre by a narrow interval; and Sissy, being at the corner of a row on the sunny side, came in for the beginning of a sunbeam, of which Bitzer, being at the corner of a row on the other side, a few rows in advance, caught the end. But, whereas the girl was so dark-eyed and dark-haired that she seemed to receive a deeper and more lustrous colour from the sun when it shone upon her, the boy was so light-eyed and light-haired that the self-same rays appeared to draw out of him what little colour he ever possessed. His cold eyes would hardly have been eyes, but for the short ends of lashes which, by bringing them into immediate contrast with something paler than themselves, expressed their form. His short-cropped hair might have been a mere continuation of the sandy freckles on his forehead and face. His skin was so unwholesomely deficient in the natural tinge, that he looked as though, if he were cut, he would bleed white.

There is no need to insist on the force – representative of Dickens's art in general in *Hard Times* – with which the moral and spiritual differences are rendered here in terms of sensation, so that the symbolic intention emerges out of metaphor and the vivid evocation of the concrete. What may, perhaps, be emphasized is that Sissy stands for vitality as well as goodness – they are seen, in fact, as one; she is generous, impulsive life, finding self-fulfilment in self-forgetfulness – all that is the antithesis of calculating self-interest. There is an essentially Laurentian suggestion about the way in which 'the dark-eyed and dark-haired' girl, contrasting with Bitzer, seemed to receive a 'deeper and more lustrous colour from the sun', so opposing the life that is lived freely and richly from the deep instinctive and emotional springs to the thin-blooded, quasi-mechanical product of Gradgrindery.

F.R. Leavis

2 Studying Poetry

Objectives

- To identify ways in which you can approach the reading of poetry
- To explore ways of writing about poetry
- To consider some of the features to look for in analysing poems
- To prepare for studying set poetry texts
- To prepare for encountering 'unseen' poetry texts

What is poetry?

The question of what exactly poetry is – what marks it out as being different from prose – is a question that poets, writers, philosophers, and critics have, over the centuries, tried to answer. In fact, there are almost as many 'definitions' of poetry as there are poets. Here are some of them:

> Poetry is the spontaneous overflow of powerful feelings: it takes its origin from emotion recollected in tranquillity.

> *William Wordsworth*

> Poetry is the sound of human speech at those times when it comes closest to the speech of angels and the speech of animals.

> *John Wain*

> Poetry: the best words in the best order.

> *Samuel Taylor Coleridge*

> Poetry is not a turning loose of emotion, but an escape from emotion; it is not the expression of personality, but an escape from personality.

> *T.S. Eliot*

You will have noticed how these 'definitions' present quite different views of what poetry actually is. Think about each of these views and what these writers, drawn from different centuries, are saying about the nature of poetry. Through your study of English you will have come into contact with a variety of poetry, perhaps ranging from the works of Chaucer and Shakespeare to those of twentieth-century writers. Are these views borne out by your experiences of poetry so far?

Activity

Make brief notes on how accurately each of these descriptions of poetry sums up your own views of poetry.

Reading poetry

The study of poetry is a central element in all AS or A level English Literature specifications. Whether you are studying a poetry set text, looking at the poetry of a Shakespeare play, writing on poetry for coursework or preparing for examinations involving 'unseen' texts, you will engage in detailed study of various poems. Even though the outcome of your work might be presented in different forms, the skills, techniques, and approaches that you need to use are essentially the same.

It is true that the poetry elements of AS and A level English Literature present particular challenges. For a number of reasons, some poetry is only fully accessible to us today if we carry out a certain amount of research such as looking up difficult words, phrases, and references. However, 'responding to poetry' cannot be 'taught' (or learned, for that matter) in the same way that some subjects can. It is no good looking for some kind of 'secret formula' that you can apply to any poem. Although most poetry is written to be read by others, and in that sense carries a 'public' voice, it can also be an intensely individual medium of communication and the responses it can evoke can be equally intense and individual. Much poetry works in a very personal way and your response to a particular poem might not be the same as another person's. Words and images carry with them connotations that might trigger different responses in the minds of different people. So while it is often possible to say what a poem 'is about' in general terms, the only really genuine response is that 'personal response' that an individual reader feels.

This does not mean that 'anything goes', of course. For example, comments like 'I haven't a clue about this' or 'This means nothing to me' may be personal responses but they are not much good in terms of a 'literary' response. At AS or A level you will be required to give what the objectives describe as 'creative, informed and relevant responses to literary texts', and to 'explore connections and comparisons between different literary texts, informed by interpretations of other readers'.

In this section we will look at some of the things that you can do to find your way into and through a poem. Here are some general strategies for improving your understanding of poetry.

- Read as much as possible – become as familiar as possible with as wide a range of poetry as possible.
- Think about how language is used and make a note of any interesting features, lines, images, etc. that you come across in your reading of poetry.
- Think about the ideas contained in the poems you read.
- Read other people's responses to poetry – not as a substitute for forming your own views but as a 'broadening' influence. (These responses can be found in various study guides, articles in literary journals, or reviews in newspapers or critical works.) They might suggest things that had not occurred to you or they might stimulate your own thoughts if you disagree with their view.
- Read poems aloud – either in company or alone. Very often reading a poem aloud helps deepen understanding and it certainly gives you a greater insight into features such as tone and rhythm.
- Adopt a questioning attitude. Whenever you read a poem ask yourself questions about it. The three key questions to ask are: 'What is this poem about?'; 'How is it written?'; 'Why has the poet chosen to write the poem in this particular way?'
- If you are studying the work of an individual poet, reading beyond the set poems will help you to understand the particular poems you are working on.

Activity

Think of other strategies that you could use to help make your study of poetry more effective. It might be helpful to discuss your ideas with a partner and make a list of them.

Although there is no set formula that can be applied to poetry to produce the required response, there are certain features of poetry that you will need to be aware of in order to begin to appreciate how a poem 'works', i.e. what the poet does to achieve the desired effect on the reader. Different critical books may refer to them in slightly different terms but basically these are the key elements that combine to create the overall effect of a poem. You will, no doubt, be familiar with some or all of these already.

Activity

Consider each of these aspects of poetry. Discuss your ideas in a small group and write notes explaining what each means.

Using these aspects of poetry to answer questions on the poems you study is really just a more detailed way of asking those three basic questions that we have already mentioned: 'What is this poem about?'; 'How is it written?'; 'Why has the poet chosen to write it in this particular way?' Answering these three questions will take you to the heart of almost any poem.

However, although we may look at elements such as content, form, and imagery in order to study their particular contributions to a poem, in reality they are completely interrelated and interdependent. The overall effect (and effectiveness) of a poem is dependent on all the individual elements within it working in unity (or acting in discord with one another if that produces the effect that the poet wants).

Content and poetic voice

In simple terms the **content** of a poem is what it is all about – the ideas, themes, and storyline that it contains.

It is useful to begin a consideration of a poem by getting a general outline of what it is about. This is sometimes referred to as the **surface meaning** of the poem. Establishing this surface meaning will give you a framework on which to build the more detailed and complex ideas that form as your analysis of the poem develops. Sometimes it is possible to respond to a poem without fully understanding every word or phrase and sometimes meaning 'evolves' as you continue to study a poem. However, having an initial idea or impression of what a poem is about can be an important first step towards a fuller and more assured understanding.

When considering the content of a poem it is also important to identify the **poetic voice** of the poem. In other words, decide who the 'speaker' of the poem is. In many cases the poetic voice may well be the poet's, but it may be that the words of the poem are 'spoken' through a character that the poet has created or a narrator figure other than the poet. This happens in *The Canterbury Tales*, where usually a particular character is telling the tale. Geoffrey Chaucer (the writer) often then interrupts his character (his fictitious narrator) to address the reader.

Identifying the 'speaker' also helps to determine a number of other aspects of the poem such as tone, mood, and the overall intention behind the poem. The poetic voice could be the poet's genuine voice expressing a heartfelt emotion or it could be the voice of a narrator expressing a view or feeling that the poet may or may not share.

Activity

Look at this poem by Carol Ann Duffy. How does an awareness of the poetic voice here help you to form an impression of what the poet is saying?

Havisham

Beloved sweetheart bastard. Not a day since then
I haven't wished him dead. Prayed for it
so hard I've dark green pebbles for eyes,
ropes on the back of my hands I could strangle with.

Spinster. I stink and remember. Whole days
in bed cawing Nooooo at the wall; the dress
yellowing, trembling if I open the wardrobe;
the slewed mirror, full-length, her, myself, who did this

to me? Puce curses that are sounds not words.
Some nights better, the lost body over me,
my fluent tongue in its mouth in its ear
then down till I suddenly bite awake. Love's

hate behind a white veil; a red balloon bursting
in my face. Bang. I stabbed at a wedding-cake.
Give me a male corpse for a long slow honeymoon.
Don't think it's only the heart that b-b-b-breaks.

Carol Ann Duffy

- -

Although this poem is written in the first person, this is clearly not Duffy writing from her own viewpoint. Here she has adopted the imagined voice and persona of Miss Havisham, a character from Charles Dickens's novel, *Great Expectations*.

In that novel Miss Havisham has been jilted by her fiancé on her wedding day, an event which deeply affects her attitudes for the rest of her life.

In the poem Duffy captures the deep bitterness that Miss Havisham feels towards the man who betrayed her, while at the same time suggesting a hint of ambiguity in her feelings towards her ex-love in the antithetical description of him as her 'Beloved sweetheart bastard'.

Activity

1 Now read the following poems through carefully.

2 Before you discuss your ideas with anyone, write down your first thoughts on what each poem is about and on the poetic voice which each presents. Spend about ten minutes setting down your ideas.

3 Now join two or three other students in a small group. Each should read out their notes to the others as a starting point for discussion on the content and poetic voice of the poems.

4 Review your notes and make any changes or additions that you wish to make in the light of the discussion. Do you find any aspect of these poems difficult to explain? If so, can you say why?

Hitcher

I'd been tired, under
the weather, but the ansaphone kept screaming:
One more sick-note, mister, and you're finished. Fired.
I thumbed a lift to where the car was parked.
A Vauxhall Astra. It was hired.

I picked him up in Leeds.
He was following the sun to west from east
with just a toothbrush and the good earth for a bed. The truth,
he said, was blowin' in the wind,
or round the next bend.

I let him have it
on the top road out of Harrogate – once
with the head, then six times with the krooklok
in the face – and didn't even swerve.
I dropped it into third

and leant across
to let him out, and saw him in the mirror
bouncing off the kerb, then disappearing down the verge.
We were the same age, give or take a week.
He'd said he liked the breeze

to run its fingers
through his hair. It was twelve noon.
The outlook for the day was moderate to fair.
Stitch that, I remember thinking,
you can walk from there.

Simon Armitage

School Dinners

Why do I dream now, of people from school?
I am not old. They are not dead.
Yet warm before waking they surface, thin,
or in Janice's case, still fat.

　　　She dyed her hair
in red rat's tails; thought brash. She hitched her skirt,
her wide thighs wobbled. She was kind as silk.
One day, chattering, tipped salad cream
over her favourite pudding;

　　　did remember
to ask the boy's address, but found it false.
They left the seaside camp. She had a daughter,

who now, I think, must be the age
of Janice in my dream; when giggling still
she reached out for the cheap gold-coloured jug.

Eight people made that table. Who do I still know?
No one who could tell me how she lives,
cooking great Sunday dinners? married? happy?
My ignorance stays perfect as the moon
dropped, like a coin through a barley field,
drowned, in all the blue waste of the sky.

Sitting by my daughter in a car
borne smooth and cool, through tunnelled trees
it strikes me, quick as shivering, that when
they must end, yet I will see them there
small and clear, in the battered jug,
their mistakes; their tails of red hair.

Alison Brackenbury

The Village Schoolmaster

Beside yon straggling fence that skirts the way,
With blossomed furze unprofitably gay,
There, in his noisy mansion, skilled to rule,
The village master taught his little school;
A man severe he was, and stern to view,
I knew him well, and every truant knew;
Well had the boding tremblers learned to trace
The day's disasters in his morning face;
Full well they laughed, with counterfeited glee,
At all his jokes, for many a joke had he:
Full well the busy whisper, circling round,
Conveyed the dismal tidings when he frowned;
Yet he was kind, or, if severe in aught,
The love he bore to learning was in fault;
The village all declared how much he knew;
'Twas certain he could write, and cipher too;
Lands he could measure, terms and tides presage,
And even the story ran that he could gauge.

In arguing, too, the parson owned his skill,
For, even though vanquished, he could argue still;
While words of learned length and thundering sound
Amazed the gazing rustics ranged around;
And still they gazed, and still the wonder grew
That one small head could carry all he knew.

Oliver Goldsmith

Tone and mood

The effect that a poem has on the reader is very closely determined by the tone and mood that it creates. As we have already discussed, a poem contains a 'voice' and like any voice it can project a certain **tone** that gives the listener (or reader) certain messages. Obviously there are many different kinds of tone. The tone might be angry or reflective, melancholy or joyful, bitter or ironic. Just as the tone of voice in which someone speaks tells us a great deal about the way they feel, so the tone of the 'poetic voice' tells us a great deal about how the poet or the narrator of the poem feels.

The **mood**, on the other hand, although very closely connected with the tone, is not quite the same thing. When we refer to the mood of a poem we are really talking about the **atmosphere** that the poem creates. Very often tone and mood in a poem are closely linked and a certain tone produces a certain mood. For example, if the poet uses a melancholy tone it is unlikely that the mood of the poem will be bright and lively. Sometimes, though, the poet may quite deliberately use a tone that does not match the mood the poem creates in order to achieve a particular effect – underlining a certain irony, for example. The overall impact of a poem stems not only from the literal meaning of the words but from the tone and mood that they create. One of the most effective ways of recognizing the tone of a poem is to hear the poem read aloud.

Try reading poems out loud for yourself, experimenting with different ways of reading each particular poem. The more practice you get at reading poems aloud and the more you are able to hear others read them, the better able you will be to 'hear' poems in your mind when you read them to yourself. The tone of a poem can be communicated to the reader or listener in many ways and it is through being sensitive to the poet's tone that we can begin to understand the intention that lies behind the words.

Here are four well-known poems for you to consider.

Upon Westminster Bridge

Sept. 3, 1802

Earth has not anything to show more fair:
Dull would he be of soul who could pass by
A sight so touching in its majesty:
This City now doth, like a garment, wear
The beauty of the morning: silent, bare,
Ships, towers, domes, theatres, and temples lie
Open unto the fields, and to the sky;
All bright and glittering in the smokeless air.
Never did sun more beautifully steep
In his first splendour, valley, rock or hill;
Ne'er saw I, never felt, a calm so deep!
The river glideth at his own sweet will:

Dear God! the very houses seem asleep;
And all that mighty heart is lying still!

William Wordsworth

Engineers' Corner

*Why isn't there an Engineers' Corner in Westminster Abbey? In Britain we've always
made more fuss of a ballad than a blueprint... How many schoolchildren dream of
becoming great engineers?*

Advertisement placed in The Times by the Engineering Council

We make more fuss of ballads than of blueprints –
That's why so many poets end up rich,
While engineers scrape by in cheerless garrets.
Who needs a bridge or dam? Who needs a ditch?

Whereas the person who can write a sonnet
Has got it made. It's always been the way,
For everybody knows that we need poems
And everybody reads them every day.

Yes, life is hard if you choose engineering –
You're sure to need another job as well;
You'll have to plan your projects in the evenings
Instead of going out. It must be hell.

While well-heeled poets ride around in Daimlers,
You'll burn the midnight oil to earn a crust,
With no hope of a statue in the Abbey,
With no hope, even, of a modest bust.

No wonder small boys dream of writing couplets
And spurn the bike, the lorry and the train.
There's far too much encouragement for poets –
That's why this country's going down the drain.

Wendy Cope

The Windhover

To Christ our Lord

I caught this morning morning's minion, king-
    dom of daylight's dauphin, dapple-dawn-drawn Falcon, in his riding
    Of the rolling level underneath him steady air, and striding
High there, how he rung upon the rein of a wimpling wing
In his ecstasy! then off, off forth on swing,
    As a skate's heel sweeps smooth on a bow-bend: the hurl and gliding
    Rebuffed the big wind. My heart in hiding
Stirred for a bird, – the achieve of, the mastery of the thing!

Brute beauty and valour and act, oh, air, pride, plume, here
    Buckle! AND the fire that breaks from thee then, a billion
Times told lovelier, more dangerous, O my chevalier!

No wonder of it: sheer plod makes plough down sillion
Shine, and blue-bleak embers, ah my dear,
    Fall, gall themselves, and gash gold-vermilion.

Gerard Manley Hopkins

Frog Autumn

Summer grows old, cold-blooded mother.
The insects are scant, skinny.
In these palustral homes we only
Croak and wither.

Mornings dissipate in somnolence.
The sun brightens tardily
Among the pithless reeds. Flies fail us.
The fen sickens.

Frost drops even the spider. Clearly
The genius of plenitude
Houses himself elsewhere. Our folk thin
Lamentably.

Sylvia Plath

Activity

1 Read each of the poems through to yourself, deciding what sort of tone of voice you would use for each.

2 In a small group, take turns to read each poem out loud. If possible, record these readings.

3 Discuss the readings and make brief notes on the kind of tone that you think is most appropriate for each poem. Describe the kind of mood that is created in each.

4 Discuss the methods used by these poets to create a specific tone and mood.

Here are some ideas of how tone and mood can be created:

* through the loudness or softness of the voice speaking the poem
* through the rhythm that is created
* through the poet's choice of words
* through the emphasis placed on particular words or phrases
* through the breaks and pauses that the poet places in the poem (often the things which go unsaid can tell you a great deal).

Imagery

Essentially the true 'meaning' of a poem lies in the total effect that it has upon the reader. Very often that effect will stimulate a response which is not just a reaction to what the poet has to say, but which draws on the reader's own intellectual and emotional experience. Imagery can be of central importance in creating this response within the reader.

The concept of imagery is a very simple one and although it is used a good deal in poetic writing it is of course found in other kinds of writing too. An **image** is language used in such a way as to help us to see, hear, taste, feel, think about or generally understand more clearly or vividly what is being said or the impression that the writer wishes to convey.

Images can work in several ways in the mind of the reader. On a simple level an image can be used literally to describe something. For example, in *Upon Westminster Bridge* (see page 48) the lines '... silent, bare/ Ships, towers, domes, theatres, and temples lie/ Open unto the fields, and to the sky;/ All bright and glittering in the smokeless air' create a literal image in our minds of the scene that Wordsworth wishes to convey.

Often, though, images are **non-literal** or **figurative**: the thing being described is compared to something else with which it has something in common to make the description more vivid to the reader. You will, no doubt, already be familiar with images, such as similes and metaphors, which work in this way. However, just in case you need it, here is a reminder of the difference between the two, along with a definition of personification.

The simile

Similes are easy to spot because they make the comparison quite clear, often by using the words 'as' or 'like'. For example, looking back at *Upon Westminster Bridge* once more, the lines 'This City now doth, like a garment, wear/ The beauty of the morning...' simply but effectively convey a sense of the beauty of the scene which 'clothes' the city but which also serves to conceal the less attractive aspects of the city which lie beneath the 'garment'.

The metaphor

In some ways a metaphor is like a simile in that it too creates a comparison. However, it is less direct than the simile in that it does not use 'as' or 'like' to create the comparison. Often the metaphor describes the subject as *being* the thing to which it is compared. For example, Wordsworth concludes *Upon Westminster Bridge* with the line: 'And all that mighty heart is lying still!'. Literally, of course, the city is not a heart, but metaphorically speaking it can be seen as the 'heart' of the country, the capital city, and the centre of government.

Personification

Personification occurs when poets attribute human qualities or actions to an inanimate object or abstract idea. For example, in *Upon Westminster Bridge*, Wordsworth speaks of the river as if it were a living person: 'The river glideth at his own sweet will'.

Aural imagery

Some kinds of images rely not upon the 'pictures' that they create in the mind of the reader but on the effect that they have on the ear, or a combination of both.

Alliteration involves the repetition of the same consonant sound, usually at the beginning of each word, over several words together. Hopkins uses this technique extensively in *The Windhover* (page 49), and much of the poem's impact lies in the effect that the repetition of the sounds creates on the reader's ear as well as the mind's eye.

Another kind of aural device is **assonance**. This involves the repetition of a vowel sound to achieve a particular kind of effect. The long, drawn out 'o' sounds in the first line of *Frog Autumn* (see page 50), 'Summer grows old, cold-blooded mother', create an impression of lethargy and lack of vitality as summer passes and winter approaches.

A third aural device is that of **onomatopoeia**. This refers to words that by their sound reflect their meaning. On a simple level words like 'bang' or 'thud' actually sound like the noises they describe. For example, Duffy uses this in *Havisham* (page 45): 'a red balloon bursting/ in my face. Bang.'

It must be stressed, however, that the important thing is not so much to be able to spot the different kinds of images that might be present in a poem but to understand why the poet has used a particular image and be able to see how it works in the mind of the reader. Being able to say 'the poet uses alliteration in stanza three' is of no value in terms of the critical appreciation of a poem, but being able to show what the alliteration contributes to the overall effect of the poem is valuable.

For more on these individual forms of imagery see the Glossary, page 329.

Activity

1 Read the poem below and list five or six images that Hughes uses. Make brief notes on what these images mean to you, what they make you think about or anything that you find striking about them.

2 Join with two or three other students and compare your ideas. Decide together the meaning of the key images and their effects in the poem.

3 Write a short essay (about two pages in length) outlining your own thoughts and responses to the poet's use of imagery here.

Wind

This house has been far out at sea all night,
The woods crashing through darkness, the booming hills,
Winds stampeding the fields under the window
Floundering black astride and blinding wet

Till day rose; then under an orange sky
The hills had new places, and wind wielded
Blade-light, luminous black and emerald,
Flexing like the lens of a mad eye.

At noon I scaled along the house-side as far as
The coal-house door. Once I looked up –
Through the brunt wind that dented the balls of my eyes
The tent of the hills drummed and strained its guyrope,

The fields quivering, the skyline a grimace,
At any second to bang and vanish with a flap:
The wind flung a magpie away and a black-
Back gull bent like an iron bar slowly. The house

Rang like some fine green goblet in the note
That any second would shatter it. Now deep
In chairs, in front of the great fire, we grip
Our hearts and cannot entertain book, thought,

Or each other. We watch the fire blazing,
And feel the roots of the house move, but sit on,
Seeing the window tremble to come in,
Hearing the stones cry out under the horizons.

Ted Hughes

Rhyme

Rhyme can make an important contribution to the 'musical quality' of a poem, and like rhythm it affects the sound and the overall impact of the piece. The system of rhyme within a poem, or **rhyme scheme**, can influence this effect in a variety of ways. It might act as a unifying influence and draw a poem together, or it could give a poem an incantatory quality or add emphasis to particular elements of the vocabulary (or diction). There are various kinds of rhymes and rhyme schemes and although most rhymes work on the basis of the rhyme occurring at the end of a line, some occur within the line. These are called **internal rhymes**.

In the same way that rhythm in a poem often follows a recognized pattern, so does rhyme. Working out the rhyme scheme is quite a straightforward business and is done by indicating lines that rhyme together through giving them the same letter of the alphabet. As an example, read the short poem that follows.

Eight O'Clock

He stood, and heard the steeple	a
Sprinkle the quarters on the morning town.	b
One, two, three, four, to market-place and people	a
It tossed them down.	b
Strapped, noosed, nighing his hour,	c
He stood and counted them and cursed his luck;	d
And then the clock collected in the tower	c
Its strength, and struck.	d

A.E. Housman

- -

Housman uses an *abab*, *cdcd* rhyme scheme, i.e. alternate lines rhyme within stanzas. Let us now consider some examples of traditional forms and patterns. Pairs of lines that rhyme are called **couplets** or **rhyming couplets**. Two lines that rhyme together and that are written in iambic pentameter (see page 56) are known as **heroic couplets**. Sometimes a whole poem can consist entirely of rhyming couplets or the couplet can be used as part of a larger rhyme scheme. A Shakespearean sonnet uses the couplet to draw the poem to an end, as in Shakespeare's Sonnet *XVIII*, for example:

So long as men can breathe or eyes can see,
So long lives this, and this gives life to thee.

Rhyming couplets tend to create a bold, assertive effect and strongly convey a point or message. They can also be used for comic effect, to deflate an argument or character.

The **quatrain** is a set of four rhyming lines. Usual rhyme schemes are *abab*, *abcb*, *aaaa, or abba*. In *Jerusalem*, William Blake uses the *abcb* scheme:

And did those feet in ancient time
Walk upon England's mountains green?
And was the holy Lamb of God
On England's pleasant pastures seen?

The quatrain is a flexible form that is used to create many effects but often, as here, it produces a sense of unity within compact and regular stanzas.

A **sestet** is a six-line stanza that can be arranged in a number of ways. The last six lines of an Italian sonnet (see page 60) are also called the sestet. In '*The lowest trees have tops, the ant her gall*', Edward Dyer uses a regular *ababcc* rhyme scheme:

> The lowest trees have tops, the ant her gall,
> The fly her spleen, the little spark his heat;
> The slender hairs cast shadows, though but small,
> And bees have stings, although they be not great;
> Seas have their source, and so have shallow springs:
> And love is love, in beggars and in kings.

The **octave** is an eight-line stanza and can be constructed in a number of ways. It can be formed by linking two quatrains together or it can have a rhyme scheme that integrates all eight lines. It is also the name given to the first eight lines of an Italian sonnet.

As with all the elements of a poem though, the important thing is not to be able to spot the use of rhymes or even to work out the rhyme scheme but to ask yourself: 'Why has the poet used rhyme in this way and what does it contribute, together with all the other features, to the overall impact of the poem?'. The answer to this question is what really matters.

Effects of rhyme

Here are some effects that rhyme might have on a poem.

- It can make a poem sound pleasing to the ear and perhaps add a musical quality. Conversely, it can create a jarring effect.

- It could serve to emphasize certain words – very often the words that rhyme are given a certain prominence.

- It can act as a kind of unifying influence on the poem, drawing lines and stanzas together through the pattern it imposes on them.

- It can give a poem an incantatory or 'ritualistic' feel.

- It can influence the rhythm of the verse.

- It can give a sense of finality – the rhyming couplet is often used to give a sense of 'ending'.

- It can exert a subconscious effect on the reader, drawing together certain words or images, affecting the sound, or adding emphasis in some way.

Activity

1 Read this poem carefully to yourself and write down your initial ideas on how the poet uses rhyme and with what effect.

2 In a small group, compare your ideas. Discuss how you think the use of rhyme affects the poem and what it contributes to its overall impact.

Ending

The love we thought would never stop
now cools like a congealing chop.
The kisses that were hot as curry
are bird-pecks taken in a hurry.

The hands that held electric charges
now lie inert as four moored barges.
The feet that ran to meet a date
are running slow and running late.
The eyes that shone and seldom shut
are victims of a power cut.
The parts that then transmitted joy
are now reserved and cold and coy.
Romance, expected once to stay,
has left a note saying GONE AWAY.

Gavin Ewart

Rhythm

When you were thinking about definitions of poetry at the beginning of this unit you might well have thought about rhythm as being one of the features that can set poetry apart from other kinds of writing. Although it is by no means true of all poems, one of the basic differences between a poem and a piece of prose is that a poem can contain some form of regular beat or rhythm.

Often this sense of rhythm can exert a profound influence on the overall effect of the poem giving it its feeling of 'movement' and life. The poet can use rhythm to create many different effects or to emphasize a certain aspect or idea in the poem. Very often it is also an important contributing factor to the mood or atmosphere and to what is sometimes referred to as the 'musical quality' of a poem. Music can be gentle and flowing, harsh or discordant, stilted and uneven in phrasing, or regular in tempo. It can have a rhythm that reflects a serious or solemn mood or a rhythm that suggests the comic or absurd. Just the same is true about the rhythms of poetry.

Here are some examples of the ways in which poets use language to create varying rhythms.

Syllable stress. The English language possesses natural rhythms which are built into it and which we use automatically every time we pronounce words. For example, if we think of a word like 'delicately', it comes quite naturally to us to stress the first syllable and not the second. Not to do so would be to mispronounce the word. Poets often use these natural rhythms within words to help contribute to the overall rhythmic effect.

Emphatic stress. Poets sometimes choose to place emphasis on a particular word or phrase in order to achieve a particular result. The stress might be shifted to reinforce a particular tone or sometimes to affect the meaning. For example, think about Wordsworth's famous line 'I wandered lonely as a cloud' and how different emphases can change the overall effect:

I wandered lonely as a cloud	I *wandered* lonely as a cloud
I wandered *lonely* as a cloud	I wandered lonely as a *cloud*

The natural rhythm of a phrase will often tell you what is right for the poem.

Phrasing and punctuation. The rhythm of a poem (or any other piece of writing) can be influenced by factors such as word order and length of phrases or sentences, and these in turn can be influenced by the choice of punctuation marks, line and stanza breaks, and use of repetition.

Metre. Technically speaking, the whole notion of rhythm in poetry is closely tied up with the idea of metre. This concept originated from the principles of classical

Greek and Latin verse and was adopted by English poets from early times. Such principles stated that a line of verse should follow a precise and regular pattern in terms of the number of syllables it contained and the stress pattern that it used. This pattern was then repeated throughout the poem. Regular patterns of these stressed and unstressed syllables are called **metres** (see also 'syllable stress', above).

On a basic level the pattern created by a regular metre can be seen in nursery rhymes and limericks. For example, each stanza of *Mary Had a Little Lamb* follows this pattern:

> Mary had a little lamb,
> Its fleece was white as snow.
> And everywhere that Mary went
> The lamb was sure to go.

In identifying the metre of a poem the first thing to do is to establish how the rhythm pattern is made up. To help do this the syllables are divided up into groups of two or three (depending on the particular pattern) and each of these groups is called a **foot**. The number of **feet** in a line can vary. Here are the main patterns:

one foot – monometer	five feet – pentameter
two feet – dimeter	six feet – hexameter
three feet – trimeter	seven feet – heptameter
four feet – tetrameter	eight feet – octameter

The process of identifying the metre is called **scansion**. In scansion a / or a — above a word indicates a stressed syllable, while a ˘ is used to denote an unstressed syllable, and feet are divided up using vertical lines |. (A double vertical line ‖ indicates a **caesura**, which simply means a brief pause in the middle of a line of poetry.) For example, look at these lines by John Keats:

> When I | have fears | that I | may cease | to be
> Before | my pen | hath gleaned | my teem | ing brain,

Each line consists of five metrical feet. Each foot consists of an unstressed and a stressed syllable. A foot that is made up in this way (˘/) is called an **iambic foot (iamb)** and a line that is made up of five feet is called a **pentameter**. These lines, therefore are written using a metrical form called **iambic pentameter**.

If you were to look at the whole of this poem you would find that Keats also uses a rhyme scheme. Verse which is written in iambic pentameter and which does not use a rhyme scheme is called blank verse. This is one of the most frequently used forms in English poetry and it has been estimated that three-quarters of all English verse is written in **blank verse**. One of its attractions is that it is a metrical form that very closely follows the patterns of natural speech and for this reason was used as the staple form by dramatists such as Shakespeare as well as by poets such as Milton and Wordsworth. It also can capture a reflective, thoughtful mood. The following example shows Wordsworth's use of the form as he describes skating on a frozen lake as a boy.

The Prelude

Book 1 (1850)

And in the frosty season, when the sun
Was set, and visible for many a mile
The cottage windows blazed through twilight gloom,
I heeded not their summons: happy time

It was indeed for all of us – for me
It was a time of rapture! Clear and loud
The village clock tolled six, – I wheeled about,
Proud and exulting like an untired horse
That cares not for his home. All shod with steel,
We hissed along the polished ice in games
Confederate, imitative of the chase
And woodland pleasures, – the resounding horn,
The pack loud chiming, and the hunted hare.
So through the darkness and the cold we flew,
And not a voice was idle; with the din,
Smitten, the precipices rang aloud;
The leafless trees and every icy crag
Tinkled like iron; while far distant hills
Into the tumult sent an alien sound
Of melancholy not unnoticed, while the stars
Eastward were sparkling clear, and in the west
The orange sky of evening died away.

William Wordsworth

- -

Although the iambic foot is the most common form there are other syllable patterns which poets use to create different effects. For example, the **trochaic foot (trochee)** consists of a stressed syllable followed by an unstressed one (/˘). A well-known poem which makes use of the trochaic foot or trochee is Blake's *The Tyger*.

Tyger! | Tyger! | burning | bright
In the | forests | of the | night

One of the effects of the trochaic metre is that the stressed first syllable adds emphasis and power to the words.

The **dactylic foot (dactyl)** consists of a stressed syllable followed by two unstressed ones (/˘˘) as in Alfred Lord Tennyson's *The Charge of the Light Brigade*:

Half a league, | half a league,
Half a league | onward

The dactylic metre reflects the rhythm of the horse at a gallop, giving a kind of 'drumming of hooves' feel to the poem. With its two unstressed syllables following the stressed one, this metre can also be used to create a sad, reflective, sometimes heavy mood.

The **anapaestic foot (anapaest)** consists of two unstressed syllables followed by a stressed one (˘˘/) while the **spondaic foot (spondee)** simply has two stressed syllables (//). Thomas Hardy uses both in his poem *A Wife Waits*.

Will's | at the dance | in the Club | -room below,
  Where | the tall liqu | or cups foam;
I | on the pave | ment up here | by the Bow,
  Wait, wait, | to | steady | him home.

The anapaests here create a sense of movement, and perhaps underlying tension, reflecting the wayward husband's revelry, whereas the spondee at the beginning of the final line gives a sense of the wife's patience and resignation as she waits to help her drunken husband home. Note how the reversal of the rhythm pattern at the end reflects the husband's return.

Twentieth-century poets have tended to move away from strict metrical forms but metre can still be an important element in modern poetry. By its nature though, metre is a mechanical and repetitive device which often is at variance with the natural rhythms that a poem may contain. Few poets stick religiously to the metrical pattern that they adopt and poetry should always be read according to the natural rhythms of the language rather than its metrical plan.

Remember when you are writing about a poem that identifying its metrical pattern is of little value in itself. You will gain little reward in an exam for simply mentioning the metre of a poem. The key thing is that you are able to say what it contributes to the effect of the poem overall. Don't worry if you can't remember the technical terms – the main thing is that you are able to describe what is happening. Technical terms are a kind of shorthand way of doing this, but they are by no means essential. What matters is your understanding of how the poem works as a piece of writing.

Activity

Read through this poem by Hardy several times. Try to get a feel of the rhythm pattern. You could try tapping it out if this helps. Try to describe the kind of rhythm pattern that Hardy uses. What kind of 'feel' do you think it gives to the poem? Write a short description of the effect that both rhyme and rhythm create in *The Voice*.

The Voice

Woman much missed, how you call to me, call to me,
Saying that now you are not as you were
When you had changed from the one who was all to me,
But as at first, when our day was fair.

Can it be you that I hear? Let me view you, then,
Standing as when I drew near to the town
Where you would wait for me: yes, as I knew you then,
Even to the original air-blue gown!

Or is it only the breeze, in its listlessness
Travelling across the wet mead to me here,
You being ever dissolved to wan wistlessness,
Heard no more again far or near?

Thus I; faltering forward,
Leaves around me falling,
Wind oozing thin through the thorn from the norward
And the woman calling.

Thomas Hardy

The Voice is one of a number of poems that Hardy wrote soon after the death of his wife, Emma. His feelings of loss were intensified by the fact that in the later years of their marriage they had grown apart. Here he remembers the love that they shared in their younger days. The poem begins with a regular rhythm created through a repetition of dactyls:

Woman much | missed, how you | call to me, | call to me,
Saying that | now you are | not as you | were
When you had | changed from the | one who was | all to me,

The dactyls help to create a mood of sad reflection and the repetition of:

call to me, | call to me

introduces a slightly haunting feel, suggestive of a calling voice being carried on the wind. The rhyming of 'call to me' with 'all to me' creates a link between the imagined caller and the poet and emphasizes how much he misses her now. Similarly, the rhyme of the second and fourth lines of the stanza emphasizes the contrast between the poet's present pain and the happiness the couple enjoyed in years past – 'you are not as you were/ … when our day was fair'.

The second stanza echoes the rhythm of the first in its repetition of dactyls:

Can it be | you that I | hear? ‖ Let me | view you, then,

and the sense of the poet's uncertainty is increased through his questioning and the caesura in the line. In stanza three again we have the repetition of the dactyls and the questioning continues as the poet wonders whether he really hears the voice of his loved one or if it is simply a trick of the wind:

Or is it | only the | breeze, in its | listlessness

Again we have the echoing rhyme, this time of 'listlessness'/'wistlessness'.

In the final stanza, however, the regular pattern the poet has established is broken. The caesura of 'Thus I; ‖ faltering forward' creates a halting, stumbling feel to the line reflecting the breakdown in the poet as his grief overwhelms him. The trochees of 'faltering forward' and 'falling' dominate the stanza and underline the sense of pain and despair that the poet feels – a pain that is made almost tangible through the image:

Wind oozing | thin through the | thorn from the | norward

There is a partial return of the dactyls here but, as the final dactyl trails away unfinished, they are dominated by the emphatic stress of the trochees in the last words of each line of this stanza. The final line itself echoes the opening line of the poem but now the dactyls have been replaced by the more emphatic trochees as the poet is left with the haunting voice in his mind:

And the | woman | calling.

We are left with the two words 'falling/calling' which create a striking effect through a combination of the rhyme and the trochaic metre, and encapsulate the poet's experience here.

This poem clearly illustrates the contribution that rhythm can make to the overall effect of the poem but its importance, as here, cannot be appreciated in isolation. Its use is inextricably bound up with the language of the poem and the ideas that the poet wants to express.

Form

There are many different ways in which poems can be structured. One thing is certain though: a poet does not simply choose a certain form at random. It will have been carefully chosen and will have a direct bearing on what the poet hopes to achieve through the poem. In considering the form of a particular poem, therefore, we are back to that central question – why? In this case, 'Why has the poet chosen to use this particular form?'.

Form can refer to the way that the poem is actually written down on the page or to the way that the lines are organized, grouped, or structured. (This is sometimes called **poetic form**.) In terms of its structure, poetry can be divided into two categories. First, there is the kind of poetry where the lines follow on one from another continuously without breaks, such as in Wordsworth's *The Prelude*, Milton's *Paradise Lost* or Keats's *Endymion*. The technical term for this is **stichic poetry**, but don't worry too much about the technical terms; the important thing is to be able to recognize that poems differ in the way they are put together.

Secondly, there is the kind of poetry where the lines are arranged in groups which are sometimes called verses but are more correctly referred to as **stanzas**. This is called **strophic poetry**. Keats uses this form in *The Eve of St Agnes* (see pages 258–263), as does Blake in *The Tyger*, Seamus Heaney in *Mid-Term Break*, and Ted Hughes in *Crow*, for example.

There are many different kinds of stanza, with variations depending on the number of lines they contain. (See the section on rhyme, page 53 and the Glossary, page 329 for further descriptions.)

The sonnet

The sonnet is a very popular form in English poetry and it is one that you are likely to come across in your studies. In basic terms a sonnet is a fourteen-line poem and the lines are usually arranged in one of two ways. First, there is the **Petrarchan** or **Italian sonnet** (so called simply because it is named after the Medieval Italian writer, Petrarch). This kind of sonnet is arranged with a first part that consists of eight lines (the octave) and a second and concluding part of six lines (the sestet). There can be variations in the rhyme scheme but generally it follows the pattern *abbaabba cdecde*. If you look back at Wordsworth's *Upon Westminster Bridge* (see page 48) you will see that it follows the pattern *abbaabba cdcdcd*.

The other form is the **Shakespearean** or **English sonnet**. The rhyme scheme of this divides into three quatrains and a concluding couplet. The rhyme scheme in this kind of sonnet usually follows the pattern *abab cdcd efef gg*.

Free verse

Although forms which adhere to a strict pattern are still frequently used by poets in the twenty-first century, there has been a trend towards poetry that does not have the constraints of metre or rhyme upon it and free verse has become predominant. This form of verse often does not have lines that are equal in length or that have a regular metre, and often it does not rhyme. To a large extent this flexibility allows poets the freedom to create forms to suit their own purposes and create the effects that they want in their writing.

Thematic form

Certain forms of poetry have been used to express themes which can be broadly grouped together. (This is sometimes called **thematic form**.) For example, the ode, the ballad, the elegy, the aubade, the pastoral, the lyric, the epic, and the song all refer to particular kinds of poetry that have a broad thematic link in common. (See the Glossary for more information on specific forms, page 329.)

Obviously the 'form' of a poem in terms of its physical structure is inseparably linked to the idea of its thematic 'form'. In turn, the whole concept of form is interlinked with other features such as rhyme, rhythm, and the poet's overall intention. What is important is that you are able to suggest reasons why a poet has chosen a particular form and comment on how it contributes, along with all these other features, in creating the poem's overall effect.

Handling 'difficult' poetry

It is, of course, far too simplistic to think in terms of 'easy' poetry and 'hard' poetry. Like some of the poems in this chapter, poetry can often be 'easy to read' but, in fact, deal with complex themes and ideas that need careful thought. However, in the course of your AS or A level study, you might come across poetry that presents you with rather different problems.

These problems can arise for a number of reasons, but here are some of the most common.

- You could encounter a problem of vocabulary – it may be that the poet uses difficult words that you do not understand or that the poem was written in a different age and so aspects of the language have changed.
- The poem could be concerned with concepts, ideas, or themes completely outside your sphere of experience.
- The poem might contain references that are difficult or obscure in some way, e.g. references based on classical mythology.
- It might use imagery that is difficult to decipher.
- The style in which the poem is written could be complex and you might need to do some detective work to unravel its meaning.

Some of these problems may be particularly apparent when studying poetry that was written in a different age. Perhaps the most extreme example of this that you might encounter in A level study would be in the study of the works of Chaucer, which we will look at later (see page 64). However, the works of writers such as Shakespeare (see Chapter 15) and Milton can also lead to feelings of apprehension.

So let us look at some examples of Milton's poetry and think about the kind of things you can do to help yourself when tackling such writers as this.

Milton lived and wrote in the seventeenth century, eventually siding with the Puritans during the English Civil War. He became their Secretary for the Foreign Tongues, translating political documents. He was also a leading author of the Puritan pamphlets which were issued to try to justify Oliver Cromwell's reign and the execution of Charles I.

Although he wrote poetry throughout his life, producing various works including *L'Allegro* (1632), *Il Penseroso* (1632), *Comus* (1634), and *Lycidas* (1637), it was in the latter part of his life that his great long, or 'epic', poems *Paradise Lost* (1667) and *Samson Agonistes* (1671) were written.

Paradise Lost concerns itself with the Fall of Adam and Eve and was originally published in ten books, although later it was issued in 12 books – the traditional number for an 'epic'. When set for A level, one or two books are usually specified for study. Here is an extract from Book I, where Satan is lying with his angels on the burning lake. This description particularly emphasizes Satan's huge size. Read it through carefully.

Paradise Lost

Book I

Thus Satan, talking to his nearest mate,
With head uplift above the wave and eyes
That sparkling blazed; his other parts besides
Prone on the flood, extended long and large,
Lay floating many a rood, in bulk as huge
As whom the fables name of monstrous size,
Titanian or Earth-born, that warred on Jove,
Briareos or Typhon, whom the den
By ancient Tarsus held, or that sea-beast
Leviathan, which God of all his works
Created hugest that swim the ocean-stream.
Him, haply slumbering on the Norway foam,
The pilot of some small night-foundered skiff
Deeming some island, oft, as seamen tell,
With fixed anchor in his scaly rind
Moors by his side under the lee, while night
Invests the sea and wished morn delays.
So stretched out huge in length the Arch-Fiend lay,
Chained on the burning lake…

John Milton

Activity

1 Write a brief summary of what Milton is saying here. (Limit this to a maximum of 45 words).

2 What immediate problems, if any, did you encounter in terms of understanding the detail of this passage?

You may find that the following cause you some problems.

- Some of Milton's vocabulary consists of words that are unfamiliar to you – words like 'rood', 'skiff' or 'under the lee'.
- Milton mentions names that you have not heard of before – 'Titanian', 'Briareos', 'Typhon', 'Tarsus' or 'Leviathan', for example.
- The word order is sometimes different from that which you are used to.
- The passage consists mainly of description with very little action.

Obviously, one of the problems in reading and understanding poetry that was written possibly hundreds of years ago is that the language we use today is not quite the same as the language that was used then. Words may have changed in meaning, hold different connotations, or may simply have become outmoded.

The second problem here is that the references or allusions used would have been understood and have held some significance to a reader in the poet's own age but often mean little to us today. These are not difficulties confined to poetry written a long time ago (a reading of T.S. Eliot's *The Wasteland* will convince you of that), but the chances of encountering them are probably greater the older the poetry is. However, good editions usually contain notes and glossaries to help the reader understand these more obscure references and so appreciate the text more fully.

Milton uses many references and allusions to classical literature and to the Bible in his work, and a knowledge of Greek and Roman mythology helps a good deal in studying his poetry. His readers in the seventeenth century would have possessed this kind of background and would understand immediately the biblical references and classical allusions. For them they would serve, as they were intended to do, to illuminate and illustrate the work. Today, most of us do not have this kind of background, and so often such references can initially act as barriers to meaning rather than assisting our understanding.

The question is – what can you do to help yourself overcome these initial difficulties? Well, three things would help to begin with:

- Buy a good dictionary if you do not possess one already, and use it. Make sure that you look up every word you come across that you do not understand. It can be a good idea to make a list of these.
- Look up and make a note of references that you do not understand. You might need to consult classical websites, dictionaries or encyclopedias for some of these.
- Ask yourself questions. Never be satisfied with ignoring difficult words or references. Always ask yourself questions like 'Why is that reference used?', 'What does it mean?', 'What does it add to the sense or effect of the poem?'

Now, let's assume that you have had the chance to do a bit of research on the passage from *Paradise Lost* on page 62. How does it help you gain a deeper understanding of the extract?

Here are some definitions or explanations of 'difficult' words and references:

rood – a measurement of about twenty feet

under the lee – sheltered from the wind

Titanian – of the Titans: in Greek mythology, Titans were giants who fought against the gods

Briareos – a mythological, hundred-armed monster

Typhon – another mythological giant monster

Tarsus – the name of a city, a great port

Leviathan – a monstrous whale referred to in the Bible

As you will see, many references are drawn from the Bible or mythology, and you will have noticed that all these references form part of an elaborate simile which Milton uses to emphasize the hugeness of Satan.

Activity

Look back at the extract on page 62 again and with a partner or in a small group discuss Milton's use of imagery here.

The simile form is an important part of the imagery of *Paradise Lost*. Some of Milton's images are drawn on a grand scale and can be elaborate and quite complicated to unravel. The key thing is that very often poetry needs working at in order to arrive at some kind of understanding of it.

Here are some suggestions to help you with that process.

- Read the piece several times and adopt a systematic approach.
- Use the parts of the poetry that you understand as clues to help you understand more difficult sections.
- Highlight particularly difficult words, phrases, lines, images, etc.
- Look up words that you do not understand in a good dictionary.
- Refer to the notes or glossary that the text contains.
- Do some background reading about the writer and his or her period.

Geoffrey Chaucer

The language of Chaucer is even further removed from that of our own modern English than Milton's, although once that language barrier has been breached students generally find his work more accessible.

Chaucer is generally considered to be the most important writer of the Middle Ages and his work, especially *The Canterbury Tales*, certainly had a great influence on our literature and language, laying the foundations for many writers who were to come after him. It is no surprise, therefore, to find Chaucer featured on a variety of AS and A level English Literature specifications.

This section will examine ways of approaching the reading of Middle English and the context within which *The Canterbury Tales* are set. The final section suggests various things that you can do in order to help develop your understanding of the particular Chaucer text that you are studying.

Reading Middle English

In the initial stages of your study of Chaucer you may encounter problems of understanding that are not present in other types of poetry. When you first open your copy of whichever Chaucer text you are studying, probably the first thing to strike you will be that it appears to be written in another language. Initially, this can be quite unsettling. Do not be put off, though, because once you have become used to the language things will seem much simpler. The language itself is nowhere near as daunting as it can look at first sight.

The first thing to bear in mind is that it is not written in another language – it is very definitely written in English. Admittedly, it is a rather different form of English from our present-day language because it is the English that was used in the fourteenth century. It is called Middle English and evolved as a mixture of different language elements. French was influential in its development. From the time of the Norman Conquest in 1066 until the mid-thirteenth century, French was the language of the court and the upper middle classes. Latin also made an important contribution to Middle English, being the language of legal and ecclesiastical documents and the preferred language of scholarly communication in the Middle Ages. These elements, combined with the predominant east Midland dialect (the dialect of Chaucer), gradually evolved into Middle English. This is the form of language from which modern English developed. In some respects modern English is similar to Middle English but there are differences too.

In studying Chaucer for the first time your first task is to become familiar with these similarities and differences. There are a number of things that you can do to help you to quickly become quite fluent in reading Chaucer in the original. So let us start by having a closer look at some of the features of Chaucer's language.

Reading Chaucer

Let us begin by looking at the opening lines of Chaucer's General Prologue to the *Canterbury Tales:*

Whan that Aprill with his shoures soote
The droghte of March hath perced to the roote,
And bathed every veyne in swich licour
Of which vertu engendred is the flour;
Whan Zephirus eek with his sweete breeth
Inspired hath in every holt and heeth
The tendre croppes,

Activity

1 Read these few lines aloud pronouncing each word just as it looks and write down a 'translation' of what you think it means. Make a note of any words that puzzle you or cause you a problem in the translation.

2 Now do exactly the same thing with these lines from the opening of *The Franklin's Tale.*

In Armorik, that called is Britayne,
Ther was a knyght that loved and dide his payne
To serve a lady in his beste wise;
And many a labour, many a greet emprise,
He for his lady wroghte er she were wonne.

Let's see how you got on. Translated literally, the lines from the *General Prologue* could read:

When that April with his showers sweet
The drought of March hath pierced to the root,
And bathed every vein in such liquor
Of which energy engendered is the flower;
When Zephirus also with his sweet breath
Has breathed in every wood and heath
Upon all the tender crops;

Here is one possible translation:

> When the sweet showers of April have pierced the drought of March to its roots and bathed every vein in the powerful moisture that gives birth to the flowers; when Zephirus too, with his sweet breath, has breathed upon the delicate shoots in every wood and heath;

How did you get on? Your version will no doubt differ slightly. There are a number of ways that this could be written down and yet the sense would remain the same. One of the reasons for this is that sometimes the sense of a particular Middle English word can be expressed through a number of modern English alternatives. For example, 'vertu' can mean *virtue* in modern English, although here it conveys the sense of the rain having the power to give life to the plants. Similarly, 'engendred' can mean *engendering* or *procreation* although here we could translate it as *gives birth*, as we have done, or even *produces* would be in keeping with the sense of the line.

Here's a translation of the opening of *The Franklin's Tale*. Compare it with your version.

> In Armorica, which is also known as Brittany, there lived a knight who loved and took trouble to serve his lady to the best of his ability. He undertook many labours and great enterprises for her before he won her.

Where did your problems with these lines occur? The place names of Armorik and Britayne perhaps caused you a little difficulty. 'Armorica' is simply another name, an ancient name, for Brittany. 'Britayne' looks very similar to Britain so this might have misled you. Perhaps certain expressions, such as '... and dide his payne', also caused you some difficulty.

You may have noticed some, or all, of the following points.

- Some words are identical to their modern English counterparts (e.g. 'bathed', 'every', 'called', 'loved').

- Some words look and sound very similar to their modern English counterparts (e.g. 'whan', 'greet', 'wonne').

- Some words look completely unfamiliar (e.g. 'soote', 'swich', 'eek').

- Some words might remind you of modern English words but actually mean something different (e.g. 'inspired', 'holt').

- Some of the words seem to be in rather a strange order.

- There are references to people, places, etc. that you might not have come across before (e.g. 'Zephirus').

The context of the tales

If you choose to study Chaucer as part of your A level studies it is likely that you will choose one of the poems which make up *The Canterbury Tales*. Whichever particular tale you are studying, though, it is important that you are able to set the tale into the wider context of *The Canterbury Tales* as a whole rather than just look at it in isolation. Each of the tales is set within the fictional framework established by Chaucer in the *General Prologue to the Canterbury Tales*, which is a kind of introduction in which Chaucer sets the scene, introduces the pilgrims, describes them, and so forth.

The basic background to the tales is straightforward. A group of pilgrims are travelling from London to Canterbury to worship at the shrine of Thomas à Becket. They meet at the Tabard Inn at Southwark in London ready to begin their journey and the landlord, or Host, as he is known, suggests that they all take part in a story-telling competition to help to pass the time on their journey. The Host will judge the stories and the winner will receive a free meal at the inn on their return from Canterbury.

You will probably find in your edition of the particular tale that you are studying other material which is not part of the tale itself but which will help you to establish some background to the character telling the tale. This material usually includes at least two extracts taken from elsewhere in *The Canterbury Tales*:

- most editions contain the section taken from the *General Prologue* which describes the particular pilgrim who is telling the tale
- most editions also contain the relevant lines that link the tale in question to the one that immediately precedes it. This often involves an exchange between the pilgrims and the Host which can help to throw light on characters and how they relate to one another.

The narrator's voice

The Canterbury Tales, then, is a story about a group of people telling stories. The characters are, of course, the invention of Chaucer but he also writes himself into the script by taking the role of one of the pilgrims. In fact, in his role as Sir Topas, he gives himself the worst tale of all to tell and is interrupted by the Host who can listen to no more, and so he never actually finishes it.

Throughout the tales there is always the sense of the presence of two narrators: first of all the character telling the story but secondly, hidden somewhere behind the first narrator, there is Chaucer himself, masterminding the whole scheme.

Activity

What do you think Chaucer gains by having his tales narrated by fictitious characters within a fictitious framework rather than simply telling the tales directly himself?

There are several factors that you might consider here.

- The idea of the group of pilgrims gives a sense of unity and structure to what might otherwise have been a loosely linked collection of stories.
- Links can be made between the character telling the tale and the tale itself, and this can add another dimension to both tale and teller.

- The whole narrative scheme is given a depth and complexity in terms of its overall effect on the audience that would have been lacking in a simple single narration scheme.

- It allows Chaucer to get away with telling stories and making comments that may be ribald or contentious by distancing himself from them and attributing them to his characters. This can add to the ironic effect he often creates.

In most parts of most of the tales Chaucer keeps to the background, but watch out for his voice coming through. Sometimes he will comment or make an aside or observation or sometimes even endow his character with a language or mode of expression which is very much Chaucer's own. In other words he has it both ways. In *The Miller's Tale*, Chaucer is able to convince his audience that the Miller is an independent character over whom he has no control, and he urges readers to choose another tale if they are likely to be offended by the Miller's bawdy offering.

The key thing throughout is to be aware of the subtlety with which Chaucer uses a variety of narrative voices to achieve just the effect that he wants. To summarize, following these steps should help you to tackle your Chaucer text confidently.

- Read the tale you are studying through fairly quickly to get a general sense of what it is about. Do not worry too much at this first stage if there are words, phrases, or sections of it that you do not understand.

- Avoid using your glossary too much during this 'first read' stage. This can interrupt your reading and make it more difficult to get the overall 'feel' of the story.

- Then look back over the tale and focus on the individual words, phrases, or sections that gave you problems and use the glossary to help form a picture of their meaning.

- Most editions of a particular tale will contain quite detailed line-referenced notes. Make full use of these – they will help you establish the meaning of more difficult sections and also fill in some useful background information that will add to your understanding of the tale.

- Try listening to a recording of the tale read by a professional. This will help you to gain an impression of the sound of the language and you will hear rhymes and rhythms that are invisible when looking at the printed page.

- Avoid using a modern English translation. If you go straight to a translation this will really inhibit you from coming to terms with the language for yourself. It is far better to be able to read the original for yourself than have to rely on a ready-made translation.

Putting it into practice

Now have a look at a quite different kind of poem and see how you handle an appreciation of it. The poem is by Samuel Taylor Coleridge, probably most famous for his narrative poem *The Ancient Mariner*. He also wrote some poems that became known as 'conversation poems' because of the way that they seem to address the reader in the style of an intimate and private talk. Read this poem through carefully.

Frost At Midnight

The Frost performs its secret ministry,
Unhelped by any wind. The owlet's cry
Came loud – and hark, again! loud as before.
The inmates of my cottage, all at rest,

Have left me to that solitude, which suits
Abstruser musings: save that at my side
My cradled infant slumbers peacefully.
'Tis calm indeed! so calm, that it disturbs
And vexes meditation with its strange
And extreme silentness. Sea, hill, and wood,
With all the numberless goings-on of life,
Inaudible as dreams! the thin blue flame
Lies on my low-burnt fire, and quivers not;
Only that film,[1] which fluttered on the grate,
Still flutters there, the sole unquiet thing.
Methinks, its motion in this hush of nature
Gives it dim sympathies with me who live,
Making it a companionable form,
Whose puny flaps and freaks the idling Spirit
By its own moods interprets, everywhere
Echo or mirror seeking of itself,
And makes a toy of Thought.

　　　　　But O! how oft,
How oft, at school, with most believing mind,
Presageful, have I gazed upon the bars,
To watch that fluttering *stranger!* and as oft
With unclosed lids, already had I dreamt
Of my sweet birth-place, and the old church-tower,
Whose bells, the poor man's only music, rang
From morn to evening, all hot Fair-day,
So sweetly, that they stirred and haunted me
With a wild pleasure, falling on mine ear
Most like articulate sounds of things to come!
So gazed I, till the soothing things, I dreamt,
Lulled me to sleep, and sleep prolonged my dreams!
And so I brooded all the following morn,
Awed by the stern preceptor's face, mine eye
Fixed with mock study on my swimming book:
Save if the door half opened, and I snatched
A hasty glance, and still my heart leaped up,
For still I hoped to see the *stranger*'s face,
Townsman, or aunt, or sister more beloved,
My play-mate when we both were clothed alike!

　　　　Dear Babe, that sleepest cradled by my side,
Whose gentle breathings, heard in this deep calm,
Fill up the interspersed vacancies
And momentary pauses of the thought!
My babe so beautiful! it thrills my heart
With tender gladness, thus to look at thee,
And think that thou shalt learn far other lore,
And in far other scenes! For I was reared
In the great city, pent 'mid cloisters dim,
And saw nought lovely but the sky and stars.
But thou, my babe! shalt wander like a breeze
By lakes and sandy shores, beneath the crags
Of ancient mountain, and beneath the clouds
Which image in their bulk both lakes and shores

And mountain crags: so shalt thou see and hear
The lovely shapes and sounds intelligible
Of that eternal language, which thy God
Utters, who from eternity doth teach
Himself in all, and all things in himself.
Great universal Teacher! he shall mould
Thy spirit, and by giving make it ask.

    Therefore all seasons shall be sweet to thee,
Whether the summer clothe the general earth
With greenness, or the redbreast sit and sing
Betwixt the tufts of snow on the bare branch
Of mossy apple-tree, while the nigh thatch
Smokes in the sun-thaw; whether the eave-drops fall
Heard only in the trances of the blast,
Or if the secret ministry of frost
Shall hang them up in silent icicles,
Quietly shining to the quiet Moon.

Samuel Taylor Coleridge

(Published 1798)

[1] *In all parts of the kingdom these films are called strangers and supposed to portend the arrival of some absent friend*

Activity

1 Discuss the poem with a partner or in a small group. Then, on your own, make a list of the key points arising from your discussion.

2 Now have a closer look at the poem. Consider the following questions about the early part of the poem. Discuss them with a partner, making notes on the following as you go.

   • Why do you think Coleridge describes the Frost's 'ministry' as 'secret'?

   • What kind of atmosphere does he create in lines 1–7?

   • What kind of scene is set within the cottage?

   • How would you describe the poet's mood here?

   • Look at lines 14–22. What is the significance of '... that film, which fluttered on the grate'?

3 Now, on your own, look at the second section of the poem. Describe what is happening here. How has the mood changed?

4 The focus shifts again in the third section. How? Comment on Coleridge's use of imagery here.

5 How effective do you find the concluding section? Refer to the text to support your comments.

6 What use do you think Coleridge has made of rhythm here and what relationship does this have with the overall form of the poem? (A consideration of the kind of poem this is may help you here.)

7 Now write your own critical appreciation of this poem covering all the aspects of it that you feel are of significance. (Your essay should be 3 to 4 pages in length.)

3 Studying Drama

Objectives

- To prepare yourself for writing about drama
- To consider some of the features to look for in evaluating drama texts
- To prepare for studying set drama texts
- To prepare for a context-based question on a drama text

What is drama?

A dictionary definition will state that:

> drama is something intended specifically for performance on stage in front of an audience.

This definition points to the fact that drama is written to be seen rather than read, and its meaning can only be fully appreciated when seen in performance. This makes it a much more 'public' form than prose or poetry in that the experience of the play in performance is a shared experience. This essential aspect of drama is easy to lose sight of when sitting in a classroom, or on your own, grappling with the language of a drama text.

Visualizing the script

It is essential, then, that you are aware in approaching a play that you are dealing with a work that is very different from, say, a novel and that you will need to employ quite different strategies to handle it. You must be able to visualize the play in your head – be able to bring the play alive in your mind and see and hear the action as if you were at the theatre. Developing the ability to do this can be difficult simply by reading from the printed page. However, there are things you can do, from the outset, to help.

- Recognize that reading a play is essentially a group activity and so work with others as much as possible.
- Go to see plays performed as often as possible. (Do not restrict yourself to the ones you are studying, or just to professional productions.)
- Keep a notebook or log of plays that you see, noting your responses – thoughts and feelings about performances and ideas on production.
- Take part in 'acting out' parts of a play – this will help you to appreciate the staging implications of a text in a way that straight reading never can.
- Listen to audio or watch video recordings of plays. (These do not replace seeing the play 'live' but they are better than only reading the script.)

With this key point in mind, let us consider some aspects of plays that you will need to examine in the texts that you study.

Opening scenes

The way that a play opens is obviously crucial to engaging the audience's attention, and writers can take many options here depending on the effects that they wish to achieve. In looking at an opening scene, whether of a text you are studying for an examination or coursework or a passage you are confronted with 'unseen', there are some key questions that are worth asking. The central questions are: 'What effect does the writer want this scene to have on the audience?' and 'What purpose does the scene serve to the play as a whole?'. Here are some possible answers to these questions.

- The scene provides an explanation of background information and details the audience needs to understand what is going on. (This is sometimes called **exposition**; see page 83.)
- The scene creates a setting or background against which the play is set.
- The scene creates a mood or creates tension which captures the audience's attention immediately (the opening scene of *Hamlet* is a good example of this).
- The scene introduces characters, situations, and relationships.
- The scene provokes a sense of intrigue which captures the audience's attention and makes them want to know more.

Activity

1 Read carefully the opening to Brian Friel's *Making History* below. Think about what Friel hopes to achieve here and what effect it would have on the audience.

2 Discuss this opening with a partner, focusing on these aspects:
- your impression of the two characters and their concerns
- the information conveyed to the audience here and the techniques that Friel uses to put it across
- the kind of atmosphere created and how Friel creates it.

Making History

Act I Scene 1

*(A large living room in **O'Neill**'s home in Dungannon, County Tyrone, Ireland. Late August in 1591. The room is spacious and scantily furnished: a large, refectory-type table; some chairs and stools; a sideboard. No attempt at decoration.*

O'Neill *moves around this comfortless room quickly and energetically, inexpertly cutting the stems off flowers, thrusting the flowers into various vases and then adding water. He is not listening to **Harry Hoveden** who consults and reads from various papers on the table.*

O'Neill *is forty-one. A private, sharp-minded man at this moment uncharacteristically outgoing and talkative. He always speaks in an upper-class English accent except on those occasions specifically scripted. **Harry Hoveden**, his personal secretary, is about the same age as **O'Neill**. **O'Neill** describes him as a man 'who has a comforting and a soothing effect'.)*

Harry: That takes care of Friday. Saturday you're free all day – so far. Then on Sunday – that'll be the fourteenth – O'Hagan's place at Tullyhogue. A big christening party. The invitation came the day you left. I've said you'll be there. All right?

(Pause)

It's young Brian's first child – you were at his wedding last year. It'll be a good day.

(Pause)

Hugh?

O'Neill: Yes?

Harry: O'Hagan's – where you were fostered.

O'Neill: Tell me the name of these again.

Harry: Broom.

O'Neill: Broom. That's it.

Harry: The Latin name is genista. Virgil mentions it somewhere.

O'Neill: Does he really?

Harry: Actually that *genista* comes from Spain.

(**O'Neill** *looks at the flowers in amazement.*)

O'Neill: Good Lord – does it? Spanish broom – magnificent name, isn't it?

Harry: Give them plenty of water.

O'Neill: Magnificent colour, isn't it?

Harry: A letter from the Lord Deputy –

O'Neill: They really transform the room. Splendid idea of yours, Harry. Thank you.

(**O'Neill** *silently mouths the word Genista again and then continues distributing the flowers.*)

Harry: A letter from the Lord Deputy 'vigorously urging you to have your eldest son attend the newly established College of the Holy and Undivided Trinity in Dublin founded by the Most Serene Queen Elizabeth'. That 'vigorously urging' sounds ominous, doesn't it?

O'Neill: Sorry?

Harry: Sir William Fitzwilliam wants you to send young Hugh to the new Trinity College. I'm told he's trying to get all the big Gaelic families to send their children there. He would like an early response.

O'Neill: This jacket – what do you think, Harry? It's not a bit... excessive, is it?

Harry: Excessive?

O'Neill: You know... a little too – too strident?

Harry: Strident?

O'Neill: All right, damn it, too bloody young?

Harry: *(Looking at his papers)* It's very becoming, Hugh.

O'Neill: Do you think so? Maybe I should have got it in maroon.

(He goes off to get more flowers.)

Harry: A reminder that the Annual Festival of Harpers takes place next month in Roscommon. They've changed the venue to Roosky. You're Patron of the Festival and they would be very honoured if you would open the event with a short –

*(He now sees that he is alone. He looks through his papers. Pause. **O'Neill** enters again with an armful of flowers.)*

Brian Friel

This opening scene starts the play off in quite a private and intimate setting. The stage directions at the beginning describe the setting and what is going on and this will help you to visualize the scene in your mind. Although the audience will not be so fully aware of what is happening here the activity taking place will capture their attention. The two characters, O'Neill and Harry, seem to have very different concerns at the opening of the play. O'Neill is immersed in the domestic – arranging the flowers in the room and seeking Harry's opinion about his attire. Harry, on the other hand, is concerned with imparting business and political news to O'Neill. Within this apparently low-key opening, Friel makes it clear that O'Neill is a prominent public figure from the details that are mentioned – his presence being requested at important domestic and public occasions and the letter from the Lord Deputy trying to persuade him to send his son to Trinity College confirm this.

Notice how Friel's economical technique allows him to give the audience a good deal of information and establishes the central character of O'Neill right at the outset. If you were to study the whole of this play you would find that Friel also establishes one of the central themes of the play here – that of the conflict between O'Neill the private man and O'Neill the public figure. He is also able to give a clear indication of O'Neill's stature and importance both as a political figure and as a man with pastoral responsibilities towards his people.

Activity

1 Read the following extract, which is the opening scene from Richard Sheridan's comedy, *The Rivals*.

2 Discuss the scene with a partner and consider these points:

   • the effect of the opening on the audience

   • the intention of the playwright

   • the techniques used

   • the purpose of any stage directions.

The Rivals

Act I Scene 1

*(Scene, a street in Bath. **Coachman** crosses the stage. Enter **Fag** looking after him.)*

Fag: What! – Thomas! – Sure 'tis he? – What! – Thomas! – Thomas!

Coachman: Hey! – Odds life! – Mr Fag! – give us your hand, my old fellow-servant.

Fag: Excuse my glove, Thomas: I'm devilish glad to see you, my lad: why, my prince of charioteers, you look as hearty! – but who the deuce thought of seeing you in Bath!

Coachman: Sure, Master, Madam Julia, Harry, Mrs Kate, and the postillion be all come!

Fag: Indeed!

Coachman: Aye! Master thought another fit of the gout was coming to make him a visit: so he'd a mind to gi't the slip, and whip we were all off at an hour's warning.

Fag: Aye, aye! hasty in everything, or it would not be Sir Anthony Absolute.

Coachman: But tell us, Mr Fag, how does young Master? Odd! Sir Anthony will stare to see the Captain here!

Fag: I do not serve Captain Absolute now –

Coachman: Why sure!

Fag: At present I am employed by Ensign Beverley.

Coachman: I doubt, Mr Fag, you ha'n't changed for the better.

Fag: I have not changed, Thomas.

Coachman: No! why didn't you say you had left young Master?

Fag: No – Well, honest Thomas, I must puzzle you no farther: briefly then – Captain Absolute and Ensign Beverley are one and the same person.

Coachman: The devil they are!

Fag: So it is indeed, Thomas; and the *Ensign* half of my master being on guard at present – the *Captain* has nothing to do with me.

Coachman: So, so! – what, this is some freak, I warrant! Do, tell us, Mr Fag, the meaning o't – you know I ha' trusted you.

Fag: You'll be secret, Thomas.

Coachman: As a coach-horse.

Fag: Why then the cause of all this is – L, O, V, E, – love, Thomas, who (as you may get read to you) has been a masquerader ever since the days of Jupiter.

Coachman: Aye, aye; I guessed there was a lady in the case: but pray, why does your master pass only for Ensign? – now if he had shammed General indeed –

Fag: Ah! Thomas, there lies the mystery o'the matter. Harkee, Thomas, my master is in love with a lady of a very singular taste: a lady who likes him better as a half-pay Ensign than if she knew he was son and heir to Sir Anthony Absolute, a baronet with three thousand a year.

Coachman: That is an odd taste indeed! – but has she got the stuff, Mr Fag; is she rich, hey?

Fag: Rich! – why, I believe she owns half the stocks! Zounds! Thomas, she could pay the national debt as easy as I could my washerwoman! She has a lap-dog that eats out of gold – she feeds her parrot with small pearls – and all her thread-papers are made of bank-notes!

Coachman: Bravo! – faith! – odd! I warrant she has a set of thousands at least: but does she draw kindly with the Captain?

Fag: As fond as pigeons.

Coachman: May one hear her name?

Fag: Miss Lydia Languish – but there is an old tough aunt in the way; though by the by – she has never seen my master – for he got acquainted with Miss while on a visit in Gloucestershire.

Coachman: Well – I wish they were once harnessed together in matrimony. But pray, Mr Fag, what kind of a place is this Bath? I ha' heard a deal of it – here's a mort o' merrymaking – hey?

Fag: Pretty well, Thomas, pretty well – 'tis a good lounge. In the morning we go to the pump-room (though neither my master nor I drink the waters); after breakfast we saunter on the parades or play a game at billiards; at night we dance: but damn the place, I'm tired of it: their regular hours stupefy me – not a fiddle nor a card after eleven! – however Mr Faulkland's gentleman and I keep it up a little in private parties; I'll introduce you there, Thomas – you'll like him much.

Coachman: Sure I know Mr Du-Peigne – you know his master is to marry Madam Julia.

Fag: I had forgot. But Thomas you must polish a little – indeed you must: here now – this wig! – what the devil do you do with a wig, Thomas? None of the London whips of any degree of ton wear wigs now.

Coachman: More's the pity! more's the pity, I say. Odds life! when I heard how the lawyers and doctors had took to their own hair, I thought how 'twould go next – odd rabbit it! when the fashion had got foot on the Bar, I guessed 'twould mount to the Box! – but 'tis all out of character, believe me, Mr Fag and lookee, I'll never gi' up mine – the lawyers and doctors may do as they will.

Fag: Well, Thomas, we'll not quarrel about that.

Coachman: Why, bless you, the gentlemen of they professions ben't all of a mind – for in our village now tho'ff Jack Gauge the exciseman has ta'en to his carrots, there's little Dick the farrier swears he'll never forsake his bob, though all the college should appear with their own heads!

Fag: Indeed! well said Dick! but hold – mark! mark! Thomas.

Coachman: Zooks! 'tis the Captain – is that the lady with him?

Fag: No! no! that is Madam Lucy – my master's mistress's maid. They lodge at that house – but I must after him to tell him the news.

Coachman: Odd! he's giving her money! – well, Mr Fag –

Fag: Goodbye, Thomas – I have an appointment in Gyde's Porch this evening at eight; meet me there, and we'll make a little party.

(Exeunt severally)

Richard Sheridan

Presenting character

A key element in the impact of a dramatic production is the extent to which the playwright achieves a convincing sense of character. However, the nature of drama is such that the playwright employs very different methods of characterization from those employed by a novelist. Novelists can provide the reader with as much background information as they wish. They can enter the minds of the characters, let their readers know what characters think, feel, are planning to do. A playwright does not have all these options.

Activity

Focusing on a play that you are studying, think carefully about the ways the characters are presented to the audience to give a full and rounded impression of them. Make a list of these methods and devices.

Perhaps the most straightforward way in which a playwright can define exactly how he or she intends a character to appear to the audience is through detailed and explicit stage directions. So it is important that when you begin to study a play you pay close attention to this information. When watching the play on the stage, of course, you will not be reading stage directions but you will be seeing them in performance.

Some playwrights give a great deal of information through their descriptions of how characters are meant to appear. Look carefully at this description from the opening of John Galsworthy's *Strife*, for example.

Strife

Act I

(It is noon. In the Underwoods' dining-room a bright fire is burning. On one side of the fireplace are double doors leading to the drawing-room, on the other side a door leading to the hall. In the centre of the room a long dining-table without cloth is set out as a board table. At the head of it in the Chairman's seat, sits **John Anthony**, *an old man, big, clean shaven, and high-coloured, with thick white hair, and thick dark eyebrows. His movements are rather slow and feeble, but his eyes are very much alive. There is a glass of water by his side. On his right sits his son,* **Edgar**, *an earnest-looking man of thirty, reading a newspaper. Next to him* **Wanklin**, *a man with jutting eyebrows, and silver-streaked light hair, is bending over transfer papers.* **Tench**, *the secretary, a short and rather humble, nervous man, with side whiskers, stands helping him. On* **Wanklin***'s right sits* **Underwood**, *the Manager, a quiet man, with a long, stiff jaw, and steady eyes. Back to the fire is* **Scantlebury**, *a very large, pale, sleepy man, with grey hair, rather bald. Between him and the Chairman are two empty chairs.)*

Wilder: *(Who is lean, cadaverous, and complaining, with drooping grey moustaches, stands before the fire)* I say, this fire's the devil! Can I have a screen, Tench?

John Galsworthy

> ### Activity
>
> In a small group, read these stage directions carefully. Imagine you are a producer discussing preliminary views of these characters with a team of actors. Think about how the characters could be presented particularly in terms of appearance and personality.

Galsworthy here presents anyone reading the text with a good deal of guidance on how to visualize the characters. Some playwrights provide little or no such direct guidance on how to interpret their characters but rely on other methods to convey a sense of character. These include:

- how characters speak (also embedded in stage directions)
- how characters are described by other characters
- what the characters say and do.

Most playwrights (including Galsworthy) use a combination of all these methods in order to give a sense of fully developed characters, although in some cases playwrights deliberately create stereotypical characters in order to achieve their particular effect. Some of the 'stock' characters to be found in Restoration comedy, or a comedy of manners such as *The Rivals*, are examples of this.

Asides and soliloquies

To succeed in creating a convincing character, the dramatist needs to give the audience some sense of deeper, inner thoughts and feelings. Unlike the novelist, however, who can describe these as fully as desired to the reader, the dramatist has much more limited means at his or her disposal.

Two methods that are often used to provide some insight into characters' minds are the aside and the soliloquy. The **aside** is a kind of 'stage whisper', a behind-the-hand comment. Sometimes it is directed to another character but often it is aimed at the audience or characters 'speak to themselves'. Asides tend to be short, often a single sentence, sometimes a single word. They are used by the playwright to convey small pieces of information concerning the plot or character to the audience. For example, in William Congreve's *The Way of the World* one of the central characters, Mirabell, has insincerely courted Lady Wishfort as a cover for his real love of her niece, Millamant. Lady Wishfort has discovered the truth and, although she gives nothing away in conversation, her aside shows that despite all she is still susceptible to his charms.

Lady Wishfort: *(Aside)* Oh, he has witchcraft in his eyes and tongue! When I did not see him, I could have bribed a villain to his assassination; but his appearance rakes the embers which have so long lain smothered in my breast.

Although asides are usually short comments, sometimes they can be more extended. In *The Rivals* the characters almost give the audience a running commentary on what is going on and how they are feeling. In the following extract, Absolute has angered his father by refusing to marry the girl his father has selected for him. He then has found out that she is in fact the girl he loves, and so he decides to appear penitent to his father (without letting him in on what is really happening!). It is worth noting that lines which can be taken as asides in performance are not always marked *(Aside)* in the script. One television adaptation of this play had the characters addressing the camera directly as though speaking confidentially and directly to the viewers, making them privy to the intrigue.

The Rivals

Act III Scene 1

*(Scene, the North Parade. Enter **Absolute**.)*

Absolute: 'Tis just as Fag told me, indeed. Whimsical enough, faith! My father wants to force me to marry the very girl I am plotting to run away with! He must not know of my connection with her yet awhile. – He has too summary a method of proceeding in these matters – and Lydia shall not yet lose her hopes of an elopement. – However, I'll read my recantation instantly. My conversion is something sudden, indeed, but I can assure him it is very sincere. – So, so – here he comes. He looks plaguy gruff.
(Steps aside)

*(Enter **Sir Anthony**.)*

Sir Anthony: No – I'll die sooner than forgive him. Die, did I say? I'll live these fifty years to plague him. – At our last meeting, his impudence had almost put me out of temper. An obstinate, passionate, self-willed boy! Who can he take after? This is my return for getting him before all his brothers and sisters! – for putting him, at twelve years old, into a marching regiment, and allowing him fifty pounds a year, besides his pay ever since! But I have done with him – he's anybody's son for me. – I never will see him more – never – never – never – never.

Absolute: Now for a penitential face.
(Advances)

Richard Sheridan

- -

The aside is an extremely useful device by which the playwright can give hints concerning plot or character to the audience. Through the **soliloquy**, the playwright has much more scope for developing a character's thoughts and feelings aloud, allowing the audience to see into the mind of the character. The soliloquy is an expanded and more fully developed speech and is usually delivered when the character is alone on the stage. Often soliloquies allow characters to reveal their true feelings, plans, or motives as they do not need to maintain any public image that they may project in front of the other characters.

Returning to *The Rivals*, the maid Lucy, who pretends to be a 'simpleton', is, in fact, a cunning operator. When she is left alone at the end of a scene, this soliloquy reveals her true nature to the audience and so adds to their amusement as they see how she is playing all the characters off against one another.

The Rivals

Act I Scene 2

Lucy: Ha! ha! ha! So, my dear simplicity, let me give you a little respite – *(Altering her manner)* let girls in my station be as fond as they please of appearing expert, and knowing in their trusts; commend me to a mask of silliness, and a pair of sharp eyes for my own interest under it! Let me see to what account I have turned my simplicity lately – *(Looks at a paper) For abetting Miss Lydia Languish in a design of running away with an ensign – in money – sundry times – twelve pound twelve – gowns, five – hats, ruffles, caps, etc., etc. – numberless! From the said Ensign, within this last month, six guineas and a half – about a quarter's pay! Item, from Mrs Malaprop, for betraying the young people to her – when I found matters were likely to be discovered – two guineas, and a black paduasoy. Item, from Mr Acres, for carrying divers letters – which I never delivered – two guineas, and a pair of buckles. Item, from Sir Lucius O'Trigger – three crowns – two gold pocket-pieces – and a silver snuff-box! – Well done, simplicity! – yet I was forced to make my Hibernian* believe, that he was corresponding, not with the aunt, but with the niece: for, though not over rich, I found he had too much pride and delicacy to sacrifice the feelings of a gentleman to the necessities of his fortune.
(Exit)

Richard Sheridan

- -

Soliloquies are frequently used at some special moment in the play or when a character is undergoing some kind of emotionally or psychologically heightened experience – for example, when a character is distressed or suffering some kind of confusion of mind or alternatively when a character is feeling exultant or wants to work through his or her own thoughts and feelings.

Although technically speaking we think of characters being alone on the stage, or at least out of earshot of other characters, when they deliver their soliloquy, a soliloquy-like effect can be created in other ways. Sometimes characters may be in the presence of others but they are so wrapped up in their own world that it is as though they are talking to themselves. Although technically speaking not a soliloquy, this can serve much the same function.

In this extract from *Hamlet*, although both Claudius and Hamlet are on stage, neither can hear what the other is saying – but the audience can. Claudius has killed Hamlet's father, the king (his own brother), taken the crown for himself and married his brother's widow, Hamlet's mother Gertrude. However, only Hamlet is aware of this. In this extract Hamlet comes across Claudius alone, apparently at prayer. Read the extract carefully.

Activity

1 What information does the audience gain from Claudius's soliloquy?

2 What thoughts are in Hamlet's mind?

3 What is the dramatic effect of the two characters being unable to hear each other but the audience being able to hear both?

4 What is the ironic effect of Claudius's final lines spoken when Hamlet has left?

Hamlet

Act III Scene 3

King Claudius: O, my offence is rank, it smells to heaven;
It hath the primal eldest curse upon't –
A brother's murder. Pray can I not,
Though inclination be as sharp as will,
My stronger guilt defeats my strong intent,
And, like a man to double business bound,
I stand in pause where I shall first begin,
And both neglect. What if this cursed hand
Were thicker than itself with brother's blood,
Is there not rain enough in the sweet heavens
To wash it white as snow? Whereto serves mercy
But to confront the visage of offence?
And what's in prayer but this twofold force,
To be forestalled ere we come to fall
Or pardon'd being down? Then I'll look up.
My fault is past – but O, what form of prayer
Can serve my turn? 'Forgive me my foul murder'?
That cannot be, since I am still possess'd
Of those effects for which I did the murder –
My crown, mine own ambition, and my queen.
May one be pardon'd and retain th'offence?
In the corrupted currents of this world
Offence's gilded hand may shove by justice,
And oft 'tis seen the wicked prize itself
Buys out the law. But 'tis not so above:
There is no shuffling, there the action lies
In his true nature, and we ourselves compell'd
Even to the teeth and forehead of our faults

To give in evidence. What then? What rests?
Try what repentance can. What can it not?
Yet what can it, when one cannot repent?
O wretched state! O bosom black as death!
O limed soul, that struggling to be free
Art more engag'd! Help, angels! Make assay.
Bow, stubborn knees; and heart with strings of steel,
Be soft as sinews of the new-born babe.
All may be well.
(He kneels)

(Enter **Hamlet***)*

Hamlet:　Now might I do it pat, now a is a-praying.
And now I'll do't. *(Draws his sword)*
　　　　　　And so a goes to heaven;
And so am I reveng'd. That would be scann'd:
A villain kills my father, and for that
I, his sole son, do this same villain send
To heaven.
Why, this is hire and salary, not revenge.
A took my father grossly, full of bread,
With all his crimes broad blown, as flush as May;
And how his audit stands who knows save heaven?
But in our circumstance and course of thought
'Tis heavy with him. And am I then reveng'd,
To take him in the purging of his soul,
When he is fit and season'd for his passage?
No.
Up, sword, and know thou a more horrid hent:
When he is drunk asleep, or in his rage,
Or in th'incestuous pleasure of his bed,
At game a-swearing, or about some act
That has no relish of salvation in't,
Then trip him, that his heels may kick at heaven
And that his soul may be as damn'd and black
As hell, whereto it goes. My mother stays.
This physic but prolongs thy sickly days.
(Exit)

King Claudius:　My words fly up, my thoughts remain below.
Words without thoughts never to heaven go.
(Exit)

William Shakespeare

- -

It has often been noted that both the aside and the soliloquy are artificial devices
and that in 'real life' people do not go around delivering speeches to themselves. In
fact, they are just two of many conventions that we accept when watching a play
which can be termed 'dramatic licence'. In the context of the theatre we forget their
artificiality and accept them quite naturally.

Activity

1 Working in pairs, select a character from a play that you are studying. One assumes the role of that character, the other the mirror image. The 'character' asks questions of the image about thoughts, feelings, motivations, etc. and the image answers. This role play should teach you as much about what your chosen character is not as what he or she is.

2 You can then select another character and swap roles.

Issues and themes

Complex though the formation and development of characters may be, they are themselves part of a more complex web that makes up the play as a whole. Within this web the playwright will have interwoven certain themes and issues. In studying a play, you will need to be able to identify these and to look at how the playwright explores them through the drama. Such ideas can be presented to the audience in two key ways. First, we can detect ideas, issues, thoughts, etc. expressed by the characters in a play. Secondly, we can detect themes, issues, or ideas that the playwright wants the play as a whole to project.

Sometimes a playwright will have major characters hold views or follow a philosophy that ultimately is shown to be counter to the message that the play as a whole conveys. This is often done to show the problems caused by or shortcomings of certain courses of action or philosophies. The issues that a play might raise can be many and varied but they are almost always presented via action centring on human relationships and conflicts.

Activity

List the major characters in a play that you are studying. Draw up a chart which shows briefly the ideas, philosophies, values etc. held by each character, as shown through the action of the play. Then think about these ideas and against each jot down the dramatist's view.

Plot and structure

Obviously plot is central to most plays although there are certain kinds of play (some of Samuel Beckett's, for example) where the very lack of a plot, or at least something that we would ordinarily recognize as a plot, is essential for the effect. At its simplest the **plot** is the story of the play – what happens. Having said that, there is much more to plot than simple 'story-line'. The whole notion of plot and its development is bound up with the way that the play is put together, with its structure. The creation of an order or pattern needs careful planning and the playwright needs to consider a number of factors. Generally speaking an effective plot should:

- maintain the interest of the audience from beginning to end
- move the action on from one episode to the next
- arouse the interest of the audience in character and situation
- create high points or moments of crisis at intervals
- create expectation and surprise.

Usually, the structure of a play follows a basic pattern which consists of a number of identifiable elements.

1 **Exposition.** This opens the play and often introduces the main characters and provides background information.

2 **Dramatic incitement.** This is the incident which provides the starting point for the main action of the play.

3 **Complication.** This usually forms the main action of the play, as the characters respond to the dramatic incitement and other developments that stem from it.

4 **Crisis.** This is the climax of the play.

5 **Resolution.** This is the final section of the play where things are worked out and some kind of conclusion is arrived at.

Let us look at this structure as applied to *The Rivals* to see how it works out. Sheridan's play, because of the complexities and confusions of the plot, may seem to have no structure at all on first reading (or viewing). However, a closer study of it reveals that it is very carefully structured indeed.

1 **Exposition.** The opening scene is a classic example of an exposition (see the script on pages 74–76). Two servants, Fag and Thomas, through their conversation provide the audience with all the information that they need to follow the action. We are introduced to the stories of the two pairs of lovers (Jack and Lydia, and Faulkland and Julia) whose fortunes run parallel to each other throughout the play and reach their resolution in the final scene.

2 **Dramatic incitement.** We are made aware of this through the exposition when we are told that Jack Absolute is wooing the beautiful Lydia Languish by pretending to be a character called Ensign Beverley.

3 **Complication.** There are many complications and twists to the plot – Jack's father, Sir Anthony, arranges for his son to marry a young woman (who happens to be Lydia); Lydia's aunt forbids her to see Ensign Beverley (although she would be happy if she knew he was, in fact, Sir Anthony's son); and many more complications develop.

4 **Crisis.** The main crisis comes when Lydia finds out who her beloved Ensign Beverley really is, thus shattering her notions of a romantic elopement, and she refuses to have any more to do with him.

5 **Resolution.** The final scene brings the reconciliation of Jack and Lydia and other strands of the plot which have created problems and complications for most of the other characters are also resolved.

In addition to the main plot involving Lydia and Jack, Sheridan makes use of various sub-plots (the most obvious being the action involving Julia and Faulkland). **Sub-plots** are secondary plots, sometimes separate from the main action but often linked to it in some way. Sub-plots tend to echo themes explored by the main plot or shed more light on them. They contribute to the interest of the play but do not detract from the main plot.

The pace of the action is also integral to the idea of plot and structure. Varying the pace at which the plot unfolds is another factor in maintaining the interest of the audience. Variations in the lengths of scenes and in mood, setting, and action can all influence a play's dramatic effectiveness.

Approaching your script

There are a number of things you can do to deepen your understanding of a drama text you are studying. Here are some suggestions.

Plays in performance

- See a live performance of the play.
- Failing that, see a video recording or a film of it.
- Make notes on performances in a play log book to help you to remember those important initial impressions.
- Read your drama text thoroughly before seeing it performed.
- Listen to the play on audio tape.
- See as many other plays as you can to broaden your experience of drama and the theatre.

Directing the text

- Work with others, dramatizing for yourselves scenes from the text.
- Talk to others about staging implications.
- Imagine you are a director – plan carefully how you would stage a production of the play, the kind of actors you would cast, how you would bring out your own interpretation on the stage, etc.
- Use diagrams, drawings and models to work out sets, stage layout, and props for selected scenes.

Studying the text

- Think about the characters – look at key speeches, look for shifts in focus, different ways of interpreting what they do and say.
- Look for various possible 'meanings' and 'patterns' in the play.
- Consider how/if the theatrical effects are signalled.
- Think about the pace and variety of the action.
- Think about the overall shape and structure of the play and the impact that this could have on an audience.
- Consider the particular characteristics and qualities of the play you are studying.
- Think about relationships between these various elements of the play and how together they present a whole.
- Apply the broader knowledge you have about the nature of plays and drama.

All these activities will help you to formulate and develop your own informed critical response to the play, and therefore fulfil the objectives which lie at the heart of your study of drama.

4 Preparing for Writing

Objectives

- To suggest a range of ways to read and make notes in preparation for writing
- To introduce different strategies for planning writing and practise using them
- To settle on the best preparation and planning methods for own writing

Applying the rules

In Willy Russell's play *Educating Rita*, Rita – a young woman from a working-class background – begins to study English literature through the Open University. She decides that an 'education' will give her more choices in life. After her first unsuccessful attempts at essays, her tutor Frank explains:

Frank: There is a way of answering examination questions that is expected. It's a sort of accepted ritual, it's a game, with rules. And you must observe those rules.

Later, the play suggests that in order to write according to the rules, Rita will have to give up some aspects of herself and her own natural, emotional responses to what she reads. Frank does not believe this will be altogether a good thing. Similarly, the challenge of writing about literature at A level is to learn the 'rules of the game' so as to write in the appropriate way for examination questions without losing the ability to respond in a personal way.

Through the chapters in Section II, we will consider those 'rules' and identify strategies for developing your language of criticism. As we work through these, we will look at some examples of planning and writing activities based on a scene from the play *A Streetcar Named Desire* by Tennessee Williams, which is often chosen for AS or A level study.

Planning strategies

Whether you are writing an essay for classwork, in an examination, or beginning a major piece of coursework, it can often be difficult to get started. However, there are several measures you can take to make this easier. There are also ways of thinking and planning beforehand that can help you feel more confident and secure about essay writing.

Many students find it best to develop their own preparing and planning methods which feel familiar and which can be used in examinations as well as for less formal pieces of writing. However, it is a good idea to try out several different methods and then choose those that work best for you. Your choice will depend on your 'learning style'. For example, some people naturally find it easier to grasp information when it is presented using pictures and diagrams, while others are more comfortable with words, and prefer information written in list or note form. The remainder of this unit presents some strategies for planning your work. Experiment to find which ones are most helpful to you.

Analysing the question

After studying the text or passage, consider the question you plan to answer very carefully. Check that you understand it fully. What are its key words and ideas? Underline them, like this:

It has been suggested that the poetry of John Clare 'is <u>not</u> a simple <u>catalogue</u> of the <u>items</u> composing a scene… but a new way of seeing the <u>movement</u> between the <u>simple</u> and the <u>vastly significant</u>.'

<u>How far</u> would you <u>agree or disagree</u> with this view?

Or

'<u>Never</u> such <u>innocence</u> again' is the concluding line of Philip Larkin's poem, *MCMXIV*. To <u>what extent</u> does this phrase <u>sum up</u> the selection of First World War poetry you have read?

Or

Referring to Extracts A and B, as well as to your <u>wider reading</u> in the literature of love, write a <u>comparison</u> of <u>the ways</u> writers write about their experiences <u>after</u> the <u>death of a loved one.</u>

The underlined words represent the ideas that you will need to keep in mind while you plan and write your answer. In addition to identifying these specific points, do not forget that the 'hidden message' in almost all questions is that you need to write about *how* the writer has used language to create effects.

Activity

Look at the following question on Scene 3 of *A Streetcar Named Desire* and decide which key words you would underline:

Write as fully as you can about Scene 3, 'The Poker Night', focusing on the way the male and female characters are presented.

Annotating the text

When you are preparing to write an essay, annotating your text can be very useful. It can help you to remember certain details and enable you to find them again, especially in a long text. This is true whether the text is a poem or a passage set in the examination, or a complete novel or play you are studying for coursework or wider reading. However, there are some factors you need to bear in mind before you fill the margins of your text with notes.

- If you are studying the text for an 'open book' examination (where you are allowed to take your text into the examination with you), you will probably need to have a 'clean copy' of the text, with no marginal notes at all. Since annotation is still a very useful aid to revision and essay preparation, you might consider buying a second copy in which you can write as many notes as you like. This will work best if the two copies of the text are the same edition, so that the general layout of the clean copy is familiar to you. Alternatively, you could perhaps make photocopies of a few key pages to annotate in detail, but check copyright regulations first. You are usually allowed to copy a small proportion of a text, provided you are using it for educational purposes. Otherwise, you will have to rely on notes written separately from the text.

- If you are studying the text for an examination where you will not have access to the text, there should be no problem about annotating your copy for practice essays or revision, unless you have borrowed the book from your college or school and they wish to keep the texts 'clean'. If that is the case, you may find it worthwhile to buy a copy of your own to annotate.

If you already have an essay question or a topic to focus on when you read and annotate, it will be easier to recognize the information, lines, and phrases from the text which are relevant for you to underline or highlight.

The following annotations on the opening stage directions for Scene 3 of *A Streetcar Named Desire*, and a brief excerpt from later in the scene, have been made in preparation for the question from the activity on page 86.

To set the scene: Blanche Dubois, a complex woman with much to hide, is staying with her sister Stella and Stella's husband Stanley in New Orleans. Their life is very different from the unrealistic expectations she carries from her girlhood as a 'Southern Belle', a pampered young lady who has grown up to expect her good looks to win her admiration. Here, she and Stella return from an evening out to find Stanley playing poker with his friends.

A Streetcar Named Desire

Scene 3
The Poker Night

*(There is a picture of Van Gogh's of a billiard-parlour at night. The kitchen now suggests that sort of lurid nocturnal brilliance, the raw colours of childhood's spectrum. Over the yellow linoleum of the kitchen table hangs an electric bulb with a vivid green glass shade. The poker players – **Stanley, Steve, Mitch,** and **Pablo** – wear coloured shirts, solid blues, a purple, a red-and-white check, a light green, and they are men at the peak of their physical manhood, as coarse and direct and powerful as the primary colours. There are vivid slices of watermelon on the table, whisky bottles, and glasses. The bedroom is relatively dim with only the light that spills between the portières and through the wide window on the street. The sisters appear around the corner of the building.) . . .*

Annotations:
- Colours bold, bright, simple, modern
- 'Raw' suggests uncultivated
- (Brilliant light where the men are)
- Colour of watermelon could suggest raw flesh
- (Where the women will be is 'dim': only light from outside)

Stella:	The game is still going on.
Blanche:	How do I look?
Stella:	Lovely, Blanche.
Blanche:	I feel so hot and frazzled. Wait till I powder before you open the door. Do I look done in?
Stella:	Why no. You are as fresh as a daisy.
	(**Stella** *opens the door and they enter.*)
Stella:	Well, well, well. I see you boys are still at it!
Stanley:	Where you been?
Stella:	Blanche and I took in a show. Blanche, this is Mr Gonzales and Mr Hubbel.
Blanche:	Please don't get up.
Stanley:	Nobody's going to get up, so don't be worried.
Stella:	How much longer is this game going to continue?
Stanley:	Till we get ready to quit.

Annotations:
- Blanche concerned with her appearance. Stella gives the answers she needs to hear
- Old-fashioned – she expects courtesy
- She doesn't get it!
- Stan takes no account of Stella's wishes. His responses to both women are abrupt, rude.

Blanche: Poker is so fascinating. Could I kibitz?

= Look over someone's shoulder and sit in on their hand of cards

Trying to get 'in' with the men

Stanley: You could not. Why don't you women go up and sit with Eunice?

Stella: Because it is nearly two-thirty.   Derogatory tone

He wants them out of the way – poker is a man's world. Women excluded

Stan will have none of it

(**Blanche** crosses into the bedroom and partially closes the portières.)

Stella: Couldn't you call it quits after one more hand?

'loud whack' – Stanley is solid, boisterous

(A chair scrapes. **Stanley** gives a loud whack of his hand on **Stella's**

Stella trying to be reasonable

thigh.)   Chauvinistic reaction – treats Stella roughly, disrespectfully, as his possession

Stella: (Sharply) That's not fun, Stanley.

(The men laugh. **Stella** goes into the bedroom.)

Tennessee Williams

She dislikes this; at least she expresses her anger – but she gets no support – the men think her annoyance is funny. All she can do is walk out

Colour coding

One additional useful way of annotating, which keeps your text fairly uncluttered but helps you to find the parts that you want quickly, especially in a longer text, is to use a system of colour-coding. Using this system you can underline or sideline references relating to different themes, topics, characters, and so on in different colours. As long as you know what the colour signifies and you do not overdo it, it can really help you to find your way around the text quickly. This is useful whether you are preparing for an essay or revising for an examination.

Making notes

There are many different ways of writing or organizing your notes on a text. Here are some to try.

Listing key points

Quickly make a list of four to six points which you would need to cover in order to answer the different aspects of the question posed on page 86. Try to arrange them in a logical order, so that you can move easily from one to another as you write. Often, it is best to begin with the most general point, and then move on to more specific ones. If you are answering an examination question, four to six points should be sufficient. (If you are writing a larger-scale essay for coursework, you will probably need a longer list.)

Taking our question on *A Streetcar Named Desire*, here is a possible list of topics, jotted down quickly.

MEN: dominant, forceful, violent

POKER: a man's world – women excluded

WOMEN: feminine – much less powerful

BLANCHE: nervous, flirtatious

SETTING: men – 'lurid' kitchen; women – 'dim' bedroom

COLOURS: men – bold; women – white, delicate

An answer which included a paragraph on each of these would cover the main points appropriate to the essay question.

Using diagrams

Try writing your key words or topic headings in the middle of a blank sheet of paper. Write words or phrases for related ideas around them, working outwards towards more detailed points, as shown in the spider diagram below. Link the words in as many ways as possible and circle or highlight ideas of most importance. Some people who use these say that you can begin your essay with any point on your diagram and find a way to work through all your ideas. Others prefer to start from one of the topic headings, for example, 'Men' or 'Women' in this case.

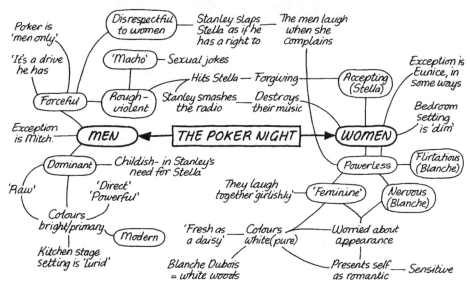

Charting information

Devise your own ways of arranging information in diagram form. For example, family trees can help sort out complex relationships, or you could use a graph to plot the ups and downs of a character's life.

If the essay question asks you to consider two 'sides' argumentatively, or involves a comparison, listing the opposing ideas like this in a table can help:

Male characters	Female characters
Dominant; powerful	Powerless; can't change the men
Rough, violent, macho	'Feminine'; Blanche presents an image of herself as sensitive and well-bred
Disrespectful to women; see them as objects, don't take them seriously and are amused when they are annoyed	Blanche flirtatious with men; Stella accepts violence as 'normal' and continues to love Stanley; strong sexual bond holds them together

Arranging ideas on cards

Write important points and related quotations, or notes for the individual paragraphs you want to include, on cards. You can then arrange these, like jigsaw pieces, in different ways until you work out the best order in which to write about them. An example, taking characters from *A Streetcar Named Desire*, is shown below.

This technique is not suitable for examination situations! It is most useful when you are working on a long text and need to collect notes and examples on a theme or character as you read. An alternative is to use a reading log for each text you study, as suggested in Chapter 1, page 4.

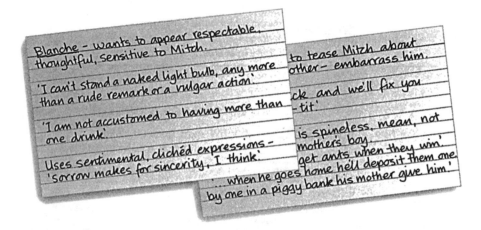

Finding your own strategies

Activity

Having seen the various strategies in action in this unit, try out at least three using an extract from one of your set texts.

As you work on each technique, decide how successful it is for you and which methods you find most fruitful in your interpretation of the text.

We do need to remember, however, that sometimes the process of writing is in itself an exploration. At times we need to throw away all our plans and plunge into the writing before we can find out exactly what our ideas are; some arguments and ideas only take shape when we have worked through them in writing. Some writers always work this way and are not comfortable with planning in advance.

The most important thing is that you discover planning strategies that work for you, and use them so that they become a natural part of your writing process. Then you will have a familiar starting point when faced with the pressure of exam conditions. (For more on planning exam essays see Chapter 16, pages 320–324.)

5 Formulating Views in Writing

Objectives

- To consider the features of clear structure in literary essays
- To use a student's written response as a model for learning
- To study the effective use of quotation in essays

Writing a considered essay

Another moment from Willy Russell's *Educating Rita* will get us thinking about what is meant by a considered essay.

Frank: In response to the question, 'Suggest how you would resolve the staging difficulties inherent in a production of Ibsen's *Peer Gynt'*, you have written, quote, 'Do it on the radio', unquote.

Rita: Precisely.

Frank: Well?

Rita: Well what?

Frank: Well I know it's probably quite naïve of me but I did think you might let me have a considered essay.

Rita's answer is not wrong, but as Frank tells her, she has not yet learned the rules she needs to follow in order to write a 'considered essay'.

> ### Activity
>
> Your understanding of essay writing will already be far more sophisticated than Rita's is at this stage! Working in a small group, create an advice sheet for her, explaining the do's and don'ts of writing essays.

Using evidence from the text effectively

Once you have done some thinking and planning for the question you will be writing about, you will have established the main points that you want to convey in your essay, and perhaps even feel you have an 'answer', as Rita does. However, as you write, it is essential that you provide some good reasons and evidence to support what you say. Evidence in this sense means examples and quotations from the text. It is not very useful, for example, to write that a poet 'uses a great deal of alliteration' in a poem. That would be to make an assertion without giving any grounds for it. All it would demonstrate is that you can recognize alliteration and that you know the technical term for it. You need to follow this statement with some quotations from the poem which contain alliteration. From there you will need to go on and *analyse* the quotation and comment on the *effect* created by the alliteration. So, broadly speaking, the process of literary comment has three stages.

Three steps to using evidence effectively

1 State the point you wish to make.

2 Follow this with your quotation, making sure the context of the quotation is clear, by briefly explaining the situation, or who is speaking and to whom. Quotations should be presented in speech marks or clearly differentiated from the rest of your writing.

3 Analyse the quotation in detail, commenting on individual words or phrases and explaining how and why they are used and with what effect.

Example

The Laboratory by Robert Browning is a poem, in the form of a monologue, spoken by a jealous woman who plans to murder the woman who is her rival. At the time she speaks she is in the laboratory of an alchemist who is mixing some arsenic for her to use, and her words are addressed to him. (Apparently this situation was not that uncommon in Renaissance France and Italy!)

1 In stanza three, as the alchemist works on preparing the poison, she comments on his actions, and seems to be enjoying the process. Her words include some alliteration which heightens this effect:

2 'Grind away, moisten and mash up thy paste,
  Pound at thy powder – I am not in haste.'

3 The repeated 'm' sounds of 'moisten' and 'mash' suggest her almost chewing these words with relish, while the 'p' sounds not only suggest the actual sound of the pestle and mortar, but, because of their explosive quality, express her spiteful pleasure at the thought of her rival's death.

Of course, you will not want to keep rigidly to this three-stage process of Statement, Quotation, Analysis; that would produce rather mechanical essays. However, it is useful to bear it in mind until it becomes integrated into your writing.

Two of the most common difficulties students have with essay-writing arise from the use of quotations.

- **Context:** not providing enough information to make sense of quotations, i.e. sprinkling quotations in essays without providing crucial details about what is going on in the text or which character is speaking, for example. However, do not fall into the trap of spending all your time paraphrasing the text. It is a fine balance to achieve.

- **Analysis:** students usually find this third stage of the process the most challenging. However, its importance is shown in the A level marking criteria where it is the ability to be analytical to a high degree that gains candidates higher grades.

In any case, you will no doubt find your study of literature more rewarding when you know how to recognize and comment on the important details of how writers use language. It will also help you to become more aware of the language choices you make when you are writing yourself.

Structuring an essay

There is no one structure that will work for every essay. Each question will demand a slightly different approach, as the following guidelines illustrate. Here is a basic suggested framework.

Essay plan

1 Introduction

Briefly outline the subject of the essay; it can be useful to refer to the question and its key words and ideas.

Sometimes in coursework it can be useful to give a very concise introduction to the text(s) you are writing about. This might include one or two sentences to establish the context of the question, for example, in terms of plot or character. It is vital that you do not tell the story at length. All your time and effort should be devoted to answering the question.

2 Main section

This could take several different forms, depending on the type of question that you are answering.

- If the question has several key words or ideas, or asks you to explore more than one aspect of the text, you may be able to see a ready-made structure for the main part of your essay.

- If you have already thought about the question and made a plan, in one of the ways suggested in Chapter 4, you can then set about working through the topics in your list or diagram, presenting them in an order which allows you to move easily from one to another.

- If the question requires you to consider two sides of an argument before concluding with your own views, you can organize your writing in one of two ways:

  either

  Present all the arguments on one side first, making sure you always support your ideas with evidence. Then repeat the process for the other side of the argument.

  or

  Make a table showing the arguments on each side of the question, then work through them 'zig-zag' fashion, presenting an argument from one side followed by one from the other side, and so on until you have covered all the points you wish to make. This may seem harder to do, but can often have more impact.

3 Conclusion

Once you have explored all the ideas or arguments you want to mention, finish by explaining the conclusion you have reached and/or briefly summing up the most important points you have made. Sometimes it is useful to restate the key words and ideas from the question in your conclusion. Try to express your conclusion clearly. An otherwise good essay can be marred by a weak ending, and you want to leave your reader with a good impression!

Whatever type of essay you are working on, it is always essential to keep the central issue(s) of the question in mind. After each point or idea you discuss, check that you have made clear how it relates to your overall argument.

If you have recently studied a GCSE English course, you will probably have learned how to make use of the 'Argument Marker' words and phrases, which are an invaluable aid to structuring arguments. As long as you don't use them too mechanically, they can help to guide the reader through your ideas and make your writing flow.

Adding more sophistication

The above essay structure is quite straightforward. You will often find, however, that in following a line of argument, it is necessary to explore a side issue or a related topic before returning to your central theme. It is vital that you can do this without becoming sidetracked and never returning to the main path, or jumping jarringly from one idea to another.

Let us look again at the question on *A Streetcar Named* Desire which featured in Chapter 4:

> Write as fully as you can about Scene 3, 'The Poker Night', focusing on the way the male and female characters are presented.

We know from the planning activities that the central theme for discussion is the contrast between the male characters – presented as dominant, hard, and forceful – and the female characters – portrayed as gentler and less powerful. Yet, in the course of the essay, we are likely to explore several side issues, some of which will contribute to the main argument while others offer exceptions to it or alternative views. It is important to find ways of incorporating these while maintaining a strong sense of direction and flow in the writing. Using connecting devices like the ones shown in the following examples can help achieve this successfully.

A   One aspect of Williams's presentation in the scene, which contributes to our sense that the men are more powerful than the women, is the way in which he uses colours...

[... discussion of the use of colour and its effect...]

Having examined the use of colours in the scene, we can see that it reinforces the impression that the men are dominant here.

B   The relative powerlessness of the female characters is demonstrated by the fact that neither Blanche nor Stella commands any respect from the poker players.

However, the two women are different in the ways in which they respond to the men...

[... comparison of the behaviour of Blanche and Stella...]

Although the female characters differ in the ways they react to the situation, they are presented in general as less forceful than the male characters.

C   Although we have seen that for the most part the men are harder and more forceful than the women, there are some exceptions...

[... First... discussion of Mitch's character ...

Second... examine how Stanley becomes like a pathetic small boy in his need for Stella once she has left...

Third... example of Eunice shouting roughly and angrily...]

There are, therefore, some occasions when male characters seem weaker. On the whole, however, they are presented as powerful.

- -

In each of these examples the writer moves temporarily away from the central line of argument to discuss a side issue, but each time returns to the central question, pointing out how the side issue relates to it. This leaves the writer back on track, ready either to continue the main argument or to explore another 'by way'.

If you are preparing to write about unseen texts or extracts these structures may still be useful. We will look in more detail at ways of organizing your ideas for close reading in Chapter 7, pages 104–110.

Activity

With a partner, look at how one student (Ian) answers the question on Scene 3, 'The Poker Night'. As you read, take note of the annotations given and discuss how this student has structured his work.

Write as fully as you can about Scene 3, 'The Poker Night', focusing on the way the male and female characters are presented.

A fair introductory paragraph which refers to the question and leads into his discussion of the characters

It has been said that Scene 3, which is the poker scene, actually represents the whole play and acts as a miniature version of the play. The Poker Night is an important scene because it shows how the male and female characters are presented by Tennessee Williams. The male characters as a group are presented as dominant and forceful because they have ordered the women out for the night so they can play poker and enjoy themselves. The group of men, Stanley, Steve, Mitch, and Pablo are presented as strong, powerful, and coarse. This is said in the stage directions:

An interesting point in this opening sentence which could do with more explanation

'They are men at the peak of their physical manhood, as coarse and direct as the primary colours.'

'The primary colours' are the colours of the shirts the men are wearing. The colours are 'solid blues, a purple, a red-and-white check, a light green'. Also from these colours and the shirts being worn these are modern men unlike the type Stella and Blanche would have been used to in their past.

The group of men are seen as brutes of men as they sit around the poker table. Here the men start to 'argue hotly':

'I didn't hear you name it.'

'Didn't I name it, Mitch?'

Several good points about the men as a group, including some discussion of the significance of the colours they wear. Next, Ian focuses on individual male characters, which makes good sense

The group of men argue over a simple game of cards. This is almost like a children's squabble.

Stanley is the prime example of a forceful modern man in a world where Stella and Blanche must do as he says. He is the most dominating male character in the group of four. Here, Stella comes in and complains to Stanley about the time they are still playing poker at. Stanley shows he isn't respectful of Stella's wishes. 'A chair scrapes. Stanley gives a loud whack of his hand on her thigh.' Stanley shows his masculinity and authority over Stella by slapping her thigh in a manly way. Stanley is showing off around his friends, proving how much of a man he is. Stanley again shows his dominance over the females when he demands Blanche turns the radio off and when she doesn't do so on his word he becomes fierce.

Structure works quite well here. Ian conveys a sense of how the men behave as a group and also draws a contrast between them

'Stanley stalks fiercely through the portières into the bedroom. He crosses to the small white radio and snatches it off the table. With a shouted oath, he tosses the instrument out of the window.'

He uses appropriate quotations and attempts more detailed analysis in places (for example, where he comments on the significance of individual words such as 'stalks')

Even the way Stanley approaches the radio before he acts presents him in a fierce and forceful light. The words 'stalks', as if he was a primitive caveman stalking his prey, and 'fiercely', which is his anger, show how Stanley is going to act before he acts. Stanley acts more like a modern barbarian around women than a modern gentleman. Mitch is the only exception to the group. Mitch is sympathetic and much more considerate to what Blanche and Stella want than Stanley. Mitch shows he is more gentle in these stage directions:

'..coughing a little shyly. He realizes he still has the towel in his hands and with an embarrassed laugh hands it to Stella.'

Quotations usually introduced quite neatly, providing enough information to place them in context, but Ian fails to do this when he quotes Mitch's moment of embarrassment. To make the situation fully clear to the reader, he needs to say: '... in these stage directions when he comes out of the bathroom and has to pass the women, who are in the bedroom...'

This is the first time we see Mitch around females and he shows he is different to the other men around him by the way he embarrassedly laughs at his little mistake. This shows a kinder and gentler side to the male populace and is a contrast to Stanley's hard, rough and ready nature. Mitch is presented as a fine character who is more suitable to Blanche and Stella and is more like the men they once knew. Here Blanche waltzes to the music with romantic gestures to Mitch.

Ian also slightly misreads Mitch's character here, not picking up that, although he is relatively gentle, he also rather naïve and undignified in the way he responds to Blanche's flirtation

'Mitch is delighted and moves in awkward imitation like a dancing bear.'

The point here is although Mitch didn't know how to waltz he gladly made a fool of himself dancing strangely just to please Blanche. Stanley, from what we know of him, would have laughed and walked away.

The female characters are quite similar in the way they are presented. Stella is presented as strong by the way she stands up to Stanley over the card game:

'Drunk – drunk – animal thing you! All of you – please go home! If any of you have one spark of decency in you...'

Stella confronts the group of males playing poker and challenges them. Also, Stella is shown as wanting to be treated with respect. Stanley slaps Stella's thigh and she reacts sharply and then tells Blanche:

'It makes me so mad when he does that in front of people.'

Stella is showing how she wants to look as if she is respected in front of people.

Stella may be presented as strong and brave and trying to gain respect, but she is also weak when it comes down to what Stanley wants. After Stanley hits her and she and Blanche go up to Eunice's, when Stanley stands downstairs crying, she gives in and goes to Stanley, showing she needs him no matter what he's done. Blanche shows or presents another image of the female which is provocative, flirty and deceitful...

... Blanche is easily older than Stella and has blatantly lied about her age so that Mitch will become more interested in her. Blanche always tries to present herself in a better light:

'I can't stand a naked light bulb, any more than I can a rude remark or a vulgar action.'

Blanche is trying to sound much more refined than she actually is. She is being provocative and flirtatious, exactly as she was in the previous scene when she was alone with Stanley.

This section is less successful: the first sentence is ambiguous. Does he mean that the women are similar to each other, or to the men? He needs to round off his discussion of the men and then lead into his discussion of the women, like this: 'Although Mitch seems different from Stanley and the others, on the whole the men are strong and rough and form a powerful group. On the other hand, the women, although different from each other, seem much less forceful...'

Ian's essay continues with a discussion of Blanche's character and actions, and concludes like this...

This is rather disappointing. The essay just stops, without a conclusion to draw the ideas together. The mention of the previous scene is a red herring – not relevant to the question here

Ian   Ian has not really made use of opportunities to analyse details in his later paragraphs. For example, Blanche's statement that she 'can't stand a naked light bulb' deserves much more attention. As Ian has pointed out, she is deceitful. The naked light bulb would reveal too much literally – she lies about her age – and metaphorically – it also represents the fact that she has a lot more to hide

Activity

1 Swap one of your recent essays for one by a partner. Assess your partner's essay. In particular, look at the structure of the essay and how evidence from the text has been used.

   • Annotate it to show where the structure is clear and informative and where this could be improved.

   • Comment on where quotations have been used effectively and where they are less successful.

2 Hand back the annotated essays and discuss the comments you have made with your partner.

6 Getting Tone and Style Right

Objectives

- To recognize the usual stylistic conventions for writing about literature
- To develop personal writing style
- To implement formal and objective elements of style

Being 'objective'

Until you are familiar with the conventions for writing literary criticism, it may be difficult to grasp exactly what kind of tone or style is appropriate. One way to approach this is to read some good critical writing to get the 'feel' of it. Collections of critical writing which contain essays and reviews relating to a particular author or to specific texts can be useful in this respect. These often illustrate widely differing points of view and so serve as good reminders that there is rarely only one way to interpret a text. As well as introducing you to some different ways of thinking about the texts you are studying, they will help you to develop your awareness of the accepted language of criticism.

Some of these points are brought out in this extract from *Educating Rita*:

Frank: Now the piece you wrote for me on – what was it called...?

Rita: *Rubyfruit Jungle.*

Frank: Yes, it was – erm...

Rita: Crap?

Frank: No. Erm – the thing is, it was an appreciation, a descriptive piece. What you have to learn is criticism.

Rita: What's the difference?

Frank: Well. You must try to remember that criticism is purely objective. It should be approached almost as a science. It must be supported by reference to established literary critique. Criticism is never subjective and should not be confused with partisan interpretation. In criticism sentiment has no place. (*He picks up the copy of* Howards End) Tell me, what did you think of *Howards End*?

Rita: It was crap.

Frank: What?

Rita: I thought it was crap!

Frank: Crap? And who are you citing in support of your thesis, F.R. Leavis?

Rita: No. Me!

Frank: What have I just said? 'Me' is subjective.

Rita: Well it's what I think.

Willy Russell

Perhaps Frank's assertion that literary criticism is 'purely objective', and like a science, is going too far. In studying A level literature there should be opportunities for you to express your own responses to texts as well as writing objectively about them. However, the more objective approach always needs to form the backbone of your critical writing, and when you do express your opinions or feelings about the effectiveness of a piece of writing, you still need to support them with reasoned evidence. Usually this evidence will take the form of quotations from the text, as was shown in Chapter 5. Beware of writing statements like 'The imagery in stanza 2 is extremely evocative and effective' or 'I found this chapter very moving' – and leaving it at that. You need to provide specific examples or quotations and explain how the lines are effective, and why.

In the extract, Frank also suggests that Rita should make 'reference to established literary critique'. In other words, she should refer to the views held by well-known academics who have already written about the text. A word of warning here. Reading the work of experienced literary critics can be useful in developing your awareness of style and also in introducing you to some different ways of approaching your text. However, it is very important that you do not write about other critics' ideas at the expense of expressing your own ideas about the text.

Examiners will always look for well-supported ideas and interpretations that you have worked out for yourself. They may also look for your understanding of other people's readings of the text, particularly if you are writing about a text in terms of its historical or critical context (see Section III). However, when you include the views of other critics, these need to be presented as quotations and acknowledged. Otherwise you run the risk of plagiarizing: 'borrowing', or even stealing, someone else's ideas and presenting them as your own. You will be penalized if you do this in exams or coursework. There is more on critical writing in Section III and on page 39 in Chapter 1.

Here is a sample of critical writing to give a sense of an appropriate tone and style and to demonstrate the use and analysis of quotations. It is an extract from an essay on Tennessee Williams's *A Streetcar Named Desire* by an American scholar, Felicia Hardison Londre, in which she comments on the scene used as an example in chapters 4 and 5.

On 'The Poker Night'

Scene 3 stands out from the others in several ways. It has its own title, 'The Poker Night.' Its pictorial atmosphere of 'lurid nocturnal brilliance, the raw colors of childhood's spectrum' is inspired by a picture of Van Gogh's of a billiard parlour at night, which Henry I. Schvey has identified as *All Night Cafe* (1888). It is one of few ensemble scenes in a play composed largely of two- or three-character sequences. And most importantly, it is the scene in which Blanche and Stanley truly begin to see each other as a threat. The opening line, spoken by one of the men at the card table, serves as a pointer: 'Anything wild in this deal?'

Stanley has been losing at cards and displays a volatile irritability even before Stella and Blanche come in. Mitch sets himself apart from the other card-players by his anxiety over his sick mother. The association with sickness and the dread of loneliness in his comment that 'I'll be alone when she goes' convey a subtle thematic linkage with Blanche, to whom he is introduced by Stella. Blanche quickly senses that Mitch is a prospective conquest. When she changes out of her dress, she deliberately stands in the light so the men can see her through the portieres. When Stella exits into the bathroom, Blanche turns on the radio and sits in a chair... as if confident of her power to attract Mitch to her. First, however, it is Stanley who crosses to the bedroom and turns off the radio, but 'stops short at the sight of Blanche in the chair. She returns his look without flinching', and he returns to the poker table. Thus with great economy of means, by a simple dramatic gesture, Williams demonstrates the staking out of territory.

Mitch soon leaves the card game to chat with Blanche. He shows her the inscription on his silver cigarette case, given to him by a girl who knew she was dying. Blanche homes in on his vulnerabilities: 'Sick people have such deep, sincere attachments.' She asks him to cover the light bulb with a paper lantern she bought on Bourbon Street: 'I can't stand a naked light bulb, any more than I can a rude remark or a vulgar action.' Her equation of the naked bulb with vulgarity implies its opposite: the soft glow of filtered light as the refined sensibility by which she identifies herself. It recalls her comment to Stanley in Scene 2: 'I know I fib a good deal. After all, a woman's charm is fifty per cent illusion...' Blanche's desire for illusion in opposition to the harsh realities that surround her is probably the play's most obvious thematic value. It is significant that Mitch is the one who both installs the paper lantern and, in Scene 9, removes it, for these actions define the period during which he sees Blanche as she wants him to see her, under the spell of an illusion she creates... Blanche... is an artist who dramatizes herself as if she were a stage character, playing roles detached from the reality of her situation, costuming herself from the trunk containing fake furs and costume jewelry, designing the lighting effects that will show her to advantage. With Mitch as her enthralled audience, she adds musical underscoring: she turns on the radio and 'waltzes to the music with romantic gestures'.

The radio galvanizes Stanley into aggressive action, though the actual source of his action undoubtedly lies deeper. Here in his own home, where he is cock of the roost and host of the poker party, the intruder Blanche has lured both his wife and his best friend into her orbit. She has appropriated his radio for her kind of music. In a drunken rage, he throws the radio out of the window.

Felicia Hardison Londre

Formality of style

As well as saying that she should be more objective, Frank hints that Rita needs to develop a more formal style of writing before her essays will be acceptable. This can be difficult to define, but there are some things to note.

Things to avoid are the following.

- **The first person.** Generally, avoid *over-using* the first person in your responses. For example, rather than saying 'I think Louisa is imaginative because...', try to use expressions like 'Dickens suggests that Louisa has a vivid imagination by...' or 'It appears that Louisa is imaginative because...'. Having said that, the occasional use of 'I' or 'me' in a piece of critical commentary to reinforce an important point or to express a personal response can be most effective.

- **Slang.** Avoid using slang expressions (unless, of course, they appear in quotations from your text!). Colloquial language is the language of informal speech. Try to develop your awareness of the differences between spoken English and written English.

- **Dialect and local usage.** Some words or expressions may be used only in some parts of the country; these are appropriate in some forms of writing, but in a formal essay, Standard English is preferable. Try to develop your awareness of your local dialect and, if you can, substitute Standard English equivalents in your essays. This will also avoid confusions in meaning. For example, 'to get wrong' (north-east England) = 'to get into trouble' (Standard English).

- **Abbreviations.** It is better not to use abbreviated forms in formal writing. For example, write 'did not' rather than 'didn't'; and avoid using 'etc.'.
- **Numbers.** These should be written in word form, for example, 'thirty-seven' rather than '37', unless the figure is very large.

However, **do** use:

- **The present tense.** Most literary criticism is written in the present tense. This is because the text itself, whether a novel or a poem, always exists in the same way, even though the narrative may be in the past tense. Aim to keep your writing in the present tense. For example, 'The opening scenes of the play take place in...' not '... took place in ...'. It is even more important to be consistent: whether you use present or past tense, make sure you use the same one throughout. There are many examples of critical responses written in the present tense throughout this book.

Activity

Here is part of a draft student essay on 'The Poker Night' scene, where the style needs quite a lot of attention. Redraft it, improving the style in as many ways as possible. Compare your version with that of another student in your group.

In the scene of the poker night the men and women were presented very differently. Stanley seems to me to be presented in a very macho style character. This is shown in the way that Stanley gets very drunk and this is seen to be the manly thing to do. Also the way he mocks Mitch about having to go home and see his Mam. Stanley says 'Hurry back and we'll fix you a sugar-tit'. He's also shown as a hard and nasty character when he hits Stella because she wants them to stop playing poker. This shows Stanley to be a harsh and hard character because he hits his wife because she asks them to stop playing poker. Whereas in contrast with the other 3 men, Mitch is shown to be a very sensitive and understanding person. This is shown in the fact that he goes home early to see his Mam because she's ill. Mitch says, 'I gotta sick mother. She don't sleep until I come in at night. She says go out, so I do, but I don't enjoy it. I just keep wondering how she is.' I think this shows Mitch is sensitive and caring and thinks about his mother a lot. Mitch also shows his sensitivity when after Stanley had hit Stella he said, 'This is terrible. Poker should not be played in a house with women.' This showed Mitch felt very sorry and awful about what had happened to Stella.

The craft in your writing

As your study of literature progresses, you will develop an awareness of the variety of ways in which writers use language. You may begin to think of writing as a 'craft', something which most writers think about and work at with great care and attention to detail, rather than something which simply happens rather haphazardly.

Try to think about your own writing in the same way.

- Make deliberate choices about the vocabulary you use, choosing the best word for the job, rather than the first one that comes to mind.
- Try out different lengths and types of sentences.
- Think about the different ideas you wish to include in your paragraphs.
- Try to weigh ideas against each other when you are writing argumentatively.

Some fortunate people – usually those who have read very widely – seem to have an innate sense of how to write appropriately for different purposes. Others only develop a sense of style with practice. The aim is to reach the point where you know you can communicate ideas clearly and that you are in complete control of your writing.

Activity

1 Re-read some of your own recent essays. What are the strengths and weaknesses of your written style? Think about this carefully yourself and/or ask a teacher for feedback. Choose one weakness (for example, not putting quotations properly in context or failing to comment on them in detail; inconsistent use of tenses; poor punctuation) and focus on correcting this in your next essay.

2 In a group of four, swap essays or other written work. Divide into pairs to read and discuss the work of each of the other pair. Consider these points:

- Is it easy to read and understand?
- Has the question been answered fully?
- Are quotations used effectively?

Make a note of positive comments as well as advice about how to improve before giving each other feedback.

7 Encountering Texts

Objectives

- To establish a strategy for approaching unprepared texts
- To practise close reading of poetry and prose texts
- To look closely at what makes a distinctive style

Close reading

Skills in close reading are essential for AS and A level literature study. Whenever you encounter a literary text for the first time – whether it is a text you are reading for coursework, a set text, or a poem or prose extract you have been asked to analyse in an examination – all the habits and skills of close reading that you have learned will enable you to discover more for yourself about the text. 'Close reading' means exactly what it says. It is the art of reading closely, paying great attention to details of language, in order to come to the best possible understanding of texts and of how writers create meaning.

For at least part of your AS or A level course, you are likely to study a selection of texts which are linked to a particular context, time period or theme. You may write about these for coursework, but for the examination you will also need to be prepared to do what used to be called 'practical criticism' or 'critical commentary'. This means that you are presented with one or more poems or short prose extracts you have not seen before, and asked to write about them, with only a short time to prepare your response.

This can be a multi-faceted task. You may be asked to compare texts with each other or relate them to other texts you have read; you will also need to recognize features that make them typical – or not typical – of their time or period; but above all, you will need to demonstrate the skills of close reading.

Developing your skills

The best way to develop your ability to read closely is to practise, by reading and analysing as wide a variety of texts as you possibly can. The more familiar you can become with a broad range of literary texts, the more you will be able to recognize the features of different types of writing and to see the similarities and differences between them. The aim is to develop skills like the following, which you can apply to all aspects of your literature studies:

- to read and make sense of a text and recognize its most important features quickly – a kind of instant 'research' where you have to 'think on your feet'
- to apply your own literary understanding as well as ideas you have read or been taught
- to know about 'how writers write', in terms of style and structure
- to organize your ideas in writing quickly.

Approaching unprepared texts

There are some methods of planning your approach which can help you feel more confident about the close reading of unprepared texts. First, it is important not to be daunted by a poem or prose extract you are given to analyse. There will be good reasons why a particular piece has been set, and with close reading you will be able to discover them. Texts about which there is nothing to say are not usually chosen!

Once you have the text in front of you, it is helpful to have a strategy that will allow you to examine it in detail. Here is a suggested checklist of the things you need to consider as you read it. As this list suggests, it is a good idea to begin with an overview or general point, such as the theme of the text, or its overall effect, and then go on to look at the details. If a written response is required, it can be structured in this way too.

1 **Subject or theme.** What is the text about? (This may seem too obvious, but it is a good broad starting point.) What other information do you have, for example the writer's name or a date?

2 **Speaker and/or situation.** Whose 'voice' do you hear in the text? Is it in the third person or the first person? If it is first-person writing, is it the voice of the author, or is the writer taking on a role? In poems, in particular, writers sometimes write with the voice of an object (for example a mountain/ the wind), an animal, or even a god, as well as with the voices of people or characters. Next, ascertain to whom the text is addressed, and the situation in which it is set. This may not always be straightforward. For example, one of Thomas Hardy's poems, *God-forgotten*, is written from the point of view of a messenger sent from earth to ask God to help the human race, only to discover God has forgotten he ever created the planet! The poem consists of the messenger's dialogue with God.

3 **Form and structure.** How does the text appear on the page? Are there any obvious ways in which it could be divided into sections? Is it in a recognizable poetic form, for example a sonnet? Usually we talk about *form* if we are looking at the technical aspects of how the text is constructed – its pattern of stanzas or paragraphs, or simply how it is set out on the page; the *structure* of the text relates to how it is constructed in terms of meaning. For example, it might break into two parts, one focusing on the past and the other on the present.

4 **Ideas and messages.** What is the writer *saying* in the text? The meaning may be different from the obvious subject matter. Think about the author's aims and purposes. These may be expressed directly or indirectly. Look for ideas which may lie below the surface. Are there any signs of irony or satire?

5 **Tone and atmosphere.** Does the text have an overall effect on you as you read it? Does it generate an atmosphere or feeling, such as sadness, gloom, or joy? If so, what is it about the writing that creates this effect? (For example, long sentences, with soft consonant sounds and repeated use of 'oo' and 'o' vowels, tend to create a sombre effect.) How would you describe the writer's 'tone of voice'?

6 **Imagery.** What kinds of visual images or 'word-pictures' does the text present? How does the writer use simile or metaphor? Comment both on individual examples and on patterns of images which you notice. Be careful to explain and analyse these examples in terms of their contribution to the overall meaning and effect of the text.

7 **Vocabulary.** What do you notice about the individual words and phrases which the writer has chosen? Are there types of words which recur? (For example, there

may be several words relating to death, or fire, or childhood.) Are there words which seem unexpected or out of place? What effect do they create?

8 **Rhyme, rhythm, and sound effects.** If the text is a poem, does it use a rhyme-scheme, and what is its effect? (Beware of simply describing a rhyme-scheme without going on to say why you think the poet has chosen it and how far this aim is achieved.) Rhythm can be important in prose as well as in poetry. Are the lines/ sentences flowing or short and jerky? Does the rhythm change at key points in the text? Other sound effects or aural images are created through the use of devices like alliteration. Remember to comment on the *effect* of these.

9 **Conclusion.** Finally, return to an overview of the text. Sum up how the effects and details of style you have analysed come together to create a 'whole' piece of writing. What has your reading of it contributed to your understanding of the subject that it deals with? Does it offer a way of looking at things which you had not considered before? If the question invites you to give a personal response to the text, this is the place for it.

Please note that this is *not* intended as a formula to be applied rigidly in every situation. Not every text requires detailed analysis of every one of these points, but this checklist can act as a starting point and you can easily omit any aspects that are not relevant.

Poetry

Let us consider a poem using this close reading strategy.

Activity

1 Working alone or with a partner, read the poem *Stars* carefully. Annotate the poem if you wish, then make notes under each of the headings 1–9 given above.

2 When you have finished, compare your notes with those that appear after the poem. What is similar and what is different about your interpretation? You may find that the poem has affected you differently or that you noticed different features. No two responses to a text will be identical.

Stars

Ah! why, because the dazzling sun
Restored our Earth to joy,
Have you departed, every one,
And left a desert sky?

All through the night, your glorious eyes
Were gazing down in mine,
And, with a full heart's thankful sighs,
I blessed that watch divine.

I was at peace, and drank your beams
As they were life to me;
And revelled in my changeful dreams,
Like petrel on the sea.

Thought followed thought, star followed star,
Through boundless regions, on;
While one sweet influence, near and far,
Thrilled through, and proved us one!

Why did the morning dawn to break
So great, so pure, a spell;
And scorch with fire the tranquil cheek,
Where your cool radiance fell?

Blood-red, he rose, and, arrow-straight,
His fierce beams struck my brow;
The soul of nature sprang, elate,
But mine sank sad and low!

My lids closed down, yet through their veil
I saw him, blazing, still,
And steep in gold the misty dale,
And flash upon the hill.

I turned me to the pillow, then,
To call back night, and see
Your worlds of solemn light, again,
Throb with my heart, and me!

It would not do – the pillow glowed,
And glowed both roof and floor;
And birds sang loudly in the wood,
And fresh winds shook the door;

The curtains waved, the wakened flies
Were murmuring round my room,
Imprisoned there, till I should rise,
And give them leave to roam.

Oh, stars, and dreams, and gentle night;
Oh, night and stars, return!
And hide me from the hostile light
That does not warm, but burn;

That drains the blood of suffering men;
Drinks tears, instead of dew;
Let me sleep through his blinding reign,
And only wake with you!

Emily Bronte, 1846

One interpretation of *Stars*

1 **Subject or theme.** As the title tells us, the poem is about stars. The poet writes of
her preference for 'gentle night' rather than the 'dazzling' light of day, contrasting
the 'cool radiance' of the stars with the 'blinding' sun.

2 **Speaker and/ or situation.** The poem is written in the first person and there is
nothing to suggest that this is not the voice of the poet herself. It is morning, the
sun has risen, and the poet speaks directly to the stars, asking why they have
gone. She laments their disappearance, which signals the end of night. Without
them, the sky seems 'a desert', and even though the sun brings 'joy' to the Earth,
it is a joy she does not share:

The soul of nature sprang, elate,
But mine sank sad and low!

3   **Form and structure.** Four-line stanzas with a regular pattern of rhyme and
    rhythm are used throughout the poem, which is quite typical for a poem of this
    era. There are no obvious structural breaks, but the poet does concentrate on
    night and the stars in stanzas 1–4, contrasting these with day and the arrival of
    the sun in stanzas 5–8. Each of these sections begins with her questioning the
    inevitable ending of night:

Why did the morning dawn to break
So great, so pure, a spell;

In the remaining four stanzas (9–12) she seems more resigned, recognizing that
she is powerless to stop day following night:

It would not do – the pillow glowed,
And glowed both roof and floor;
And birds sang loudly in the wood,
And fresh winds shook the door;

Finally she begs the stars to return, to protect her from the 'hostile light' of day.
Meanwhile, she hopes to sleep through the day's 'blinding reign', waking only
when the stars are once more in the sky.

4   **Ideas and messages.** This poem does not appear to contain any hidden messages,
    though it does ask us to think a little differently about day and night, light and
    darkness. Emily Brontë rejects the sun, presenting it as brash and 'fierce'. It has
    the power to 'burn' and 'scorch' and has no compassion; it

… drains the blood of suffering men;
Drinks tears, instead of dew;

It is also associated with imprisonment, when she describes the flies trapped
behind her closed window. Night and the stars, however, seem to offer peace
and the freedom of 'boundless regions' for her imagination and her dreams. She
experiences night as a time of spiritual or mystical experience, when she feels
connected with all of creation:

… one sweet influence, near and far,
Thrilled through, and proved us one!

Night brings her to life, making her heart 'throb'; by day, all she wants is oblivion.

5   **Tone and atmosphere.** The poem is pervaded by sadness, even grief. Daybreak
    may bring joy to the 'soul of nature', but the poet's 'sank sad and low'. However,
    her language is strong and passionate, suggesting an intense feeling of aliveness,
    when she describes both the night landscape where the stars 'Throb with my
    heart', and the destructive power of the sun, which 'does not warm, but burn'.
    Her tone is one of complaint, or rebellion, but it is as if she is resisting the
    inevitable. The energetic onward movement of the poem reflects the inexorable
    cycle of night and day and perhaps in spite of herself, she makes day sound
    attractively full of life too:

And birds sang loudly in the wood,
And fresh winds shook the door;

6   **Imagery.** The poet chooses her images to intensify the contrast of night and day.
    Both the stars and the sun are personified. The stars are 'glorious eyes' which
    gaze protectively down at her in a 'watch divine', while the sun attacks her with

its 'fierce' and 'arrow-straight' beams and becomes a monster, or vampire, 'That drains the blood of suffering men' and saps her strength. The storm petrel is a sea-bird that is most at home at sea, rarely returning to land. It flies above the water, 'riding' the wind and waves, and provides an effective simile for the poet who is most at home at night and 'revels' in the waves and storms of her

… changeful dreams,
Like petrel on the sea.

7   **Vocabulary.** The same contrast is sustained in Brontë's choice of words all through the poem. Night is 'gentle' and 'pure', but day is 'hostile'; the stars offer 'cool radiance', the sun has 'fierce beams' which 'scorch with fire.' Mystical and religious vocabulary is used to describe the stars – they are 'glorious', 'divine', 'solemn' and they create 'a spell' that is 'great' and 'pure'. The sun, on the other hand, is 'Blood-red' and associated with violence and cruelty. However, in the middle of the poem, perhaps in spite of herself, the poet's words suggest beauty in the morning light too. She sees it 'steep in gold the misty dale', her 'pillow glowed' and the winds are 'fresh'.

8   **Rhyme, rhythm and aural imagery/ sound effects.** As we noted earlier, the poem adheres to a four-line stanza pattern, with alternating rhyme (*abab*) and a more or less regular rhythm (iambic tetrameter alternating with iambic trimeter). This is a fairly simple, traditional form, but it does, perhaps give a sense of regularity and a forward momentum that reinforces the sense of the inevitable passage of time which the poet resists. Aural imagery is not a feature of the poem, although the poet uses occasional subtle alliteration and assonance. For example, we hear in the soft 'w', 'r' and 'm' consonants how

The curtains waved, the wakened flies
Were murmuring round my room

Her dispirited feeling is captured in the sound of the words 'sank sad', and contrasted with the liveliness of 'nature sprang, elate', while the repeated sounds in 'hide me from the hostile light' give emphasis to her plea.

9   **Conclusion.** Overall, Brontë's poem is like a hymn in praise of the night world of stars, dreams and imagination, compared to the mundane demands of day, which she finds threatening and painful. Her choice of words and images all contribute to this powerful contrast.

If you were to omit the headings from these notes and adapt them slightly, you would have a reasonable analysis of the poem in essay form. Of course, not every detail of the poem has been examined here; you may well find that you have noted other ideas or examples that you would include in an answer.

Activity

Now try applying the same procedure to the poem which follows. It was written in the early nineteenth century by John Clare. (For more about him, see Chapter 9.) Make notes under each of the nine headings, before writing a short critical essay to answer the following question:

How does John Clare present the skylark and its nest, the boys, and the landscape around them?

The Skylark

The rolls and harrows lie at rest beside
The battered road and, spreading far and wide
Above the russet clods, the corn is seen
Sprouting its spiry points of tender green,
Where squats the hare to terrors wide awake
Like some brown clod the harrows failed to break,
While neath the warm hedge boys stray far from home
To crop the early blossoms as they come;
Where buttercups will make them eager run
Opening their golden caskets to the sun
To see who shall be first to pluck the prize;
And from their hurry up the skylark flies
And o'er her half-formed nest with happy wings
Winnows the air – till in the clouds she sings,
Then hangs a dust spot in the sunny skies
And drops and drops till in her nest she lies
Where boys unheeding passed – ne'er dreaming then
That birds which flew so high – would drop again
To nests upon the ground where any thing
May come at to destroy. Had they the wing
Like such a bird, themselves would be too proud
And build on nothing but a passing cloud,
As free from danger as the heavens are free
From pain and toil – there would they build and be
And sail about the world to scenes unheard
Of and unseen – O were they but a bird.
So think they while they listen to its song
And smile and fancy and so pass along
While its low nest moist with the dews of morn
Lie safely with the leveret in the corn.

John Clare

Comparing poems

This approach can also be used when two or more poems or short texts are to be compared. Notes can be made on the poems individually at first, or you can create a table like the one below or a diagram to enable you to see the similarities and differences more clearly.

Comparison	Poem 1	Poem 2
Subject		
Who speaks/ situation		
Form Rhyme Rhythm Structure		
Ideas and messages		
Tone/ feeling/ atmosphere		

(Continued)

Imagery Similes/ metaphors Sound effects		
Vocabulary		

Activity

1 On your own, or with a partner, read the two poems which follow. Both were written during the First World War. Use the close reading strategy to make notes on them, separately, or using a table like the one above.

2 Compare your ideas with the table that follows the poems.

3 Use your notes to write a short essay to answer the question:

Compare the ways in which these poets express despair about the effects of war, explaining which you find more effective.

Rain

Rain, midnight rain, nothing but the wild rain
On this bleak hut, and solitude, and me
Remembering again that I shall die
And neither hear the rain nor give it thanks
For washing me cleaner than I have been
Since I was born into this solitude.
Blessed are the dead that the rain rains upon:
But here I pray that none whom once I loved
Is dying tonight or lying still awake
Solitary, listening to the rain,
Either in pain or thus in sympathy
Helpless among the living and the dead,
Like a cold water among broken reeds,
Myriads of broken reeds all still and stiff,
Like me who have no love which this wild rain
Has not dissolved except the love of death,
If love it be towards what is perfect and
Cannot, the tempest tells me, disappoint.

Edward Thomas

'There Will Come Soft Rains'

There will come soft rains and the smell of the ground,
And swallows calling with their shimmering sound;

And frogs in the pools singing at night,
And wild-plum trees in tremulous white;

Robins will wear their feathery fire
Whistling their whims on a low fence-wire;

And not one will know of the war, not one
Will care at last when it is done.

Not one would mind, neither bird nor tree,
If mankind perished utterly;

And Spring herself, when she woke at dawn,
Would scarcely know that we were gone.

Sara Teasdale

Comparison	Edward Thomas: *Rain*	Sara Teasdale: *'There Will Come Soft Rains'*
Subject	Despair about war, evoked by the sound of heavy rain at night; the numbing effect of war; death.	Despair about war and the fate of the human race; the regeneration of nature after the war; nature is beautiful, but indifferent to war and human life.
Who speaks/ situation	First person; the poet describes his own experience, alone in a 'bleak hut' on a stormy night. Though he never mentions war directly, we surmise that his hut is on the battlefield or in the war zone. He imagines and prays for others, the dead, and those he has loved; he looks forward only to his own death.	Descriptive, general voice; the poet imagines a post-war future, in which birds and wildlife return to the battlefields and trees blossom again – but also the possibility that when the war eventually ends, 'mankind' will have 'perished utterly'.
Form Rhyme Rhythm Structure	One stanza, 18 lines, each line has 10 syllables; no rhyme or regular rhythmic pattern. Some internal rhyme. Flows as one train of thought, from his personal experience to a more general view.	Six 2-line stanzas, with fairly regular rhythm (four stressed syllables in each line) and rhyme. Stanzas 1–3 describe aspects of nature, while 4–6 focus on nature's indifference.
Ideas and messages	♦ Isolation of his experience of war; 'Since I was born into this solitude' suggests it feels like a whole lifetime, separate from his previous existence or normal life. ♦ War (or the rain) takes away power to feel love and emotion – the 'Myriads' of soldiers, living and dead, 'have no love which this wild rain/ Has not dissolved'. ♦ Death is the only thing left that is 'perfect' and cannot 'disappoint' or lead to any further loss or pain.	♦ Spring will return, nature will regenerate, covering the devastation left by war. ♦ The rest of the natural world would not notice or care if the human race was wiped out entirely – 'Not one would mind'; nature is blind and will regenerate, regardless of what has gone before. ♦ A warning, perhaps, that if the war and destruction continue, this will be the result – a beautiful planet minus any human presence. Human life will cease to matter.

(Continued)

Tone/ feeling/ atmosphere	Dark, grim, painful and despairing; no hope for life; insistent repetition of 'rain' in the first line emphasizes the relentlessness of the weather; gives way to a sense of cold resignation to his fate, of giving in to death, which seems inevitable and almost soothing by the end of the poem – a release from a life that has ceased to matter to him.	Initially gentle – 'soft rains'; 'shimmering sound' – delicate but lively; hopeful.\n\nTone more bitter, or perhaps just wistful, at possibility that human life will cease to matter.
Imagery\n\n**Similes/ metaphors**\n\n**Sound effects**	Image of the rain, after his death, 'washing [him] cleaner' is perhaps both a literal reference to the mud of the battlefield and a suggestion that it offers a kind of baptism, or a washing away of sins.\n\n'Like a cold water among broken reeds' – very desolate simile, perhaps suggesting the many 'broken' bodies in the mud, the devastated landscape; the 'Myriads of broken reeds all still and stiff' may represent the soldiers numbed by the relentless horror, unable to feel, with alliteration and assonance giving emphasis to the sombre image.\n\nThere is no end rhyme, but internal rhyme and assonance in several lines, along with repetition of 'rain' adds to feeling of weight, or of a measured, prayer-like pace: 'washing me cleaner than I have been'; 'dying tonight or lying still awake'.	Series of sensual images – sights, smells, sounds and the 'soft' feel of the rain.\n\nPersonification of Spring, and anthropomorphism, as birds/ trees are given human characteristics or motives. 'Wild-plum trees in tremulous white' suggests a nervous bride, or innocent young girls making a debut in white dresses, while the robins 'Whistling their whims' sound carefree. Interesting irony as poem is about nature's lack of awareness of humanity.\n\nAlliteration of 's', 'f', 'w' and other soft consonants in stanzas 1–3 represent sound of rain/ swallows/ robins and add to gentle, delicate feel of new life: 'Robins will wear their feathery fire/ Whistling their whims…'

Vocabulary	Words like 'wild' and 'bleak' suggest the harshness of the environment. Pattern of religious vocabulary: 'washing me cleaner' sounds sacramental, while 'Blessed are the dead' and 'the living and the dead' are phrases from the mass for the dead or funeral service. The idea of love for something that 'is perfect' hints at something divine, but all he desires is death, giving an ironic flavour to the religious language.	Description of beauties of nature contains a few ironic word choices, which hint at war. The robins sit on 'fence-wire' and their plumage is 'fire'. Repetition of 'not one will know… not one/ Will care… Not one would mind' reinforces the bitterness of her lack of hope for the future; 'mankind perished utterly' emphasizes the finality of this.

Prose extracts

The close reading strategy can also be applied to prose passages, although you may find you need to focus on different aspects of the texts. You will be examining many of the same literary techniques, such as imagery, choice of vocabulary, and rhythm, but these will probably be more 'dilute' in prose writings than in poetry. You will also need to think about the effects of different sentence lengths or structures, or the use of dialogue.

For the most part, prose passages will be extracts from longer works rather than complete texts, although occasionally you might encounter very short essays or short stories. The next piece we will look at is from the novel *Small Island*, by Andrea Levy.

This episode is set during the Second World War. Gilbert, from Jamaica, then a British colony, has volunteered to join the RAF to fight for the 'Mother country'. Newly arrived at a training camp in Yorkshire, he and some friends venture out to the local village.

Activity

First, read the following extract carefully. Make notes using the close reading strategy, then draft a short essay to answer the following question:

How does Andrea Levy present the airmen's first encounter with English civilian life?

Small Island

Now see this, a fine day: a weak, heatless sun resting in a blue sky. We are out of the camp for the first time, six, maybe seven of the boys and me. Walking in our RAF blue through the English village of Hunmanby. No order to follow, no command to hear, just us boys. We are remarking on the pretty neatness of the gardens – a flower still in bloom, which someone, I forget who, insists they know the name of. Shutting his eye and biting his lip he tries to recall it. 'A rose,' he says.

'Cha, that is not a rose,' someone else says. 'Every flower is rose to you.'

'That is a rose.'

'It is not a rose.'

This argument is going on as we walk on past the post office and shop. The display in the window, piled up high with tins and boxes, still manages to proclaim that there is a lot of nothing to buy inside. Hubert is trying to persuade James, a strict Presbyterian and teetotal, to come into the pub. 'You think one little beer gonna keep you outta heaven?'

It was I who first noticed. Leaning urgently into our group I whispered, 'Man, everyone looking at us.'

The entire village had come out to play dog with gecko. Staring out from dusty windows, gawping from shop doors, gaping at the edge of the pavement, craning at gates and peering round corners. The villagers kept their distance but held that gaze of curious trepidation firmly on we West Indian RAF volunteers. Under this scrutiny we darkies moved with the awkwardness of thieves caught in a sunbeam.

'Gilbert, ask them what the problem,' Hubert told me.

From every point of the compass eyes were on us. 'You have a megaphone for me, man?' I said. When I scratched my head the whole village knew. If any one of those people had a stick long enough, I swear they would have poked us with it.

It was some while before the more daring among them took cautious steps toward us, the unfamiliar. A young woman – curling brunette hair, dark eyes, pretty and plump at the hips – finally stood within an arm's distance to ask, 'Are you lot American?' She had her mind on feeling some nylon stockings on her graceful leg. Which, as she stood pert and feminine before us, every one of us boys had our mind on too.

'No, we are from Jamaica,' I told her.

'The West Indies,' the Trinidadian among us corrected.

Like a chink in a dam, a trickle of villagers approached us. Most merely nodded as they passed. An old man with a face as cracked as a dry riverbed shook us all hearty by the hand in turn saying, 'We're all in this together, lad. We're glad to have you here – glad to have ya.'

An elderly couple tapping on James's shoulder asked, 'Would you mind, duck – would you mind saying something? Only my husband here says it's not English you're speaking.'

When James replied, 'Certainly, madam, but please tell me what you require me to say,' her husband shouted, 'Bloody hell, Norma, you're right.'

As Norma concluded: 'There, I told you. They speak it just like us, only funnier. Ta, ducks, sorry to bother ya.'

A middle-aged man, not in uniform, kept his hands resolutely in his pockets before addressing me. Eyeing intently the young woman, who was by now getting on very nicely with a lucky Fulton – consorting with him as we had been assured no white woman would – this man, not looking on my face as he spoke, asked me, 'Why would you leave a nice sunny place to come here if you didn't have to?'

When I said, 'To fight for my country, sir' his eyebrows jumped like two caterpillars in a polka.

'Humph. Your country?' he asked without need of an answer. He then took the young woman's arm, guiding her, reluctant as she was, away from Fulton and our group.

✳   ✳   ✳

Let me ask you to imagine this. Living far from you is a beloved relation whom you have never met. Yet this relation is so dear a kin she is known as Mother. Your own mummy talks of Mother all the time. 'Oh, Mother is a beautiful woman – refined, mannerly and cultured.' Your daddy tells you, 'Mother thinks of you as her children; like the Lord above she takes care of you from afar.' There are many valorous stories told of her, which enthral grown men as well as children. Her photographs are cherished, pinned in your own family album to be admired over and over. Your finest, your best, everything you have that is worthy is sent to Mother as gifts. And on her birthday you sing-song and party.

Then one day you hear Mother calling – she is troubled, she need your help. Your mummy, your daddy say go. Leave home, leave familiar, leave love. Travel seas with waves that swell about you as substantial as concrete building. Shiver, tire, hunger – for no sacrifice is too much to see you at Mother's needy side. This surely is adventure. After all you have heard, can you imagine, can you believe, soon, soon you will meet Mother?

The filthy tramp that eventually greets you is she. Ragged, old and dusty as the long dead. Mother has a blackened eye, bad breath and one lone tooth that waves in her head when she speaks. Can this be that fabled relation you heard so much of? This twisted-crooked weary woman. This stinking cantankerous hag. She offers you no comfort after your journey. No smile. No welcome. Yet she looks down at you through lordly eyes and says, 'Who the bloody hell are you?'

Andrea Levy

Examining writers' styles

Throughout this book you are being asked to think not only about what writers are saying – the content of their work – but also about *how* they write. This means examining the particular combination of literary devices, structures, and vocabulary which a writer uses and which go together to form that writer's individual 'style'. From your own reading you will know that some writers' work is easy to recognize immediately because they have a distinctive 'style'. However, it can be more difficult to explain exactly which characteristics make a writer's style recognizable.

As a student of A level literature, you will need to develop the ability to analyse and write about style. One shortcoming noted by examiners is that students fail to take account of this and do not engage in enough detailed analysis of how texts are written. It is easier to concentrate on the writer's use of language when studying poetry, but it can be tempting, when writing about novels or other longer prose works, to focus on the plot or the ideas and neglect to examine the features that make up the author's style.

Try thinking of 'style' as the product of many choices the writer makes about the elements in the following diagram.

THEME
General or specific?
Banal or profound?
Accessible or hidden?

RHYTHM
Rugged or smooth?
Flowing or staccato?
Varied or monotonous?

VOCABULARY
Simple or complex?
Poetic or matter-of-fact?
Emotive or neutral?

STYLE

IMAGERY
Visual or sensual?
Vivid or subtle?
Original or conventional?

SOUND
Harsh or mellifluous?
Gutteral or sibilant?
Use of rhyme?

SENTENCE CONSTRUCTION
Short or long and elaborate?
Varied or patterned?

Thinking or feeling

'Style' can also be viewed as the expression of a writer's personality and preoccupations. The ways in which writers experience the world and the things which are most important to them are bound to affect how and what they write.

The psychologist Carl Jung puts forward the theory that people tend towards being **introverted** (more concerned with the 'inner' world of thought or imagination) or **extraverted** (more grounded in the external world of physical reality and other people). Stemming from this, he maintains that some people are *thinking* types, most at home with thoughts and ideas and perhaps less comfortable with the experience and expression of emotions, while others tend to be more *intuitive*. A third group are *feeling* types, relying on their feelings more than their thoughts to guide them through life, and a final group are *sensation* types, experiencing the world via their physical senses.

This is a partial and simplistic explanation of Jung's ideas, and many other people have created models to try to understand human personality types. However, factors like these are bound to influence the choices authors make when they write, in terms of content and style. They may also account for the fact that most of us respond or 'relate' better to some writers than others. We naturally feel more at home with the work of a writer who experiences the world as we do, while reading the work of a writer who experiences it very differently may feel like struggling to understand a foreign culture.

Of course, most writing – the act of putting ideas and experiences into words – involves a rather cerebral or 'thinking' activity. Most writers 'craft' their work carefully even if their aim is to use words to convey emotional or sensual experiences, but there are some who use more intuitive or free-writing techniques, allowing their words to flow without judging or altering them.

Now let us consider how these ideas might help us in gaining a sense of an author's personal 'style'.

First, read the following passage from *The Rainbow*. This novel by D.H. Lawrence traces the patterns of love and relationships through three generations of the Brangwens, a family of farmers in the East Midlands. Here, in the early part of the book, Tom Brangwen struggles with his sense of being both close to and distant from the woman he will marry.

The Rainbow

Chapter 1

Then, as he sat there, all mused and wondering, she came near to him, looking at him with wide, grey eyes that almost smiled with a low light. But her ugly-beautiful mouth was unmoved and sad. He was afraid.

His eyes, strained and roused with unusedness, quailed a little before her, he felt himself quailing and yet he rose, as if obedient to her, he bent and kissed her heavy, sad, wide mouth, that was kissed, and did not alter. Fear was too strong in him. Again he had not got her.

She turned away. The vicarage kitchen was untidy, and yet to him beautiful with the untidiness of her and her child. Such a wonderful remoteness there was about her, and then something in touch with him, that made his heart knock in his chest. He stood there and waited, suspended.

Again she came to him, as he stood in his black clothes, with blue eyes very bright and puzzled for her, his face tensely alive, his hair dishevelled. She came close up to him, to his intent, black-clothed body, and laid her hand on his arm. He remained unmoved. Her eyes, with a blackness of memory struggling with passion, primitive and electric away at the back of them, rejected him and absorbed him at once. But he remained himself. He breathed with difficulty, and sweat came out at the roots of his hair, on his forehead.

'Do you want to marry me?' she asked slowly, always uncertain.

He was afraid lest he could not speak. He drew breath hard, saying:

'I do.'

Then again, what was agony to him, with one hand lightly resting on his arm, she leaned forward a little, and with a strange, primeval suggestion of embrace, held him her mouth. It was ugly-beautiful, and he could not bear it. He put his mouth on hers, and slowly, slowly the response came, gathering force and passion, till it seemed to him she was thundering at him till he could bear no more. He drew away, white, unbreathing. Only, in his blue eyes, was something of himself concentrated. And in her eyes was a little smile upon a black void.

She was drifting away from him again. And he wanted to go away. It was intolerable. He could bear no more. He must go. Yet he was irresolute. But she turned away from him.

With a little pang of anguish, of denial, it was decided.

'I'll come an' speak to the vicar to-morrow,' he said, taking his hat.

She looked at him, her eyes expressionless and full of darkness. He could see no answer.

'That'll do, won't it?' he said.

'Yes,' she answered, mere echo without body or meaning.

'Good night,' he said.

'Good night.'

He left her standing there, expressionless and void as she was. Then she went on laying the tray for the vicar. Needing the table, she put the daffodils aside on the dresser without noticing them. Only their coolness, touching her hand, remained echoing there a long while.

They were such strangers, they must for ever be such strangers, that his passion was a clanging torment to him. Such intimacy of embrace, and such utter foreignness of contact! It was unbearable. He could not bear to be near her, and know the utter foreignness between them, know how entirely they were strangers to each other. He went out into the wind. Big holes were blown into the sky, the moonlight blew about. Sometimes a high moon, liquid-brilliant, scudded across a hollow space and took cover under electric, brown-iridescent cloud-edges. Then there was a blot of cloud, and shadow. Then somewhere in the night a radiance again, like a vapour. And all the sky was teeming and tearing along, a vast disorder of flying shapes and darkness and ragged fumes of light and a great brown circling halo, then the terror of a moon running liquid-brilliant into the open for a moment, hurting the eyes before she plunged under cover of cloud again.

D.H. Lawrence

> **Activity**
>
> After reading the passage carefully, make notes on the following questions:
>
> 1 To what extent is Lawrence concerned with
>   - his characters' thoughts and ideas?
>   - his characters' feelings and emotions?
>   - his characters' experience of the physical world around them?
>   - relationships between characters?
> 2 What choices does Lawrence make relating to
>   - theme
>   - vocabulary
>   - sentence structure
>   - rhythm
>   - sound?

Lawrence is a writer deeply concerned with human relationships, particularly those between men and women. He tries to articulate the effect people have on each other and presents an ambivalent view of close relationships, which can bring great happiness, but may also be very threatening or destructive.

You will probably have noticed in this extract that he seems to be chiefly aiming to convey Brangwen's feelings, both in a physical and in an emotional sense. Brangwen feels sexual desire for the woman, but is also fearful of losing himself in love, of being 'absorbed' by it. Lawrence sometimes describes this in terms of the actual physical sensations in his body:

> He breathed with difficulty, and sweat came out at the roots of his hair, on his forehead.

However, when he describes their kiss, he can no longer be quite so concrete. To convey the emotional and physical sensations Brangwen feels here, Lawrence uses the image of her seeming to be 'thundering at him', which suggests something both powerful and threatening, but is much less direct. It is the nearest he can get to an impression of his character's feelings.

Some of Lawrence's work was originally banned for being too sexually explicit, but often, as he tries to convey his characters' experiences of love and sex, his descriptions have this rather impressionistic quality. Powerful images and metaphors from nature are used to portray emotional and sexual needs as something almost mystical. Something of this is present in the final paragraph of the extract above, where his description of the stormy night sky mirrors Brangwen's experience with the woman. The moon, which scuds behind the clouds, appears intermittently, 'hurting the eyes' and causing 'terror', reminds us of the moments when he fully feels the presence of the woman and their mutual desire, or looks into her eyes and sees 'a little smile upon a black void'. Both are elusive, beautiful, and frightening.

Having recognized that Lawrence's 'style' has its basis in the emotional, physical, and sensual exploration of life, we can go on to examine in detail some of the choices he makes in using language. You may have noticed some of these:

- Predictably, perhaps, he uses 'feeling' words in almost every sentence: 'unmoved and sad', 'afraid', 'fear', 'agony', and 'anguish' are just a few.
- Although this is a third-person narrative, everything is filtered through Brangwen's emotional responses.

- Colours, and other adjectives, are sometimes used repeatedly, reinforcing their effect, creating patterns, or even giving a ritualistic effect. His eyes are blue and 'very bright', while hers are grey, black, or 'full of darkness' and her 'sad, wide' mouth is 'ugly-beautiful'.

- Sentence lengths are varied. This too contributes to the portrayal of Brangwen's feelings. Moments of tension and uncertainty are made up of short or incomplete sentences, which give a sense of pain, urgency, and indecision:

She was drifting away from him again. And he wanted to go away. It was intolerable. He could bear no more. He must go. Yet he was irresolute.

- The description of the ragged sky is similarly broken up, but there are other moments when the sentences flow more freely, usually when the two characters seem more connected. The use of sentence patterns to enhance a sense of drama is typical of Lawrence.

- The sound qualities of the words are fairly varied, with a few alliterative patterns. Hard consonants are used and, in the case of the image of the disordered sky 'teeming and tearing along', add to the sense of confusion.

Exaggerating style

One interesting – and amusing – way of becoming more aware of a writer's style is to look at a pastiche or parody. The parodist usually takes the most obvious features of a writer's style and exaggerates them, as a cartoonist exaggerates physical features in visual images. A successful parody can make it obvious what a writer's stylistic 'habits' are and help you to recognize them when you return to the original. Writing parody yourself encourages you to concentrate hard on the features which make a writer's style distinctive.

Activity

What features of Lawrence's writing do you recognize in this short parody?

Sons and Aztecs

She lay, motionless, in the burning heat. She gave herself to the sun in an act of supreme worship. Her body was the sacrament. He watched and was thrilled to the soul. A dark primeval shout resounded through his whole being. To him, she was the true female spirituality. Not the whimpering, cloying, tendrilled feminine grasp of demand and duty, not the empty ache of sentiment, but the pure lambent flame of passion. He warmed to her flame. She basked in his primitive mooncold light. She was the sun, and he the moon. He lay down beside her. Then he climbed on top of her and did it to her.

Richard Curtis

A 'thinking' style

Now we will look at how a very different writer, Henry James, presents a scene of courtship. In his novel *Washington Square*, Catherine Sloper, a likeable, but rather plain and naïve young woman who is heiress to a great fortune, receives a visit from her 'lover' Morris Townsend, of whom her father disapproves. Mrs Penniman is her sentimental, meddling aunt.

Washington Square

Chapter 10

Catherine received the young man the next day on the ground she had chosen – amidst the chaste upholstery of a New York drawing-room furnished in the fashion of fifty years ago. Morris had swallowed his pride, and made the effort necessary to cross the threshold of her too derisive parent – an act of magnanimity which could not fail to render him doubly interesting.

'We must settle something – we must take a line,' he declared, passing his hand through his hair and giving a glance at the long, narrow mirror which adorned the space between the two windows... If Morris had been pleased to describe the master of the house as a heartless scoffer, it is because he thought him too much on his guard, and this was the easiest way to express his own dissatisfaction – a dissatisfaction which he had made a point of concealing from the Doctor. It will probably seem to the reader, however, that the Doctor's vigilance was by no means excessive, and that these two young people had an open field. Their intimacy was now considerable, and it may appear that, for a shrinking and retiring person, our heroine had been liberal of her favours. The young man, within a few days, had made her listen to things for which she had not supposed that she was prepared; having a lively foreboding of difficulties, he proceeded to gain as much ground as possible in the present. He remembered that fortune favours the brave, and even if he had forgotten it, Mrs Penniman would have remembered it for him. Mrs Penniman delighted of all things in a drama, and she flattered herself that a drama would now be enacted. Combining as she did the zeal of the prompter with the impatience of the spectator, she had long since done her utmost to pull up the curtain. She, too, expected to figure in the performance – to be the confidante, the Chorus, to speak the epilogue. It may even be said that there were times when she lost sight altogether of the modest heroine of the play in the contemplation of certain great scenes which would naturally occur between the hero and herself.

What Morris had told Catherine at last was simply that he loved her, or rather adored her. Virtually, he had made known as much already – his visits had been a series of eloquent intimations of it. But now he had affirmed it in lover's vows, and, as a memorable sign of it, he had passed his arm round the girl's waist and taken a kiss. This happy certitude had come sooner than Catherine expected, and she had regarded it, very naturally, as a priceless treasure. It may even be doubted whether she had ever definitely expected to possess it; she had not been waiting for it, and she had never said to herself that at a given moment it must come. As I have tried to explain, she was not eager and exacting; she took what was given her from day to day; and if the delightful custom of her lover's visits, which yielded her a happiness in which confidence and timidity were strangely blended, had suddenly come to an end, she would not only not have spoken of herself as one of the forsaken, but she would not have thought of herself as one of the disappointed. After Morris had kissed her, the last time he was with her, as a ripe assurance of his devotion, she begged him to go away, to leave her alone, to let her think. Morris went away, taking another kiss first. But Catherine's meditations had lacked a certain coherence. She felt his kisses on her lips and on her cheeks for a long time afterwards; the sensation was rather an obstacle than an aid to reflection. She would have liked to see her situation all clearly before her, to make up her mind what she should do if, as she feared, her father should tell her that he disapproved of Morris Townsend.

Henry James

Activity

Now ask yourself these questions about the style of this extract.

1 To what extent, would you say, is James concerned with:
   • his characters' thoughts and ideas?
   • his characters' feelings and emotions?
2 Where do you think he stands in relation to his characters? What is his attitude towards them?

Probably you will have noticed the enormous difference between this extract and the one from *The Rainbow*. Both depict an encounter between a man and a woman where marriage is in question, yet the writers are poles apart in the ways they approach this subject. Where Lawrence is so intent on conveying a sense of his characters' emotions and sensations, James is much more concerned with what they are thinking, or with analysing what is going on.

The effect is that reading Lawrence can be a powerful emotional experience: we are presented with such a close view of the characters that it can almost feel as if we are inside their skins. Reading James, however, is often more of an intellectual challenge. It is not that his characters do not have feelings, but that they stop and think about them – or James does – for several pages sometimes. Situations are weighed up and the rights and wrongs of their responses pondered. James maintains a good distance between himself and his characters, leaving himself space to comment and judge, to use irony, or to gently mock. (It is almost impossible, incidentally, to imagine Lawrence being ironic or mocking his characters.) As a result, we as readers also feel more remote from James's characters.

There are other factors in James's writing which contribute to this very different style. Asking some further questions about the details of how he uses language should reveal these.

Activity

Look again at the passage from *Washington Square*.

1 What are James's choices with respect to:
   • vocabulary
   • imagery
   • sentence structures
   • sound?
2 What do these choices contribute to his style? What words would you use to describe his style?

These are some of the points you may have noted:

• James's vocabulary tends to be demanding or 'inflated': he often deliberately chooses words which are complex or Latinate (derived from Latin), when simpler words would convey his meaning equally well. Morris is not 'worried', for example, but has 'a lively foreboding of difficulties' (and this extract is a relatively straightforward example!) This gives a sense of formality, and adds to the feeling of distance mentioned earlier: only someone who steps back and weighs his words would make these choices. Also, James's tone becomes ironic or mocking as he uses long words when his characters and subjects do not really merit them. They may be foolish, like Mrs Penniman, or dishonest or ordinary, but think themselves grander than they really are.

- There is little imagery in the extract, but what there is is deliberately clever. For example, the extended metaphor which describes Mrs Penniman's propensity for acting as if life is a stage drama ('Combining as she did the zeal of the prompter... between the hero and herself') goes on a bit, as we may imagine Mrs Penniman herself does.

- On the whole, James's sentence structures also tend to be complex. (More extreme examples can be found elsewhere in his work.) He is renowned for producing sentences with multiple clauses which temporarily digress from their subject. These require us to hold several ideas in mind simultaneously, which demands concentration. You will find this aspect of his style particularly noticeable if you read the passage aloud.

- There is no evidence that James chooses words in order to create deliberate sound effects. However, the complex and Latinate vocabulary does perhaps give a rather dry, crisp effect to his style, but precision in meaning is his chief aim.

- There can be little doubt that James's main purpose is to present us with something to think about. It is the meanings and ideas contained in his long, precisely constructed sentences, carefully chosen vocabulary, and clever metaphors which are important, never sensual effects like alliteration or visual imagery. It is as difficult to imagine James writing to appeal to the senses as it is to imagine Lawrence being ironic.

Activity

Write a short essay in which you compare the ways in which D.H. Lawrence and Henry James present the encounters and courtship between these two pairs of lovers.

8 Texts in Context

Objectives

- To learn about various ways of placing texts in context
- To develop the ability to recognize and make use of relevant contextual information
- To prepare for studying and writing about the literature of a particular historical era or literary period

What do we mean by context?

When we study a poem, a play, a novel or any other piece of writing we may initially give most of our attention to exploring and analysing the text we see in front of us. However, no literary text can exist in a vacuum, or entirely on its own. All kinds of factors influence the way authors write and affect the way we read their work. Becoming aware of this background information can enhance our understanding and enjoyment of texts by enabling us to see them as part of a wider picture. In other words, we place them in context.

There are several ways in which we can begin to place texts in context. We can consider:

- how a text interrelates with the events of the **author's life**
- the place of a particular text in the **author's** *oeuvre* or **writings as a whole**
- how the text reflects the **historical period** and/or the **place** in which it was written
- the text as an example of its **genre** or of a particular **literary style** or **period**
- the ways in which the **language** of a particular time or place is reflected in the text
- how our reading of the text might be influenced by the way other readers or critics have reacted to it recently or in the past, that is, its **reception**
- the place and significance in the work as a whole of an **extract**, such as a passage from a novel or one poem from a collection.

Relevant contexts

At AS level, at least part of your study of literature will be integrated with the study of a particular context – a historical era or literary period. This involves becoming familiar not only with the events, but also the beliefs, ideas and concerns that have influenced or inspired the writers of that time. It works both ways, however. As you study the literary works, they themselves will reveal a lot about how society functioned at the time when they were written. You will be expected to recognize features that make a text typical – or atypical – of its context and to make your understanding clear by linking it with other texts you have read.

At A2 level, you will study literature relating to a particular theme across the whole sweep of English literature from Chaucer to the present day. In doing so, you should develop an awareness of the differences between the literary styles and conventions of different times and contexts and learn to draw comparisons between them.

Each of the other chapters in this section will introduce you to the literature of a particular period or context which is set for A level study. First, though, we will look more generally at some ways into exploring literature from a contextual point of view.

The author's biography

It can certainly be interesting and increase our enjoyment of texts if we learn something about the lives of the people who wrote them. Indeed, it can be difficult to make any sense at all of some writing without any such knowledge. There can be two sides to this issue, however. Some critics believe that a text should stand alone and that as students of literature we should concern ourselves only with the words on the page, while others suggest that we should learn as much as possible about an author's life and times in order to understand the work fully. For AS and A level, we are aiming to achieve a balance between these two approaches.

Some awareness of a writer's biography may be invaluable for understanding what lies behind the work, but it cannot take the place of thorough knowledge of the text itself and it can create some pitfalls. For example, in essays or exam answers, it may be tempting to include more of the writer's life story than necessary, if you have spent time learning about it. Unless you have specifically been asked to write about the text in this way, too much biographical information can waste valuable time and words that would be better spent focusing on the text itself. It is more likely that you will want to demonstrate your understanding in more subtle ways, including facts or background details only when they are clearly relevant or they support points you want to make about the text.

Finding biographical information

As a starting point, editions intended for study, particularly of classics or older texts, often include an introduction with some biographical material. The best way to gain a deeper understanding of an author's life and times, however, is to read a good biography, or if one exists, an autobiography.

Biographies can vary enormously. Some can be thoroughly researched and packed with information but very dry and dull to read, while others may be enjoyable – even scandalous – but less accurate. It is worth dipping into a few, if they are available. It can be particularly interesting to compare the different viewpoints found in biographies written by contemporaries of the author with those written more recently. For example, *The Life of Charlotte Brontë* by Elizabeth Gaskell, published in 1857, gives not only a fascinating and personal account of her friend's life, but provides an inside view of society in the Victorian era. There are plenty of more recent biographies of the Brontës to read for a modern perspective.

You could also try the following:

- **Encyclopaedias**
- **Diaries** or **letters** from the author, published in book form. These can give fascinating insights into a writer's life, and how and why he or she writes, as well as reflecting the events and concerns of the time. In studying the literature of the First World War, for example, there are many such documents to explore.
- **Television documentaries** or **films** about the lives and times of famous writers.

- The **Internet**. Contemporary writers, and associations of people interested in particular authors, such as The Brontë Society, often have websites, although you may have to search carefully for genuinely useful information.

The author's *oeuvre*

It can be important to know not only about the lives of writers but about their other works, so that you can see whether the text you are studying is typical of its author or whether it stands out for some reason. You may be asked to show that you are aware that authors can have 'favourite' themes or features of style, which crop up regularly in their writings. For example, *The Handmaid's Tale* (see Chapter 1) is typical of Margaret Atwood's work in that she frequently writes prose fiction about the roles and experiences of women in modern society. It is unusual, however, because it is the only novel in which she chooses to explore these ideas in a futuristic or 'science fiction' setting.

Activity

1 Choose a writer whose work you are currently studying. Arrange for each member of your group to research one possible source of information about this author and make notes to bring to your next session. Aim to cover a range of sources, past and present, if that is relevant.

2 Discuss what you have discovered, noting any differences in your findings. Combine your information and create a handout on the life, work and times of your chosen writer.

Time and place

When you are studying texts in context, knowledge of the historical period and the location in which they were written is an essential tool for understanding the literature. Different times and places or cultures have conventions, styles or variations of language which, with experience, we can learn to recognize. The poet Shelley tries to explain how this comes about in this short extract:

> There must be a resemblance, which does not depend upon their own will, between all the writers of any particular age. They cannot escape from subjection to a common influence which arises out of an infinite combination of circumstances belonging to the times in which they live; though each is in a degree the author of the very influence by which his being is thus pervaded.

> *Percy Bysshe Shelley* (from his introduction to *Laon and Cythna*)

Shelley points out that not only are writers moulded – whether they like it or not – by the historical period in which they live and work, but they have the power to influence that age and contribute to creating the culture in which they live. It is a two-way process.

Activity

At the back of this book (see page 334) there is a Chronology listing important historical, political and social events in parallel with literary developments. Choose some texts you are studying or have read recently and make sure that you know the dates when they were written and/or published. Refer to the

Chronology to find out some of the key historical events that occurred around that time. Use other reference materials to expand your knowledge. Discuss whether you can find any evidence that your texts reflect what was happening at the time they were written.

'Place' can be as important as time. In recent decades there has been a surge of interest in the work of British writers who can trace their roots to other cultures, and in the literature of other English-speaking countries. Some of this is what we call 'post-colonial' writing, by authors from nations which were previously colonies under the rule of European powers like the British Empire. Writers from the West Indies, India, and several African states, as well as from Canada and Australia, may fit this category. In a colony, the 'native' or indigenous culture may have been partly suppressed to make way for that which was imposed by the European invaders. With independence, there may be efforts to reassert the original culture. In any case, such societies are complex mixtures, often carrying the weight of the memory of oppression. The struggle to find a true sense of identity is a frequent theme.

If you are studying texts from this sort of background, find out as much as you can about the writer's cultural situation and/or the setting of the text. You will also need to be aware that some of these writers use non-standard forms of the English language. (For more on this, see Chapter 11.)

Literary period, style and genre

As well as relating texts to a historical period, we sometimes put them in the context of a **literary period** or style, which is not quite the same thing. Texts written around the same time are likely to have at least some similarities, as Shelley suggested in the passage above, but texts from a particular literary period are connected at a deeper level. Their authors are likely to share particular ideas about life, art and literature which are reflected in their work. They may be part of a 'movement' – a group of people who share a philosophy or belief system. Such groups tend to arise in response to political or social events, or out of a desire for change. For example, in the late eighteenth century, the Romantic movement was a reaction against the dry, formal, rather artificial styles of the previous decades. Writers embraced the spirit of revolution that was sweeping through Europe and America, and literature reflected a greater concern with nature, imagination and individual experience. A century or so later, in the years after the First World War, the Modernists experimented with artistic forms and styles. The old styles of art and writing no longer seemed appropriate in a world that had changed beyond recognition and had ceased to make sense in the way it had done in the past.

When we talk about **literary genre,** we simply mean the particular kind or form of text we are reading: a play, a novel, a short story, a biography or a poem, for example. We might also focus on narrower categories, such as the Gothic novel, or Shakespearean tragedy.

Language

Language evolves continuously over time. We can see enormous differences between the language of our time and that of Chaucer or Shakespeare, but even in relatively recent texts, vocabulary and usage may be unfamiliar.

Language also alters with place. Within the British Isles, there are many varieties of English and quite a number of writers have experimented with these, from

Emily Brontë's representation of Yorkshire dialect in *Wuthering Heights* to James Joyce's Irish English, or from Lewis Grassic Gibbon's Lowland Scots in *Sunset Song* to the broad Glaswegian of Irvine Welsh's *Trainspotting*. Also, as we have already mentioned, writers from other cultures may use forms of English other than Standard English. These are not 'wrong' or 'inferior', but are languages in their own right, with their own rules and structures.

Activity

Read the following poem with a partner. Try reading it aloud, or at least try to imagine how it would sound. You may even be able to listen to a recorded performance by the author. Discuss how the language differs from Standard English – but enjoy the poem too!

The poet, Grace Nichols, was born in Guyana in the West Indies in 1950, but came to live in the United Kingdom in her twenties. Often, she writes about the challenges of keeping a sense of identity while living in a culture very different from that of her past. Her work is written to be heard, not just to be read, and is best appreciated in live performance.

The Fat Black Woman Goes Shopping

Shopping in London winter
is a real drag for the fat black woman
going from store to store
in search of accommodating clothes
and de weather so cold

Look at the frozen thin mannequins
fixing her with grin
and de pretty face salesgals
exchanging slimming glances
thinking she don't notice

Lord is aggravating

Nothing soft and bright and billowing
to flow like breezy sunlight
when she walking

The fat black woman curses in Swahili/Yoruba
and nation language under her breathing
all this journeying and journeying

The fat black woman could only conclude
that when it come to fashion
the choice is lean

Nothing much beyond size 14

Grace Nichols (from *The Fat Black Woman's Poems*)

Working on an extract

Examination questions on texts in context usually ask you to write analytically about extracts, while also using them as a 'sample' to demonstrate your understanding of the literature of the period you have been studying. Extracts are likely to be taken from non-fiction texts, such as biographies, essays, diaries or letters, which comment on some aspect of life and society or reflect ways of thinking particular to that period. They could also include passages from novels or plays. In another type of question, you may also be asked to consider whether an individual poem is typical of the collection in which it is published, or whether it differs from the 'norm'.

To succeed in tasks like these, you will need good close reading skills (see Chapter 7) as well as a thorough understanding of the wider picture in order to be able to assess this 'sample' in relation to its context.

Reception and critical context

As well as knowing something about the context in which a text is *written*, we also need to be aware that there is someone else in the equation: the *reader*. The background, culture or period in which we read a text may significantly influence how we react to it and what we 'receive' from it. If we think for a minute about texts written in our own time, such as very recent novels, we will see that it is not really possible to categorize them or place them in context in quite the same way as we do with texts from the past, which have already been allocated to a 'period' that has been given a name, like 'Romantic' or 'Victorian'. With older texts, we can also read the comments of critics, both those who wrote their responses when the text was first published and those who write with many years of hindsight, and all these ideas contribute something to our overall impression of the text. For example, it is interesting to learn that some of the first readers of Emily Brontë's famous novel *Wuthering Heights* called it respectively:

> 'The weirdest story in the English Language...'
> 'A nightmare.'
> 'A world of brilliant figures in an atmosphere of mist...'
> 'One of the most repellent books we ever read.'
> [A book that] 'shows more genius... than you will find in a thousand novels.'

Critics and readers ever since have continued to respond to the novel in different ways, depending on their own backgrounds and ideas.

When we turn to a modern text, however, we may have the remarks of a few reviewers or literary scholars to consider, along with contemporary journalism and social commentary, but we cannot yet see how readers of the future might read and categorize it. There is less established critical material to influence our opinions, but also less to get in the way of our own responses. At the same time, ever-growing forms of mass communication generate huge amounts of information and comment. The Internet makes it possible for almost anyone to express their opinions to a global audience. We have to treat this with some caution, accepting that we cannot know how much is significant and how much will be short-lived or ephemeral.

Reading the 'critics'

Reading critical writing brings you into contact with different interpretations of literary texts and these can throw interesting light on texts you are reading yourself, but this needs to be approached in a balanced way. It is vital that you develop confidence in your own ability to assess and respond to texts. Reading other people's opinions can help in this process, but it is important not to allow the ideas of critics to confuse or take the place of your own thoughts and feelings about a text.

If you go on to study literature at a higher level, you will have more exposure to the writings of literary critics and also to various literary **theories**. The ideas and approaches that these offer can be useful in stimulating new ways of looking at texts and can often prompt ideas that might not have occurred to you had you not read them. It does not matter whether you agree or disagree with the ideas you read. Challenging the things that you read is just as important as agreeing with them when you are developing your ideas about the texts you are studying.

Literary theory

Many of the critics you will read, in studying literature at a higher level, will approach their analysis of the text using a particular theory that they apply to all texts. There are many of these literary theories, most of which have been developed by academics over the past three or four decades, and sometimes they run counter to one another. The main thing to remember is that each one looks at a text from a particular point of view or focuses on a particular aspect of it. This is because the theory regards one particular aspect of the text as being more significant than anything else. It is important to keep this in mind when reading literary analysis based on individual literary theories. The following are brief descriptions of the more important literary theories. You may well have already come across some of these. (Bear in mind, though, that these descriptions only give you a very simple definition of very complex theories.)

Structuralism

This is a complex theory but basically it involves the reader giving up his or her right to a personal response or interpretation and focusing on the text alone, describing how the text operates. The theory involves taking a much more 'scientific' approach by looking at texts with the view that all texts attempt to create a view of the world by ordering it through the structure of language. The effect of a structuralist approach can be to look closely at the language structures of a text and to place less emphasis on the ideas of what a text tells us about life, the world, and the characteristics of human nature; the latter are more common approaches at A level.

Post-structuralism or deconstructive criticism

Post-structuralism covers a whole range of activities, so again the ideas are very much simplified here. Post-structuralism questions the structuralist idea that the reader must have knowledge of the 'literary code' of language in order to gain access to the 'meaning' of a text. It does not regard the meaning in language as being stable. It also argues that the reader's perceptions of a text are necessarily subjective so that the idea of any kind of literary objectivity is brought into question. Although post-structuralist criticism seeks to 'destabilize' the text by, among other means, demonstrating its contradictions and problems – and as such has sometimes been regarded as a quite destructive form of criticism – it can have more positive aspects. For example, it can encourage you to consider alternative meanings and treat the text as something that is dynamic and not as something that has finite or 'closed' meanings.

Psychoanalytical theory

Psychoanalytical theory has made a major contribution to post-structuralist theory, taking as its starting point the ideas of Sigmund Freud, who sought to provide universal models and explanations for the unconscious drives and desires that motivate human behaviour. Jacques Lacan developed Freud's theories further through his view that language is the major force in shaping human identity. These theories have been applied to literature study and can provide new angles on the ways in which texts are constructed and presented.

Marxist criticism

Unlike structuralist and post-structuralist literary theories, which have nothing to do with history, society, and class in relation to a text, the Marxist critic brings to a text Karl Marx's view of history in which the idea of class struggle is central. It promotes analysis of a text by creating connections between the text itself and the social and economic structure of the society in which it was written. The theory regards these connections as being fundamental to the nature of the literature produced. Necessarily, Marxist criticism challenges many of the traditional views of texts which interpret them according to the values of a bourgeois or middle-class culture. It seeks to get away from the idea that texts present universal truths about human nature, looking instead to question and reinterpret a text in the light of the period in which it was written and the nature of the society within which it was produced and which influenced it.

Feminist criticism

Like Marxist criticism, feminist criticism also concerns itself with social and political issues, in this case with the presentation of women in literature. The feminist critic is particularly interested in seeking to affirm feminine qualities within what is regarded as a male-dominated society. Most feminist criticism takes as its starting point the idea that society is and always has been patriarchal (i.e. men assume the dominant role) and examines texts from this perspective.

An important element within feminist criticism is that of black, women-of-colour, and lesbian critical theory. Writers and critics involved in this area are very much concerned with the interrelationship between race, sexuality, and oppression of one kind or another.

An overview

This very brief look at some of the key critical theories that you might come across shows just a few examples of the varying ways in which texts can be considered through different critical theories. Your understanding of such theories can contribute to your overall understanding of literature but you should always be aware that they all approach the analysis of texts from a very particular, even partisan, point of view.

As you take your studies further, your awareness and sensitivity to the layers of meaning within literary texts will continue to grow, but never forget that the fundamental element in this process is to develop your own view. Your view of a text is as valid as anyone else's, so long as it is based firmly on a study of the text itself – a view that presents your 'creative, informed, and relevant responses' is vital.

9 Victorian Literature

Objectives

- To understand the requirements of the Victorian literature option of Unit 1 – Texts in Context
- To gain an overview of the Victorian period as a context for literature
- To understand what you will need to do to prepare yourself for Section A of the examination paper – Contextual Linking
- To develop an understanding of the work of the poet you have chosen for study and prepare yourself for Section B of the examination paper

The Victorian literature option

In studying this option you will need to study a variety of texts for AS level.

Unit 1: Texts in Context

This unit will be assessed through one two-hour exam paper. The paper will consist of two sections and you will need to answer one question in each section.

Section A: Contextual Linking

In this section you will be given one question which will consist of a short extract related to Victorian literature. This may be taken from a variety of sources such as a diary, a letter, biography, commentary on the social or cultural aspects of the period, or from a critical work on the period. You will be asked to link your reading in Victorian literature to the extract given.

Section B: Poetry

You will be given a choice of two questions on each of the set poetry texts. One of the questions will focus on one particular poem and its relation to the whole text, and the other will ask you to discuss some aspect of the poems you have studied. You will answer one of these two questions.

The set texts to choose from are as follows:

Selected Poems: John Clare ed. Thornton (Everyman)

Selected Poems: The Brontës ed. Norris (Everyman)

Selected Poems: Thomas Hardy ed. Page (Everyman)

Assessment Objectives

The Assessment Objectives that you will be assessed on in this unit are as follows:

- **AO1** Articulate creative, informed and relevant responses to literary texts, using appropriate terminology and concepts, and coherent, accurate written expression (assessed in Sections A and B)
- **AO2** Demonstrate detailed critical understanding in analysing the ways in which structure, form and language shape meanings in literary texts (assessed in Sections A and B)

- **AO3** Explore connections and comparisons between different literary texts, informed by interpretations of other readers
  (assessed in Sections A and B)
- **AO4** Demonstrate understanding of the significance and influence of the contexts in which literary texts are written and received
  (assessed in Section A)

Unit 2: Creative Study

For this unit you will need to produce a coursework portfolio which, together with your work for Unit 1, will form a coherent course of study of Victorian literature. For your portfolio you will need to study one prose text and one drama text.

You will need to produce two pieces of writing:

- the first piece of writing should present a personal, informed response to the prose text, and will be a creative piece
- the second piece of writing should be on your chosen drama text, and should focus either on its dramatic context or link it to your prose text, covering aspects such as theme, structure, characterization, etc.

Your two pieces of work should be 2000–2500 words in total.

Assessment Objectives

The Assessment Objectives that you will be tested on in this unit are the same as those in Unit 1 – all the objectives are assessed in both pieces of work.

You will find more on the Creative Study unit and a list of the set texts for the Victorian literature option in Chapter 12.

Wider reading

In addition to the set texts you have studied, you should also choose at least three texts covering poetry, prose and drama for wider reading. If you can study further short pieces or extracts, this will enhance your understanding of the context.

The Victorian context

When Victoria became queen in June 1837, it marked the beginning of a reign that was to last more than 63 years and a period marked by many significant developments, both material and intellectual. It was a time that saw a revolution in commerce with a huge expansion of available markets, which in turn led to enormous advances in a whole range of technology and mechanization. The Great Exhibition of 1851 provided a showcase for many of these new developments, heralding a new era of commercial success and prosperity.

On the other hand, for those less fortunate it was a time of poverty and deprivation. Social conditions in the rapidly developing new industrial towns and cities were often appalling and the many squalid slums provided fertile breeding grounds for disease. Mortality rates, especially among children, were high. The poor provided a ready source of cheap labour, including very young children, for the labour-intensive mills and factories. Some enlightened employers such as Joseph Rowntree and Sir Titus Salt, and reformers such as Matthew Arnold and Charles Kingsley, sought to improve the conditions of the poor, and writers such as Charles Dickens and Elizabeth Gaskell painted vivid pictures in their novels of the plight of the poor in the industrialized towns.

The Victorian era was also an age of great developments in thought and ideas. The commercial revolution was matched with an equally far-reaching revolution in scientific thinking. It was the age in which Charles Darwin put forward his theory of evolution in *The Origin of Species* in 1859, and there was a great upsurge in social and political ideas presented through the writings of such figures as John Stuart Mill and Thomas Carlyle. In terms of education, many major developments took place during Victoria's reign, but perhaps one of the most important was the Elementary Education Act of 1870, which laid the foundations for compulsory education for all children. By 1880 all children had to attend school until the age of ten.

It is natural that during a period of such great change, there was also a wealth and variety of literary writing. Alfred Lord Tennyson, Robert Browning, Elizabeth Barrett Browning, Dante Gabriel Rossetti, Christina Rossetti and Gerard Manley Hopkins are among some eminent poets of this period. Novelists such as Dickens, Gaskell, William Thackeray, George Eliot and Robert Louis Stevenson explored various aspects of Victorian society through their works, while dramatists such as Oscar Wilde and John Galsworthy, in their very different ways, exposed the hypocrisies, pretensions and idiosyncrasies they saw around them.

Contextual linking

The following extract is from *Cambridge Cultural History of Britain*, 1989, Volume 7, 'Victorian Britain', edited by Boris Ford.

Activity

1 Read the extract carefully and then discuss it in a small group, making notes on the following:

- the importance of the word 'energy' as applied to Victorian Britain
- the writer's view of the features which typified Britain during this period
- the prose and verse of the period.

2 Now think about how this picture of Britain in Victorian times compares with the view you have formed through your wider reading.

The best synoptic guide to the general quality of life, and also of literature, in England in the 1850s and 1860s, is Hippolyte Taine's *Notes sur l'Angleterre* of 1872; and in Taine's account, there is one particular word which is eye-catchingly recurrent. That is the word 'energy'. 'This need for action and striving... will supply the necessary *energy*'; 'an Englishman needs to be doing something...: he... has a surplus of *energy*'; 'that persevering attentiveness and *energy* which I have noticed so often'; 'each speaker trumpeted his own little fanfare in honour of Anglo-Saxon *energy*'. I pass over the many places where Taine identifies the thing, without happening to use the word. But besides this, one need look no further than simplest statistics of the time: annual output of published books more quadrupled between 1840 and 1870; civil public expenditure nearly trebled; woollen exports more than quadrupled; coal exports increased ten times over; rail travel, and exports of iron and steel, more than twelve times.

The 1850s and 1860s were years of success, prosperity and expansion (though one should never forget that the prosperity included terrible poverty), and the writing of the time reflects that basic reality. There are the glittering portraits of grandiose financial speculators like Mr Merdle in Dickens's *Little Dorrit* (1855–7) or, somewhat later, Trollope's Mr Melmotte in *The Way we Live Now* (1875), where the very title hints at a newer, brasher, more plutocratic order.

That both of those characters crashed in the end was but part of the hectic exuberance of the time. Charlotte Brontë's *Shirley* (1849) depicts this energy-crammed productivity scramble in a northern industrial context, and so does Elizabeth Gaskell's *North and South* (1855); while Dickens's *Hard Times* (1854), set in Preston (which is called Coketown in the novel) shows something of a southerner's reaction to the northern industrial scene, and to the materialism and 'gospel-of-work' ethic as well as, more widely, to the Benthamite 'utilitarianism' that seemed to be its ultimate rationale: the 'greatest good of the greatest number' easily seeming to equate with the greatest volume of goods, and nothing more than that.

In the prose of this period, and indeed before it, this condition of life and society was reflected clearly: as in Carlyle's 'gospel of work' – 'know what thou canst *work* at'. Likewise in the verse. Elizabeth Barrett Browning in her 1861 poem entitled 'The North and the South' (of Europe though, not England) wrote:

> Now give us men from the sunless plain...
> By need of work in the snow and the rain,
> Made strong, and brave by familiar pain!
>   Cried the South to the North.

That is to see the matter much as Taine did, on his visits to England of 1859 and (in all probability) 1862: 'cold, rain, bad weather... are enemies against which he [the Englishman] is obliged to struggle unceasingly'. In the verse of the period, possibly the clearest evidence of the sense of energy is in the work of Gerard Manley Hopkins. What, after all, was his conception of 'instress' but the intrinsic energy of being of every individual reality, considered by itself as a part of Nature, radiating out into the rest of Nature its own irresistible selfhood? –

> Each mortal thing does one thing and the same:
> Deals out that being indoors each one dwells;
> Selves – goes itself: *myself* it speaks and spells;
> Crying *What I do is me: for that I came.*

- -

In the 1840s the journalist and sociologist Henry Mayhew carried out an in-depth study of the lives and conditions of the working-class people of London, first published as a series of articles in the *Morning Chronicle* newspaper. These were collected together and published in three volumes in 1851 under the title *London Labour and the London Poor*. Later a fourth volume covering the lives of beggars, thieves and prostitutes was also published. Mayhew's accounts were based on detailed interviews he carried out with a wide variety of people.

Below is his account of the life of a flower seller he interviewed.

Activity

1 Read the account through carefully and discuss your responses to it with a partner.

2 Make a note of any features of Mayhew's description that struck you for any reason.

3 Compare the picture of Victorian life presented here with the one you have gained from your wider reading.

4 Comment on Mayhew's style of writing and the ways in which he expresses his ideas.

5 Do you think the writer's personal view comes across in his writing, or is he completely impartial? Give reasons for your ideas.

Some of these girls are, as I have stated, of an immoral character, and some of them are sent out by their parents to make out a livelihood by prostitution. One of this class, whom I saw, had come out of prison a short time previously. She was not nineteen, and had been sentenced about a twelvemonth before to three months' imprisonment with hard labour, 'for heaving her shoe', as she said, 'at the Lord Mayor, to get a comfortable lodging, for she was tired of being about the streets'. After this she was locked up for breaking the lamps in the street. She alleged that her motive for this was a belief that by committing some such act she might be able to get into an asylum for females. She was sent out into the streets by her father and mother, at the age of nine, to sell flowers. Her father used to supply her with the money to buy the flowers, and she used to take the proceeds of the day's work home to her parents. She used to be out frequently till past midnight, and seldom or never got home before nine. She associated only with flower-girls of loose character. The result may be imagined. She could not state positively that her parents were aware of the manner in which she got the money she took home to them. She supposes that they must have imagined what her practices were. He used to give her no supper if she 'didn't bring home a good bit of money'. Her father and mother did little or no work all this while. They lived on what she brought home. At thirteen years old she was sent to prison (she stated) 'for selling combs in the street' (it was winter, and there were no flowers to be had). She was incarcerated fourteen days, and when liberated she returned to her former practices. The very night that she came home from gaol her father sent her out into the streets again. She continued in this state, her father and mother living upon her, until about twelve months before I received this account from her, when her father turned her out of his house, because she didn't bring home money enough. She then went into Kent, hop-picking, and there fell in with a beggar, who accosted her while she was sitting under a tree. He said, 'You have got a very bad pair of shoes on; come with me, and you shall have some better ones.' She consented, and walked with him into the village close by, where they stood out in the middle of the streets, and the man began addressing the people, 'My kind good Christians, me and my poor wife here is ashamed to appear before you in the state we are in.' She remained with this person all the winter, and travelled with him through the country, begging. He was a beggar by trade. In the spring she returned to the flower-selling, but scarcely got any money either by that or other means. At last she grew desperate, and wanted to get back to prison. She broke the lamps outside the Mansion-house, and was sentenced to fourteen days' imprisonment. She had been out of prison nearly three weeks when I saw her, and was in training to go into an asylum. She was sick and tired, she said, of her life.

Henry Mayhew, *London Labour and the London Poor,* Volume 1

During the Victorian period many people became involved in campaigning for better social conditions for the poor, exploited and less fortunate. There are many eminent reformers of this period. One of them was Richard Oastler of Fixby Hall near Huddersfield, West Yorkshire. He was a prominent campaigner for the 'Ten Hours Bill', eventually leading to the Factory Act of 1847, which restricted children's working hours in factories to a maximum of ten hours a day.

Below are extracts from a letter he wrote to the *Leeds Mercury* in September 1830. It was printed on 16 October 1830.

Activity

1 Read the letter through carefully. Make a list of the key points that Oastler makes in his letter.

2 Pick out four examples of Oastler's use of imagery here, and comment on the effects he creates.

3 Comment on other stylistic features he uses to add impact to his letter (e.g. rhetorical features, choices of vocabulary).

4 Compare this text to your wider reading, commenting on how typical you think it is of Victorian literature.

To the editors of the *Leeds Mercury*

'It is the pride of Britain that a slave cannot exist on her soil; and if I read the genius of her constitution aright, I find that slavery is most abhorrent to it – that the air which Britons breathe is free – the ground on which they tread is sacred to liberty.' Rev. R. W. Hamilton's Speech at the Meeting held in the Cloth-hall Yard, September 22d, 1830.

Gentlemen, – No heart responded with truer accents to the sounds of liberty which were heard in the Leeds Cloth-hall Yard, on the 22d instant, than did mine, and from none could more sincere and earnest prayers arise to the throne of Heaven, that hereafter slavery might only be known to Britain in the pages of her history. One shade alone obscured my pleasure, arising not from any difference in principle, but from the want of application of the general principle to the whole empire. The pious and able champions of negro liberty and colonial rights should, if I mistake not, have gone farther than they did; or perhaps, to speak more correctly, before they had travelled so far as the West Indies, should, at least for a few moments, have sojourned in our own immediate neighbourhood, and have directed the attention of the meeting to scenes of misery, acts of oppression, and victims of slavery, even on the threshold of our homes.

Let truth speak out, appalling as the statement may appear. The fact is true. Thousands of our fellow-creatures and fellow-subjects, both male and female, the miserable inhabitants of a Yorkshire town, (Yorkshire now represented in Parliament by the giant of anti-slavery principles) are this very moment existing in a state of slavery, more horrid than are the victims of that hellish system 'colonial' slavery. These innocent creatures drawl out, unpitied, their short but miserable existence, in a place famed for its profession of religious zeal, whose inhabitants are ever foremost in professing 'temperance' and 'reformation', and are striving to outrun their neighbours in missionary exertions, and would fain send the Bible to the farthest corner of the globe – aye, in the very place where the anti-slavery fever rages most furiously, her apparent charity is not more admired on earth, than her real cruelty is abhorred in Heaven. The very streets which receive the droppings of an 'Anti-Slavery Society' are every morning wet by the tears of innocent victims at the accursed shrine of avarice, who are compelled (not by the cart-whip of the negro slave-driver) but by the dread of the equally appalling thong or strap of the over-looker, to hasten, half-dressed, but not half-fed, to those magazines of British infantile slavery – the worsted mills in the town and neighbourhood of Bradford!

Would that I had Brougham's eloquence, that I might rouse the hearts of the nation, and make every Briton swear, 'These innocents shall be free!'

Thousands of little children, both male and female, but principally female, from seven to fourteen years of age, are daily compelled to labour from six o'clock in the morning to seven in the evening, with only – Britons, blush while you read it! with only thirty minutes allowed for eating and recreation. Poor infants! ye are indeed sacrificed at the shrine of avarice, without even the solace of the negro slave; ye are no more than he is, free agents; ye are compelled to work as long as the necessity of your needy parents may require, or the coldblooded avarice of your worse than barbarian masters may demand! Ye live in the boasted land of freedom, and feel and mourn that ye are slaves, and slaves without the only comfort which the negro has. He knows it is his sordid, mercenary master's interest that he should live, be strong and healthy. Not so with you. Ye are doomed to labour from morning to night for one who cares not how soon your weak and tender frames are stretched to breaking! You are not mercifully valued at so much per head; this would assure you at least (even with the worst and most cruel masters) of the mercy shown to their own labouring beasts. No, no! your soft and delicate limbs are tired and fagged, and jaded, at only so much per week, and when your joints can act no longer, your emaciated frames are cast aside, the boards on which you lately toiled and wasted life away, are instantly supplied with other victims, who in this boasted land of liberty are HIRED – not sold – as slaves and daily forced to hear that they are free…

The nation is now most resolutely determined that negroes shall be free. Let them, however, not forget that Britons have common rights with Afric's sons.

The blacks may be fairly compared to beasts of burden, kept for their master's use; the whites, to those which others keep and let for hire. If I have succeeded in calling the attention of your readers to the horrid and abominable system on which the worsted mills in and near Bradford is conducted, I have done some good. Why should not children working in them be protected by legislative enactments, as well as those who work in cotton mills? Christians should feel and act for those whom Christ so eminently loved, and declared that, of such is the Kingdom of Heaven. I remain, yours, etc.,

A Briton.

Fixby Hall, near Huddersfield, Sept. 29, 1830

Examination practice

In Section A of the exam you will be presented with one compulsory question which will ask you to read a short extract related to Victorian literature. This short extract could be taken from a variety of sources such as letters, biography, literary criticism, social commentary, diaries, etc.

Activity

Read the following extract carefully. It has been taken from Francis Turner Palgrave's dedication at the beginning of his anthology of English poetry, *Palgrave's Golden Treasury*, first published in 1861.

In your answer you should:

- consider the writer's thoughts and feelings about Tennyson and poetry and the ways in which he expresses them
- compare this extract to your wider reading, saying how typical you think it is of Victorian literature. You should consider both subject matter and style.

TO ALFRED TENNYSON

POET LAUREATE

This book in its progress has recalled often to my memory a man with whose friendship we were once honoured, to whom no region of English Literature was unfamiliar, and who, whilst rich in all the noble gifts of Nature, was most eminently distinguished by the noblest and the rarest, – just judgment and high-hearted patriotism. It would have been hence a peculiar pleasure and pride to dedicate what I have endeavoured to make a true national Anthology of three centuries to Henry Hallam. But he is beyond the reach of any human tokens of love and reverence; and I desire therefore to place before it a name united with his by associations which, whilst Poetry retains her hold on the minds of Englishmen, are not likely to be forgotten.

Your encouragement, given while traversing the wild scenery of Treryn Dinas, led me to begin the work; and it has been completed under your advice and assistance. For the favour now asked I have thus a second reason: and to this I may add, the homage which is your right as a Poet, and the gratitude due to a Friend, whose regard I rate at no common value.

Permit me, then, to inscribe to yourself a book which, I hope, may be found by many a lifelong fountain of innocent and exalted pleasure; a source of animation to friends when they meet; and able to sweeten solitude itself with best society, – with the companionship of the wise and the good, with the beauty which the eye cannot see, and the music only heard in silence. If this collection proves a storehouse of delight to Labour and to Poverty, – if it teaches those indifferent to the Poets to love them, and those who love them to love them more, the aim and the desire entertained in framing it will be fully accomplished.

F.T.P.

May, 1861

Activity

Read the following extract carefully. It has been taken from a letter written by Charlotte Brontë to her publisher and friend William Smith Williams, in which she expresses her views on the poet Robert Southey. It was written on 12 April 1850.

In your answer you should:

- consider the writer's thoughts and feelings about Southey and the ways in which she expresses them

- compare this extract to your wider reading, saying how typical you think it is of Victorian literature. You should consider both subject matter and style.

The perusal of Southey's Life has lately afforded me much pleasure; the autobiography with which it commences is deeply interesting and the letters which follow are scarcely less so, disclosing as they do a character most estimable in its integrity and a nature most amiable in its benevolence, as well as a mind admirable in its talent. Some people assert that Genius is inconsistent with domestic happiness, and yet Southey was happy at home and made his home happy; he not only loved his wife and children *though* he was a poet, but he loved them the better *because* he was a poet. He seems to have been without taint of worldliness; London, with its pomp and vanities, learned coteries with their dry pedantry rather scared than attracted him; he found his prime glory in his genius, and his chief felicity in home-affections. I like Southey.

Charlotte Brontë

Poetry

John Clare

Clare was born in the village of Helpstone in Northamptonshire in 1793, the son of an agricultural labourer, and he remained in this area all his life; his poetry is deeply rooted in it. Although he had little formal education after the age of 12 he was, from an early age, a voracious and wide reader. He had a variety of jobs including hedge-setter, labourer, ploughboy, bar-tender and even, for a brief spell, soldier. However, he continued to read and educate himself to the point where he was able to give private lessons to his neighbours' children.

He began writing poetry as a boy; right from the start he developed a deep interest in nature and, being a countryman, he had a detailed and first-hand knowledge of it. Nature, the countryside and its people are at the heart of his poetry and all his writings.

In 1820 he published *Poems Descriptive of Rural Life and Scenery* and also married Martha Turner, although he never forgot his first love, Mary Joyce, from whom he had earlier parted – probably because her family felt that he was a poor match for her.

His first volume of poetry was a success and he followed this with *The Village Minstrel* (1821), *The Shepherd's Calendar* (1827) and *The Rural Muse* (1835).

In 1832 Clare moved from his cottage to Northborough. Although this was only four miles away Clare, being a man deeply rooted in place, was very unsettled by the move and it impacted on his work, accentuating the theme of loss and sense of melancholy. In 1837 he was admitted to an asylum in Epping, although he escaped from there in 1841 and walked all the way home to Northamptonshire, where he hoped to be reunited with Mary who, in his disturbed state, he thought he had married.

He was again certified insane and admitted to Northampton General Lunatic Asylum, where he remained for the rest of his life, although he had considerable freedom there and continued to write poetry.

Clare is usually considered to be one of the Romantic poets, although has never gained the acclaim of Wordsworth, Coleridge, Keats or Byron. He shared with the Romantics a passion for the natural world, although his interest manifests itself more through a detailed observation of many facets of nature rather than through more abstract philosophical musings.

Here are some of the themes and ideas that he explores through his poetry:

- the country and the seasons
- birds and beasts
- love
- loss and dispossession
- Clare himself.

The country and the seasons in Clare's poetry

His sonnet *The Barn Door is Open* clearly illustrates the simple style that Clare adopts in some of his poems.

Sonnet: The Barn Door is Open

The barn door is open and ready to winnow,
The woodman is resting and getting his dinner
And calls to the maiden with little to say
Who takes the hot dinner and hurries away.
The hen's in the dust and the hog's in the dirt,
The mower is busy and stripped in his shirt,
The waggon is empty and ready to start,
The ploughman is merry and drinking his quart,
The men are at work and the schoolboy at play,
The maid's in the meadow a-making the hay;
The ducks are a-feeding and running about,
The hogs are a-noising and try to get out;
The dog's at his bone and the ass at his tether,
And cows in the pasture all feeding together.

Here are some points you might have noted:

- Most of the lines begin with 'The' – this repetition gives a kind of cohesion to the various images of the community that the poem presents.
- The simple but vivid visual images work collectively to give an overall impression of the scene.
- The close observation and sense of detail are simply presented.
- The poem uses rhyming couplets.
- The use of a tetrameter rhythm gives a jaunty, bright tone to the poem.

The *Wheat Ripening* is a very descriptive poem, but this time the effect is quite different.

The Wheat Ripening

What time the wheat field tinges rusty brown
And barley bleaches in its mellow grey,
'Tis sweet some smooth-mown balk to wander down

Or cross the fields on footpath's narrow way
Just in the mealy light of waking day
As glittering dewdrops moise the maiden's gown
And sparkling bounces from her nimble feet
Journeying to milking from the neighbouring town
Making life light with song – and it is sweet
To mark the grazing herds and list the clown
Urge on his ploughing team with cheering calls
And merry shepherd's whistling toils begun
And hoarse-tongued birdboy whose unceasing calls
Joint the lark's ditty to the rising sun.

- -

You may have noted some of the following:

- the use of the sonnet form
- Clare's presentation of the scenes is more detailed and complex, e.g. the use of colour is very specific
- it captures a range of moods
- it uses poetic techniques in a more sophisticated way, e.g. the use of alliteration, assonance, enjambment and repetition
- the *abab* rhyme scheme coupled with Clare's use of iambic pentameter produces a tone that is more suggestive of the expression of more profound ideas.

Sport in the Meadows is a longer poem and again reflects Clare's close attention to detail. He describes the natural life that springs forth in May, but his focus is not just on nature – he is also interested in the effects the children have on the natural scene.

Activity

Read the poem *Sport in the Meadows* carefully. In a pair or a small group, discuss the following points:

- Clare's use of vocabulary to create a sense of place; note the effect of his dialect expressions or the use of representation of local accent
- the effect created by his introduction of the children
- his description of and attitude towards the children
- his use of rhyme and rhythm
- the structure of the poem.

Sport in the Meadows

Maytime is to the meadows coming in
And cowslip peeps have gotten e'er so big
And water-blobs and all their golden kin
Crowd round the shallows by the striding brig.
Daisies and buttercups and lady-smocks
Are all abouten shining here and there,
Nodding about their gold and yellow locks
Like morts of folken flocking at a fair.
The sheep and cows are crowding for a share
And snatch the blossoms in such eager haste

That basket-bearing childern running there
Do think within their hearts they'll get them all
And hoot and drive them from their graceless waste
As though there wa'n't a cowslip peep to spare
– For they want some for tea and some for wine
And some to maken up a cuckaball
To throw across the garland's silken line
That reaches o'er the street from wall to wall
– Good gracious me, how merrily they fare.
One sees a fairer cowslip than the rest
And off they shout – the foremost bidding fair
To get the prize – and earnest half and jest
The next one pops her down – and from her hand
Her basket falls and out her cowslips all
Tumble and litter there – the merry band
In laughing friendship round about her fall
To helpen gather up the littered flowers
That she no loss may mourn – and now the wind
In frolic mood among the merry hours
Wakens with sudden start and tosses off
Some untied bonnet on its dancing wings.
Away they follow with a scream and laugh
And aye the youngest ever lags behind
Till on the deep lake's very brink it hings.
They shout and catch it and then off they start
To chase for cowslips merry as before;
And each one seems so anxious at the heart
As they would even get them all and more.
One climbs a molehill for a bunch of May,
One stands on tiptoe for a linnet's nest
And pricks her hand and throws her flowers away
And runs for plantain leaves to have it dressed.
So do they run abouten all the day
And tease the grass-hid larks from getting rest
– Scare give they time in their unruly haste
To tie a shoestring that the grass unties,
And thus they run the meadow's bloom to waste
Till even comes and dulls their phantasies,
When one finds losses out to stifle smiles
Of silken bonnet strings – and others sigh
O'er garments renten clambering over stiles.
Yet in the morning fresh afield they hie
Bidding the last day's troubles all goodbye,
When red-pied cow again their coming hears
And, ere they clap the gate, she tosses up
Her head and hastens from the sport she fears;
The old ewe calls her lamb nor cares to stoop
To crop a cowslip in their company.
Thus merrily the little noisy troop
Along the grass as rude marauders hie
For ever noisy and forever gay
While keeping in the meadows holiday.

Birds and beasts in Clare's poetry

In *The Skylark* (see Chapter 7, page 109) Clare uses the idea of the skylark and the boys to create a link between man and nature. In *The Yellowhammer's Nest* (see below) Clare describes another scene from the natural world, this time focusing on the yellowhammer's struggle for survival.

Activity

Read through the poem carefully and make notes on the ways in which Clare creates an impression of the yellowhammer, its habits and its vulnerability.

The Yellowhammer's Nest

Just by the wooden brig a bird flew up,
Frit by the cow-boy as he scrambled down
To reach the misty dewberry – let us stoop
And seek its nest – the brook we need not dread;
'Tis scarcely deep enough a bee to drown,
So it sings harmless o'er its pebbly bed
– Aye, here it is, stuck close beside the bank
Beneath the bunch of grass that spindles rank
Its husk seeds tall and high – 'tis rudely planned
Of bleached stubbles and the withered fare
That last year's harvest left upon the land,
Lined thinly with the horse's sable hair
– Five eggs pen-scribbled over lilac shells
Resembling writing scrawls, which fancy reads
As nature's poesy and pastoral spells;
They are the yellowhammer's and she dwells
A poet-like – where brooks and flowery weeds
As sweet as Castaly to fancy seems
And that old molehill like as Parnass hill
On which her partner haply sits and dreams
O'er all his joy of song – so leave it still,
A happy home of sunshine, flowers and streams.
Yet in the sweetest places cometh ill.
A noisome weed that burthens every soil,
For snakes are known with chill and deadly coil
To watch such nests and seize the helpless young
And like as though the plague became a guest,
Leaving a houseless home a ruined nest
And mournful hath the little warblers sung
When such like woes hath rent its little breast.

The hedgehog too is presented by Clare as a vulnerable creature, but this time it is man and not nature that is the threat.

Activity

Make notes on how Clare presents the hedgehog and the threat that man poses to it in the sonnets below.

Focus on the following features:

- Clare's vocabulary
- his use of imagery
- his attitude towards those who hunt the hedgehog and how he conveys this
- your own responses to these sonnets.

Sonnets: The Hedgehog

The hedgehog hides beneath the rotten hedge
And makes a great round nest of grass and sedge,
Or in a bush or in a hollow tree,
And many often stoops and say they see
Him roll and fill his prickles full of crabs
And creep away and, where the magpie dabs
His wing at muddy dyke in aged root,
He makes a nest and fills it full of fruit;
On the hedge-bottom hunts for crabs and sloes
And whistles like a cricket as he goes.
It rolls up like a ball, a shapeless hog,
When gipsies hunt it with their noisy dogs.
I've seen it in their camps; they call it sweet,
Though black and bitter and unsavoury meat.

But they who hunt the fields for rotten meat
And wash in muddy dyke and call it sweet
And eat what dogs refuse where'er they dwell,
Care little either for the taste or smell.
They say they milk the cows and when they lie
Nibble their fleshy teats and make them dry;
But they who've seen the small head like a hog,
Rolled up to meet the savage of a dog
With mouth scarce big enough to hold a straw,
Will ne'er believe what no one ever saw.
But still they hunt the hedges all about
And shepherd dogs are trained to hunt them out.
They hurl with savage force the stick and stone
And no one cares and still the strife goes on.

Love in Clare's poetry

Clare's poems focusing on the idea of love take various forms. In *Ballad: I dreamt not what it was to woo* he adopts the persona of a woman who has felt both the pleasure and the pain of the uncertainty of love.

Activity

Read through the poem carefully and discuss your initial responses to it with a partner. Focus in particular on the following points:

- the effect of each stanza
- the use of vocabulary
- the change of tone in the final stanza
- Clare's message.

Ballad: I dreamt not what it was to woo

I dreamt not what it was to woo
And felt my heart secure
Till Robin dropped a word or two
Last evening on the moor.
Though with no flattering words the while
His suit he urged to move,
Fond ways informed me with a smile
How sweet it was to love.

He left the path to let me pass,
The dropping dews to shun,
And walked himself among the grass;
I deemed it kindly done.
And when his hand was held to me
As o'er each stile we went,
I deemed it rude to say him nay
And manners to consent.

He saw me to the town and then
He sighed but kissed me not,
And whispered 'We shall meet again'
But didn't say for what;
Yet on my breast his cheek had lain
And, though it gently pressed,
It bruised my heart and left a pain
That robs it of its rest.

In the following two poems Clare presents contrasting ideas of love. *Song: Say what is love* is an expression of the pain he feels at the loss of his first love, Mary Joyce. In *Song: Love lives beyond*, though, he expresses rather different sentiments towards the idea of love.

> ## Activity
>
> Write a detailed comparison of the two poems below, exploring the ways in which Clare presents his ideas about love.

Song: Say what is love

Say what is love – to live in vain:
To live and die and live again.

Say what is love – is it to be
In prison still and still be free

Or seem as free – alone and prove
The hopeless hopes of real love?

Does real love on earth exist?
'Tis like a sunbeam on the mist

That fades and nowhere will remain
And nowhere is o'ertook again.

Say what is love – a blooming name,
A rose leaf on the page of fame

That blooms, then fades – to cheat no more
And is what nothing was before.

Say what is love – whate'er it be,
It centres Mary still with thee.

Song: Love lives beyond

Love lives beyond
The tomb – the earth – which fades like dew.
I love the fond,
The faithful and the true.

Love lives in sleep;
The happiness of healthy dreams
Eve's dews may weep
But love delightful seems.

'Tis seen in flowers
And in the even's pearly dew,
On earth's green hours
And in the heaven's eternal blue.

'Tis heard in Spring
When light and sunbeams warm and kind
On angel's wing
Bring love and music to the mind;

And where is voice
So young and beautifully sweet
As nature's choice
When Spring and lovers meet?

Love lives beyond
The tomb, the earth, the flowers and dew;
I love the fond,
The faithful, young and true.

Loss and the politics of nature in Clare's poetry

In the following poem Clare imagines the end of all things.

Activity

Read the poem carefully and make notes on the ideas that Clare presents here and the ways in which he creates the overall tone and effect of the poem.

Note down at least five images, words or phrases that he uses and explain the effects that they create.

Song: Last Day

There is a day, a dreadful day,
Still following the past,
When sun and moon are past away
And mingle with the blast.
There is a vision in my eye,
A vacuum o'er my mind,
Sometimes as on the sea I lie
'Mid roaring waves and wind,

When valleys rise to mountain waves
And mountains sink to seas,
When towns and cities, temples, graves
All vanish like a breeze.
The skies that was are past and o'er;
That almanac of days,
Year chronicles are kept no more;
Oblivion's ruin pays,

Pays in destruction shades and hell;
Sin goes in darkness down,
And there in sulphur's shadows dwell.
Worth wins and wears the crown.
The very shore, if shore I see,
All shrivelled to a scroll;
The Heavens rend away from me
And thunder's sulphurs roll.

Black as the deadly thunder cloud
The stars shall turn to dun
And heaven by that darkness bowed
Shall make day's light be done.
When stars and skies shall all decay
And earth no more shall be,
When heaven itself shall pass away
Then thou'lt remember me.

- -

Clare uses a range of techniques here. You might have noted some of these:

- vocabulary suggestive of doom
- alliteration
- imagery of destruction
- pathetic fallacy
- repetition of words and images to do with darkness.

Poems about John Clare, poet

In several of the poems in the collection, Clare questions and examines the nature of his own self.

Activity

Read through the poem *I Am* and make notes on the following aspects:

- Clare's questioning of his own existence
- how he feels about himself
- the vocabulary he uses
- the imagery he uses
- the overall tone of the poem.

I Am

I am – yet what I am, none cares or knows;
    My friends forsake me like a memory lost: –
I am the self-consumer of my woes; –
    They rise and vanish in oblivion's host,
Like shadows in love's frenzied stifled throes: –
And yet I am, and live – like vapours tossed

Into the nothingness of scorn and noise, –
    Into the living sea of waking dreams,
Where there is neither sense of life or joys,
    But the vast shipwreck of my life's esteems;
Even the dearest, that I love the best
Are strange – nay, rather stranger than the rest.

I long for scenes, where man hath never trod,
    A place where woman never smiled or wept,
There to abide with my Creator, God;
    And sleep as I in childhood, sweetly slept,
Untroubling, and untroubled where I lie,
The grass below – above the vaulted sky.

In *The Peasant Poet*, Clare uses the third person to refer to himself as he explores how he has developed from a boy to a man.

Activity

Read the poem through carefully. Compare it with I Am, making a note of any differences in tone, language and ideas.

The Peasant Poet

He loved the brook's soft sound,
The swallow swimming by;
He loved the daisy-covered ground,
The cloud-bedappled sky.
To him the dismal storm appeared
The very voice of God,
And where the Evening rock was reared
Stood Moses with his rod;

And every thing his eyes surveyed –
The insects i' the brake –
Were creatures God almighty made;
He loved them for his sake.
A silent man in life's affairs,
A thinker from a Boy,
A Peasant in his daily cares –
The Poet in his joy.

Examination practice

Answer either question 1 or question 2 below.

Activity

1 A critic has written that Clare '...is almost more like a twentieth-century poet than a nineteenth-century poet.' To what extent do you agree with this view? In your answer, you should **either** refer to **two** or **three** poems in detail **or** range more widely through the whole collection.

You may wish to use the poem entitled *Remembrances* as the starting point for your answer.

2 To what extent do you feel that *The Cottager* is typical, in terms of subject matter and style, of Clare's writing?

Thomas Hardy

Thomas Hardy was born at Higher Bockhampton, near Dorchester, in 1840. He was the son of a stonemason and builder. His formal education ended at 16 when he was apprenticed to a local architect named John Hicks (although his mother, who had ambitions for her son and whose own wide reading included the Latin poets, had an input to his education). He began his training as an architect in the Dorchester office, specializing in church restoration. He moved to London in 1862 where he continued his architectural training at the firm of Arthur Blomfield, while reading extensively and continuing to educate himself in the broadest sense.

In 1867 he returned to Dorchester having decided to pursue a career in writing. However, he also continued to work for Hicks and in 1868 was sent to St Juliot in Cornwall to assess a church restoration project. Here he met and fell in love with the rector's sister-in-law, Emma Lavinia Gifford, whom he married in 1874.

His first published novel, *Desperate Remedies,* appeared in 1871, followed by *Under the Greenwood Tree* (1872), *A Pair of Blue Eyes* (1873), and *Far From the Madding Crowd* (1874). These novels were a great success and provided him with the financial security to give up architecture and pursue his interest in writing. He went on to write a number of other novels: *Tess of the D'Urbervilles* was published in 1891 and his final novel, *Jude the Obscure,* in 1895. This met with much moral criticism because of the presentation of its themes, and Hardy gave up fiction writing to devote himself to poetry, which he had written throughout his life and had always regarded as superior to fiction writing.

In later life his marriage underwent much strain, and he and Emma effectively became estranged although they continued to live in the same house. Her death in 1912, however, had a profound effect on him and gave rise to a series of poems known as *Poems 1912–13* in which he deals with his remorse and grief by exploring through his poetry his memories of their early days in Cornwall and their life together.

In 1914 he married his secretary, Florence Dugdale, who had done much to protect Hardy from publicity in his later years, although Emma's death still remained in the forefront of his mind. After a short illness he died in January 1928. He is buried in Poet's Corner at Westminster Abbey, although his heart is buried in the same grave as his first wife Emma at Stinsford churchyard in Dorset.

Although Hardy wrote poetry for most of his life, very little was published until after 1898 when his first volume of poetry, *Wessex Poems,* was published. This was a collection of poems that had been written over a period of more than 30 years.

His poems explore a wide variety of themes and ideas. Here are some of them:

- love in various moods
- love as a response to the death of his wife, Emma
- regret, disillusionment and disappointment
- ballad-style poems that tell a story
- nature as a source of inspiration, and rural life
- the pointlessness of war
- satirical poems
- people, places and events.

Love in Hardy's poetry

In the poem *Neutral Tones*, he explores the effects of a love that has died.

Activity

Read the poem through carefully.

1 What mood does Hardy create here?
2 How does he use language to create the mood? Pick out five examples to illustrate your ideas.

Neutral Tones

We stood by a pond that winter day,
And the sun was white, as though chidden of God,
And a few leaves lay on the starving sod;
 —They had fallen from an ash, and were gray.

Your eyes on me were, as eyes that rove
Over tedious riddles of years ago;
And some words played between us to and fro
 On which lost the more by our love.

The smile on your mouth was the deadest thing
Alive enough to have strength to die;
And a grin of bitterness swept thereby
 Like an ominous bird a-wing…

Since then, keen lessons that love deceives,
And wrings with wrong, have shaped to me
Your face, and the God-curst sun, and a tree,
 And a pond edged with grayish leaves.

Here are some ideas:

- The very setting of the poem creates a sense of coldness and lack of feeling reflecting the lack of feeling that the couple now experience, e.g. the 'winter day'. The sun itself lacks warmth and colour, and the use of words like 'ash' and 'gray' emphasize this lack of colour and life.
- The image of 'tedious riddles of years ago' suggests the love that is now dead.
- This is further heightened by the lines: 'The smile on your mouth was the deadest thing/Alive enough to have strength to die'.
- Vocabulary such as 'bitterness', 'ominous' and 'God-curst' emphasizes the 'keen lessons that love deceives'.

A rather different tone is created in the next two poems. These are two of the poems that Hardy wrote in response to the death of his wife Emma. (Another one can be found in Chapter 2 on page 58.) In *I Found Her Out There*, Hardy recalls scenes in Cornwall where he first met Emma, how he brought her back to Dorset with him, and has now laid her to rest. In *Your Last Drive* he recalls her going on an outing, little knowing, of course, that it would be her last.

Activity

Make detailed notes on these two poems, comparing the following:

- Hardy's thoughts and feelings as expressed through the poems
- his use of vocabulary
- his use of imagery
- the use of nature
- the use of poetic techniques.

I Found Her Out There

I found her out there
On a slope few see,
That falls westwardly
To the sharp-edged air,
Where the ocean breaks
On the purple strand,
And the hurricane shakes
The solid land.

I brought her here,
And have laid her to rest
In a noiseless nest
No sea beats near.
She will never be stirred
In her loamy cell
By the waves long heard
And loved so well.

So she does not sleep
By those haunted heights
The Atlantic smites
And the blind gales sweep,

Whence she often would gaze
At Dundagel's far head,
While the dipping blaze
Dyed her face fire-red;

And would sigh at the tale
Of sunk Lyonnesse,
As a wind-tugged tress
Flapped her cheek like a flail;
Or listen at whiles
With a thought-bound brow
To the murmuring miles
She is far from now.

Yet her shade, maybe,
Will creep underground
Till it catch the sound
Of that western sea
As it swells and sobs
Where she once domiciled,
And joy in its throbs
With the heart of a child.

Your Last Drive

Here by the moorway you returned,
And saw the borough lights ahead
That lit your face – all undiscerned
To be in a week the face of the dead,
And you told of the charm of that haloed view
That never again would beam on you.

And on your left you passed the spot
Where eight days later you were to lie,
And be spoken of as one who was not;
Beholding it with a heedless eye
As alien from you, though under its tree
You soon would halt everlastingly.

I drove not with you… Yet had I sat
At your side that eve I should not have seen
That the countenance I was glancing at
Had a last-time look in the flickering sheen,
Nor have read the writing upon your face,
'I go hence soon to my resting-place;

'You may miss me then. But I shall not know
How many times you visit me there,
Or what your thoughts are, of if you go
There never at all. And I shall not care.
Should you censure me I shall take no heed,
And even your praises no more shall need.'

True: never you'll know. And you will not mind.
But shall I then slight you because of such?

Dear ghost, in the past did you ever find
The thought 'What profit,' move me much?
Yet abides the fact, indeed, the same, –
You are past love, praise, indifference, blame.

December 1912

War in Hardy's poetry

Although not a pacifist, Hardy was aware of the waste of life that war involved, and felt keenly what Wilfred Owen was later to call 'the pity of war'. This sense is nowhere more evident in Hardy's poetry than in *Drummer Hodge*, where he describes the burial of a young drummer boy, one of the many casualties of the Boer War, far from home in an unmarked grave.

Activity

Read the poem through carefully and discuss your initial responses to it with a partner. Now make notes on the following questions.

1 What is the effect of the opening two lines of the poem?

2 What do the words 'kopje-crest', 'veldt' and 'Karoo' mean? Why do you think Hardy uses these words?

3 How does Hardy create the sense that the young drummer is far from home in the second stanza?

4 Why does he call the stars 'Strange' and use the phrase 'strange-eyed constellations'?

5 What is the effect of his grave being unmarked?

6 How would you sum up Hardy's attitude towards war from this poem?

Drummer Hodge

i   They throw in Drummer Hodge, to rest
        Uncoffined – just as found:
    His landmark is a kopje-crest
        That breaks the veldt around;
    And foreign constellations west
        Each night above his mound.

ii   Young Hodge the Drummer never knew –
        Fresh from his Wessex home –
    The meaning of the broad Karoo,
        The Bush, the dusty loam,
    And why uprose to nightly view
        Strange stars amid the gloam.

iii Yet portion of that unknown plain
        Will Hodge for ever be;
    His homely Northern breast and brain
        Grow to some Southern tree,
    And strange-eyed constellations reign
        His stars eternally.

In *The Man He Killed* Hardy also explores ideas on war but in a very different way. This poem is written in the form of a dramatic monologue and the poetic voice is that of a soldier recently returned from the fighting.

Activity

Read the poem carefully.

1 What do you notice about the 'voice' of the poem?

2 Comment on the vocabulary used in the poem.

3 What is the attitude of the soldier towards war?

The Man He Killed

'Had he and I but met
    By some old ancient inn,
We should have sat us down to wet
    Right many a nipperkin!

'But ranged as infantry
    And staring face to face,
I shot at him as he at me,
    And killed him in his place.

'I shot him dead because –
    Because he was my foe,
Just so: my foe of course he was;
    That's clear enough; although

'He thought he'd 'list, perhaps,
    Off-hand like – just as I –
Was out of work – had sold his traps –
    No other reason why.

'Yes; quaint and curious war is!
    You shoot a fellow down
You'd treat if met where any bar is,
    Or help to half-a-crown.'

- -

Here are some ideas:

- The language is simple and the expression of the soldier hesitant and halting as he grapples with a difficult idea. The voice comes across as that of a simple soldier.

- The vocabulary is simple, with no complex words used. A dialect expression is used in 'traps' meaning possessions, again in keeping with the persona Hardy has used.

- There is a sense that he is bewildered by the situation and struggles to come to an understanding of it. Do you think he succeeds?

Other Hardy poems

> **Activity**
>
> Now read *The Darkling Thrush.*
>
> In a small group discuss your ideas about it and the ways in which Hardy uses language to achieve his effects.
>
> What do you think Hardy is saying through the poem?

The Darkling Thrush

I leant upon a coppice gate
    When Frost was spectre-gray,
And Winter's dregs made desolate
    The weakening eye of day.
The tangled bine-stems scored the sky
    Like strings of broken lyres,
And all mankind that haunted nigh
    Had sought their household fires.

The land's sharp features seemed to be
    The Century's corpse outleant,
His crypt the cloudy canopy,
    The wind his death-lament.
The ancient pulse of germ and birth
    Was shrunken hard and dry,
And every spirit upon earth
    Seemed fervourless as I.

At once a voice arose among
    The bleak twigs overhead
In a full-hearted evensong
    Of joy illimited;
An aged thrush, frail, gaunt, and small,
    In blast-beruffled plume,
Had chosen thus to fling his soul
    Upon the growing gloom.

So little cause for carolings
    Of such ecstatic sound
Was written on terrestrial things
    Afar or nigh around,
That I could think there trembled through
    His happy good-night air
Some blessed Hope, whereof he knew
    And I was unaware.

The Ruined Maid presents a very different kind of poem. It is both humorous and satirical, as the naïve country girl newly arrived in London meets an old acquaintance who has been transformed into a quite different figure.

Activity

Read the poem aloud and you will find the humorous effect is even more marked.

1 What do you find amusing about the poem?

2 How effective do you find Hardy's handling of the dialogue?

3 Now think about the form of the poem. How does this have an important part to play in the overall effect of the poem?

4 Do you think the poem has a more serious underlying message?

The Ruined Maid

'O 'Melia, my dear, this does everything crown!
Who could have supposed I should meet you in Town?
And whence such fair garments, such prosperi-ty?' –
'O didn't you know I'd been ruined?' said she.

– 'You left us in tatters, without shoes or socks,
Tired of digging potatoes, and spudding up docks;
And now you've gay bracelets and bright feathers three!' –
'Yes: that's how we dress when we're ruined,' said she.

– 'At home in the barton you said "thee" and "thou",
And "thik oon", and "theäs oon", and "t'other"; but now
Your talking quite fits 'ee for high compa-ny!' –
'Some polish is gained with one's ruin,' said she.

– 'Your hands were like paws then, your face blue and bleak
But now I'm bewitched by your delicate cheek,
And your little gloves fit as on any la-dy!' –
'We never do work when we're ruined,' said she.

– 'You used to call home-life a hag-ridden dream,
And you'd sigh, and you'd sock; but at present you seem
To know not of megrims or melancho-ly!' –
'True. One's pretty lively when ruined,' said she.

– 'I wish I had feathers, a fine sweeping gown,
And a delicate face, and could strut about Town!' –
'My dear – a raw country girl, such as you be,
Cannot quite expect that. You ain't ruined,' said she.

- -

Here are some ideas you might have thought about:

* the contrast between the voices of the two speakers, one very naïve and the other very street-wise, creates an important effect

* it is written in simple rhyming couplets in straightforward quatrains

* the anapaestic metre (see page 57) creates a lilting rhythm commonly used in comic ballads

* dialect words are used to accentuate the contrast.

One of the momentous events that happened during Hardy's lifetime was the sinking of the *Titanic*. Hardy wrote these lines only days after the *Titanic* went down on 15 April 1912. They were first printed in the programme of a Covent Garden charity concert in support of the disaster fund that had been set up.

Activity

Read the poem through carefully and discuss your initial responses to it in a small group.

Think about the following points:

- Hardy's attitude towards the tragedy
- his use of imagery and vocabulary
- the form and structure of the poem.

The Convergence of the Twain

(*Lines on the loss of the* Titanic)

i

In a solitude of the sea
Deep from human vanity,
And the Pride of Life that planned her, stilly couches she.

ii

Steel chambers, late the pyres
Of her salamandrine fires,
Cold currents thrid, and turn to rhythmic tidal lyres.

iii

Over the mirrors meant
To glass the opulent
The sea-worm crawls – grotesque, slimed, dumb, indifferent.

iv

Jewels in joy designed
To ravish the sensuous mind
Lie lightless, all their sparkles bleared and black and blind.

v

Dim moon-eyed fishes near
Gaze at the gilded gear
And query: 'What does this vaingloriousness down here?'…

vi

Well: while was fashioning
This creature of cleaving wing,
The Immanent Will that stirs and urges everything

vii

Prepared a sinister mate
For her – so gaily great –
A Shape of Ice, for the time far and dissociate.

viii

And as the smart ship grew
In stature, grace and hue,
In shadowy silent distance grew the Iceberg too.

ix

    Alien they seemed to be:
    No mortal eye could see
The intimate welding of their later history,

x

    Or sign that they were bent
    By paths coincident
On being anon twin halves of one august event,

xi

    Till the Spinner of the Years
    Said 'Now!' And each one hears,
And consummation comes, and jars two hemispheres.

Examination practice

Answer either question 1 or question 2 below.

Activity

1 A critic has written of Hardy's poetry: 'Much of Hardy's characteristic strength... derives from his steady refusal to write one kind of poetry... to the exclusion of another.'

How far do you agree with this view?

In your answer, you should **either** refer to **two** or **three** poems in detail **or** range more widely through the whole collection.

2 Remind yourself of the poem *Great Things*.

To what extent do you feel that, in terms of subject matter and style, this poem is typical of Hardy's poetry?

The Brontës

Charlotte (born 1816), Branwell (1817), Emily (1818), and Anne (1820) were the youngest four of the six children of Patrick and Maria Brontë. Their father Patrick was a clergyman and shortly after Anne's birth the family moved to Haworth, Yorkshire where he had been appointed as curate. However, a little more than a year later their mother died, and their aunt joined the household to help care for the children. In 1825 the two eldest, Maria and her sister Elizabeth, both died of tuberculosis contracted at school.

Six years after the death of her sisters, Charlotte started attending Roe Head School at Mirfield, West Yorkshire, where she made a number of friends. When she left the school she had so impressed the principal, Miss Wooler, that she was invited back as a teacher and one of her sisters was offered a free place at the school. Emily attended the school but illness forced her to return to Haworth and her place was taken by Anne.

At this time all four of the Brontës had ambitions to be poets, and Charlotte sent some of her verses to the poet Robert Southey, asking him to comment on them. However, he did not approve of women earning a living through writing and his response was not encouraging. Branwell was hoping to pursue a career as an artist and had taken lessons from a professional portrait painter, while Charlotte had taken up a post as a private governess. Emily spent several months as a teacher near Halifax and Anne became a governess in Mirfield. However, none of these positions lasted very long. Emily accompanied Charlotte to Brussels in 1842 where they taught English and music at a boarding school in return for language tuition. However, Emily always preferred to remain at home and took the opportunity to return to Haworth to keep house for her father when her aunt fell ill and died. Charlotte returned to Brussels alone for a while.

From childhood the Brontë children had written stories based on their imaginary kingdoms of Angria and Gondal, and many of their poems had their origins in this make-believe world. However, when Charlotte, Emily and Anne published their volume of *Poems* under the names of Currer, Ellis and Acton Bell (names chosen to disguise the fact that they were women), much re-editing had taken place to remove evidence of the imaginary world. They published at their own expense, but only two copies were sold. They did, however, receive some favourable reviews. The sisters from this point turned their attention to writing prose.

Themes and ideas in the poetry of the Brontës

As might be expected, the poetry of the Brontës varies between the individuals.

It has been said that Charlotte's poetic expression often suffers because of her strict adherence to the rules of rhythm and metre, and that her best poems are those inspired by personal experience rather than the imaginary worlds of Angria and Gondal.

Branwell's poems reveal his talent for observing nature and capturing an individual scene, although human life often provides the inspiration for his poetry.

Emily is often regarded as the most successful of the poets and certainly is the one whose poems are most widely recognized. Much of her work focuses on the natural world and has elements of pantheism about it. On the other hand, clear Christian beliefs are at the heart of Anne's poetry.

Although they are very different poets, they do share interests and ideas, and similar themes arise in their poems, even if they approach them in very different ways. Here are some general areas of interest:

- love
- nature
- liberty
- the idea of a lost paradise
- death.

Charlotte Brontë

Parting is a very personal poem which Charlotte wrote on the last day of the Christmas holidays before she returned to Roe Head School.

Activity

Read the poem carefully.

1 What does Charlotte Brontë have to say here?
2 How would you describe the tone and voice of her poem? Why?
3 Who do you think it is addressed to?
4 What techniques does she use to express her message?

Parting

There's no use in weeping,
Though we are condemned to part:
There's such a thing as keeping
A remembrance in one's heart:

There's such a thing as dwelling
On the thought ourselves have nurs'd,
And with scorn and courage telling
The world to do its worst.

We'll not let its follies grieve us,
We'll just take them as they come;
And then every day will leave us
A merry laugh for home.

When we've left each friend and brother,
When we're parted wide and far,
We will think of one another,
As even better than we are.

Every glorious sight above us,
Every pleasant sight beneath,
We'll connect with those that love us,
Whom we truly love till death!

In the evening, when we're sitting
By the fire perchance alone,
Then shall heart with warm heart meeting,
Give responsive tone for tone.

We can burst the bonds which chain us,
Which cold human hands have wrought,
And where none shall dare restrain us
We can meet again, in thought.

So there's no use in weeping,
Bear a cheerful spirit still;
Never doubt that Fate is keeping
Future good for present ill!

- -

Here are some ideas.

- She knows the parting is inevitable and that they must accept it.
- The tone seems designed to give comfort both to herself and those she is parting from, although there is an underlying sense of sadness. The cheerfulness of tone is not quite convincing and does not quite hide the pain of parting.
- Her use of the first person plural creates a very personal tone and binds her and those she is parting from together.
- Her use of language creates a sense of fortitude in the face of adversity through a series of contrasts, e.g. 'condemned to part… remembrance in one's heart'; 'follies grieve us… A merry laugh'; 'the bonds which chain us… none shall dare restrain us'.
- Her repetition of the word 'love' accentuates the closeness they feel for one another and therefore intensifies the sense of pain in parting.

Charlotte wrote *Life* at a time when all her family, with the exception of Branwell, were at home together.

Activity

What view of life does Charlotte express here? How would you describe the tone?

Make notes on the following:

- her use of vocabulary and imagery
- the structure of the poem and the use of rhyme.

Life

Life, believe, is not a dream
  So dark as sages say;
Oft a little morning rain
  Foretells a pleasant day.
Sometimes there are clouds of gloom,
  But these are transient all;
If the shower will make the roses bloom,
  O why lament its fall?
    Rapidly, merrily,
  Life's sunny hours flit by,
    Gratefully, cheerily,
  Enjoy them as they fly!

What though Death at times steps in
  And calls our Best away?
What though sorrow seems to win,
  O'er hope, a heavy sway?
Yet hope again elastic springs,
  Unconquered, though she fell;
Still buoyant are her golden wings,
  Still strong to bear us well.
    Manfully, fearlessly,
  The day of trial bear,
    For gloriously, victoriously,
  Can courage quell despair!

Less than two weeks after Emily had died on 19 December 1848, Anne was diagnosed as suffering from tuberculosis, the same disease that had killed her sister. Although at first there seemed to be some hope for Anne as the disease was in its early stages, the advance of the illness was relentless. Charlotte, together with her friend Ellen Nussey, took Anne to Scarborough in the hope that the sea air would improve her condition. It was a vain hope, and on 28 May 1849 Anne died at the age of 29. She was buried in Scarborough.

Activity

Read the following poem carefully.

Considering the language, style and structure of the poem, examine the ways in which Charlotte Brontë expresses her feelings at the death of her sister.

On the Death of Anne Brontë

There's little joy in life for me,
    And little terror in the grave;
I've lived the parting hour to see
    Of one I would have died to save.

Calmly to watch the failing breath,
    Wishing each sigh might be the last;
Longing to see the shade of death
    O'er those beloved features passed.

The cloud, the stillness that must part
    The darling of my life from me;
And then to thank God from my heart,
    To thank Him well and fervently;

Although I knew that we had lost
    The hope and glory of our life;
And now, benighted, tempest-tossed,
    Must bear alone the weary strife.

Patrick Branwell Brontë

It is thought that the following poem by Branwell came about as a result of a feeling that his friend, Francis Grundy, had been distant towards him at a party; but the poem clearly has a broader message too.

Activity

Read the poem carefully and make notes on the following, thinking about the effect they have:

- the rhyme and rhythm pattern of the poem
- the structure
- the tone
- the poem as a response to Grundy and the broader message it delivers.

'The man who will not know another'

The man who will not know another,
    Whose heart can never sympathise,
Who loves not comrade, friend or brother,
    Unhonoured lives – unnoticed dies.
His frozen eye, his bloodless heart,
Nature, repugnant, bids depart.

O Grundy! born for nobler aim,
    Be thine the task to shun such shame;
And henceforth never think that he
    Who gives his hand in courtesy
To one who kindly feels to him,
His gentle birth or name can dim.

However mean a man may be,
    Know man *is* man as well as thee;
However high thy gentle line,
    Know he who writes can rank with thine;
And though his frame be worn and dead,
Some light still glitters round his head.

Yes! though his tottering limbs seem old,
    His heart and blood are not yet cold.
Ah, Grundy! shun his evil ways,
    His restless nights, his troubled days;
But never slight his mind, which flies,
Instinct with noble sympathies,
Afar from spleen and treachery,
To thought, to kindness and to thee.

- -

You might have commented on the following.

- The sophisticated poetic structure – three six-line stanzas and a concluding eight-line stanza, which give a formal pattern to the poem. It builds up to the final stanza, which urges his friend and more broadly people in general not to judge others by rank or appearance.

- The rhyme scheme is equally sophisticated and adds emphasis to the formality of the structure. Branwell uses an *ababcc* scheme for the first stanza, but the final message and appeal is given added emphasis by being delivered in rhyming couplets.

- There is direct address to Grundy, but this character is used as a vehicle to deliver a wider message concerning how people treat one another.

Emily Brontë

Activity

Read *The Night Wind* by Emily Brontë.

1 Make a list of the adjectives that Brontë uses in the first two stanzas. What effect do these have?

2 How does Brontë create an impression of a dream-like state?

3 What is the effect of the personification of the night wind, and what effect does the night wind have on the poet?

4 How does Brontë convey the benign, seductive nature of the night wind?

5 What do you think the night wind represents to Brontë?

6 What is the effect of the final stanza?

The Night Wind

In summer's mellow midnight,
A cloudless moon shone through
Our open parlour window
And rosetrees wet with dew –

I sat in silent musing –
The soft wind waved my hair,
It told me Heaven was glorious
And sleeping Earth was fair –

I needed not its breathing
To bring such thoughts to me,
But still it whispered lowly;
'How dark the woods will be! –

'The thick leaves in my murmur
Are rustling like a dream,
And all their myriad voices
Instinct with spirits seem.'

I said, 'Go, gentle singer,
Thy wooing voice is kind
But do not think its music
Has power to reach my mind –

'Play with the scented flower,
The young tree's supple bough –
And leave my human feelings
In their own course to flow.'

The Wanderer would not leave me,
Its kiss grew warmer still –
'O come,' it sighed so sweetly,
'I'll win thee 'gainst thy will –

'Have we not been from childhood friends?
Have I not loved thee long?
As long as thou hast loved the night
Whose silence wakes my song?

'And when thy heart is laid at rest
Beneath the church-yard stone
I shall have time enough to mourn
And thou to be alone –'

- -

You may have noted some of these ideas:

- The adjectives 'mellow', 'silent', 'soft', and 'sleeping' create a gentle and
  peaceful effect and give a calm, soft tone to the poem.
- The reader is given the impression of seeing into Brontë's mind. The simile
  'thick leaves in my murmur/ Are rustling like a dream' creates the sense of a
  dream-like state.
- The personification of the night wind creates a mystical effect in the poem.
  It creates an image of the wind as a living being, entering through the open
  window, addressing Brontë directly and beginning a dialogue with her.
- Although Brontë resists the urgings of the night wind, it will not leave her mind
  and its urgings become more insistent as it attempts to seduce her thoughts. Note
  the soft imploring tone of '"O come," it sighed so sweetly' and its reminder that
  'Have we not been from childhood friends?'

- Brontë often used the idea of what she referred to elsewhere as the 'life-giving wind' to symbolize the muse or imaginative force that was fundamental to her spiritual beliefs and the importance of nature to her being. Here the imaginative force is drawing her back to nature and the spiritual, creative state.

- The final stanza presents a stark reminder that when she dies the night wind will no longer be able to visit her, and when that happens the night wind will 'have time enough to mourn' and Brontë will have time enough 'to be alone', the implication being that she should make the most of her ability to experience the state induced by the night wind while she can.

Activity

Now read the poems *Death* and *Remembrance* by Emily Brontë.

1 Make notes on your responses to the poem *Death*, focusing particularly on the following ideas:

- Brontë's view of death as presented here
- her use of metaphor to present the idea of the mourner's life
- the use of natural imagery
- the cyclical structure of the poem.

2 Look at *Remembrance*, focusing particularly on the following ideas:

- Brontë's view of death as presented here
- her use of repetition and alliteration
- the use of imagery
- the structure of the poem.

3 Now write an essay comparing the language and style of these two poems.

Death

Death! that struck when I was most confiding
In my certain faith of joy to be –
Strike again, Time's withered branch dividing
From the fresh root of Eternity!

Leaves, upon Time's branch, were growing brightly,
Full of sap, and full of silver dew;
Birds beneath its shelter gathered nightly;
Daily round its flowers the wild bees flew.

Sorrow passed, and plucked the golden blossom;
Guilt stripped off the foliage in its pride;
But, within its parent's kindly bosom,
Flowed for ever Life's restoring tide.

Little mourned I for the parted gladness,
For the vacant nest and silent song –
Hope was there, and laughed me out of sadness;
Whispering, 'Winter will not linger long!'

And, behold! with tenfold increase blessing,
Spring adorned the beauty-burdened spray;
Wind and rain and fervent heat, caressing,
Lavished glory on that second May!

High it rose – no winged grief could sweep it;
Sin was scared to distance with its shine;
Love, and its own life, had power to keep it
From all wrong – from every blight but thine!

Cruel Death! The young leaves droop and languish;
Evening's gentle air may still restore –
No! the morning sunshine mocks my anguish –
Time, for me, must never blossom more!

Strike it down, that other boughs may flourish
Where that perished sapling used to be;
Thus, at least, its mouldering corpse will nourish
That from which it sprung – Eternity.

Remembrance

Cold in the earth – and the deep snow piled above thee,
Far, far, removed, cold in the dreary grave!
Have I forgot, my only Love, to love thee,
Severed at last by Time's all-severing wave?

Now, when alone, do my thoughts no longer hover
Over the mountains, on that northern shore,
Resting their wings where heath and fern-leaves cover
Thy noble heart for ever, ever more?

Cold in the earth – and fifteen wild Decembers,
From those brown hills, have melted into spring:
Faithful, indeed, is the spirit that remembers
After such years of change and suffering!

Sweet Love of youth, forgive, if I forget thee,
While the world's tide is bearing me along;
Other desires and other hopes beset me,
Hopes which obscure, but cannot do thee wrong!

No later light has lighten'd up my heaven,
No second morn has ever shone for me;
All my life's bliss from thy dear life was given,
All my life's bliss is in the grave with thee.

But when the days of golden dreams had perished,
And even Despair was powerless to destroy;
Then did I learn how existence could be cherished,
Strengthened, and fed without the aid of joy.

Then did I check the tears of useless passion –
Weaned my young soul from yearning after thine;
Sternly denied its burning wish to hasten
Down to that tomb already more than mine.

And, even yet, I dare not let it languish,
Dare not indulge in memory's rapturous pain;
Once drinking deep of that divinest anguish,
How could I seek the empty world again?

Anne Brontë

The following poem was written by Anne Brontë while she was a governess to the Robinson family at Thorp Green near York. When she wrote this poem she had four months to go before her next holiday, when she could return to her family.

Activity

Read the poem through carefully and write down your ideas of what it is about.

Now compare your ideas with a partner and look at the poem in detail, focusing on the following points.

- What mood is Anne in here?
- Make a list of words which are used to create an impression of this mood.
- How does she use nature and natural images in the poem?
- What message does she give in the final stanza?

Lines Written at Thorp Green

That summer sun, whose genial glow
Now cheers my drooping spirit so,
    Must cold and silent be,
And only light our northern clime
With feeble ray, before the time
    I long so much to see.

And this soft, whispering breeze, that now
So gently cools my fevered brow,
    This too, alas! must turn
To a wild blast, whose icy dart
Pierces and chills me to the heart,
    Before I cease to mourn.

And these bright flowers I love so well,
Verbena, rose, and sweet bluebell,
    Must droop and die away;
Those thick, green leaves, with all their shade
And rustling music, they must fade,
    And every one decay.

But if the sunny, summer time,
And woods and meadows in their prime,
    Are sweet to them that roam;
Far sweeter is the winter bare,
With long, dark nights, and landscape drear,
    To them that are at Home!

Here are some ideas:

- She appears lonely, unhappy, even depressed. She seems to long to return home.

- This mood is created through the use of words and phrases such as 'drooping spirit', 'feeble ray', 'fevered brow', 'wild blast', 'icy dart', 'decay'.

- To create an impression of the depth of her unhappiness, Brontë uses natural images that would normally give comfort and warm the spirit, and turns them around to emphasize that even they cannot console her. For example, 'That summer sun' and its 'genial glow' must become 'cold and silent' with 'feeble ray' before the time arrives when she can return home. Similarly the 'whispering breeze… must turn/ To a wild blast'. The 'bright flowers I love so well… Must droop and die away'. Instead of providing her with comfort these aspects of nature only remind her how long must pass before she can return to her home.

- She makes the point that if roaming in the meadows in the 'sunny, summer time' is sweet, it is 'Far sweeter' to spend dark winter nights at home. The Brontë sisters particularly enjoyed winter nights at home together as it was a time when they did much of their writing.

In literature the image of the caged bird was commonly used to symbolize the idea of imprisonment, or lack of physical or spiritual liberty. Emily had used the same image in her poem *The Caged Bird*. In *The Captive Dove*, Anne uses the image in a slightly different way.

Activity

Read the poem carefully.

How does Anne Brontë create the sense of being trapped in this poem? Give examples to illustrate your ideas.

The Captive Dove

Poor restless dove, I pity thee;
And when I hear thy plaintive moan,
I mourn for thy captivity,
And in thy woes forget mine own.

To see thee stand prepared to fly,
And flap those useless wings of thine,
And gaze into the distant sky,
Would melt a harder heart than mine.

In vain – in vain! Thou canst not rise:
Thy prison roof confines thee there;
Its slender wires delude thine eyes,
And quench thy longings with despair.

Oh, thou wert made to wander free
In sunny mead and shady grove,
And, far beyond the rolling sea,
In distant climes, at will to rove!

Yet, hadst thou but one gentle mate
Thy little drooping heart to cheer,
And share with thee thy captive state,
Thou couldst be happy even there.

Yes, even there, if, listening by,
One faithful dear companion stood,
While gazing on her full bright eye,
Thou mightst forget thy native wood.

But thou, poor solitary dove,
Must make, unheard, thy joyless moan;
The heart, that Nature formed to love,
Must pine, neglected, and alone.

Examination practice

Answer either question 1 or question 2 below.

Activity

1 It has being said that 'At his best, Branwell Brontë easily rivals Emily as a poet'.

   How far do you agree with this view?

   In your answer, you should **either** refer to **two** or **three** poems in detail or range more widely through the whole collection.

2 Remind yourself of Emily Brontë's poem *Alone I Sat*.

   To what extent do you agree with the view that, in terms of subject matter and style, this poem is typical of the poetry of the Brontës?

10 First World War Literature

Objectives

- To gain an overview of the First World War as a context for literature
- To recognize features which are typical of First World War literature
- To understand how views of the war alter with different times of writing
- To understand what you will need to do to prepare yourself for Section A of the examination paper – Contextual Linking
- To develop an understanding of the poetry you have chosen for study and prepare yourself for Section B of the examination paper

The World War One literature option

In studying this option you will need to study a variety of texts for AS level.

Unit 1: Texts in Context

This unit will be assessed through one two-hour exam paper. The paper will consist of two sections and you will need to answer one question in each section.

Section A: Contextual Linking

In this section you will be given one question which will consist of a short extract related to First World War literature. This may be taken from a variety of sources such as a diary, a letter, biography or commentary on the period. You will be asked to link your reading in First World War literature to the extract given.

Section B: Poetry

You will be given a choice of two questions on each of the set poetry texts. One of the questions will focus on one particular poem and its relation to the whole text, and the other will ask you to discuss some aspect of the poems you have studied. You will answer one of these two questions.

The set texts to choose from are as follows:

Up the Line to Death: The War Poets 1914–1918, selected by Brian Gardner (Methuen, 1964)

Scars Upon My Heart: Women's Poetry and Verse of the First World War, selected by Catherine Reilly (Virago, 1981)

The Oxford Book of War Poetry, edited by Jon Stallworthy (Oxford University Press, 1984), pages 176–225

Assessment Objectives

The Assessment Objectives that you will be assessed on in this unit are as follows:

- **AO1** Articulate creative, informed and relevant responses to literary texts, using appropriate terminology and concepts, and coherent, accurate written expression (assessed in Sections A and B)

- **AO2** Demonstrate detailed critical understanding in analysing the ways in which structure, form and language shape meanings in literary texts (assessed in Sections A and B)
- **AO3** Explore connections and comparisons between different literary texts, informed by interpretations of other readers (assessed in Sections A and B)
- **AO4** Demonstrate understanding of the significance and influence of the contexts in which literary texts are written and received (assessed in Section A)

Unit 2: Creative Study

For this unit you will need to produce a coursework portfolio which, together with your work for Unit 1, will form a coherent course of study of First World War literature. For your portfolio you will need to study one prose text and one drama text.

You will need to produce two pieces of writing:

- the first piece of writing should present a personal, informed response to the prose text, and will be a creative piece
- the second piece of writing should be on your chosen drama text, and should focus either on its dramatic context or link it to your prose text, covering aspects such as theme, structure, characterization, etc.

Your two pieces of work should be 2000–2500 words in total.

Assessment Objectives

The Assessment Objectives that you will be tested on in this unit are the same as those in Unit 1 – all the objectives are assessed in both pieces of work.

You will find more on the Creative Study unit and a list of the set texts for the World War One literature option in Chapter 12.

Wider reading

In addition to the set texts you have studied, you should also choose at least three texts covering poetry, prose and drama for wider reading. If you can study further short pieces or extracts, this will enhance your understanding of the context.

The historical context

The 'Great War' of 1914–1918, one of the greatest catastrophes of modern times, cast a long shadow over twentieth-century Europe. This so-called 'war to end wars' did nothing of the kind, but it did bring about profound changes in society, culture and ways of thinking. It is said to have marked the true beginning of the 'modern age'.

You may already have some knowledge of the events of the First World War. If not, you will find it useful to read a straightforward account in an encyclopaedia or textbook, to get to know basic names and dates that are likely to be mentioned in the literary texts you read. Television documentaries or history programmes are also useful, as are historical websites. The BBC 'World War One' website offers a wealth of informative articles, film clips and interactive material, for example.

To start you off, here is a brief summary from Paul Fussell's introduction to *The Bloody Game*, a huge, fascinating anthology of the literature of modern war.

It had all begun in June 1914, when Archduke Francis Ferdinand, heir to the throne of Austria-Hungary, was assassinated in Sarajevo, Bosnia-Herzegovina, by a Serbian patriot fed up with Austrian domination of his country. Austria-Hungary used the occasion to pick a long-desired quarrel with Serbia and to issue an ultimatum that could only produce war. At this point the system of European alliances, negotiated over many decades, had to be honored: Russia came to the aid of Serbia, whereupon Germany jumped in on the side of Austria-Hungary. France then honored her treaty with Russia, Britain hers with France. By October 1914, Turkey had joined the side of Germany and Austria-Hungary (the 'Central Powers'). By the end of the year the notorious trench system was emplaced in Belgium and France, running 400 miles from its northern anchor at the North Sea to its southern end at the Swiss border, while in the east, another front developed along the Russian border with Austria-Hungary. Italy came in on the side of the Allies in 1915, opening a front against Austria. And in April 1917, the United States, exasperated by German sinking of its ships, joined the Allies… The Americans… were generally credited with supplying the needed weight to win the war.

Paul Fussell

An unprecedented catastrophe

Wars have always been horrific, but there were certain aspects of the First World War that made it shockingly different from anything that had gone before.

- The **vast scale of the conflict**. The First World War was truly a world war. It involved all the major powers of Europe and America and fighting extended to Russia, Africa, Turkey, Palestine and the Persian Gulf as well as both the Atlantic and Pacific Oceans. Much of the literature you read is likely to relate to events on the Western Front, in Belgium and France, but bear in mind that this selection may not fully reflect the huge, international scale of the hostilities.

- The sheer **number of casualties**. Over 37 million people died or were wounded.

- War as a **mass activity**. For the first time, all eligible (male) civilians were called up or conscripted to fight, where previously wars had been fought by professional armies at a distance from civilian life. The concept of 'total war', in which all the resources of the nation, at home and abroad, were concentrated on the war effort, became a reality. The first ever air raids – from Zeppelin airships – also brought war much closer to home.

- **Technology**. Machine guns, tanks, barbed wire and poison gas were all used for the first time, along with new and ever more deadly varieties of bombs, shells and grenades. These new weapons killed indiscriminately, regardless of whether soldiers were 'brave' or not. Early in the war soldiers were still taught to fight face-to-face, with bayonets, but as time went on and technology became more sophisticated, enemies no longer had to see each other and the personal element of combat was removed. It became easier, literally and psychologically, to kill.

- **Trench warfare**. Much of the war was fought in a system of deep, muddy ditches in which soldiers lived, in appalling conditions, for months on end, facing the 'enemy' across 50 yards of 'no man's land'. The trench system on the Western Front was put in place late in 1914 and fighting there stagnated, with little progress on either side, until 1918.

- **Gender issues**. Women did not participate directly in the fighting – although some did experience the war at close quarters through serving as army nurses – but the war had a drastic effect on their lives. The loss of so many men left gaps in the workforce and caused an imbalance between the genders. Some women took on roles that had never been open to them before; many worked in munitions factories, for example, while countless others, who had lost husbands or lovers, had no choice but to remain single. During the war, women over 30 gained the right to vote for the first time. Gender roles were never again as fixed as they had been previously.

In the table that follows, you will find a summary of events which are most likely to be mentioned in English literature of the war.

Date		Events on the war fronts	The British home front
1914	July–August	War is declared. German armies advance in Belgium and against the Russians in Galicia	Defence of the Realm Act
	September	Battle of the Marne	Recruiting campaigns begin
	November	Trench warfare begins on the Western Front	
	December	First mines are exploded	People opposing the war set up the Union of Democratic Control
1915	March–April	War against Turkey; the Dardanelles campaign and the landings at Gallipoli; German submarine campaign in the Atlantic	
	April	First use of gas at the Battle of Ypres, on the Western Front; Italy joins the war	
	May	The Germans inflict further defeats on the Russians, who lose 1 million soldiers; the liner *Lusitania* sunk by German submarine	Coalition government takes over from the Liberals; government takes control of munitions factories
	July	Zeppelin raids on England begin	National Registration Act – all men eligible for military service are registered
	September–November	British and French offensive on the Western Front makes little headway	British nurse Edith Cavell executed by the Germans
1916	January	Allied troops are evacuated from Gallipoli	Conscription is introduced
	February	Battle of Verdun	
	April	British troops in Turkey forced to surrender	Easter Uprising in Dublin – part of a campaign for Irish independence

(Continued)

	July	Battle of the Somme begins	
	September	The Russians lose another million men; first use of tanks	
	December		Lloyd George becomes prime minister
1917	February	Submarine warfare a growing threat; ships sail in convoys for protection	Food shortages; bread and other foods are rationed; Women's Land Army is formed; air raids on east coast towns
	April	US enters the war; French offensive fails	
	May	Mutiny in French army	
	July	British offensive – Third Battle of Ypres (Passchendaele) – no progress; terrible conditions in trenches continue	
	October	Bolshevik revolution in Russia	
	November	British victory at Cambrai and small advance	
	December	Russia pulls out of the war	
1918	February		Women over 30 are given the vote
	March	Treaty of Brest-Litovsk forces Russians to give up huge amounts of land in the Ukraine, Finland and the Baltic states; Germans begin huge 'Spring Offensive' and advance towards Paris	Ministry of Information is created to 'improve morale'; meat rationing
	May	French and American troops stop the German advance	
	July	Allied counter offensive begins – Germans now in retreat; disintegration of the Austro-Hungarian Empire	Education Act raises the school leaving age to 14

| August | Allies on the offensive; battles of the Marne and Amiens; the Germans are forced to retreat towards the border | |
| 11 November | The war ends with the signing of the Armistice at 11 am | |

Writing the war: The literary context

The war occurred at a time when literature flourished and was highly respected, and it prompted a great outpouring of writing of all sorts. Writing was not just the preferred mode of communication, but really the only way for those involved in the war to make their experiences known. Even in the midst of battle, apparently, the post reached its destination quite rapidly and almost every soldier corresponded regularly, if not every day, with those at home, generating huge numbers of letters, ranging from the standard 'field postcard' to sophisticated literary accounts. Confined to trenches for long periods, often with little to do but wait, many men who might not otherwise have done so tried their hands at poetry, which was considered a 'safe' way to express one's view of the war.

However, the literary context of the First World War includes a great deal more than the enormous amount of writing produced by men on the Western Front between 1914 and 1918. It embraces literature ranging from that written in the years leading up to the war right up to the present day, and it is an ever-growing field. Authors have been fascinated by the subject ever since, and have continued to re-present the war in drama, poetry and fiction, through the lens of later decades.

The First World War seems to hold a special, almost archetypal or mythical, significance. When we think of war, it is images of that war which tend to spring to mind first, as Vernon Scannell suggests in his poem *The Great War*.

Activity

1 Think about your own perceptions of war in general and the First World War in particular. What images and associations come to mind? If you wish, write freely for about ten minutes, in any form you like, about the ideas that come to mind.

2 In your group, brainstorm your ideas and images and discuss where you think they have come from (e.g. history or English lessons, films, books you have read, television programmes).

3 With a partner or in a group, read the poem *The Great War*, on the next page, and discuss the following points.

• Underline or note images which you consider typical of the First World War.

• Look closely at the language he uses. Which senses and colours does he use? Which does he not use? What is the reason for these choices, do you think? (What do the colours 'grey' and 'sepia' suggest about his description, for example?)

• What attitudes and feelings about the war does the poet reveal here?

4 When you have worked through the poems, extracts and activities in this chapter and/or done some wider reading and study, return to this poem and write a short essay on the following topic:

In what ways can you relate Scannell's *The Great War* to the poetry (and other literature) of the First World War that you have read so far?

The Great War

Whenever war is spoken of
I find
The war that was called Great invades the mind:
The grey militia marches over land
A darker mood of grey
Where fractured tree-trunks stand
And shells, exploding, open sudden fans
Of smoke and earth.
Blind murders scythe
The deathscape where the iron brambles writhe;
The sky at night
Is honoured with rosettes of fire,
Flares that define the corpses on the wire
As terror ticks on wrists at zero hour.
These things I see,
But they are only part
Of what it is that slyly probes the heart:
Less vivid images and words excite
The sensuous memory
And, even as I write,
Fear and a kind of love collaborate
To call each simple conscript up
For quick inspection:
Trenches' parapets
Paunchy with sandbags; bandoliers, tin-hats.
Candles in dug-outs,
Duckboards, mud and rats.
Then, like patrols, tunes creep into the mind:
A long, long trail, The Rose of No-Man's Land,
Home Fire and *Tipperary:*
And through the misty keening of a band
Of Scottish pipes the proper names are heard
Like fateful commentary of distant guns:
Passchendaele, Bapaume, and Loos, and Mons.
And now,
Whenever the November sky
Quivers with a bugle's hoarse, sweet cry,
The reason darkens; in its evening gleam
Crosses and flares, tormented wire, grey earth
Splattered with crimson flowers,
And I remember,
Not the war I fought in
But the one called Great

Which ended in a sepia November
Four years before my birth.

Vernon Scannell (included in *The Oxford Book of War Poetry*)

Time perspectives

When you study the literature of the First World War, it is important to be aware
of just how much writers' perspectives can differ, depending on when they were
writing. Attitudes to the war altered drastically, from the enthusiasm of the early
months of the war to the disillusionment of hindsight. The following summary
suggests some of the main time perspectives or categories you are likely to encounter.

- **Pre-war.** From 1912 onwards, the work of a group known as the **Georgian** poets
  was popular. Unlike either the formal, traditional work of the Victorian writers
  who came before, or the challenging, experimental work of the Modernists who
  followed, Georgian writing is associated with a rather old-fashioned, romantic
  and somewhat sentimental presentation of 'Englishness', which captures
  something of the spirit of the pre-war years. Some of the best-known war poets,
  including Siegfried Sassoon, contributed to collections of Georgian poetry before
  they became involved in the war.

- **The spirit of 1914.** The beginning of the war sparked an effusion of patriotic
  feeling, which was expressed in the exalted, romantic language of poets like
  Rupert Brooke and Laurence Binyon. Idealized images of war and the hero's
  death, along with the writing of propagandists and recruiters, who portrayed
  war as an exciting game, inspired many young men 'ardent for some desperate
  glory'. With the wisdom of hindsight, we tend to view this kind of writing as
  poignantly naïve, or hypocritical, or ironic in the face of what was to come, but
  at the time, the sentiments were genuine enough.

- **1916–1918: Disillusionment.** By the end of the war, this innocence was well
  and truly shattered, replaced by anger, bitterness and despair. The Battle of the
  Somme, in the summer of 1916, with its catastrophic but futile loss of life, is
  regarded as a turning point. For the remainder of the war, critical and dissenting
  voices became more prominent. Writers like Wilfred Owen, Siegfried Sassoon
  and many other 'trench poets' who aimed to expose the horror and pity of war,
  tend to be the first to come to mind when we think of First World War literature.

- **1920s–1930s: Time to reflect.** Society, along with the lives of countless
  individuals, had been irrevocably altered by the war. These decades saw many
  survivors attempting to come to terms with their experience or make sense of
  it through writing memoirs. Writers like Sassoon, Edmund Blunden and Vera
  Brittain, along with novelists like Virginia Woolf and Ernest Hemingway, wrote
  reflectively about the war and its effects with the wider perspective of hindsight.

- **1940s: A war to end wars?** Only one generation later, attention was focused on
  the new conflict of 1939–1945. Not surprisingly, little First World War literature
  was produced at this time, but some writers inevitably pointed out the irony that
  it had been called 'the war to end wars'.

- **1950s–1980s: The nuclear age.** The 'Cold War' era involved the polarization
  of East and West, Communism and Capitalism, Russia and America. With its
  recurrent crises, it was a time of tension. The fear of nuclear holocaust was
  widespread and anti-war feeling was strong. Renewed interest in the First
  World War as an 'archetypal' war emerged in literature. At the same time, now
  that most of the survivors were dead, it became acceptable to use the war as a

subject for satire and black comedy. The musical *Oh What a Lovely War* (1963) was highly successful at a time when people were torn between fear, protest and despair.

- **Post-1990.** Many more documents, such as letters, diaries, and new biographies have been researched and published. Understanding of the psychology of war and trauma is more sophisticated, and what was once 'unspeakable' has become almost commonplace. Graphic descriptions of horrific events are less unusual than they once were, and television images of war reach our homes daily. Now that there is almost no one alive who remembers the war, there is more freedom to offer fictional interpretations and many novelists have returned to the First World War for inspiration.

Themes and motifs

As well as knowing something about the events and impact of the war, it is vital that you develop some understanding of how people typically thought and felt, both at the time and afterwards, so that you are able to recognize the recurring themes, ideas and 'motifs' of First World War literature. Here are some things to look out for:

- Features of First World War combat, mentioned earlier, are reflected in an increasing sense of **depersonalization**. As war became more mechanized, soldiers became mere numbers, not individuals. Literary accounts of the **dehumanizing** experience of the trenches became more graphic as the war went on, while contemporary authors like Pat Barker and Sebastian Faulks continue the trend. Look out for language and imagery that reflect this.

- **Dichotomies.** First World War literature is full of starkly contrasted images. The war generated a tendency to see things in 'black and white', in terms of two-sided 'splits' or contrasts, between for example:

  – 'us' and 'them' (the 'enemy')

  – people who fought and people who stayed at home

  – soldiers at the front and high-ranking officials who gave their orders from safe places

  – middle-class officers and working-class soldiers or 'Tommies'

  – men and women – men could not communicate the full horror of their experiences to women who had stayed at home, which caused misunderstanding and resentment

  – the horror of war and the comfort of home; the smart restaurants and theatres of London were sometimes no more than 70 miles from the trenches

  – the ugliness and devastation of the war-torn landscape and the beauty of nature; for example the irony of glorious sunsets over the battlefield.

- **Loss of innocence** or **faith.** With the idealism of 1914, young men susceptible to propaganda saw the war as a 'big picnic', and dying for one's country as an honour, or a religious duty. By the time the war ended, those who were left felt resigned or cynical. Religion no longer offered consolation, and soldiers had little to rely on except the comradeship they shared.

- **Comradeship.** In such terrible conditions and isolated from other sources of support, fierce loyalty and friendship among the soldiers is a recurrent theme.

- **Propaganda** and **censorship.** Away from the front, governments and the press – which was heavily censored – continued to present the war to the public in old-fashioned, idealized language. Soldiers were still 'gallant warriors' and horses were 'steeds'.

- **Language.** Trench warfare generated a language of its own. As well as vocabulary associated with the trenches themselves ('dugouts', 'funk-holes') and the technology of war ('whizz-bangs', 'five-nines'), soldiers had their own codes and euphemisms to describe their activities. Some who were stationed in France also developed a kind of 'pidgin' French.
- **Social class.** The war threw together many people from different backgrounds who would not otherwise have met. Language differences also reflect differences in social class. For example, you may notice how writers portray middle-class officers, compared with working-class soldiers whose speech is often more colloquial, accented, or in dialect.

The First World War: A sample anthology

The texts and extracts that follow have been selected to help you start your exploration of First World War literature, and to demonstrate a range of different genres, styles and points of view. You can approach the pieces in various ways.

- Read them as an introduction to the literature of the period.
- Make notes on any or all of them, using the close reading strategy outlined in Chapter 7. The poems are to be found in the three set anthologies, one of which you will be studying in depth. You may like to concentrate your close reading work on the poems that appear in the anthology you are studying.
- Note the many ways in which the texts can be connected, compared and contrasted.
- Use the questions and activities to explore how these texts reflect the themes and motifs suggested above, and to practise writing about this kind of material.

1 'Never such innocence again'

The two poems which follow were written early in the war and capture the mood of religious, idealized, patriotic fervour which inspired young people in 1914. Binyon's famous poem is still sometimes read at funerals, while Rupert Brooke's five *Sonnets 1914* won huge popularity early in the war.

For the Fallen (September 1914)

With proud thanksgiving, a mother for her children,
England mourns for her dead across the sea.
Flesh of her flesh they were, spirit of her spirit.
Fallen in the cause of the free.

Solemn the drums thrill: Death august and royal
Sings sorrow up into immortal spheres.
There is music in the midst of desolation
And a glory that shines upon our tears.

They went with songs to the battle, they were young,
Straight of limb, true of eye, steady and aglow.
They were staunch to the end against odds uncounted,
They fell with their faces to the foe.

They shall grow not old, as we that are left grow old:
Age shall not weary them, nor the years condemn.
At the going down of the sun and in the morning
We will remember them.

They mingle not with their laughing comrades again;
They sit no more at familiar tables of home;
They have no lot in our labour of the day-time;
They sleep beyond England's foam.

But where our desires are and our hopes profound,
Felt as a well-spring that is hidden from sight,
To the innermost heart of their own land they are known
As the stars are known to the night.

As the stars that shall be bright when we are dust,
Moving in marches upon the heavenly plain,
As the stars that are starry in the time of our darkness,
To the end, to the end, they remain.

Laurence Binyon (included in *The Oxford Book of War Poetry*)

Activity

1 Working on your own or with a partner, read the poem carefully and make notes. In particular, think about:

- how England and death are presented in the poem
- how the soldiers are described in stanza 3
- Binyon's use of 'we' for the voice of the poem
- the effect of the form, rhyme and rhythm of the poem
- the imagery of stars in stanzas 6 and 7
- whether the ideas in the poem are 'concrete' (real, down to earth) or 'abstract'
- how imagery and vocabulary are chosen to create the atmosphere of the poem and to reinforce the message Binyon wishes to convey.

2 Now read *Peace*, by Rupert Brooke. Make notes on the poem, paying particular attention to how the poet makes use of imagery, vocabulary and contrast. What atmosphere or feeling does this poem generate?

3 Write a short essay in which you explore the ways in which the spirit of 1914 is presented in these two poems.

Peace

Now, God be thanked Who has matched us with His hour,
    And caught our youth, and wakened us from sleeping,
With hand made sure, clear eye, and sharpened power,
    To turn, as swimmers into cleanness leaping,
Glad from a world grown old and cold and weary,
    Leave the sick hearts that honour could not move,
And half-men, and their dirty songs and dreary,
    And all the little emptiness of love!

Oh! We, who have known shame, we have found release there,
    Where there's no ill, no grief, but sleep has mending,
        Naught broken save this body, lost but breath;

Nothing to shake the laughing heart's long peace there
But only agony, and that has ending;
And the worst friend and enemy is but Death.

Rupert Brooke (included in *The Oxford Book of War Poetry* and *Up the Line to Death*)

2 Letters home

These two letters, in which young officer poets relate some of their experiences to loved ones at home, illustrate the change in attitude that occurred between the excitement of the early months of the war and the disillusionment of the later years, as well as the different personalities of the writers. The first is from Rupert Brooke to his friend Katharine Cox, and was written from a transport ship in the Aegean Sea, between Greece and North Africa. His use of the word 'romantic' is interesting. It sounds as if he is talking about the 'glamour' of war, but it also suggests a private 'code' to disguise his involvement in military manoeuvres.

In the second letter, Wilfred Owen writes to his mother of the realities of 'Flanders'. Both letters show evidence of the censorship that prevented soldiers from giving away too much about their activities. Neither of these young men survived the war: Brooke died at sea in April 1915 and was buried on a small Greek island, and Owen was killed only days before the Armistice in 1918.

A

To KATHARINE COX   19–24 March [1915]

Somewhere (some way from the front)

Dear Ka,

Your letter of the 3rd of March has just reached me. Fairly quick. There are said to be 80 bags of mail still (parcels, if anything, I suspect) at headquarters (here). But your letter is the only letter I've had since we sailed. It is fun getting letters. Tell people – Dudley and such – to write occasionally. I can't write much. There's very little I could, of interest. And that, as a rule, I mayn't. This letter is to be censored by the Brigade Chaplain. ... Here three quarters of the day is dullish – routine – and the society is unnatural – over a long period – all men. Anyway, it's nice to hear.

... Yes: this is romantic. (But I won't admit that Flanders isn't.) But I'm afraid I can't tell you most of the romantic things, at present.

My own lot have seen no fighting yet, and very likely won't for months. The only thing that seems almost certain is that one doesn't know from day to day what's to happen. The other day we – some of us – were told that we sailed next day to make a landing. A few thousand of us. Off we stole that night through the phosphorescent Aegean, scribbling farewell letters, and snatching periods of dream-broken, excited sleep. At four we rose, buckled on our panoply[1], hung ourselves with glasses compasses periscopes revolvers food and the rest, and had a stealthy large breakfast. *That* was a mistake. It is ruinous to load up one's belly four or five hours before it expects it: it throws the machinery out of gear for a week. I felt extremely ill the rest of that day.

We paraded in silence, under paling stars, along the sides of the ship. The darkness on the sea was full of scattered flashing lights, hinting at our fellow-transports and the rest. Slowly the day became wan and green and the sea opal. Everyone's face looked drawn and ghastly. If we landed, my company was to be the first to land... We made out that we were only a mile or two from a dim shore. I was seized with an agony of remorse that I hadn't taught my platoon a thousand things more energetically and competently. The light grew. The shore looked to be crammed with Fate, and most ominously silent. One man thought he saw a camel through his glasses...

There were some hours of silence.

About seven someone said 'We're going home.' We dismissed the stokers, who said, quietly, 'When's the next battle?'; and disempanoplied, and had another breakfast. If we were a 'feint', or if it was too rough to land, or, in general, what little part we blindly played, we never knew, and shall not. Still, we did our bit; not ignobly, I trust. We did not see the enemy. We did not fire at them; nor they at us. It seemed improbable they saw us. One of B Company – she was rolling very slightly – was sick on parade. Otherwise no casualties. A notable battle.

All is well. Good-bye.

Rupert

[1] *Panoply: full suit of armour (old-fashioned word; suggests what knights would wear)*

B

To Susan Owen

Friday, 19 January 1917   2nd Manchester Regiment,
                                                           British Expeditionary Force.

We are now a long way back in a ruined village, all huddled together in a farm. We all sleep in the same room where we eat and try to live. My bed is a hammock of rabbit-wire stuck up beside a great shell hole in the wall. Snow is deep about, and melts through the gaping roof, on to my blanket. We are wretched beyond my previous imagination – but safe.

Last night indeed I had to 'go up' with a party. We got lost in the snow. I went on ahead to scout – foolishly – alone – and when half a mile away from the party, got overtaken by

GAS

It was only tear-gas from a shell, and I got safely back (to the party) in my helmet, with nothing worse than a severe fright! And a few tears, some natural, some unnatural.

Here is an Addition to my List of Wants:

Safety Razor (in my drawer) & Blades

Socks (2 pairs)

6 handkerchiefs

Celluloid Soap Box (Boots)

Cigarette Holder (Bone, 3d. or 6d.)

Paraffin for Hair.

(I can't wash hair and have taken to washing my face with snow.)

Coal, water, candles, accommodation, everything is scarce. We have not always air! When I took my helmet off last night – O Air it was a heavenly thing!

Please thank uncle for his letter, and send the Compass. I scattered abroad some 50 Field Post Cards from the Base, which should bring forth a good harvest of letters. But nothing but a daily one from you will keep me up.

I think Colin might try a weekly letter. And Father?

We have a Gramophone, and so musical does it seem now that I shall never more disparage one. Indeed I can never disparage anything in Blighty again for a long time except certain parvenus living in a street of the same name as you take to go to the Abbey. [i.e. Westminster.]

They want to call No Man's Land 'England' because we keep supremacy there.

It is like the eternal place of gnashing of teeth; the Slough of Despond could be contained in one of its crater-holes; the fires of Sodom and Gomorrah could not light a candle to it – to find the way to Babylon the Fallen.

It is pock-marked like a body of foulest disease and its odour is the breath of cancer.

I have not seen any dead. I have done worse. In the dank air I have <u>perceived</u> it, and in the darkness, <u>felt</u>. Those 'Somme Pictures' are the laughing stock of the army – like the trenches on exhibition in Kensington.

No Man's Land under snow is like the face of the moon, chaotic, crater-ridden, uninhabitable, awful, the abode of madness.

To call it 'England'!

... Now I have let myself tell you more facts than I should, in the exuberance of having already done '<u>a Bit</u>.' <u>It is done</u>, and we are all going still farther back for a long time. A long time. The people of England needn't hope. They must agitate. But they are not yet agitated even. Let them imagine 50 strong men trembling as with ague for 50 hours!

Dearer & stronger love than ever.
W.E.O.

Activity

1 Read the letters carefully, thinking about and making notes in response to the following questions:

- What are the main topics and concerns of each writer?
- What is each writer's attitude to his experience of war?
- What are their attitudes to people at home – their family and friends and/or public figures?
- How is each letter influenced by the time at which it was written?
- How does each writer reveal that his letter is subject to censorship?
- What evidence can you detect, from the ways they use language, that these two young soldiers are also poets?

2 Write as fully as you can about these two letters, exploring the similarities and differences between the ways these young men portray their experience of war.

3 'A sunlit picture of hell': 1 July 1916

The Battle of the Somme is generally considered to be one of the worst calamities of modern warfare and marks the point at which attitudes to the war began to change. The Allies launched a huge offensive, but the strength of the German defences had been underestimated, planning and preparation were poor, and very little was achieved. Overall, more than a million lives were lost; on the first day, there were almost 60,000 British casualties alone. Whole battalions were wiped out as they attempted to advance, in broad daylight, into no man's land. That day's glorious summer weather provided an ironic backdrop to unspeakable slaughter.

Activity

1 Read the two extracts about the beginning of the Battle of the Somme, which follow. One is an eye-witness account, the other an attempt to re-create the experience in fiction.

2 With a partner, or in a small group, discuss the ways in which each author approaches the task of describing the battle. Some points to consider are:

- the narrative viewpoint and perspective adopted by each writer
- how genre (diary/novel) affects style in each case
- the details each writer chooses to include; in particular, what is *added* in the fictional portrayal
- how graphic the description is in each case
- the way each writer uses imagery, colour, and the senses
- the extent to which each account shocks or moves you, and why.

3 Now write a comparison of the two extracts, explaining which you found the more effective and why. Support your answer with detailed reference to the text.

Siegfried Sassoon watched from a distance as the campaign was launched, on the morning of 1 July. In his semi-fictional autobiography, *Memoirs of an Infantry Officer*, he quotes directly from his diary for that day. A few lines earlier, he exclaims, 'I hadn't expected the Battle of the Somme to be quite like this...'

Memoirs of an Infantry Officer

From the support-trench, which Barton called 'our opera box', I observed as much of the battle as the formation of the country allowed, the rising ground on the right making it impossible to see anything of the attack towards Mametz. A small shiny black notebook contains my pencilled particulars, and nothing will be gained by embroidering them with afterthoughts. I cannot turn my field-glasses onto the past.

*   *   *

7.45   The barrage is now working to the right of Fricourt and beyond. I can see the 21st Division advancing about three-quarters of a mile away on the left and a few Germans coming to meet them, apparently surrendering. Our men in small parties (not extended in line) go steadily on to the German front-line. Brilliant sunshine and a haze of smoke drifting along the landscape. Some Yorkshires a little way below on the left, watching the show and cheering as if at a football match. The noise almost as bad as ever.

9.30   Came back to the dug-out and had a shave. 21st Division still going across the open, apparently without casualties. The sunlight flashes on bayonets as the tiny figures move quietly forward and disappear beyond mounds of trench débris. A few runners come back and ammunition parties go across. Trench-mortars are knocking hell out of Sunken Road Trench and the ground where the Manchesters will attack soon. Noise not so bad now and very little retaliation.

9.50   Fricourt half-hidden by clouds of drifting smoke, blue, pinkish and grey. Shrapnel bursting in small bluish-white puffs with tiny flashes. The birds seem bewildered; a lark begins to go up and then flies feebly along, thinking better of it. Others flutter above the trench with querulous cries, weak on the wing. I can see seven of our balloons, on the right. On the left our men still filing across in twenties and thirties. Another huge explosion in Fricourt and a cloud of brown-pink smoke. Some bursts are yellowish.

10.05   I can see the Manchesters down in New Trench, getting ready to go over. Figures filing down the trench. Two of them have gone out to look at our wire gaps! Have just eaten my last orange… I am staring at a sunlit picture of Hell, and still the breeze shakes the yellow weeds, and the poppies glow under Crawley Ridge where some shells fell a few minutes ago. Manchesters are sending forward some scouts. A bayonet glitters. A runner comes back across the open to their Battalion Headquarters close here on the right. 21st Division still trotting along the skyline toward La Boisselle. Barrage going strong to the right of Contalmaison Ridge. Heavy shelling toward Mametz.

12.15   Quieter the last two hours. Manchesters still waiting. Germans putting over a few shrapnel shells. Silly if I got hit! Weather cloudless and hot. A lark singing confidently overhead.

1.30   Manchesters attack at 2.30. Mametz and Montauban reported taken. Mametz consolidated.

2.30   Manchesters left New Trench and apparently took Sunken Road Trench, bearing rather to the right. Could see about 400. Many walked casually across with sloped arms. There were about forty casualties on the left (from machine-gun in Fricourt). Through my glasses I could see one man moving his left arm up and down as he lay on his side; his face was a crimson patch. Others lay still in the sunlight while the swarm of figures disappeared over the hill. Fricourt was a cloud of pinkish smoke. Lively machine-gun fire on the far side of the hill. At 2.50 no one to be seen in no-man's-land except the casualties (about half-way across). Our dug-out shelled again since 2.30.

5.00   I saw about thirty of our A Company crawl across to Sunken Road from New Trench. Germans put a few big shells on the Cemetery and traversed Kingston Road with machine-gun. Manchester wounded still out there. Remainder of A Company went across – about 100 altogether. Manchesters reported held up in Bois Français Support. Their Colonel went across and was killed.

8.00   Staff Captain of our Brigade has been along. Told Barton that Seventh Division has reached its objectives with some difficulty, except on this Brigade front. Manchesters are in trouble, and Fricourt attack has failed. Several hundred prisoners brought in on our sector.

9.30   Our A Company holds Rectangle and Sunken Road. Jenkins gone off in charge of a carrying-party. Seemed all right again. C Company now reduced to six runners, two stretcher-bearers, Company Sergeant-Major, signallers, and Barton's servant. Flook away on carrying-party. Sky cloudy westward. Red sunset. Heavy gun-fire on the left.

2.30 (Next afternoon) Adjutant has just been up here, excited, optimistic, and unshaven. He went across last night to ginger up A Company who did very well, thanks to the bombers. About 40 casualties; only 4 killed. Fricourt and Rose Trench occupied this morning without resistance. I am now lying out in front of our trench in the long grass, basking in sunshine where yesterday there were bullets. Our new front-line on the hill is being shelled. Fricourt is full of troops wandering about in search of souvenirs. The village was a ruin and is now a dust heap. A gunner (Forward Observation Officer) has just been along here with a German helmet in his hand. Said Fricourt is full of dead; he saw one officer lying across a smashed machine-gun with his head bashed in –'a fine looking chap', he said, with some emotion, which rather surprised me.

8.15 Queer feeling, seeing people moving about freely between here and Fricourt. Dumps being made. Shacks and shelters being put up under skeleton trees and all sorts of transport arriving at Cemetery Cross Roads. We stay here till to-morrow morning. Feel a bit of a fraud.

Siegfried Sassoon

- -

In his novel *Birdsong*, contemporary author Sebastian Faulks includes a fictional portrayal of the Battle of the Somme, as seen through the eyes of his character Captain Stephen Wraysford. Here, on the morning of 1 July, Stephen waits for the exact moment when he must order his men to go 'over the top'.

Birdsong

The mine went up on the ridge, a great leaping core of compacted soil, the earth eviscerated. Flames rose to more than a hundred feet. It was too big, Stephen thought. The scale appalled him. Shock waves from the explosion ran through the trench. Brennan was pitched forward off the firestep and broke his leg.

We must go now, thought Stephen. No word came. Byrne looked questioningly at him. Stephen shook his head. Still ten minutes.

German fire began at once. The lip of the British trench leapt and spat soil where machine guns raked it. Stephen ducked. Men shouting.

'Not yet.' Stephen screaming. The air above the trench now solid.

The second hand of his watch in slow motion. Twenty-nine past. The whistle in his mouth. His foot on the ladder. He swallowed hard and blew.

He clambered out and looked around him. It was for a moment completely quiet as the bombardment ended and the German guns also stopped. Skylarks wheeled and sang high in the cloudless sky. He felt alone, as though he had stumbled on this fresh world at the instant of its creation.

Then the artillery began to lay down the first barrage and the German machine guns resumed. To his left Stephen saw men trying to emerge from the trench but being smashed by bullets before they could stand. The gaps in the wire became jammed with bodies. Behind him the men were coming up. He saw Gray run along the top of the trench, shouting encouragement.

He walked hesitatingly forward, his skin tensed for the feeling of metal tearing flesh. He turned his body sideways, tenderly, to protect his eyes. He was hunched like an old woman in the cocoon of tearing noise.

Byrne was walking beside him at the slow pace required by their orders. Stephen glanced to his right. He could see a long, wavering line of khaki, primitive dolls progressing in tense deliberate steps, going down with a silent flap of arms, replaced, falling, continuing as though walking into a gale. He tried to catch Byrne's eye but failed. The sound of machine guns was varied by the crack of snipers and the roar of the barrage ahead of them.

He saw Hunt fall to his right. Studd bent to help him and Stephen saw his head opening up bright red under machine gun bullets as his helmet fell away.

His feet pressed onwards gingerly over the broken ground. After twenty or thirty yards there came a feeling that he was floating above his body, that it had taken on an automatic life of its own over which he had no power. It was as though he had become detached, in a dream, from the metal air through which his flesh was walking. In this trance there was a kind of relief, something close to hilarity.

Ten yards ahead and to the right was Colonel Barclay. He was carrying a sword.

Stephen went down. Some force had blown him. He was in a dip in the ground with a bleeding man, shivering. The barrage was too far ahead. Now the German guns were placing a curtain of their own. Shrapnel was blasting its jagged cones through any air space not filled by the machine guns.

All that metal will not find room enough, Stephen thought. It must crash and strike sparks above them. The man with him was screaming inaudibly. Stephen wrapped his dressing round the man's leg, then looked at himself. There was no wound. He crawled to the rim of the shellhole. There were others ahead of him. He stood up and began to walk again.

Perhaps with them he would be safer. He felt nothing as he crossed the pitted land on which humps of khaki lay every few yards. The load on his back was heavy. He looked behind and saw a second line walking into the barrage in no man's land. They were hurled up like waves breaking backwards into the sea. Bodies were starting to pile and clog the progress.

There was a man beside him missing part of his face, but walking in the same dreamlike state, his rifle pressing forward. His nose dangled and Stephen could see his teeth through the missing cheek. The noise was unlike anything he had heard before. It lay against his skin, shaking his bones. Remembering his order not to stop for those behind him, he pressed slowly on, and as the smoke lifted in front of him he saw the German wire.

It had not been cut.

Sebastian Faulks

4 'Was it for this…?'

Now look at the next two poems, each of which describes a soldier's experience of the death of a comrade. *In Parenthesis* is a memoir of the war years written in the form of a prose-poem, by the Welsh artist and writer David Jones. ('In parenthesis' means 'in brackets' – as if his wartime experience was bracketed off from the rest of his life.)

From **In Parenthesis**

The First Field Dressing is futile as frantic as seaman's shift
bunged to stoved bulwark, so soon the darking flood percolates
and he dies in your arms.
    And get back to that digging can't yer –
this ain't a bloody Wake
        for these dead, who will soon have their dead
for burial clods heaped over.

Nor time for halsing
nor to clip green wounds
nor weeping Maries bringing anointments
neither any word spoken
nor no decent nor appropriate sowing of this seed
nor remembrance of the harvesting
of the renascent cycle
and return
nor shaving of the head nor ritual incising for these *viriles*
     under each tree
  No one sings: Lully lully
for the mate whose blood runs down.

David Jones (included in *Up the Line to Death*)

halsing (archaic) – cleansing wounds; healing
viriles (Latin) – young men

Futility

Move him into the sun –
Gently its touch awoke him once,
At home, whispering of fields unsown.
Always it woke him, even in France,
Until this morning and this snow.
If anything might rouse him now
The kind old sun will know.

Think how it wakes the seeds, –
Woke, once, the clays of a cold star.
Are limbs, so dear-achieved, are sides,
Full-nerved – still warm – too hard to stir?
Was it for this the clay grew tall?
– O what made fatuous sunbeams toil
To break earth's sleep at all?

Wilfred Owen (included in *The Oxford Book of War Poetry*)

Activity

1 Read the poems carefully. Think about:
   - the situation each poem describes
   - the different types of language each poet uses (e.g. formal, colloquial, religious)
   - the way each uses simile and/or metaphor
   - the feelings and attitudes of the poets
   - which poem you find most moving.

2 Wilfred Owen wrote, 'My subject is war and the pity of war. The poetry is in the pity.'

   Write about the ways in which these two poets confront us with 'the pity of war'. If you wish, you can also extend this to include a comparison of these poems with others you have studied.

5 'Keep the homefires burning'?

Unless they volunteered for active service as nurses or in the women's sections of the army and navy, women were unlikely to have any direct experience of the war. Even then, they could never share the horror of trench warfare. However, the war made a huge impact on the lives of women as well as men. The extracts and poems which follow reflect some of the ways women experienced the war.

Sometimes, during the great recruiting campaigns, all the young men of a town who were eligible to fight joined up together, forming what were known as 'Pals' Battalions'. Some of these battalions were almost entirely wiped out, which made the war particularly devastating for the communities involved. Here, in the play *The Accrington Pals*, the women of the Lancashire town react to news of the Battle of the Somme.

The Accrington Pals

Bertha: Oh May have you seen Sarah?

May: Not since this morning.

Bertha: I knocked at her door. She wasn't back.

May: (*to* **Reggie**) Take them. Make sure she has her sleeping draught. If you need me shout for me.

Reggie: Thank you, miss. *(He goes.)*

Bertha: That's funny. She set out before me. She went to the station. I went to the Town Hall.

May: What for?

Bertha: To see what we could find out.

May: Turn that lamp down for me love, or I'll be had up for showing too much light.

Bertha: There was quite a few at Town Hall, but they said we was to clear off and stop spreading rumour.

May: Quite right.

Bertha: But everyone's going up and down, round and round, they'll go out of their minds. Who's that over there? Sarah? No. All the nurses have been stopped their leave, have you heard? Jessie Bains had only just got home and there was a bobby round at their home with an order for her to go back. She'd only time for a cup of tea and she was back on the train. Listen! There's people shouting down the hill. People running.

Sarah: *(off)* Bertha!

Bertha: Sarah!

(**Sarah** *runs on, white and breathless. During what she says* **Eva** *will enter quietly, to one side.)*

Sarah: Seven... seven... there's only seven of them left. The Pals. Only seven of them left alive. Out of nearly seven hundred men.

Bertha: Oh no God... don't... don't...

Sarah: We talked to the railwaymen that had been at Manchester Central. There's crowds there trying to find out what they can from the drivers and people coming from London. Well apparently it's certain because down in London they've spoken with stretcher bearers that crossed with the wounded yesterday into Dover. They asked them were any from up here. They said there were wounded Manchesters but there were not likely to be any Accringtons for they were wiped out... except for seven.

May: How could they know for sure?

Sarah: They were there! They still had the dirt and mess on their uniforms. And there was a young officer. He said he wasn't supposed to confirm it… but he did. And he was a big well-spoken young man but he was crying.

Eva: They treat us like children but we'll not behave like children. D'you believe it now May? I've been thinking and talking to one or two up the street. There's a general opinion that we should force them to tell us properly at the Town Hall. And we should all go there in the morning and make sure they do. And I mean everybody. Will you two go round with me and knock on doors?

Sarah: Yes. That's good. Bertha and me'll do all Waterloo Street if you like…

Bertha: I couldn't…

Sarah: You can! We'll get that bloody Mayor stood in front of us and if he says he doesn't know he can get on his telephone to wherever and find out! We'll march there! Come on Bertha. Let's get started.

Bertha: If only they could be alive!

Peter Whelan

Jessie Pope is best known for writing patriotic and jingoistic 'recruiting poems', in which she compares fighting in the war to sports, exhorting young men to 'play the game' for their team. Here she turns her attention to the 'girls':

War Girls

There's the girl who clips your ticket for the train,
    And the girl who speeds the lift from floor to floor,
There's the girl who does a milk-round in the rain,
    And the girl who calls for orders at your door.
        Strong, sensible, and fit,
        They're out to show their grit,
    And tackle jobs with energy and knack.
        No longer caged and penned up,
        They're going to keep their end up
    Till the khaki soldier boys come marching back.

There's the motor girl who drives a heavy van,
    There's the butcher girl who brings your joint of meat,
There's the girl who cries 'All fares, please!' like a man,
    And the girl who whistles taxis up the street.
        Beneath each uniform
        Beats a heart that's soft and warm,
    Though of canny mother-wit they show no lack;
        But a solemn statement this is,
        They've no time for love and kisses
    Till the khaki soldier boys come marching back.

Jessie Pope (included in Scars Upon My Heart)

Women who did serve often struggled to combine their new roles with meeting the stereotypical expectations of their families and friends. In this excerpt from her autobiography of the war years, *Testament of Youth*, Vera Brittain explores this feeling of dividing her loyalty between the army and the needs of her middle-class parents.

She had fought long and hard to gain a place at Oxford University, but when her fiancé Roland, her brother Edward and their friends had all gone to the Front, Brittain left her studies to become a Voluntary Aid Detachment (VAD) nurse in an army hospital in London. After Roland was killed on the very day he was due home for Christmas leave, she considered returning to college, but a visit to Oxford convinced her that she should continue nursing until after the war.

Testament of Youth

Back at Camberwell, I found a notice pinned to the board in the dining-hall asking for volunteers for foreign service. Now that Roland was irretrievably gone and my decision about Oxford had finally been made, there seemed to be no reason for withholding my name. It was the logical conclusion, I thought, of service in England, though quite a number of V.A.D.s refused to sign because their parents wouldn't like it, or they were too inexperienced, or had had pneumonia when they were five years old.

Their calm readiness to admit their fears amazed me. Not being composed in even the smallest measure of the stuff of which heroines are made, I was terrified of going abroad – so much publicity was now given to the German submarine campaign that the possibility of being torpedoed was a nightmare to me – but I was even more afraid of acknowledging my cowardice to myself, let alone to others. ... If once I allowed myself to recognise my fear of foreign service, and especially of submarines, all kinds of alarming things that I had survived quite tolerably – such as Zeppelin raids, and pitch-black slum streets, and being alone in a large hut on night-duty – would become impossible.

So I put down my name on the active service list, and never permitted my conscious self to hear the dastardly prayer of my unconscious that when my orders came they might be for anywhere but a hospital ship or the Mediterranean.

*   *   *

The final and worst stage of my refusal to be reconciled to my world after the loss of Roland was precipitated by quite a trivial event.

When the bitter Christmas weeks were over, my parents, for the sake of economy, had moved from the Grand Hotel to a smaller one, where the service was indifferent and the wartime cooking atrocious. As the result of its cold draughtiness, its bad food, and her anxiety over Edward, my mother, in the middle of March, was overcome by an acute species of chill. Believing herself, in sudden panic, to be worse than she was, she wrote begging me to get leave and come down to Brighton and nurse her.

After much difficulty and two or three interviews, I managed to obtain the grudging and sceptical leave of absence granted to V.A.D.s who had sick relatives – always regarded as a form of shirking, since the Army was supposed to be above all but the most vital domestic obligations. When I arrived at the hotel to find that my mother, in more stoical mood, had already struggled out of bed and was in no urgent need of me, I felt that I was perpetrating exactly the deceit of which I had been suspected. Forgetting that parents who had been brought up by their own forebears to regard young women as perpetually at the disposal of husbands or fathers, could hardly be expected to realise that Army discipline – so demonstrably implacable in the case of men – now operated with the same stern rigidity for daughters as for sons, I gave way to an outburst of inconsiderate fury that plunged me back into the depths of despondency from which I had been struggling to climb.

Wretched, remorseful, and still feeling horribly guilty of obtaining leave on false pretences, I stayed in Brighton for the two days that I had demanded. But the episode had pushed my misery to the point of mental crisis, and the first time that I was off duty after returning to Camberwell, I went up to Denmark Hill to try to think out in solitude all the implications of my spasmodic angers, my furious, uncontrolled resentments.

It was a bitter, grey afternoon, and an icy wind drove flurries of snow into my face as I got off the tram and hastened into the hostel. Huddling into a coat in my cheerless cubicle, I watched the snowflakes falling, and wondered how ever I was going to get through the weary remainder of life. I was only at the beginning of my twenties; I might have another forty, perhaps even fifty, years to live. The prospect seemed appalling, and I shuddered with cold and desolation as my numbed fingers wrote in my diary an abject, incoherent confession of self-hatred and despair.

Vera Brittain

Perhaps

(To R.A.L. Died of Wounds in France, December 23rd, 1915)

Perhaps some day the sun will shine again,
    And I shall see that still the skies are blue,
And feel once more I do not live in vain,
    Although bereft of You.

Perhaps the golden meadows at my feet
    Will make the sunny hours of Spring seem gay,
And I shall find the white May blossoms sweet,
    Though You have passed away.

Perhaps the summer woods will shimmer bright,
    And crimson roses once again be fair,
And autumn harvest fields a rich delight,
    Although You are not there.

Perhaps some day I shall not shrink in pain
    To see the passing of the dying year,
And listen to the Christmas songs again,
    Although You cannot hear.

But, though kind Time may many joys renew,
    There is one greatest joy I shall not know
Again, because my heart for loss of You
    Was broken, long ago.

Vera Brittain (included in *Scars Upon My Heart*)

Activity

1 On your own, or in a group, read through all four of the texts above. Discuss and/or make notes about

- what each text reveals about the ways that the lives of women were affected by the war

- the wide differences they demonstrate in style, point of view and language.

2 Using evidence from these texts (and others you have read, if you wish) write an essay about how women's experience of the First World War is presented in literature.

6 'We still can dance...'

The apparent insensitivity and indifference of those who were not directly involved in the conflict was an issue that sparked some bitter responses. Army commanders who ordered soldiers into battle from a safe distance, and civilians who continued 'partying' back home, are the targets in these two short poems.

Base Details

If I were fierce, and bald, and short of breath,
    I'd live with scarlet Majors at the Base,
And speed glum heroes up the line to death.
    You'd see me with my puffy petulant face,
Guzzling and gulping in the best hotel,
    Reading the Roll of Honour. 'Poor young chap,'
I'd say – 'I used to know his father well;
    Yes, we've lost heavily in this last scrap.'
And when the war is done and youth stone dead,
    I'd toddle safely home and die – in bed.

Siegfried Sassoon (included in *Up the Line to Death*)

The Dancers

(During a Great Battle, 1916)

The floors are slippery with blood:
The world gyrates too. God is good
That while His wind blows out the light
For those who hourly die for us –
We still can dance, each night.

The music has grown numb with death –
But we will suck their dying breath,
The whispered name they breathed to chance,
To swell our music, make it loud
That we may dance, – may dance.

We are the dull blind carrion-fly
That dance and batten. Though God die
Mad from the horror of the light –
The light is mad, too, flecked with blood, –
We dance, we dance, each night.

Edith Sitwell (included in *Scars Upon My Heart*)

Activity

These poems are designed to shock. Read them closely and/or discuss them with a partner, before writing a comparison of the tactics used by each poet to make people take notice.

Examination practice: Contextual Linking

In Section A of the exam you will be presented with one compulsory question which will ask you to read a short extract related to the First World War. This short extract could be taken from a variety of sources such as letters, biography, literary criticism, social commentary, or diaries.

Activity

Read the following extracts carefully. They are taken from an account of the Battle of the Somme by the historian R.H. Tawney, which was written in August 1916 and published in the *Westminster Gazette*.

Then write an essay in which you:

- explore the writer's thoughts and feelings about his experience of fighting

- compare this extract to your wider reading, saying how typical you think it is of First World War literature. You should consider both subject matter and style.

The Attack

It was a glorious morning, and, as though there were some mysterious sympathy between the wonders of the ear and of the eye, the bewildering tumult seemed to grow more insistent with the growing brilliance of the atmosphere and the intenser blue of the July sky. The sound was different, not only in magnitude, but in quality, from anything known to me. It was not a succession of explosions or a continuous roar; I, at least, never heard either a gun or a bursting shell. It was not a noise; it was a symphony. It did not move; it hung over us. It was as though the air were full of a vast and agonized passion, bursting now into groans and sighs, now into shrill screams and pitiful whimpers, shuddering beneath terrible blows, torn by unearthly whips, vibrating with the solemn pulse of enormous wings. And the supernatural tumult did not pass in this direction or that. It did not begin, intensify, decline, and end. It was poised in the air, a stationary panorama of sound, a condition of the atmosphere, not the creation of man. It seemed that one had only to lift one's eyes to be appalled by the writhing of the tormented element above one, that a hand raised ever so little above the level of the trench would be sucked away into a whirlpool revolving with cruel and incredible velocity over infinite depths. And this feeling, while it filled one with awe, filled one also with triumphant exultation, the exultation of struggling against a storm in mountains, or watching the irresistible course of a swift and destructive river. Yet at the same time one was intent on practical details, wiping the trench dirt off the bolt of one's rifle, reminding the men of what each was to do, and when the message went round, 'five minutes to go', seeing that all bayonets were fixed. My captain, a brave man and a good officer, came along and borrowed a spare watch off me. It was the last time I saw him. At 7.30 we went up the ladders, doubled through the gaps in the wire, and lay down, waiting for the line to form up on each side of us. When it was ready we went forward, not doubling, but at a walk. For we had nine hundred yards of rough ground to the trench which was our first objective, and about fifteen hundred to a further trench where we were to wait for orders. There was a bright light in the air, and the tufts of coarse grass were gray with dew.

I hadn't gone ten yards before I felt a load fall from me. There's a sentence at the end of *The Pilgrim's Progress* which has always struck me as one of the most awful things imagined by man: 'Then I saw that there was a way to Hell, even from the Gates of

Heaven, as well as from the City of Destruction.' To have gone so far and be rejected at last! Yet undoubtedly man walks between precipices, and no one knows the rottenness in him till he cracks, and then it's too late. I had been worried by the thought: 'Suppose one should lose one's head and get other men cut up! Suppose one's legs should take fright and refuse to move!' Now I knew it was all right. I shouldn't be frightened and I shouldn't lose my head. Imagine the joy of that discovery! I felt quite happy and self-possessed. It wasn't courage. That, I imagine, is the quality of facing danger which one knows to be danger, of making one's spirit triumph over the bestial desire to live in this body. But I knew that I was in no danger. I knew I shouldn't be hurt; knew it positively, much more positively than I know most things I'm paid for knowing.

*   *   *

In crossing No Man's Land we must have lost many more men than I realized then. For the moment the sight of the Germans drove everything else out of my head. Most men, I suppose, have a Paleolithic savage somewhere in them, a beast that occasionally shouts to be given a chance of showing his joyful cunning in destruction. I have, anyway, and from the age of catapults to that of shot-guns always enjoyed aiming at anything that moved, though since manhood the pleasure has been sneaking and shamefaced. Now it was a duty to shoot, and there was an easy target. For the Germans were brave men, as brave as lions. Some of them actually knelt – one for a moment even stood – on the top of their parapet, to shoot, within not much more than a hundred yards of us. It was insane. It seemed one couldn't miss them. Every man I fired at dropped, except one. Him, the boldest of the lost, I missed more than once. I was puzzled and angry. Three hundred years ago I should have tried a silver bullet. Not that I wanted to hurt him or anyone else. It was missing I hated. That's the beastliest thing in war, the damnable frivolity. One's like a merry, mischievous ape tearing up the image of God. When I read now the babble of journalists about the 'sporting spirit of our soldiers', it makes me almost sick. God forgive us all! But then it was as I say.

*   *   *

We attacked, I think, about 820 strong. I've no official figures of casualties. A friend, an officer in 'C' Company, which was in support and shelled to pieces before it could start, told me in hospital that we lost 450 men that day, and that, after being put in again a day or two later, we had 54 left. I suppose it's worth it.

R.H. Tawney

Examination practice: Poetry

In Section B of the exam you will have a choice of two questions on your set poetry text. The activities below will give you practice in answering the type of questions involved.

Activity

1 'Never such innocence again' is how Philip Larkin concludes his poem *MCMXIV*, published in 1974, which looks back on the early months of the war.

   How well does this phrase sum up the selection of First World War poetry you have read? Refer to three poems in detail.

2 Read the poem *Attack*, by Siegfried Sassoon, which follows. How typical is it of First World War poetry (and other literature)? Write a detailed analysis of this poem, comparing it with two others from the collection you have studied.

Attack

At dawn the ridge emerges massed and dun
In the wild purple of the glow'ring sun,
Smouldering through spouts of drifting smoke that shroud
The menacing scarred slope; and, one by one,
Tanks creep and topple forward to the wire.
The barrage roars and lifts. Then, clumsily bowed
With bombs and guns and shovel and battle-gear,
Men jostle and climb to meet the bristling fire.
Lines of grey, muttering faces, masked with fear,
They leave their trenches, going over the top,
While time ticks blank and busy on their wrists,
And hope, with furtive eyes and grappling fists,
Flounders in mud. O Jesus, make it stop!

Siegfried Sassoon (included in *Up the Line to Death*)

1 The Struggle for Identity in Modern Literature

Objectives

- To understand the requirements of the modern literature option of Unit 1 – Texts in Context
- To gain an overview of the twentieth and twenty-first centuries as a context for literature
- To understand what you will need to do to prepare yourself for Section A of the examination paper – Contextual Linking
- To develop an understanding of the work of the poet you have chosen for study and prepare yourself for Section B of the examination paper

The modern literature option

In studying this option you will need to study a variety of texts for AS level.

Unit 1: Texts in Context

This unit will be assessed through one two-hour exam paper. The paper will consist of two sections and you will need to answer one question in each section.

Section A: Contextual Linking

In this section you will be given one question which will consist of a short extract related to modern literature. This may be taken from a variety of sources such as a diary, a letter, biography, commentary on the social or cultural aspects of the period, or from a critical work on the period. You will be asked to link your reading in modern literature to the extract given.

Section B: Poetry

You will be given a choice of two questions on each of the set poetry texts. One of the questions will focus on one particular poem and its relation to the whole text, and the other will ask you to discuss some aspect of the poems you have studied. You will answer one of these two questions.

The set texts to choose from are as follows:

And Still I Rise: Maya Angelou (Virago)
The World's Wife: Carol Ann Duffy (Picador)
Skirrid Hill: Owen Sheers (Seren)

Assessment Objectives

The Assessment Objectives that you will be assessed on in this unit are as follows:

- **AO1** Articulate creative, informed and relevant responses to literary texts, using appropriate terminology and concepts, and coherent, accurate written expression assessed in Sections A and B)

- **AO2** Demonstrate detailed critical understanding in analysing the ways in which structure, form and language shape meanings in literary texts
(assessed in Sections A and B)

- **AO3** Explore connections and comparisons between different literary texts, informed by interpretations of other readers
(assessed in Sections A and B)

- **AO4** Demonstrate understanding of the significance and influence of the contexts in which literary texts are written and received
(assessed in Section A)

Unit 2: Creative Study

For this unit you will need to produce a coursework portfolio which, together with your work for Unit 1, will form a coherent course of study of modern literature. For your portfolio you will need to study one prose text and one drama text.

You will need to produce two pieces of writing:

- the first piece of writing should present a personal, informed response to the prose text, and will be a creative piece

- the second piece of writing should be on your chosen drama text, and should focus either on its dramatic context or link it to your prose text, covering aspects such as theme, structure, characterization, etc.

Your two pieces of work should be 2000–2500 words in total.

Assessment Objectives

The Assessment Objectives that you will be tested on in this unit are the same as those in Unit 1 – all the objectives are assessed in both pieces of work.

You will find more on the Creative Study unit and a list of the set texts for the modern literature option in Chapter 12.

Wider reading

In addition to the texts you have studied, you should also choose at least three texts covering poetry, prose and drama for wider reading. If you can study further short pieces or extracts, this will enhance your understanding of the context.

The modern context

The period from the beginning of the twentieth century to the present day has been a time of tremendous change and of many momentous events. Obviously the First World War had an enormous impact on the social fabric of Britain as a generation of young men had perished, and following the war there began a gradual breakdown of established patterns of social order. Among many people a distrust of 'authority' developed, and the 1920s became, in some ways, an age of revolt against established convention. Increased knowledge and educational opportunities contributed towards a questioning attitude about many aspects of social and political life; in particular women, who during the war had taken over many of the roles traditionally reserved for men, sought more freedom and independence.

The Second World War lasted from 1939–1945, and the post-war world seemed fundamentally changed. This had been a people's war with civilian casualties in Britain accounting for almost a quarter of the total casualties of the war. After it ended there was much pressure for social change. The 1944 Education Act had guaranteed secondary education up to the age of 15 for all, and post-war measures were put in place to create a National Health Service, with an expanded contributory National Insurance scheme to provide individuals with some financial security throughout life. The coal and steel industries and the railways were taken into public ownership. The granting of independence to India marked the beginning of the break-up of the British Empire.

Soon after the Second World War tensions with the Soviet bloc and the increasing dangers posed by the nuclear arms race polarized nations, and pitted democratic socialism against the dangers posed by totalitarianism. This theme is evident in much writing of the time, most notably in George Orwell's *Nineteen Eighty-Four* (1949) in which he gives his nightmare vision of a future world dominated by totalitarianism. A little later, 'cold war' themes were explored in popular fiction through the novels of writers such as Ian Fleming and John Le Carre.

During the 1950s a new breed of dramatists and novelists emerged, with radical views and a style of literature that challenged the social norms. One journalist described them as 'the angry young men', as their writing often contained a sense of resentment, betrayal and futility, and focused on the idea of alienation from society. This was often founded in the perception that the post-war promises of a 'new world' had not materialized. John Osborne's play *Look Back in Anger* (1956), John Wain's *Hurry on Down* (1953), Kingsley Amis's *Lucky Jim* (1954), and Alan Sillitoe's *Saturday Night and Sunday Morning* (1958) exemplify the work of such writers.

The post-war years also saw a significant increase in the prominence of women writers in all genres, many of whom focused on issues of particular relevance to women. The creation of the publishing houses The Women's Press and Virago encouraged new writers, and new critical approaches reassessed the work of earlier women writers such as Charlotte Perkins Gilman and Jean Rhys as well as that of well-known writers such as Muriel Spark, Doris Lessing and Iris Murdoch.

The years since the Second World War have also seen a great increase in interest in poetry. The work of well-known poets such as Philip Larkin, Ted Hughes and John Betjeman did much in the 1950s, 1960s and 1970s to capture the imaginations of the people; poetry readings, festivals and competitions have promoted the genre and added to its popularity. In the latter part of the twentieth century and the beginning of the twenty-first, this popularity has been sustained through a new generation of poets such as Simon Armitage, Carol Ann Duffy, Gillian Clarke and Wendy Cope who have the ability to connect with the people and capture the popular imagination.

From the latter part of the twentieth century English literature in all genres has been further enriched through the contributions of writers drawing on a background of other cultures and traditions, such as Grace Nichols, Alice Walker, Moniza Alvi, Linton Kwesi Johnson, Wole Soyinka and Ken Saro-Wiwa.

Contextual linking

The following extract is from the *Cambridge Cultural History of Britain*, Volume 9, 'Modern Britain', edited by Boris Ford. The writer discusses the features which show that literature in Britain is flourishing. Here he focuses on the status of poetry.

Activity

1 Read the extract carefully and then discuss it in a small group, making notes on the following:

  • the writer's overall view of the state of poetry in Britain

- the evidence he presents to support his view
- the kinds of poetry he is critical of.

2 Now think about how the view of British post-war poetry presented here compares with the view you have formed through your own study of modern literature.

Another phenomenon which seems at first sight to suggest that post-war British culture is in a flourishing condition has been the marked upsurge of interest in poetry. The public have bought the verse of their favourite poets to an extent unprecedented in modern times: Philip Larkin's *The Whitsun Weddings* (1964), for example, sold 70,000 copies; Ted Hughes' *Crow* (1970), 50,000; and Seamus Heaney's *North* (1975), 30,000, while John Betjeman's volumes, beginning with *Summoned by Bells* (1960) moved into the best-seller class. These are figures which rival those achieved by Scott, Byron and Tom Moore in the early nineteenth century. In addition, poetry readings and festivals have drawn big audiences, and poetry programmes on BBC radio attract many listeners. There have also been numerous poetry magazines, especially during the 1950s and early 1960s, many of them edited outside London, like Hull's *Listen* and *Wave* and Edinburgh's *Lines Review*, and although in recent years economic factors have forced many of them out of business, they still come and go, and some, like Newcastle-upon-Tyne's *Stand* (which contains criticism and prose as well as new verse) persist.

Moreover many more people are apparently writing poetry – as witness the startling scale of entries for the various annual poetry competitions, no less than 40,000 in one recent case. It would appear that the sense of almost continuous political and social crisis, the threat of nuclear warfare, and the loss of faith not only in religion but also in general ethical standards and in social and political institutions which had once seemed tested and proved, has created a mood of anxiety and impotence which has led more and more people to look to poetry to provide answers, or at least to impose some sort of order on the chaos.

There has certainly been no lack of established poets to cater for the demand. Few of these write less than decent poetry, and some of them do very much better than that. What has become rare is the production of a really solid body of poetic work, marked by variety and steady progression. With a few notable exceptions, long poems that seek to probe deeply into the contemporary human situation have become equally rare. Short poems or lyrics are the general rule, and the term 'occasional' – not necessarily in a pejorative sense – often seems the appropriate one.

At first sight the adjective is particularly applicable to Betjeman's poetry, with its tremendous popularity. Some of it is undoubtedly light verse like the famous 'Miss Joan Hunter Dunn, Miss Joan Hunter Dunn': but the pre-war suburban world which many of Betjeman's poems conjure up – with their tennis courts, vicarage garden parties, and old-style railway stations – is a far more stable and therefore comforting one than our own. At its best, the easy lyrical measures of Betjeman's poetry are the result of considerable artistic subtlety, as Auden among others observed; while the emotions with which he deals – the remembered joys and terrors of childhood, the fear of death, a hard-won religious faith, and the belief in simple pieties and virtues – sometimes have a genuine dramatic urgency and the kind of innocence that commands respect because of its complete freedom from self-conscious cleverness or intellectual faking.

This kind of appeal is in many ways a healthier phenomenon than some of the post-war trends in the popularising of poetry. One of these has been a movement towards a concept of poetry that regards it primarily as performance or group activity. Christopher Logue's frequently stimulating experiments with poetry and jazz in the 1950s pointed the way; the first considerable breakthrough was the Albert Hall reading of 1965, which Michael Horovitz, one of its organisers, described as 'a sacramental jubilee'. If the work of the 'pop' poets is often worth reading, that can hardly be said of the 'rants' of other poets – vituperatively anarchic doggerel, full of obscenities, usually accompanied by a violently aggressive and amplified musical backing. These writers challenge the traditional idea of the permanence of poetry, from a standpoint which regards considerations of quality and evaluation as the remnants of an anachronistic bourgeois and patriarchal society.

In the following piece the novelist Margaret Atwood explores the creative process that faces a writer.

Activity

Read the text through carefully.

1 What view of the creative process does Atwood present here?

2 Pick out four examples of Atwood's use of imagery here and comment on the effects she creates.

3 Comment on other stylistic features she uses to add impact (e.g. choices of vocabulary, structure).

4 Compare this text to your wider reading, commenting on how far you think the views presented here differ from or are reflected in other texts you have read.

The Page

Good bones and simple murders

1   The page waits, pretending to be blank. Is that its appeal, its blankness? What else is this smooth and white, this terrifyingly innocent? A snowfall, a glacier? It's a desert, totally arid, without life. But people venture into such places. Why? To see how much they can endure, how much dry light?

2   I've said the page is white, and it is: white as wedding dresses, rare whales, seagulls, angels, ice and death. Some say that like sunlight it contains all colours; others, that it's white because it's hot, it will burn out your optic nerves; that those who stare at the page too long go blind.

3   The page itself has no dimensions and no directions. There's no up or down except what you yourself mark, there's no thickness and weight but those you put there, north and south do not exist unless you're certain of them. The page is without vistas and without sounds, without centres or edges. Because of this you can become lost in it forever. Have you never seen the look of gratitude, the look of joy, on the faces of those who have managed to return from the page? Despite their faintness, their loss of blood, they fall on their knees, they push their hands into the earth, they clasp the bodies of those they love, or, in a pinch, any bodies they can get, with an urgency unknown to those who have never experienced the full horror of a journey into the page.

4   If you decide to enter the page, take a knife and some matches, and something that will float. Take something you can hold onto, and a prism to split the light and a talisman that works, which should be hung on a chain around your neck: that's for getting back. It doesn't matter what kind of shoes, but your hands should be bare. You should never go into the page with gloves on. Such decisions, needless to say, should not be made lightly.

There are those, of course, who enter the page without deciding, without meaning to. Some of these have charmed lives and no difficulty, but most never make it out at all. For them the page appears as a well, a lovely pool in which they catch sight of a face, their own but better. These unfortunates do not jump: rather they fall, and the page closes over their heads without a sound, without a seam, and is immediately as whole and empty, as glassy, as enticing as before.

5 The question about the page is: what is beneath it? It seems to have only two dimensions, you can pick it up and turn it over and the back is the same as the front. Nothing, you say, disappointed.

But you were looking in the wrong place, you were looking *on the back* instead of *beneath*. *Beneath the page* is another story. Beneath the page is a story. Beneath the page is everything that has ever happened, most of which you would rather not hear about.

The page is not a pool but a skin, a skin is there to hold in and it can feel you touching it. Did you really think it would just lie there and do nothing?

Touch the page at your peril: it is you who are blank and innocent, not the page. Nevertheless you want to know, nothing will stop you. You touch the page, it's as if you've drawn a knife across it, the page has been hurt now, a sinuous wound opens, a thin incision. Darkness wells through.

One of the features of modern literature is the way in which much of it centres on establishing a sense of identity. Throughout the twentieth century, feminist writers have explored the nature of womanhood and woman's position in what was, and in many respects still remains, a predominantly male-oriented society.

In the following article Judy Syfers, a prominent feminist, uses satire to explore the status of women in marriage. The article appeared in the very first edition of the feminist magazine *Ms* in December 1971.

Activity

Read the article through carefully and discuss your responses to it with a partner.

1 What is the main point of Syfers's article?
2 Make a note of any aspects of it that you find particularly interesting.
3 Comment on Syfers's style of writing and the ways in which she expresses her ideas.
4 Compare the views presented here with others you have gained from your wider reading.

Why I Want a Wife

I belong to that classification of people known as wives. I am A Wife.

And, not altogether incidentally, I am a mother. Not too long ago a male friend of mine appeared on the scene fresh from a recent divorce. He had one child, who is, of course, with his ex-wife. He is looking for another wife. As I thought about him while I was ironing one evening, it suddenly occurred to me that I, too, would like to have a wife. Why do I want a wife?

I would like to go back to school so that I can become economically independent, support myself, and, if need be, support those dependent upon me. I want a wife who will work and send me to school. And while I am going to school I want a wife to take care of my children.

I want a wife to keep track of the children's doctor and dentist appointments. And to keep track of mine, too. I want a wife to make sure my children eat properly and are kept clean. I want a wife who will wash the children's clothes and keep them mended. I want a wife who is a good nurturing attendant to my children, who arranges for their schooling, makes sure that they have an adequate social life with their peers, takes them to the park, the zoo, etc. I want a wife who takes care of the children when they are sick, a wife who arranges to be around when the children need special care, because, of course, I cannot miss classes at school. My wife must arrange to lose time at work and not lose the job. It may mean a small cut in my wife's income from time to time, but I guess I can tolerate that. Needless to say, my wife will arrange and pay for the care of the children while my wife is working.

I want a wife who will take care of my physical needs. I want a wife who will keep my house clean. A wife who will pick up after my children, a wife who will pick up after me. I want a wife who will keep my clothes clean, ironed, mended, replaced when need be, and who will see to it that my personal things are kept in their proper places so that I can find what I need the minute I need it. I want a wife who cooks the meals, a wife who is a good cook. I want a wife who will plan the menus, do the necessary grocery shopping, prepare the meals, serve them pleasantly, and then do the cleaning up while I do my studying. I want a wife who will care for me when I am sick and sympathize with my pain and loss of time from school. I want a wife to go along when our family takes a vacation so that someone can continue to care for me and my children when I need a rest and change of scene.

I want a wife who will not bother me with rambling complaints about a wife's duties. But I want a wife who will listen to me when I feel the need to explain a rather difficult point I have come across in my course of studies. And I want a wife who will type my papers for me when I have written them.

I want a wife who will take care of the details of my social life. When my wife and I are invited out by my friends, I want a wife who will take care of the baby-sitting arrangements. When I meet people at school that I like and want to entertain, I want a wife who will have the house clean, will prepare a special meal, serve it to me and my friends, and not interrupt when I talk about things that interest me and my friends. I want a wife who will have arranged that the children are fed and ready for bed before my guests arrive so that the children do not bother us. I want a wife who takes care of the needs of my guests so that they feel comfortable, who makes sure that they have an ashtray, that they are passed the hors d'oeuvres, that they are offered a second helping of the food, that their wine glasses are replenished when necessary, that their coffee is served to them as they like it. And I want a wife who knows that sometimes I need a night out by myself.

I want a wife who is sensitive to my sexual needs, a wife who makes love passionately and eagerly when I feel like it, a wife who makes sure that I am satisfied. And, of course, I want a wife who will not demand sexual attention when I am not in the mood for it. I want a wife who assumes the complete responsibility for birth control, because I do not want more children. I want a wife who will remain sexually faithful to me so that I do not have to clutter up my intellectual life with jealousies. And I want a wife who understands that my sexual needs may entail more than strict adherence to monogamy. I must, after all, be able to relate to people as fully as possible.

If, by chance, I find another person more suitable as a wife than the wife I already have, I want the liberty to replace my present wife with another one. Naturally, I will expect a fresh, new life; my wife will take the children and be solely responsible for them so that I am left free.

When I am through with school and have a job, I want my wife to quit working and remain at home so that my wife can more fully and completely take care of a wife's duties.

My God, who wouldn't want a wife?

Examination practice

In Section A of the exam you will be presented with one compulsory question which will ask you to read a short extract related to modern literature. This short extract could be taken from a variety of sources such as letters, biography, literary criticism, social commentary, diary, etc.

Activity

Read the following extract carefully. It is taken from Stephen Fry's autobiography *Moab Is My Washpot*, first published in 1997.

In your answer you should:

- consider the writer's thoughts and feelings about himself and his writing, and the ways in which he expresses them
- compare this extract to your wider reading, saying how typical you think it is of literature about the struggle for identity. You should consider both subject matter and style.

To Myself: Not to Be Read Until I Am Twenty-five

I know what you will think when you read this. You will be embarrassed. You will scoff and sneer. Well I tell you now that everything I feel now, everything I am now is truer and better than anything I shall ever be. Ever. This is me now, the real me. Every day that I grow away from the me that is writing this now is a betrayal and a defeat. I expect you will screw this up into a ball with sophisticated disgust, or at best with tolerant amusement but deep down you will know, you will know that you are smothering what you really, really were. This is the age when I truly am. From now on my life will be behind me. I will tell you now, THIS IS TRUE – truer than anything else I will ever write, feel or know. WHAT I AM NOW IS ME, WHAT I WILL BE IS A LIE.

I can dimly, just dimly, recall writing it. A whole condition of mind swims back into me every time I look at it, and swam back all the more strongly when I typed it out for you just now. I won't go so far as to call it a Proustian *petite madeleine,* one of those epiphanic memory revivifiers, for the memory has always been there, but it still has the power to create a feeling like hot lead leaking into my stomach, a feel-good pain that was both the dreaded demon and the welcome companion of my adolescence. It was a strange piece of writing to happen upon as I did recently, going through all my old papers, writings, poems and scrapbooks, and it's a strange thing to look at now. What would you think if you read such a message to yourself?

Activity

Read the following extract carefully. It is taken from Malcolm Bradbury's book *The Modern British Novel.* Here he gives his views on the state of British fiction in the 1980s and 1990s.

In your answer you should:

- consider the writer's thoughts and feelings about British fiction and the ways in which he expresses them

> - compare this extract to your wider reading, saying how typical you think it is of literature about the struggle for identity. You should consider both subject matter and style.

In British fiction, the Eighties opened in an atmosphere of political dismay but great artistic excitement. The Nineties started on a note of gloom, perhaps the inevitable bitter reflection of an increasingly recessionary time which has affected the marketplace, making publishers cautious, readers fewer, critics more savage. When, in 1993, the magazine *Granta* announced its second select list of the twenty 'best of young British novelists', the familiar gloomy reports did not take a long time to come in. 'Contemporary British fiction, as everyone knows... is in a sad state,' announced the *Guardian* newspaper darkly. Other critics and newspapers echoed the despondency; 'we have failed even to produce a handful of novelists of any real stature', noted one young writer (Nick Hornby) of his contemporaries. The now usual complaints were widely rehearsed: British fiction was poor in comparison with American or Latin American writing, had no sense of world history and no wide view of contemporary Britain, no social and reportorial excitement, no strong voice, no moral force, no deep themes.

Poetry

Maya Angelou

Maya Angelou was born Marguerite Johnson in 1928 in St Louis, USA (she took the name Maya Angelou in her early twenties after her debut performance as a dancer in a cabaret club). She was brought up in rural Arkansas at a time when segregation was still the norm. By the time she had reached her early twenties she had already had numerous jobs including cook, waitress, dancer and streetcar conductor. She later became a successful singer, actor and playwright. She travelled widely, living for a time in Egypt, where she edited *The Arab Observer*, and Ghana where she was features editor of the *African Review* and lectured at the University of Ghana. She returned to the United States in the mid 1960s and took up a position as lecturer at the University of California in Los Angeles in 1966.

She was active as a civil rights campaigner and in the 1960s Martin Luther King asked her to become the northern co-ordinator for the Southern Christian Leadership Conference; she has been awarded numerous honours and honorary degrees. She has also worked in the film industry, script writing, producing and directing, has written and produced several prize-winning documentaries, and was nominated for an Emmy award for her role in the film *Roots*.

However, for many it is her writing for which she is most well-known, perhaps most of all for *I Know Why the Caged Bird Sings* (1969), the first volume of her autobiography which recounts her life up to the age of 16. The life she presents here is often hard and grim, set against the deep-seated racist attitudes prevalent in the Southern states during the 1930s, and includes the harrowing account of being raped at the age of eight by her mother's boyfriend. It was with this book that she became the first African-American woman writer to be placed in the best-seller lists. She has also published a number of volumes of poetry, including *And Still I Rise*, which have been equally highly acclaimed.

Thematic ideas

Angelou's life, experiences and beliefs are at the centre of and provide the driving force for her poetry, as with her autobiographical writing, and critics have often praised it more for its content than for poetic form. However, it is clearly the ideas and message that the poems convey that is the central issue to Angelou. Here are some of the ideas she explores through her poems:

- overcoming life's struggles
- the strength of women and the human spirit
- social justice
- love
- the sense of self – pride in black roots
- the lives of black people in the United States from the time of slavery.

In the title poem of the anthology, Angelou presents ideas that are at the centre of her poetry.

Activity

Read the poem through carefully.

1 Make notes on the ideas that Angelou explores in the poem.
2 Do you notice anything unusual about the vocabulary she uses?
3 What particular techniques does she use to create her effects in the poem?
4 Comment on the structure of the poem. Why do you think Angelou organizes her poem in this way?

Still I Rise

You may write me down in history
With your bitter, twisted lies,
You may trod me in the very dirt
But still, like dust, I'll rise.

Does my sassiness upset you?
Why are you beset with gloom?
'Cause I walk like I've got oil wells
Pumping in my living room.

Just like moons and like suns,
With the certainty of tides,
Just like hopes springing high,
Still I'll rise.

Did you want to see me broken?
Bowed head and lowered eyes?
Shoulders falling down like teardrops,
Weakened by my soulful cries.

Does my haughtiness offend you?
Don't you take it awful hard
'Cause I laugh like I've got gold mines
Diggin' in my own back yard.

You may shoot me with your words,
You may cut me with your eyes,
You may kill me with your hatefulness,
But still, like air, I'll rise.

Does my sexiness upset you?
Does it come as a surprise
That I dance like I've got diamonds
At the meeting of my thighs?

Out of the huts of history's shame
I rise
Up from a past that's rooted in pain
I rise
I'm a black ocean, leaping and wide,
Welling and swelling I bear in the tide.

Leaving behind nights of terror and fear
I rise
Into a daybreak that's wondrously clear
I rise
Bringing the gifts my ancestors gave,
I am the dream and the hope of the slave.
I rise
I rise
I rise.

Here are some ideas that you might have noted.

- In the poem Angelou asserts her pride in being black and in her strength to withstand all kinds of attack, pressures and misfortunes without submitting to them. She rejects prejudice and those who would attempt to demean and humiliate her. In a broader sense the poem addresses all who might suffer oppression and prejudice or those who would humiliate and attempt to crush the individual.

- There are colloquialisms and non-standard constructions, e.g. 'sassiness', 'You may trod me in the very dirt', 'Don't you take it awful hard', and clipped words, e.g. ''Cause' and 'Diggin' – all of which help to create a sense of the individual, personal voice of the poet.

- Similes are used – some linked to the idea of rising, e.g. 'But still, like dust, I'll rise', 'But still, like air, I'll rise' and some to emphasize the description, e.g. ''Cause I laugh like I've got goldmines', 'I dance like I've got diamonds/ At the meeting of my thighs'.

- The phrase 'Still I'll rise' is repeated, which emphasizes the sense that nothing can succeed in repressing the poet – no matter what happens, what pressures or blows she endures, she will rise again.

- The repeated use of questions almost seems to challenge the unseen 'You' to whom the poem is addressed, e.g. 'Did you want to see me broken?', 'Does my haughtiness offend you?', which contain the unspoken implication 'if it does, that is more your problem than mine – I am as I am, and nothing will prevent me being myself'.

- The first seven fairly regular four-line stanzas contain the questions and also the images of oppression against which the poet will continue to rise. The final stanzas break this pattern and conclude with fifteen irregular lines which signal a switch in focus. These lines look back to the age of slavery and to the roots and ancestors of the poet. Rhyme is used here to accentuate the words, e.g. 'shame/ pain', 'fear/ clear', 'gave/ slave'. The repeated 'I rise' (seven times in this section) gives a kind of incantatory effect so that it presents an unchallengeable mantra; the final triple repetition concludes the poem.

In *Phenomenal Woman*, the persona of the poem also comes across as a confident and strong woman.

Activity

Read *Phenomenal Woman* through carefully and make notes on the following areas:

- the use of imagery
- the use of repetition
- the structure of the poem.

Phenomenal Woman

Pretty women wonder where my secret lies.
I'm not cute or built to suit a fashion model's size
But when I start to tell them,
They think I'm telling lies.
I say,
It's in the reach of my arms,
The span of my hips,
The stride of my step,
The curl of my lips.
I'm a woman
Phenomenally.
Phenomenal woman,
That's me.

I walk into a room
Just as cool as you please,
And to a man,
The fellows stand or
Fall down on their knees.
Then they swarm around me,
A hive of honey bees.
I say,
It's the fire in my eyes,
And the flash of my teeth,
The swing in my waist,
And the joy in my feet.
I'm a woman
Phenomenally.
Phenomenal woman,
That's me.

Men themselves have wondered
What they see in me.
They try so much
But they can't touch
My inner mystery.
When I try to show them,
They say they still can't see.

I say,
It's in the arch of my back,
The sun of my smile,
The ride of my breasts,
The grace of my style.
I'm a woman
Phenomenally.
Phenomenal woman,
That's me.

Now you understand
Just why my head's not bowed.
I don't shout or jump about
Or have to talk real loud.
When you see me passing
It ought to make you proud.
I say,
It's in the click of my heels,
The bend of my hair,
The palm of my hand,
The need for my care.
'Cause I'm a woman
Phenomenally.
Phenomenal woman,
That's me.

- -

Here are some points that you might have noted.

- Imagery is used to give an impression of what the 'Phenomenal Woman' looks like, e.g. 'the fire in my eyes', 'The sun of my smile'.

- The metaphor 'Then they swarm around me,/ A hive of honey bees' gives a strong impression of the interest men show in her when she enters a room.

- Repetition is used to stress certain words and phrases – the word 'Phenomenally', and the phrase 'Phenomenal woman' followed by the phrase 'That's me', are repeatedly used to stress the key idea of the poem, as is the phrase 'I'm a woman'. Repetition of words or phrases at the beginnings of lines (anaphora) is also used to stress ideas and images, e.g. 'The span of my hips,/ The stride of my step', or the repeated use of 'I say'.

It has been said that in some of her poems Angelou 'speaks of love, longing and parting'. In the following three poems Angelou presents ideas and feelings about love.

Activity

1 In a group, take a poem each and read it through carefully, making detailed notes on what Angelou has to say in the poem and the techniques that she uses for effectively conveying her ideas to her reader. Note features such as her use of imagery, vocabulary, structure, etc.

2 Read the poem you have worked on aloud to the rest of the group and then present your ideas on it. Now discuss your ideas on the poem with the others in your group.

Just for a Time

Oh how you used to walk
With that insouciant smile
I liked to hear you talk
And your style
Pleased me for a while.

You were my early love
New as a day breaking in Spring
You were the image of
Everything
That caused me to sing.

I don't like reminiscing
Nostalgia is not my forté
I don't spill tears
On yesterday's years
But honesty makes me say,
You were a precious pearl
How I loved to see you shine,
You were the perfect girl.
And you were mine.
For a time.
For a time.
Just for a time.

A Kind of Love, Some Say

Is it true the ribs can tell
The kick of a beast from a
Lover's fist? The bruised
Bones recorded well
The sudden shock, the
Hard impact. Then swollen lids,
Sorry eyes, spoke not
Of lost romance, but hurt.

Hate often is confused. Its
Limits are in zones beyond itself. And
Sadists will not learn that
Love by nature, exacts a pain
Unequalled on the rack.

Where We Belong, A Duet

In every town and village,
In every city square,
In crowded places

I searched the faces
Hoping to find
Someone to care.

I read mysterious meanings
In the distant stars,
Then I went to schoolrooms
And poolrooms
And half-lighted cocktail bars.
Braving dangers,
Going with strangers,
I don't even remember their names.
I was quick and breezy
And always easy
Playing romantic games.

I wined and dined a thousand exotic Joans and Janes
In dusty dance halls, at debutante balls,
On lonely country lanes.
I fell in love forever,
Twice every year or so.
I wooed them sweetly, was theirs completely,
But they always let me go.
Saying bye now, no need to try now,
You don't have the proper charms.
Too sentimental and much too gentle
I don't tremble in your arms.

Then you rose into my life
Like a promised sunrise.
Brightening my days with the light in your eyes.
I've never been so strong,
Now I'm where I belong.

- -

In the following poem Angelou looks at the lot of many women in life.

Activity

Read the poem through carefully.

1 What do you think the poem is about?
2 What techniques does Angelou use to convey the life of the woman?
3 What do you notice about the structure and rhyme in the first part of the poem?
4 How does the language change in the second half of the poem?

Woman Work

I've got the children to tend
The clothes to mend
The floor to mop
The food to shop
Then the chicken to fry

The baby to dry
I got company to feed
The garden to weed
I've got shirts to press
The tots to dress
The cane to be cut
I gotta clean up this hut
Then see about the sick
And the cotton to pick.

Shine on me, sunshine
Rain on me, rain
Fall softly, dewdrops
And cool my brow again.

Storm, blow me from here
With your fiercest wind
Let me float across the sky
'Til I can rest again.

Fall gently, snowflakes
Cover me with white
Cold icy kisses and
Let me rest tonight.

Sun, rain, curving sky
Mountain, oceans, leaf and stone
Star shine, moon glow
You're all that I can call my own.

Here are some points you might have noticed.

- The poem presents the life of not one woman but a life that is representative of some women the world over who have to perform the dull, dreary and uninspiring everyday tasks of running the home for their families. Often the women perform these tasks uncomplainingly out of a sense of duty. Sometimes, though, the persona of the poem needs more than the drab routine her life provides her with and she find comfort in thinking of the elements of nature that surround her. She views the natural beauties of nature and they give her the strength to carry on.

- In the first part of the poem she conveys the dreary life of the woman by listing all the tasks she has to perform. The catalogue of tasks creates a cumulative effect to emphasize the burden of the drudgery. The repetition of 'The' to begin a number of the lines helps to create this sense of monotony.

- The first part of the poem is not divided into stanzas, again to increase the sense of monotony and repetition of her tasks and her life. This first section is written in rhyming couplets, which sometimes can give a sense of pace and lightness, but here are used as a further device for increasing the sense of the routine and the monotonous predictability of her life.

- The language, tone and structure of the poem change in the second half. The monotony of routine disappears and is replaced with positive images of nature – note the comforting tone of the language here, e.g. 'rain/ Fall softly', 'cool my brow again', 'Fall gently, snowflakes'.

Now read *Through the Inner City to the Suburbs.* Write an essay on this poem analysing the techniques that Angelou uses to create her effects.

Through the Inner City to the Suburbs

Secured by sooted windows
And amazement, it is
Delicious. Frosting filched
From a company cake.

People. Black and fast. Scattered
Watermelon seeds on
A summer street. Grinning in
ritual, sassy in pomp.

From a slow moving train
They are precious. Stolen gems
Unsaleable and dear. Those
Dusky undulations sweat of forest
Nights, damp dancing, the juicy
secrets of black thighs.

Images framed picture perfect
Do not move beyond the window
Siding.

Strong delectation:
Dirty stories in the changing rooms
Accompany the slap of wet towels and
Toilet seats.
Poli-talk of politician
Parents: 'They need shoes and
cooze and a private
warm latrine. I had a colored
Mammy…'

The train, bound for green lawns
Double garages and sullen women
in dreaded homes, settles down
On its habit track.
Leaving
The dark figures dancing
And grinning. Still
Grinning.

Examination practice

Answer either question 1 or question 2 below.

Activity

1 How far do you agree with the view that one of the most striking things about Angelou's poetry is its honesty?

In your answer, you should **either** refer to **two** or **three** poems in detail **or** range more widely through the whole selection.

> **2** Remind yourself of *I Know Why the Caged Bird Sings*. How far do you agree that, in terms of subject matter and style, this poem is central to the whole selection?

Carol Ann Duffy

Carol Ann Duffy was born in Glasgow in 1955. She grew up in Stafford and later moved to Liverpool. She graduated from Liverpool University with a degree in philosophy and now lives in London where she works as a freelance writer. In 1977, she embarked on a career as a playwright and two of her plays were performed at Liverpool Playhouse. This led her into television where she worked as a freelance scriptwriter. However, it is for her poetry that Carol Ann Duffy is best known and it has gained acclaim, winning the Dylan Thomas Award in 1989, the Whitbread Poetry Award in 1993 and the T.S. Eliot Award in 2005. She was awarded an OBE in 1995, a CBE in 2002 and became a Fellow of the Royal Society of Literature in 1999.

She is regarded now as one of Britain's leading contemporary poets, her work dealing with themes that have universal significance touching on the concerns of all people. Although it is easy to see some of her poetry reflecting her own life, in reading her work it is a mistake to see it as autobiographical and to look for clues to its significance in Duffy's own life. The poems should be viewed in a much wider context than this and the voice of the poems should be seen as expressing concerns, experiences and emotions that lie deep within us all.

She has written several collections of poetry and her fifth volume, *The World's Wife*, was published in 1999.

Thematic ideas

The title *The World's Wife* gives a strong clue as to the central focus of the poems in this collection. In the poems here, Duffy presents and recasts a wide range of mythical and historical events from a woman's point of view. Every poem is written in the voice of a wife of a well-known figure from history or mythology or in the persona of a female version of a male figure.

The personas in the poems can be grouped as follows:

- folk myth (e.g. Little Red Ridinghood – i.e. Little Red-cap)
- the Bible (e.g. Delilah, Salome, Pilate's wife, Lazarus)
- historical figures (e.g. Pope Joan, Anne Hathaway, Mrs Darwin, Frau Freud)
- classical figures (e.g. Midas, Tiresias, Aesop, Sisyphus, Pygmalion, Icarus)
- literary (e.g. Faust, Quasimodo, Rip Van Winkle, the Beast)
- female versions of male figures (e.g. Queen Herod, Queen Kong, the Kray sisters, Elvis's twin sister).

In her poems she creates personalities which she explores, through the form of a dramatic monologue written in the voice of the persona. The result is sometimes humorous, sometimes serious, sometimes violent; all reveal the female perspective, opening up new insights as these personas are freed from the male figure who hitherto has defined their role.

The Language of *The World's Wife*

When we examine Duffy's use of language in her poetry, every poem needs to be looked at individually to determine how exactly the poem works in order to achieve its effects. Here are some specific features that you might like to keep in mind when looking in detail at her work:

- her use of rhyme
- her use of 'echoes' and assonance

- the form of her poetry – the ways in which stanzas are organized to give an ordered shape to the poems
- the use of imagery
- the use of a language and vocabulary of her time
- the use of personas.

Now look at *Anne Hathaway*. It is written from the point of view of Shakespeare's widow.

Activity

Read the poem through carefully several times. What is it about? What do you notice about the ways in which Duffy uses language and form here? What effect is achieved by adopting the persona of Shakespeare's widow?

Anne Hathaway

'Item I gyve unto my wife my second best bed...'
(from Shakespeare's will)

The bed we loved in was a spinning world
of forests, castles, torchlight, clifftops, seas
where we would dive for pearls. My lover's words
were shooting stars which fell to earth as kisses
on these lips; my body now a softer rhyme
to his, now echo, assonance; his touch
a verb dancing in the centre of a noun.
Some nights, I dreamed he'd written me, the bed
a page beneath his writer's hands. Romance
and drama played by touch, by scent, by taste.
In the other bed, the best, our guests dozed on,
dribbling their prose. My living laughing love –
I hold him in the casket of my widow's head
as he held me upon that next best bed.

Here are some ideas you might have thought of:

- In the poem Duffy writes using the voice of Shakespeare's widow, Anne Hathaway, as she remembers the love that she and her husband shared.
- The poem begins with an epigraph quoted from Shakespeare's will, which makes reference to his 'second best bed'. (This might sound odd, but it was the convention of the time that the best bed was kept for guests.)
- The idea of the bed is at the centre of the imaginative world that Duffy's persona creates. Note how 'forests', 'castles', and 'clifftops' suggest some of the settings of Shakespeare's plays, while the metaphor of the 'spinning world' gives a striking opening which is suggestive of the giddiness of love.
- The references to the technical details of language such as 'assonance', 'verb', and 'noun' connect with Shakespeare's occupation as a writer – a wordsmith.
- The poem is written in the form of a sonnet, which again is in keeping with the Shakespearean flavour of the poem, as is the fact that it concludes with a rhyming couplet – the usual way in which Shakespeare finished his own sonnets.

- Duffy's adoption of the persona of Anne Hathaway gives the poem a very personal sense, and also presents the ideas from the perspective of a woman and a wife.

Activity

Make a list of the techniques that Duffy uses here to create her effects.

Here are some points you might have thought of:

- the use of a specific persona
- the use of a particular form
- the use of imagery
- the use of rhyme
- the use of vocabulary
- the use of tone.

The poem *Salome* is based on the story of Salome in the New Testament. Salome danced before the ruler, Herod, who promised to grant any request she wanted to make. John the Baptist had criticized Salome's mother for having an affair and so, prompted by her mother, Salome asked Herod for the head of John the Baptist. He was immediately arrested and executed, and Salome was presented with his head.

Activity

Read the poem through carefully. Make a note of any details from the poem that strike you as interesting or unusual.

Salome

I'd done it before
(and doubtless I'll do it again,
sooner or later)
woke up with a head on the pillow beside me – whose? –
what did it matter?
Good-looking, of course, dark hair, rather matted;
the reddish beard several shades lighter;
with very deep lines round the eyes,
from pain, I'd guess, maybe laughter;
and a beautiful crimson mouth that obviously knew
how to flatter…
which I kissed…
Colder than pewter.
Strange. What was his name? Peter?

Simon? Andrew? John? I knew I'd feel better
for tea, dry toast, no butter,
so rang for the maid.
And, indeed, her innocent clatter
of cups and plates,
her clearing of clutter,

her regional patter,
were just what I needed –
hungover and wrecked as I was from a night on the batter.

Never again!
I needed to clean up my act,
get fitter,
cut out the booze and the fags and the sex.

Yes. And as for the latter,
it was time to turf out the blighter,
the beater or biter,
who'd come like a lamb to the slaughter
to Salome's bed.

In the mirror, I saw my eyes glitter.
I flung back the sticky red sheets,
and there, like I said – and ain't life a bitch –
was his head on a platter.

Here are some points you might have noticed:

- Her adaptation of the original story.
- The use of the persona of Salome and the personal, informal tone of the opening of the poem.
- The sexual connotations of waking up 'with a head on the pillow beside me'.
- The description of the head on the pillow with the emphasis on the good looks.
- The attempts to remember his name.
- The introduction into the poem of contemporary details, such as suffering from a hangover.
- The use of slang expressions such as 'wrecked as I was from a night on the batter', 'clean up my act'.
- The impact of the final stanza and the expression 'and ain't life a bitch'.

In *Pilate's Wife*, Duffy adopts the persona of the wife of Pontius Pilate, the Roman governor of Judea, who allowed the crucifixion of Christ.

Activity

Read the poem *Pilate's Wife*. Look carefully at the form and structure and Duffy's use of imagery here. What effects do the poet's choice of imagery and the overall form and structure create?

Pilate's Wife

Firstly, his hands – a woman's. Softer than mine,
with pearly nails, like shells from Galilee.
Indolent hands. Camp hands that clapped for grapes.
Their pale, mothy touch made me flinch. Pontius.

I longed for Rome, home, someone else. When the Nazarene
entered Jerusalem, my maid and I crept out,
bored stiff, disguised, and joined the frenzied crowd.
I tripped, clutched the bridle of an ass, looked up

and there he was. His face? Ugly. Talented.
He looked at me. I mean he looked at me. My God.
His eyes were eyes to die for. Then he was gone,
his rough men shouldering a pathway to the gates.

The night before his trial, I dreamt of him.
His brown hands touched me. Then it hurt.
Then blood. I saw that each tough palm was skewered
by a nail. I woke up, sweating, sexual, terrified.

Leave him alone. I sent a warning note, then quickly-dressed.
When I arrived, the Nazarene was crowned with thorns.
The crowd was baying for Barabbas. Pilate saw me,
looked away, then carefully turned up his sleeves

and slowly washed his useless, perfumed hands.
They seized the prophet then and dragged him out,
up to the Place of Skulls. My maid knows all the rest.
Was he God? Of course not. Pilate believed he was.

Activity

Now read the following two poems, *Demeter* and *Frau Freud*.

Compare these two poems, examining the following:

- the ideas explored in the poems
- the ways in which Duffy uses imagery
- the form and structure of the poems.

Demeter

Where I lived – winter and hard earth.
I sat in my cold stone room
choosing tough words, granite, flint,

to break the ice. My broken heart –
I tried that, but it skimmed,
flat, over the frozen lake.

She came from a long, long way,
but I saw her at last, walking,
my daughter, my girl, across the fields,

in bare feet, bringing all spring's flowers
to her mother's house. I swear
the air softened and warmed as she moved,

the blue sky smiling, none too soon,
with the small shy mouth of a new moon.

Frau Freud

Ladies, for argument's sake, let us say
that I've seen my fair share of ding-a-ling, member and jock,
of todger and nudger and percy and cock, of tackle,
of three-for-a-bob, of willy and winky; in fact,
you could say, I'm as au fait with Hunt-the-Salami

as Ms M. Lewinsky – equally sick up to here
with the beef bayonet, the pork sword, the saveloy,
love-muscle, night-crawler, dong, the dick, prick,
dipstick and wick, the rammer, the slammer, the rupert,
the shlong. Don't get me wrong, I've no axe to grind
with the snake in the trousers, the wife's best friend,
the weapon, the python – I suppose what I mean is,
ladies, dear ladies, the average penis – not pretty…
the squint of its envious solitary eye… one's feeling of pity…

Mrs Darwin is the shortest poem that Duffy has published. It forms quite a contrast to the other poems in the collection, most of which are two pages or more long.

Activity

Read *Mrs Darwin* and think about it carefully.

1 Is it simply a light-hearted joke, or do you think there is more to it?
2 Why do you think Duffy included it in the anthology?

Mrs Darwin

7 April 1852

Went to the Zoo.
I said to Him –
Something about that Chimpanzee over there
reminds me of you

In *Delilah*, Duffy presents a different slant on the Samson and Delilah story.

Activity

1 Research the Samson and Delilah story and make a note of the key points.
2 How closely does Duffy's poem follow the actual story?
3 How does Duffy's presentation of Delilah in her poem differ from the way in which she is presented in the accounts of the story you have read?
4 What impression of Delilah do you form from having read Duffy's poem?
5 How does Duffy use language, imagery and a sense of detail to create her effects? Pick out five examples to illustrate your points.

Delilah

Teach me, he said –
we were lying in bed –
how to care.
I nibbled the purse of his ear.
What do you mean? Tell me more.
He sat up and reached for his beer.
I can rip out the roar

from the throat of a tiger,
or gargle with fire,
or sleep one whole night in the minotaur's lair,
or flay the bellowing fur
from a bear,
all for a dare.
There's nothing I fear.
Put your hand here –
he guided my fingers over the scar
over his heart,
a four-medal wound from the war –
but I cannot be gentle, or loving, or tender.
I have to be strong.
What is the cure?
He fucked me again,
until he was sore,
then we both took a shower.
Then he lay with his head on my lap
for a darkening hour;
his voice, for a change, a soft burr
I could just about hear.
And, yes, I was sure
that he wanted to change,
my warrior.
I was there.
So when I felt him soften and sleep,
when he started, as usual, to snore,
I let him slip and slide and sprawl, handsome and huge,
on the floor.
And before I fetched and sharpened my scissors –
snipping first at the black and biblical air –
I fastened the chain to the door.
That's the how and the why and the where.
Then with deliberate, passionate hands
I cut every lock of his hair.

Examination practice

Answer either question 1 or question 2 below.

Activity

1 A critic has expressed the view that *Mrs Beast* is '…a conscious summation of the themes of the book'. How far do you agree with this view?

2 *The World's Wife* has become one of poetry's biggest sellers. Why do you think this is?

In your answer, you should **either** refer to **two** or **three** poems in detail or range more widely through the whole collection.

Owen Sheers

Owen Sheers was born in Fiji in 1974 and brought up in Abergavenny, South Wales. He was educated at King Henry VIII comprehensive school and went on to read English at New College, Oxford. He later gained an MA in Creative Writing from the University of East Anglia. He was the winner of an Eric Gregory Award and the

Vogue Young Writers' Award in 1999. His first collection of poetry, *The Blue Book*, was published in 2000 and was short-listed for the Arts Council Forward Prize for the best first collection of poetry in 2001. He was named by *The Independent on Sunday* as one of Britain's top 30 young writers.

His first prose work, *The Dust Diaries*, was published in 2004 and is a non-fiction narrative in which he explores the life of his distant relative, Arthur Shearly Cripps, a missionary to what is now Zimbabwe in the early years of the twentieth century. For this work he was short-listed for the Royal Society of Literature's Ondaatje Prize and won the Welsh Book of the Year prize for 2005. In 2004 he was Writer in Residence at the Wordsworth Trust and was picked as one of the Poetry Book Society's '20 Next Generation Poets.'

Skirrid Hill is his second volume of poetry and was published in 2005. His first novel, *Resistance*, was published in 2007. He has also written for radio and TV and has written several plays, one of which, called *Unicorns, Almost* (based on the life of the Second World War poet Keith Douglas) was produced by Old Vic New Voices as part of their summer programme in 2006.

Thematic ideas

At the beginning of the collection we are told that 'Skirrid' is derived from a Welsh word meaning divorce or separation, and the metaphor of Skirrid Hill runs throughout the collection, giving some hint of one of Sheers's focuses. The poems here are wide-ranging and take their settings or starting points from widely different parts of the world, from Los Angeles to Fiji, from Paris to Zimbabwe. But taken together the poems are linked by what the *Guardian* describes as a 'gorgeously elegiac' quality. Here are some of the ideas that inspire Sheers's poems in this volume:

- death in one form or another, sometimes through war, suicide or illness
- grief and loss
- estrangement or separation between people or from places
- various places, e.g. Fiji, Los Angeles, Wales
- beginnings and endings.

Mametz Wood was written as a result of a visit Sheers made to the Somme battlefield to make a short film about two Welsh writers who had fought there. While he was visiting the battlefield a shallow grave was uncovered, containing the remains of 20 Allied soldiers who had been buried quickly after the battle. However, despite the circumstances of their burial, whoever buried them had taken the trouble to link the bodies, arm-in-arm.

Activity

Read the poem through carefully. Write down your ideas on the following:

- the ideas explored in the poem
- the ways in which Sheers uses imagery
- the form and structure of the poem.

Mametz Wood

For years afterwards the farmers found them –
the wasted young, turning up under their plough blades
as they tended the land back into itself.

A chit of bone, the china plate of a shoulder blade,
the relic of a finger, the blown
and broken bird's egg of a skull,

all mimicked now in flint, breaking blue in white
across this field where they were told to walk, not run,
towards the wood and its nesting machine guns.

And even now the earth stands sentinel,
reaching back into itself for reminders of what happened
like a wound working a foreign body to the surface of the skin.

This morning, twenty men buried in one long grave,
a broken mosaic of bone linked arm in arm,
their skeletons paused mid dance-macabre

in boots that outlasted them,
their socketed heads tilted back at an angle
and their jaws, those that have them, dropped open.

As if the notes they had sung
have only now, with this unearthing,
slipped from their absent tongues.

- -

Here are some ideas you might have noted:

- the waste of young lives and the passage of time between their deaths and the discovery of their bodies, e.g. the irony of 'boots that outlasted them'
- the contrast of their death in war and the 'plough blades' uncovering their bodies – perhaps the contrast of war and peace, with the idea of 'turning swords into ploughshares'
- the union of the soldiers and the earth
- the use of a variety of images, e.g. the metaphor of 'the blown/ and broken bird's egg of a skull' emphasizing the fragility of the skull; the personification of 'the earth stands sentinel'; and the simile of 'reminders of what happened/ like a wound working a foreign body to the surface of the skin'
- the use of enjambment.

Some of Sheers's poems have been described as 'bruised, awkward poems, less of love than of tenderness'. In the following three poems Sheers presents ideas and feelings about love and relationships.

Activity

1 In a group, take a poem each and read it through carefully, making detailed notes on what Sheers has to say in the poem and the techniques that he uses for effectively conveying his ideas to the reader. Note features such as the use of imagery, vocabulary, structure, etc.

2 Read the poem you have worked on aloud to the rest of the group and then present your ideas on it. Now discuss your ideas on the poem with the others in your group.

Night Windows

That night we turned some of them off
but left the hall bulb bright,
sending one bar of light into the living room,
so we could see.

Which of course meant they could too –
us impressionist through the thin white drapes
as you lowered yourself to me,
the curves of a distant landscape

opening across your pelvis,
your body slick and valleyed
in the August heat
and your back arching like a bow

drawn by an invisible tendon
strung from the top of your head
to the ends of your toes,
loading you with our meeting.

The night windows opposite performed
their Morse codes,
side-swipes of curtains,
until eventually every one of them went dark

and the only light left was a siren's,
sending its blue strobe across the rooftops
like lightning in the corner of my eye,
somewhere far away yet near,

as with a sigh you rose from me
and walked into the lit hallway,
trailing the dress of your shadow behind you.

Marking Time

That mark upon your back is finally fading
in the way our memory will,
of that night our lust wouldn't wait for bed
so laid us out upon the floor instead
where we worked up that scar –
two tattered flags flying from your spine's mast,
a brand-burn secret in the small of your back.

I trace them now and feel the disturbance again.
The still waters of your skin broken, the *volte* engaging
as we made our marks like lovers who carve trees,
the equation of their names equalled by an arrow
that buckles under time but never leaves,
and so though changed, under the bark, the skin,
the loving scar remains.

Valentine

The water torture of your heels
emptying before me down that Paris street,
evacuated as the channels of our hearts.

That will be one memory.

The swing of the tassels on your skirt
each step filling out the curve of your hip;
your wet lashes, the loss of everything we'd learnt.

That will be another.

Then later – holding each other on the hotel bed
like a pair of wrecked voyagers
who had thought themselves done for,

only to wake washed up on the shore
uncertain in their exhaustion
whether to laugh or weep.

That my valentine, will be the one I'll keep.

If the idea of partings figures prominently in the poems you have just looked at, *The Wake* presents a parting of a different kind.

Activity

Read the poem through carefully.

1 What is the poem about?

2 Sheers makes use of an extended metaphor in the poem. Explain the nature of this metaphor.

3 Make a list of words, phrases or images which Sheers links together to create this metaphor.

4 How do you respond to the ending of the poem?

The Wake

He looks me straight in the eye,
ninety years old,
folded into his favourite chair

and tells me he doesn't want this,
to watch himself die, to have the doctor
plumb any further in the depths of his scarred lungs.

He, who himself spent so many years
holding the chests of others up to the light
to forecast the storms gathering there,

the squalls and depressions
smudging those two pale oceans,
rising and falling in the rib cage's hull.

Here then is the old curse
of too much knowledge, driftwood
collected along the shore of a century.

He settles himself in the chair
and I say what I can, but my words are spoken
into a coastal wind long after the ship has sailed.

Later he shows me to the door
and as he stands in its frame to wave me away
we both know there has already been a passing,

one that has left a wake as that of a great ship
that disturbs the sea for miles either side
but leaves the water directly at its stern

strangely settled, turned, fresh
and somehow new,
like the first sea there ever was

or that ever will be.

- -

Here are some ideas.

- In the poem an old man, perhaps the poet's grandfather, explains to him that he is dying. The old man faces his impending death unflinchingly – note the sense of directness as he looks the poet 'straight in the eye', and the sense of comfort created by the phrase 'folded into his favourite chair'. He doesn't want the doctors to treat him further – he knows what to expect, the suggestion being that he himself was in the medical profession, perhaps a doctor –

  He, who himself spent so many years
  holding the chests of others up to the light
  to forecast the storms gathering there.

- The extended metaphor to do with the sea uses a range of images that link together, e.g. 'plumb any further in the depths', 'forecast the storms gathering', 'squalls and depressions', 'pale oceans', 'the rib cage's hull', 'driftwood', 'the shore of a century', 'coastal wind', 'the ship has sailed', 'a wake as that of a great ship', 'disturbs the sea', 'at its stern', 'the first sea'.

- Although the old man is not yet dead, the poet senses that they 'both know there has already been a passing'. The image of that passing being as the 'wake… of a great ship' suggests the deeply moving and far-reaching effect on the poet. The other meaning of 'wake' (a vigil for the dead) perhaps also comes into play here. But a sense of life, even re-birth, or the universality of the human cycle, is suggested in the vocabulary of the closing lines: 'fresh', 'somehow new,/ like the first sea there ever was'.

Activity

Now read the following two poems, *Skirrid Fawr* and *Farther*. Compare these two poems, examining the following:

- the ideas explored in the poems
- the ways in which Sheers uses imagery
- the form and structure of the poems.

Skirrid Fawr

Just like the farmers who once came to scoop
handfuls of soil from her holy scar,

so I am still drawn to her back for the answers
to every question I have never known.

To the sentence of her slopes,
the blunt wind glancing from her withers,

to the split view she reveals
with every step along her broken spine.

This edge of her cleft palate,
part hill, part field,

rising from a low mist, a lonely hulk
adrift through Wales.

Her east-west flanks, one dark, one sunlit,
her vernacular of borders.

Her weight, the unspoken words
of an unlearned tongue.

Farther

I don't know if the day after Boxing Day has a name
but it was then we climbed the Skirrid again,
choosing the long way round,
through the wood, simplified by snow,
along the dry stone wall, its puzzle solved by moss,
and out of the trees into that cleft of earth
split they say by a father's grief
at the loss of his son to man.
We stopped there at an altar of rock and rested,
watching the dog shrink over the hill before continuing ourselves,
finding the slope steeper than expected.
A blade of wind from the east
and the broken stone giving under our feet
with the sound of a crowd sighing.
Half way up and I turned to look at you,
your bent head the colour of the rocks,
your breath reaching me, short and sharp and solitary,
and again I felt the tipping in the scales of us,
the intersection of our ages.
The dog returns having caught nothing but his own tongue
and you are with me again, so together we climbed to the top
and shared the shock of a country unrolled before us,
the hedged fields breaking on the edge of Wales.
Pulling a camera from my pocket I placed it on the trig point
and leant my cheek against the stone to find you in its frame,
before joining you and waiting for the shutter's blink
that would tell me I had caught this:
the sky rubbed raw over the mountains,

us standing on the edge of the world, together against the view
and me reaching for some kind of purchase
or at least a shallow handhold in the thought
that with every step apart, I'm another closer to you.

- -

While travelling in Zimbabwe gathering material for *The Dust Diaries*, Sheers found
himself drinking in a bar in Harare with Dr Chenjerai 'Hitler' Hunzvi, the brutal
leader of the Zimbabwean 'war veterans'. Sheers and Hunzvi had a disagreement and
the situation became potentially dangerous for Sheers. Fortunately Hunzvi and his
bodyguards eventually left. Sheers captures the scene in his poem *Drinking with Hitler*.

Activity

Read the poem through carefully.

1 How does Sheers use language here to create an impression of Hunzvi? Give
   specific examples to support your ideas.

2 What message do you think Sheers want to convey to his reader through this
   poem?

Drinking with Hitler*

Harare, Zimbabwe, July 2000

He wears his power like an aftershave,
so thick the women about him flounder in it,
their unsure eyes switching in their heads
as they try out their smiles, brief as fireworks on the night.

Turning to me his own slides into place – a CD selected
with play pressed across his lips.
But I've heard about the burned workers' homes,
the scorched huts like cauterised wounds,

the men who cradle the fruit of their bruises,
the 5th brigade trucks that come in the night
and finding no-one in particular,
beat the first two hundred instead.

So finished with me, he turns away
to the Zambian businesswoman at his side –
film pretty, delicate among her jewellery,
long-fingered, dark and quiet.

Conducting asked-for laughter from the bar,
he leans in close, then leaves, as quick as he came
in a flourish of cards,
following his driver out of the door and into his world.

She returns to her drink, lightly touching her leg
where he laid his hand on her thigh,
before looking up into the bar's mirror and washing him away
with one slow blink of her blue-painted eyes.

*The late Dr 'Hitler' Hunzvi, Zanu PF MP and leader of the Zimbabwe 'War Veterans'

Answer either question 1 or question 2 below.

Activity

1 How far do you agree with the view that *The Wake* typifies Sheers's poetry in *Skirrid Hill*?

   You should consider both subject matter and style.

2 A critic has described Sheers's poetry as being 'adept at probing wounds'. To what extent do you agree with this view of *Skirrid Hill*?

   You may use *Y Gaer* as a starting point if you wish.

12 Creative Study

Objectives

- To think about the requirements of your written coursework portfolio
- To consider the kinds of tasks you will need to undertake
- To think about the use of secondary sources and a bibliography

Unit 2 of your AS course is a coursework unit based on texts that you will choose from those within the option you are studying for AS: Victorian Literature, World War One Literature or The Struggle for Identity in Modern Literature.

What are the benefits of coursework?

The benefits that the coursework element can bring to a course and the breadth that it can give to your studies are well acknowledged.

In particular coursework can:

- offer you freedom in terms of choice of texts and more of a say in the nature of the work you undertake
- provide you with opportunities to set your own tasks and goals and pursue particular literary interests, so developing more independence in your learning
- allow you to produce work free of the constraints of exam conditions so that you can present more carefully planned and considered responses and employ the drafting process
- develop skills which will help you perform more effectively in the exams
- help you to gain experience in undertaking research and wider reading in preparation for studying English at degree level.

Coursework portfolio requirements

You will study two texts, one prose text and one drama text chosen from the texts listed for your option. The texts that you study for this unit can also be used in your response to question 1 in the Unit 1 examination if you wish. Similarly, your wider reading in drama may be used in your coursework for your drama task. This unit will present you with opportunities to explore creative interpretations of your texts, transformational writing and drawing connections between texts.

You will need to complete **two** pieces of writing, one on your prose text and one on your drama text. The two pieces of work together should total between 2000 and 2500 words.

The texts choices you will have are as follows (* indicates texts written after 1990).

Victorian Literature

Prose

Jane Eyre   Charlotte Brontë

Wuthering Heights   Emily Brontë

Possession   A.S. Byatt

Heart of Darkness   Joseph Conrad

Hard Times   Charles Dickens

Middlemarch   George Eliot

The French Lieutenant's Woman   John Fowles

Tess of the D'Urbervilles   Thomas Hardy

*English Passengers   Matthew Kneale

The Picture of Dorian Gray   Oscar Wilde

Drama

A Woman of No Importance   Oscar Wilde

A Doll's House   Henrik Ibsen

*Arcadia   Tom Stoppard

World War One Literature

Prose

Strange Meeting   Susan Hill

*Birdsong   Sebastian Faulks

*Regeneration   Pat Barker

*The Eye in the Door   Pat Barker

*The Ghost Road   Pat Barker

Her Privates We   Frederic Manning

*A Long, Long Way   Sebastian Barry

Memoirs of an Infantry Officer   Siegfried Sassoon

Not So Quiet   Helena Zenna Smith

Return of the Soldier   Rebecca West

Drama

Journey's End   R.C. Sherriff

The Accrington Pals   Peter Whelan

Not About Heroes   Stephen MacDonald

The Struggle for Identity in Modern Literature

Prose

The Handmaid's Tale   Margaret Atwood

*Wise Children   Angela Carter

*Hullaballoo in the Guava Orchard   Kiran Desai

*The Woman Who Walked into Doors   Roddy Doyle

*Spies   Michael Frayn

*Snow Falling on Cedars   David Guterson

*Trumpet   Jackie Kay

*Paradise   Toni Morrison

Vernon God Little   D.B.C. Pierre

The Color Purple   Alice Walker

Drama

Top Girls   Caryl Churchill

Making History   Brian Friel

Death and the King's Horseman   Wole Soyinka

Coursework tasks

An essential difference between an exam essay and a coursework essay is that examination questions are specifically designed to be answered in a very limited time under exam conditions, whereas you might work on a coursework task for several weeks, using various research skills, reference to other writers, and critical works.

For your coursework folder for Unit 2 you will need to produce two pieces of work.

Piece 1

This will focus on the prose text and you will need to give a personal and informed response to it. You have a choice as to exactly what form this response takes. It can be **either**:

a) a creative response which gives a personal and original interpretation of your text

or

b) creative/transformational writing.

Here are some examples of the kind of tasks that could be suitable for either a) or b).

Victorian Literature: *Wuthering Heights*

a) How does Brontë's use of multiple narrators affect your interpretation of *Wuthering Heights*?

b) Write Catherine Linton's account of her return from The Grange at Christmas, creating Catherine's voice, capturing Brontë's style and tone and building on Brontë's presentation of the character.

World War One Literature: *The Ghost Road*

a) How does Barker's use of narrative structure in *The Ghost Road* affect your interpretation of the novel?

b) Write Rivers' account of his experiences in Melanesia, creating Rivers' voice, capturing Barker's style and tone and building on her realization of the character.

The Struggle for Identity in Modern Literature: *The Color Purple*

a) How does Walker's use of letters to structure her narrative affect your interpretation of the novel?

b) Write Shug Avery's account of her relationship with Celie, creating Shug's voice, capturing Walker's style and tone and building on Walker's presentation of the character.

Piece 2

The second piece of writing in your folder will be on your chosen drama text. Your piece of writing should focus either on placing it in its **dramatic context** or **link it to your prose text** in some way. Some possible links you may explore are aspects such as theme, structure or characterization.

Here are some examples of the kind of tasks that could be suitable here.

Victorian Literature: *A Doll's House*

Explore the ways in which Ibsen uses setting for dramatic effect.

Then, **either**:

Compare the ways *A Doll's House* and other Victorian plays you have read use setting

or

Compare the ways Ibsen uses setting in *A Doll's House* with the way in which Charlotte Brontë uses setting in *Jane Eyre*.

World War One Literature: *Journey's End*

Explore the ways in which Sherriff uses characters to create dramatic effect.

Then, **either**:

Compare the ways *Journey's End* and other World War One plays you have read use characters

or

Compare the ways Sherriff uses characters in *Journey's End* with the ways in which Hill uses characters in *Strange Meeting*.

The Struggle for Identity in Modern Literature: *Making History*

Explore the ways in which Friel use the structure of his play to create dramatic effect.

Then, **either**:

Compare the ways *Making History* and any other modern plays you have read use structure

or

Compare the ways in which Friel uses structure in *Making History* with the ways in which Guterson uses structure in *Snow Falling on Cedars*.

Assessment Objectives

Your work for this unit will be assessed against the following Assessment Objectives. Both pieces of work are assessed against each of the objectives.

AO1 Articulate creative, informed and relevant responses to literary texts, using appropriate terminology and concepts, and coherent, accurate written expression

AO2 Demonstrate detailed critical understanding in analysing the ways in which structure, form and language shape meanings in literary texts

AO3 Explore connections and comparisons between different literary texts, informed by interpretations of other readers

AO4 Demonstrate understanding of the significance and influence of the contexts in which literary texts are written and received

Potential problem areas

Overall, examiners report that a high standard of work is produced by students through coursework. However, here are some points that they have highlighted as weaknesses or problem areas in some of the work they have assessed:

- inappropriately framed or worded assignments
- tasks that focus on a general discussion of themes or 'character studies'; these tend to lack interest and focus
- titles that do not require close attention to the text and critical judgement
- the inclusion of too much biographical or historical background
- too much narrative retelling of the plot or events.

It is important that your assignment titles are carefully constructed to allow you to meet the Assessment Objectives against which they will be judged. Your teacher has an important role to play in helping you frame your assignment titles in the right way and you must make sure that your response addresses the issues that are focused on in your title.

Activity

Devise a coursework title for a text or texts that you have studied. Think very carefully about the wording of your title. When you have written it, add a brief description (about 50 words or so) explaining how you would tackle the piece of work. Include the main ideas you would put forward. In a small group, look at your titles individually and discuss their strengths and weaknesses, drawing up a master list of good and bad points.

The use of secondary sources

In producing coursework it is important that, if you use secondary sources, you learn how to refer to and acknowledge them correctly. Clearly, the primary source for your work is the text that you are studying. The secondary sources are any other materials that help you in your work, such as study aids, critical books, or articles about the text. It can also be useful to 'read around the text' – to learn about the history, the art, and the music of the time it was written. (The Chronology on pages 334–346 provides a starting point for this.)

Certainly use secondary sources if you wish and they will form part of your wider reading around the texts you are studying. They can help to broaden your view of the text and show you other ways of looking at it. It does not matter whether you agree or disagree with the views and interpretations you read, because they will all help you to arrive at what you think. Remember that there are rarely right answers as far as literature is concerned – all texts are open to a variety of interpretations. Your view can be 'informed' by other sources but never let other views substitute for your own. Have confidence in your view, develop your own voice, and avoid plagiarism (even accidental) at all costs. This means that if you use secondary source material you must make sure that you acknowledge every text you have used and list it in the bibliography at the end of your assignment.

Bibliography

In order to acknowledge appropriately the books and other materials that you have read or consulted while writing your coursework essay, it is important to understand the conventions of bibliography writing.

Even if you have read only a part of a particular book or article it should be included in your bibliography. If you have used only the text that you are studying, you should still include a bibliography simply consisting of relevant details about the edition you used. This will clearly show the examiner that you have used nothing other than the text itself and it will also give information about the particular edition.

Your bibliography should be arranged in the following format:

- surname of the author (authors listed alphabetically)
- initials of the author
- title of the book (italics or underlined) or article (inverted commas) and source
- publisher's name
- date of publication (usually the date when first published).

Here is an example of how to record the texts you have used in your bibliography.

Bibliography

Chilcott, T., *A Critical Study of the Poetry of John Clare*, Hull University Press, 1985

Drabble, M. (ed.) *The Oxford Companion to English Literature*, Oxford University Press, 1985

Ford, B. (ed.) *Victorian Britain*, Cambridge University Press, 1989

Gibson, J. and Johnson, T. (eds.), *Thomas Hardy Poems: A Casebook*, Macmillan, 1979

Johnson, T., *A Critical Introduction to the Poems of Thomas Hardy*, St Martin's Press, 1991

Activity

Using your library or learning resource centre, find at least five books or articles on a particular topic, text or author. Find the information that you would need for a bibliography, such as author, publisher, publication date, etc., and then, using the examples above as a guide, order them in the way you would if you were creating a bibliography for a piece of coursework.

13 Reading for Meaning: Love Through the Ages

Objectives

- To consider a theme-based approach to texts
- To introduce literature on the theme of love through the ages
- To explore a variety of texts covering a range of genres and periods
- To practise comparing short texts and extracts linked by theme

Reading round a theme

The 'Reading for Meaning' module specifies a particular theme, which you will study in advance, familiarizing yourself with a variety of texts covering a range of genres and literary periods. You will study at least three main texts, but you should also aim to read round the subject more widely, to gain the fullest possible sense of how the theme has been represented in literature in different times and places.

The module is assessed in an examination paper in which you are presented with two pairs of extracts or short texts and asked to write about them in detail, comparing them and setting them within the framework of your knowledge of the theme. There will be two questions:

1   You are asked to compare two texts of the **same genre**. This question will require close reading of the texts and will also ask you to relate them to your wider reading where this is appropriate.

2   You are asked to compare two further extracts, this time of **different genres**. Here you will be expected to show how your wider reading has influenced or contributed to your understanding and interpretation of the extracts.

Any genre may be used in Question 1; whichever is chosen, Question 2 will be based on the remaining two genres. For example, if Question 1 asks you to compare two poems, Question 2 will involve comparing prose and drama extracts.

You are not expected to have read the particular texts given, although if you have read widely and prepared thoroughly, you should find that you are able to tell approximately where they belong in the wider context of literature through the ages. It is best, however, to be ready to encounter them initially as unprepared texts for close reading.

When you are preparing to analyse unfamiliar texts in this way, you may find it useful to remind yourself of the strategies suggested in Chapter 7, but there are some additional factors to consider.

- As well as analysing unseen texts in detail, the questions will require you to compare them with each other *and* to relate them to other texts you have read. You will also be expected to demonstrate that you can recognize features of texts which are typical of particular literary periods and contexts.

- You will improve your chances of success by carefully studying your set theme and reading widely, so that you become aware of recurring ideas and conventions and are familiar with the key authors and their works.

- The wider your reading around the topic, the more likely you are to be able to make interesting connections with other texts. You may find that you have already read the 'unprepared' texts, which can give you a real advantage.

A word of warning is necessary too. You should still give a large part of your attention to *in-depth exploration of the texts in front of you* and *the connections and differences between them*. Don't spend *more* of your time writing about your wider reading than you spend on these, however much you think it may impress the examiner. Use your knowledge, but only when it is *relevant*! When you do refer to your wider reading, the aim is to make detailed and specific connections with the extracts you are given. The point of this exercise is for you to demonstrate your skills of close reading and comparison *as well as* your wider reading.

Love through the ages

From the very earliest times, writers have shown a deep preoccupation with the idea of 'love' in all its forms. Chaucer's pilgrims exhibit a variety of attitudes towards it, from the courtly idealism of the Knight and the pragmatism of the Wife of Bath, to the earthiness of the Miller. In one form or another, love is central to most of Shakespeare's plays; sonnets have been written on it, novels have explored its complexities, plays have examined attitudes towards it, and it continues to fascinate writers and readers alike.

Of course, we should not be surprised by this, because love is a basic human emotion that we all share. It is a common thread that binds us together and allows us to understand and share in the experiences of others, despite differences of class or culture, race or religion, society or time.

Activity

In your group, discuss some of your own ideas about love.

- What does the word 'love' bring to mind first? What are your expectations about studying the literature of love?
- Brainstorm or list some of the great stories of love you know from books, children's stories or fairy tales, films, plays, and television.
- What forms of love do they depict?
- What attitudes to love do they show?

Initially, perhaps, your thoughts turned to romantic or sexual love relationships – and there are certainly plenty of those in literature – but we do need to remember that love exists in many other forms too. For example, parent–child relationships, close friendships, and religious devotion have all provided inspiration for writers.

Writers explore all the different stages of love too, the ups and downs, and the emotions that colour relationships. They write not only about falling in love, but also about disillusionment, jealousy, despair and the grief of separation or bereavement.

'What then is love?'

So much has been written about love, yet writers – and their characters – have often complained that they struggle to express what love is, or to put into words what it feels like to love, or to be in love.

Early in Shakespeare's *Romeo and Juliet*, perhaps the most famous love story in English literature, Romeo tries to express his feelings about love. At this point, he has not yet set eyes on Juliet, and is still infatuated with another girl, who does not return his love:

Romeo: Why then, O brawling love! O loving hate!
O any thing! Of nothing first create.
O heavy lightness! Serious vanity!
Mis-shapen chaos of well-seeming forms!
Feather of lead, bright smoke, cold fire, sick health!
Still-waking sleep, that is not what it is!
This love feel I…

Activity

Make brief notes on and/or discuss the language Romeo uses here. Now read these excerpts from song lyrics, and the poem that follows. What similarities do you notice? List some of the images used in each text.

Burning for Love

I'm burning for love
Filled with desire
I can't stand the heat
And my heart's on fire

Bon Jovi

The Window

Lost in the rages of fragrance
Lost in the rags of remorse
Lost in the waves of a sickness
That loosens the high silver nerves

Oh chosen love, Oh frozen love
Oh tangle of matter and ghost
Oh darling of angels, demons and saints
And the whole broken-hearted host…

Leonard Cohen

- -

The next poem is the text of an Elizabethan song by Thomas Ford. The names of the characters, Corydon and Phillida, are typical of the tradition of pastoral poetry, in which shepherds woo shepherdesses and nymphs in an idealized countryside (pastoral) landscape.

What Then is Love?

What then is love, sings Corydon,
      Since Phillida is grown so coy?
A flatt'ring glass to gaze upon;
      A busy jest, a serious toy;
A flow'r still budding, never blown;
      A scanty dearth in fullest store;
Yielding least fruit where most is sown.
      My daily note shall be therefore
      Heigh ho! Heigh ho! 'chill love no more.

'Tis like a morning dewy rose
      Spread fairly to the sun's arise,
But when his beams he doth disclose,
      That which then flourish'd quickly dies.
It is a self-fed dying hope,
      A promised bliss, a salveless sore,
An aimless mark, an erring scope,
      My daily note shall be therefore,
      Heigh ho! Heigh ho! 'chill love no more.

'Tis like a lamp shining to all,
      Whilst in itself it doth decay,
It seems to free, whom it doth thrall,
      And leads our pathless thoughts astray.
It is the Spring of wintered hearts,
      Parched by the summer's heat before,
Faint hope to kindly warmth converts,
      My daily note shall be therefore
      Heigh ho! Heigh ho! 'chill love no more.

'chill love no more: I will love no more.
An aimless mark, an erring scope: from sailing; the land-'mark' and the tele-'scope' would be means of navigating. The sailor will be lost if these are 'aimless' or 'erring'.

Here are some points you may have noted:

- In their attempts to express what love is, or what it feels like, both Romeo and Corydon use a string of **metaphors** or **similes** rather than any sort of direct description of their feelings, e.g. 'A flatt'ring glass to gaze upon'.
- Both are reduced to using **oxymoron** and **paradox** – impossible combinations, opposites, or words and ideas that seem to cancel each other out, such as 'cold fire' or 'a serious toy'.
- Images of light and darkness, heat and cold, happiness and misery, time and the seasons are used frequently.
- These features convey the sense that love is a confusing and bewildering experience, not easily put into words.

This sort of language is very common in the literature of love. It is not confined to poetry, or to Elizabethan times. Writers still have characters going hot and cold or 'burning' with love or desire in contemporary novels, poems and songs, as you saw in the modern examples above.

Other common patterns to look out for are:

- similes, metaphors or extended metaphors which compare love to a battle, or war
- the idea of love as a 'sickness' or illness
- the use of religious or cosmic language to describe human, physical love, or to make sex sound like a spiritual experience
- connecting sex with death. Sometimes poets beg to 'die', when what they really want is the ecstasy of sexual love. Both sex and death mean a kind of 'letting go' of yourself, or losing touch with ordinary reality.

Activity

Have a look at the lyrics of some love songs you know or which are currently popular. Can you find examples of these patterns or images?

Great literary lovers

Some of the greatest love stories of all time have taken on the status of myths, or have become part of our everyday language. For example, we may call a man a 'Romeo' if he is young, attractive and rather dreamily or passionately romantic, or a 'Don Juan' or 'a bit of a Casanova' if he is a womanizer who likes to make many conquests.

In earlier centuries, most British writers, and educated readers, too, would have been familiar with the great stories of ancient and classical times – the myths and epic poems of the Greeks and Romans. They would also have known the Bible thoroughly, and would probably also have read the most important literary works of their own times and earlier. This meant that writers could mention stories, characters or events from these sources and expect their readers to instantly recognize these **allusions**, and automatically make connections with what they were reading.

Allusions sometimes add an extra layer of meaning to the text, and because this kind of knowledge is not normally part of our education today, twenty-first century readers can sometimes find themselves at a disadvantage. If you are reading more recent or post-colonial literature, you are also likely to find references to the myths and religious texts of other cultures. Good student editions of older texts should provide you with plenty of explanatory notes to help make sense of these; with modern texts you may need to do your own research. It can be useful to know a little about some of the most famous mythological characters and literary lovers, so here are a few to get you started.

Ancient Greece and Rome

- The Greek goddess of love was **Aphrodite**; for the Romans, she was **Venus**.
- **Cupid**, son of Venus, is the winged god armed with a bow, and arrows which have the power to make anyone struck by them fall in love. Arrows and hearts still appear on Valentine cards and graffiti. He was known as **Eros** in Greece.
- **Helen of Troy**, the wife of a Greek general, Menelaus, was abducted by Paris, one of the sons of King Priam of Troy. Her beautiful face is said to have 'launched a thousand ships' when the Greeks set off to ransack Troy in retaliation.
- **Antony and Cleopatra** are one of the most famous pairs of lovers. Mark Antony (Marcus Antonius) was one of the three Roman 'triumvirs' who shared power after the murder of Julius Caesar. In Shakespeare's version, he becomes besotted with Cleopatra, the beautiful and exotic queen of Egypt, and neglects his duties

in Rome. In the end, when Antony and Cleopatra are defeated in battle, suicide is the only honourable option for both of them.

Activity

Use an encyclopedia or the Internet to find out more about mythology. If you can, read some stories retelling the Greek and Roman myths.

Love through the ages: a rough guide

The selection of texts which follows is intended to give you a brief tour of some of the main periods of English literature. On the way, we will look at some of the ways in which authors have explored the experience of love.

Of course, this is a huge subject. Love and the situations that it gives rise to in literature can take many forms and these extracts can only present a glimpse of some of them.

Geoffrey Chaucer (fourteenth century)

Text suggestions

The Canterbury Tales:

The Knight's Tale

The Wife of Bath's Tale

The Miller's Tale

Troilus and Criseyde (selected passages)

For an introduction to Chaucer, and some suggestions about how to read his work, see Chapter 2, pages 64–68. On an A level course, you are most likely to read one of *The Canterbury Tales*, but he is also famous for another long narrative poem, *Troilus and Criseyde.*

Troilus and Criseyde is a fairly complicated tale of love and betrayal, set during the Trojan war. In this extract, at a festival in honour of Palladion, Criseyde, a young widow, attracts the attention of Troilus, a Trojan prince.

Activity

1 With a partner, take turns to read the stanzas aloud. It is often much easier to recognize Chaucer's meaning when we hear it, rather than just seeing it on the page. Don't worry if the words and spellings are unfamiliar or you don't understand all of it.

2 See if you can work out the gist of the story and, alone or with a partner, create a rough modern translation of the text.

3 Discuss and make notes on what you learn about the two characters.

   • Criseyde (stanzas 3–4 and 12–13): What sort of language does Chaucer use to describe her, among the crowd of other people, on this occasion?

   • Troilus (stanzas 5–15): In particular, how does Chaucer present his attitude to love?

from Troilus and Criseyde

[1] And so bifel, whan comen was the tyme
     Of Aperil, whan clothed is the mede
     With newe grene, of lusty Veer the pryme,
     And swote smellen floures whyte and rede,
     In sondry wises shewed, as I rede,
     The folk of Troie hire observaunces olde,
     Palladiones feste for to holde.

[2] And to the temple, in al hir beste wise,
     In general ther wente many a wight,
     To herknen of Palladions servyce;
     And namely, so many a lusty knyght,
     So many a lady fressh and mayden bright,
     Ful wel arayed, bothe meeste, mene, and leste,
     Ye, bothe for the seson and the feste.

[3] Among thise othere folk was Criseyda,
     In widewes habit blak; but natheles,
     Right as our firste lettre is now an A,
     In beaute first so stood she, makeles.
     Hire goodly lokyng gladed al the prees.
     Nas nevere yet seyn thyng to ben preysed derre,
     Nor under cloude blak so bright a sterre

[4] As was Criseyde, as folk seyde everichone
     That hir behelden in hir blake wede.
     And yet she stood ful lowe and stille allone,
     Byhynden other folk, in litel brede,
     And neigh the dore, ay undre shames drede,
     Simple of atir and debonaire of chere,
     With ful assured lokyng and manere.

[5] This Troilus, as he was wont to gide
     His yonge knyghtes, lad hem up and down
     In thilke large temple on every side,
     Byholding ay the ladies of the town,
     Now here, now there; for no devocioun
     Hadde he to non, to reven hym his reste,
     But gan to preise and lakken whom hym leste.

[6] And in his walk ful faste he gan to wayten
     If knyght or squyer of his compaignie
     Gan for to syke, or lete his eighen baiten
     On any womman that he koude espye.
     He wolde smyle and holden it folye,
     And seye hym thus, 'God woot, she slepeth softe
     For love of the, whan thow turnest ful ofte!

[7] 'I have herd told, pardieux, of youre lyvynge,
     Ye loveres, and youre lewed observaunces,
     And which a labour folk han in wynnynge
     Of love, and in the kepyng, which doutaunces;
     And whan youre prey is lost, woo and penaunces.

O veray fooles, nyce and blynde be ye!
Ther nys nat oon kan war by other be.'

[8] And with that word he gan caste up the browe,
Ascaunces, 'Loo! is this naught wisely spoken?'
At which the God of Love gan loken rowe
Right for despit, and shop for to ben wroken.
He kidde anon his bowe nas naught broken;
For sodeynly he hitte hym atte fulle –
And yet as proud a pekok kan he pulle.

[9] O blynde world, O blynde entencioun!
How often falleth al the effect contraire
Of surquidrie and foul presumpcioun;
For kaught is proud, and kaught is debonaire.
This Troilus is clomben on the staire,
And litel weneth that he moot descenden;
But alday faileth thing that fooles wenden.

                *   *   *

[10] Withinne the temple he wente hym forth pleyinge,
This Troilus, of every wight aboute,
On this lady, and now on that, lokynge,
Wher so she were of town or of withoute;
And upon cas bifel that thorugh a route
His eye percede, and so depe it wente,
Til on Criseyde it smot, and ther it stente.

[11] And sodeynly he wax therwith astoned,
And gan hir bet biholde in thrifty wise.
'O mercy, God!' thoughte he, 'wher hastow woned,
That art so feyr and goodly to devise?'
Therwith his herte gan to sprede and rise,
And softe sighed, lest men myghte hym here,
And caught ayeyn his firste pleyinge chere.

[12] She nas nat with the leste of hire stature,
But alle hire lymes so wel answerynge
Weren to wommanhod, that creature
Was nevere lasse mannyssh in semynge;
And ek the pure wise of hire mevynge
Shewed wel that men myght in hire gesse
Honour, estat, and wommanly noblesse.

[13] To Troilus right wonder wel with alle
Gan for to like hire mevynge and hire chere,
Which somdel deignous was, for she let falle
Hire look a lite aside, in swich manere,
Ascaunces, 'What, may I nat stonden here?'
And after that hir lokynge gan she lighte,
That nevere thoughte hym seen so good a syghte.

[14] And of hire look in him ther gan to quyken
So gret desir and such affeccioun,
That in his herte botme gan to stiken

Of hir his fixe and depe impressioun.
And though he erst hadde poured up and down,
He was tho glad his hornes in to shrinke:
Unnethes wiste he how to loke or wynke.

[15]   Lo, he that leet hymselven so konnynge,
And scorned hem that Loves peynes dryen,
Was ful unwar that Love hadde his dwellynge
Withinne the subtile stremes of hire yen;
That sodeynly hym thoughte he felte dyen,
Right with hire look, the spirit in his herte:
Blissed be Love, that kan thus folk converte!

Geoffrey Chaucer

The Elizabethan era (1558–1603)

Text suggestions

Drama

Shakespeare: *Romeo and Juliet*
The Taming of the Shrew
Much Ado about Nothing
Hamlet
Twelfth Night

Poetry

Shakespeare: Selections from the *Sonnets*
Selections from anthologies of Elizabethan poetry

The reign of Queen Elizabeth I was a time when literature, theatre, music and the other arts blossomed. The first public theatres were opened and the work of playwrights such as Shakespeare, Christopher Marlowe and Ben Jonson became highly popular. Great epic poems, like Sir Philip Sidney's *Arcadia* and Edmund Spenser's *The Faerie Queene* used the old classical, pastoral style and **allegory** as ways of glorifying Elizabeth's reign, as if it were a 'Golden Age', and countless short poems and songs of love were written.

First, we will look briefly at how Shakespeare depicts Romeo falling in love – with Juliet this time. He is an uninvited guest at a ball hosted by Juliet's father, Capulet. There is a long-standing family feud between his own family, the Montagues, and the Capulets, but as soon as he notices Juliet, it is love at first sight:

Romeo and Juliet

Romeo: What lady is that which doth enrich the hand
Of yonder knight?

Servant: I know not, sir.

Romeo: O! she doth teach the torches to burn bright.
It seems she hangs upon the cheek of night
Like a rich jewel in an Ethiop's ear;

Beauty too rich for use, for earth too dear!
So shows a snowy dove trooping with crows,
As yonder lady o'er her fellows shows.
The measure done, I'll watch her place of stand,
And, touching hers, make blessed my rude hand.
Did my heart love till now? forswear it, sight!
For I ne'er saw true beauty till this night.

Activity

Read the short passage, looking closely at the images Romeo uses to describe Juliet. Make a note of some of these.

Now look back at the extract from *Troilus and Criseyde* on page 241. What similarities can you find between the ways these two writers describe falling in love?

There is a long tradition of lovers using simile and metaphor to describe or flatter the beloved. The images and comparisons range from the unusual or extravagant to the predictable clichés we find in Valentine cards. But are these true compliments? The two sonnets which follow give us a chance to decide. The first is a fairly typical Elizabethan love poem by Edmund Spenser. In the second sonnet, Shakespeare does things rather differently.

Activity

Read the two poems and make notes about the images used by each poet. Discuss the similarities and differences between the two poems. Which do you consider the more effective as an expression of love?

The Garden of Beauty

Coming to kiss her lips (such grace I found),
Me seem'd I smelt a garden of sweet flow'rs
That dainty odours from them threw around,
For damsels fit to deck their lovers' bow'rs.
Her lips did smell like unto gillyflowers,
Her ruddy cheeks like unto roses red,
Her snowy brows like budded bellamoures,
Her lovely eyes like pinks but newly spread,
Her goodly bosom like a strawberry bed,
Her neck like to a bunch of cullambines,
Her breast like lilies ere their leaves be shed,
Her nipples like young blossom'd jessamines:
Such fragrant flow'rs do give most odorous smell,
But her sweet odour did them all excel.

Edmund Spenser

Sonnet 130

My mistress' eyes are nothing like the sun;
Coral is far more red than her lips' red;
If snow be white, why then her breasts are dun;
If hairs be wires, black wires grow on her head;

I have seen roses damasked, red and white,
But no such roses see I in her cheeks,
And in some perfumes is there more delight
Than in the breath that from my mistress reeks.
I love to hear her speak, yet well I know
That music hath a far more pleasing sound.
I grant I never saw a goddess go;
My mistress when she walks treads on the ground.
And yet, by heaven, I think my love as rare
As any she belied with false compare.

William Shakespeare

- -

Francis Bacon published an important collection of essays, on a wide range of
topics, in 1597. He was a man of strong opinions, and expressed his views on
everything from practical matters like education, or marriage, to abstract ideas
like truth and faith. His essays tend to be beautifully constructed, using careful
arguments, and rhetorical devices such as balanced sentences or ideas neatly
arranged in threes, which can be satisfying and memorable to read. Here we have
his thoughts about love.

Of love

The stage is more beholding to love, than the life of man. For as to the stage, love is ever
matter of comedies, and now and then of tragedies; but in life it doth much mischief;
sometimes like a siren, sometimes like a fury. You may observe, that amongst all the great
and worthy persons (whereof the memory remaineth, either ancient or recent) there is not
one, that hath been transported to the mad degree of love: which shows that great spirits,
and great business, do keep out this weak passion. You must except, nevertheless, Marcus
Antonius, the half partner of the empire of Rome, and Appius Claudius, the decemvir and
lawgiver; whereof the former was indeed a voluptuous man, and inordinate; but the latter
was an austere and wise man: and therefore it seems (though rarely) that love can find
entrance, not only into an open heart, but also into a heart well fortified, if watch be not
well kept. It is a poor saying of Epicurus, *Satis magnum alter alteri theatrum sumus*: as
if man, made for the contemplation of heaven, and all noble objects, should do nothing
but kneel before a little idol and make himself a subject, though not of the mouth (as
beasts are), yet of the eye; which was given him for higher purposes. It is a strange thing,
to note the excess of this passion, and how it braves the nature, and value of things, by
this; that the speaking in a perpetual hyperbole, is comely in nothing but in love. Neither
is it merely in the phrase; for whereas it hath been well said, that the arch-flatterer, with
whom all the petty flatterers have intelligence, is a man's self; certainly the lover is more.
For there was never proud man thought so absurdly well of himself, as the lover doth of
the person loved; and therefore it was well said, *That it is impossible to love and to be
wise*. Neither doth this weakness appear to others only, and not to the party loved; but to
the loved most of all, except the love be reciproque. For it is a true rule, that love is ever
rewarded, either with the reciproque, or with an inward and secret contempt. By how
much the more, men ought to beware of this passion, which loseth not only other things,
but itself! As for the other losses, the poet's relation doth well figure them: that he that
preferred Helena, quitted the gifts of Juno and Pallas. For whosoever esteemeth too much
of amorous affection, quitteth both riches and wisdom. This passion hath his floods, in
very times of weakness; which are great prosperity, and great adversity; though this latter
hath been less observed: both which times kindle love, and make it more fervent, and
therefore show it to be the child of folly. They do best, who if they cannot but admit love,

yet make it keep quarters; and sever it wholly from their serious affairs, and actions, of life; for if it check once with business, it troubleth men's fortunes, and maketh men, that they can no ways be true to their own ends. I know not how, but martial men are given to love: I think, it is but as they are given to wine; for perils commonly ask to be paid in pleasures. There is in man's nature, a secret inclination and motion, towards love of others, which if it be not spent upon some one or a few, doth naturally spread itself towards many, and maketh men become humane and charitable; as it is seen sometime in friars. Nuptial love maketh mankind; friendly love perfecteth it; but wanton love corrupteth, and embaseth it.

Francis Bacon

Activity

1 First, read the essay carefully. As with other older texts, don't worry too much if you do not understand every word at first.

2 Bacon expresses some strong opinions. Discuss with a partner what you understand about Bacon's view of love. To start you off, look at the following:

- his opening sentence
- the phrases and sentences which have been underlined here
- his final statement about love.

3 Do you agree with any of his views, or can you relate his ideas about the effects of love to any situations from the literature of love you have read so far? For example, have you noticed any writers or characters 'speaking in a perpetual hyperbole' or lovers who quit 'both riches and wisdom'?

The Jacobean age (1603–1625)

Text suggestions

Drama

Shakespeare: *Othello*

King Lear

Antony and Cleopatra

John Webster: T*he Duchess of Malfi*

Poetry

John Donne: *Selected Poems*

Selections from anthologies of metaphysical poetry

The time of King James I is known in particular for the many great tragic dramas that were written and performed. Shakespeare's Globe Theatre was flourishing and his great late tragedies were written at this time, along with his 'last plays', such as *The Tempest* and *The Winter's Tale*, which do not fit neatly into the categories of tragedy or comedy. John Webster's powerful tragedies were popular too. Love, in some form, features in the plots of most of these.

Many writers point out that it is difficult to put genuine love into words; others use many words in an attempt to express their feelings. Shakespeare's great tragedy,

King Lear, focuses on love between parents and children, in two families. Lear, the elderly king, has three daughters, and the Duke of Gloucester has two sons. The tragedy comes about because neither father is able to see which of his children genuinely loves him and which are merely presenting a façade of love, in order to profit from their position.

Lear sets up his own downfall in the opening scene of the play. He has decided to 'retire' as king, and to divide up his kingdom among his three daughters. However, he sets up a rather bizarre ritual, or competition, in which each daughter has to declare how much she loves him, in order to secure a bigger share of the kingdom than her sisters. His elder daughters, Goneril (married to the Duke of Albany) and Regan (wife of the Duke of Cornwall), have no difficulty in playing this game, but for their younger sister, Cordelia, it is a different matter.

King Lear

Lear: Give me the map there. Know that we have divided
In three our kingdom; and 'tis our fast intent
To shake all cares and business from our age,
Conferring them on younger strengths, while we
Unburden'd crawl toward death. Our son of Cornwall
And you, our no less loving son of Albany,
We have this hour a constant will to publish
Our daughters' several dowers, that future strife
May be prevented now. The princes, France and Burgundy,
Great rivals in our youngest daughter's love,
Long in our court have made their amorous sojourn,
And here are to be answer'd. Tell me, my daughters, –
Since now we will divest us both of rule,
Interest of territory, cares of state, –
Which of you shall we say doth love us most?
That our largest bounty may extend
Where nature doth with merit challenge. Goneril
Our eldest born, speak first.

Goneril: Sir, I love you more than word can wield the matter;
Dearer than eye-sight, space and liberty;
Beyond what can be valued rich or rare;
No less than life, with grace, health, beauty, honour;
As much as child e'er loved, or father found;
A love that makes breath poor and speech unable;
Beyond all manner of so much I love you.

Cordelia: *(Aside)* What shall Cordelia speak? Love, and be silent.

Lear: Of all these bounds, even from this line to this,
With shadowy forests and with champains riched,
With plenteous rivers and wide-skirted meads,
We make thee lady: to thine and Albany's issues
Be this perpetual. What says our second daughter
Our dearest Regan, wife of Cornwall?

Regan: I am made of that self metal as my sister,
And prize me at her worth. In my true heart
I find she names my very deed of love;
Only she comes too short: that I profess

Myself an enemy to all other joys
Which the most precious square of sense possesses,
And find I am alone felicitate
In your dear highness' love.

Cordelia: *(Aside)*   Then poor Cordelia!
And yet not so; since I am sure my love's
More ponderous than my tongue.

Lear: To thee and thine, hereditary ever,
Remain this ample third of our fair kingdom,
No less in space, validity, and pleasure,
Than that conferred on Goneril. Now, our joy,
Although our last, and least; to whose young love
The vines of France and milk of Burgundy
Strive to be interested; what can you say to draw
A third more opulent than your sisters? Speak.

Cordelia: Nothing, my lord.

Lear: Nothing?

Cordelia: Nothing.

Lear: Nothing will come of nothing: speak again.

Cordelia: Unhappy that I am, I cannot heave
My heart into my mouth: I love your Majesty
According to my bond; no more nor less.

Lear: How, how, Cordelia! Mend your speech a little,
Lest you may mar your fortunes.

Cordelia: Good my Lord,
You have begot me, bred me, loved me: I
Return those duties back as are right fit,
Obey you, love you, and most honour you.
Why have my sisters husbands, if they say
They love you all? Happily, when I shall wed,
That lord whose hand must take my plight shall carry
Half my love with him, half my care and duty:
Sure I shall never marry like my sisters,
To love my father all.

Lear: But goes thy heart with this?

Cordelia: Ay, my good Lord.

Lear: So young, and so untender?

Cordelia: So young, my Lord, and true.

Lear: Let it be so; thy truth then be thy dower:
For, by the sacred radiance of the sun,
The mysteries of Hecate and the night,
By all the operation of the orbs
From whom we do exist and cease to be,
Here I disclaim all my paternal care,
Propinquity and property of blood,
And as a stranger to my heart and me
Hold me from this for ever.

In a small group, read through the extract from *King Lear* and discuss the following points:

- What do you think of Lear's idea? Is it a realistic way to test his children's love for him? Give reasons for your answer. Can you detect any difference, initially, between his attitudes to his daughters?

- Look closely at the language the two elder daughters, Goneril and Regan, use to describe their love. Comment on their style and choice of vocabulary.

- Now compare this with Cordelia's speeches. What do you think of her response? Is she right not to tell her father what he wants to hear?

- What is your opinion of Lear's reaction to what happens? Why do you think Cordelia's behaviour here makes him so angry that he forgets how much she has loved him in the past?

A group of writers of this time became known as the **metaphysical poets**, because they tended to explore ideas and images which were *meta*-physical, or beyond everyday, physical reality, and more to do with religious beliefs, or with attempts to understand how the universe works. It was a time when knowledge was advancing and changing people's view of the world in ways that were quite disorientating. New continents were being 'discovered', and 'exotic' countries explored, while the understanding that the earth was a spherical planet, rather than a flat disc at the centre of the universe, with an infinite heaven above and an infinite hell below, was forcing people to question beliefs that had been held for centuries.

John Donne (1572–1631) is one of the most celebrated metaphysical poets. He was a man actively involved in many spheres of life – he sailed on expeditions to Spain and the Azores, was elected an MP, and had 12 children as well as being ordained as a priest and eventually becoming Dean of St Paul's Cathedral. He wrote many sermons and longer poems as well as the *Songs and Sonnets* which are his best-known works. His love poetry is varied, from explorations of love on a spiritual level to quite earthy celebrations of physical love, and from delight in newfound love to deep mourning at death and loss. He often uses the **conceit**: a complex or far-fetched metaphor, using unlikely comparisons, worked out in detail and sometimes rather like a clever or cryptic game.

- Look back at the strategy for close reading suggested in Chapter 7, pages 104–105.

- Read the text of the following poem, *The Sun Rising*, carefully, alone or with a partner, and use the headings suggested in Chapter 7 to make notes.

- Use your notes to write a short essay based on the following question: Explore how Donne presents the experience of love in his poem *The Sun Rising*.

The Sun Rising

> Busy old fool, unruly sun,
> Why dost thou thus,
> Through windows, and through curtains call on us?
> Must to thy motions lovers' seasons run?
> Saucy pedantic wretch, go chide
> Late school-boys, and sour prentices,
> Go tell court-huntsmen, that the King will ride,
> Call country ants to harvest offices;
> Love, all alike, no season knows, nor clime,
> Nor hours, days, months, which are the rags of time.
>
> Thy beams, so reverend, and strong
> Why shouldst thou think?
> I could eclipse and cloud them with a wink,
> But that I would not lose her sight so long:
> If her eyes have not blinded thine,
> Look, and tomorrow late, tell me,
> Whether both th'Indias of spice and mine
> Be where thou left'st them, or lie here with me.
> Ask for those kings whom thou saw'st yesterday,
> And thou shalt hear, All here in one bed lay.
>
> She'is all states, and all princes, I,
> Nothing else is.
> Princes do but play us; compared to this,
> All honour's mimic; all wealth alchemy.
> Thou sun art half as happy as we,
> In that the world's contracted thus;
> Thine age asks ease, and since thy duties be
> To warm the world, that's done in warming us.
> Shine here to us, and thou art everywhere;
> This bed thy centre is, these walls, thy sphere.

John Donne

Activity

Now compare your essay with the student response that follows. Although it does not examine every detail of the poem, it is an effective response to the task. It is clearly written and points are supported with evidence from the text and some close analysis of Donne's use of language. It also shows some knowledge of the context of the poem.

- What has this student included, or emphasized, that you have not?
- What other points have you written about, which are not covered here?

Donne's *The Sun Rising* is a poem about how powerful and wonderful the experience of love is, making him feel as if the whole world is at his command. It is morning, and a lover and his mistress are in bed, when they are interrupted in their love-making by the rising sun, which shines in the window. The poet, in the character of the lover, speaks directly to the sun, personifying it as a 'Busy old fool' as if it is a nosey old man, or a spoilsport, for interrupting their pleasure. The whole poem then goes on to talk about how the lovers are richer, happier and stronger than 'kings', 'princes', or even than the sun itself, because of the power of love.

The lover's tone of voice towards the sun is impatient, irreverent and rather cheeky. This is quite humorous. He calls it a 'Saucy pedantic wretch', which gives three ideas, first that it is the sun which is being cheeky or impudent for getting in the way of love, then 'pedantic' suggests it is rather boring and perhaps obsessive, because the sun always follows the rules and rises on time, while it is also a 'wretch', which makes it sound rather useless. He dismisses the sun to go and wake up other, less important people, like 'late school-boys' or people who work on farms, who he calls 'country ants', making them sound very small and insignificant.

As the poem goes on, his tone becomes more and more boastful. In the second stanza, he challenges the sun, claiming that he could easily 'eclipse' the sun, but his view is very egocentric. What he means is that he could shut out the sun's light by blinking, 'a wink' – he feels that the whole world is contained in the bed where he is and anyone else's experience doesn't count. In the final stanza, he shows that love makes him feel as if he and his mistress are the most important people in the world, at the centre of the universe, and nothing and nobody else even exists for them. Now he is even patronizing to the sun, saying that because it is old, it needs to rest:

Thine age asks ease.

All it needs to do is to shine on him and his mistress, because they *are* the whole world. She is the world to him, and he is its ruler. This makes him sound rather dominating.

She 'is all states, and all princes, I,
Nothing else is.

The poem has three stanzas with the same rhyming pattern, but at the beginning of each stanza, the number of stressed syllables is uneven, and together with the punctuation, this makes the effect more like the rhythm of speech, especially in the first and third stanzas.

Busy old fool, unruly sun…

And when he says 'Nothing else is', the full stop halts the rhythm and really draws attention to this bold, megalomaniac statement.

By the end of each stanza the rhythm and rhyme have become steadier and more regular, ending in a smooth couplet, as if he has become calmer, or more sure of himself.

All through the poem, the main idea or conceit is that love makes him more powerful than the sun and he argues this in various ways, based on the old belief that the sun travelled round the earth rather than vice versa. This fits very well with his egocentric view that the world revolves round him and his lover. He imagines the sun's journey round the earth and the rich things it will have seen on the way, like 'th'Indias of spice and mine', which seemed very exotic in Donne's time when new continents were only just being discovered. But then he claims that everything rich or important in the world is actually right here in his bed.

In the third stanza he diminishes the sun further by pointing out that the sun can only ever see half the world at a time:

Thou sun art half as happy as we,
In that the world's contracted thus;

whereas for the lovers, it is as if the whole world is in their possession at once. He suggests the 'old' sun must be weary and could retire and rest after all its travelling and do just as good a job by staying put and shining only on them,

> … since thy duties be
> To warm the world, that's done in warming us.

The sun's orbit or 'sphere' can be contained within 'these walls' of his bedroom.

Overall, the message of the poem is that love is – or makes him feel – supremely powerful; more powerful than the sun itself, and immune to the passage of time, almost as if love makes them immortal. The experience of love is above and beyond the things that usually rule our lives:

> Love, all alike, no season knows, nor clime,
> Nor hours, days, months, which are the rags of time.

Donne also used poetry to explore and express his religious faith. The poem which follows is one of his *Holy Sonnets*. Critical of his own imperfect faith, he begs God to 'work harder' to get through to him the true strength of divine love and keep him on the path of faith.

Activity

Read Holy Sonnet 14 carefully. Make notes on the vocabulary and imagery Donne uses to describe divine love and his struggle to have enough faith in God.

- What do you make of the first line of the poem?
- What do you notice about lines 2–4?
- What extended metaphors does Donne use in lines 5–8 and lines 9–14?
- What is Donne's meaning when he says he is 'betrothed unto your enemy'?

Discuss your findings. What is surprising about this language, for a poem about religious faith?

Holy Sonnet 14

Batter my heart, three-personed God; for, you
As yet but knock, breathe, shine, and seek to mend;
That I may rise, and stand, o'erthrow me, and bend
Your force, to break, blow, burn, and make me new.
I, like an usurped town, to another due,
Labour to admit you, but oh, to no end,
Reason your viceroy in me, me should defend,
But is captived, and proves weak or untrue,
Yet dearly'I love you, and would be loved fain,
But am betrothed unto your enemy,
Divorce me, untie, or break that knot again,
Take me to you, imprison me, for I
Except you enthral me, never shall be free,
Nor ever chaste, except you ravish me.

John Donne

Text suggestions

Drama

William Wycherley: *The Country Wife*

William Congreve: *The Way of the World*

Aphra Behn: *The Rover*

Prose

Daniel Defoe: *Moll Flanders*

Henry Fielding: *Tom Jones*

      Joseph Andrews

Poetry

John Milton: Selections from *Paradise Lost*

Alexander Pope: *The Rape of the Lock*

King Charles II was restored to the throne of England in 1660, after a period of great change and instability. Civil war, the execution of King Charles I, religious conflicts and the bloody and puritanical regime of Oliver Cromwell had all left their mark on society.

In literature, the Restoration period is known for its comic plays, which reflect – or criticize – the new, rather superficial and sceptical mood of a time when many beliefs and certainties had been undermined. Plays by John Dryden, Aphra Behn, William Wycherley and William Congreve present cynical views of love and marriage and make a hero of the 'rake' or 'libertine' character, sometimes charming, sometimes disreputable, who is unwilling to be tied down or bound by traditional morals. The plays make use of rather complicated, farcical plots and witty language to amuse the audience, as well as including elaborate songs, which were an opportunity to 'showcase' celebrity singers/actors of the day.

Activity

1 With a partner, or in a small group, read the following extract from *The Way of the World*.

2 Discuss the attitudes of these characters to love, marriage and the opposite sex – and what do they give away about themselves?

3 Make a note of some of the words and phrases that are used to talk about love.

4 What stage directions, for actions and manners of speech, would you add to bring out the humour in the scene?

5 Act out the scene again, exaggerate, and enjoy it!

The Way of the World

(St James's Park)

*(Enter **Mrs Fainall** and **Mrs Marwood**)*

Mrs Fainall: Ay, ay, dear Marwood, if we will be happy, we must find the means in ourselves, and among ourselves. Men are ever in Extremes; either doating or averse. While they are Lovers, if they have Fire and Sense, their Jealousies are insupportable. And when they cease to Love, (we ought to think at least) they loath; they look upon us with Horror and Distaste; they meet us like the Ghosts of what we were, and as such, fly from us.

Mrs Marwood: True, 'tis an unhappy Circumstance of Life, that Love shou'd ever die before us; and that the Man so often shou'd out-live the Lover. But say what you will, 'tis better to be left than never to have been lov'd. To pass our Youth in dull Indifference, to refuse the Sweets of Life because they once must leave us, is as preposterous as to wish to have been born Old, because we one Day must be Old. For my part, my Youth may wear and waste, but it shall never rust in my Possession.

Mrs Fainall: Then it seems you dissemble an Aversion to Mankind, only in compliance with my Mother's Humour.

Mrs Marwood: Certainly. To be free, I have no Taste of those insipid dry Discourses with which our Sex of force must entertain themselves, apart from Men. We may affect Endearments to each other, profess eternal Friendships, and seem to doat like Lovers; but 'tis not in our Natures long to persevere. Love will resume his Empire in our Breasts, and every Heart, or soon or late receive and readmit him as its lawful tyrant.

Mrs Fainall: Bless me, how have I been deceived! Why you profess a Libertine!

Mrs Marwood: You see my Friendship by my Freedom. Come, be as sincere, acknowledge that your Sentiments agree with mine.

Mrs Fainall: Never!

Mrs Marwood: You hate Mankind?

Mrs Fainall: Heartily, inveterately.

Mrs Marwood: Your Husband?

Mrs Fainall: Most transcendently; ay, tho' I say it, meritoriously.

Mrs Marwood: Give me your Hand upon it.

Mrs Fainall: There.

Mrs Marwood: I join with you; what I have said has been to try you.

Mrs Fainall: Is it possible? Dost thou hate those Vipers Men?

Mrs Marwood: I have done hating 'em, and am now come to despise 'em; the next thing I have to do is eternally to forget 'em.

Mrs Fainall: There spoke the Spirit of an *Amazon*, a *Penthesilea*!

Mrs Marwood: And yet I am thinking sometimes to carry my Aversion further.

Mrs Fainall: How?

Mrs Marwood: Faith, by Marrying; if I cou'd but find one that lov'd me very well and would be thoroughly sensible of ill usage, I think I shou'd do myself the violence of undergoing the Ceremony.

Mrs Fainall: You would not make him a cuckold?

Mrs Marwood: No, but I'd make him believe I did, and that's as bad.

Mrs Fainall: Why, had not you as good do it?

Mrs Marwood: Oh, if he shou'd ever discover it, he wou'd then know the worst, and be out of his Pain; but I wou'd have him ever to continue upon the Rack of Fear and Jealousy.

Mrs Fainall: Ingenious Mischief! Wou'd thou wert married to *Mirabell*.

Mrs Marwood:	Wou'd I were!
Mrs Fainall:	You change Colour.
Mrs Marwood:	Because I hate him.
Mrs Fainall:	So do I; but I can hear him nam'd. But what Reason have you to hate him in particular?
Mrs Marwood:	I never lov'd him; he is, and always was, insufferably proud.
Mrs Fainall:	By the Reason you give for your Aversion, one wou'd think it dissembl'd; for you have laid a Fault to his Charge of which his Enemies must acquit him.
Mrs Marwood:	Oh, then it seems you are one of his favourable Enemies. Methinks you look a little pale, and now you flush again.
Mrs Fainall:	Do I? I think I am a little sick o'the sudden.
Mrs Marwood:	What ails you?
Mrs Fainall:	My Husband. Don't you see him? He turn'd short upon me unawares, and has almost overcome me.
	(*Enter* **Fainall** *and* **Mirabell**)
Mrs Marwood:	Ha, ha, ha; he comes opportunely for you.
Mrs Fainall:	For you, for he has brought *Mirabell* with him.
Fainall:	My Dear.
Mrs Fainall:	My Soul.

William Congreve

- -

Later in the Restoration period, Alexander Pope, Jonathan Swift and others highlighted the artificiality and hypocrisy of society in a great deal of powerful satirical writing. They were known as **Augustan** writers, because they had a high regard for the classical literature of ancient Rome, particularly poetry from the time of the Emperor Augustus. They often wrote in **heroic couplets** (rhymed couplets of iambic pentameter) in the style of the Latin poets. Much of their work deals with politics, religion, or social issues, but in *The Rape of the Lock*, Pope writes a more gentle satire, dedicated to young ladies who can laugh at their own 'little unguarded follies'.

The plot of the poem is based on a real incident, and concerns the theft, by an admirer, of one lock of a girl's hair, and the quarrel that ensued. He wrote the poem 'to make a jest of it and laugh them together again'. The story is told with much 'heroi-comical' exaggeration, using the language of the classical pastoral world of nymphs and shepherds. This style is known as **mock-heroic**. The humour arises from using the high-flown vocabulary and style of great epic poems to describe something quite down to earth or even ridiculous.

In this extract, the admirer, the Baron, first catches sight of the tempting ringlet, or 'lock'.

The Rape of the Lock (Canto II)

Not with more glories, in th'ethereal plain,
The Sun first rises o'er the purpled main,
Than issuing forth, the rival of his beams
Launch'd on the bosom of the silver *Thames*.
Fair Nymphs, and well-drest Youths around her shone,
But ev'ry eye was fix'd on her alone.
On her white breast a sparkling Cross she wore,
Which Jews might kiss, and Infidels adore.
Her lively looks a sprightly mind disclose,

Quick as her eyes, and as unfix'd as those:
Favours to none, to all she smiles extends,
Oft she rejects, but never once offends.
Bright as the sun, her eyes the gazers strike,
And, like the sun, they shine on all alike.
Yet graceful ease, and sweetness void of pride,
Might hide her faults, if *Belles* had faults to hide:
If to her share some female errors fall,
Look on her face, and you'll forget'em all.

This Nymph, to the destruction of mankind,
Nourish'd two Locks which graceful hung behind
In equal curls, and well conspir'd to deck
With shining ringlets the smooth iv'ry neck:
Love in these labyrinths his slaves detains,
And mighty hearts are held in slender chains.
With hairy sprindges we the birds betray,
Slight lines of hair surprise the finny prey,
Fair tresses man's imperial race insnare,
And beauty draws us with a single hair.

Th' advent'rous Baron the bright locks admir'd,
He saw, he wish'd, and to the prize aspir'd.
Resolv'd to win, he meditates the way,
By force to ravish, or by fraud betray;
For when success a Lover's toil attends,
Few ask, if fraud or force attain'd his ends.

Alexander Pope

Activity

Make notes on Pope's use of language here, picking out examples of pastoral language, comic exaggeration, and features which make it like classical poetry.

Write a short commentary, showing how the mock-heroic style is demonstrated in the extract.

The Romantic period (1780–1830)

Text suggestions

Drama

Richard Sheridan: *The Rivals*

Prose

Jane Austen: *Pride and Prejudice*
    Emma
    Northanger Abbey

Poetry

John Keats: Poetry and letters

Selections from anthologies of Romantic poetry

'Romanticism' refers to a new set of ways of thinking and feeling about the world which swept through Europe in the later part of the eighteenth century and remained important for much of the nineteenth. These ideas influenced most aspects of life, including politics, religion and science as well as music, painting and literature. This was a stormy age of war and revolution. The French Revolution, with its ideals of liberty, equality and the brotherhood of man, captured the imagination of many people in Britain, until it turned into a violent reign of terror.

Political revolution was about making people more equal, and with it came a taste for what was simpler and more natural. Romantic literature reflects this change and is very different from the artificial, cynical or inflated styles that had been fashionable before. The key Romantic authors are William Blake, William Wordsworth, Samuel Taylor Coleridge, Lord Byron, John Keats and Percy Shelley. Wordsworth sets out what is important in Romantic poetry: nature, imagination, the expression of feeling which is genuine and spontaneous, the experience of ordinary individuals, and clear, simple language.

However, bear in mind that not all literature written at this time is considered 'Romantic'. Jane Austen's novels, for example, are not Romantic in this sense. They are, however, important in the literature of love, and you are very likely to read one as part of your A level course. Her novel *Emma* is featured in Chapter 1. Like her other works, it is an entertaining story of the interplay between relationships, love, money and social class.

John Keats (1795–1821)

More than any other writer, Keats has been idealized as the typical Romantic poet – the young genius who dies young – and many people respond warmly to his work. Keats's life was shadowed by life-threatening illness. In his early twenties, he developed tuberculosis, which had already killed his beloved younger brother. He made a voyage to Italy in the hope that the warmer climate would be beneficial, but he died aged only 25. He was painfully aware of the transience and fragility of human life, and this is the central theme of his poetry, together with the message that since life is short and things change, we should 'sieze the day', live life to the full and find what joy we can in the time we have.

A few years before his death, he fell deeply in love with a young woman, Fanny Brawne. The letters he wrote to her from Italy, in his last months, when he knew he was doomed, are heart-breaking. They are among the most famous love letters ever written.

Activity

Read the letter which follows carefully. Discuss and make notes on:

- his thoughts and feelings about love
- the language he uses to write about love, and any vocabulary, imagery or other features that strike you
- his expectations of Fanny. What is your response to what he requires of her? What might be the feelings of someone receiving a letter like this?

Letter to Fanny Brawne

May (?)1820
Tuesday Morn –
My dearest Girl,

I wrote a Letter for you yesterday expecting to have seen your mother. I shall be selfish enough to send it though I know it may give you a little pain, because I wish you to see how unhappy I am for love of you, and endeavour as much as I can to entice you to give up your whole heart to me whose whole existence hangs upon you. You could not step or move an eyelid but it would shoot to my heart – I am greedy of you – Do not think of any thing but me. Do not live as if I was not existing – Do not forget me – But have I any right to say you forget me? Perhaps you think of me all day. Have I any right to wish you to be unhappy for me? You would forgive me for wishing it, if you knew the extreme passion I have that you should love me – and for you to love me as I do you, you must think of no one but me, much less write that sentence. Yesterday and this morning I have been haunted with a sweet vision – I have seen you the whole time in your shepherdess dress. How my senses have ached at it! How my heart has been devoted to it! How my eyes have been full of Tears at it! I[n]deed I think a real Love is enough to occupy the widest heart – Your going to town alone, when I heard of it was a shock to me – yet I expected it – *promise me you will not for some time, till I get better*. Promise me this and fill the paper full of the most endearing mames [*for* names]. If you cannot do so with good will, do my Love tell me – say what you think – confess if your heart is too much fasten'd on the world. Perhaps then I may see you at a greater distance, I may not be able to appropriate you so closely to myself. Were you to loose a favorite bird from the cage, how would your eyes ache after it as long as it was in sight; when out of sight you would recover a little. Perhaps if you would, if so it is, confess to me how many things are necessary to you besides me, I might be happier, by being less tantaliz'd. Well may you exclaim, how selfish, how cruel, not to let me enjoy my youth! to wish me to be unhappy! You must be so if you love me – upon my Soul I can be contented with nothing else. If you could really what is call'd enjoy yourself at a Party – if you can smile in peoples faces, and wish them to admire you now, you never have nor ever will love me – I see life in nothing but the cerrtainty of your Love – convince me of it my sweetest. If I am not somehow convinc'd I shall die of agony. If we love we must not live as other men and women do – I cannot brook the wolfsbane of fashion and foppery and tattle. You must be mine to die upon the rack if I want you. I do not pretend to say I have more feeling than my fellows – but I wish you seriously to look over my letters kind and unkind and consider whether the Person who wrote them can be able to endure much longer the agonies and uncertainties which you are so peculiarly made to create – My recovery of bodily hea[l]th will be of no benefit to me if you are not all mine when I am well. For god's sake save me – or tell me my passion is of too awful a nature for you. Again God bless you

J.K.

No – my sweet Fanny – I am wrong. I do not want you to be unhappy – and yet I do, I must while there is so sweet a Beauty – my loveliest my darling! Good bye! I kiss you – O the torments!

John Keats

- -

The narrative poem *The Eve of Saint Agnes* is considered to be one of Keats's best works. It is an exploration of some of his ideas about life, death and love rather than pure storytelling. The tale has parallels with Shakespeare's *Romeo and Juliet*. It concerns lovers, Madeline and Porphyro, who are kept apart by her family's hatred of him, and includes a scene where he wakens her from sleep before they elope – without mishap, unlike Romeo and Juliet. Other significant members of the 'cast' are an old nurse, Angela, and an ancient 'beadsman' or holy man.

According to an old superstition, if on St Agnes' Eve a young woman fasts and goes straight to bed without speaking or looking around, her future husband may appear to her in a dream. Madeline tries this and is rewarded with a dream of her lover, Porphyro. Porphyro, meanwhile, has gained access to her chamber. She awakens to find her dream has become reality, and they run away to start a new life together. The 'romance' is set within a contrasting frame. The poem begins – and ends – with the elderly beadsman who prays in the bitter cold, and with thoughts of death. He passes the statues of knights and ladies of the past. It seems that no amount of praying can keep death at bay.

The Eve of St Agnes

I   St Agnes' Eve – Ah, bitter chill it was!
The owl, for all his feathers, was a-cold;
The hare limped trembling through the frozen grass,
And silent was the flock in woolly fold:
Numb were the Beadsman's fingers, while he told
His rosary, and while his frosted breath,
Like pious incense from a censer old,
Seemed taking flight for heaven, without a death,
Past the Sweet Virgin's picture, while his prayer he saith.

II   His prayer he saith, this patient, holy man;
Then takes his lamp, and riseth from his knees,
And back returneth, meagre, barefoot, wan,
Along the chapel aisle by slow degrees:
The sculptured dead, on each side, seem to freeze,
Emprisoned in black, purgatorial rails;
Knights, ladies, praying in dumb orat'ries,
He passeth by; and his weak spirit fails
To think how they may ache in icy hoods and mails.

- -

Inside the castle, meanwhile, the scene is entirely different. A celebration is in progress, although Madeline's mind is elsewhere:

V   At length burst in the argent revelry,
With plume, tiara, and all rich array,
Numerous as shadows haunting faerily
The brain, new-stuffed, in youth, with triumphs gay
Of old romance. These let us wish away,
And turn, sole-thoughted, to one Lady there,
Whose heart had brooded, all that wintry day,
On love, and winged St Agnes' saintly care,
As she had heard old dames full many times declare.

VI   They told her how, upon St Agnes' Eve,
Young virgins might have visions of delight,
And soft adorings from their loves receive
Upon the honeyed middle of the night,
If ceremonies due they did aright;
As, supperless to bed they must retire,
And couch supine their beauties, lily white;

Nor look behind, nor sideways, but require
Of Heaven with upward eyes for all that they desire.

Activity

1 Compare the way Keats presents the 'outside world' in the two opening stanzas with his language and imagery here, inside the castle.

2 Compare Madeline's 'prayers' with the beadsman's.

While she lingers half-heartedly at the ball, Porphyro arrives. He too is 'praying':

IX So, purposing each moment to retire,
She lingered still. Meantime, across the moors,
Had come young Porphyro, with heart on fire
For Madeline. Beside the portal doors,
Buttressed from moonlight, stands he, and implores
All saints to give him sight of Madeline
But for one moment in the tedious hours,
That he might gaze and worship all unseen;
Perchance speak, kneel, touch, kiss – in sooth such things have been.

Porphyro risks his life to enter the castle of his 'Hyena foemen', where 'not one breast affords/ Him any mercy' except an old woman, Angela. She takes some persuading, but eventually 'Angela gives promise she will do/ Whatever he shall wish'.

XVI Sudden a thought came like a full-blown rose,
Flushing his brow, and in his painèd heart
Made purple riot; then doth he propose
A stratagem, that makes the beldame start:
...

XIX Which was, to lead him, in close secrecy,
Even to Madeline's chamber, and there hide
Him in a closet, of such privacy
That he might see her beauty unespied,
And win perhaps that night a peerless bride,
While legioned faeries paced the coverlet,
And pale enchantment held her sleepy-eyed.

Activity

Look closely at the language Keats uses to describe Porphyro's feelings when his idea comes to him.

Having gained entrance to Madeline's chamber, Porphyro looks around. This is the stereotypical castle of Gothic romance and the moon lends further 'enchantment'. The description is incredibly rich and sumptuous. It is language like this that creates the atmosphere for which this poem is famous.

Activity

With a partner, read the following stanzas and discuss how Keats uses visual description, imagery and colour to create a sense of atmosphere.

XXIV   A casement high and triple-arched there was,
              All garlanded with carven imag'ries
              Of fruits, and flowers, and bunches of knot-grass,
              And diamonded with panes of quaint device,
              Innumerable of stains and splendid dyes,
              As are the tiger-moth's deep-damasked wings;
              And in the midsts, 'mong thousand heraldries,
              And twilight saints, and dim emblazonings,
              A shielded scutcheon blushed with blood of queens and kings.

XXV   Full on this casement shone the wintry moon,
              And threw warm gules on Madeline's fair breast,
              As down she knelt for heaven's grace and boon;
              Rose-bloom fell on her hands, together pressed,
              And on her silver cross soft amethyst,
              And on her hair a glory, like a saint:
              She seemed a splendid angel, newly dressed,
              Save wings, for Heaven – Porphyro grew faint;
              She knelt, so pure a thing, so free from mortal taint.

- -

At the climax of the poem, Porphyro has watched Madeline sleep for some time, when, desperate for her to wake, he takes up her 'lute/ Tumultuous, and, in chords that tenderest be,' he plays an old song, *La belle dame sans mercy*. She does wake, but her reaction is interesting, and perhaps a little unexpected:

XXXIV Her eyes were open, but she still beheld,
              Now wide awake, the vision of her sleep –
              There was a painful change, that nigh expelled
              The blisses of her dream so pure and deep.
              At which fair Madeline began to weep,
              And moan forth witless words with many a sigh,
              While still her gaze on Porphyro would keep;
              Who knelt, with joined hands and piteous eye,
              Fearing to move or speak, she looked so dreamingly.

XXXV   'Ah, Porphyro!' said she, 'but even now
              Thy voice was a sweet tremble in mine ear,
              Made tuneable with every sweetest vow,
              And those sad eyes were spiritual and clear:
              How changed thou art! How pallid, chill, and drear!
              Give me that voice again, my Porphyro,
              Those looks immortal, those complainings dear!
              O leave me not in this eternal woe,
              For if thou diest, my Love, I know not where to go.'

Activity

1 Madeline's dream has apparently come true. Why, then, do you think she begins to 'weep' and 'moan'? What point might Keats be making here?

2 Now read the ending of the poem. In what ways does this ending fit the pattern of the conventional romance? Can you see any ways in which it is different or unexpected?

XXXVI   Beyond a mortal man impassioned far
At these voluptuous accents, he arose,
Ethereal, flushed, and like a throbbing star
Seen mid the sapphire heaven's deep repose;
Into her dream he melted, as the rose
Blended its odour with the violet –
Solution sweet. Meantime the frost-wind blows
Like Love's alarum pattering the sharp sleet
Against the window-panes; St Agnes' moon hath set.
   ...

XXXIX   'Hark! 'tis an elfin-storm from faery land,
Of haggard seeming, but a boon indeed:
Arise – arise! the morning is at hand.
The bloated wassaillers will never heed –
Let us away, my love, with happy speed –
There are no ears to hear, or eyes to see,
Drowned all in Rhenish and the sleepy mead;
Awake! arise! my love, and fearless be,
For o'er the southern moors I have a home for thee.'

XL   She hurried at his words, beset with fears,
For there were sleeping dragons all around,
At glaring watch, perhaps with ready spears –
Down the wide stairs a darkling way they found.
In all the house was heard no human sound.
A chain-drooped lamp was flickering by each door;
The arras, rich with horseman, hawk and hound,
Fluttered in the besieging wind's uproar;
And the long carpets rose along the gusty floor.

XLI   They glide, like phantoms, into the wide hall;
Like phantoms, to the iron porch, they glide;
Where lay the Porter, in uneasy sprawl,
With a huge empty flaggon by his side:
The wakeful bloodhound rose, and shook his hide,
But his sagacious eye an inmate owns.
By one, and one, the bolts full easy slide –
The chains lie silent on the footworn stones –
The key turns, and the door upon its hinges groans.

XLII   And they are gone – ay, ages long ago
These lovers fled away into the storm.
That night the Baron dreamt of many a woe,
And all his warrior-guests, with shade and form
Of witch, and demon, and large coffin-worm,
Were long be-nightmared. Angela the old
Died palsy-twitched, with meagre face deform;
The Beadsman, after thousand aves told,
For aye unsought for slept among his ashes cold.

John Keats

Summary

- In Madeline's dream, the Porphyro who came to her was not real, but an enchanted, perfect version of her lover, with eyes that were 'spiritual and clear' and whose voice was a 'sweet tremble'. When she wakes, the man before her cannot match this image. He is disappointingly 'pallid, chill, and drear', a physical, mortal, reality. She calls for the 'immortal' image which is everlasting, unlike the real man, who could die and leave her.

- In stanza XXXVI, the strength of his love seems to enable Porphyro to transcend – or go 'beyond' – the limits of 'mortal man', and he 'melts into her dream'. (This version of the poem leaves things vague. Though originally Keats made it clear that the lovers come together sexually at this point, the poem was censored by his publisher, who thought it 'unfit for Ladies'.) The lovers run off together, to a new life 'o'er the southern moors', escaping from the castle in a scene typical of Gothic romance, past the tapestries of 'horseman, hawk, and hound' and with the long carpets rising off the floor in the draughty halls. However, Keats's ending is not quite the conventional happy one. The lovers are not seen heading out into the sunshine of an ideal future, but into a very real, wintry storm. Once the enchantment of St Agnes' Eve has passed, and 'St Agnes' moon hath set', their romance, like Madeline's idealized image of Porphyro, must be replaced with reality.

- What Keats seems to be saying is that it is all very well having high-flown, spiritual visions of love, but when it comes down to it, love can only have a reality if it is between real, flesh-and-blood people, who have to live in an imperfect, harsh world. By setting his 'romance' between images of age and death, he shows that Madeline and Porphyro have to go out of the enchanted castle and make the most of love and life here on earth, before death overtakes them, as it inevitably must.

The Victorians

> ### Text suggestions
>
> **Drama**
>
> Oscar Wilde: *An Ideal Husband*
>
>   *The Importance of being Ernest*
>
> **Prose**
>
> Charlotte Brontë: *Jane Eyre*
>
>   *Villette*
>
> Emily Brontë: *Wuthering Heights*
>
> Elizabeth Gaskell: *Mary Barton*
>
> George Eliot: *Adam Bede*
>
>   *Middlemarch*
>
> Thomas Hardy: *Tess of the D'Urbervilles*
>
>   *Jude the Obscure*
>
>   *Far from the Madding Crowd*
>
> **Poetry**
>
> Elizabeth Barrett Browning: *Sonnets*
>
> Selections from anthologies of Victorian poetry, e.g. Robert Browning, Alfred Lord Tennyson, the Brontës

Although we may tend to think of issues such as industrial change or the stark differences between rich and poor as especially typical of Victorian literature, love still features in many important Victorian texts. Poets like Robert Browning and his wife Elizabeth Barrett wrote about love. The novels of the Brontë sisters, George Eliot and Thomas Hardy have plots that revolve around themes of loving relationships, while even those writers like Charles Dickens, Elizabeth Gaskell or Benjamin Disraeli, who were particularly concerned with making their readers think about social and political issues, still make use of plenty of 'love interest'.

Compared to the times both before and after, Victorian society is considered to have been quite repressive. The accepted views about love and sex tended to be moralistic, and people who deviated from society's rules were judged harshly. For example, women who had 'fallen' by engaging in sex outside marriage – whatever the reason – were often treated as outcasts. This is an interesting theme to explore in novels like *Adam Bede*, *Mary Barton* and *Tess of the d'Urbervilles*, which show attitudes just beginning to change.

You may already have studied Victorian literature at AS level, and Chapter 9 contains a full overview of the Victorian era.

Activity

1 Read the following sonnet by Elizabeth Barrett Browning. What is she asking of her lover?

2 Now remind yourself of Sonnet 130, by Shakespeare, on pages 244–245.

3 Make notes on the connections, similarities and differences between the two poems, before writing a short comparative essay:

Compare the ways in which these two poets present what they believe to be most important about loving someone.

Sonnet

If thou must love me, let it be for nought
Except for love's sake only. Do not say
'I love her for her smile – her look – her way
Of speaking gently, – for a trick of thought
That falls in well with mine, and certes brought
A sense of pleasant ease on such a day' –
For these things in themselves, Beloved, may
Be changed, or change for thee, – and love, so wrought,
May be unwrought so. Neither love me for
Thine own dear pity's wiping my cheeks dry, –
A creature might forget to weep, who bore
Thy comfort long, and lose thy love thereby!
But love me for love's sake, that evermore
Thou may'st love on, through love's eternity.

Elizabeth Barrett Browning

certes: certainly

Read the following passage from George Eliot's novel *Middlemarch*. In a group, or with a partner, discuss:

- the ways in which the author describes the environment and creates a sense of atmosphere
- your response to Dorothea and her situation. What are your expectations for her marriage?

Dorothea Brooke, an 'open, ardent', imaginative young woman has recently married Mr Casaubon, a much older, scholarly man, whom she has idealized. They have just returned from their honeymoon in Italy.

Middlemarch

Mr and Mrs Casaubon, returning home from their wedding journey, arrived at Lowick Manor in the middle of January. A light snow was falling as they descended at the door, and in the morning, when Dorothea passed from her dressing-room into the blue-green boudoir that we know of, she saw the long avenue of limes lifting their trunks from a white earth, and spreading white branches against the dun and motionless sky. The distant flat shrank in uniform whiteness and low-hanging uniformity of cloud. The very furniture in the room seemed to have shrunk since she saw it before: the stag in the tapestry looked more like a ghost in his ghostly blue-green world; the volumes of polite literature in the bookcase looked more like immovable imitations of books. The bright fire of dry oak-boughs burning on the dogs seemed an incongruous renewal of life and glow – like the figure of Dorothea herself as she entered carrying the red-leather cases containing the cameos for Celia.

She was glowing from her morning toilette as only healthful youth can glow; there was gem-like brightness on her coiled hair and in her hazel eyes; there was warm red life in her lips; her throat had a breathing whiteness above the differing white of the fur which itself seemed to wind about her neck and cling down her blue-grey pelisse with a tenderness gathered from her own, a sentient commingled innocence which kept its loveliness against the crystalline purity of the out-door snow. As she laid the cameo-cases on the table in the bow-window, she unconsciously kept her hands on them, immediately absorbed in looking out on the still, white enclosure which made her visible world.

Mr Casaubon, who had risen early complaining of palpitation, was in the library giving audience to his curate Mr Tucker. By-and-by Celia would come in her quality of bridesmaid as well as sister, and through the next weeks there would be wedding visits received and given; all in continuance of that transitional life understood to correspond with the excitement of bridal felicity, and keeping up the sense of busy ineffectiveness, as of a dream which the dreamer begins to suspect. The duties of her married life, contemplated as so great beforehand, seemed to be shrinking with the furniture and the white vapour-walled landscape. The clear heights where she expected to walk in full communion had become difficult to see even in her imagination; the delicious repose of the soul on a complete superior had been shaken into uneasy effort and alarmed with dim presentiment. When would the days begin of that active wifely devotion which was to strengthen her husband's life and exalt her own? Never perhaps, as she had preconceived them; but somehow – still somehow. In this solemnly pledged union of her life, duty would present itself in some new form of inspiration and give a new meaning to wifely love.

Meanwhile there was the snow and the low arch of dun vapour – there was the stifling oppression of that gentlewoman's world, where everything was done for her and none asked for her aid – where the sense of connection with a manifold pregnant existence had to be kept up painfully as an inward vision, instead of coming from without in claims that would have shaped her energies. – 'What shall I do?' 'Whatever you please, my dear': that had been her brief history since she had left off learning morning lessons and practising silly rhythms on the hated piano. Marriage, which was to bring guidance into worthy and imperative occupation, had not yet freed her from the gentlewoman's oppressive liberty: it had not even filled her leisure with the ruminant joy of unchecked tenderness. Her blooming full-pulsed youth stood there in a moral imprisonment which made itself one with the chill, colourless, narrowed landscape, with the shrunken furniture, the never-read books, and the ghostly stag in a pale fantastic world that seemed to be vanishing from the daylight.

George Eliot

'Modern' Literature

Text suggestions

Drama

Tennessee Williams: *The Glass Menagerie*

Prose

E.M. Forster: *A Room with a View*

D.H. Lawrence: *Sons and Lovers*

Poetry

Selections from:

>   *New Faber Book of Love Poems* (ed. James Fenton)
>   *Virago Book of Love Poetry*

In the early part of the twentieth century, writers began to challenge accepted conventions in a variety of ways. Subject matter became more daring, forms became freer or were discarded altogether, and some writers like T.S. Eliot, James Joyce and Virginia Woolf experimented and were deliberately 'modern'. The First World War had an enormous impact, sweeping away many of the beliefs and assumptions people had held onto in the past, and changing society irrevocably. As you will have seen if you studied 'The Struggle for Identity in Modern Literature' (see Chapter 11) at AS level, literature in the twentieth century has reflected a loss of innocence and a questioning on almost every level. Beliefs and conventions about love were no exception to this. Sex, homosexuality and unconventional relationships began to be explored much more freely in literature, although it was several decades before this became acceptable in open society. Books like D.H. Lawrence's *Lady Chatterley's Lover* and James Joyce's *Ulysses* were banned in the UK until the 1930s.

In Chapter 7, on pages 116–122, you will find a discussion and comparison of two extracts which present themes of courtship, from *The Rainbow* by D.H. Lawrence and *Washington Square* by Henry James. Both were written during this era, but are very different in style and approach.

Funeral Blues

Stop all the clocks, cut off the telephone,
Prevent the dog from barking with a juicy bone,
Silence the pianos and with muffled drum
Bring out the coffin, let the mourners come.

Let aeroplanes circle moaning overhead
Scribbling on the sky the message He Is Dead,
Put crêpe bows round the white necks of the public doves,
Let the traffic policemen wear black cotton gloves.

He was my North, my South, my East and West,
My working week and my Sunday rest,
My noon, my midnight, my talk, my song;
I thought that love would last forever: I was wrong.

The stars are not wanted now: put out every one;
Pack up the moon and dismantle the sun;
Pour away the ocean and sweep up the wood,
For nothing now can ever come to any good.

W. H. Auden

Time does not bring relief

Time does not bring relief; you all have lied
Who told me time would ease me of my pain!
I miss him in the weeping of the rain;
I want him at the shrinking of the tide;
The old snows melt from every mountain-side;
And last year's leaves are smoke in every lane;
But last year's bitter loving must remain
Heaped on my heart, and my old thoughts abide.
There are a hundred places where I fear
To go – so with his memory they brim.
And entering with relief some quiet place
Where never fell his foot or shone his face
I say, 'There is no memory of him here!'
And so stand stricken, so remembering him.

Edna St Vincent Millay

After Great Pain

After great pain, a formal feeling comes –
The Nerves sit ceremonious, like Tombs –
The stiff Heart questions was it He, that bore,
And Yesterday, or Centuries before?

The Feet, mechanical, go round –
Of Ground, or Air, or Ought –
A Wooden way
Regardless grown,
A Quartz contentment, like a stone –

This is the Hour of Lead –
Remembered, if outlived,
As Freezing persons, recollect the Snow –
First – Chill – then Stupor – then the letting go –

Emily Dickinson

Activity

1 On your own or working with a partner, read the drama extract from *The Glass Menagerie* which follows. Pay close attention to the stage directions as well as to the words of the characters. As we saw in Chapter 4, these are very important in Tennessee Williams's plays, giving us insight into the thoughts and feelings of the characters as well as the atmosphere and dramatic effect he wants to create.

2 Make notes before writing an account of the extract in which you explore:

- how Tennessee Williams presents the characters and their experiences
- the ways in which he creates dramatic and emotional effects
- your own response to the extract.

This play is set in the mid-western US city of St Louis, during the depression of the 1930s. Laura Wingfield is a painfully shy young woman. She has a slight disability, but is more crippled by lack of confidence than by her damaged leg. She rarely goes out and her chief pleasure in life is her collection of tiny glass animals. Williams tells us that she has become 'like a piece of her own glass collection, too exquisitely fragile to move from the shelf'. At the insistence of their mother, her brother Tom has invited one of his workmates to dinner, to meet Laura. The young man, Jim, turns out to be someone Laura had liked when they were at school, and who had nicknamed her 'Blue Roses' when she had been ill with pleurosis. Here, near the end of the play, they are left alone together after the meal.

The Glass Menagerie

Jim: You know – you're – well – very different! Surprisingly different from anyone else I know!
(*His voice becomes soft and hesitant with a genuine feeling.*)
Do you mind me telling you that?
(**Laura** *is abashed beyond speech.*)
I mean it in a nice way...
(**Laura** *nods shyly, looking away.*)

You make me feel sort of – I don't know how to put it! I'm usually pretty good at expressing things, but – This is something that I don't know how to say!
(**Laura** *touches her throat and clears it – turns the broken unicorn in her hands. Even softer.*)
Has anyone ever told you that you were pretty?
(*Pause: Music.*)
(**Laura** *looks up slowly, with wonder, and shakes her head.*)
Well, you are! In a very different way from anyone else. And all the nicer because of the difference, too.
(*His voice becomes low and husky.* **Laura** *turns away, nearly faint with the novelty of her emotions.*)
I wish that you were my sister. I'd teach you to have some confidence in yourself. The different people are not like other people, but being different is nothing to be ashamed of. Because other people are not such wonderful people. They're one hundred times one thousand. You're one times one! They walk all over the earth. You just stay here. They're common as – weeds, – but – you – well, you're – Blue Roses!
(*Music changes.*)

Laura: But blue is wrong for – roses…

Jim: It's right for you! – You're – pretty!

Laura: In what respect am I pretty?

Jim: In all respects – believe me! Your eyes – your hair – are pretty! Your hands are pretty!
(*He catches hold of her hand.*)
You think I'm making this up because I'm invited to dinner and have to be nice. Oh, I could do that! I could put on an act for you, Laura, and say lots of things without being very sincere. But this time I am. I'm talking to you sincerely. I happened to notice you had this inferiority complex that keeps you from feeling comfortable with people. Somebody needs to build your confidence up and make you proud instead of shy and turning away and – blushing –
Somebody ought to –
Ought to – *kiss* you, Laura!
(*His hand slips slowly up her arm to her shoulder.*
Music swells tumultuously.
He suddenly turns her about and kisses her on the lips.
When he releases her, **Laura** *sinks on the sofa with a bright, dazed look.*
Jim *backs away and fishes in his pocket for a cigarette.*)
Stumble-john!
(*He lights the cigarette, avoiding her look.*
There is a peal of girlish laughter from **Amanda** *in the kitchen.*
Laura *slowly raises and opens her hand. It still contains the little broken glass animal. She looks at it with a tender, bewildered expression.*)
Stumble-john!
I shouldn't have done that – That was way off the beam.
You don't smoke, do you?
(*She looks up, smiling, not hearing the question.*
He sits beside her a little gingerly. She looks at him speechlessly – waiting.
He coughs decorously and moves a little farther aside as he considers the situation and senses her feelings, dimly, with perturbation. Gently.)
Would you – care for a – mint?
(*She doesn't seem to hear him but her look grows brighter even.*)
Peppermint – Life-Saver?
My pocket's a regular drug store – wherever I go…
(*He pops a mint in his mouth. Then gulps and decides to make a clean breast of it. He speaks slowly and gingerly.*)

Laura, you know, if I had a sister like you, I'd do the same thing as Tom. I'd bring out fellows and – introduce her to them. The right type of boys of a type to – appreciate her

Only – well – he made a mistake about me.

Maybe I've got no call to be saying this. That may not have been the idea in having me over. But what if it was?

There's nothing wrong about that. The only trouble is that in my case – I'm not in a situation to – do the right thing.

I can't take down your number and say I'll phone.

I can't call up next week and – ask for a date.

I thought I had better explain the situation in case you – misunderstand it and – hurt your feelings...

(Pause.

Slowly, very slowly, **Laura**'s *look changes, her eyes returning slowly from his to the ornament in her palm.*

Amanda *utters another gay laugh in the kitchen.)*

Laura: *(faintly)* You – won't – call again?

Jim: No, Laura, I can't.

(He rises from the sofa.)

As I was just explaining, I've – got strings on me.

Laura, I've – been going steady!

I go out all of the time with a girl named Betty. She's a home-girl like you, and Catholic, and Irish, and in a great many ways we – get along fine.

I met her last summer on a moonlight boat trip up the river to Alton, on the *Majestic.*

Well – right away from the start it was – love!

(Laura sways slightly forward and grips the arm of the sofa. He fails to notice, now enrapt in his own comfortable being.)

Being in love has made a new man of me!

(Leaning stiffly forward, clutching the arm of the sofa, **Laura** *struggles visibly with her storm. But* **Jim** *is oblivious, she is a long way off.)*

The power of love is really pretty tremendous!

Love is something that – changes the whole world, Laura!

(The storm abates a little and **Laura** *leans back. He notices her again.)*

It happened that Betty's aunt took sick, she got a wire and had to go to Centralia. So Tom – when he asked me to dinner – I naturally just accepted the invitation, not knowing that you – that he – that I –

(He stops awkwardly.)

Huh – I'm a stumble-john!

(He flops back on the sofa.

The holy candles in the altar of **Laura's** *face have been snuffed out.*

There is a look of almost infinite desolation.

Jim *glances at her uneasily.)*

I wish that you would – say something. *(She bites her lip which was trembling and then bravely smiles. She opens her hand again on the broken glass ornament. Then she gently takes his hand and raises it level with her own. She carefully places the unicorn in the palm of his hand, then pushes his fingers closed upon it.)* What are you – doing that for? You want me to have him? – Laura? *(She nods.)* What for?

Laura: A – souvenir...

Tennessee Williams

Contemporary writers

> **Text suggestions**
>
> **Poetry**
>
> Selections from:
>
>   *Virago Book of Love Poetry* (ed. Wendy Mulford)
>
>   *Hand in Hand: An anthology of love poems* (ed. Carol Ann Duffy)
>
> **Prose**
>
> Ian McEwan: *Enduring Love*
>
> Alice Walker: *The Color Purple*
>
> Kiran Desai: *The Inheritance of Loss*
>
> Zadie Smith: *On Beauty*

The texts suggested here represent only a very small selection of the possibilities. Contemporary writers come from a wide variety of backgrounds and new works which explore the themes of love and relationships often reflect also the complexities of life in the culturally mixed communities of Britain and the United States.

Activity

1 The novel extract and the poem which follow both portray couples in the early stages of falling in love. Read both texts carefully, making notes on the way each writer uses language and imagery. In particular, think about:
   - whose point of view is being represented
   - the ways in which the lovers are described or presented
   - the effect of the weather and surroundings in the novel extract
   - the way the different forms of the texts shape your responses.

2 Now use your notes to write a comparison of the ways Kiran Desai and C.K. Williams present the experience of new love. You should also consider how your wider reading in the literature of love has contributed to your understanding of the extracts. (For example, you could look back at some of the other extracts which present people falling in love, earlier in this chapter.)

3 You could also look back at the extract from *The Glass Menagerie* on page 268 and compare the ways in which Tennessee Williams and Kiran Desai present the rather different encounters which take place when these two couples find themselves alone together for the first time.

Kiran Desai was born in India in 1971 and educated in India, England and the United States. *The Inheritance of Loss* is her second novel and won the Booker Prize in 2006. In it she explores the experience of love and other cultures. Here, Sai is supposed to be having a maths lesson with her new tutor, Gyan.

The Inheritance of Loss

In the drawing room, sitting with the newspapers, Sai and Gyan were left alone, quite alone, for the first time.

Kiki De Costa's recipe column: marvels with potatoes. Tasty treat with meat. Noodles with doodles and doodles of sauce and oodles and oodles of cheese.

Fleur Hussein's beauty tips.

The handsome baldy competition at the Calcutta Gymkhana Club had given out prizes to Mr Sunshine, Mr Moonshine, and Mr Will Shine.

Their eyes read on industriously, but their thoughts didn't cleave to such discipline, and finally Gyan, unable to bear this any longer, this tightrope tension between them, put down his paper with a crashing sound, turned abruptly toward her, and blurted:

'Do you put oil in you hair?'

'No,' she said, startled. 'I never do.'

After a bit of silence, 'Why?' she asked. Was there something wrong with her hair?

'I can't hear you – the rain is so loud,' he said, moving closer. 'What?'

'Why?'

'It looks so shiny I thought you might.'

'No.'

'It looks very soft,' he observed. 'Do you wash it with shampoo?'

'Yes.'

'What kind?'

'Sunsilk.'

Oh, the unbearable intimacy of brand names, the boldness of the questions.

'What soap?'

'Lux.'

'Beauty bar of the film stars?'

But they were too scared to laugh.

More silence.

'You?'

'Whatever is in the house. It doesn't matter for boys.'

He couldn't admit that his mother bought the homemade brown soap that was sold in large rectangles in the market, blocks sliced off and sold cheap.

The questions grew worse: 'Let me see your hands. They are so small.'

'Are they?'

'Yes.' He held his own out by hers. 'See?'

Fingers. Nails.

'*Hm.* What long fingers. Little nails. But look, you bite them.'

He weighed her hand.

'Light as a sparrow. The bones must be hollow.'

These words that took direct aim at something elusive had the deliberateness of previous consideration, she realized with a thud of joy.

*   *   *

Rainy season beetles flew by in many colors. From each hole in the floor came a mouse as if tailored for size, tiny mice from the tiny holes, big mice from big holes, and the termites came teeming forth from the furniture, so many of them that when you looked, the furniture, the floor, the ceiling, all seemed to be wobbling.

But Gyan did not see them. His gaze itself was a mouse; it disappeared into the belladonna sleeve of Sai's kimono and spotted her elbow.

'A sharp point,' he commented. 'You could do some harm with that.'

Arms they measured and legs. Catching sight of her foot –

'Let me see.'

'He took off his own shoe and then the threadbare sock of which he immediately felt ashamed and which he bundled into his pocket. They examined the nakedness side by side of those little tubers in the semidark.

Her eyes, he noted, were extraordinarily glamorous: huge, wet, full of theatre, capturing all the light in the room.

But he couldn't bring himself to mention them; it was easier to stick to what moved him less, to a more scientific approach.

With the palm of his hand, he cupped her head…

'Is it flat or is it curved?'

With an unsteady finger, he embarked on the arch of an eyebrow…

Oh, he could not believe his bravery; it drove him on and wouldn't heed the fear that called him back; he was brave despite himself. His finger moved down her nose.

The sound of water came from every direction: fat upon the window, a popgun off the bananas and the tin roof, lighter and messier on the patio stones, a low-throated gurgle in the gutter that surrounded the house like a moat. There was the sound of the *jhora* rushing and of water drowning itself in this water, of drainpipes disgorging into the rain barrels, the rain barrels brimming over, little sipping sounds from the moss.

The growing impossibility of speech would make other intimacies easier.

As his finger was about to leap from the tip of Sai's nose to her perfectly arched lips –

Up she jumped.

'*Owwaaa*,' she shouted.

He thought it was a mouse.

It wasn't. She was used to mice.

'*Oooph*,' she said. She couldn't stand a moment longer, that peppery feeling of being traced by another's finger and all that green romance burgeoning forth. Wiping her face bluntly with her hands, she shook out her kimono, as if to rid the evening of this trembling delicacy.

'Well, good night,' she said formally, taking Gyan by surprise. Placing her feet one before the other with the deliberateness of a drunk, she made her way toward the door, reached the rectangle of the doorway, and dove into the merciful dark with Gyan's bereft eyes following her.

She didn't return.

Kiran Desai

American poet C.K. Williams was awarded the Pulitzer Prize in 2000.

Love: Beginnings

They're at the stage where so much desire steams between them,
    so much frank need and want,

so much absorption in the other and the self and the self-admiring
    entity and unity they make –

her mouth so full, breast so lifted, head thrown back *so* far
    in her laughter at his laughter,

he so solid, planted, oaky, firm, so resonantly factual in the
    headiness of being craved so,

she almost wreathed upon him as they intertwine again, touch
    again, cheek, lip, shoulder, brow,

every glance moving toward the sexual, every glance away soaring
    back in the flame into the sexual –

that just to watch them is to feel that hitching in the groin,
    that filling of the heart,

the old, sore heart, the battered, foundered, faithful heart,
    snorting again, stamping in its stall.

C.K. Williams

Examination practice

Comparing two texts of the same genre

1 Read the two poems A and B carefully. They were written at different times by different writers.

Basing your answer on the poems and, where appropriate, your wider reading in the poetry of love, compare the ways the two poets have used poetic form, structure and language to express their thoughts and ideas.

A The Parting

Since there's no help, come let us kiss and part;
Nay, I have done, you get no more of me.
And I am glad, yea, glad with all my heart,
That thus so cleanly I myself can free.
Shake hands for ever, cancel all our vows,
And when we meet at any time again,
Be it not seen in either of our brows
That we one jot of former love retain.
Now at the last gasp of Love's latest breath,
When, his pulse failing, Passion speechless lies,
When Faith is kneeling by his bed of death,
And innocence is closing up his eyes.
Now if thou would'st, when all have given him over,
From death to life thou might'st him yet recover.

Michael Drayton

B *From* **The North Ship XXIV**

Love, we must part now: do not let it be
Calamitous and bitter. In the past
There has been too much moonlight and self-pity:
Let us have done with it: for now at last
Never has sun more boldly paced the sky,
Never were hearts more eager to be free,
To kick down worlds, lash forests; you and I
No longer hold them; we are husks, that see
The grain going forward to a different use.

There is regret. Always there is regret.
But it is better that our lives unloose,
As two tall ships, wind-mastered, wet with light,
Break from an estuary with their courses set,
And waving part, and waving drop from sight.

Philip Larkin

- -

2 Read the two drama extracts A and B carefully. They were written at different times by different writers.

Basing your answer on the extracts and, where appropriate, your wider reading in the literature of love, compare the ways the two dramatists have used language, dialogue, stage directions or other techniques to present their ideas and have an effect on the audience.

A The Double Dealer

Mellefont:	You're thoughtful, *Cynthia*?
Cynthia:	I'm thinking, that tho' Marriage makes Man and Wife One Flesh, it leaves 'em still Two Fools; and they become more Conspicuous by setting off one another.
Mellefont:	That's only when Two Fools meet, and their follies are oppos'd.
Cynthia:	Nay, I have known Two Wits meet, and by the opposition of their Wits, render themselves as ridiculous as Fools. 'Tis an odd Game we're going to Play at; what think you of drawing Stakes, and giving over in time?
Mellefont:	No, hang't, that's not endeavouring to Win, because it's possible we may lose; since we have Shuffled and Cut, let's e'en turn up Trump now.
Cynthia:	Then I fine it's like Cards: if either of us have a good Hand, it is an Accident of Fortune.
Mellefont:	No, Marriage is rather like a Game at Bowls; fortune indeed makes the match, and the Two nearest, and sometimes the Two farthest are together, but the Game depends entirely upon Judgment.
Cynthia:	Still, it is a Game, and Consequently one of us must be a Loser.
Mellefont:	Not at all; only a Friendly Trial of Skill, and the Winnings to be Shared between us. –

William Congreve

B Stags and Hens

Frances: It's great the way the music gets to y'though, isn't it? Y'can come to a disco or a dance an' be feelin' really last. But once y'walk into the music it gives y'a lift doesn't it? Makes y'feel special.

Linda: Yeh. *(After a pause.)* I get lost in music I do.

Frances: Yeh I do that.

Linda: I become someone else when the music's playin'. I do y'know.

Frances: Yeh I'm like that.

Linda: D'y'know if it wasn't for music I wouldn't be gettin' married tomorrow.

Frances: *(laughing)* Oh don't be stupid Linda. You're nuts sometimes. Y'are y'know.

Linda: I'm not bein' stupid. We were dancin' when he asked me to marry him. 'When A Man Loves A Woman' it was. I heard this voice in me ear, like it was part of the music, sayin' 'Will y'marry me?' So I said yeh. I would've said yeh if I'd been dancin' with Dracula's ugly brother.

Frances: Linda, stop bein' soft.

Linda: When the music stopped I looked up an' there was Dave, beamin' down at me, talkin' about gettin' married an' I'm wonderin' what he's on about, then I remembered. An' the next thing y'know I'm here, tonight.

Frances: Linda!

Linda: Oh come on, hurry up an' get me hair done. All I wanna do is get out there an' dance the night away. There mightn't be another opportunity after tonight.

Frances: Linda, you're gettin' married, not gettin' locked up! There y'go. *(She begins putting her implements away.)*

Linda: *(looking at herself in the mirror)* Y'do get frightened y'know. I mean if it was just gettin' married to Dave it'd be OK, he's all right Dave is. But it's like, honest, it's like I'm gettin' married to a town.

Frances: To a what?

Linda: It's not just like I'm marryin' Dave. It's like if I marry him I marry everythin'. Like, I could sit down now an' draw you a chart of everythin' that'll happen in my life after tomorrow.

Frances: *(Looking at her)* D'y'know something Linda, you're my best mate, but half the time I think you're a looney!

Linda: *(going into an exaggerated looney routine)* I am… *(She plays it up)*

Frances: *(laughing)* Linda… don't mess y'hair up…

Linda: *(quickly knocking her hair back into place, preparing to leave)* Well… look at it this way, after tomorrow I'll have me own Hoover, me own colour telly an' enough equipment to set up a chain of coffee bars.
(They go into the corridor and exit.)

Willy Russell

Comparing two texts of different genres

Write a comparison of the ways in which Wordsworth and Brittain write about the impact of the death of a loved one.

You should consider:

- the ways the writers' choices of language, form and structure shape your response to the extracts

- how your wider reading in the literature of love has contributed to your understanding and interpretation of the extracts.

C Sonnet

Surprized by joy – impatient as the Wind
I wished to share the transport – Oh! with whom
But Thee, long buried in the silent Tomb,
That spot which no vicissitude can find?
Love, faithful love recalled thee to my mind –
But how could I forget thee! – Through what power
Even for the least division of an hour,
Have I been so beguiled as to be blind
To my most grievous loss? – That thought's return
Was the worst pang that sorrow ever bore,
Save one, one only, when I stood forlorn,
Knowing my heart's best treasure was no more;
That neither present time, nor years unborn
Could to my sight that heavenly face restore.

William Wordsworth

D 'When the Vision Dies...' from Testament of Youth

Whenever I think of the weeks that followed the news of Roland's death, a series of pictures, disconnected but crystal clear, unroll themselves like a kaleidoscope through my mind.

A solitary cup of coffee stands before me on a hotel breakfast-table; I try to drink it, but fail ignominiously.

Outside, in front of the promenade, dismal grey waves tumble angrily over one another on the windy Brighton shore, and, like a slaughtered animal that still twists after life has been extinguished, I go on mechanically worrying because his channel-crossing must have been so rough.

In an omnibus, going to Keymer, I look fixedly at the sky; suddenly the pale light of a watery sun streams out between the dark, swollen clouds, and I think for one crazy moment that I have seen the heavens opened...

At Keymer a fierce gale is blowing and I am out alone on the brown winter ploughlands, where I have been driven by a desperate desire to escape from the others. Shivering violently, and convinced that I am going to be sick, I take refuge behind a wet bank of grass from the icy sea-wind that rushes, screaming, across the sodden fields.

It is late afternoon; at the organ of the small village church, Edward is improvising a haunting memorial hymn for Roland, and the words: 'God walked in the garden in the cool of evening', flash irrelevantly into my mind.

I am back on night-duty at Camberwell after my leave; in the chapel, as the evening voluntary is played, I stare with swimming eyes at the lettered wall, and remember reading the words: 'I am the Resurrection and the Life', at the early morning communion service before going to Brighton.

I am buying some small accessories for my uniform in a big Victoria Street store, when I stop, petrified, before a vase of the tall pink roses that Roland gave me on the way to *David Copperfield*; in the warm room their melting sweetness brings back the memory of that New Year's Eve, and suddenly, to the perturbation of the shop-assistants, I burst into uncontrollable tears, and find myself, helpless and humiliated, unable to stop crying in the tram all the way back to the hospital.

It is Sunday, and I am out for a solitary walk through the dreary streets of Camberwell before going to bed after the night's work. In front of me on the frozen pavement a long red worm wriggles slimily. I remember that, after our death, worms destroy this body – however lovely, however beloved – and I run from the obscene thing in horror.

It is Wednesday, and I am walking up the Brixton Road on a mild, fresh morning of early spring. Half-consciously I am repeating a line from Rupert Brooke:

The deep night, and birds singing, and clouds flying...

For a moment I have become conscious of the old joy in rainwashed skies and scuttling, fleecy clouds, when suddenly I remember – Roland is dead and I am not keeping faith with him; it is mean and cruel, even for a second, to feel glad to be alive.

Vera Brittain

14 The Extended Essay

Objectives

- To prepare for the task of writing an extended essay, and successfully complete the various steps needed in the process
- To build the ability to work independently and make informed choices of texts, topics and questions
- To further develop the skill of exploring relationships and comparisons between literary texts

Working on an extended essay for coursework offers you an opportunity to work more independently than you may have done in other parts of the course, and to develop skills that will be very useful if you go on to study literature or other arts subjects at a higher level. Teachers or lecturers may organize this in different ways, but usually you will have the chance to make your own choice of some of the texts that you study and to devise your own question or theme to explore. This may seem daunting at first, if you are used to being told which texts to study and guided through them, but teachers or lecturers will offer help and support as you go through the process. In the end, most students gain a sense of great satisfaction and 'ownership' from completing an extended essay. It can help you to develop confidence in your own ideas, which is invaluable if you plan to study at university, where you will be expected to organize your own work and think for yourself.

The extended essay requires you to undertake the comparison of three texts of your own choice, linked either by the theme of 'Love Through the Ages' or by a theme of your own choice. One of the texts must be a Shakespeare play. The other two texts for comparison can be of any genre or period.

Making connections

Becoming skilful at making connections between things which may on the surface seem unrelated can be a useful way of making sense of some of the situations you encounter in real life, as well as in literature. In another conversation from Willy Russell's play *Educating Rita*, Rita reveals that, like many people, she has a natural ability to do this:

Rita: ... everyone behaves as though it's normal, y'know inevitable that there's vandalism an' violence an' houses burnt out an' wrecked by the people they were built for. There's somethin' wrong. An' like the worst thing is that y'know the people who are supposed to like represent the people on our estate, y'know the Daily Mirror an' the Sun, an' ITV an' the Unions, what are they tellin' people to do? They just tell them to go out an' get more money; it's like me, isn't it? y'know, buyin' new dresses all the time, isn't it? The Unions tell them to go out an' get more money an' ITV an' the papers tell them what to spend it on so the disease is always covered up.
*(**Frank** swivels round in his chair to face **Rita**.)*

Frank: *(after a pause)* Why didn't you take a course in politics?

Rita: Politics? Go way, I hate politics. I'm just tellin' y' about round our way. I wanna be on this course findin' out. You know what I learn from you, about art an' literature, it feeds me, inside. I can get through the rest of the week if I know I've got coming here to look forward to. Denny tried to stop me comin' tonight. He tried to get me to go out to the pub with him an' his mates. He hates me comin' here. It's like drug addicts, isn't it? They hate it when one of them tries to break away. It makes me stronger comin' here. That's what Denny's frightened of.

Frank: 'Only connect.'

Rita: Oh, not friggin' Forster again.

Frank: 'Only connect.' You see what you've been doing?

Rita: Just tellin' y' about home.

Frank: Yes, and connecting, your dresses/ ITV and the Daily Mirror. Addicts/ You and your husband.

Rita is hardly aware of what she is doing, but the study of literature provides you with the opportunity to practise making connections more consciously. Learning to relate literary texts to each other by linking their themes, or spotting how the human situations they present can appear to be very different and yet be parallel, or by analysing how authors can deal with the same topic in radically different ways, can be fascinating.

For Advanced Level courses, particularly at A2 level, you will be expected to demonstrate that you can recognize and understand literary connections like these and explore them effectively in writing. There are several situations in which your ability to compare texts will be assessed, but in the extended essay, it will be your chief concern.

Prepare to compare

It is likely that you will undertake the study of one or more Shakespeare plays with a teacher, as part of your exploration of 'Love Through the Ages' for Unit 3. You will also have studied plays by Shakespeare for GCSE and KS3. A Shakespeare play will be the starting point for your extended essay. (See Chapter 15 for some approaches to studying Shakespeare at A level.)

You may also prepare the other texts for the extended essay as a group. The suggestions offered here are intended to help you in situations where you are working more independently, on a topic of your own choice, with the support of a teacher or supervisor. The tasks you will need to complete can be broken down into the following stages:

Preparation

1 Choosing suitable texts

2 Getting to know your material

3 Clarifying your ideas

4 Formulating a question

5 Research and note-taking

1 Choose your texts

The first step in the process is to choose the texts that you are going to study and write about. You need to bear in mind that the texts you choose should be 'literary' and of sufficient quality to justify the effort you will put into studying them. However, because you are likely to be working on your extended essay over a period of several months, and will need to get to know your chosen books very well, it is also important that you choose texts that you enjoy and find interesting or inspiring in some way. You are likely to enjoy the task more and produce a much more effective essay if you are studying a subject that is personally meaningful to you.

Above all, the texts need to have some clear connections that will enable you to write an effective comparative study. They should not only give you the chance to discuss interesting links and parallels in plot, characters and theme, but should also provide you with opportunities to explore and comment on:

- the writers' styles and techniques
- choices of genre
- different narrative techniques
- individual choices of language and their effects
- the different ways writers structure ideas and develop similar themes.

You may already have some ideas about texts that interest you, but here are some suggestions to aid the process.

- Use one of the Shakespeare plays you have studied as a starting point. Brainstorm or list the themes that are highlighted in the play. For example, *Romeo and Juliet* is about tragic love, love and conflict, forbidden love, love between people from divided backgrounds; *King Lear* involves themes of youth versus old age, madness, conflict between parents and children, misperceptions of reality, loyalty; *Othello* includes mixed-race marriage, jealousy, and deceit. Choose one of these themes and look for texts by other writers who have explored it in their work in similar or contrasting ways.

- Teachers may set up a special session or meeting where there will be lots of texts available for you to browse through and a chance to discuss your ideas and interests individually. They can help to suggest texts that will interest you and point out possible connections between them.

- You may have read a book that you particularly enjoyed and want to use in your essay, but need some help with choosing other texts. Think about what made the book interesting to you and ask your teachers for suggestions.

- Do some research on your own. If your school or college has a library, set aside some time to explore the books that are available. Browsing in public libraries and bookshops can be useful too.

- Ask around. Friends, family and fellow students may be able to recommend books they have enjoyed.

Examples

The table below shows just a few of the possibilities open to you – there are many more.

Shakespeare	Texts for comparison	Themes and connections
Romeo and Juliet	Emily Brontë: *Wuthering Heights* John Keats: *Selected Poems*	How writers present passionate love
	Kiran Desai: *The Inheritance of Loss* Marguerite Duras: *The Lover* Edna O'Brien: *Girl with Green Eyes*	Love and passion set against a background of conflict
King Lear	Rohinton Mistry: *Family Matters* Thomas Hardy: *The Mayor of Casterbridge*	Families; relationships between parents and children; conflict between the generations
	Jane Smiley: *A Thousand Acres* Edward Bond: *Lear*	Versions of the 'Lear' story
Othello	Ian McEwan: *Enduring Love* Thomas Hardy: *Tess of the D'Urbervilles*	Love, jealousy and rejection
	Ruth Prawer Jhabvala: *Heat and Dust* Marguerite Duras: *The Lover*	Cross-cultural relationships
	Andrea Levy: *Small Island* Lemn Sissay (editor): *The Fire People: A Collection of Contemporary Black British Poets*	Black experience
The Tempest	Chinua Achebe: *Things Fall Apart* Brian Friel: *Translations*	Colonialism; language and power
The Merchant of Venice	George Eliot: *Daniel Deronda* Primo Levi: *If This Is a Man* Primo Levi: *If Not Now, When?* Thomas Keneally: *Schindler's Ark*	The experience and treatment of Jewish people
The Taming of the Shrew	George Bernard Shaw: *Pygmalion* George Eliot: *Middlemarch* Charlotte Brontë: *Jane Eyre* Jean Rhys: *Wide Sargasso Sea* Marilyn French: *The Women's Room*	The 'perfect wife'; women's experience of marriage
Measure for Measure	David Hare: *Murmuring Judges* Charles Dickens: *Bleak House*	Justice and the legal system

2 Get to know your material

Once you have chosen your texts, you need to become very familiar with them. Your aim is to know them well enough to be able to find material as you need it and to be comfortable moving backwards and forwards from one to the other.

- Start by reading each of your texts straight through to gain an overview – and for enjoyment. If you have already studied the Shakespeare play, watch a film version of it or try to see a live performance. You will already have ideas about some of the connections between your texts, or themes you plan to write about, so keep these in the back of your mind as you read.

- Do some research about the contexts of your texts. When were they written? What was going on at the time? How may this have influenced the authors? How do the contexts of your other texts differ from the age of Shakespeare? How is this apparent in their content and/or in the way they are written?

- Once you know your way around the texts and their main themes, you will also wish to read some critical material and interpretations of your texts. This can help you see the texts in different ways and spark ideas for essay questions, but, as always, remember that other people's views are only a part of the exercise – they can never be a substitute for your own considered opinions, based on your own careful reading of the texts.

3 Clarify your ideas

Once you have a good overview of each text, you need to find ways of focusing your thoughts and ideas effectively, not just about one text at a time but about all three together. This will help you in the process of formulating connections and contrasts.

It is usually helpful to focus first on the **connections**. Establish the major links between the texts first, making sure that you are clear about any similarities in themes, characters or their situations.

You can then go on to note more specific or detailed similarities. These may be to do with:

- the contexts in which the texts were written
- the settings or 'worlds' the texts present
- the writers' attitudes to the same subject or theme
- the narrative viewpoints they use
- how the texts are structured
- the tone of the writing, e.g. serious, humorous, satirical, ironic, tragic, etc.
- the use of imagery or its absence
- vocabulary
- other stylistic features.

Then turn your attention to the **contrasts**. Concentrate on noting what makes the texts **different** in any of the above ways.

For example, below are a few of the ways we can connect and contrast three texts which can be said to explore the experience of living in territories which have been colonized:

- Shakespeare: *The Tempest*
- Chinua Achebe: *Things Fall Apart*
- Brian Friel: *Translations*

Connections

- All three texts present situations where there is conflict between the indigenous people of a country or territory and outsiders who have usurped power or assumed control. (Although this is not Shakespeare's central or only theme in *The Tempest*, the play offers enough material to provide interesting parallels.)
- Language is an issue in all of the texts. Each shows how language may be used as a means of subduing indigenous cultures and controlling those who are less powerful; each also shows how people resist such control.
- Each text features a character who is a leader or representative of the native community; each also includes a contrasting character who represents the incomers.
- The incomers all believe themselves superior and that the 'natives' benefit from their presence.
- The native 'culture' or community in each case breaks down or is damaged in some way.

Contrasts

- The texts have very different contexts and settings. *The Tempest*, one of Shakespeare's 'last plays', was first performed around 1612, and is a fantasy tale, set on an imaginary island. *Things Fall Apart* is a twentieth-century novel which explores the impact of British missionaries on an Ibo tribal community in Nigeria. Friel's play *Translations* was first performed in 1980, but portrays life in an Irish village in 1830, when Ireland was under English rule.
- The different genres of the texts mean that the stories and themes are presented in very different ways.
- Different viewpoints are offered in the texts. In *Translations*, the audience is invited into the village community of Baile Beag, and for the most part, shares the point of view of the villagers rather than the English soldiers. While Achebe uses a straightforward third-person narrative, the missionaries and their white leader are described from the point of view of the Ibo. In *The Tempest*, in Shakespeare's time at least, the audience would have been expected to side with Prospero in viewing the native Caliban as a monster.
- Language styles in the three texts are very different. Shakespeare's language is typically poetic and full of imagery; Achebe's clear, direct prose is intended to give a flavour of how the story would be told in a culture which has an oral rather than a written tradition; Friel's play uses a combination of languages in his dialogue.

Sometimes, you will find that the contrasts between texts become more apparent once you have made the connections. The differences grow out of the similarities. Here is an example, of some of the ways we can connect and contrast three more related texts.

- Shakespeare: *Romeo and Juliet*
- Emily Brontë: *Wuthering Heights*
- Kiran Desai: *The Inheritance of Loss*

Connections	Contrasts
All three texts present passionate love stories	**But** they were written at different times, in different genres, and have different settings. *Romeo and Juliet* is an Elizabethan play set in Renaissance Italy; *Wuthering Heights* is a Victorian novel, set in a small community on the Yorkshire moors; *The Inheritance of Loss* is a contemporary novel, set in Kalimpong, at the edge of the Himalayas, in India.
All three love stories are set against a background of conflict, violence and hatred	**But** *Romeo and Juliet* takes place amid an ongoing feud between 'two households both alike in dignity', while *Wuthering Heights* illustrates conflict both between and within two families of very different social class and character, the dark, passionate, stormy Earnshaws, and the fair, refined, gentle Lintons. *The Inheritance of Loss* also revolves around two families of different status, the Judge and his granddaughter, Sai, on one hand, and their cook and his son, Biju, who struggles to make a life for himself in New York, but it is conflict between Nepalese insurgents and the English-speaking authorities which tears apart the relationship of Sai and Gyan.
Each text enables the audience or reader to share the point of view of more than one character or see events from different perspectives	**But** different genres allow different possibilities and different dramatic and narrative techniques are used in each case. Through the dramatic presentation of different scenes, and dialogue, Shakespeare can allow the audience to understand the intentions and motives of different characters, such as Paris, or Friar Lawrence, as well as Romeo and Juliet themselves. The two novels use very different approaches to narrative. In *Wuthering Heights*, Emily Brontë uses two first-person narrators, Lockwood and Nelly Dean, neither of whom is a central character. They are onlookers, who nevertheless influence the action and impose their very different personalities on the style of the narrative. Kiran Desai opts for an unobtrusive 'omniscient' third-person narrative, which allows us to enter into the thoughts and feelings of different characters.

(Continued)

The authors use a range of ways to engage the audience or reader and maintain interest or tension	**But** this is achieved in different ways. Shakespeare uses various hints early in the play to signal to the audience that the outcome will be tragic and also makes use of dramatic irony, for example in the fight in Act 3, which is partly triggered by the characters' ignorance of the marriage of Romeo and Juliet, to which the audience have been party in Act 2. *Wuthering Heights* is a 'fractured' narrative, which departs from chronological order and uses various flashbacks, creating interest and tension for the reader. In *The Inheritance of Loss*, the narrative is also fractured, with two parallel, but related storylines, some flashbacks, and many shifts of perspective, which keep the reader waiting for the next stage in each thread of the narrative.
All three writers make use of imagery and description of the natural world to enhance their portrayal of passionate love	**But** their styles are very different. Simile and metaphor feature when Romeo and Juliet first meet (e.g. see the extract in Chapter 13, page 243) and religious metaphors represent their first kiss, while the lovers refer to the natural world around them when they have to part after their first night together. The imagery of the love of Catherine and Heathcliff in *Wuthering Heights* is extremely powerful, even violent, and rooted in the natural world of the moors. The natural world and the surroundings also feature in *The Inheritance of Loss*. For example, the romance of Sai and Gyan blossoms against the background of the monsoon rains. The colours and sounds of the rain and the insects and animals it brings forth enhance or symbolize the sense of new life and growth in their relationship (see the extract on page 271).

4 Formulate your question

So far, we have looked at a whole range of ways in which connections can be made between texts that share a theme. However, in your extended essay, you will not be required to write about all those aspects of the texts at the same time, but to choose one area to focus on in depth. From this, you will create your question. This needs careful thought, as a good question can make all the difference between a highly effective extended essay and a weak piece of writing with no clear direction. Your teacher should be able to help you to word your question in a way that will enable you to succeed.

The best questions:

- are well focused, on a limited, specific topic which you can explore in depth
- are challenging, but not too complex
- require you to analyse and compare the ways the writers have used language and literary techniques as well as themes; this is vital for achieving good grades.

Sample questions

As an example, we will look again at the theme of love in *Romeo and Juliet*, *Wuthering Heights* and *The Inheritance of Loss*. Here is a selection of questions based on some of the starting points for comparison we considered above. Question A is the most general and open-ended; the others require an increasingly narrow focus. Any one of them would offer the potential for a successful extended essay. However, Question A might be slightly too broad in focus, while Question E could be too limiting.

A Looking closely at the language used by each author, discuss the ways in which love is presented by Shakespeare in *Romeo and Juliet*, Brontë in *Wuthering Heights* and Desai in *The Inheritance of Loss*.

B In each of these texts, love is threatened or destroyed by conflict. Compare the different ways in which the authors handle this theme.

C Compare and contrast the settings of these three texts, exploring how the setting is presented and how it inter-relates with the central love story in each case.

D How does each of these authors 'tell the story'? Discuss the narrative techniques used by each of the novelists, and compare them with the strategies Shakespeare uses to present his story dramatically. Consider the effect on the reader or audience in each case.

E Explore the different ways in which these three very different authors use imagery to enhance their presentation of the experience of love.

Key words and phrases in questions can be used to guide you through the comparison, to help structure your response, and to keep your answer relevant.

Activity

1 Look at Questions B, C and D above, and decide which are the key words or phrases in each case (e.g. 'threatened', 'conflict'). Think about the meaning of each of the key words in relation to each of the texts, and about any questions that might arise from them.

2 If you have not already done so, devise your own extended essay question, making sure you are clear about the key words and the ideas you intend to explore.

5 Research and note-taking

Now that you have a clear idea of your question, you will need to re-read the texts, but this time making careful notes, using annotations, highlighting, and any other methods you find helpful. Your aim is to find the material you will need to make detailed comparisons. (Look back at Chapter 4 for suggestions.) It is useful to have your own copies of texts for this task, so that you can make as many notes on them as you wish. In particular, look out for and highlight passages or scenes which are relevant to your theme, and which will provide you with examples and quotations to discuss. Passages that demonstrate clear parallels or contrasts between the texts will be especially useful.

For example, here are three short extracts from our sample texts, which would provide some useful material for questions A, D, or E above.

Activity

1 Read the extracts which follow, each of which presents a kiss between lovers. Even if you have not read the whole texts, you will be able to see that the texts have some parallels – and some contrasts too.

2 In a group of three, choose one text each and make detailed notes on how language and imagery are used in your extract. Look at

   • your response to the characters
   • dialogue
   • structure/ form
   • choice of vocabulary
   • use of simile/ metaphor
   • the overall 'feeling', tone or atmosphere that is generated.

3 Now present your ideas to the other members of your group, share your notes and discuss the similarities and differences between your findings.

4 Use your notes to write a short essay, based on the extracts, in response to this question:

   Compare and contrast the ways in which these three moments of intimacy are presented.

At the ball given by Juliet's father, Romeo has fallen in love with Juliet at first sight. (See Chapter 13, page 243). Here, a few moments later, they speak to each other – and kiss – for the first time.

Romeo and Juliet

Romeo: If I profane with my unworthiest hand
This holy shrine, the gentle sin is this;
My lips, two blushing pilgrims, ready stand
To smooth that rough touch with a tender kiss.

Juliet: Good pilgrim, you do wrong your hand too much,
Which mannerly devotion shows in this;
For saints have hands that pilgrims' hands do touch,
And palm to palm is holy palmers' kiss.

Romeo: Have not saints lips, and holy palmers too?

Juliet: Ay, pilgrim, lips that they must use in prayer.

Romeo: O! then, dear saint, let lips do what hands do;
They pray, grant thou, lest faith turn to despair.

Juliet: Saints do not move, though grant for prayers' sake.

Romeo: Then move not, while my prayers' effect I take.
Thus from my lips, by thine, my sin is purg'd.
(Kissing her.)

Juliet: Then have my lips the sin that they have took.

Romeo: Sin from my lips? O trespass sweetly urg'd!
Give me my sin again.

Juliet: You kiss by th'book.

William Shakespeare

- -

This is the first kiss of Sai and Gyan, whom we met in Chapter 13, on page 271.

The Inheritance of Loss

'Kiss me!' he pleaded.
'No,' she said, delighted and terrified.
She would hold herself ransom.
Oh, but she had never been able to stand suspense.
A fine drizzle spelled an ellipsis on the tin roof…
Moments clocked by precisely, and finally she couldn't bear it – she closed her eyes and felt the terrified measure of his lips on hers, trying to match one shape with the other.

*   *   *

Just a week or two later, they were shameless as beggars, pleading for more.
'Nose?' He kissed it.
'Eyes?' Eyes.
'Ears?' Ears.
'Cheek?' Cheek.
'Fingers.' One, two, three, four, five.
'The other hand, please.' Ten kisses.
'Toes?'
They linked word, object, and affection in a recovery of childhood, a confirmation of wholeness, as at the beginning –
Arms legs heart –
All their parts, they reassured each other, were where they should be.

Kiran Desai

- -

Emily Brontë's dark novel portrays the deep and stormy relationship between Heathcliff and Catherine Earnshaw. Earlier in the novel, Catherine underestimated the power of this bond and married the more refined Edgar Linton. In this episode, when she is ill and dying, Heathcliff returns.

Wuthering Heights

In her eagerness she rose, and supported herself on the arm of the chair. At that earnest appeal, he turned to her, looking absolutely desperate. His eyes wide, and wet at last, flashed fiercely on her; his breast heaved convulsively. An instant they held asunder; and then how they met I hardly saw, but Catherine made a spring, and he caught her, and they were locked in an embrace from which I thought my mistress would never be released alive. In fact, to my eyes, she seemed directly insensible. He flung himself into the nearest seat, and on my approaching hurriedly to ascertain if she had fainted, he gnashed at me, and foamed like a mad dog, and gathered her to him with greedy jealousy. I did not feel as if I were in the company of a creature of my own species; it appeared that he would not understand, though I spoke to him; so, I stood off and held my tongue, in great perplexity.

A movement of Catherine's relieved me a little presently: she put up her hand to clasp his neck, and bring her cheek to his, as he held her: while he, in return, covering her with frantic caresses, said wildly –

'You teach me now how cruel you've been – cruel and false. *Why* did you despise me? *Why* did you betray your own heart, Cathy? I have not one word of comfort – you deserve this. You have killed yourself. Yes, you may kiss me, and cry; and wring out my kisses and tears. They'll blight you – they'll damn you. You loved me – then what *right* had you to leave me? What right – answer me – for the poor fancy you felt for Linton? Because misery, and degradation, and death, and nothing that God or Satan could inflict would have parted us, *you*, of your own will, did it. I have not broken your heart – *you* have broken it – and in breaking it, you have broken mine. So much the worse for me, that I am strong. Do I want to live? What kind of living will it be when you – oh God! Would you like to live with your soul in the grave?'

'Let me alone. Let me alone,' sobbed Catherine. 'If I've done wrong, I'm dying for it. It is enough! You left me too; but I won't upbraid you! I forgive you. Forgive me!'

'It is hard to forgive, and to look at those eyes, and feel those wasted hands,' he answered. 'Kiss me again; and don't let me see your eyes! I forgive what you have done to me. I love my murderer – but yours! How can I?'

They were silent – their faces hid against each other, and washed by each other's tears.

Emily Brontë

Activity

1 Find passages, scenes or poems from each of the texts you have chosen for your own extended essay, which offer you a clear opportunity to make detailed comparisons.

2 Carry out the same process as we have done with these examples. You may find it useful to relate the ideas from the close reading strategy in Chapter 7 to extracts or poems from your texts.

3 Save your notes and any practice essays to help you when you write your extended essay.

Writing your essay

Now that you have become familiar with your texts, formulated your question, made notes and gathered your ideas, you are ready to begin the process of writing your extended essay. At this point, it may be useful to remind yourself of the advice on planning, structuring and writing essays in Chapters 5 and 6. All of this is particularly relevant to the extended essay.

Writing comparatively about three texts is inevitably a more complex process than writing about a single one. Sometimes it may seem easier to resort to writing about one text at a time, perhaps making an attempt to link them in the final stages of your essay. However, this is not true comparative writing and rarely produces a satisfactory result. It is much better to develop the skill of weaving together your ideas and arguments about all three texts throughout your writing, even if this seems more difficult initially.

The writing process involves several stages:

1 Planning

First, you need to structure your ideas and make a plan for your essay. Always keeping your question in mind, make a list of the main ideas and points you are going to explore, and then arrange them in an order that will allow you to link them in a logical way. An outline plan is suggested on page 93.

2 The first draft

Very often, students find actually starting to write the essay quite difficult. In particular, it is common to get stuck when deciding on the exact starting point or the exact form of words of the first paragraph. The main thing at this stage, though, is to let go of the idea of perfection and get something down on paper that you can begin to develop. It is worth taking this approach to the essay as a whole, too. This is only the first draft of your essay and it is likely that quite extensive revision and editing will take place before you are happy with your final version. In fact, it would be extremely unusual – and not advisable – for a student to submit the first draft of an extended essay for assessment without any changes or revisions having been made.

Once you have completed the first draft, you can ask your teacher or supervisor to read it and give you some feedback. This will normally be in the form of general guidance. They will not be able to edit your essay in detail, but can point out which aspects of your work are successful and which need further development or improvement.

3 Revising and editing

Now you are ready to begin the task of revising and editing your work. Many students find at this point that they are trying to handle too much material, and need to use the revising and editing stage to select and organize their work more effectively. Be prepared to re-draft as much as you need to in order to produce a 'polished' final piece of work.

Different students have different ways of approaching revision and editing but it can be useful to read through your work marking any alterations, deletions, amendments, etc. with a different coloured pen. Sections that require more extensive re-writing or alterations can be asterisked and numbered and new sections written and inserted.

If you are using a computer, it is possible to edit your work directly on-screen, but you will probably find it easier to work on a printed copy, which allows you to see all your work at once, rather than endlessly scrolling up and down. When your revisions are complete, you are ready to begin your final version.

4 The final version

Working from your revisions you now need to write your final version. However, it is worth remembering when you are writing it that you can still make alterations to it even at this stage. If, in the course of your writing, you come across a section you are not happy with or a new idea strikes you that would improve your work further, then you can still make changes. The 'final' version is only really 'final' when you have handed it in!

5 Presenting your essay

This is a major piece of coursework and it is important to present it in a way that will make a good impression. As well as being accurate, and typed or legibly written, it is good practice to acknowledge the sources you have used and any references you have made, directly or indirectly, to the words of someone else.

Obviously, in a literature essay, you will quote often from the texts you are comparing. As long as you show those quotations clearly, using quotation marks, or for longer quotations, by indenting and separating them from the main body of your writing, you do not need to acknowledge them further.

If you have used information or critical writing from books other than the texts you are comparing, or from Internet sources, you must acknowledge this clearly. Using material from sources without acknowledgement is known as plagiarism and is a form of malpractice that can have serious consequences. If plagiarism is discovered, the candidate concerned will not be awarded a qualification.

Sources are acknowledged using **references**, which can be presented in various ways.

- Number each reference as it crops up in your work. At the end of your essay make a numbered list of references, each linked to the corresponding number in the text. Each reference should give: the name of the author or editor of the book, the title of the book, the name of the publisher, the year it was published, and the page reference. It is rarely advisable to use references from the Internet, but if you do, you need to include the whole web address, followed by the date on which you accessed the site.

- Alternatively, place the details of the reference in brackets in the main body of your essay, immediately after the quotation or reference.

Finally, add your **bibliography**. This should list all the books and other material that you have used in producing your essay. These should be in alphabetical order of the authors' surnames, and for each text, you should give details of: author(s)/ editor; title; date; place of publication; publisher.

Your teacher or supervisor will give you advice about how to do this if necessary.

How your work will be assessed

Your teacher will make an initial assessment of your essay, then it will be passed on to an external moderator or examiner who will finalize your grade.

Four Assessment Objectives will be used to assess your work. The most important of these are:

- **AO1** Articulate creative, informed and relevant responses to literary texts, using appropriate terminology and concepts, and coherent, accurate written expression.

- **AO2** Demonstrate detailed critical understanding in analysing the ways in which structure, form and language shape meanings in literary texts.

- **AO3** Explore connections and comparisons between different literary texts, informed by interpretations of other readers.

Examiners are also looking for some evidence that you recognize the importance of context, though this is given less weight in the extended essay than in other parts of the course:

- **AO4** Demonstrate understanding of the significance and influence of the contexts in which literary texts are written and received.

15 Shakespeare Study

Objectives

- To understand the relationship between your study of a Shakespeare play and the other texts you will study for Unit 4
- To identify ways in which you can approach the study of a Shakespeare play
- To prepare yourself for writing about Shakespeare
- To consider some of the features to look for in Shakespearean drama

Shakespeare has always held a dominant position in the drama element of English literature at AS and A level. By the time you reach this stage in your studies you will probably have encountered several Shakespeare plays already. It is likely that you will have studied Shakespeare for Key Stage 3 and Key Stage 4, so you will already be aware of some of the features that characterize his plays.

Exactly which play you study may depend on which particular text is selected by your teacher or lecturer, or your teacher or lecturer may, with guidance, help you to select your own text. However you arrive at the text that you will study, ultimately you will need to compare your Shakespeare text with two other texts you have studied for this unit and produce a 3000-word comparative essay linking them through theme. What you need to do to successfully complete your extended essay is explored in Chapter 14. Obviously, though, before you can compare your Shakespeare text with other texts you must know and understand your Shakespeare well.

Shakespeare and drama

Since Shakespeare is a dramatist, it follows that his plays have a great deal in common with those of other dramatists. In this respect, much of what you learned from the chapter on drama is applicable to Shakespeare's plays too.

They follow the clear structural pattern that we discussed in some detail earlier:

EXPOSITION → DRAMATIC INCITEMENT → COMPLICATION → CRISIS → RESOLUTION

Similarly, Shakespeare's plays also make use of sub-plots or secondary plots which, although separate from the main action, link with it in some way.

Approaching your text

In approaching the Shakespeare text you are studying, make use of the knowledge you already possess as to the nature of drama generally. This can help you understand the plot of your Shakespeare text when reading it for the first time. For example, it will help if you know that Shakespeare's plays follow this pattern:

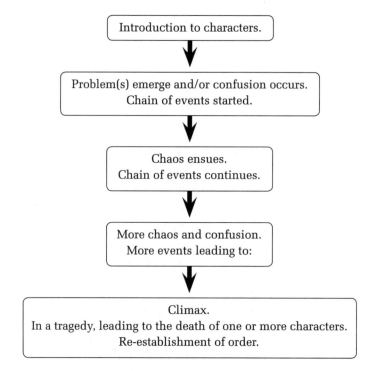

Knowledge of this general structure can help you to follow the storyline of any play, but more than this, it can provide you with a framework for your analysis of the play as a whole. One of the problems that students frequently encounter when studying a Shakespeare text is that they focus so closely on detailed summaries of scene, character and theme that they sometimes lose sight of the fact that the play is an integrated whole. Being able to see the play in terms of its overall framework can help you to appreciate the broad pattern of the text, thus helping you to make sense of the detail when it emerges through more detailed study.

Shakespeare's plays

There are various ways in which the plays of Shakespeare can be categorized, but a useful and simple method is to divide them into histories, tragedies and comedies.

The texts most frequently studied for AS and A level are as follows:

Histories	Tragedies	Comedies
Richard II	Hamlet	The Taming of the Shrew
Henry IV (Part 1)	Macbeth	Love's Labour's Lost
Henry IV (Part 2)	Othello	A Midsummer Night's Dream
Henry V	King Lear	Much Ado About Nothing
Richard III	Romeo and Juliet	The Merchant of Venice
Antony and Cleopatra		As You Like It
Coriolanus		Twelfth Night
Julius Caesar		

In addition, there are two further categories for a handful of plays that do not fit easily into the three broad areas.

Problem comedies	Romances
Troilus and Cressida	*Cymbeline*
All's Well That Ends Well	*The Winter's Tale*
Measure for Measure	*The Tempest*

Let's have a closer look at some of the features of plays in each of these categories.

The histories

The main history plays that you are likely to encounter in studying English at AS or A level are *Richard II*, *Henry IV Part 1*, *Henry IV Part 2*, *Henry V*, and *Richard III*, all of which focus on a specific period of English history. Added to these five are the Roman history plays, *Coriolanus*, *Julius Caesar*, and *Antony and Cleopatra*. It appears that Shakespeare was the first playwright to write a real history play and to treat his material as a drama rather than a mere chronicle of events. His development of character, ideas and themes in these plays makes them far more than simple chronicles, because he adapts historical facts to suit his dramatic purpose.

Although each of Shakespeare's histories is very different from the others in many respects, they do have certain features in common. For example, history plays usually:

- present famous historical figures at moments of crisis in their lives
- concern themselves with the order and stability of the state
- portray rebels who create problems
- have heroes who are fallible
- examine the gap between an ideal notion of kingship and the less tidy reality
- accept the inevitability of disorder
- show that the failings and ambitions of individuals can disrupt the social order.

Activity

If you are studying a history play, think about these points and decide how many of them you can identify in it. Make a note of how each feature can be seen in your play.

The tragedies

The idea of disorder also lies at the heart of the tragedies. The Roman history plays are often included in the list of tragedies. The four plays that are regarded as 'the great' tragedies are *Hamlet*, *King Lear*, *Othello*, and *Macbeth*. These plays are very frequently set for study at A level. At the heart of each of these plays is the central character after whom the play is named – the **eponymous hero**, to give the technical term – and the action focuses very much on this character. However, other characters are important too, and often several innocent victims are claimed before the play reaches its end.

Overall, Shakespeare's tragedies have many of the key features we associate with the concept of dramatic tragedy in general.

- At the beginning of the play something occurs that disrupts the normal order of things.
- Chaos or disorder in society results.
- Extreme emotions are involved.
- Social restraint disintegrates.

A climax is reached, usually with the death of the main character (and several others) before order is restored. The purging of emotions that affects the audience at the end of a tragedy is sometimes referred to as **catharsis**.

Activity

If you are studying one of Shakespeare's tragedies, think about how the play fits this general pattern. Note down one thing that happens in the play which corresponds to each of the above features.

The comedies

The term 'comedy' in modern usage tends to be associated with something fairly lightweight that makes us laugh. However, in its original sense, and certainly as applied to the plays of Shakespeare, the term simply means a play that has a happy ending; the action that leads to this ending may be funny and light in tone, but equally it could deal with serious, even dangerous and life-threatening situations. Shakespearean comedy can deal with issues that are just as serious as those raised by other kinds of plays.

Shakespeare's comedies vary considerably both in style and the mood the play creates. Early comedies such as *The Taming of the Shrew, Love's Labour's Lost, A Midsummer Night's Dream*, and *Much Ado About Nothing*, or the later comedies, *As You Like It* and *Twelfth Night*, might reasonably be called romantic comedies, as love plays a central role in them. The general pattern for these comedies is as follows.

- Life is going on as normal.
- Characters fall in love.
- Various mishaps and misunderstandings threaten the happy outcome.
- The problems are resolved.
- The play ends happily with the various lovers united.

However, in some – notably *Much Ado About Nothing* – a good deal in the play verges on the tragic and in some ways is reminiscent of *Romeo and Juliet*. This serious edge is clearly there in *The Merchant of Venice* too, so much so that although the play ends happily for all except Shylock – almost a tragic figure at the end – the term tragicomedy has been applied to it. The basic pattern, then, is very similar to that of the tragedies.

- An event occurs.
- This leads to disorder and disruption.
- Confusion results.
- The problems are resolved.

The difference comes in the way that the action is resolved and the focus that is maintained. In a comedy, serious issues may be raised and addressed but the focus is very much on the foolishness of human behaviour, and the audience usually feels confident that all will turn out well. However, within this structure evil influences may be at work and the play may deal with the powerful negative forces that motivate characters – sexual appetite, lust for power, greed, and envy. These forces are nowhere more evident than in what are referred to as the problem comedies.

The problem comedies

Generally the problem comedies are taken to be *Measure for Measure*, *Troilus and Cressida*, and *All's Well That Ends Well*. In many ways these plays fall somewhere between tragedy and comedy – they avoid becoming tragic because they end 'happily', at least in so far as no one dies at the end of the play. They are also known as the **problem plays** or **dark comedies**.

A dark tone and flawed characters are typical of these plays. They are more likely to disturb the audience than amuse them, as they raise unsettling issues about the darker side of human nature. Like the other types of plays we have looked at, they centre on disorder within society, but whereas the comedies operate in a world of fantasy and make-believe, these plays take place in a very much bleaker and often coldly realistic environment.

It has been said that in writing these plays Shakespeare was experimenting with a dramatic form which brought together comedy and tragedy. If this is so, his experimentation culminated in the romance plays, written towards the end of his career.

The romance plays

The romances (or 'last plays'), *Pericles*, *Cymbeline*, *The Winter's Tale*, and *The Tempest*, are once again concerned with the idea of disorder. Unlike the problem comedies, which have a harshly realistic setting, these plays make much use of fantasy elements and magic to explore their central ideas. They operate in make-believe worlds and the plots often take improbable or incredible turns and twists. However, these features of the plays are essential to the effects that they create and the purpose they hope to achieve.

Certain key ideas can be seen emerging through all four of these plays.

- The play centres on a noble family and a king.
- An evil or misguided deed is done.
- This causes great suffering to characters and they endure years of separation.
- Through the suffering, something new and positive begins to emerge.
- In the end this new element transforms the old evil.
- An act of forgiveness resolves the problems, and reconciliation takes place. In simple terms the general pattern can be seen as:

PROSPERITY → DESTRUCTION → RE-CREATION

In many ways the unusual (sometimes bizarre) events that occur in the romances can present added difficulties when you are trying to establish the plot and characters in your mind. However, at their heart are the same features that are present in the other kinds of plays we have discussed. There is order versus disorder; love and harmony versus conflict and discord; and life falls short of the ideal because of human imperfection.

What type of Shakespeare play are you studying? Draw up a table of the key events and describe the plot structure, thinking about the overall pattern that is created.

Shakespeare's plots

As we have seen, the plots of Shakespeare's plays adhere to a general pattern common to many plays. However, when studying your text one of the first things you will need to do is to get to grips with the details of the plot. Very often your first encounter with the play will be through a reading, perhaps in class, with students taking the various parts. When reading the play either to yourself or as part of a group, though, it is easy to lose sight of the fact that you are studying a drama. The text you are reading was written to be performed and therefore brought to life on the stage. Although we now read Shakespeare's plays as 'literary texts', we must not forget this central fact, and you should view the 'text' as a 'script'. A 'script' suggests something that in itself is incomplete because it needs a dramatic enactment to achieve its purpose. This opens up the whole question of how the play is to be enacted, and touches on the fact that the play has many rather than a single meaning.

In coming to terms with the plot of a Shakespeare play, therefore, you first need to understand generally what is happening, and then think about ways in which this could be enacted on the stage. To help you appreciate the variety of ways that a play can be interpreted, you should try to see as many performances of it (live in the theatre, on film, or video, etc.) as you can.

In ten sentences, summarize the plot of the Shakespeare play you are studying. Then take the opening scene of that play and describe two possible, but contrasting, ways in which that scene could be enacted on the stage.

Structure

The structure of each play is integral to the way in which Shakespeare develops its central issues. The structure of his plays (or any play) can be viewed in two ways. What is sometimes called the **dynamic structure** of the play consists of the sequence of events which builds up in a 'cause and effect' fashion to create the plot of the play, and so drives the play forward.

Underlying this obvious structure, however, it is often possible to detect another that is less prominent but just as important. This second structure consists of various parallels and cross-references, or repeated images, symbols, and language that create a network of threads running through the play. This kind of structure is sometimes called the **symmetric structure**, and it can exert a powerful influence on the overall effect of a play.

In *Hamlet*, for example, the repeated parallels between Hamlet and Laertes as avenging sons, and Hamlet's repeated contemplation of death with its associated imagery, are just two elements that help to form a web of patterning developed throughout the play. Similarly, in *King Lear*, the theme of 'blindness' to the truth as well as physical blindness, presented through Gloucester and Lear, create parallels that give another kind of structure to the play.

> ## Activity
> Draw two diagrams, one to represent the dynamic structure of the Shakespeare play you are studying, the other to represent the symmetric structure.

Character in Shakespeare's plays

An essential part of the study of any play will be to study the characters and Shakespeare's methods of creating and presenting them.

To put it simply, Shakespeare uses three main techniques to create characters. They reveal themselves:

- through their actions
- by what others say about them
- through their own language.

Let's have a look at this in practice.

> ## Activity
> Examine the following extracts from *Othello*. Iago is the focus of them all.

Othello

Act II Scene 1

Iago: That Cassio loves her, I do well believe't:
That she loves him, 'tis apt and of great credit.
The Moor – howbeit that I endure him not –
Is of a constant, loving, noble nature,
And, I dare think, he'll prove to Desdemona
A most dear husband. Now, I do love her too;
Not out of absolute lust – though peradventure
I stand accountant for as great a sin –
But partly led to diet my revenge
For that I do suspect the lusty Moor
Hath leaped into my seat, the thought whereof
Doth, like a poisonous mineral, gnaw my inwards,
And nothing can, or shall, content my soul
Till I am evened with him, wife for wife;
Or failing so, yet that I put the Moor
At least into a jealousy so strong
That judgement cannot cure. Which thing to do
If this poor trash of Venice, whom I leash
For his quick hunting, stand the putting on,
I'll have our Michael Cassio on the hip,
Abuse him to the Moor in the rank garb –
For I fear Cassio with my night-cap too –
Make the Moor thank me, love me, and reward me
For making him egregiously an ass,
And practising upon his peace and quiet,
Even to madness. 'Tis here, but yet confused:
Knavery's plain face is never seen till used.

(*Exit*)

Act III Scene 3

(Enter Othello and Iago)

Emilia: Madam, here comes my lord.

Cassio: Madam, I'll take my leave.

Desdemona: Why, stay and hear me speak.

Cassio: Madam, not now: I am very ill at ease,
Unfit for mine own purposes.

Desdemona: Well, do your discretion.

*(Exit **Cassio**)*

Iago: Ha! I like not that.

Othello: What dost thou say?

Iago: Nothing, my lord; or if – I know not what.

Othello: Was not that Cassio parted from my wife?

Iago: Cassio, my lord? No, sure, I cannot think it
That he would sneak away so guilty-like,
Seeing you coming.

Othello: I do believe 'twas he.

Desdemona: How now, my lord?
I have been talking with a suitor here,
A man that languishes in your displeasure.

Act V Scene 1

*(He wounds **Roderigo**)*

Roderigo: O, I am slain!
*(**Iago** wounds **Cassio** in the leg, and exit)*

Cassio: I am maimed for ever. Help, ho! Murder, murder!
*(Enter **Othello**, above)*

Othello: The voice of Cassio: Iago keeps his word.

Roderigo: O, villain that I am!

Othello: It is even so.

Cassio: O, help, ho! A surgeon!

Othello: 'Tis he! O brave Iago, honest and just,
That hast such noble sense of thy friend's wrong,
Thou teachest me! Minion, your dear lies dead,
And your unblest fate lies. Strumpet, I come!
Forth of my heart those charms, thine eyes, are blotted;
Thy bed, lust-stained, shall with lust's blood be spotted.

*(Exit **Othello**)*

*(Enter **Lodovico** and **Gratiano**)*

Cassio: What, ho! No watch? No passage? Murder, murder!

Gratiano: 'Tis some mischance: the cry is very direful.

Cassio: O, help!

Lodovico: Hark!

Roderigo: O wretched villain!

Lodovico: Two or three groan. It is a heavy night.
These may be counterfeits. Let's think't unsafe
To come in to the cry without more help.

Roderigo: Nobody come? Then shall I bleed to death.

Lodovico: Hark!

*(Enter **Iago**, with a light)*

Gratiano: Here's one comes in his shirt, with light and weapons.

Iago: Who's there? Whose noise is this that cries on murder?

Lodovico: We do not know.

Iago: Did you not hear a cry?

Cassio: Here, here: for heaven's sake help me!

Iago: What's the matter?

Gratiano: This is Othello's Ancient, as I take it.

Lodovico: The same indeed, a very valiant fellow.

Iago: What are you here, that cry so grievously?

Cassio: Iago? O, I am spoiled, undone by villains!
Give me some help.

Act V Scene 2

Lodovico: Where is this rash and most unfortunate man?

Othello: That's he that was Othello: here I am.

Lodovico: Where is that viper? Bring the villain forth.

Othello: I look down towards his feet; but that's a fable.
If that thou be'st a devil, I cannot kill thee.

*(He wounds **Iago**)*

Lodovico: Wrench his sword from him.

Iago: I bleed, sir, but not killed.

Othello: I am not sorry neither; I'd have thee live,
For in my sense 'tis happiness to die.

Lodovico: O, thou Othello, that wast once so good,
Fallen in the practice of a damned slave,
What shall be said to thee?

Othello: Why, anything:
An honourable murderer, if you will:
For naught did I in hate, but all in honour.

Lodovico: This wretch hath part confessed his villainy.
Did you and he consent in Cassio's death?

Othello: Ay.

Cassio: Dear General, I never gave you cause.

Othello: I do believe it, and I ask your pardon.
Will you, I pray, demand that demi-devil
Why he hath thus ensnared my soul and body?

Iago: Demand me nothing; what you know, you know:
From this time forth I never will speak word.

1 What does each of the extracts tell you about the nature of Iago's character and the nature of Othello's character? Make a note how each feature is revealed.

2 Choose one of the central characters from the Shakespeare play that you are studying. Imagine that you are an actor who has been offered that part in a forthcoming production. Collect evidence from the play to support your view of the character and the way that you intend to play him or her on stage. Your evidence should consist of the following:

- what the character says about himself or herself
- what others say about the character
- what the character does when speaking
- what the character does when silent
- how the character's words match his or her actual deeds or underlying motives
- how the character is viewed by those around him or her.

This activity should help you form your own view of a character. Remember, though, there is more than one way of looking at a character. Characters in plays, like living people, can rarely be seen in clear-cut, black-and-white terms. As part of your preparation for writing about your play, it would be useful for you to make notes on each of the characters in the play you are studying, making sure that you cover the points in the following list.

- Consider all possible interpretations of the character.
- Assess the role or function that the character performs in the play.
- Examine in detail the key speeches the character makes and the scenes in which he or she appears.
- Gather a range of evidence from the play to support your view of the character.

Soliloquies and asides

In most of his plays Shakespeare makes full use of the dramatic devices of asides and soliloquies as a means of developing aspects of character.

In Shakespeare's *Othello* there is substantial use of both long and short asides. Often they reveal to the audience the wicked plan developing in Iago's mind, and give a glimpse into his thoughts and the delight he takes in his evil. In this unusually long aside we are shown his thoughts taking shape as he watches Desdemona and Cassio.

Othello

Act II Scene 1

Iago: *(Aside)* He takes her by the palm. Ay, well said, whisper. With as little web as this will I ensnare as great a fly as Cassio. Ay, smile upon her, do. I will gyve thee in thine own courtship. You say true, 'tis so indeed. If such tricks as these strip you out of your lieutenantry, it had been better you had not kissed your three fingers so oft, which now again you are most apt to play the sir in. Very good: well kissed, an excellent courtesy! 'Tis so indeed. Yet again your fingers to your lips? Would they were clyster-pipes for your sake!

The repeated use of asides also gives us an insight into Othello's growing torment. For example, in the following extract Iago urges him to secretly observe his conversation with Cassio, to convince Othello (quite wrongly) that Cassio and Desdemona are having an affair. In fact, he and Cassio are talking about Bianca.

Act IV Scene 1

Othello: *(Aside)* Look, how he laughs already!

Iago: I never knew a woman love man so.

Cassio: Alas, poor rogue! I think i'faith she loves me.

Othello: *(Aside)* Now he denies it faintly, and laughs it out.

Iago: Do you hear, Cassio?

Othello: *(Aside)* Now he importunes him to tell it o'er.
Go to, well said, well said!

Iago: She gives it out that you shall marry her.
Do you intend it?

Cassio: Ha, ha, ha!

Othello: *(Aside)* Do you triumph, Roman? Do you triumph?

Cassio: I marry her! What! A customer! Prithee bear some charity to my wit: do not think it so unwholesome. Ha, ha, ha!

Othello: *(Aside)* So, so, so, so: they laugh that win.

- -

And so Othello's jealousy builds and is communicated to the audience through the cumulative tension created by the asides.

Soliloquies, too, are used extensively to convey both information and inward emotion to the audience. In *Hamlet*, for example, it is possible to trace the development of Hamlet's shifting emotions during the course of the play through the sequence of soliloquies he delivers at various points in the action.

In *Henry IV Part 1* the following soliloquy allows us, the audience, to see the true nature of Prince Hal early on in the play. We see him in a light that none of the other characters can see. He has been a complete disappointment to his father, King Henry, and all the 'responsible' authority figures in the play, because of the wild and dissolute life he has been leading in the company of an old reprobate, Falstaff, and his dubious tavern and whorehouse companions. However, at the end of Act I Scene 2, after bantering with these companions in the tavern and becoming involved in the planning of a robbery, the Prince is left alone on the stage and delivers this soliloquy.

Henry IV Part 1

Act I Scene 2

Prince: I know you all, and will awhile uphold
The unyok'd humour of your idleness.
Yet herein will I imitate the sun,
Who doth permit the base contagious clouds
To smother up his beauty from the world,
That, when he please again to be himself,
Being wanted he may be more wonder'd at

By breaking through the foul and ugly mists
Of vapours that did seem to strangle him.
If all the year were playing holidays,
To sport would be as tedious as to work;
But when they seldom come, they wish'd-for come,
And nothing pleaseth but rare accidents:
So, when this loose behaviour I throw off,
And pay the debt I never promised,
By how much better than my word I am,
By so much shall I falsify men's hopes;
And, like bright metal on a sullen ground,
My reformation, glittering o'er my fault,
Shall show more goodly, and attract more eyes
Than that which hath no foil to set it off.
I'll so offend to make offence a skill,
Redeeming time when men think least I will.

In the second soliloquy, taken from *Henry IV Part 2*, we see the Prince at the bedside of his father as he sleeps. His father is ill and the Prince is likely to succeed to the throne.

Henry IV Part 2

Act IV Scene 5

Prince: Why doth the crown lie there upon his pillow,
Being so troublesome a bedfellow?
O polish'd perturbation! golden care!
That keep'st the ports of slumber open wide
To many a watchful night! Sleep with it now!
Yet not so sound and half so deeply sweet
As he whose brow with homely biggen bound
Snores out the watch of night. O majesty!
When thou dost pinch thy bearer, thou dost sit
Like a rich armour worn in the heat of day
That scald'st with safety. By his gates of breath
There lies a downy feather which stirs not.
Did he suspire, that light and weightless down
Perforce must move. My gracious lord! my father!
This sleep is sound indeed; this is a sleep
That from this golden rigol hath divorc'd
So many English kings. Thy due from me
Is tears and heavy sorrows of blood
Which nature, love, and filial tenderness,
Shall, O dear father, pay thee plenteously.
My due from thee is this imperial crown,
Which, as immediate from thy place and blood,
Derives itself to me. (*Putting on crown.*) Lo where it sits –
Which God shall guard; and put the world's whole strength
Into one giant arm, it shall not force
This lineal honour from me. This from thee
Will I to mine leave as 'tis left to me.

The soliloquy, then, is one key way in which Shakespeare lets us, the audience,
know what a character is really like. Through a soliloquy characters tell us directly
about themselves and can inform us about a whole range of issues, such as what is
in their minds, why they are acting as they are, what they intend to do in the future.

Othello

Act I Scene 3

Iago: Thus do I ever make my fool my purse:
        For I mine own gained knowledge should profane
        If I would time expend with such a snipe
        But for my sport and profit. I hate the Moor,
        And it is thought abroad that 'twixt my sheets
        He's done my office. I know not if't be true
        But I, for mere suspicion in that kind,
        Will do as if for surety. He holds me well:
        The better shall my purpose work on him.
        Cassio's a proper man: let me see now;
        To get his place and to plume up my will
        In double knavery. How? How? Let's see.
        After some time, to abuse Othello's ear
        That he is too familiar with his wife;
        He hath a person and a smooth dispose
        To be suspected, framed to make women false.
        The Moor is of a free and open nature,
        That thinks men honest that but seem to be so,
        And will as tenderly be led by th'nose
        As asses are.
        I have't. It is engendered. Hell and night
        Must bring this monstrous birth to the world's light.

                                                        (Exit)

Shakespeare's themes and ideas

Each of Shakespeare's plays is concerned with certain ideas or issues that recur and develop as the play progresses. These topics with which the play is preoccupied are the play's 'themes'. They are the subject that Shakespeare explores through the events, characters and language of the play. It is the themes that give a shape and pattern to the play and give it a significance beyond the events it describes.

The themes are developed through the language of the play, and often Shakespeare creates powerful images. For example, in *Othello* one of the themes of the play is 'honesty' and Iago's 'dishonesty'. The language itself draws attention to this theme in a variety of ways, one of which is the repetition of the word 'honest' to emphasize Othello's complete belief in Iago's 'honesty' and Desdemona's 'dishonesty'.

It has often been said that one of the reasons that Shakespeare's plays have remained so popular for so long, lies in the fact that they deal with great and universal themes that were of concern to people in Shakespeare's time, and are of no less significance to us today. His plays often deal with themes such as love, hate, envy, jealousy, death, revenge, guilt, corruption, destiny.

Certain themes seem to have particularly interested Shakespeare and can be seen in one form or another in all of his plays. These themes are:

- conflict
- appearance and reality
- order and disorder
- change
- love.

Conflict

Conflict, of one type or another, is the starting point for many dramas, and it can take many forms. In *Othello*, for example, we have the conflict between Iago and Othello (a conflict that Othello is unaware of until it is too late), and the inner conflict that Othello experiences as he battles to control his growing jealousy. In *Henry IV Part 2*, conflict exists externally as Henry faces rebellion.

Appearance and reality

In all of Shakespeare's plays there is a mis-match between how things seem to be and how they actually are. In *Othello*, for example, everyone thinks Iago is 'honest' but in fact he is completely the opposite. In *Twelfth Night*, Viola disguises herself as a boy, while in *Hamlet* the apparently popular and effective King, Claudius, is in reality guilty of the murder of his brother and seduction of his brother's wife. *Measure for Measure* is very concerned with 'seeming' as the Duke leaves his apparently incorruptible deputy, Angelo, in charge of the state, to see 'If power change purpose, what our seemers be'. He certainly finds out, when it is revealed that Angelo attempted to seduce the innocent Isabella.

Order and disorder

In all of Shakespeare's plays there is some kind of breakdown in order, and some form of confusion temporarily gains the upper hand. Sometimes the breakdown is in the order of the state, as in *Macbeth*, where the murder of Duncan plunges the state into turmoil and war. In *Henry IV* (Parts 1 and 2), King Henry faces rebellion and civil war, while *Twelfth Night* begins with Olivia's rejection of Orsino's suit and Viola shipwrecked on the coast of Illyria. The causes of the disruption vary from play to play, but they tend to include key causes such as jealousy, love, hate, and ambition. Very often the protagonist undergoes some kind of learning process during the course of the play before order is re-established.

Change

In all Shakespeare plays the characters undergo some kind of change. Sometimes the ultimate result of this change is death, as in *Othello*, where Othello changes from a respected military leader to a man eaten away by jealousy who murders his wife and then, realizing the terrible mistake he has made, takes his own life. In *Twelfth Night*, Malvolio changes from a puritan figure into a foolish lover.

Love

For Shakespeare, one of the instruments of change is love, which has a transforming power and is often at the heart of his plays. *Twelfth Night* begins with the words 'If music be the food of love, play on'. It goes on to present a world of romantic love. In *A Midsummer Night's Dream* we see young men and women who love each other but who also have to endure crosses and frustrations in love. In *Othello* we see a quite different portrayal of love, as Othello's love for Desdemona is corrupted into jealousy and hate by the scheming Iago.

Development of themes

Of course, there are many specific themes that can be traced in individual plays, but in one way or another they will relate to the four key areas discussed above.

The themes in Shakespeare's plays often develop in one of three ways:

*   An individual character or characters experience some personal difficulties or inner turmoil, perhaps moral or spiritual, that causes some mental conflict. For example, Hamlet struggles to come to terms with events and revenge his father.
*   The family, society, or the country is affected by turmoil. For example, the feuding Capulets and Montagues disrupt Verona in *Romeo and Juliet*, and Rome is at war with Egypt in *Antony and Cleopatra*.
*   Nature or the universe may be disordered, or supernatural events may be involved. Examples are the appearance of the witches and Banquo's ghost in *Macbeth*, or the storm imagery in *King Lear*.

At the heart of the development of the themes of a play is Shakespeare's rich and complex use of language.

Shakespeare's language

Often students encounter difficulties when first studying a Shakespeare play because they find the language of Shakespeare different in a number of ways from the kind of English they are used to. This difficulty is particularly evident when reading the text rather than watching the play being performed, when actions are brought to life and give the words much more meaning.

At first, concentrate on arriving at a broad understanding of what is happening, in terms of the plot of the play. Once this basic knowledge has been established, you will very soon progress to a more detailed study of the language of the play and the effects that it creates to bring the drama to life.

Here are some of the uses to which Shakespeare puts language:

- creating atmosphere
- opening scenes
- in songs
- in dialogue
- in puns and wordplay.

Creating atmosphere

You should remember that in Shakespeare's time theatres did not have the elaborate scenery, backdrops and the sophisticated technology that is used to create effects in modern theatres. If you have ever visited Shakespeare's Globe in London or seen drawings of the Elizabethan theatre, you will know that they had little more than a bare stage, and in that sense theatregoers went to 'hear' a play rather than to 'see' a play as we would say today. The plays would also usually take place in daylight, without the elaborate lighting effects we are used to today.

Apart from all its other important functions, language was therefore essential to the creation of setting and atmosphere. In a Shakespeare play the atmosphere and setting are created through words.

Look at the following extract from the opening scene of *Hamlet*.

Hamlet

Act I Scene 1
*(Enter **Barnardo** and **Francisco**, two sentinels)*

Barnardo: Who's there?

Francisco: Nay, answer me. Stand and unfold yourself.

Barnardo: Long live the King.

Francisco: Barnardo?

Barnardo: He.

Francisco: You come most carefully upon your hour.

Barnardo: 'Tis now struck twelve. Get thee to bed, Francisco.

Francisco: For this relief much thanks. 'Tis bitter cold,
And I am sick at heart.

Barnardo: Have you had quiet guard?

Francisco: Not a mouse stirring.

Barnardo: Well, good night.
If you do meet Horatio and Marcellus,
The rivals of my watch, bid them make haste.

*(Enter **Horatio** and **Marcellus**)*

Francisco: I think I hear them. Stand, ho! Who is there?

Horatio: Friends to this ground.

Marcellus: And liegemen to the Dane.

Francisco:	Give you good night.
Marcellus:	O, farewell honest soldier, Who hath relieved you?
Francisco:	Barnardo hath my place. Give you good night.

(Exit)

Marcellus:	Holla, Barnardo!
Barnardo:	Say, What, is Horatio there?
Horatio:	A piece of him.
Barnardo:	Welcome, Horatio. Welcome, good Marcellus.
Marcellus:	What, has this thing appeared again tonight?
Barnardo:	I have seen nothing.
Marcellus:	Horatio says 'tis but our fantasy, And will not let belief take hold of him Touching this dreaded sight, twice seen of us. Therefore I have intreated him along With us to watch the minutes of this night, That, if again this apparition come, He may approve our eyes and speak to it.
Horatio:	Tush, tush, 'twill not appear.
Barnardo:	Sit down awhile, And let us once again assail your ears, That are so fortified against our story, What we have two nights seen.
Horatio:	Well, sit we down, And let us hear Barnardo speak of this.
Barnardo:	Last night of all, When yon same star that's westward from the pole, Had made his course t'illume that part of heaven Where now it burns, Marcellus and myself, The bell then beating one –

Activity

Read the extract carefully and try to 'feel' the atmosphere that is being created.

Identify the ways in which Shakespeare creates a sense of the atmosphere through the language.

Here are some points you may have noted:

- The opening challenge 'Who's there?' creates a sense of tension.
- The darkness (remember, Shakespeare's plays were performed in daylight) is created through the language.
- There is a sense of fear about what is to happen next.
- The fact that it is midnight is clearly signalled.

Opening scenes

Shakespeare was very aware of the necessity to capture the audience's attention at
the beginning of the play, and the opening of *Hamlet*, which you have just looked
at, is a prime example of this. Obviously the creation of atmosphere is an integral
part of the impact of the opening of the play in terms of capturing the audience's
interest right from the outset.

Look now at the opening of *Antony and Cleopatra*.

Antony and Cleopatra

Act I Scene 1

*(Alexandria, **Cleopatra**'s palace.)*

*(Enter **Demetrius** and **Philo**)*

Philo: Nay, but this dotage of our General's
O'erflows the measure. Those his goodly eyes
That o'er the files and musters of the war
Have glowed like plated Mars, now bend, now turn
The office and devotion of their view
Upon a tawny front. His captain's heart,
Which in the scuffles of great fights hath burst
The buckles on his breast, reneges all temper
And is become the bellows and the fan
To cool a gypsy's lust.

*(Flourish. Enter **Antony**, **Cleopatra**, her **Ladies**, The Train, with Eunuchs fanning her.)*

Look where they come:
Take but good note, and you shall see in him
The triple pillar of the world transformed
Into a strumpet's fool. Behold and see.

Cleopatra: If it be love indeed, tell me how much.

Antony: There's beggary in the love that can be reckoned.

Cleopatra: I'll set a bourn how far to be beloved.

Antony: Then must thou needs find out new heaven, new earth.

*(Enter a **Messenger**)*

Messenger: News, my good lord, from Rome.

Antony: Grates me! The sum.

Cleopatra: Nay, hear them, Antony.
Fulvia perchance is angry; or who knows
If the scarce-bearded Caesar have not sent
His pow'rful mandate to you, 'Do this, or this;
Take in that kingdom, and enfranchise that.
Perform't, or else we damn thee.'

Antony: How, my love?

Cleopatra: Perchance? Nay, and most like:
You must not stay here longer, your dismission
Is come from Caesar; therefore hear it, Antony.
Where's Fulvia's process? Caesar's I would say? Both?
Call in the messengers. As I am Egypt's Queen,
Though blushest, Antony, and that blood of thine
Is Caesar's homager: else so thy cheek pays shame
When shrill-tongued Fulvia scolds. The messengers!

Antony: Let Rome in Tiber melt, and the wide arch
Of the ranged empire fall! Here is my space,
Kingdoms are clay: our dungy earth alike
Feeds beast as man. The nobleness of life
Is to do thus; when such a mutual pair
And such a twain can do't, in which I bind,
On pain of punishment, the world to weet
We stand up peerless.

Cleopatra: Excellent falsehood!
Why did he marry Fulvia, and not love her?
I'll seem the fool I am not. Antony
Will be – himself.

Antony: But stirred by Cleopatra.
Now for the love of Love and her soft hours,
Let's not confound the time with conference harsh.
There's not a minute of our lives should stretch
Without some pleasure now. What sport tonight?

Cleopatra: Hear the ambassadors.

Antony: Fie, wrangling queen!
Whom everything becomes – to chide, to laugh,
To weep; whose every passion fully strives
To make itself, in thee, fair and admired.
No messenger but thine; and all alone
Tonight we'll wander through the streets and note
The qualities of people. Come, my queen;
Last night you did desire it. (*To Attendants*) Speak not to us.

(Exeunt **Antony** *and* **Cleopatra** *with the Train)*

Demetrius: Is Caesar with Antonius prized so slight?

Philo: Sir, sometimes, when he is not Antony,
He comes too short of that great property
Which still should go with Antony.

Demetrius: I am full sorry
That he approves the common liar, who
Thus speaks of him at Rome; but I will hope
Of better deeds tomorrow. Rest you happy!

Activity

How does Shakespeare capture the audience's attention at the outset of the play?

This scene is particularly interesting as an opening to the play because it presents, in terms of language, theme and technique, a kind of summary of the play itself.

Here are some points you might have noticed about Shakespeare's use of language in the opening speech here:

- Philo's 'Look where they come:/ Take but good note' invites us to view the scene as if through his eyes.
- His introductory speech creates a picture of Antony as a man with mythic rather than human qualities.
- There is vivid imagery in the description, for example he 'glowed like plated Mars' in his armour.
- At the same time, Philo disparages him in vulgar terms, describing him as being no more than the 'bellows and the fan/ To cool a gypsy's lust.'
- The use of the word 'gypsy' derived from 'Egyptian', presents us with the Rome/ Egypt contrast.
- Contemptuous terms are used to describe Cleopatra.

Activity

Now look at the opening scene of the play you are studying and write about the kind of impact it would have on an audience and how Shakespeare achieves this through his use of language.

Songs

At first sight, songs may not seem particularly important in the plays of Shakespeare, but it is interesting to note that 26 of his 37 plays contain songs or parts of songs. Each of these is used quite deliberately to create a particular effect such as influencing the mood, giving us an insight into character, or echoing a theme.

In *The Tempest*, for example, the spirit Ariel sings the following song to Ferdinand:

Full fathom five thy father lies,
Of his bones are coral made;
Those are pearls that were his eyes:
Nothing of him that doth fade,
But doth suffer a sea-change
Into something rich and strange.
Sea-nymphs hourly ring his knell:
(Burden: Ding-dong)
Hark! Now I hear them – Ding-dong, bell.

Activity

Look carefully at the words of this song. Write down the themes that it seems to deal with.

You may have noted the following:

- The song addresses the theme of death.
- It deals with something being magically transformed into something else.

This gives a forecast of what will happen in the play, where Alonso and several other characters will be transformed through suffering into something better and will come to regret past wrongdoings.

> **Activity**
>
> Look at the play you are studying as part of your course. Does it have any songs in it? If it does, look at them carefully and make notes on why Shakespeare uses a song or songs, and what they contribute to the play.

Dialogue

Dialogue is the means by which the characters communicate with each other, and it can take many different forms. For example, in *Othello*, Shakespeare uses the technique of rapidly alternating single lines in the scene where Othello accuses Desdemona of being unfaithful, and she responds.

Othello

Act V Scene 2

Othello: That handkerchief which I so loved and gave thee,
Thou gav'st to Cassio.

Desdemona: No, by my life and soul!
Send for the man and ask him.

Othello: Sweet soul, take heed,
Take heed of perjury; thou art on thy death-bed.

Desdemona: Ay, but not yet to die.

Othello: Yes, presently.
Therefore confess thee freely of thy sin;
For to deny each article with oath
Cannot remove nor choke the strong conception
That I do groan withal. Thou art to die.

Desdemona: Then Lord have mercy on me!

Othello: I say, amen.

Desdemona: And have you mercy too! I never did
Offend you in my life; never loved Cassio
But with such general warranty of heaven
As I might love. I never gave him token.

Othello: By heaven, I saw my handkerchief in's hand!
O perjured woman! Thou dost stone my heart,
And mak'st me call what I intended to do
A murder, which I thought a sacrifice.
I saw the handkerchief.

Desdemona: He found it then.
I never gave it to him. Send for him hither.
Let him confess a truth.

Othello: He hath confessed.

Desdemona: What, my lord?

Othello: That he hath used thee.

Desdemona: How? Unlawfully?

Othello: Ay.

Desdemona: He will not say so.

Othello: No, his mouth is stopped:
Honest Iago hath ta'en order for't.

Desdemona: O, my fear interprets! What, is he dead?

Othello: Had all his hairs been lives, my great revenge
Had stomach for them all.

Desdemona: Alas, he is betrayed, and I undone.

Othello: Out, strumpet! Weep'st thou for him to my face?

Desdemona: O banish me, my lord, but kill me not!

Othello: Down, strumpet!

Desdemona: Kill me tomorrow: let me live tonight!

Othello: Nay, if you strive –

Desdemona: But half an hour!

Othello: Being done, there is no pause.

Desdemona: But while I say one prayer.

Othello: It is too late

The sharpness of Othello's words here, and the increasing desperation of Desdemona's pleading, clearly work to increase the tension as it builds towards the climax.

By contrast, the following extract of dialogue from *Romeo and Juliet* shows the tender expression of the love between them.

Romeo and Juliet

Act II Scene 1

Juliet: My ears have not yet drunk a hundred words
Of thy tongue's uttering, yet I know the sound
Art thou not Romeo, and a Montague?

Romeo: Neither, fair maid, if either thee dislike.

Juliet: How cam'st thou hither, tell me, and wherefore?
The orchard walls are high, and hard to climb,
And the place death, considering who thou art,
If any of my kinsmen find thee here.

Romeo: With love's light wings did I o'erperch these walls,
For stony limits cannot hold love out,
And what love can do, that dares love attempt.
Therefore thy kinsmen are no stop to me.

Juliet: If they do see thee, they will murder thee.

Romeo: Alack there lies more peril in thine eye
Than twenty of their swords; look thou but sweet,
And I am proof against their enmity.

Juliet: I would not for the world they saw thee here.

Romeo: I have night's cloak to hide me from their eyes,
And but thou love me, let them find me here.
My life were better ended by their hate,
Than death prorogued, wanting of thy love.

Juliet:	By whose direction found'st thou out this place?
Romeo:	By love that first did prompt me to inquire;
	He lent me counsel, and I lent him eyes.
	I am no pilot, yet wert thou as far
	As that vast shore washed with the farthest sea,
	I should adventure for such merchandise.

Every exchange is different, with rhythm patterns, tone and vocabulary suited to the context and the mood that Shakespeare wants to express.

> ## Activity
>
> Look at the play you are studying and find three or four examples of contrasting uses of dialogue.

Puns and wordplay

Wordplay was much admired in Elizabethan England, and so it is no surprise that it is frequently used in the plays of Shakespeare. Puns were a particularly popular kind of wordplay. A pun is created when a word has two or more different meanings and the ambiguity is used to witty effect.

An example in *The Taming of the Shrew* is where Petruchio tells his servant, Grumio, to knock on the door of Hortensio. Grumio deliberately misunderstands his master's order.

The Taming of the Shrew

Act I Scene 2

Petruchio:	Verona, for awhile I take my leave,
	To see my friends in Padua; but, of all,
	My best beloved and approved friend,
	Hortensio; and I trow this is his house, –
	Here, sirrah Grumio, knock, I say.
Grumio:	Knock sir! Whom should I knock? Is there any man has rebused your worship?
Petruchio:	Villain, I say, knock me here soundly.
Grumio:	Knock you here, sir! Why, sir, what am I, sir, that I should
	Knock you here, sir?
Petruchio:	Villain, I say, knock me at this gate.
	And rap me well, or I'll knock your knave's pate
Grumio:	My master is grown quarrelsome. – I should knock you first,
	And then I know after who comes by the worst.
Petruchio:	Will it not be?
	Faith, sirrah, an you'll not knock, I'll wring it;
	I'll try how you can sol, fa, and sing it.
	(He wrings him by the ears)

In *Hamlet*, the gravedigger insists on a precise interpretation of words.

Hamlet

Act V Scene 1

Hamlet: Whose grave's this, sirrah?

Clown: Mine, sir –
(sings)
O, a pit of clay for to be made
For such a guest is meet.

Hamlet: I think it be thine, indeed, for thou liest in't.

Clown: You lie out on't sir, and therefore 'tis not yours; for my part I do not lie in't, and yet it is mine.

Hamlet: Thou dost lie in't, to be in't and say it is thine.
'Tis for the dead, not for the quick – therefore thou liest.

Clown: 'Tis a quick lie, sir, 'twill away again from me to you.

Hamlet: What man dost thou dig it for?

Clown: For no man, sir.

Hamlet: What woman then?

Clown: For none neither.

Hamlet: Who is it to be buried in't?

Clown: One that was a woman, sir, but rest her soul she's dead.

Hamlet: How absolute the knave is! We must speak by the card or equivocation will undo us.

Activity

Now look at the play you are studying and find some examples of wordplay. Explain what the wordplay consists of. What function does the wordplay serve in the context of the play?

Shakespeare's imagery

The use of imagery, designed to conjure up vivid images in the mind, is a very important aspect of the way in which Shakespeare works with language. Such imagery plays a key part in every Shakespeare play and very often it is closely linked to central themes of the play. For example, as Othello becomes convinced of Desdemona's infidelity, his jealousy is expressed in increasingly unpleasant animal imagery.

In *King Lear*, certain images recur time and again. Here, too, there is an abundance of animal imagery, often used to stress the inhuman behaviour of Lear's daughters. Here, Lear complains to Regan about the treatment he has received from Goneril.

King Lear

Act II Scene 4

Regan: Good sir, no more; these are unsightly tricks.
Return you to my sister.

Lear: *(Rising)* Never, Regan.
She hath abated me of half my train;
Looked black upon me; struck me with her tongue,

Most serpent-like, upon the very heart.
All the stored vengeances of Heaven fall
On her ungrateful top! Strike her young bones,
You taking airs, with lameness!

Cornwall: Fie, sir, fie!

Lear: You nimble lightnings, dart your blinding flames
Into her scornful eyes! Infect her beauty,
You fen-sucked fogs, drawn by the pow'rful sun,
To fall and blister her!

Regan: O the blest Gods! so will you wish on me,
When the rash moods is on.

Lear: No, Regan, thou shalt never have my curse:
Thy tender-hefted nature shall not give
Thee o'er to harshness: her eyes are fierce, but thine
Do comfort and not burn. 'Tis not in thee
To grudge my pleasures, to cut off my train,
To bandy hasty words, to scant my sizes,
And, in conclusion to oppose the bolt
Against my coming in:

Storm imagery also plays an important part in the language of the play, reflecting the chaos and breakdown caused to society and the mental chaos created within Lear's mind.

King Lear

Act III Scene 2
*(Another part of the heath. Storm still. Enter **Lear** and **Fool**.)*

Lear: Blow, winds, and crack your cheeks! rage! blow!
You cataracts and hurricanoes, spout
Till you have drenched our steeples, drowned the cocks!
You sulph'rous and thought-executing fires,
Vaunt-couriers of oak-cleaving thunderbolts,
Singe my white head! And thou, all-shaking thunder,
Strike flat the thick rotundity o'th'world!
Crack Nature's moulds, all germens spill at once
That makes ungrateful man!

Fool: O Nuncle, court holy-water in a dry house is better than this rain-water out o'door. Good Nuncle, in, ask thy daughters blessing; here's a night pities neither wise men nor Fools.

Fool: Rumble thy bellyful! Spit, fire! spout, rain!
Nor rain, wind, thunder, fire, are my daughters:
I tax you not, you elements, with unkindness;
I never gave you kingdom, called you children,
You owe me no subscription: then let fall
Your horrible pleasure; here I stand, your slave,
A poor, infirm, weak, and despised old man.
But yet I call you servile ministers,
That will with two pernicious daughters join
Your high-engendered battles 'gainst a head
So old and white as this. O, ho! 'tis foul.

Activity

1 Find examples of vivid imagery in the play you are studying.

2 Are there any links between the kind of imagery the play contains and the themes of the play?

3 Pick **two** examples of imagery and analyse the ways in which Shakespeare uses language to achieve his effects.

4 Now write an essay in which you analyse the imagery patterns in the play you are studying.

Verse and prose

It has often been said that Shakespeare's greatness is rooted in his ability to use language to suit all moods, occasions, and characters. Much of his work is written in blank verse (see Chapter 2, page 56) – a flexible form which he adapts to suit many purposes, from moments of intense passion to bawdy bantering. However, we must not lose sight of the fact that Shakespeare makes substantial use of prose, too, which prompts the question 'Why does he switch between verse and prose in his plays?'

A common answer to this question is that the 'high' characters use poetry, in keeping with their elevated natures and the substance of their dialogue, while the 'low' or comic characters use the more plebeian prose. An alternative answer is that Shakespeare uses prose for sub-plots, or to indicate madness or a highly-wrought emotional state in a character. It is easy to find examples to support these ideas, but it is also easy to find examples to disprove them. The truth is that all these explanations are too general and simplistic to help us much, and the real explanation is rather more complex.

For example, *Hamlet* begins with the guards, Francisco and Barnardo, who are 'ordinary' and minor characters, speaking in verse (see page 308). This helps to create a solemn and dignified tone with which to open the play, in keeping with the serious events that are about to unfold with the appearance of the Ghost. When Ophelia becomes mad she speaks prose but she also speaks prose in the 'play-within-the-play' scene where she is perfectly sane. Hamlet himself speaks both prose and verse depending on the situation and who he is speaking to. The Players speak prose when they are not performing and verse when they are in role.

In looking at Shakespeare's use of verse and prose, therefore, you need to look at the context of the specific episode to determine why Shakespeare has chosen to use language in the form he has. In every instance there will be a good dramatic reason on which his decision is based. Remember also that Shakespeare's prose is not an unplanned, casual form of writing. It is as much an art-form as his verse, and is just as carefully structured and organized.

Activity

Make a note of where switches between verse and prose occur in the text you are studying. Choose four of these points. Give reasons why you think the switch is made in each case.

Critical notes and commentaries

There have probably been more critical works written on Shakespeare than any other writer. This can give the impression that in order to understand his plays it is necessary to be familiar with the massive body of scholarship that attaches itself to his works. This is not true.

When studying a Shakespeare play for AS or A level the first thing to do is to try to make sense of it in your own terms. Reading the writings of literary critics can help to show the range of views that it is possible to take on almost any aspect of a Shakespeare play, but you must not let these views become substitutes for your own. Be aware that other views exist, and often can be well supported. Use them to help form your own ideas and sometimes to revise them, but do not be overawed by them. Words in print are not automatically 'true'. If you support your view with direct reference to the text, then you have a valid view.

Many students seek the security of prepared commentaries, particularly in the early stages of their studies. There are various commentaries on the market but most of them have the same basic format of a scene-by-scene summary of the play and then sections on basic features such as 'themes', 'character', and 'style'. Most include some kind of 'specimen questions'. This type of commentary is sometimes frowned upon by teachers, but nevertheless many students do use them, and providing you are aware of their limitations they can help you come to terms with a text early on in your studies. Be aware, however, that in order to be successful at A level you need to go far beyond the level of discussion that they provide.

Which edition?

If you are working on AS or A level literature in a class, the edition of the Shakespeare text may well be chosen for you by your teacher. If you are working in isolation or if you are providing your own text for your class, then you might find yourself puzzling over which edition to choose. The Arden edition is usually regarded as the most 'academic' and is packed with detailed notes covering a whole variety of issues. Many of these notes can be useful, but a great many of them are more relevant to undergraduate study and beyond.

There are several editions (New Penguin, New Swan, Cambridge, Oxford, etc.) which contain some notes, usually at the back of the book, in a more accessible form. Some are specifically aimed at school or college students and contain activities, suggested essay questions, etc. Finally, there are editions that simply contain the text alone. There are no notes or other 'trimmings' in these editions, and they are very inexpensive.

The key thing to remember is that although notes might help, they are by no means essential. Indeed, sometimes they can even interfere with you coming to grips with the text itself. It would be easy to get the impression that Shakespeare study is so arcane that you can only understand it and engage with it if you have notes to unlock the meaning for you. That would be a wrong impression. The two essential requirements are your mind and the text itself.

16 Revising for the Examination

Objectives

- To plan the revision for your examinations
- To consider approaches to essay planning and working under timed conditions

A key role

The texts you have studied obviously play a key role in your final assessment for either the AS or A level course, and it is essential that you revise them very carefully in readiness for the exam. Your grade in these examinations will depend on the quality and effectiveness of this preparation, so it is well worth planning how you intend to revise in good time. This is not a matter that you should put off until the last minute; hasty, inadequate revision could well damage your chances of getting the grade you want. Students who do well will show an independence of mind which reveals the ability to think for themselves, and to think clearly under the pressure of exam conditions. Revision is key to these skills.

Now let us have a look at some of the things that you can do to help revise your set texts and prepare yourself for the exam.

Reading, re-reading, and re-reading again

By this stage you will, no doubt, have read your texts a number of times. This reading and re-reading of the texts is essential to the development of your understanding and appreciation of them.

However, different kinds of reading are appropriate depending on why you are doing the reading. You may first read the text quickly, before you start to study it in detail. The next time you read it you will probably do so quite slowly and carefully, in order to follow the plot carefully, to examine the ways in which the characters emerge, and to get used to the style and language used. Subsequent reads will be different again. You may skim through the text to quickly refresh your memory of the whole thing, or you may scan the text looking for particular references to images or ideas. These various readings are extremely important for a number of reasons:

- They help you to become very familiar with the text, not just in terms of the plot (although some books do need to be read several times just to sort out what is happening), but also in terms of picking up on the details of the text. Most texts chosen for AS and A level are very complex, and every time you read them you notice something new, something that you had not picked up the first, second, or even third time round.

- You tend to come to an understanding of a text over a period of time. You do not just read it, understand it, and that is that, you are ready for the exam. The kinds of texts that you will have encountered in your AS and A level studies need thinking about. You need to allow yourself this thinking time in order to reflect on what you have read, to absorb the material, and then return to it again.

Obviously this kind of reading is part of a developmental process which enhances your knowledge and understanding of your set texts and, therefore, it needs to be planned for over a period of time.

Time management

Time is a crucial factor in your revision programme. Building time into your programme for sufficient practice on a variety of tasks is vital. To make sure that you do this, it is advisable to draw up a revision programme to cover the build-up to the final exams. This can be quite loose in the initial stages but the closer you get to the exams, the tighter it needs to be. Make sure that you cover every aspect of assessment that you need to. Here are some basic principles to think about when drawing up your revision programme.

- Be realistic – do not overestimate how much you can get through in a given time. It is far better to start your revision programme earlier than to try to cram everything in at the last minute.
- Make sure that your programme gives the necessary attention to every text. Do not rely on the 'I know that one well enough so I needn't revise it' approach. Often, when you come to revise a text that you studied months before, you remember things about it that you had forgotten or that had become hazy.
- Aim for variety in your revision tasks. Create a balance between revision activities which are reading-based and those which involve writing tasks. For example, as well as the various reading activities there are those involving written responses, such as practice on specimen papers, timed essays, essay planning, etc., which are described in the rest of this chapter. If possible, you should also watch videos related to your texts, or listen to recordings of them.
- Build in to your programme some time off to relax. You will not work at your best if you spend all your time studying. Revision is best done with a fresh mind and in relatively short sessions with breaks. You can only take in so much at one sitting. One to two hours at a stretch is enough.

It is important to keep a good balance between texts. Even if you feel you know a text really well, do not skimp on the revision of it. Remember, though, that a revision programme will need to be flexible in order to cater for the unexpected. Allow yourself time to think about questions and ideas. Also, beware of wasting too much valuable revision time trying to create the 'perfect programme'.

Activity

Try planning out a short revision programme for yourself lasting a week, taking account of all the points mentioned above.

Past-paper and specimen paper questions

As part of your revision programme, try to look at as many questions from past or specimen papers as you can. The value of this lies in giving you the flavour of the question types that Chief Examiners set. Certainly, looking at past-paper questions on your texts will show you a range of topics that questions have focused on in the past, and sometimes similar questions do appear again. However, do not learn 'model' answers and hope to be able to use these in the exam. If you come across specimen or model answers, regard them critically and as one possible way of answering, but do not take them to be the definitive answer. Remember, in the exam you will be expected to respond using your own ideas and thoughts, and examiners can tell immediately if you are parroting a 'model' answer you have learned.

As well as giving you ideas of the types of things that have been asked about before, looking at past-paper questions will also give you a clear idea of how questions can be worded and the style in which they are presented. The more you know in this respect, the less likely you are to be thrown by question phrasing or terminology. Looking at past papers can also show up gaps in your knowledge of a set text and allow you to remedy them.

Timed essays

One of the main worries that students have in terms of answering on their set texts is how they are going to get all their ideas down in the time allowed. Certainly one of the most common problems students encounter in AS and A level English literature exams is running out of time. Often this is due to too much time being spent on one question in particular (usually the first one) and so not allowing enough time to deal adequately with the rest of the paper.

For this reason it is extremely important that you get a good deal of practice writing under timed conditions. You will, no doubt, do some timed pieces in class, but there is no reason why you should not practise them at home as well. All you need are some suitable questions, a quiet place, and some time. In one sense it does not even matter if the work is not marked (although obviously you will get even more benefit from it if it is) – what really matters with this is building up your experience of writing against the clock. One thing is certain – the more you practise, the quicker you will get. It really will help you to speed up and it will also show you how much information you can deal with in a specified time and how well you can plan your work under time pressures.

Essay planning

Practice in essay planning should form another key part in your revision process. The best essays are those where students have thought about what they want to say before they actually start to write. By planning essays you can ensure that your argument is coherent and that you are using your knowledge and evidence to best effect. Essays that are not planned can easily drift away from the main point of the question or become rambling and jumbled.

In the exam itself you will have little time to spend on planning; you will feel an in-built pressure to start writing as soon as possible. However, what you do in that first two or three minutes after reading the question can be vital to the success of your answer. Practice in the build-up to the exam will help you to develop the skills to plan quickly and effectively. There are a number of things you can do to help.

- Read the question very carefully and make sure that you understand all parts of it.
- Analyse the question and note down the key topic areas it deals with.
- Briefly plan how you intend to deal with these areas – this may mean only three or four points each summed up in a few words. The main thing is that you will have a checklist of the points you are going to cover before you begin writing your essay.

Immediately after reading the question it is likely that ideas will whiz through your mind very quickly. If you do not get these down on paper in the form of a rough plan, there is a chance you might miss out an important point in the finished essay.

As well as doing your timed essays it will also be useful preparation if you can do essay plans for as many questions as you can. This will help to get you into the routine of planning but it will also give you the opportunity to think about a wide variety of issues related to your set texts.

There are many ways in which you can create your essay plans. Some students prefer to create a 'spidergram' or 'pattern notes' (see page 89 for an example), while others prefer a linear or flow-diagram approach. Many students find a straightforward list of points the most helpful.

You will need to find the method that suits your way of thinking best, and which allows you to plan your work most effectively. For more methods of planning essays in detail, see Chapter 4, pages 85–90.

Writing your essay

Having completed your plan you are ready to write your essay. Here are some things to bear in mind.

- Always begin your essay by addressing the question directly. It can be a very useful technique to actually use some of the words of the question in your introduction. Your introduction should give a general indication of your response to the question or summarize the approach you intend to take, perhaps stating your viewpoint. The introduction might consist of your basic essay plan, expanded a little. However, keep the introduction brief and never include biographical information or plot summary.
- An alternative way to begin your essay, and one that can be very effective, is to respond to the question by starting with a strong, perhaps contentious idea that captures the reader's attention immediately. This will launch you straight into points that will support your argument.
- Develop your points clearly using evidence and references to the text to support your ideas.
- Assume that the examiner has read the text you are writing about and knows it extremely well, so there is no need to explain the plot or who the characters are.
- Make sure that your essay deals with all parts of the question.
- If your answer is similar to an essay you have written before, make sure that you are being relevant at all times and are not simply regurgitating a 'set' answer that is in your mind. Also, avoid rehashing your notes as an answer to a question.
- If you use quotation, make sure that it is short and relevant. Do not copy out chunks of the text.

- Make sure that your essay has a conclusion in which you sum up your arguments and analysis. It is often through the conclusion that the relevance of certain points you have made is brought into focus and the essay is given a sense of unity and completeness.

Throughout your revision period, bear in mind what you will be expected to show in the exam. Some factual knowledge will be required, but not much. That you know the 'facts' about a text, the story-line, who the characters are, etc., will be taken as read. The emphasis will be much more on showing judgement, analysis, sensitivity, and perception in your responses.

17 The Examiner's View

Objectives

- To think about the things examiners and moderators look for in the work they mark
- To understand how your work will be assessed

What the examiner looks for

An important person in the process of your assessment at AS or A level is the examiner who will mark or moderate your work. 'Examiners' are not some special breed of people who spend their lives marking examination scripts. For the most part, they are practising teachers who work with students like yourself helping them to prepare for exams. However, they can only mark the work that you present them with, and the mark that is awarded depends *solely* on its quality.

It is a fallacy that one examiner might be more generous with you than another. Careful procedures are followed to ensure that the mark you receive from one examiner is just the same as the mark you would receive if another assessed your work. Indeed, it is not simply a case of one examiner looking at your work, giving a mark and that is the end of it. Exam scripts go through a number of processes which involve responses being looked at by several people before a final mark is awarded. How well you do is up to you, not the examiner.

It is also worth dispelling another misconception that some students have concerning the role of the examiner. They picture the examiner as some kind of merciless inquisitor who takes delight in catching them out. Examiners, so the thinking goes, look only for negative aspects in responses and ruthlessly dismantle every essay that they come across. Questions are their tools, designed to catch students out.

In fact, nothing could be further from the truth. Questions are designed to let you show your knowledge to the best of your ability. Obviously examiners will not reward qualities which are not present in your responses, but they will look for the positive features in your work. Examiners take far more pleasure and satisfaction in reading good quality material that they can reward than they do in poor work that must be awarded poor marks. Think of the examiner as an interested and positive audience for your writing, who will award marks fairly and look positively on responses wherever there are positive qualities to be found.

Bearing in mind the large number of students who sit exams in AS and A level literature each year, it is very encouraging that examiners report that very few candidates reveal lack of knowledge, skills, or preparation, and very weak answers are extremely uncommon. The vast majority of students show that they have prepared themselves to the best of their abilities for the papers. Having said that, there are aspects of the exam that examiners often comment on as areas that need more careful preparation. We will now go on to consider some of these.

The questions

The questions that you will be asked will not be prescriptive. They are 'open' so as to invite you to debate the issues or express an opinion on a particular view, and to encourage you to develop informed judgements on the texts and the issues they raise. It is these judgements that the examiner is interested in reading about.

Where the question contains some kind of proposition, you are never expected to simply accept it. Acceptance or rejection needs to be supported with evidence and justification. One criticism frequently made by examiners is where a student simply agrees with or rejects the proposition and then goes on to write about something else entirely. This still happens with worrying regularity. The key thing in all this is to read the question and do what it says.

Unseen texts

Part of your examination will require you to write on unprepared material that you have not seen before. In relation to writing about unseen material, examiners often stress that students need to develop effective close reading skills in order to answer this kind of task well. The best advice is to get as much practice as you can on this type of work (see chapters 7 and 13 for more on this).

As part of this practice, examiners recommend that you actively seek out meaning from the unseen texts and pay particular attention to organizing your responses. (Of course, these skills can also be applied to the set texts – see below.)

In tackling unseen texts, examiners recommend a detached perspective so that you focus on the text you have been given. It is better not to emphasize biographical or other background knowledge that you might have about the authors, or the complete text, for example.

Set texts

On this specification there is a wide degree of choice in which texts you study and so there are few 'set' texts as such. However, you will study your poetry text for Unit 1 and you will also study a number of other texts throughout the course as part your wider reading or coursework.

Technical accuracy

Clearly the ideas that you express in your answers or your coursework are of primary importance. However, these ideas will be not presented most effectively if your writing suffers from various technical inaccuracies. It is, therefore, crucial that your answers are as free from technical errors as you can make them.

There are several points that examiners draw attention to in this respect.

- **Punctuation**. Ensure that you use full stops, commas, quotation marks, etc. where appropriate. It is easy for these things to be forgotten in the heat of the exam but poor punctuation can mean that your ideas are communicated to the reader less effectively and this may affect your mark.
- **Sentences**. Make sure that you write in sentences and that you avoid long, convoluted ones.
- **Paragraphing**. Few candidates fail to use paragraphs at all, but examiners often point to the inappropriate use of paragraphs. For example, one-sentence paragraphs should be avoided and so should excessively long paragraphs.

- **Vocabulary**. Try to vary your vocabulary without becoming verbose simply to make your essay sound more 'impressive'.

- **Spelling**. Obviously you should try to make your work free of spelling errors. However, in the heat of writing under exam conditions some errors may well creep in. You should do your best to check each answer as you complete it to keep these to a minimum. If nothing else, though, make sure that you are spelling the titles of the texts, the names of the characters, and the names of the authors correctly. It does not give a good impression if, after two years' study, you are still writing about 'Shakespear's play' or 'Jayne Austin's novel'.

- **Cliché, flattery, and slang**. Avoid the use of well-worn phrases such as 'Jane Eyre is a victim of male domination' or 'Lear acts like a man possessed'. Flattery towards authors, such as 'Shakespeare's portrayal of a man in emotional turmoil is second to none' or 'It is clear that Hardy is one of the giants of English poetry' are equally to be avoided; so are slang expressions, such as 'Oskar Schindler is a bit of a Del-boy character' or 'Laertes goes ballistic when he hears about his father's death'.

- **Quotation**. If you are using quotation, make sure it is accurate. If you have the book with you in the exam there is really no excuse for misquoting (although it still happens). If you are relying on memory, it is very easy to misquote. Perhaps all that needs to be said is that it is better not to use a quotation than to misquote, or worse still 'invent' a quote based on a rough idea of how it goes.

Model and prepared answers

Examiners report that they do not see model or prepared answers anywhere near as frequently as they used to in student responses. However, they do still crop up from time to time. There is nothing wrong with reading model answers during the course of your study, as long as you use them wisely. They can be useful in presenting you with new ideas, but be aware that they present just one way of answering a question. The examiner is interested in what *you* have to say on a particular topic or question, not what the writer of a prepared answer has to say.

Remember that the best responses are those in which your own voice can be heard. The whole point of the course that you are studying is to develop your ability to write confidently, relevantly, and thoughtfully about your ideas on the texts you have studied. Do not be afraid to use the pronoun 'I' occasionally in your essays and do not be afraid to respond genuinely to a question. Attempts to memorize prepared answers never work.

How the examiner will mark your work

Above all, examiners marking AS or A level English literature scripts are trained to be positive and flexible.

The examiners (each of your exam papers is usually marked by a separate examiner) will look for the positive qualities in your work. They will not approach your response with a preconceived idea of an 'ideal answer' but will have an open mind. They will evaluate your efforts to provide an informed personal response to the question.

Answering the question

Examiners are always aware of students who do not read the questions carefully enough. You should make absolutely sure that you are well trained in studying carefully the exact wording of the question or task. Remember that the question or task set should be the whole basis and framework of your response.

You will remember the Assessment Objectives that we examined in the Introduction are at the centre of your studies and the work you produce for assessment. All the questions and tasks that you will encounter on your course have been specifically designed to give you the opportunity to meet these objectives as effectively as possible. The views, opinions and ideas you explore are up to you (providing you can support them through close reference and analysis of the text, and they fulfil the demands of the task you have been set).

Length

In written examination answers, examiners do not award marks on the basis of the length of your essay but they will look for what you have achieved in your writing. An essay may appear brief but on closer inspection it may be a succinct and well-argued response and therefore worthy of a high mark. It is true to say, though, that essays that are very short often lack sufficient depth in the development of ideas. On the other hand, over-long essays can become repetitive, rambling and lacking in a coherent structure. Do your best to create a balanced answer.

With your coursework, as you have already seen, you are given clear guidance on the length of the pieces you should produce.

Descriptors

In addition to the question-specific guidance that examiners are given, exam boards also provide them with 'descriptors' to help them to place your essay in a particular mark band. These describe the typical features of responses at different levels, and are linked to the Assessment Objectives being tested. You can access them for yourself on the AQA website (www.aqa.org.uk).

In reading the descriptors you will see the key features that can bring you success in the exam, and to achieve them there are some basic things you can do. In fact if you are to achieve success there are certain things that you *must* do. You must make sure that:

- you have read your texts carefully several times
- you know your texts thoroughly
- you are fully aware of the issues, ideas, themes, etc. they contain
- you are aware of the stylistic features of the texts you have studied
- you can support your ideas and comments effectively.

Remember: The secret of success is to be well prepared. Know your material and know what you think about it. Know the Assessment Objectives that you are being tested on, and make sure that what you have written addresses these objectives.

Glossary

Allegory: an allegory is a story or narrative, often told at some length, which has a deeper meaning below the surface. *The Pilgrim's Progress* by John Bunyan is a well-known allegory. A more modern example is George Orwell's *Animal Farm*, which on a surface level is about a group of animals who take over their farm but on a deeper level is an allegory of the Russian Revolution and the shortcomings of Communism.

Alliteration: the repetition of the same consonant sound, especially at the beginnings of words. For example, 'Five miles meandering with a mazy motion' (*Kubla Khan* by S.T. Coleridge).

Allusion: a reference to another event, person, place, or work of literature – the allusion is usually implied rather than explicit and often provides another layer of meaning to what is being said.

Ambiguity: use of language where the meaning is unclear or has two or more possible interpretations or meanings. It could be created through a weakness in the way the writer has expressed himself or herself but often it is used by writers quite deliberately to create layers of meaning in the mind of the reader.

Ambivalence: this indicates more than one possible attitude is being displayed by the writer towards a character, theme, or idea, etc.

Anachronism: something that is historically inaccurate, for example the reference to a clock chiming in Shakespeare's *Julius Caesar*.

Anthropomorphism: the endowment of something that is not human with human characteristics.

Antithesis: contrasting ideas or words that are balanced against each other.

Apostrophe: an interruption in a poem or narrative so that the speaker or writer can address a dead or absent person or particular audience directly.

Archaic: language that is old-fashioned – not completely obsolete but no longer in current modern use.

Assonance: the repetition of similar vowel sounds. For example: 'There must be Gods thrown down and trumpets blown' (*Hyperion* by John Keats). This shows the paired assonance of 'must', 'trum-', 'thrown', 'blown'.

Atmosphere: the prevailing mood created by a piece of writing.

Ballad: a narrative poem that tells a story (traditional ballads were songs), usually in a straightforward way. The theme is often tragic or containing a whimsical, supernatural, or fantastical element.

Bathos: an anti-climax or sudden descent from the serious to the ridiculous – sometimes deliberate, sometimes unintentional on the part of the writer.

Blank verse: unrhymed poetry that adheres to a strict pattern in that each line is an iambic pentameter (a ten-syllable line with five stresses). It is close to the rhythm of speech or prose and is used a great deal by many writers including Shakespeare and Milton.

Caesura: a conscious break in a line of poetry (see Chapter 2, page 56).

Caricature: a character often described through the exaggeration of a small number of features that he or she possesses.

Catharsis: a purging of the emotions which takes place at the end of a tragedy.

Cliché: a phrase, idea, or image that has been used so much that is has lost much of its original meaning, impact, and freshness.

Colloquial: ordinary, everyday speech and language.

Comedy: originally simply a play or other work which ended happily. Now we use this term to describe something that is funny and which makes us laugh. In literature the comedy is not a necessarily a lightweight form. A play like *Measure for Measure*, for example, is for the most part a serious and dark play, but as it ends happily, it is described as a comedy.

Conceit: an elaborate, extended, and sometimes surprising comparison between things that, at first sight, do not have much in common.

Connotation: an implication or association attached to a word or phrase. A connotation is suggested or felt rather than being explicit.

Consonance: the repetition of the same consonant sounds in two or more words in which the vowel sounds are different. For example: 'And by his smile, I knew that sullen hall,/ By his dead smile I knew we stood in Hell' (*Strange Meeting* by Wilfred Owen). Where consonance replaces the rhyme, as here, it is called half-rhyme.

Couplet: two consecutive lines of verse that rhyme.

Dénouement: the ending of a play, novel, or drama where 'all is revealed' and the plot is unravelled.

Diction: the choice of words that a writer makes. Another term for 'vocabulary'.

Didactic: intending to preach or teach; didactic works often contain a particular moral or political point.

Dramatic monologue: a poem or prose piece in which a character addresses an audience. Often the monologue is complete in itself, as in Alan Bennett's *Talking Heads*.

Elegy: a meditative poem, usually sad and reflective in nature. Sometimes, though not always, it is concerned with the theme of death.

Empathy: a feeling on the part of the reader of sharing the particular experience being described by the character or writer.

End stopping: ending a verse line with a pause or a stop.

Enjambement: where a line of verse flows on into the next line without a pause.

Epic: a long narrative poem, written in an elevated style and usually dealing with a heroic theme or story. Homer's *The Iliad* and Milton's *Paradise Lost* are examples of this.

Euphemism: the expression of an unpleasant or unsavoury idea in a less blunt and more pleasant way.

Euphony: use of pleasant or melodious sounds.

Exemplum: a story that contains or illustrates a moral point, put forward as an 'example'.

Fable: a short story that presents a clear moral lesson.

Fabliau: a short comic tale with a bawdy element, akin to the 'dirty story'. Chaucer's *The Miller's Tale* contains strong elements of the fabliau.

Farce: a play that aims to entertain the audience through absurd and ridiculous characters and actions.

Feminine ending: an extra unstressed syllable at the end of a line of poetry. (Contrast with a stressed syllable, a masculine ending.)

Figurative language: language that is symbolic or metaphorical and not meant to be taken literally.

Foot: a group of syllables forming a unit of verse – the basic unit of 'metre'. (See Chapter 2, pages 55–60.)

Free verse: verse written without any fixed structure (either in metre or rhyme).

Genre: a particular type of writing, e.g. prose, poetry, drama.

Heptameter: a verse line containing seven feet.

Hexameter: a verse line containing six feet.

Hyperbole: deliberate and extravagant exaggeration.

Iamb: the most common metrical foot in English poetry, consisting of an unstressed syllable followed by a stressed syllable.

Idyll: a story, often written in verse, usually concerning innocent and rustic characters in rural, idealized surroundings. This form can also deal with more heroic subjects, as in Tennyson's *Idylls of the King*. (See **Pastoral**.)

Imagery: the use of words to create a picture or 'image' in the mind of the reader. Images can relate to any of the senses, not just sight, but also hearing, taste, touch, and smell. It is often used to refer to the use of descriptive language, particularly to the use of metaphors and similes.

Internal rhyme: rhyming words within a line rather than at the end of lines.

Inter-textual: having clear links with other texts through the themes, ideas, or issues which are explored.

Irony: at its simplest level, irony means saying one thing while meaning another. It occurs where a word or phrase has one surface meaning but another contradictory, possibly opposite meaning is implied. Irony is frequently confused with sarcasm. Sarcasm is spoken, often relying on tone of voice, and is much more blunt than irony.

Lament: a poem expressing intense grief.

Lyric: originally a song performed to the accompaniment of a lyre (an early harp-like instrument), but now it can mean a song-like poem or a short poem expressing personal feeling.

Metaphor: a comparison of one thing to another in order to make description more vivid. The metaphor actually states that one thing *is* the other. For example, the simile would be: 'The huge knight stood like an impregnable tower in the ranks of the enemy', whereas the metaphor would be: 'The huge knight was an impregnable tower in the ranks of the enemy'. (See **Simile** and **Personification**.)

Metre: the regular use of stressed and unstressed syllables in poetry. (See **Foot** and Chapter 2, pages 55–60.)

Mock heroic: a poem that treats trivial subject matter in the grand and elevated style of epic poetry. The effect produced is often satirical, as in Pope's *The Rape of the Lock*.

Monometer: a verse line consisting of only one metrical foot.

Motif: a dominant theme, subject or idea which runs through a piece of literature. Often a 'motif' can assume a symbolic importance.

Narrative: a piece of writing that tells a story.

Octameter: a verse line consisting of eight feet.

Octave: the first eight lines of a sonnet.

Ode: a verse form similar to a lyric but often more lengthy and containing more serious and elevated thoughts.

Onomatopoeia: the use of words whose sound copies the sound of the thing or process that they describe. On a simple level, words like 'bang', 'hiss', and 'splash' are onomatopoeic, but the device also has more subtle uses.

Oxymoron: a figure of speech which joins together words of opposite meanings, e.g. 'the living dead', 'bitter sweet', etc.

Paradox: a statement that appears contradictory, but when considered more closely is seen to contain a good deal of truth.

Parody: a work that is written in imitation of another work, very often with the intention of making fun of the original.

Pastoral: generally literature concerning rural life with idealized settings and rustic characters. Often pastorals are concerned with the lives of shepherds and shepherdesses presented in idyllic and unrealistic ways. (See **Idyll**.)

Pathos: the effect in literature which makes the reader feel sadness or pity.

Pentameter: a line of verse containing five feet.

Periphrasis: an indirect, roundabout or long-winded way of expressing something.

Personification: the attribution of human feelings, emotions, or sensations to an inanimate object. Personification is a kind of metaphor where human qualities are given to things or abstract ideas.

Plot: the sequence of events in a poem, play, novel, or short story that make up the main storyline.

Prose: any kind of writing which is not verse – usually divided into fiction and non-fiction.

Protagonist: the main character or speaker in a poem, monologue, play, or story.

Pun: a play on words that have similar sounds but quite different meanings.

Quatrain: a stanza of four lines, which can have various rhyme schemes.

Refrain: repetition throughout a poem of a phrase, line, or series of lines, as in the 'chorus' of a song.

Rhetoric: originally the art of speaking and writing in such a way as to persuade an audience to a particular point of view. Now it is often used to imply grand words that have no substance to them. There are a variety of rhetorical devices such as the rhetorical question – a question which does not require an answer as the answer is either obvious or implied in the question itself. (See **Apostrophe**, **Exemplum**.)

Rhyme: corresponding sounds in words, usually at the end of each line but not always. (See **Internal Rhyme**.)

Rhyme scheme: the pattern of the rhymes in a poem.

Rhythm: the 'movement' of the poem as created through the metre and the way that language is stressed within the poem.

Satire: the highlighting or exposing of human failings or foolishness within a society through ridiculing them. Satire can range from being gentle and light to being extremely biting and bitter in tone, e.g. Swift's *Gulliver's Travels* or *A Modest Proposal* and George Orwell's *Animal Farm*.

Scansion: the analysis of metrical patterns in poetry. (See Chapter 2, pages 55–60.)

Septet: a seven-line stanza.

Sestet: the last six lines of a sonnet.

Simile: a comparison of one thing to another in order to make description more vivid. Similes use the words 'like' or 'as' in this comparison. (See **Metaphor**.)

Soliloquy: a speech in which a character, alone on stage, expresses his or her thoughts and feelings aloud for the benefit of the audience, often in a revealing way.

Sonnet: a fourteen-line poem, usually with ten syllables in each line. There are several ways in which the lines can be organized, but often they consist of an octave and a sestet.

Stanza: the blocks of lines into which a poem is divided. (Sometimes these are, less precisely, referred to as verses, which can lead to confusion as poetry is sometimes called 'verse'.)

Stream of consciousness: a technique in which the writer writes down thoughts and emotions in a 'stream' as they come to mind, without giving order or structure.

Structure: the way that a poem or play or other piece of writing has been put together. This can include the metre pattern, stanza arrangement, and the way the ideas are developed, etc.

Style: the individual way in which a writer has used language to express his or her ideas.

Sub-plot: a secondary storyline in a story or play. Often, as in some Shakespeare plays, the sub-plot can provide some comic relief from the main action, but sub-plots can also relate in quite complex ways to the main plot of a text.

Sub-text: ideas, themes, or issues that are not dealt with overtly by a text but which exist below the surface meaning of it.

Symbol: like images, symbols represent something else. In very simple terms a red rose is often used to symbolize love; distant thunder is often symbolic of approaching trouble. Symbols can be very subtle and multi-layered in their significance.

Syntax: the way in which sentences are structured. Sentences can be structured in different ways to achieve different effects.

Tetrameter: a verse line of four feet.

Theme: the central idea or ideas that the writer explores through a text.

Tone: the tone of a text is created through the combined effects of a number of features, such as diction, syntax, rhythm, etc. The tone is a major factor in establishing the overall impression of the piece of writing.

Trimeter: a verse line consisting of three feet.

Zeugma: a device that joins together two apparently incongruous things by applying a verb or adjective to them which only really applies to one of them, e.g. 'Kill the boys and the luggage' (Shakespeare's *Henry V*).

Chronology

This chronology features texts that are often set for study at AS and A level. Some of the publication dates given, where no definitive date is known (as in the works of Shakespeare), should be taken as approximate. This is not an exhaustive list of important literary works but, along with the social and political landmarks, it is intended to give the flavour of the times.

Significant social and political events		Significant literary events	
1327	Accession of Edward III.		
1337	Beginning of the Hundred Years' War.		
		c.1340	Geoffrey Chaucer born.
1348	First occurrence of Black Death in England.		
		c.1369	Chaucer, *The Book of the Duchess*.
1377	Death of Edward III. Accession of Richard II.	1377	William Langland, *Piers Plowman*.
1381	Peasants' Revolt.	c.1381	Chaucer, *House of Fame*.
		c.1385	Chaucer, *The Parlement of Fowles* and *Troilus and Criseyde*.
		1387–1400	Chaucer, *The Canterbury Tales*.
1399	Death of Richard II. Accession of Henry IV (Earl of Bolingbroke).		
		1400	Chaucer dies.
1413	Death of Henry IV. Accession of Henry V.		
1415	Battle of Agincourt.		
1422	Henry V dies of fever. Accession of Henry VI.		
1455	First battle in The Wars of the Roses.		
1461	Henry VI put to death. Accession of Edward IV.		
		1474	William Caxton prints first book in English.
1483	Death of Edward IV. Richard, Duke of Gloucester appointed as Protector. Murder of the Princes in the Tower. Accession of Richard of Gloucester as Richard III.		
1485	Richard III defeated at Battle of Bosworth. Succeeded by Henry VII.	1485	Sir Thomas Mallory, *Morte D'Arthur*.

		1501	English poet Thomas Wyatt born.
1503	Leonardo Da Vinci, the 'Mona Lisa'.		
1509	Death of Henry VII. Accession of Henry VIII.		
		1510	*Everyman* – English morality play.
1512	Michelangelo finishes work on Sistine Chapel.		
1513	Battle of Flodden.		
		1516	Thomas More, *Utopia*.
1533–5	Henry VIII excommunicated: Acts of Succession and Supremacy. Henry makes himself Head of the Church of England. Thomas More executed.		
1540	Thomas Cromwell executed.		
1547	Death of Henry VIII. Accession of Edward VI.		
1549	The Book of Common Prayer.		
1553	Edward VI dies. Accession of Mary I.		
1558	Death of Mary I. Accession of Elizabeth I.		
		1564	William Shakespeare and Christopher Marlowe born.
1570	Elizabeth I excommunicated by Pope Pius V.		
		1572	Ben Jonson and John Donne born.
		1575	Cyril Tourneur born.
1576	London's first playhouse, The Theatre, opens.		
1577	Sir Francis Drake begins voyage round the world. London's second playhouse, 'The Curtain' opens.	1577	Raphael Holinshed, *Chronicles of England, Scotland and Ireland, a History in Two Volumes* published.
		1579	Edmund Spenser, *The Shepherd's Calender*.
		1581	Sir Philip Sidney, *Astrophil and Stella*.
		1585	Shakespeare leaves Stratford for London.
1588	Spanish Armada defeated.	1588–92	Shakespeare's early plays, including *Henry VI (pts 1,2 and 3), Richard III, A Comedy of Errors, The Taming of the Shrew, Love's Labour's Lost.* Marlowe, *Doctor Faustus*.

		1590	Marlowe, *The Jew of Malta*. Spenser, *The Faerie Queene (Books 1–3)*.
1592	Plague closes the London theatres.	1592	Thomas Kyd, *The Spanish Tragedy*.
		1593	Marlowe killed in tavern brawl.
		1593–1600	Shakespeare, *Titus Andronicus, Two Gentlemen of Verona, Romeo and Juliet, Henry IV (pts 1 and 2), Richard II, A Midsummer Night's Dream, The Merchant of Venice, Henry V, Much Ado About Nothing*.
1594	Theatres reopen.		
		1596	Spenser, *The Faerie Queene (Books 4–6)*.
		1597	Francis Bacon, *Essays*.
		1598	Jonson, *Every Man in His Humour*.
1599	Globe Theatre built at Southwark. Shakespeare's plays performed here.		
		1601–4	Shakespeare, *Hamlet, Twelfth Night, All's Well That Ends Well, Measure for Measure, The Merry Wives of Windsor, Troilus and Cressida*.
		1602	Thomas Campion, *Observations in the Art of English Poesie*.
1603	Death of Elizabeth I. Accession of James I.		
		1604–8	Shakespeare, *Othello, King Lear, Macbeth, Antony and Cleopatra, Coriolanus*.
1605	The Gunpowder Plot.	1605	Bacon, *Advancement of Learning*.
1606	Rembrandt born.	1606	Jonson, *Volpone*.
		1608–13	Shakespeare, *Cymbeline, The Winter's Tale, The Tempest*.
		1610	Jonson, *The Alchemist*.
		1611	Donne, *An Anatomy of the World*.
		1612	John Webster, *The White Devil*.
1613	Globe Theatre burns down.		
1614	Globe re-built.	1614	Webster, *The Duchess of Malfi*.
		1616	Shakespeare dies.
1618	Sir Walter Raleigh executed. The Thirty Years' War begins.		
1624	Frans Hals, 'The Laughing Cavalier'.		

1625	James I dies. Accession of Charles I.	1625	Michael Drayton, *Nymphidia*.
1629	Dissolution of Parliament.	1629	John Ford, *The Lover's Melancholy*.
		1633	Donne, *Poems* (posth.). Ford, *'Tis Pity She's a Whore*.
		1634	John Milton's *Comus* performed.
		1637	Jonson dies. Milton, *Lycidas*.
1640	Long Parliament summoned.		
1642	Civil War begins. All theatres in England closed by order of the Puritans.		
1649	Trial and execution of Charles I.		
1653	Oliver Cromwell becomes Lord Protector.		
1658	Cromwell dies. Succeeded by his son Richard.	1658	John Dryden, *Heroic Stanzas on Cromwell's Death*.
1660	Charles II restored to throne. Theatres re-open.	1660	Samuel Pepys begins his diary.
1663	Theatre Royal, Drury Lane opens.		
		1664	Dryden, *The Rival Ladies*.
1665	Great Plague of London.		
1666	Great Fire of London.		
		1667	Milton, *Paradise Lost*.
		1669	Last entry in Pepys's diary.
		1670	Dryden appointed historiographer royal and Poet Laureate.
		1671	Aphra Behn, *The Forced Marriage*. Milton, *Paradise Regained*.
		1672	William Wycherley, *Love in a Wood*.
		1674	Milton dies.
1675	Wren begins rebuilding St Paul's Cathedral.	1675	Wycherley, *The Country Wife*.
		1677	Behn, *The Rover*.
		1678	Dryden, *All For Love*. John Bunyan, *Pilgrim's Progress (pt 1)*.
		1684	Bunyan, *Pilgrim's Progress (pt 2)*.
1685	Charles II dies. Accession of James II. Monmouth invades and is defeated.		
1688	'The Glorious Revolution'. James II flees and William III and Mary succeed.		
		1700	William Congreve, *The Way of the World*.

1701	War of Spanish Succession begins. Act of Settlement provides for Protestant succession of House of Hanover.		
1702	William III dies. Accession of Queen Anne.		
1704	Battle of Blenheim. J.S. Bach writes first cantata.		
		1706	George Farquhar, *The Recruiting Officer.*
1707	Union of England and Scotland.	1707	Farquhar, *The Beaux' Stratagem.*
		1711	*The Spectator* begun by Joseph Addison and Richard Steele. Alexander Pope, *Essay on Criticism.*
		1712	Pope, *The Rape of the Lock.*
1713	Peace of Utrecht ends War of Spanish Succession.		
1714	Queen Anne dies. George I succeeds.		
1715	Jacobite Rebellion in support of James Edward Stuart, the 'Old Pretender'. Jacobites defeated.		
		1719	Daniel Defoe, *Robinson Crusoe.*
		1722	Defoe, *Moll Flanders, Journal of the Plague Year.*
		1726	Jonathan Swift, *Gulliver's Travels.*
1727	George I dies. George II succeeds.		
		1728	Pope, *The Dunciad.*
		1740	Samuel Richardson, *Pamela.*
		1742	Henry Fielding, *Joseph Andrews.*
1745	Second Jacobite Rebellion led by Charles Edward Stuart, the 'Young Pretender' or 'Bonnie Prince Charlie'.		
1746	After initial success the rebellion is crushed at Battle of Culloden. Charles flees to France.		
		1748	Richardson, *Clarissa.*
		1749	Fielding, *The History of Tom Jones, a Foundling.*
		1750	Thomas Gray, *Elegy Written in an English Country Church Yard.*
1754	Anglo-French War in North America.		
		1755–73	Dr Samuel Johnson, *Dictionary of the English Language.*

Year	Event	Year	Literary
1756	Britain declares war on France. 120 Britons die in 'Black Hole of Calcutta'.		
1760	George II dies. Accession of his grandson, George III.		
		1763	James Boswell (biographer) meets Johnson for first time.
1764	Mozart (age 8) writes his first symphony.	1764	The Literary Club founded in London by Dr Johnson, Burke, Gibbon, Goldsmith, Reynolds, and others.
		1766	Oliver Goldsmith, *The Vicar of Wakefield*.
		1767	Laurence Sterne, *Tristram Shandy*.
		1773	Goldsmith, *She Stoops to Conquer*.
1775	American Revolution begins. J.M.W. Turner born.	1775	Dr Johnson, *A Journey to the Western Isles of Scotland*. Richard Sheridan, *The Rivals*.
1776	American Declaration of Independence.		
		1777	Sheridan, *The School for Scandal*.
1781	British defeated at Yorktown.		
1783	Britain and America proclaim cessation of hostilities. Peace of Versailles – Britain recognizes independence of the United States.	1783	William Blake, *Poetical Sketches*. George Crabbe, *The Village*.
1784	Invention of steam engine by James Watt.		
		1785	William Cowper, *The Task, John Gilpin*.
1789	The French Revolution. The Bastille falls (14 July), the Declaration of the Rights of Man (4 August).	1789	Blake, *Songs of Innocence*.
		1790	Robert Burns, *Tam O'Shanter*.
1791	Louis XVI tries to leave France with his family but is caught and returned to Paris.		
1792	Louis is tried. The first guillotine execution in Paris. Massacres take place.		
1793	Louis is executed. 'The Terror' begins. Britain joins war against France. Queen Marie Antoinette executed.	1793	John Clare born.
1794	Habeas Corpus Act suspended in Britain.	1794	Blake, *Songs of Experience*.
		1795	Robert Southey, *Poems*.
1797	Napoleon appointed to command forces for invasion of Britain.	1797	Samuel Taylor Coleridge, *Kubla Khan* (pub. 1816).

1798	French defeated by Nelson at the Battle of the Nile.	1798	William Wordsworth and Coleridge, *The Lyrical Ballads*.
1804	Spain declares war on Britain. Napoleon becomes Emperor Napoleon I.		
1805	Combined French and Spanish fleet destroyed by Nelson at Trafalgar.	1805	Sir Walter Scott, *The Lay of the Last Minstrel*.
1807	Abolition of the slave trade in the British Empire.	1807	Lord Byron, *Hours of Idleness*. Charles and Mary Lamb, *Tales From Shakespeare*.
1808	Beethoven's symphonies 5 and 6.	1808	Scott, *Marmion*.
1811	Luddite riots.	1811	Jane Austen, *Sense and Sensibility*.
1812	French retreat from Moscow.	1812	Byron, *Childe Harold's Pilgrimage*.
		1813	Austen, *Pride and Prejudice*.
1814	Napoleon abdicates and is banished to Elba.	1814	Austen, *Mansfield Park*. Scott, *Waverley*. Wordsworth, *The Excursion*.
1815	Napoleon leaves Elba and is defeated by Wellington at Waterloo. Corn Laws are passed.		
		1816	Austen, *Emma*.
		1817	Austen dies.
		1818	Austen, *Northanger Abbey* and *Persuasion* (posth.).
1819	'Peterloo' massacre in Manchester.	1819	John Keats, *Hyperion* (pub. 1856).
1820	Death of George III. Succeeded by the Prince Regent, George IV.	1820	Keats, *Ode to a Nightingale*. Scott, *Ivanhoe*. P.B. Shelley, *Prometheus Unbound*.
		1821	William Hazlitt, *Table Talk*. Keats dies. Shelley, *Adonais*.
		1822	Shelley drowns.
1824	The National Gallery opens.	1824	Byron dies at Missolonghi, in Turko-Greek war. Scott, *Redgauntlet*.
1825	The Stockton to Darlington railway opens – the first passenger-carrying line.	1825	Hazlitt, *The Spirit of the Age*. *The Diaries of Samuel Pepys* (1633–1703) published.
1829	New Act of Parliament establishes an effective police force in London.		
1830	George IV dies. Succeeded by William IV. Agitation for reform.	1830	Alfred Lord Tennyson, *Poems, Chiefly Lyrical*.
		1835	Clare, *The Rural Muse*
		1836–7	Charles Dickens, *Pickwick Papers* serialized.
1837	Death of William IV. Accession of Queen Victoria.		

1838	Anti-Corn Law League established in Manchester.	1838	Elizabeth Barrett Browning, *The Seraphim and Other Poems.*
1840	Queen Victoria marries Prince Albert. Afghan War ends. Penny postage established.		
1842	Chartist Riots – riots and strikes in industrial areas in North of England.		
		1843	Robert Browning, *A Blot in the Scutcheon.* Dickens, *A Christmas Carol* and *Martin Chuzzlewit.* Tennyson, *Morte d'Arthur, Locksley Hall.*
1844	Turner's 'Rain, Steam and Speed'.	1844	Elizabeth Barrett Browning, *Poems.* W.M. Thackeray, *Barry Lyndon.*
1846	Repeal of Corn Laws. Famine in Ireland.		
1847	Factory Act restricts working day for women and children to ten hours.	1847	Charlotte Brontë, *Jane Eyre.* Emily Brontë, *Wuthering Heights.* Anne Brontë, *Agnes Grey.* W.M. Thackeray, *Vanity Fair.*
		1848	Elizabeth Gaskell, *Mary Barton.*
		1849	Dickens, *David Copperfield.*
		1850	Wordsworth dies.
1851	The Great Exhibition.		
		1853	Matthew Arnold, *The Scholar Gypsy.* Charlotte Brontë, *Villette.*
1854	Crimean War begins. Battles of Alma, Inkerman, and Balaclava.	1854	Charles Kingsley, *Westward Ho!* Tennyson, *The Charge of the Light Brigade.*
1856	Peace of Paris ends Crimean War.		
1857	Indian Mutiny. Siege of Delhi.	1857	Anthony Trollope, *Barchester Towers.*
1858	Peace proclaimed in India.		
		1859	Dickens, *A Tale of Two Cities.* George Eliot, *Adam Bede.* Tennyson, *Idylls of the King.*
		1860	Wilkie Collins, *The Woman in White.* George Eliot, *The Mill on the Floss.*
1861	Prince Albert dies. Start of American Civil War.	1861	Dickens, *Great Expectations.* George Eliot, *Silas Marner.*
1864	Geneva Convention established.		
1865	President Lincoln assassinated. American Civil War ends.		
1867	The Second Reform Act. North America Act establishes dominion of Canada.		

		1868	Collins, *The Moonstone*.
1870	Forster's Education Act. Franco-Prussian War.	1870	Dickens dies.
		1871	George Eliot, *Middlemarch*.
		1872	Thomas Hardy, *Under the Greenwood Tree*.
1874	First Impressionist exhibition.	1874	Hardy, *Far From the Madding Crowd*.
		1878	Hardy, *The Return of the Native*. Walter Swinburne, *Poems and Ballads*.
1879	Zulu War. British massacred at Isandhlwana. Public granted unrestricted admission to British Museum.		
1885	The Mahdi takes Khartoum, General Gordon killed. Benz builds first internal combustion engine for motor car. Radio waves discovered.		
1886	Georges Seurat, 'Sunday Afternoon on the Grande Jatte'.	1886	R.L. Stevenson, *Dr Jekyll and Mr Hyde, Kidnapped*.
		1890	Oscar Wilde, *The Picture of Dorian Gray*.
		1891	Hardy, *Tess of the D'Urbervilles*.
		1894	Rudyard Kipling, *The Jungle Book*. George Bernard Shaw, *Arms and the Man*.
1895	X-rays discovered. Marconi invents radio telegraphy. *Tchaikovsky, Swan Lake*.	1895	H.G. Wells, *The Time Machine*. Hardy, *Jude the Obscure*.
		1896	A.E. Housman, *A Shropshire Lad*.
1897	Queen Victoria's Diamond Jubilee.	1897	Wells, *The Invisible Man*. W.B. Yeats, *Adoration of the Magi*.
1898	Kitchener wins Battle of Omdurman. Zeppelin builds his airship.	1898	Wells, *The War of the Worlds*. Hardy, *Wessex Poems*. Oscar Wilde, *The Ballad of Reading Gaol*.
1899–1902	Boer War.	1899	Wilde, *The Importance of Being Ernest*. Rudyard Kipling, *Stalkey and Co*.
1900	Edward Elgar, *Dream of Gerontius*, Giacomo Puccini, *Tosca*.		
1901	Queen Victoria dies. Succeeded by her son Edward VII.		
		1902	Joseph Conrad, *Youth*.
1903	First aeroplane flight.		
		1904	Conrad, *Nostromo*. J.M. Synge, *Riders to the Sea*.
		1906	John Galsworthy, *Man of Property, The Silver Box*.

		1908	E.M. Forster, *A Room With a View*.
1909	Louis Bleriot flies across English Channel.		
1910	Edward VII dies. Accession of George V.		
		1910	Arnold Bennett, *Clayhanger*. Forster, *Howards End*. Wells, *The History of Mr Polly*.
1912	Sinking of Titanic.	1912	Synge, *Playboy of the Western World*.
		1913	D.H. Lawrence, *Son and Lovers*.
1914–18	The First World War.	1914	James Joyce, *Dubliners*.
		1915	D.H. Lawrence, *The Rainbow*. W. Somerset Maugham, *Of Human Bondage*.
1916	The Easter Rising in Dublin. Battle of the Somme.	1916	Joyce, *Portrait of the Artist as a Young Man*.
1917	Russian Revolution.	1917	T.S. Eliot, *Prufrock and Other Observations*.
1918	Germany surrenders and Armistice signed to end First World War.	1918	Lytton Strachey, *Eminent Victorians*.
1919	First flight across Atlantic by Alcock and Brown.	1919	Hardy, *Collected Poems*.
1921	Irish Free State established.	1921	D.H. Lawrence, *Women in Love*. Shaw, *Heartbreak House*.
		1922	T.S. Eliot, *The Waste Land*. Joyce, *Ulysses*. Katherine Mansfield, *The Garden Party*.
1924	First Labour government elected.	1924	Forster, *A Passage to India*. Sean O'Casey, *Juno and the Paycock*.
1926	General Strike.	1926	T.E. Lawrence, *Seven Pillars of Wisdom*.
		1927	Virginia Woolf, *To the Lighthouse*.
1929	Salvador Dali joins surrealist group.	1929	Robert Graves, *Goodbye to All That*. Ernest Hemingway, *A Farewell to Arms*. J.B. Priestley, *The Good Companions*. Erich Maria Remarque, *All Quiet on the Western Front*. R.C. Sherriff, *Journey's End*.
1930	World economic depression.	1930	W.H. Auden, *Poems*. Noel Coward, *Private Lives*. T.S. Eliot, *Ash Wednesday*.
1932	Shakespeare Memorial Theatre opens in Stratford-upon-Avon.	1932	Aldous Huxley, *Brave New World*.
1933	Hitler becomes Chancellor of Germany. The first concentration camps erected by Nazis.		

		1934	Graves, *I Claudius*, and *Claudius the God*.
		1935	T.S. Eliot, *Murder in the Cathedral*.
1936	Spanish Civil War. George V dies. Succeeded by his son Edward VIII. Edward abdicates and is succeeded by his brother, George VI.		
1937	Picasso, 'Guernica'.		
1938	Germany mobilizes forces and occupies Sudetenland. Munich Agreement.		
1939	Spanish Civil War ends. Germany invades Poland and Britain and France declare war. Second World War begins.	1939	Joyce, *Finnegan's Wake*. John Steinbeck, *Grapes of Wrath*.
1940	British Army retreats from Dunkirk. Battle of Britain.	1940	Graham Greene, *The Power and the Glory*. Hemingway, *For Whom the Bell Tolls*.
1941	Japanese bomb Pearl Harbour. US enters war.	1941	Coward, *Blithe Spirit*.
1944	D-Day landings in Normandy.	1944	H.E. Bates, *Fair Stood the Wind for France*. T.S. Eliot, *Four Quartets*.
1945	Germany surrenders, ending war in Europe. Japan surrenders, and Second World War ends.	1945	Evelyn Waugh, *Brideshead Revisited*. John Betjeman, *New Bats in Old Belfries*. George Orwell, *Animal Farm*.
1946	Coal industry nationalized. The National Health Service founded.	1946	Arthur Miller, *All My Sons*. Eugene O'Neill, *The Iceman Cometh*. Terence Rattigan, *The Winslow Boy*. Priestley, *An Inspector Calls*.
1947	Independence of India and Pakistan.	1947	Tennessee Williams, *A Streetcar Named Desire*.
		1949	T.S. Eliot, *The Cocktail Party*. Miller, *Death of a Salesman*. Orwell, *Nineteen Eighty-four*.
1950	Britain recognizes Israel. North Korea invades South Korea.	1950	Christopher Fry, *The Lady's Not For Burning*.
		1951	J.D. Salinger, *The Catcher in the Rye*. John Wyndham, *The Day of the Triffids*.
1952	Winston Churchill announces that Britain has produced an atomic bomb. King George VI dies and is succeeded by his daughter Queen Elizabeth II.	1952	Dylan Thomas, *Collected Poems*. Samuel Beckett, *Waiting for Godot*.
1953	Korean War ends.	1953	Miller, *The Crucible*.
		1954	Kingsley Amis, *Lucky Jim*. William Golding, *Lord of the Flies*. Dylan Thomas, *Under Milk Wood*.
		1955	Philip Larkin, *The Less Deceived*.

1956	Egypt nationalizes Suez Canal. Attempted intervention by Britain, France, and Israel.	1956	John Osborne, *Look Back in Anger*. Angus Wilson, *Anglo-Saxon Attitudes*.
		1957	Ted Hughes, *The Hawk in the Rain*. Jack Kerouac, *On the Road*. Beckett, *Endgame*. Osborne, *The Entertainer*.
		1958	Truman Capote, *Breakfast at Tiffany's*. Harold Pinter, *The Birthday Party*. Iris Murdoch, *The Bell*.
		1959	Colin MacInnes, *Absolute Beginners*.
		1960	Robert Bolt, *A Man For All Seasons*. Harper Lee, *To Kill a Mockingbird*. Pinter, *The Caretaker*.
1961	Attempted invasion of Cuba – 'Bay of Pigs' fiasco.	1961	Joseph Heller, *Catch 22*. Greene, *A Burnt-Out Case*.
1962	Cuban missile crisis.	1962	Edward Albee, *Who's Afraid of Virginia Woolf?*
1963	US President Kennedy assassinated.	1963	Sylvia Plath, *The Bell Jar*. Margaret Drabble, *A Summer Birdcage*. Murdoch, *The Unicorn*.
1964	US aircraft attack North Vietnamese bases.	1964	Peter Schaffer, *The Royal Hunt of the Sun*. Larkin, *The Whitsun Weddings*.
1965	Churchill dies.		
		1966	Jean Rhys, *Wide Sargasso Sea*.
1967	Homosexuality and abortion legalized.	1967	Angela Carter, *The Magic Toyshop*.
1969	'Troubles' in Northern Ireland. British troops sent in. Abolition of capital punishment.	1969	Margaret Atwood, *The Edible Woman*. John Fowles, *The French Lieutenant's Woman*.
1970	Voting age reduced from 21 to 18.	1970	Hughes, *Crow*.
1973	Britain joins European Economic Community.	1973	Schaffer, *Equus*. Martin Amis, *The Rachel Papers*.
		1974	Larkin, *High Windows*. W.H. Auden, *Thank You Fog: Last Poems*.
1975	South Vietnam surrenders to North Vietnam. US withdrawal and end of Vietnam War.	1975	Malcolm Bradbury, *The History Man*.
		1977	Paul Scott, *Staying On*.
1979	First direct election to European Parliament.		
		1980	Golding, *Rites of Passage*.
1981	Wedding of HRH the Prince of Wales and Lady Diana Spencer.		
1982	The Falklands War.	1982	Thomas Keneally, *Schindler's Ark*. Paul Theroux, *The Mosquito Coast*.

		1983	Susan Hill, *The Woman in Black*.
1984	Worldwide reaction to famine in Ethiopia – 'Band Aid'.	1984	J.G. Ballard, *Empire of the Sun*. Anita Brookner, *Hotel du Lac*. Carter, *Nights at the Circus*. Iain Banks, *The Wasp Factory*.
		1987	Alan Bennett, *Talking Heads*. Toni Morrison, *The Beloved*.
		1989	Kazuo Ishiguro, *The Remains of the Day*. Martin Amis, *London Fields*.
1990	Reunification of Germany. Iraq invades Kuwait.	1990	A.S. Byatt, *Possession*. Brookner, *Brief Lives*.
		1991	Hill, *Air and Angels*.
		1992	Michael Ondaatje, *The English Patient*. Adam Thorpe, *Ulverton*. Banks, *The Crow Road*.
		1993	John Banville, *Ghosts*. A.N. Wilson, *The Vicar of Sorrows*.
1994	Opening of Channel Tunnel.	1994	Margaret Atwood, *The Robber Bride*. Bennett, *Writing Home*. Brookner, *A Private View*.
1997	Election of first Labour government for 18 years. Death of Diana, Princess of Wales.		
		1999	Appointment of Andrew Motion as Poet Laureate, after the death of Ted Hughes. Carol Ann Duffy, *The World's Wife*.
2001	11 September terrorist attacks on US.		
2003	Invasion of Iraq by US and its allies.		

Index

Headings in *italics* refer to the titles of prose, drama and poetical works. Page numbers in **bold** type refer to definitions; those in *italics* refer to extracts from texts.